Building
TEACHERS

This work is dedicated to

Marilyn Kern Loomis and A. Reeve Loomis, Jr.

Shannon, Katelynn, and Joshua Martin

And all the teachers, professors, colleagues, and students who have taught us

Building TEACHERS

A Constructivist Approach to Introducing Education

David Jerner Martin
Kennesaw State University

Kimberly S. Loomis
Kennesaw State University

WADSWORTH
CENGAGE Learning™

Australia • Brazil • Japan • Korea • Mexico • Singapore • Spain • United Kingdom • United States

WADSWORTH
CENGAGE Learning™

Building Teachers: A Constructivist Approach to Introducing Education
David Jerner Martin and Kimberly S. Loomis

Executive Editor: Vicki Knight

Acquisitions Editor: Dan Alpert

Development Editor: Tangelique Williams

Assistant Editor: Dan Moneypenny

Editorial Assistant: Ann Lee Richards

Technology Project Manager: Amanda Kaufmann

Marketing Manager: Terra Schultz

Marketing Communications Manager:
    Tami Strang

Project Manager, Editorial Production:
    Matt Ballantyne

Creative Director: Rob Hugel

Art Director: Maria Epes

Print Buyer: Judy Inouye

Permissions Editor: Roberta Broyer

Production Service: Graphic World Publishing
    Services

Text Designer: Brian Molloy

Photo Researcher: Terri Wright Design

Illustrator: Patricia McDermond

Cover Designer: Brian Molloy

Cover Image: Copyright © Getty Images

Compositor: Graphic World Inc.

For product information and technology assistance, contact us at
Cengage Learning Customer & Sales Support, 1-800-354-9706

For permission to use material from this text or product,
submit all requests online at cengage.com/permissions
Further permissions questions can be emailed to
permissionrequest@cengage.com

Library of Congress Control Number: 2006921034

ISBN-13: 978-0-534-60849-1

ISBN-10: 0-534-60849-3

Wadsworth
10 Davis Drive
Belmont, CA 94002-3098
USA

Cengage Learning is a leading provider of customized learning solutions with office locations around the globe, including Singapore, the United Kingdom, Australia, Mexico, Brazil, and Japan. Locate your local office at: **international.cengage.com/region**

Cengage Learning products are represented in Canada by Nelson Education, Ltd.

For your course and learning solutions, visit **www.cengage.com**

Purchase any of our products at your local college store or at our preferred online store **www.ichapters.com**

Printed in China by China Translation & Printing Services Limited
3 4 5 6 7 11 10 09 08

BRIEF CONTENTS

CONTENTS

CHAPTER 12   Social Issues and the School's Response   315

Welcome to *Building Teachers: A Constructivist Approach to Introducing Education*. This book is markedly different from other Introduction to Education textbooks. From the ground up, we designed it around a constructivist framework that reflects our sincere belief that people learn best when they are able to construct their own knowledge and understandings of any given topic. Its purpose is to encourage students who are interested in becoming teachers to construct basic understandings of what it means to be a teacher. We wrote it to help the instructor and students actually implement the constructivist approach. This means that the book is interactive in nature and inductive in approach.

We included all the topics normally found in an introduction to education course, although they might not be in the same order as in a traditional textbook.

We begin each chapter by asking students to explore what they already know about the topic at hand, and we encourage them to build on that knowledge by investigating additional information from the research, the media, government agencies, professional societies, psychologists, philosophers, other teachers, and many other sources. We then ask students to construct new understandings by combining the new information with their existing information.

Overview of the Text

The overall scheme of the text can be represented by a set of concentric circles in which the *Self* is in the center, and the *Student*, *School*, and *Society* occupy larger circles that encompass the inner ones (see inside front cover). Thus, the student continually refers to the Self during the exploration of the other topics.

The text begins with Chapter Zero, a short chapter designed to familiarize the student with the nature of the book, how to use it to develop their own understandings, and how to use its various features.

Part I deals with the *Self*—the individual student and his or her beliefs and informed opinions about education. In Chapter 1, students examine the characteristics of excellent teachers and exemplary teaching. In Chapter 2, students consider the conclusions they developed in Chapter 1 together with research findings, contemporary thinking about education, and philosophies and psychologies. They use their beliefs and this new information to develop their own philosophy of education that will provide a personal and flexible framework to guide them through the rest of the text.

Part II extends the explorations beyond the Self to the *Student* in the classroom. It asks readers to think about how students are alike, how they are different, and how these characteristics factor into the complex relationships teachers have with students. In Chapter 3, readers explore ways in which students are alike, their common needs, and general motivational factors. Chapter 4 asks readers to explore the unique perspectives of students such as cultural, language, and religious diversity; socioeconomic status; gender;

and sexual orientation. In Chapter 5, they explore the unique abilities of students in such areas as learning disabilities, intelligence, and learning styles and preferences.

Part III helps students expand their awareness of the Self and Students to the context of the *School*. In Chapter 6, they examine purposes of schools, and in Chapter 7 they look at how the purpose of a school is reflected in its structure. Chapter 8 guides the exploration of what schools expect of students and what students expect of schools, including an investigation of behavior management techniques. Chapter 9 focuses on what schools expect of teachers and what teachers expect of schools.

Part IV further broadens students' understandings by looking at education in the context of our *Society*. Chapter 10 deals with the historical foundations of education in the United States. In Chapter 11, students explore broad concepts of governance and finance. In Chapter 12, they consider additional social issues to which schools feel they should respond, and Chapter 13 guides students through an exploration of the legal and ethical issues to which schools, teachers, and students are accountable. Finally, Chapter 14 considers contemporary trends and issues in curriculum and educational reform.

Part V (Chapter 15) returns students to their thinking about what makes excellent teachers and exemplary teaching and asks them to examine their motives for wanting—or not wanting—to be a teacher.

Distinctive Features of *Building Teachers*

This textbook contains many unique features. The **Building Blocks** comprise the basic tools of learning and serve as inquiry activities for student explorations. Some Building Blocks ask students to reflect on existing knowledge, some ask them to reflect on contemporary problems and issues, and some ask them to put new knowledge together with their existing knowledge and describe and give reasons for their conclusions. The Building Blocks can be used in several ways—as assignments before reading the textual material, as short beginning-of-class activities, as springboards for class discussions, as homework assignments, as tools for assessment, and so on. The Building Blocks are intended to foster the constructivist nature of the book; student responses to the Building Blocks are one of the better ways of seeing how they are constructing information. For the most part, the Building Blocks do not presuppose any "right" or "wrong" answers; they are intended to enable students to express and examine their own thinking. Some ask students to compare their conclusions with those of the authors. Hopefully there will be a degree of congruence.

The topics students explore in this book are interdependent. To this end, you will find that we have integrated important themes throughout several chapters instead of treating them as independent topics. For example, the material on diversity, social issues, and current trends in education are addressed as appropriate in the context of several different chapters. And, instead of occupying a single chapter, curriculum is addressed in the contexts of philosophy (Chapter 2), history (Chapter 10), educational reform (Chapter 14), and in several other places.

The material on technology is infused throughout the text, and individual elements of technology are addressed contextually where the elements are most meaningful. Technology is covered in several ways. Major discussions on elements of technology are found in sections of the main text as well as in **Technology & Education** features. Many Internet sites are highlighted and can be accessed through direct links on the *Building Teachers* companion website. The companion website also contains hotlinks to all the electronic references used (identified with the WWW icon), the Instructor's Manual, and other interesting and useful sites not necessarily referenced in the text. To access the companion website, type the following address in your Internet browser: http://www.cengage.com/education.

The textbook supports the INTASC (Interstate New Teacher Assessment and Support Consortium) principles. In the **Deconstructing the Standards** features at the end of each chapter, students are asked to analyze ways in which their investigations helped them meet the principles. The text also supports the NCATE (National Council for Accreditation of Teacher Education) standards and the propositions of the National Board for Professional Teaching Standards (NBPTS).

Other features include the following:

- The *No Child Left Behind* legislation is addressed throughout the text and gives students the opportunity to explore its effects on education in the United States today, as well as the mixed thoughts educators and other stakeholders have about its implementation.
- A CD-ROM developed specifically for use with *Building Teachers* contains 15 original video segments of excellent teachers; video interviews with teachers, administrators, and parents; and multimedia tools that continue to draw students into the learning process. A separate instructor's video contains additional classroom-based segments.
- **From the Teacher** elements feature the first-person testimony of practicing teachers from across the United States, nearly all of whom are recent state-wide Teacher-of-the-Year winners.
- The **Your Portfolio** features contain suggestions for artifacts that can be included in the student's learning portfolio.
- The **Field Experience** features reference activities in the *Field Experience Companion* that are designed to expand students' explorations of certain topics into the field.

This book is about helping education students learn what teaching is all about in an exploratory, inquiry, constructivist-based manner so they, in turn, can help the students in their classrooms learn meaningfully. It is about process rather than product. It is about exploring, wondering, giving in to curiosity, and thinking. It is about constructing sound and valid conceptualizations from new experiences that foster the desire to continue constructing and reconstructing personal and valid conceptualizations.

In this practical textbook, we have taken the bold and uncompromising position that constructivist-oriented inquiry must be fostered in our schools. Preservice teachers who construct their conceptualizations about education through the guidance offered in this textbook will find teaching to be fun, stimulating, rewarding, and extremely successful. We sincerely hope that future teachers will use their convictions and the value of the constructivist approach to education as the primary basis of their teaching.

Acknowledgments

This work would not have been possible without the support and help of a great many people. We are especially grateful to the following:

- Editors Dan Alpert and Tangelique Williams of Wadsworth, a part of Cengage Learning, who offered strong ideas, gentle guidance, and a tremendous amount of help in every aspect of this work
- All the instructors of the Introduction to Education course at Kennesaw State University, especially the course coordinator, Professor Beth Marks, who graciously agreed to use pilot editions of this textbook and provided suggestions for content, organization, and editing
- Dr. Linda Webb, who reviewed and critiqued countless drafts in addition to writing Chapter 13, Teachers, Students, and the Law
- Dr. Marjorie Economopoulos and Dr. Nita Paris, who provided help in organizing the chapters in Part II

- Dr. Rick Breault, who read and critiqued the material on the history of American education
- Dr. T. C. Chan, who provided much assistance with the material on school structure and facilities
- Dr. Alice Snyder and Dr. Debra Coffey, who helped with the material on the language arts
- Dr. Maurice Wilson, who helped with the material on mathematics
- Dr. Lynn Stallings and Mary Martin, who provided great support and encouragement through the whole process of writing this book
- All the many professional colleagues who have supported our work through the years
- The students in our introduction to education classes who have used parts of this text in draft form and have shown us what works and what doesn't; we have used many of their ideas and vignettes in this book

David Jerner Martin
Kimberly S. Loomis

REVIEWERS

Thank you to all of the professors who reviewed *Building Teachers* and provided invaluable feedback and suggestions at various stages in the writing and revising:

Harvey Alvy, Eastern Washington University

Lloyd Anderson, Bismarck State College

Patricia Bason, Elon University

John J. Bertalan, Hillsborough Community College

Robert E. Bleicher, California State University–Channel Islands

John Bruno, Florida State University

Ted Bulling, Jr., Nebraska Wesleyan University

Susan Carson, Grand Valley State University

Margaret Denny, Louisiana State University

Elizabeth D. Dore, Radford University

John A. Ellis, Valparaiso University

Steven R. Greenberg, Bridgewater State College

Susan Allen Gulledge, University of North Carolina, Chapel Hill

Gwendolyn Guy, East Carolina University

Ann S. Hernandez, University of St. Francis

Charles Howell, Minnesota State University, Moorhead

Edward Janak, University of Wyoming

Robert Leahy, Stetson University

William Patrick Leedom, Shawnee State University

Delinda Dent Lybrand, Eastern Kentucky University

Helena Mariella-Walrond, Bethune-Cookman College

Wendy L. McCarty, University of Nebraska, Kearney

Anthony P. Murphy, College of St. Catherine

Raja T. Nasr, Marymount University

Terry Nourie, Illinois State University

Melvin J. Pedras, University of Idaho

Rachel G. Ragland, Lake Forest College

Dutchie S. Riggsby, Columbus State University

Rochelle P. Ripple, Columbus State University

Richard F. Rodriguez, Western New Mexico University

Robert Shearer, Miami University

Rosemary Traoré, Florida State University

Cara Livingstone Turner, University of Charleston

Alexander Urbiel, Ramapo University

Laura M. Wendling, California State University–San Marcos

Carol S. Whelan, Tulane University

Ginger Williams, Oglethorpe University

Henry S. Williams, Sr., Central Washington University

Carlisle E. Womack, Bainbridge College

We also wish to extend a note of thanks to the following individuals who served as specialist reviewers for specific chapters of the manuscript:

Richard M. Gargiulo, University of Alabama, Birmingham

Paul Gorski, Hamline University

Gerald Gutek, Loyola University

Leslie S. Kaplan, Newport News Public Schools

William Owings, Old Dominion University

CHAPTER 0

Building a Foundation for This Book

> What we see depends mainly on what we look for.
>
> SIR JOHN LUBBOCK

Welcome to your textbook! This textbook differs from others you have read. Most textbooks tell you the information you are supposed to learn, but this one asks you to come to your own conclusions. To be sure, there is a great deal of information in this book to be learned about education, but our primary goal is for you to use this information to build your own ideas rather than simply memorizing the ideas of others.

This text is written from a constructivist viewpoint, which means you will be asked to construct your own conceptualizations about education by combining the information presented with your own prior experiences. Because no two people have the same prior experiences, we expect each individual will construct something different. How is this idea reflected in the opening quote by Lubbock?

The text is new and different; the way you will study it is also new and different. Therefore, we would like you to become familiar with the way this book is organized.

What Is in a Textbook?

What do you look for in a textbook?

Stop reading for a moment and consider this question seriously. What do you look for in a textbook? Maybe jotting down a few words or phrases will help you arrange your thoughts. Also think seriously about the next two questions:

1. Why do you think your instructors require you to purchase textbooks?

2. What do you expect from your textbook?

Your answers to the preceding questions probably are not unlike the answers of the rest of the people in your class and in college classes like yours all over the world. For the most part, students look for information in their textbooks—facts, concepts, theories, explanations, and ideas and thoughts of others. They suppose that instructors require the purchase of textbooks to supplement lecture material, and they expect the textbooks to tell them what they need to know for the purpose of passing the tests and thereby passing the course. But consider this next proposition:

> A master can tell you what he expects of you. A teacher, though, awakens your own expectations.
>
> PATRICIA NEAL

Who writes textbooks? Would you consider these people to be masters in the sense that Neal describes a master? Probably. But the quote says that a teacher awakens your own expectations. Because textbooks are required for classes, you ought to be able to assume that they can teach you something and thereby awaken your expectations. You should expect to learn from all textbooks, and you should expect to learn from this textbook.

We believe the organization of a textbook used in a course designed for future teachers should be especially conducive to learning and should model the best way of teaching. Most textbooks assume the reader has limited or no knowledge about the topics presented. However, we know you already have a great deal of information about education. You amassed this information through being a student yourself, through discussions with family members or friends who work in the field of education, through watching public portrayals of education in movies and TV shows, through hearing about education on the news, through reading about education in newspapers and magazines, and through many other sources.

The way people learn is by attaching new information to the information they already have, thereby building their own personal conceptualizations. Accordingly, we have written a book that enables you to do just that. It encourages you to bring the information you already know about teaching and schools to the surface of your mind, introduces new ideas, and helps you put the two together. Learning in this manner is consistent with a learning theory called *constructivism*.

This book is constructivist in nature, which means you will look at your own ideas and the ideas of others before you come to new and informed conclusions. This book also is field-based, which means you will combine the experiences you develop from the text and in the classroom with your field experiences to augment your conclusions. Your venture into this method of learning consists of three main steps:

1. You will use your prior knowledge and experiences to help establish your familiarity with the material presented.
2. You will obtain new information and experiences from the text, your class work, your fieldwork, and other sources.
3. You will draw your own personal conclusions by combining your prior knowledge with the new information and experiences. These conclusions will likely be different from the conclusions of others because each person has different prior experiences.

By using this text, you will approach this course in a manner similar to the way you will approach the act of teaching. It is our conviction that you will become a better teacher as a result of using this book because you will be learning the basic material about education in a way that parallels the best way of teaching.

Traditional Textbooks

Think about the textbooks you have used during your academic career. Do any stand out as being exceptionally "good reads"? Other than being particularly interested in the subject matter, can you recall being *actively* involved with any text?

How is this student using her textbook?

The dictionary defines *textbook* as "a book used in the study of a subject . . . one containing a presentation of the principles of a subject." A typical textbook is a means of transferring information from the mind of one person or a group of people to the mind of someone else through the written word, thereby increasing the knowledge of the person using the textbook. Students normally are required to read the textbook to learn the information presented so that they can participate in class discussions, do the homework, and pass tests about the material.

The information presented in such a textbook may differ from that presented in class. It may be more detailed, or it may come from different sources. In the typical class, your instructor reinforces or adds to what you read in the text or offers a different "spin" on the information.

This Textbook

If what you expect in a text is information, you will find it in this book; it includes all the topics typically covered in an introduction to education course. However, the topics might not be presented as you expect them to be. As teachers ourselves, we would rather awaken your own expectations by having you first explore what you already know about teaching, learning, schools, students, and education. Then, we will give you opportunities to obtain information from other sources, such as other students, teachers and experts in the field, professional standards, research, governmental agencies, and the like. Rather than simply telling you what you should know of other people's ideas, we want you to construct your own understanding by merging what you already know with the ideas of others. It is this treatment that separates this book from a traditional textbook. This book does not contain "right answers" to be regurgitated on tests. What you *will* find is that you are asked to formulate *your* answers—answers that you have constructed from your experiences, your knowledge, your beliefs, and the ideas of others that are presented in this book. Your own answer is much more powerful and meaningful than any information that passes from the pages of a book through you onto a test paper without ever really spending time in your brain, because *you* have developed it. Let us take a look at how this powerful and meaningful construction of knowledge works.

An Example—Building a Table

Suppose you were to sign up for a woodworking class in which you are to learn how to build a wooden table, the kind you might have in your living room or den. No carpentry expertise or prior experience is necessary for this class. From your past experience in attending classes, what would you expect to do on the first day of class? What would you expect to see in your classroom that would help you build the table? What tools and materials would you expect to get? Let us look at two different scenarios.

Method 1

In the first scenario, suppose that when you walk into the classroom, all that is present are the teacher and the other students. Imagine that you are given no tools or materials whatever, and the teacher simply says, "Build a table."

Where would you start? Remember that no experience was necessary to enroll in this class. Your instructor assures you that to begin the task, you need only to be familiar with tables, which you definitely are (even if this experience has consisted only of sitting at one).

Where would you start? What would you tell the teacher you need? What would you do? Before you continue reading, stop for a moment and consider your responses to these questions.

Do you suppose you can answer the preceding questions? Yes, you absolutely can, regardless of any experience you may or may not have had in woodworking! How do you know the answers to the questions about where to start, what you would need to build a table, and what you would do? You know because of your prior experience with tables. You have seen tables before, and you have used them. Maybe you have even built one. We bet that with the teacher's help, you would be able to get started designing your table and creating a list of needed tools and materials on the very first day of class.

But how can that be? You're not a furniture builder. You don't know how to build a table.

Surely the teacher, who is a master carpenter, could tell you what you need to know. But instead of having these ready solutions, in this situation, you must recall what you already know about tables. And, in the process of this thinking, a table is beginning to take shape in your mind. As it does, you can make a list of tools and materials you think you will need. If you are not experienced in woodworking and have not used woodworking tools before, you will probably want to build a table that does not require complicated tools—maybe a saw, a drill, and a hammer are all you would want to deal with at first.

Now, imagine that on the second day of class, your teacher has supplied you with the tools and materials you have requested. After a demonstration on safety in the woodworking shop, you begin construction. How would you know if you had all the tools and materials you will need? What would you do if something did not quite work out the way you thought it might?

Having been given the tools and materials you requested, you begin working. While you are building your table, your teacher circulates among the students, discussing with them their plans, progress, skills, and choices of materials and offering suggestions and ideas. At certain points, your teacher encourages you to look at what other students in your class are doing. What do you suppose the purpose of this is? What impact might it have on your work with your own table? What impact would it have on your knowledge of how to build a table?

One day when you arrive at your class, your teacher hands you a book written by a master carpenter about building tables. As you flip through the pages, looking at the pictures and diagrams and reading the text, what is happening in your mind? What impact does the information from the master carpenter have on your work? What impact does it have on your knowledge of how to build a table?

What is this student building? What is her teacher doing?

Finally, the last day of class comes. Everyone has constructed a table. How would you expect the tables to look? What factors might influence the designs of different students' tables? What would you know about building tables now that you have finished yours? How have you learned it? What do you suppose your next experience with making something out of wood would be like?

Method 2

Now let us look at the second scenario. Pretend again that it is the first day of class. This time, as you enter the classroom, you see a woodworking shop equipped with table saws, routers, sanders, and other power tools. You see a large supply of fine hardwood and a supply of hardware, including nails and screws. You take a seat at one of the tables, and soon the teacher distributes a textbook about building tables, complete with drawings and "blueprints" created by a master carpenter. The teacher gives you a list of materials you will need and tells you where those materials are located in the shop. After a demonstration on woodworking shop safety, your teacher tells you where to begin in the book and helps you follow the instructions for building a table, step by step.

After a period of time, you have built your table. What does this table look like? What do the other tables in your class look like? What do you know about building tables now that you are done? How have you learned it? What would your next experience with making something out of wood be like?

Comparing Methods of Learning

Let us think about the two different ways in which you learned how to build a table. Consider the following questions. Take time to formulate your answer to each question before you move on to the next one. Your goal is to make some important conclusions.

- How does the time it would take to make a table using method 1 compare with the time it would take using method 2?
- When you completed building your table using method 1, could you pass a test on how to make tables? Could you pass a test on how to make tables if you had used method 2?
- What kind of test questions (multiple-choice, true/false, fill-in-the-blank, matching, or essay questions) could you answer if you made your table as a student using method 1? Using method 2?

The *Building Teachers* companion website has direct links to several Internet sites that show how to build wood tables.

- Who constructed the knowledge you used to answer the test questions? Where did you get the knowledge?
- Which method do you think would allow you to build another table successfully several years later?

We hope you have drawn some significant conclusions about the advantages of the two different teaching methods described. You probably concluded that building a table on your own would take a lot more time than following step-by-step instructions from a book but that the actual act of learning by discovery would make the learning more meaningful and much more powerful. The experience itself gives ownership of the knowledge. Following the prescribed steps in a book means applying someone else's knowledge. There is a danger of this knowledge remaining forever "outside" the learner. The student might recall it for the test but forget it from then on.

Think about the types of test questions you said you would be able to answer relative to method 1 and method 2. Low-level questions on tests are those that ask you to recall information by means such as choosing a "correct" answer from a multiple-choice list, deciding whether a statement is true or false, filling in the blanks, or matching words with their definitions. Do you think you could answer low-level questions if you had participated in method 1? What if you had participated in method 2?

Suppose an essay question asks you to describe the process of selecting the way you used to attach the legs of the table to its top. This type of question is called a high-level question. It requires you to think. There may be more than one right answer. You may not have acquired sufficient information to provide a good answer to this high-level question if you had participated in a class taught using method 2. You probably would know only one answer—that of the author of the text you used. In comparison, think of the rich answer you could provide if you had been in the method 1 class. You could offer some insightful information gained by experience. Even better, it would be *your* knowledge, not the knowledge of some "master" you had memorized. *You* would be the master of the information. As the famous ancient Chinese proverb puts it:

> I hear and I forget;
>
> I see and I remember;
>
> I do and I understand.

It is usually the high-level questions that we encounter in real-life situations. High-level thinking skills are required for answering high-level questions, solving problems, evaluating, formulating hypotheses, and drawing conclusions, among other tasks. Can you see how you would have had the opportunity to use and practice these high-level thinking skills if you had been a student in the class using method 1, where you had to figure out how to build the best table you could? To what extent are these skills used in the method 2 class?

Which class would you rather participate in? Why?

Suppose that, rather than building a table, the subject of the class was building a teacher. Which instructional method would you prefer?

This Book Is a Little Like Building a Table

We assume that you are reading this textbook because you are enrolled in a class designed to introduce you to education in the United States. You are most likely taking this class at the beginning of a program intended to promote your development as a teacher. To stay with our analogy, you could say that you are starting to build yourself as a teacher—thus the title of this book.

Based on what you already have done in this introductory chapter, it may not surprise you that, as authors, we want this book to contribute to your learning in a fashion consistent with the strategies employed in method 1 of our table-building example. Let us examine how this book is set up, how it correlates with the method 1 class, and how it compares with the method 2 class and other texts (see Table 0.1).

In this text, you are asked to recall and use what you already know to begin to build your knowledge about American education. This is analogous to the shop teacher in the method 1 class asking the students to recall and use what they already knew about tables to design and build one. However, in standard textbooks, you are given information to learn; this is analogous to having to follow specific directions to build a table, as required in method 2.

This text provides you with information from many sources, such as other students, experts in the field, and research, which you use to augment your previous ideas; this is analogous to talking with other students and reading authoritative books about building tables in method 1. On the other hand, if you are given a traditional text, you would not have the opportunity to interact with it; instead, you would read and try to absorb the material the author intended to transmit. This is analogous to building a table by following specific directions, as required in method 2.

In this text, you are encouraged to compare your existing thoughts and ideas with new information that is introduced; this is analogous to comparing your table with the

TABLE 0.1 Comparison of Texts with Table-Construction Classes

This Text	Method 1	Other Texts	Method 2
Readers are asked to recall and use what they already know to begin to build knowledge about American education.	Students are asked to recall and use what they already know to begin to design and build a table.	Readers are given information from masters about American education.	Students are given instructions from masters on how to build a table.
Readers are provided with additional information about education from other students, experts, and research.	Students are provided with additional information about building tables from other students and books by master carpenters.	Readers read and/or listen to the information.	Students build tables following the instructions.
Readers compare their thoughts and ideas with the new information.	Students compare what they have done with the work of other students and books by master craftspeople.		
Readers draw conclusions and modify their knowledge to construct new knowledge.	Students draw conclusions and modify their tables using their new knowledge.		
Readers' understandings may or may not be the same as those of other readers, but each reader's ideas work for him or her. Readers are able to use higher-level thinking skills to answer high-level questions.	Students' tables may or may not resemble each other, but each table works. Students are able to use higher-level thinking skills to answer high-level questions.	Readers' understandings are expected to be identical to those presented in the text (and by the teacher). Students are able to recall the knowledge of the masters in the book.	Students' tables are identical. Students are able to answer low-level questions that ask them to recall the knowledge of the master carpenter.

tables others have built and with the work of master craftspeople. In this text, you are encouraged to draw conclusions and construct your own conceptualizations. This corresponds to the woodworking class taught using method 1, where you can expect to learn from your table-building experience and make modifications to your table based on your new understandings. Each person learns something different. For some, it might be how to use a power saw or how to hammer small nails without damaging the wood; for others, it might be how to put a scalloped edge on the tabletop or how to include a medallion on it.

As a result of your active thinking while studying this text, you will develop your own personal conceptualizations. These conceptualizations may or may not be the same as those of others, but they are valid and they reflect your own best thinking. You will have used higher-level thinking skills to arrive at your conclusions. This is analogous to each person in the method 1 woodworking class crafting a unique table that reflected him or her as an individual. In the traditional text, however, all learners are expected to recall the same knowledge from the text, often in the same way, as in the method 2 woodworking class, in which all students built identical tables.

Using Building Blocks

As we indicated earlier, in each chapter you will first be asked to recall what you already know about the topic. Usually, you will be prompted to do this in sections called Building Blocks. For example, the first Building Block for the method 1 class described might be as follows.

BUILDING BLOCK 0.1

Building a Table

Suppose you were to sign up for a woodworking class in which you are to learn how to build a wooden table. No carpentry expertise or prior experience is necessary for this class.

- From your past experience in attending classes, what would you expect to do on the first day of class?
- What would you expect to see in your classroom that would help you build the table?
- What tools and materials would you expect to get?

Now, suppose that when you walk into the classroom, all that is present are the teacher and the other students. Imagine that you are given no tools or materials whatever, and the teacher simply says, "Build a table."

- Where would you start?
- What would you tell the teacher you need?
- What would you do?

The words are the same as those used before, but the scenario is set apart as a Building Block to encourage you to pause in your reading, seriously consider the questions, and formulate your responses. Other Building Blocks ask you to think and draw conclusions. Be sure to pay particular attention to these Building Blocks and to do the reflecting, thinking, and writing suggested. When you get to class, your instructor might ask you what you thought about the questions and invite you and your classmates to share your knowledge and experience. Doing so would be analogous to the teacher in the method 1 table-building class encouraging you to look at the other students' tables. In that way, you are getting new information that may reinforce your ideas, cause you to modify your ideas, or maybe even influence you to revise your ideas completely.

Many sources of information are cited in this book, including students in classes like yours, experts in the field, educational research, books, journals, magazines, newspapers, and the Internet. As in the method 1 table-building class, we expect that you will compare this information with your existing knowledge to reinforce and/or modify it as you draw your conclusions. Because you begin the study of each topic by bringing your own ideas to the surface of your mind, and because you use the higher-level thinking skills in processing the information, you take ownership in powerful and meaningful learning.

This Is Constructivism

Consider the title of this book—*Building Teachers*. It says this book takes a *constructivist* approach to the introduction of education. From what you have looked at so far, can you begin to formulate a definition of *constructivism*? Think back to the method 1 table-building class and the format of this textbook as described in Table 0.1. Where is the student constructing knowledge? How is this process happening?

We are not going to give you a specific definition of *constructivism* right now. We want you to construct your own definition as you go through the experience of using this constructivist-based textbook. You will address constructivism in later chapters when you consider it in relation to teaching your future students. However, simply by reading and interacting with the material in this chapter, you have already begun to construct an understanding of constructivist methods. Meanwhile, let us explore the other features you can expect to see in this textbook.

Other Features

We have already mentioned the Building Blocks you will find in every chapter. Remember that Building Blocks ask you to recall prior knowledge and experience so that you will have something to which you can attach the new material. As you progress through this book, your course, and your field experiences, your knowledge base will grow. You will obtain more and more knowledge and experience to which you can attach new material. You will have more and more to offer, share, and compare. Your understandings will grow like a giant web.

You will find other features in this text that provide information and allow you to investigate further, apply what you have learned, and practice higher-level thinking skills. Biographies provide personal and professional information about experts in the field.

BIOGRAPHY

Courtesy Kim Loomis

Kimberly S. Loomis is an associate professor of middle grades science education in the Department of Secondary and Middle Grades Education at Kennesaw State University. She has taught science and education courses for 17 years at the middle grades through college levels. Many of her presentations and publications focus on inquiry teaching strategies, which are grounded in constructivist learning theory. Currently, her work is focused on using inquiry teaching to foster attitude changes in the field of wolf education.

David Jerner Martin is professor of science education in the Department of Elementary and Early Childhood Education at Kennesaw State University. He was a teacher of science and mathematics for 18 years at the elementary, middle grades, and high school levels. He is author of *Elementary Science Methods: A Constructivist Approach,* currently in its fourth edition, and *Constructing Early Childhood Science.* He has made numerous presentations fostering process-oriented constructivist inquiry science teaching and has consulted on this topic in Indonesia and South Korea.

The *From the Teacher* features contain thoughts and ideas from actual teachers.

from the TEACHER — From a Student

have just now finished reading Chapter 1 of our new textbook, and I wanted to make a few comments. First of all, reading this chapter has in some way put a greater desire in me to teach, and not only to teach but to be the best teacher there is! The section that lists the basic conditions of teaching was very interesting, and I found the five "beliefs" very helpful as well. Something I am really enjoying about this book is that the authors have taken many quotes and ideas from other people, enabling the reader to think about multiple ideas and methods of teaching. When I was in school, I remember the teachers always had quotes all over the room. You have provided some really thought-provoking quotes in this book that one day may be seen on the walls of my classroom. The Building Blocks are a really interesting and unique aspect of this book and one I haven't seen in this form in any other book I have read. I really like the idea of the Building Blocks, and I believe they challenge the reader to think!

Rebecca, a teacher education student who used a preliminary edition of Building Teachers

Web icons direct you to the Internet for additional information or to the *Building Teachers* companion website, where you can find direct links to websites referred to in the text.

Technology & Education features contain descriptions of specific kinds of technology that are used in education, their applications to teaching and learning, and some exercises you can do to gain familiarity with that technology.

The *CD* that comes with *Building Teachers* is an extremely valuable resource. It contains video clips and other information to help you make your constructions.

Margin questions ask you to think about the information you are reading and apply it to specific situations.

The *Construct and Apply* questions at the end of each chapter help you solidify your conclusions and apply them to new situations.

Like other professions, the field of teaching has standards for performance. There are standards for general teaching performance, and there are standards for teaching performance in each grade level or discipline. In this text, we focus on the general teaching performance standards developed by the Interstate New Teacher Assessment and Support Consortium (INTASC). INTASC has developed a set of 10 standards, which they call "principles," that state what teachers should know and be able to do as a result of their teacher preparation program (see inside back cover). At the end of each chapter, we present one or two of these INTASC principles in *Deconstructing the Standards* and ask you to analyze ways in which the material you investigated has helped you meet those principles, providing you an opportunity to assess your progress toward becoming a highly skilled teacher.

You will find Field Experience and Portfolio suggestions at the end of each chapter. These activities are meant to focus your observations and participation in your field experience so that you can have the best learning experience possible.

In teacher education programs, students are often asked to document their learning experience in the form of a portfolio. Just as an artist's portfolio displays his or her best work as evidence of talent, your portfolio should provide evidence that you are achieving the standards and proficiencies for teachers designated by your college, your state, and the nation. Portfolio suggestions at the end of each chapter provide suggestions of opportunities of which you might take advantage to generate some of this evidence.

Conclusion

In this chapter, you have begun to explore the constructivist way of teaching and learning. Constructivism involves combining new information and experiences with information the learner already has, enabling the learner to construct new conceptualizations that are meaningful to him or her. The text is arranged in a manner that encourages you to *interact* with the material presented rather than memorize its content. By using this text, you will be learning in a way that parallels the most effective way of teaching—the constructivist way. Enjoy your explorations!

▣ Construct and Apply

1. This chapter is organized in a constructivist-oriented format. Identify the points in the chapter at which you:
   a. Assessed your own knowledge.
   b. Obtained new information.
   c. Constructed new knowledge and understandings.

2. How would you teach a student to do tricks with a yo-yo using strategies like those in the method 1 table-building class? How would you teach a student to do tricks with a yo-yo using strategies like those in the method 2 class? What would you expect about the level of knowledge for each of these two students?

3. What goals do you have for your future students and their learning? How can constructivist methods foster these goals?

▣ Deconstructing the Standards

INTASC Principle #1 says:

> The teacher understands the central concepts, tools of inquiry, and structures of the discipline(s) he or she teaches and creates learning experiences that make these aspects of subject matter meaningful for students.

- What part(s) of this principle does this chapter address?
- How does this chapter address this principle?
- How will the concepts in this chapter help you apply this principle as a teacher?

▣ Field Experience

You will probably begin a field experience associated with this course very shortly. Do you think you will see teaching most like method 1 or method 2?

■ Your Portfolio

Activities suggested by the Building Blocks or Field Experience activities frequently provide good evidence of your progress in becoming a teacher. Start your portfolio now by obtaining a notebook or a folder and designating it as the holding place for evidence from this course. Be sure to keep graded assignments; whenever possible, keep electronic copies of the work you do.

Remember, the reflections you make about what you are learning in class and what you are learning and observing in your field placement are very valuable. Keeping track of your thoughts as you progress through your program can offer insight into your development of knowledge, skills, and professionalism.

PART I

Self

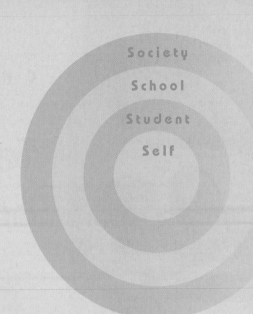

Society

School

Student

Self

Part I deals with your *self*. You already know a lot about effective teaching. In the two chapters that make up Part I, you will look at yourself as a prospective teacher. You will investigate the characteristics of excellent teachers and effective teaching, comparing your beliefs with the beliefs of others and the results of research, and using these comparisons to augment and refine your existing ideas of what it means to be an excellent teacher. In addition, you will examine your philosophical and psychological convictions about high-quality teaching, and you will compare your beliefs with the major philosophies and psychologies that form the foundation for education. Using these comparisons, you will continue to augment and refine your personal ideas of what it means to be an excellent teacher.

The primary goal of Part I is for you to construct personal and valid conceptualizations about the role of the teacher.

1

Teaching Excellence and You

> Once the classroom door closes, once the lesson begins, once the student steps toward the teacher asking for help, it is all up to the teacher, not the school. Good schools help; great schools help more; but great teachers are the far more precious commodity.
>
> PETER TEMES, PRESIDENT, THE GREAT BOOKS FOUNDATION

Schools are wonderfully rich and exciting. Students walk in the footsteps of great thinkers, explore the natural world, master and expand numerous aspects of literacy, experience the joys and inspirations of the arts, and participate in many other enriching activities.

How does this happen? Through a good teacher.

You have decided that you might want to be a teacher, and you probably believe you will be a good one. But considering the tremendous amount of information and experiences—often conflicting—to which you have been exposed, you may be asking yourself, "Just what is good teaching, anyway?"

Research shows that the teacher is the most important factor in the classroom (Legler, 2000; "Questions of Quality," 1999; "Teacher Quality," 2000). Sanders and Rivers (1996) found that not only is the teacher the single most dominant factor affecting student achievement, but that the effects of both very effective and ineffective teachers remained for at least 2 years, regardless of the effectiveness of the later teachers. In fact, according to David Imig, president and chief executive officer of the American Association of Colleges for Teacher Education, the quality of the teacher is 20 times more important in student learning than any other factor (2002). A high-quality teacher is more important to student learning than class size, funding, academic specialty, the school building or campus, the makeup of the student population, or anything else. What do you suppose Peter Temes, author of the quotation cited at the opening of this chapter, believes about the importance of teachers?

The purpose of this chapter is to help you identify qualities of teaching excellence possessed by effective teachers. You will begin by examining these factors from the perspective of your own familiarity with education. Everyone has had experiences with schools—as students, employees, volunteers, parents, concerned citizens, and just plain onlookers. From your experiences, you have acquired much knowledge and many feelings about excellence in teaching. This chapter invites you to participate in several activities designed to help you to bring your current thinking to the surface. You will be amazed at how much you already know about good teaching!

Then, you will examine public portrayals of education, as in movies, television shows, and newspaper and magazine articles—both old and new—and you will explore relationships between these portrayals and your own thoughts and feelings about teaching and education. Finally, you will compare all this with research, expert opinion, and the positions taken by professional education societies to refine your personal conceptualizations of excellent teachers and effective teaching.

As you found in Chapter 0, the constructivist perspective suggests that learning occurs best when you question your own preconceived ideas. This happens through exposure to experiences you must reconcile with the understandings you already have. This chapter sets the stage for you to identify your current understandings of excellent teachers and effective teaching and begin to question, enlarge, and refine these understandings in light of new experiences. These experiences include listening to others; watching movies and television newscasts and programs; reading newspapers and magazines; studying the work of researchers, educational experts, and psychologists; and familiarizing yourself with current standards for high-quality teachers. At the end of the chapter, you will put all this information together as you reconsider and refine your ideas about what it means to be an excellent teacher.

CHAPTER GOALS

As a result of your work in this chapter, you will:

1. Examine your beliefs about effective teaching.
2. Investigate others' beliefs about effective teaching.
3. Look at the results of research on effective teaching.
4. Consider educational experts' theories about effective teaching.
5. Survey the standards for effective teaching established by professional educational organizations.
6. Formulate your conclusions about characteristics of effective teaching.

Characteristics of Excellent Teachers and Effective Teaching: Your Beliefs

Everyone has favorite teachers. Your experience as a student has given you invaluable insight into factors that characterize excellent teachers and excellence in teaching. In fact, you may have decided to consider teaching because you were affected by a particular teacher. To begin, look at your beliefs about the characteristics of excellent teachers and effective teaching.

Your Favorite Teachers

BUILDING BLOCK
1.1

Think back to your precollege years (elementary school, middle school, junior high, or high school) or your previous college experience.

- Who were your favorite teachers? Why?
- In whose classes did you learn the most? What did these teachers do to help you learn?

- Were your favorite teachers also the teachers in whose classes you learned the most? (You may have identified the same person in your answers to both questions, or you may have identified different individuals.)
- Which characteristics on your list relate to personality?
- Which characteristics on your list relate to the teaching itself?

Now look at the opposite side.

- Who were your least favorite teachers? Why?
- In whose classes did you learn the least? Why?
- Were your least favorite teachers also the teachers in whose classes you learned the least?
- Which characteristics on your list relate to personality?
- Which characteristics on your list relate to the teaching itself?

Save this list; you will use it again later.

You probably ended up with a fairly long list of your favorite teachers' attributes. Note that you have been considering two separate but related notions: personality characteristics and teaching characteristics. Students in introductory education classes similar to yours have come up with many characteristics they identify with excellent teachers and effective teaching. Words used by these students to identify *personality* characteristics are shown in Figure 1.1.

Characteristics of *effective teaching* described by students are shown in Figure 1.2.

What can you conclude about the characteristics of excellent teachers and effective teaching? It seems clear that several characteristics identify excellent teachers and effective teaching, and that different students identify different characteristics. Some of these characteristics reflect the teacher's personality and some reflect the teacher's instructional skill.

Personality plays a large role in teaching. Perhaps someone who knows you well has told you, "You'd be a good teacher!" Has this person ever seen you teach in a classroom? Probably not. What made this person think you would be a good teacher? It must be something about your personality. Maybe you have had experience working with young people. Some people seem to attract small children; others seem able to establish an immediate rapport with young adults. Maybe you are a "good explainer" and have found that others understand ideas better thanks to something you said or demonstrated. People who possess this connection with children and young adults have not necessarily had

Courtesy of David Ottenstein Photography

What are the characteristics of an excellent teacher?

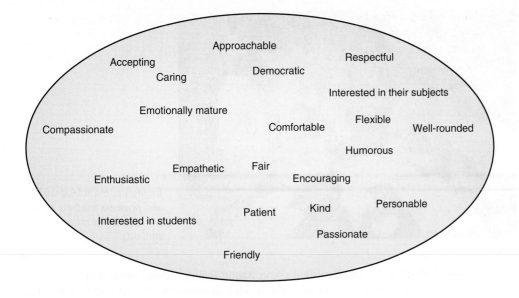

figure 1.1
Personality characteristics of excellent teachers identified by students.

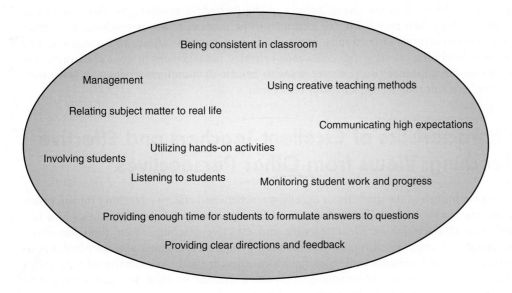

figure 1.2
Characteristics of effective teaching identified by students.

actual teaching experience. Yet something about their personalities enables them to establish the kind of relationship that is foundational in creating a learning environment.

Instructional skills also factor into effective teaching. Berliner (1985) identifies three components of instructional skills:

- **Planning:** Skills that occur before the instruction, including planning for content, time allocation, grouping, pacing, and student activities.
- **Implementation:** Skills that occur during the instruction, including monitoring student understanding during the lesson, adjusting the lesson to meet unexpected requirements, questioning, communicating high expectations, managing small and large group activities, and minimizing off-task behaviors.
- **Reflection and assessment:** Skills that occur after the instruction, including assessment of student performance, feedback, reflection, and management of tests and grades.

These skills can be learned, practiced, and refined. You will focus on developing the full array of teaching skills in your teacher preparation program.

Engaging, knowledgeable, and positive teachers make learning enjoyable for students.

In Building Block 1.1, you identified some strong feelings about what qualities effective and ineffective *teachers* possess and about what constitutes effective and ineffective *teaching*. The characteristics you remember of the effective teachers are those you most want to emulate. And the characteristics of the ineffective teachers are those you most want to avoid. You may want, for example, to be passionate about teaching; to explain concepts so everyone understands; and to be caring, compassionate, and communicative while maintaining effective and consistent behavior management in your classroom. But under *no* circumstances do you ever want to belittle or humiliate students or have ineffective behavior management in your classroom.

Characteristics of Excellent Teachers and Effective Teaching: Views from Other Perspectives

You have looked at the qualities of excellent teachers and effective teaching through your experiences as a student. Those experiences have given you invaluable insights into factors that characterize excellent teachers and effective teaching. Your thoughts about teaching and education also may be influenced by other experiences you have had. Let us look at teacher excellence and teaching effectiveness from the perspective of a parent, a teacher's aide, a school volunteer, a company executive or local business owner who might hire graduates from the local school system, or a concerned, tax-paying citizen.

BUILDING BLOCK 1.2

Other Perspectives

Think of teachers from the viewpoint of an outsider. You might want to imagine you are a specific outsider, such as a parent, or you might want to consider your own parents when they were in school.

- Taking the outsider's viewpoint, list the characteristics about teachers you would consider to be effective.
- Taking the outsider's viewpoint, list the characteristics about the teachers you consider to be the least effective.
- Did you identify new characteristics or any characteristics different from the ones you cited in Building Block 1.1?
- What concerns influenced your perspective in this Building Block?

Save your list; you will use it again later.

Are the characteristics of quality teaching you identified from the perspective of an outsider the same as those you identified from the perspective of a student? In all probability, there were differences. As students, we value certain characteristics of teachers; as parents or other outsiders, we may find we value other attributes. For example, as a student, you may put very high value on mutual respect between teacher and student and on classroom order. As a parent, however, you may place higher priority on attributes such as communication with the home and student performance on achievement tests.

As you have seen, there are different ways of looking at what constitutes quality in teaching. Perspective is influenced by the stakes someone has in education. A student's perspective is likely to be different from a parent's; the stakes are different. Can you see how they are different?

Components of Effective Teaching

We have been discussing two aspects of effective teaching: attributes of excellent *teachers* (personality) and attributes of effective *teaching* (instructional skill). We can construct a Venn diagram showing these two categories in two overlapping circles. (See Figure 1.3.) One circle is labeled *Personality Characteristics* and contains the personality traits that you indicated are associated with effective teaching. For example, the attributes of *caring, fair,* and *friendly* would be listed in this circle. The other circle is labeled *Instructional Skills* and contains the instructional abilities that you indicated are associated with effective teaching, such as providing clear directions and utilizing hands-on materials.

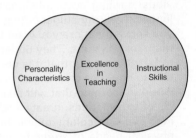

Figure 1.3
Venn diagram showing attributes of personality and instructional skill.

Many attributes we associate with excellence in teaching are functions of both personality and instructional skill; these attributes occupy the area of intersection of the two circles, which is labeled *Excellence in Teaching*. For example, teachers whose lessons are clear and understandable know how to teach the concepts in the lessons, and also act in an understanding and encouraging way while they teach the lessons. Teachers who succeed in engaging students in their learning also are accepting and **empathetic**. Teachers whose students have a sincere desire to learn also are fair, reliable, and often humorous.

It is important to realize that you do *not* have to possess all the personality characteristics that have been identified to be an effective teacher. However, if any are identified that you feel might help you become a more effective teacher, by all means try to assimilate them. For example, if you learned that effective teachers exhibit a sense of humor, you might try to kid or joke with your students a bit more.

This Venn diagram may also be used to show how the art of teaching and the science of teaching come together to form excellence. The art of teaching often is considered a function of personality, and the science of teaching often is considered a function of instructional skill. When both are effective, we have an effective teacher.

Characteristics of Excellent Teachers and Effective Teaching: Views from Teachers

Some of the best information about the desirable characteristics of teachers comes from teachers themselves. Throughout this textbook we include "From the Teacher" features, in which outstanding teachers from across the United States describe their thoughts about various topics from the point of view of the classroom teacher. Nearly all of these teachers have been named Teacher of the Year in their respective states as testimony to their excellence. Let us see what one Teacher of the Year has to say about effective teachers and teaching.

In a world of rapidly shrinking education budgets and ever-increasing concerns about new government mandates, my philosophy behind what I do every day in the classroom does not change—teach all children! Albert Einstein said what is so applicable in my classroom: "It is the supreme art of the teacher to awaken joy in creative expression and knowledge." It is this thinking that drives me to inspire young minds and empower them to seek creative expression and knowledge in a student-centered, engaging classroom. I believe that I, as a teacher, must recognize and develop the potential in all students through challenging and stimulating material that is directly related to their lives. I build on their previous learning accomplishments and tackle their challenges. I tell my students that the quotation "the more you know, the more you want to grow" will ring true for them for a lifetime. They understand that it is not wrong to be ignorant but that it is wrong to stay ignorant. Students should be challenged to immerse themselves in a world of learning that will take them to the highest levels of expectations, greatest wisdom, and lifelong striving. The curriculum meets the academic, social, and physical needs of students, while challenging them to discover their inherent curiosities in a world that is constantly changing.

I know that I must actively involve parents as co-teachers in the classroom by providing varied opportunities to engage in my classroom as curriculum presenters, field study chaperones, writing coaches, mock trial attorney coaches, and service project supporters. As teachers we must understand that parents are their child's first teacher. We must see our students through the eyes of the parents and build relationships with families. Meeting students and families on their playing fields of life bridges the world of school to the world of family and community and unites us as scholars in a quest for a common goal— lifelong learning in an ever-changing, global world, while maximizing each child's potential.

I know students must learn to think critically and then develop conclusions that will result in more questions and a quest for more answers. "The one real object of education is to have a man in the condition of continually asking questions" (Creighton). This happens when teachers challenge students' thinking and then offer a safe environment for inquiry. I do this best when I open myself to building relationships with my students—sharing my own challenges and celebrations and allowing them to share theirs.

It happens when I welcome students with a smile and personal comment into a classroom filled with warm, glowing lamps, framed prints, and rugs; as I sit among them in a group discussion listening and questioning; and as I learn along with my students and admit that we can research the answer together. It happens, too, as I understand that no two students learn the same way, and I vary my teaching style and differentiate learning.

I know that teachers must respect students and seek to understand their complex world of emotional highs and lows. If a teacher backs a child into a corner, that child will come out fighting. I rely on the philosophy in my classroom that I used with my own four children—give children choices, but make sure that all the choices are good ones. I know this works; I have not written a discipline notice in my classroom in years. My students understand that they have control of their learning and behavior.

I know my personal teaching style and philosophy. Both were acknowledged by a student teacher who said to me, "I've never seen so much learning in such a creative classroom. Students are actively participating by researching, questioning, discussing, and moving from activity to activity, and even actively involved in teacher instruction." This style reflects my philosophy about awakening the joy in creative expression and knowledge. It is not one that came easily or overnight.

Teachers must constantly research new strategies in order to facilitate learning and bring the curriculum to life. We must be willing to recognize that students' explorations and investigations may lead a lesson in another direction—we must celebrate their insights! We must adopt a philosophy of teaching that says we can make a difference in our students' lives—one child at a time! We do this as we facilitate a classroom that leads students to understand the challenges of a constantly changing world and as we lead them to discover for themselves new and deeper truths with real problems that are relevant to the past, present, and future.

2005 South Carolina Teacher of the Year
Summit Parkway Middle School
Richland School District Two
Columbia, South Carolina

Characteristics of Excellent Teachers and Effective Teaching: The Media

You have examined teaching from your personal experience as a student and from experiences that you may have had in other roles in schools. But there is still more information to consider in thinking about excellence in teaching.

Let us look at the issue of effective teaching from the perspective of the media.

Teachers in Films

Movies sometimes portray fictional conceptualizations of teachers and teaching based on true stories. Although intended for entertainment, these movies present some insight into society's general views of what teachers do, and they may depict examples of both effective and ineffective teaching. For example, *Dangerous Minds* (Smith, 1995), based on fact, stars Michelle Pfeiffer as Lou Ann Johnson, an ex-Marine who wants to become a high school English teacher. Her first class comprises supposed troublemakers who seem to have more important things to take care of than learning poetry. To gain control and the ability to teach, Ms. Johnson uses unconventional techniques, such as teaching karate and reciting Bob Dylan lyrics, as she tries to associate school with her students' lives. This film shows many characteristics of excellence in teaching, such as relating subject matter to real life; involving students and listening to them; and being caring, accepting, compassionate, and mature.

© Barbara Laing/Time Life Pictures/Getty Images

Lou Ann Johnson (center) with former students

Jaime Escalante

Stand and Deliver (Menendez, 1988) is the true story of Jaime Escalante, a tough high school mathematics teacher who motivates his classes of potential losers to amazing achievements. Mr. Escalante believes in his students; holds extremely high expectations; and exhibits great enthusiasm, interest, and passion for his subject—all qualities of an excellent teacher.

BUILDING
BLOCK
1.3

Movies about Teachers

Do you remember watching movies that deal with teaching? What specific characteristics of effective teaching can you recall? It is well known that Hollywood often skews reality. What do these movies tell the public about teachers and teaching? Based on the understandings of teaching you have developed so far, do you believe that the teaching characteristics portrayed are realistic?

You might enjoy watching one or more movies that portray teachers. A few examples include *The Breakfast Club*; *The Emperor's Club*; *Fast Times at Ridgemont High*; *Ferris Bueller's Day Off*; *Good Morning, Miss Toliver* (available through the Public Broadcasting System, PBS); *Kindergarten Cop*; *October Sky*; *Summer School*; *Teachers*; and *To Sir, with Love*.

While you are watching these movies, ask yourself questions such as the following, which are based on the material you have been studying so far:

- How is the teaching done?
- What are the movie teacher's most effective characteristics?
- What are the teacher's least effective characteristics?
- What are the most and the least effective lessons?
- What makes them so?

Teachers on TV and in the News

The information you get from journalists may play a role in forming your opinions about the characteristics of effective teaching. You get this information from television shows, TV newscasts and news programs, newspapers, magazines, radio, and the Internet. Television is an important source of information. For example, you may have seen episodes of the popular teacher-focused television show *Boston Public*. This show offered a fictional, behind-the-scenes look at the professional and personal lives of teachers and ad-

Student Reactions to the Portrayal of Teachers in Films

Dead Poets Society (1989) stars Robin Williams. In this movie, Mr. Keating, a literature teacher, pushes his students to be involved, to think, and to use their minds. His teaching style is unconventional and opposes the traditional lecture method, with its requirements for accurate recitation.

Below are reactions from students in introductory education classes, written in response to *Dead Poets Society*:

When I become a teacher, I would like to mimic some of Mr. Keating's teaching styles. I like the idea of his unconventional methods of teaching. He was always able to maintain the interest of the class. Lessons were taught in an interesting and fun way. I liked the idea of eliminating the parts of the curriculum that seem to be irrelevant to real life. I think Mr. Keating had good intentions. He knew how to get the students to learn and want to participate. However, I think he seemed to want to be more their peer than their teacher.

The underlying current in Mr. Keating's philosophy is that he is creative, if not wildly creative. He constantly keeps his students guessing what he will do next and he constantly challenges the students to question what they know or what they think they know. I believe that as educators, when we encounter uncertain territory, we tend to fall back on what we know or how we were taught—lecturing to the class, telling them what they should know, asking mindless questions, and doing exercises from the back of the chapter. When I teach I want to be unafraid, bold, and ambitious.

In *Mr. Holland's Opus* (1995, starring Richard Dreyfuss), Mr. Holland, a music teacher, has been trying all year to teach his music students to appreciate the classics, with little success. He is frustrated; his students are bored. In an attempt to relate the material to his students' lives, he begins a lesson by playing what the students think are excerpts from a popular song. All the students can name the song and the artist. They are surprised, however, when Mr. Holland reveals that the piece was actually written by a classical composer and then used by the popular band. Following this, the students are eager to learn more.

College students wrote the following reactions to Mr. Holland and his qualities as a teacher:

At the beginning of the movie, Mr. Holland personified many of those qualities that are not wanted in a teacher. He had poor lecture skills, taught straight out of the book, was not enthusiastic, and did not want to be in the classroom. As he learned the tricks of the trade, he began to incorporate many interesting techniques into his teaching. He involved the students, included real-life scenarios, was creative, and was very passionate about his profession. His transformation from one of the worst teachers to one of the greatest teachers shows that while he didn't have the qualities of a good teacher in the beginning, he still had the heart—and that is what made him a good teacher.

In the beginning of the movie, Mr. Holland showed many weaknesses and was less than a dedicated teacher. He came to school just to teach his classes, and he left immediately after classes were over each day. He didn't spend one minute longer in school than was absolutely necessary. Although at first he seemed to be harsh with his students, there were some teaching strengths that were evident right away. He was extremely knowledgeable in what he taught, and he seemed to want his students to love music as much as he did. As time went on, he found ways to involve students by showing them the connections and similarities between the pop music they were familiar with and classical music. This reinforces my idea that you, the teacher, must create new, fresh, and exciting ways to teach or you will not be able to hold the interests of the students. You must keep trying until you find a method that works. I hope my future students will see me as a vital part of their lives and as someone who cared and made a difference.

ministrators at a mid-size high school. Examples of both effective and ineffective teaching practices were shown in each episode.

Network and local TV stations frequently report on teachers and school activities and sometimes present opposing sides of controversial issues, such as the growing controversy over the benefits of the Head Start program discussed on National Public Radio (Jones, 2005).

Print material also is a very important source of information about education. Newspapers and popular magazines regularly report on educational issues and offer pros and cons related to education, for example, the controversy surrounding the use of standardized tests in making high-stakes education decisions.

You will have many opportunities to think through educational issues during this course. Be sure to keep up with the current news and opinions about education given by

Can you think of other TV shows about schools and teachers or other aspects of education? How are the teachers portrayed?

the media. For each, ask yourself, "Is this news story realistic? Does this item *really* portray education as we know it?"

Characteristics of Excellent Teachers and Effective Teaching: The Experts

You have looked at effective and ineffective teachers and teaching from three viewpoints: yourself as a student, yourself in other roles, and the media. You have also heard ideas from students in your class and read ideas generated by students in other classes and by a practicing teacher. You have identified what you believe are the most important attributes of effective teachers and teaching and of ineffective teachers and teaching, thereby becoming conscious of your thoughts about what constitutes good and bad teaching. How do your thoughts compare with those of the experts?

Several quotations written by individuals deeply involved with education follow. How strongly do you agree or disagree with each?

> That type of scholarship which is bent on remembering things in order to answer people's questions does not qualify one to be a teacher.
>
> CONFUCIUS

> The teacher's job is limited to offering the materials, and it suffices if she demonstrates their use; after that, she leaves the child with his work. Our goal is not so much the imparting of knowledge as the unveiling and developing of spiritual energy.
>
> MARIA MONTESSORI

> The man who can make hard things easy is the educator.
>
> RALPH WALDO EMERSON

> I have one rule—attention. They give me theirs and I give them mine.
>
> SISTER EVANGELIST, RSM, TEACHER IN MONTANA

> I had learned to respect the intelligence, integrity, creativity, and capacity for deep thought and hard work latent somewhere in every child; they had learned that I differed from them only in years and experience, and that I, an ordinary human being, loved and respected them. I expected payment in kind.
>
> SYBIL MARSHALL, ON 18 YEARS AS A TEACHER IN A ONE-ROOM SCHOOLHOUSE IN RURAL ENGLAND

> You cannot teach a man anything; you can only help him find it within himself.
>
> GALILEO

> A child must feel the flush of victory and the heart-sinking of disappointment before he takes with a will to the tasks distasteful to him and resolves to dance his way through a dull routine of textbooks.
>
> HELEN KELLER

A teacher must believe in the value and interest of his subject as a doctor believes in health.

GILBERT HIGHET, *THE ART OF TEACHING*

Teaching is an instinctual art, mindful of potential, craving of realization, a pausing, seamless process.

A. BARTLETT GIAMATTI, PRESIDENT, YALE UNIVERSITY, 1978–1986,
AND PRESIDENT, NATIONAL BASEBALL LEAGUE, 1986–1989

Much that passes for education is not education at all but ritual.

DAVID P. GARDNER, PRESIDENT, UNIVERSITY OF UTAH, 1973–1983

We don't receive wisdom; we discover it for ourselves after a journey that no one can take for us or spare us.

MARCEL PROUST

The extent to which you agree or disagree with these statements may be an indicator of how you are constructing your ideas about effective teaching. All these quotations are from outstanding educators. Were any of them particularly meaningful to you? There are literally thousands of memorable quotations on education by outstanding individuals. You will find many scattered throughout this book. Consider starting a collection of meaningful quotations to read when you want inspiration or when the going gets tough.

Many prominent educators have suggested basic qualities of effective teaching. Gurney Chambers, former dean of the College of Education at Western Carolina University, identified five fundamental traits common to what he called "great teachers" (Chambers, 2000):

1. Great teachers are empathetic and see things from the students' perspectives.
2. Great teachers are energetic.
3. Great teachers have high expectations.
4. Great teachers are concerned with the whole child.
5. Great teachers perceive the hidden curriculum (the learning that goes on but that is not part of the daily course of study) in the classroom.

Parker Palmer, senior associate of the American Association for Higher Education and designer of the Teacher Formation Program for K–12 teachers, reinforces the observation that excellent teachers demonstrate a variety of personality traits and classroom skills. Additionally, Palmer says excellent teachers show that they value academic and personal relationships with their students, whereas poor teachers seem disconnected from their students and seem to work at keeping the academic material disconnected with the result that students can neither establish relationships with the information nor take ownership of it (Palmer, 1998).

Characteristics of Excellent Teachers and Effective Teaching: The Research

Let us look at what researchers have said about effective teachers and teaching. We refer to educational research throughout this textbook. Educational research takes many forms and serves many functions, but its primary purpose is to inform the educator on issues of best practice. As a student preparing to enter the field of education, you are advised to study the referenced material, question the usefulness of its results to classroom practice, and determine whether you accept its conclusions. Questioning is the key to intelligent consumption of research. When you question, you become a proactive consumer of research. Ask yourself some questions, such as those that follow, as you review research reports:

- What is the purpose of the research?
- Who is the intended audience?
- What methodology did the researchers use?
- Does the analysis seem valid?
- Is the research useful to teachers?

Much educational research has focused on characteristics of quality teaching from the perspectives of different groups of people. From the accounts that follow, try to gain an idea of some of the commonalities and some of the differences in thinking among different groups about the characteristics of excellence in teaching.

Research Involving Perceptions

A considerable amount of the research involving characteristics of effective teaching has dealt with the **perceptions** students have of their teachers. Minor et al. (2000) asked students in introductory education classes to identify the characteristics of excellent teachers. The authors grouped the characteristics identified by the students into seven basic categories:

- Student-centeredness
- Effective classroom and behavior management
- Competent instruction
- Ethics
- Enthusiasm about teaching
- Knowledge of subject
- Personableness

Young et al. (1998) examined characteristics of effective teachers perceived by students at different levels of maturity: high school, college freshmen, and college seniors.

© Photodisc Collection/Getty Images

Students appreciate teachers who are inspiring, communicative, enthusiastic, knowledgeable, and caring.

These researchers found that the two most important indicators of teacher effectiveness according to these students are how knowledgeable the teacher is and how much the students learn. They also identified humor in the classroom, the ability to inspire students, effective parent–teacher communications, and friendliness as important attributes.

Some educational research has involved practicing teachers. In one study, Norton (1997) found that first-year teachers described effective teachers in the following ways:

- Caring
- Committed
- Highly creative
- Reflective
- Having a "strong internal **locus of control**" (believing in one's own abilities)

Other educational research has focused on the perceptions of people of different nationalities, affiliations, **socioeconomic** groups, and **ethnicities.** For example, Papandreou (1995) conducted a survey of graduating high school seniors in Greece. The survey was similar to the activities you did earlier, drawing on your experiences as a student in recalling your most effective teachers. These high school seniors identified the following characteristics as the most important in effective teaching:

- Correcting student errors
- Displaying liveliness during lessons
- Ending the lesson with a content review
- Giving clear and complete directions
- Including variety in teaching practices
- Making eye contact with students
- Moving around the room
- Using appropriate student ideas

McDermott and Rothenberg (2000) studied the perceptions of effective teachers in a high-poverty urban neighborhood. They found that exemplary urban teachers are those who build respectful and trusting relationships with students and their families. Students felt that effective teachers are those who show respect, provide comfort, provide personal connections, exhibit humor, and use a variety of learning techniques. Parents felt that effective teachers are those who have positive relationships with the children and good communication with the parents.

> How are the characteristics of effective teachers identified through research similar to those you identified?

Positive student-teacher relationships are essential for optimal student motivation and achievement.

© Stewart Cohen/Getty Images

Prater et al. (1995) studied perceptions of Native American students in grades 3–12 regarding effective practices of non-Native teachers. They found that the following characteristics were most valued:

- Avoiding talking too fast
- Having a positive attitude
- Not giving boring lectures
- Not making fun of Native culture
- Showing a sense of humor
- Showing respect, kindness, and patience
- Teaching the concepts of responsibility, honesty, tolerance, and the Golden Rule
- Treating students with respect
- Using a variety of learning methods
- Using hands-on projects

How do the characteristics of effective teachers identified by students in cultures different from yours resemble or differ from the characteristics you identified? Are there commonalities? What does this imply about teaching effectively in a multicultural classroom?

Research Involving Student Achievement

Research on effective teachers and teaching often is tied to student achievement. In this view, the measure of a teacher's excellence is how well his or her students perform. As Ballou (1999) writes, everything a teacher does should be aimed at improving student learning. In a study that **correlated** effective teaching practices with student achievement, Kemp and Hall (1992) found that achievement is linked to these issues:

- Teacher competence
- Lesson presentation
- Review
- Skill practice
- Teacher questioning techniques
- Discipline
- Effective patterns of instruction

Kemp and Hall also stressed the importance of a teacher's recognition of the dignity and worth of each student and expression of the belief that each student has the ability to achieve if taught effectively.

As you review this abbreviated collection of information presented by research and prominent educators, you can see that effective teaching is characterized by myriad factors, many of which you have already identified. These factors seem to center on instructional skill and the teacher's relationship with students.

Characteristics of Excellent Teachers and Effective Teaching: Psychologists

What do psychologists say about effective teachers? Educational psychologists are psychologists whose primary interest is in the area of education. Some educational psychologists work with students in schools, some work with school accountability and administrative programs, and some specialize in research. We will focus our attention on the psychologists who specialize in research. More detail about major psychologies of learning is given in Chapter 2.

Glasser and the Quality School

William Glasser (pictured here) is one of America's pioneer educational psychologists. Trained as a psychiatrist, he became interested in education in the 1960s and 1970s. He developed the Quality School approach in which he holds that all human beings have five basic needs: love, power, freedom, fun, and survival. In Glasser's approach, the basic premise of quality education is that "we will work hard for those we care for [*love*], for those we respect and who respect us (*power*), for those who allow us to think and act for ourselves (*freedom*), for those with whom we laugh (*fun*), and for those who help us make our lives secure (*survival*)" (Glasser, 1993, p. 30). He identifies six basic conditions under which quality teaching is done in school:

© Craig Ferre Photography/Courtesy W. Glasser Institute

1. There must be a warm, supportive classroom environment.
2. Students should be asked to do only meaningful work.
3. Students are always asked to do the best they can do.
4. Students are asked to evaluate their own work and improve it.
5. Quality work is always good.
6. Quality work is never destructive. (Glasser, 1993, p. 22–25)

Glasser believes that good teachers are those who design lessons and create learning environments that are relevant and satisfying to students.

 The *Building Teachers* companion website has a direct link to the Glasser Institute website, where you can find out more about Glasser's ideas about effective teaching.

The Quality School

Look again at the six conditions of the Quality School outlined by Glasser. How do these conditions compare with the characteristics of effective teaching you have listed?

BUILDING BLOCK 1.4

Combs and Perceptual Psychology

Arthur Combs (1993) investigated what makes people good "helpers" (including teachers, counselors, clergy, nurses, and therapists). Combs (pictured here) concluded that what makes an effective helper is *not* knowledge and *not* methodology. Rather, the effectiveness of a helping professional is a result primarily of that individual's *beliefs* (or perceptions). Teachers and other helping professionals behave in terms of their beliefs. Combs identified five areas of beliefs:

Courtesy of The Field Psych Trust

Beliefs about the kind of data to which we should be tuned: Good helpers tune into data concerned with *people* questions; poor helpers tune into data concerned with *things* questions.

Beliefs about what people are like: Good helpers believe people are *able*; poor helpers *doubt* that people are able.

Beliefs about self (self-concept): Good helpers see the self in essentially positive ways and are self-actualizing; poor helpers see the self in essentially negative ways.

Beliefs about purpose (what is truly important): Good helpers see their purpose to be essentially a *freeing* behavior; poor helpers see their purpose to be essentially a *controlling* behavior.

Beliefs about methods: Good helpers utilize *self-revealing* methods; poor helpers utilize *self-concealing* methods.

Beliefs are innate and are integrated into one's personality. They are based on the life experiences that occur from earliest childhood onward. We cling to our beliefs because they are deeply rooted in our experience. Beliefs drive people's actions. Combs tells the story of a little boy who was lost in the halls of his elementary school on the first day of school. The principal saw the boy and escorted him to his classroom. The teacher, who was in the middle of a lesson, stopped and went to greet the boy, who was worried about being late. She showed she believed that this boy was important when she said, "Welcome! I am so glad you are here!" rather than scolding him for being late.

If a teacher believes Melissa is a troublemaker, the teacher unconsciously will interpret some of Melissa's behaviors as disruptive and will act accordingly. Similarly, if you, the teacher, believe that each student can learn, you will act differently from the teacher who believes there always will be one or two students each year who simply do not have what it takes to learn.

What do you believe about students? Do you believe all students are capable and can learn? What do you believe about yourself as a teacher? How do your beliefs compare with those identified by Combs as integral to effective teachers?

Good teachers examine their beliefs and change them in light of new evidence. Is this difficult? Yes. It is possible? Most assuredly. Because teacher beliefs are so crucial to professional behavior, we ask you to examine your beliefs on a number of issues and factors throughout this textbook.

The quotations that follow about the power of beliefs seem appropriate.

Whatever one believes to be true either is true or becomes true in one's mind.

JOHN C. LILLY

The real difficulty in changing the course of any enterprise lies not in developing new ideas but in escaping from the old ones.

JOHN MAYNARD KEYES

There is a principle which is a bar against all information, which is proof against all arguments, and which cannot fail to keep a man in everlasting ignorance—that principle is contempt prior to investigation.

HERBERT SPENCER

Perhaps the most important single cause of a person's success or failure educationally has to do with the question of what he believes about himself.

ARTHUR COMBS

Characteristics of Excellent Teachers and Effective Teaching: The Federal Government

Even the federal government has become involved in the discussion of the characteristics of effective teachers and teaching. On January 8, 2002, President George W. Bush signed into law the No Child Left Behind Act of 2001. This Act increases the federal role in K–12 education and aims to close the achievement gap between disadvantaged and minority students and their peers. The Act is based on four basic principles (U.S. Department of Education, 2002):

1. Stronger accountability for results
2. More choices for parents and students
3. Increased flexibility and local control
4. Emphasis on teaching methods that have been proved to work

The Act specifically addresses the quality of American teachers and aims to increase the academic achievement of all students by enhancing the quality of their teachers. High-quality teachers are defined as those who demonstrate subject matter knowledge and skills in basic subject areas. It requires that all teachers in core academic areas meet the requirement of being "highly qualified" by 2006. "Highly qualified" in the Act means that all teachers in core academic subjects must be licensed by the state in which they teach, hold at least a bachelor's degree, and demonstrate competence in their subject area as determined by the state. You will investigate many of the provisions of this legislation in this course.

Direct links to the *No Child Left Behind* Executive Summary and the NCLB home page are available on the *Building Teachers* companion website.

Characteristics of Excellent Teachers and Effective Teaching: Professional Standards

You have done a great deal of work constructing your understanding of what effective teaching is. Now, let us look at statements from professional bodies within the teaching profession itself. After all, it is those in the teaching profession who set the professional standards. Over the past decade, education professionals have worked to build a quality system to assure that every child is taught by a caring and competent teacher. Several important groups have established standards for quality teaching and the preparation of high-quality teachers. These groups include the National Council for Accreditation of Teacher Education (NCATE), the Interstate New Teacher Assessment and Support Consortium (INTASC), the National Board for Professional Teaching Standards (NBPTS), and individual state licensing agencies. These groups are staffed by educators and obtain extensive input from other educators in shaping their standards. They all have one interest in mind—to staff every classroom with high-quality teachers.

Let us look at the standards of these national organizations. As you are examining the standards, compare them with the ideas you constructed about the characteristics and attributes of excellent teachers and excellent teaching. Are they similar?

National Council for Accreditation of Teacher Education (NCATE)

NCATE is one of the primary bodies responsible for accrediting teacher preparation institutions. **Accreditation** means that an institution has met all formal official requirements of excellence described in professional standards developed by the professionals in that discipline. Institutions accredited by NCATE have met rigorous, NCATE-established standards for the preparation of teachers. In many states, teacher preparation institutions are required to be accredited by NCATE in order for their graduates to be eligible for teaching certification in that state. The Teacher Education Accreditation Council (TEAC) also accredits teacher preparation institutions, and the American Association of Colleges for Teacher Education (AACTE) is developing standards for the preparation of teachers. However, NCATE is the largest and most well known accreditation body.

NCATE is a coalition of more than 30 national associations that represent all aspects of the education profession. Its mission is to employ peer review processes to ensure that NCATE-accredited institutions produce "competent, caring, and qualified teachers and other professional school personnel who can help all students learn" (National Council

A direct link to the website of the National Association for the Accreditation of Teacher Education, where you can find complete information about NCATE, is available on the *Building Teachers* companion website.

for the Accreditation of Teacher Education, 2002, p.1). In 2005, 702 (50%) of the 1,399 teacher preparation institutions in the United States were accredited by or were candidates for accreditation by NCATE. Institutions are reviewed every 5 or 7 years for compliance with the standards, depending on the agreements between NCATE and the state. Reviews are made by a committee of professors from other NCATE-accredited teacher preparation institutions, who are trained by NCATE and who are assembled as a team to review a specific institution.

NCATE requires teacher preparation institutions to meet the criteria inherent in six broad standards. The standards (NCATE, 2002) were developed by professionals in the field of teacher education and deal with

1. candidate knowledge, skills, and dispositions;
2. assessment system and unit evaluation;
3. field experience and clinical practice;
4. diversity;
5. faculty qualifications, performance, and development; and
6. unit governance and resources.

Standard 1 identifies standards for effective teacher candidates. The standards describe basic characteristics of excellent teachers.

NCATE Standards for Effective Teacher Candidates

1. *Content knowledge.* Teacher candidates know the subject matter that they plan to teach and can explain important principles and concepts delineated in professional, state, and institutional standards.
2. *Pedagogical content knowledge.* Teacher candidates have a broad knowledge of instructional strategies that draws upon content and pedagogical knowledge and skills delineated in professional, state, and institutional standards to help all students learn. They facilitate student learning of the subject matter through presentation of the content in clear and meaningful ways and through the integration of technology.
3. *Professional and pedagogical knowledge and skills.* Teacher candidates can apply their professional and pedagogical knowledge and skills delineated in professional, state, and institutional standards to facili-

tate learning. They consider the school, family, and community contexts in which they work and the prior experience of students to develop meaningful learning experiences.

4. *Dispositions.* Candidates are familiar with the dispositions expected of professionals. Their work with students, families, and communities reflects the dispositions delineated in professional, state, and institutional standards.
5. *Student learning.* Teacher candidates focus on student learning as shown in their assessment of student learning, use of assessments in instruction, and development of meaningful learning experiences for students based on their developmental levels and prior experience. (National Council for the Accreditation of Teacher Education, 2002)

How are the NCATE standards consistent with the characteristics of effective teachers you identified?

Interstate New Teacher Assessment and Support Consortium (INTASC)

INTASC is a group of educators representing state education agencies, higher education institutions, and national educational organizations. As described in Chapter 0, INTASC has developed a set of standards that represent state and professional views of proficient teaching (Interstate New Teacher Assessment and Support Consortium, 1992). The standards are summarized in 10 principles that characterize effective teachers and teaching. These principles are designed to be compatible with the certification standards of the National Board for Professional Teaching Standards (next section) and are used by many institutions as benchmarks for effective teacher preparation programs. Indeed, many institutions show how their programs are aligned with the INTASC principles. The principles are listed inside the back cover.

National Board for Professional Teaching Standards (NBPTS)

Teachers can acquire certification at the national level after they have been certified at the state level and have taught for at least three years. National certification, recognized in all states, shows that the teacher has demonstrated characteristics and competence of the highest order. National certification is a long and demanding process administered by NBPTS. It requires passing a difficult multiple-choice examination and receiving passing scores on a series of portfolios demonstrating the candidate's teaching of certain lessons, reflections on the planning and results of the lessons, proposed changes, and interpretations of the instructional activity in terms of sound instructional practice. Review of these materials is carried out by groups of teachers and other education professionals who have been trained in the rubrics used to assess the materials.

The NBPTS consists of classroom teachers and public school administrators. Its mission is to advance the quality of teaching and learning through the following activities:

- Maintaining high and rigorous standards for what accomplished teachers should know and be able to do
- Providing a national voluntary system certifying teachers who meet these standards
- Advocating related education reforms to integrate national board certification in American education and to capitalize on the expertise of national board–certified teachers (National Board for Professional Teaching Standards, 1999)

NBPTS identifies five core propositions that describe the knowledge, skills, and dispositions that characterize accomplished teaching.

> Direct links to the websites of the Interstate New Teacher Assessment and Support Consortium (INTASC) and the National Board for Professional Teaching Standards (NBPTS) are available on the *Building Teachers* companion website.

The Five Core Propositions of the National Board for Professional Teaching Standards

- Teachers are committed to students and their learning.
- Teachers know the subjects they teach and how to teach those subjects to students.
- Teachers are responsible for managing and monitoring student learning.
- Teachers think systematically about their practice and learn from experience.
- Teachers are members of National Board for Professional Teaching Standards of learning communities.

Competency Standards

BUILDING BLOCK 1.5

Each institution with teacher preparation programs develops or subscribes to standards that describe the competencies the institution expects its teacher candidate graduates to demonstrate.

Obtain a copy of your institution's teacher preparation competency standards. Compare them with the NCATE and the INTASC standards.

- How are they similar?
- How are they different?

Keep these standards to help you focus your thinking as you progress through this course.

State Certification Requirements

Each state has its own set of initial certification requirements. Find your state's education preparation and certification requirements; these requirements have great influence on the nature and content of your teacher preparation program. Compare these requirements to the competencies and dispositions you will be required to demonstrate as you progress through your program. You will satisfy some of these requirements in this course. You will satisfy others in future courses. You will satisfy still others in your field experiences.

BUILDING BLOCK 1.6

Assessment of Your Field Experiences

As teacher candidates progress through their programs, the teaching and professional behavior they exhibit during field experiences and student teaching are evaluated using criteria that correlate with standards developed by state and national accreditation agencies.

- What competencies are you expected to demonstrate in your field experiences?
- How do these competencies compare with the professional standards?

Putting It All Together

From your explorations in this chapter, you can see that many characteristics contribute to excellence in teachers and teaching. You have investigated these characteristics from numerous sources: yourselves as students, yourselves as outsiders, the media, some research, some expert educators, some psychologists, the federal government, and professional education organizations. Now it is time for you to summarize all this material. In so doing, you will continue to construct your own ideas as to what constitutes a good teacher and good teaching.

Your conclusions are entirely your own, formed on the basis of your personal experiences and previous knowledge, as well as the new information to which you have been exposed in class and by reading this chapter. There are no right or wrong responses to this activity. Your response is yours and yours alone. However, there are valid conclusions. You can validate your conclusions by reflecting on the progression of your thinking as you read through this chapter and participated in the suggested activities. Perhaps your ideas about effective teaching have been reinforced. Perhaps you have integrated some new ideas into your original understanding. Perhaps your original understanding has undergone radical revisions. Whatever the case, you are now ready to draw some definite conclusions.

This is the first of many situations you will encounter in this book where there are no right or wrong answers. In this case, there simply is no consensus on the attributes all excellent teachers possess. What is important is that you have brought your own experiences and ideas together with those of others and constructed your own understanding.

BUILDING BLOCK 1.7

Putting It All Together: Attributes of Effective Teachers

Use the lists you developed in Building Blocks 1.1 and 1.2 together with the new information you explored in this chapter.

- List the most important attributes you now believe characterize an effective teacher.
- Explain why you selected these attributes and why you believe they are important.
- Compare these attributes with those you selected in the earlier activities. Which attributes do you still believe to be important? Which do you believe less important that you originally thought? Which have you added?

Keep the work you do in this building block; you will use it again in later chapters.

How have you seen teachers use technology effectively? How have you seen teachers use technology ineffectively? If you consider the pervasiveness of technology in today's society, it should not surprise you that effective teachers know how to integrate technologies into classroom instruction and management.

In this chapter, you have identified some characteristics of effective teachers. How can technology contribute to effective teaching? Remember that merely using technology does not make teaching effective. The *teacher* makes the technology effective. When a teacher directs students to a flashy website or has them create a fancy electronic slide show, these assignments do not necessarily enhance the lesson. The use of technology in instruction must be guided by the teacher's professional knowledge and skills.

Teachers should not separate technology from other instructional tools, such as textbooks and manipulatives, as if it were an effective tool in and of itself. Technology does not automatically engage students, nor does it automatically improve learning. The teacher must determine where and how the use of technology would be most appropriate in any given lesson, based on learning objectives, state standards, and students' needs. You must apply what you know about students and how they learn when making decisions about *when*, *how*, or even *if* you should use technology to teach.

Effective teachers possess such characteristics as strong content area knowledge, efficient organizational skills, and a repertoire of teaching methods and activities that keep learners engaged. How can technology help teachers express these characteristics in their teaching?

As you already know, the Internet is a vast source of content information and instructional ideas. You can find almost anything by searching on the Internet. Many teachers share their lessons, classroom management, and discipline plans by posting these online. It is necessary, however, to evaluate all Internet-accessible information in terms of credibility, accuracy, and applicability for use in your classroom. You must verify the credibility of all web-based content information by checking the site author's credentials. Is the author an individual, an organization, or a company? If the author is an individual, what are his or her credentials regarding the content? Is the author (whether an individual or an organization) biased in any way that might affect the presentation, inclusion, or exclusion of content on the site?

Similarly, not all classroom management or discipline plans posted on the Internet are good. How will you know if a particular plan is good? Some websites review information before they will post it. In all cases, however, you must use your knowledge and skills in your content area and pedagogy to evaluate what you find, judging its appropriateness for use in your classroom. Remember, though: If something doesn't "fit" your needs exactly, you don't have to reject it outright.

Teachers can also use technology to present instruction, produce instructional materials, and manage classroom records. Besides the Internet, teachers can use other technologies, such as the following, to enhance their teaching effectiveness:

- Television and DVDs for students to view educational programs
- Electronic slide shows with color, graphics, sound, video, and animation to present content
- Content area software on CD-ROMs for students to use independently or in groups
- Content-related Internet sites projected for the class or viewed on individual computers
- Teacher-made websites
- Word processing programs to create neat and colorful handouts, worksheets, signs, and bulletin boards
- Assistive and adaptive technologies for students with special needs

Technology can help teachers add to their professional knowledge when it serves a resource for content information and provides teaching ideas, and it can help teachers present the information effectively and in a variety of engaging ways. Technology also can help teachers be more productive. Creating handouts, quizzes, and tests using a word processing application is certainly more efficient than writing them out by hand. Teachers may use a database program to manage student records, a spreadsheet program to calculate student grades, and e-mail to communicate with students and parents. When used together with the student record database, a word processing program can generate personalized letters asking parents to volunteer, informing them of classroom events, or sharing good news. How does being a more efficient teacher contribute to being a more effective teacher?

The use of technology can contribute to teacher effectiveness by helping a teacher increase professional knowledge, present information, and increase productivity.

Conclusion

A great deal of information is available about the qualities of effective teachers and teaching. You have looked at your own ideas. You have considered the ideas of other students, the media, researchers, exemplary educators, psychologists, and professional organizations. You have compared this information with your own preliminary ideas to construct a new and more complete characterization of effective teachers and effective teaching.

You have found that your beliefs exert strong influences on the characteristics you bring to the classroom, and you have seen the necessity of examining your beliefs to see whether they are compatible with your vision of excellence in teaching. You have found that different people value different characteristics in assessing teaching effectiveness.

Yet several common characteristics seem to emerge, and these describe what teachers do to ensure student achievement. Effective teachers are personable, good communicators, caring, and patient. They relate the information taught to students' lives. They are respectful of students and teach in such a manner that *all* students can learn.

Key Terms and Concepts

Accreditation, 31

Empathetic, 19

Locus of control, 27

Correlation, 28

Ethnicity, 27

Socioeconomic, 27

Construct and Apply

1. List the characteristics of excellent teachers and effective teaching that are common to all the groups you investigated.
2. What do you think is the ultimate measure of a teacher's effectiveness? Explain your response.
3. To what extent do you believe an individual's personality characteristics can be learned and refined?
4. Which characteristics of an effective teacher would you like to develop within yourself? What kinds of experiences could help you develop these characteristics?
5. Which skills do you expect to learn as you participate in your teacher preparation program?
6. Where and how do you expect to gain experience in developing these skills?

Deconstructing the Standards

INTASC Principle #1 says:

> The teacher understands the central concepts, tools of inquiry, and structures of the discipline(s) he or she teaches and creates learning experiences that make these aspects of subject matter meaningful for students.

What part(s) of this principle does this chapter address?
How does this chapter address this principle?
How will the concepts in this chapter help you apply this principle as a teacher?

Field Experience

Field experiences occur when you are assigned to real classes of students in real schools to observe or to work under the general direction of real teachers. You will have the opportunity to participate in many field experiences during your teacher preparation program. The field experience suggestions made in this textbook refer to field experiences associated with this course. They are outlined in detail by chapter in the *Field Experience Companion* that accompanies this textbook.

While you are in a field experience, observe your collaborating teacher. (This teacher, sometimes called the *cooperating teacher,* is the person to whom you are assigned for your field experience.)

- How does the teacher show qualities that are congruent with your ideas of effective teaching?
- Does your cooperating teacher utilize any of Glasser's six conditions of quality education in the classroom?

Obtain copies of the instruments used to evaluate field experiences and student teaching at your institution.

- How do the evaluation criteria compare to the national standards presented previously?
- Are there similarities in focus and in terminology?
- Can you find representations of the characteristics you identified in the first part of this chapter?
- Which attributes can you begin to develop during this course?

■ Your Portfolio

During your teacher preparation program, you will be asked to demonstrate your achievement of certain competencies. Many education departments ask students to demonstrate their competencies through *portfolios*. A portfolio demonstrates the student's mastery of various concepts and skills. It is not a scrapbook; it is a record of the student's achievements.

In this chapter, you have considered numerous factors dealing with qualities of effective teachers and teaching. Begin to develop your portfolio by selecting one or two pieces of evidence that show your mastery of this topic and putting them in your portfolio. This evidence may come from work done in class, work done out of class, class discussions, or field experiences.

Also include a copy of the requirements for the teacher preparation program you plan to pursue and a copy of your state's requirements for the certification you plan to seek.

Keep your portfolio in a safe place, and be ready to add to it throughout this course.

■ Technology Resources

 Check out the *Building Teachers* companion website for more information about effective teacher qualities. Links to the following sites are accessible via the companion website, http://www.education.wadsworth.com/martinloomis1:

- Glasser Institute
- *No Child Left Behind* Executive Summary
- National Association for the Accreditation of Teacher Education
- Interstate New Teacher Assessment and Support Consortium
- National Board for Professional Teaching Standards

 See video footage of effective teachers in action on the *Building Teachers* CD-ROM that accompanies your textbook.

 Also link to InfoTrac College Edition through the *Building Teachers* companion website. Use InfoTrac College Edition to search for articles to enhance your study.

CHAPTER 2

Your Philosophy of Education

Men are by no means agreed about the things to be taught, whether we aim at virtue or the best in life. Neither is it clear whether education should be more concerned with intellectual or moral virtue. Existing practice is perplexing; no one knows on what principle we should proceed . . . about method there is no agreement; for different persons, starting with different ideas about the nature of virtue, naturally disagree about the practice of it.

ARISTOTLE

In Chapter 1, you looked at qualities of effective teachers and effective teaching. You examined these attributes from several perspectives: your own thoughts and feelings, the ideas of classmates and other preservice teachers, the media, educational research, educational psychologists, and professional associations. After considering this new information and using it to augment your own initial ideas, you developed a list of the most important attributes you believe characterize effective teachers.

Your work in Chapter 1 may have left you with the impression that all teachers should have the same qualities and should teach in the same way if they are to achieve excellence. Nothing could be further from the truth.

Doubtless, there are areas where your thoughts about teaching excellence are decidedly different from those of others, even though you may agree in principle on the qualities that characterize effective teachers. These thoughts are based in large measure on your beliefs and predispositions. Can you see the perplexity of the educational questions that concerned Aristotle in the opening quote?

Your beliefs and predispositions about teaching and education have a profound impact on how you teach and what you teach, just as your beliefs and predispositions about living have a profound impact on how you live your life. As human beings, we carry beliefs from tradition, experience, education, religion, and socialization, and we revise and refine them through experience. Over time, these beliefs become stronger as we find they serve us well and prove to be true for us. These beliefs ultimately become our philosophy of life.

The same can be said about teaching. You have current beliefs about which you are beginning to think and which you are beginning to modify in response to new experiences and your explorations of new information. What you know and come to believe about education will become stronger through the experiences you will have in your teacher preparation program. Over time, you will learn more and more about education and will revise and refine your beliefs as a result of your experiences. These beliefs will form the basis of your ever-evolving philosophy of education.

There are many different philosophies in education that motivate the approaches exhibited by excellent teachers. In this chapter you will consider several prominent philosophies that guide American education and find where your current beliefs fit. You will examine your own philosophical beliefs, compare them with these basic philosophies of education, study the applications of these philosophies in schools, investigate prominent psychologies that seek to explain the mechanism of learning, and put all this together as you develop your own tentative philosophy of education that will guide your inquiries through the rest of this course.

CHAPTER GOALS

As a result of your work in this chapter, you will:

1. Describe the main branches of philosophy and how they relate to educational issues.
2. Categorize your beliefs about what is most important in education.
3. Investigate the nature of basic philosophies of education and your thoughts about each.
4. Describe the primary characteristics of humanist, behaviorist, information processing, and constructivist approaches to education.
5. Develop your personal preliminary philosophy of education.
6. Select a metaphor that represents your beliefs about the role of a teacher.

The Nature of Educational Philosophy

Let us eavesdrop on a conversation between two students who have just finished their explorations in Chapter 1 of this text.

> *"Sure,"* says one, *"I agree that teachers should be respectful, listen to the kids, and show a sense of humor. But, that doesn't mean I am going to let them run my classroom. I am the authority, and I am going to run it my way."*
>
> *The other preservice teacher responds, "I agree that teachers should respect to students, should listen to students, and should have a sense of humor. But if they are to learn anything at all, they have to have a say-so about what goes on in the classroom."*

Here are two people with the same thoughts about the qualities of effective teachers but opposite thoughts about how to run the classroom. One believes teachers must have total control of the classroom if students are to learn; the other believes teachers must allow students to have a great deal of input into what goes on in the classroom if they are to learn.

These two people differ fundamentally in their beliefs about the most effective practices in the classroom. They have different views about human beings and human nature, and they have different beliefs and concepts about how people learn, especially in schools. In short, they have different philosophies of education.

What Is Philosophy?

The word *philosophy* comes from two Greek words *philos*, which means "love," and *sophy*, which means "wisdom." Literally speaking, then, *philosophy* means "love of wisdom." In common use, *philosophy* refers to the general beliefs, concepts, and attitudes possessed by an individual or group. You have a philosophy of life that consists of a set of general beliefs, concepts, and attitudes about life, and you probably have a philosophy of education in which you have a set of general beliefs, concepts, and attitudes about education.

Throughout history, people have struggled to find answers to fundamental questions such as:

- What is real?
- What do we know?
- How do we know what we know?
- What is of value?
- What is logical?
- What is beautiful?
- What is right? What is wrong?

There are many complex and elusive questions about life, education, and other areas of our existence that are similar to these questions. There are also many different, complex, and elusive answers to these questions. The study of these kinds of questions is the substance of philosophy.

Branches of Philosophy

To facilitate the studies of these kinds of questions, philosophy has been arranged into several branches, each addressing different, but related, questions. The chief branches are **metaphysics, epistemology, axiology,** and **logic** (see Figure 2.1).

Metaphysics

Metaphysics is the branch of philosophy that addresses questions of reality. Metaphysics is concerned with such philosophical questions as:

- What is reality?
- Are people basically good or bad?
- What is the nature of the world in which we live?
- What is the nature of being and of reality? (a branch of metaphysics called **ontology**)
- What is the origin and what is the structure of the universe? (a branch of metaphysics called **cosmology**)
- What or who is God? What are the relations among God, humankind, and the universe? (a branch of metaphysics called **theology**)

In classrooms, teachers invoke metaphysical issues regularly when they make decisions about what they should teach on any particular day, how they should organize the classroom to facilitate maximum learning, and what motivational strategies they should use. Several metaphysical questions related to educational situations are shown in Figure 2.1.

Branch of Philosophy		Chief Topic	Questions Related to Education
Metaphysics	Ontology	Reality	• What is knowledge? • Are students basically capable people or incapable people? • How does our view of knowledge determine what should be taught?
	Cosmology	The Universe	• How orderly should my classroom be? • Should the curriculum be structured or determined by students? • Should I teach the theory of evolution or creationism? • What texts should I use as authoritative?
	Theology	God	• Is it possible to motivate all students to want to learn? • Is a student's ability to learn innate or acquired? • Should all people have the same access to education?
Epistemology		Knowledge	• Should teachers lecture, ask questions, provide experiences, or encourage activities to enable students to learn? • How do scientists do science?
Axiology		Values Ethics Aesthetics	• Are students basically good or bad? • How should I treat students? • How should students treat others and me? • Should my behavior management system be punitive or encouraging? • What different understandings of "beautiful" might there be in my classroom? • What values should be taught in character education? • What is the importance of art education and music education in schools?
Logic		Reasoning	• Should I use deductive or inductive reasoning in my lessons? • How can I understand the ways my students are reasoning?

Figure 2.1
Branches of Philosophy and Representative Educational Questions Associated with Each.

Epistemology

Epistemology is the study of knowledge and how we come to know. This branch of philosophy seeks to answer several basic questions, such as:

■ What is knowledge?

■ What is truth?

■ Where did knowledge originate?

■ How do we come to know?

■ How do we learn?

As you can imagine, much of your teacher preparation program will deal with epistemological topics. For educators, epistemology (the nature of knowledge and learning) and its cousin, **pedagogy** (ways of teaching), are the primary areas of concern. These are the teacher's profession. A few education-related questions that deal with epistemological ideas are shown in Figure 2.1.

Axiology

Axiology is the branch of philosophy that deals with values. Axiology seeks to answer such questions as:

- What is of value?
- What values are essential?
- What is morality? Is morality defined by our actions or our thoughts? (a branch of axiology called *ethics*)
- What is beauty? (a branch of axiology called *aesthetics*)
- What is beautiful?

Axiology addresses our thinking about what teacher-student interactions should be and how teachers should behave toward students. As you will learn, according to Abraham Maslow, axiology also addresses one of the basic needs of human beings—the need for aesthetic satisfaction. A few education-related questions dealing with axiological concerns are shown in Figure 2.1.

Logic

What characteristics of this text make it inductive in approach rather than deductive?

Logic is the branch of philosophy that deals with reasoning. There are two basic types of reasoning: **deductive reasoning** and **inductive reasoning.** In *deductive* reasoning, thinking proceeds from the most general concepts to the most specific examples. In *inductive* reasoning, thinking proceeds from the most specific examples to the most general concepts; generalizations are derived from the specific examples (see Figure 2.2).

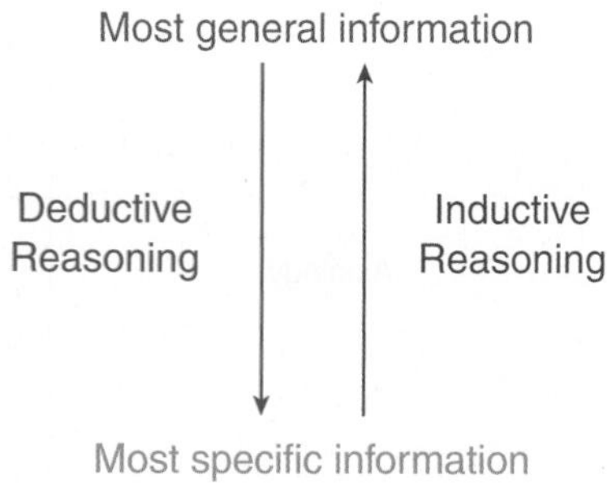

As you may have observed, this entire text uses an inductive approach.

The following sets illustrate deductive and inductive reasoning.

Most general information

Deductive Reasoning | Inductive Reasoning

Most specific information

Figure 2.2
Deductive versus Inductive Reasoning.

A famous puzzle in deductive logic, "Who Owns the Zebra?" was published by *Life* magazine in 1962. You can access this puzzle through the direct link available on the *Building Teachers* companion website.

Deductive reasoning	*Inductive reasoning*
All humans are mortal.	I am mortal.
I am human.	You are mortal.
Therefore I am mortal.	We are humans.
	Therefore humans are mortal.

A few education-related questions dealing with concerns of logic are shown in Figure 2.1.

Educational Philosophy

Whereas general philosophy seeks to answer questions about metaphysics, epistemology, axiology, and logic, educational philosophies extend to questions about the general beliefs, concepts, and attitudes people have about education. You have already looked at some general philosophical questions as they apply to education. In this chapter, we narrow our focus to six basic questions:

- What should be taught?
- Who should decide what should be taught?
- Why should this material be taught?
- How should this material be taught?
- What should the teacher's role be?
- What should the student's role be?

There are many possible answers to these questions. The answers differ according to who is considering the questions and what that person's beliefs are. They differ from one historical time period to another, from region to region, and among different kinds of schools, such as public, private, parochial, charter schools, and home schools. They change as the cultural makeup of our country becomes increasingly diversified.

What are *your* responses to these questions? You probably have some initial thoughts and ideas based on your beliefs and your past experiences. These thoughts represent the beginnings of your philosophy of education.

Your Personal Beliefs about Education

To help you move toward finding your own personal niche in the world of educational philosophy, let us start with an examination of your personal beliefs about what is important and what is not important in education.

Characteristics of Educational Philosophies

Study the statements in each of the following groups and circle the numbers of the statements with which you agree. Then consider the questions that follow the final group.

GROUP I

1. The most important knowledge for students to learn in school are the profound truths discovered and developed in the past.
2. Above all, schools should develop students' abilities to think deeply, analytically, and creatively.
3. Drill and acquisition of factual knowledge are very important components of the learning environment.
4. There is certain basic information that everyone must know.
5. When it comes to knowledge, the teacher is the most authoritative person in the classroom.
6. Students should study great works that have been validated by society over time.
7. Students should focus primarily on learning the knowledge and insights their teachers impart.
8. The teacher should be a strong authority figure in the classroom.
9. Ideal teachers present knowledge to students and interpret it for them to ensure that they understand it correctly.
10. The curriculum in a given grade or subject should be the same for everyone.

GROUP II

1. The student is the receiver of knowledge.
2. The curriculum of schools should center on the basic subjects of reading, writing, history, mathematics, and science.
3. Students should not be promoted from one grade to the next until they have mastered certain key material.
4. Recitation and demonstration of acquired knowledge are essential components of learning.
5. The curriculum of a school should consist primarily of the skills and subjects that are essential for all students to know.

6. Schools should reflect the social and economic needs of the society they serve.
7. Lecture-discussion is the most effective teaching technique.
8. Memorization, drill, and practice are the keys to learning skills.
9. Teaching by subject area is the most effective approach.
10. Effective classrooms are quiet and orderly.

GROUP III

1. Schools should prepare students for analyzing and solving the types of problems they will face outside the classroom.
2. New material is best taught through facilitating students in their own investigations.
3. Teachers must stress the relevance of what students are learning to their lives outside, as well as inside, the classroom.
4. Many students learn best by engaging in real-world activities rather than by reading.
5. Art lessons should focus primarily on individual expression and creativity.
6. Students should be active participants in the learning process.
7. The curriculum of a school should be built around the personal experiences and needs of students.
8. Teachers should be seen as facilitators of learning.
9. Students should have substantial input into the curriculum being studied.
10. Classrooms should have areas for large group discussion and small group inquiries.

GROUP IV

1. Students should be permitted to determine their own rules in the educational process.
2. Schools should offer students choices in what to study and when classes are held.
3. Ideal teachers are constant questioners.
4. Effective learning can be unstructured, informal, and open.
5. The purpose of the school is to help students understand and define themselves and find the meaning of their existence.
6. It is more important for a student to develop a positive self-concept than to learn specific subject matter.
7. Students should be permitted to determine their own curriculum.
8. The ideal teacher helps students identify their most effective methods of study.
9. The furniture in the classroom should be movable by both students and teachers to meet multiple and flexible purposes.
10. Teachers function as facilitators and resource persons rather than as instructors.

GROUP V

1. Schools should foster change through orderly means when dealing with controversial issues.
2. Schools must place more emphasis on teaching about the concerns of minorities and women.
3. The United States must become more cooperative economically with countries such as Japan, China, and Mexico, and schools have an obligation to provide the education students need to facilitate such change.
4. Schools should plan substantial social interactions in their curriculum.
5. The primary aim of schools is to prepare students to accomplish social reform.
6. Education should focus on injustices and inequities in society and ways of solving these difficulties.
7. Teachers should be committed to achieving a new social order.
8. Students should learn to identify problems and situations that affect society.
9. Students should focus on community building in their classes rather than obedience of the teacher's directions.
10. Community service and involvement with community projects are essential components of education.

Each group represents a particular philosophy of education—a set of beliefs, concepts, and attitudes about what should happen in schools. Different philosophies contend that education ought to be handled in ways that are markedly different from the contentions of other philosophies.

These five philosophies of education are the primary sets of educational beliefs that govern education in the United States. Although many other philosophies of education exist and many philosophies originate from non-European roots, the five presented here represent the mainstream of American thinking about education.

- Is there a group in which you agreed with all or most statements? Which one?
- Is there a group in which you disagreed with all or most statements? Which one?
- In which group or groups did you agree with some of the statements and disagree with others?
- If you had to select only one group that represents your beliefs about education, which would it be? What is its name?

Schools of Philosophic Thought

In Building Block 2.1, group I contains statements with which *perennialists* strongly agree. Group II contains statements with which *essentialists* strongly agree. Group III contains statements with which *progressivists* strongly agree. Group IV contains statements with which *existentialists* strongly agree. Group V contains statements with which *social reconstructionists* strongly agree.

From this activity, you can identify one or more labels for your philosophic thoughts. Does any one of the philosophies represent your personal beliefs completely?

Let us examine these five philosophies in a bit more detail. While you are doing this, compare the inventory you took in Building Block 2.1 with the discussions of each philosophy. Ask yourself where you agree and where you disagree. In this manner, you can interpret your thoughts about educational philosophies and you can judge whether your label or labels are well suited.

Exploring Educational Philosophies

BUILDING BLOCK 2.2

In this Building Block, you will become better acquainted with the major philosophies of education. Answer the six questions we raised earlier for each philosophy shown in the table below. Use your exploration of philosophies in Building Block 2.1 and your current understandings of what should occur in schools to help you in your thinking.

What are the root words for the terms *perennialism, essentialism, existentialism,* and *social reconstructionism?*

Based on the root words for each of the four philosophies, what inferences can you make about the following questions?

	Perennialism	Essentialism	Progressivism	Existentialism	Social Reconstructionism
What should be taught?					
Who should decide what is taught?	society				
Why should this material be taught?					
How should this material be taught?					

	Perennialism	Essentialism	Progressivism	Existentialism	Social Reconstructionism
What should the teacher's role be?					
What should the student's role be?					

Perennialism

As you doubtless have surmised, the root word of *perennialism* is "perennial." The philosophy of perennialism advances the idea that the focus of education should be the universal truths conveyed through the classic and profound thoughts and works that have lasted through the centuries and have recurred in each generation. Like a perennial plant that returns year after year, these thoughts and works are everlasting. They have withstood the test of time and are as important and relevant today as they were when first conceived. The enduring wisdom of the past is a guide to the present.

Examples of these classic materials include works of great literature, findings of great scientists, and timeless concepts of history. High school students study Shakespeare's plays, Homer's *Iliad*, Melville's *Moby Dick*, Newton's laws of motion, Einstein's theories, and other works that have become part of today's classic repertoire. Students take courses that focus on the traditional subjects of reading, writing, language, mathematics, science, history, and the arts. Elementary and middle school students prepare for more advanced work by studying basic subjects from the perspective of the classic tradition in a tightly controlled and well-disciplined atmosphere. The perennialist believes the emphasis of school should be the mastery of content and the development of reasoning skills in the arts and sciences and that thoughtful consideration of the classical works is the way these goals can be achieved.

Perennialists believe that truth does not depend on time or place but rather is the same for all people. They believe the same curriculum should be required of all students. Their reasoning is twofold: (1) Because the goal of school is to teach the truth, and the truth is the same for everyone, the curriculum must be the same. (2) Because people are born equal and have the same opportunities, to give some students a curriculum that is different from that of others is to treat them differently and is a form of discrimination.

Who decides what should be taught? Society at large makes these decisions because it is society that has validated the importance of these works over time and has continued to hold these classics in high esteem. Many individuals have assembled canons of material they believe should be taught. Noteworthy is Mortimer Adler, whose 1982 work *The Paideia Proposal* describes a system of education based on the classics. His book has led to the development of an innovative school model called the Paideia (pronounced py-DEE-a) program, which several hundred schools in all grade levels throughout the United States have adopted. The Paideia program calls for all students to study a single rigorous curriculum in which the only elective is foreign language. Teachers in the program use three basic methods of teaching: (1) didactic teaching in which the teacher lectures (10% to 15% of the time), (2) Socratic seminars in which the teacher uses directed questioning to help students arrive at desirable answers (15% to 20% of the time), and (3) coaching in which the teacher coaches students in the academic subjects (60% to 70% of the time) (Brandt & Voke, 2002; National Paideia Center, 2005).

The Socratic method is patterned after the way Socrates taught. He believed people were born with all the information they need in life and that all people were born with the same basic information. This information was already present at birth, but it was

How is the Socratic method of questioning used in schools today?

hidden. He believed that through skillful question and discussion sessions with students, he was able to get his students to bring this hidden information to the surface.

In the 1930s, Adler and Robert Maynard Hutchins, then president of the University of Chicago, organized the classics into a set of more than 400 works titled *Great Books of the Western World* (1952), which they believed would enable students to become independent and critical thinkers. They held that people can discover the truths through their senses and their reasoning—that they do not construct truths because they are already in existence. The *Great Books of the Western World* represent the fruit of these discoveries made by other people; as students read and discuss them, they, too, can encounter the great truths of the universe.

Of course, because the perennialist believes the primary goal of school is for students to learn what others have created and to use this knowledge in their own lives, the teacher is expected to present this material to the students. There is little or no room for students to venture into tangents of their own interest; the curriculum must be covered. The teacher's role is to impart knowledge. To do this, teachers hold seminars, engage students in Socratic discussions, foster directed readings of great books, explain principles and concepts, and lecture as effectively as possible, presenting dynamic lessons with all the interest-grabbing devices available. The work is demanding, and the classroom is disciplined.

The student's role is to discuss, examine, and reexamine the information presented by the teacher with the ultimate goal of learning the content.

www Links to the National Paideia Center website, a Mortimer Adler biography, and sites about Adler's work are available on the *Building Teachers* companion website.

Have you taken a course in classic literature or philosophy? How did the requirements of this course reflect the arguments of Adler?

Of the five philosophies of education—perennialism, essentialism, existentialism, progressivism, or social reconstructionism—which is demonstrated in this elementary classroom?

© ImageState/Alamy

© Center for the Study of The Great Ideas

BIOGRAPHY

Mortimer Jerome Adler

(1902–2001) was born in New York City, the son of an immigrant jewelry salesman. He dropped out of school at the age of 14 to become a copy boy for a New York newspaper, but hoping to become a journalist, he took courses in writing at Columbia University. While there, he became intensely interested in philosophy. He completed his course work but did not graduate because he had not completed the physical education requirement. He later earned his Ph.D. at Columbia. Adler served as a professor of psychology at Columbia during the 1920s, and he taught at the University of Chicago during the 1930s. At the University of Chicago, he advocated the adoption of the classics as a main part of the curriculum, although the rest of the faculty disagreed.

Adler believed in providing the same liberal education without electives or vocational classes for all people. He believed education should teach people (1) to think critically, (2) to use their leisure time well, (3) to earn their living ethically, and (4) to be responsible citizens in a democracy. He believed that people should become lifelong learners.

Mortimer Adler is best known in the education community for his devotion to the adoption of the classics as the mainstream of education, the Paideia schools, and his insistence that students read key works of Western literature and philosophy.

Your Thoughts about Perennialism

- Review the statements in Building Block 2.1 associated with perennialism (group I). How well do these statements describe the perennialist philosophy of education?
- How did the inferences you made about perennialism in Building Block 2.2 compare with the description of this educational philosophy?
- What do you think are the strengths of perennialism as applied to education?
- What do you think are the weaknesses of perennialism as applied to education?

Essentialism

The philosophy of essentialism takes its name from the word *essential*. The essentialist believes there are certain basic or essential knowledge, skills, and understandings students should master. Essentialists assert that, over time, society has found that certain skills, such as reading, writing, computing, and, in today's world, computer skills, are needed for people to function effectively. Accordingly, certain subjects, such as the language arts, mathematics, science, history, and, in today's world, computer training, are essential for people to gain the knowledge and skills they need. According to the essentialist viewpoint, this knowledge and these skills will always be needed. Thus, we can say that society at large decides in general what these essentials are. Businesses, banks, manufacturers, retailers, and others provide input to the institutions of education, detailing the strengths and weaknesses they see in high school graduates. The educators, in turn, use this input to help them develop programs of study that will prepare students to enter the workforce. Because most of the people who provide input into the educational system are concerned with students mastering the basic skills of reading, writing, and basic mathematics (the "3 Rs"), the programs developed naturally reflect these concerns. Thus, essentialism can be termed the "Back to Basics" approach to education.

Essentialism has been the guiding philosophy of American education for a very long time. (You will consider this again in Chapter 10, when you investigate the history of American education.) The Soviet launching of Sputnik in October 1957 rekindled this thinking. The United States felt deeply humiliated by the Soviet success. American scientists had been working on launching an American spacecraft for a number of years. Americans asked, "How did this happen? How did the United States, with all its technological capabilities, all its talent, and all its money, not achieve the goal of being first in space?" As so often happens, education took much of the blame.

Two opposing views addressed the seeming weaknesses in American education. One advocated an increased emphasis on education in science, mathematics, and technology and an increase in inquiry teaching strategies. This thrust was strengthened by the Woods Hole Conference of 1959, chaired by Jerome Bruner and attended by scientists, mathematicians, psychologists, and technology specialists (Bruner, 1965). The conference affirmed the increasing momentum in science, mathematics, and technology education and called for studying less material but studying it in greater depth and requiring students to inquire and figure things out for themselves.

The other view was a growing concern that American students were not mastering the basic material of reading, writing, mathematics, science, and other areas. This concern was later highlighted in *A Nation at Risk,* the 1983 report of the President's Commission on Excellence in Education (National Commission on Excellence in Education, 1983). The report essentially said that American children were at risk for lagging behind other nations in achievement of basic subjects and that we had better teach our children to read, write, and do mathematics—and we had better do it *now.* In 1998, the Center for Education Reform reaffirmed these findings in *A Nation Still at Risk.* These same concerns are the chief underliers of the No Child Left Behind Act of 2001 (*The No Child Left Behind Executive*

Summary, 2001). This wide support for a back-to-basics curriculum and the emphasis on basic subjects has eclipsed the recommendations made at the Woods Hole Conference.

In essentialist education, students receive instruction in the basic subjects of reading, writing, mathematics, science, history, foreign language, and technology. Unlike perennialism, which emphasizes a canon of great works and classics, essentialism emphasizes fundamental knowledge and skills that business and political leaders believe members of today's society need to know to be productive in the workplace.

Teachers transmit this essential knowledge and expect students to learn it. The teacher is considered the repository of knowledge to be transmitted. This means educators develop and employ a sequence of topics in each subject that progresses from less complex to more complex material through successive grade levels. It also means using lecture and recitation, discussion, drill and practice, and a variety of teaching and learning materials to ensure that students learn the content. For example, a middle grades social studies teacher might give a lecture on why large cities are located where they are, using maps and videos as aids, rather than having students investigate the phenomenon for themselves by engaging in map exploration activities.

The role of the students is to learn the content and skills being taught and to demonstrate their mastery of them on achievement tests, often in the form of standardized tests that are used to make local, regional, statewide, and national comparisons.

E. D. Hirsch, Jr., has written extensively on what should be included in essentialist education. His works include *Cultural Literacy: What Every American Needs to Know* (Turtleback Books, 1988), *The Dictionary of Cultural Literacy: What Every American Needs to Know* (Houghton Mifflin, 1987), and *A First Dictionary of Cultural Literacy: What Our Children Need to Know* (Turtleback Books, 1991). In addition, he has published several volumes in his *Core Knowledge Series* that deal with what children in elementary grades should know (Hirsch, 1994–1999). Hirsch's work could be considered perennialist in nature except for its emphasis on science, which reflects the essentialist viewpoint.

 Direct links to the full texts of *A Nation At Risk* and *The No Child Left Behind Executive Summary*, as well as a link to the Core Knowledge Foundation established by E. D. Hirsch, Jr., are available on the *Building Teachers* companion website.

How important do you think it is to teach a basic core curriculum to all students?

Your Thoughts about Essentialism

BUILDING BLOCK 2.4

- Review the statements in Building Block 2.1 associated with essentialism (group II). How well do these statements describe the essentialist philosophy of education?
- How did the inferences you made about essentialism in Building Block 2.2 compare with the description of this educational philosophy?
- What do you think are the strengths of essentialism as applied to education?
- What do you think are the weaknesses of essentialism as applied to education?

BIOGRAPHY

Courtesy Hoover Institution

E. D. Hirsch, Jr. (b. 1928), is a prominent figure in the theories underlying essentialist education. He holds degrees from Cornell and Yale and is a professor of education and the humanities at the University of West Virginia. He is founder and chairman of the Core Knowledge Foundation, a nonprofit organization dedicated to the establishment of a curriculum of Core Knowledge, a sequenced body of knowledge recommended by the Foundation to be taught in preschool through eighth grade. The Foundation is a major source of research, theory, and practical lessons and assessments for all recommended subjects in pre-K–8 schools. Although his Core Knowledge schools operate nationwide, critics have challenged Hirsch's essentialist theories, contending that students who use the Core Knowledge curriculum are taught *what* to think rather than *how* to think and that the perspective is Eurocentric, giving only minor attention to non-Eurocentric influences.

Progressivism

The educational philosophy of progressivism takes its name from the word *progressive*. The dictionary defines *progressive* as "making use of or interested in new ideas, findings, or opportunities" and ". . . an educational theory marked by emphasis on the individual child, informality of classroom procedure, and encouragement of self-expression" (Merriam-Webster, 2003). Thus, the philosophy of progressivism espouses the idea that the focus of education should be students rather than content and that whatever is taught should be meaningful. To the progressivist, the purpose of education is to prepare students to be lifelong learners in an ever-changing society.

One of the key figures in the progressivist movement was John Dewey. Dewey's writings and his work at the Laboratory School at the University of Chicago, where he tested and refined his educational ideas, have produced tremendous innovations in American education. To Dewey, the traditional school where students sat in rows and passively received information imparted by the teacher was ineffective. He argued that if students are to learn, they must be involved with real problems and meaningful questions, must solve problems according to a scientific method, must be free to develop their own theories and their own conceptualizations, and must be encouraged to test their conclusions in real situations. The progressivist movement focused on several basic principles*:

1. Students should be free to develop naturally.
2. Student interest should guide the teaching.
3. The teacher should be a guide, not a taskmaster.
4. Student development should involve the *whole* student, and should include physical, mental, moral, and social growth.
5. Schools should attend to the physical development of students.
6. There should be school-home cooperation to meet the needs of students realistically.

> How does Dewey's philosophy of education compare with the constructivist view described in Chapter 0?

© Hulton Archive/Getty Images

Born on a farm near Burlington, Vermont, **John Dewey** (1859–1952) was arguably the most influential American educator in the 20th century. He graduated from the University of Vermont, and after 3 years of teaching, he earned his doctorate at Johns Hopkins University. Dewey taught philosophy at the University of Michigan and the University of Minnesota before becoming chair of the Department of Philosophy, Psychology, and Pedagogy at the University of Chicago. He developed the university's Laboratory School in 1896 and directed it for the next 7 years, pioneering experimental efforts and translating their results into practice. Because of disagreements with the university over the Laboratory School, Dewey left in 1904 to become a professor of philosophy at Columbia University.

In addition to his contributions in the areas of philosophy, psychology, politics, and social thought, Dewey was instrumental in developing modern education theory. His was a prominent voice in educational philosophy, with an emphasis on progressivism. He rejected authoritarian teaching methods and advocated the importance of experiential education—learning by doing. He also stressed the importance of the development of the person.

Dewey's ideas were adopted by the "progressivist education" movement, but they frequently were distorted, with the result that, contrary to Dewey's intentions, subject matter education was often neglected in favor of classroom entertainment or vocational education.

To some of Dewey's admirers, he was the greatest educator who ever lived. On the other hand, many attribute the "ills" of American education to the influence of his ideas. Whatever one believes about John Dewey, there is no mistaking the fact that he taught generations of students to examine ideas carefully and objectively before deciding on their own conclusions or course of action.

Several of Dewey's quotes are apropos:

- Anyone who has begun to think places some portion of the world in jeopardy.
- Education is not preparation for life; education is life itself.
- Every great advance in science has issued from a new audacity of the imagination.

---

*From "The Principles of Education" stated by the Progressive Education Association in 1924; cited in Tyack, 1967, pp. 347–348.

Progressivists focus the curriculum on the needs of students. These needs include academic, social, and physical needs and are fueled by the interests of the students. Therefore, the material to be studied is determined jointly among the school, the teacher, and the students. Learning is considered a natural response to curiosity and the need to solve problems. In the progressivist school, teachers expose students to many new developments in science, technology, literature, and the arts to show that knowledge is constantly changing. Progressivists believe there are great ideas and thoughts of the past that students should study, but they also believe knowledge is changing and the job of students is to learn *how* to learn so that they can cope successfully with new challenges in life and discover what truths are relevant to the present.

Of prime importance is the idea that knowledge that is true in the present may not be true in the future. Costa and Liebman (1995) estimate that by the year 2020, the amount of knowledge in the world will double every 73 days. Not only is knowledge expected to grow exponentially, but new knowledge will replace old knowledge and old knowledge will become obsolete.

The progressivist teacher engages students in inquiries that the students themselves develop. Students learn from one another, so the progressivist classroom fosters social learning by having students working in cooperative groups. The progressivist teacher is a facilitator, a resource person, and a co-inquirer. The primary role of students is to develop new and deeper understandings continuously through their own investigation. Thus, in an elementary education progressivist mathematics class dealing with place value, we see children in small groups using various kinds of manipulatives to develop their own understandings of place value and helping each other clarify their ideas. The teacher facilitates these activities but does not lecture.

© Richard Hutchings/PhotoEdit

Which philosophy of education encourages active, hands-on learning, like using mathematics manipulatives in a math lesson—perennialism, essentialism, existentialism, progressivism, or social reconstructionism?

Your Thoughts about Progressivism

■ Review the statements in Building Block 2.1 associated with progressivism (group III). How well do these statements describe the progressivist philosophy of education?

■ How did the inferences you made about progressivism in Building Block 2.2 compare with the description of this educational philosophy?

■ What do you think are the strengths of progressivism as applied to education?

■ What do you think are the weaknesses of progressivism as applied to education?

Existentialism

Existentialism focuses on the *existence* of the individual. Existentialists emphasize that people are responsible for defining themselves. To exist is to choose, and the choices people make define who they are. According to the existentialist point of view, people have two choices: they can either define themselves, or they can choose to be defined by others. The existentialist believes the only "truth" is the "truth" determined by the individual. Individuals determine for themselves what is meant by such terms as *right, wrong, beautiful, ugly, true, false,* and the like. The existentialist truly believes "beauty is in the eye of the beholder." The existentialist believes that, whereas the great thinkers of the past had their own ways of thinking about life and the natural world, their thoughts were uniquely theirs, and today's students need to find their own ways of thinking and develop their own conclusions.

In the existentialist classroom, students determine what they need to study, guided, of course, by the teacher. The idea is for students to come to their own understandings. Because every student is different, no single set of learning outcomes is appropriate for all students. Teachers and the school lay out the topics that are considered appropriate for the students at each grade level to study, and the students make their own meaningful choices.

The teacher is a facilitator, working with each student to help him or her find appropriate materials and the best methods of study. The teacher is a resource—one of many resources that also include other students, books, great works, contemporary works, the Internet and other technological resources, television programs, newspapers and magazines, and other people.

In the existentialist classroom, students do many different things and study many different topics at the same time. For example, in a science class, a group of three or four students might be dissecting a frog, using models, manuals, and drawings to guide their work; another group might be watching a video on the human circulatory system (using headphones); and yet another group might be recording the observations they had previously

Jean Paul Sartre (1905–1980), a leader of existentialism, was born in Paris. After earning his doctorate, he taught philosophy in French high schools until he was drafted into the army at the start of World War II. He was captured by the Germans but escaped and became a leader in the resistance movement.

The philosophy of existentialism became very popular in Europe after the war. According to existentialism, we first exist and then we define ourselves through the choices we make. Sartre believed man's responsibility is vested in man, himself. People are entitled to be human with dignity, and a human is a human only when he or she is entirely free and accepts responsibility for this freedom. Sartre's basic premise was that life has no meaning or purpose except for the personal goals each person sets. This philosophy captured the attention of post–World War II Europeans who were yearning for freedom, and it is embraced today by people who believe they have the freedom to take responsibility for their own actions.

Although Sartre was principally a novelist, essayist, and playwright, his works captured the essence of his philosophy and have become the underpinnings of today's application of existentialism to education.

made of the night sky in chart form. The teacher moves from group to group, working to facilitate the investigations, probing for understandings, and challenging students' conclusions.

The role of the student is to pursue his or her investigations of the chosen topic until the desired learnings and understandings have taken place.

BUILDING BLOCK 2.6

Your Thoughts about Existentialism

- Review the statements in Building Block 2.1 associated with existentialism (group IV). How well do these statements describe the existentialist philosophy of education?
- How did the inferences you made about existentialism in Building Block 2.2 compare with the description of this educational philosophy?
- What do you think are the strengths of existentialism as applied to education?
- What do you think are the weaknesses of existentialism as applied to education?

Social Reconstructionism

Social reconstructionism is particularly germane in today's shrinking world. As its name suggests, the social reconstructionist philosophy of education asserts that society needs to be changed (reconstructed) and that schools are the ideal instrument to foster such changes. Social reconstructionists believe that world crises require the use of education to facilitate the development of a new social order, one that is truly democratic in nature. Schools are seen as agents of the reformation of society rather than as transmitters of knowledge.

To this end, teachers help their students understand the validity and urgency of social problems. The determination of which of the many important and controversial social problems should be studied is made through democratic consensus of the students under the leadership of the teacher. There is an abundance of social problems at the local, national, and global levels that can be the focus of the curriculum. Examples include violence, hunger, poverty, terrorism, inflation, inequality, racism, sexism, homophobia, acquired immunodeficiency syndrome (AIDS), pollution, homelessness, substance abuse, and many others. In social reconstructionism, the students select the social priorities to be studied and decide on the educational objectives to be attained from the study. The curriculum integrates all the traditional subjects into single thematic interdisciplinary units. The students and teacher work together to uncover, solve, and propose solutions to the selected problems. The teacher helps students explore the problems, suggests alternative perspectives, and facilitates student analysis and conclusion formation. Throughout the study, the teacher models the democratic process. Teaching methodologies include simulation, role-playing, group work, internships, work-study programs, and other forms of cooperation with the community and its resources.

Similar to their role in the existentialist classroom, students in a social reconstructionist class engage in many different activities to study the agreed-on topic, such as researching through the Internet, reading case histories, analyzing multiple aspects of the topic, formulating predictions, proposing and justifying workable revisions and solutions, and taking action to implement these solutions.

A good example of a social reconstructionist issue is a problem that captured the attention of a university class in 1999. Northwestern University journalism students teamed with the *Chicago Tribune* to investigate the trials and backgrounds of death row inmates in Illinois. Their work showed that some of the inmates were innocent; this uncovered serious flaws in the state's death penalty system and resulted in the release of several death row inmates. This series of investigations has prompted additional investigations, which, in turn, have freed numerous death row convicts, and has changed the way the United States thinks about capital punishment (American Civil Liberties Union, 2002; CBS News, 2002). In another example, social reconstructionists have fostered the development of nationwide literacy programs, especially for students in urban schools, "helping poor, urban students to become resilient, to change their communities, and thus improve their lives" (Reed & Davis, 1999, p. 293).

A social reconstructionist curriculum can help students become successful in school by encouraging them to develop a sense of self-worth (Reed & Davis, 1999). This can occur by engaging students in activities that instill purpose to their lives, providing them with a sense of accomplishment, and providing them with a support system. Among these activities are service learning and experiential learning activities that simultaneously foster students' academic achievement and respond to community needs. As you can infer, social reconstructionist principles are important in helping guide schools, teachers, and students toward a multicultural emphasis.

Social reconstructionism is a very influential and powerful philosophy, especially when its goals of social reform are combined with other philosophies such as progressivism and existentialism. Critics of social reconstructionism are concerned with its singularity of purpose (the formation of a utopian democratic world society) and the indoctrination of students into this purpose. However, the new world order of the 21st century may well need the type of impact that can be given by students whose education is provided in a social reconstructionist environment.

> How are social reconstructionism, progressivism, and existentialism as educational philosophies similar? How are Freire's beliefs similar to the constructivist approach to education?

BUILDING BLOCK 2.7

Your Thoughts about Social Reconstructionism

- Review the statements in Building Block 2.1 associated with social reconstructionism (group V). How well do these statements describe the social reconstructionist philosophy of education?
- How did the inferences you made about social reconstructionism in Building Block 2.2 compare with the description of this educational philosophy?
- What do you think are the strengths of social reconstructionism as applied to education?
- What do you think are the weaknesses of social reconstructionism as applied to education?

www A direct link to a summary of Paolo Freire's *Pedagogy of the Oppressed* is available on the *Building Teachers* companion website.

BIOGRAPHY

Courtesy of the Paulo Freire Institute

Paulo Freire (1921–1997) was a Brazilian educator who, although educated in law, became interested in education after he had children. He worked in literacy campaigns with the poor in Brazil to help them overcome their sense of powerlessness and empower themselves. Because he challenged the ruling elite, he was exiled from Brazil during a military coup in 1964. He taught at Harvard University from 1969 until 1979, when he was able to return to Brazil. In 1988, he assumed the position of Minister of Education for the City of Sao Paulo, a large city that contains two-thirds of Brazil's schools.

Freire is considered among the most influential educational thinkers in the late 20th century. He has been a major figure in progressive education, especially as it relates to empowering poor and oppressed adults. In his *Pedagogy of the Oppressed,* a significant and highly popular education book, he discussed his belief that education must involve dialogue and mutual understanding and must nurture respect between student and teacher, stressing that this was the key to the liberation of the oppressed. According to Freire, education is a two-way exchange of beliefs, thoughts, and ideas, unlike the traditional system of schooling, which he called a "banking approach" in which the teacher makes deposits of information into the students. He believed that true knowledge can result only from experiences in which students inquire into unknown phenomena and thereby establish their need for further knowledge. He believed that teachers must be sensitive to their students' viewpoints and lifestyles.

According to Freire, students must be viewed as being in charge of their own education and destinies. Once they arrive at this point, they can find their own ideas and then begin to reconstruct the society they knew on the basis of their new and validated conclusions.

Freire's contributions to education are firmly grounded in the progressivist approach and have helped expand progressivism to encompass the investigation and resolution of social problems and the subsequent reconstruction of a new and meaningful social order.

Come observe my classroom. Students have assigned seats. They receive a list of upcoming assignments once every 3 weeks. On the board are posted the assignments due the previous class meeting, the assignments due that day, and the assignments due during the next week. Papers to be handed back are in the center of each table, and materials we will be using during the class period are stacked neatly in a pile at the edge of the table. I determine the curriculum. The first 45 minutes are mine to present information, take questions, and facilitate teacher-directed activities; the last 45 minutes constitute student work time. Sounds pretty structured doesn't it? *Perennialism perhaps?*

Take a closer look. The students are seated at hexagonal tables scattered throughout the room, not desks in a straight row. If seats weren't assigned, students would sit at the same table, in the same chair, usually by a friend, all semester long. Instead, I change the seating arrangements every 4 weeks so that by the end of the semester, students will have sat at each table and with every person in the class. Most likely they will have met classmates they never knew before (and I still have control over seating arrangements if there are conflicts). *Is it looking more like progressivism?*

Students have a 3-week list of assignments so that they can see what is coming up, have time to think about their approach to the assignments, budget their time, and work ahead should they choose. If they were absent, the board reminds them of what was due the day they missed. Today's assignments tell everyone what will be covered that day, and the upcoming assignments allow them to work ahead should they finish the work due that day. Students budget their own time and have total control over what they accomplish. *Students have total control? Is this existentialism?*

As soon as the students are seated at their tables, they look through the corrected papers and take theirs, so corrected work is retrieved by each student before the tardy bell rings; no time is wasted distributing handouts to the class because they are already at the individual tables. Organization is modeled, and one by one, students begin to pick up on that mode of operation. *One by one? Progressivism or existentialism?*

Although I determine the curriculum, it is based on what postsecondary school admissions and scholarship committees require. Each student determines his or her approach to the assignments. I assign a personal essay for use with school or scholarship applications, but each student begins by listing his or her three most outstanding character traits. The student then asks two acquaintances to list what they consider to be his or her three most outstanding traits. Each student then chooses on which of the nine traits he or she will focus and how he or she will develop the essay. *Is this progressivism with an emphasis on the individual child and encouragement of self-expression, or is it existentialism where the truth is determined by the individual and the thoughts uniquely their own?*

Students finish their personal essay and go on to a goals essay, which can also be used with school and scholarship applications. After individual exploration and listening to essays developed by former students, each student outlines his or her career goal, education goal (2-year, 4-year, vocational, technical, military, or apprenticeship), major, and choice of school(s), as *no single set of curricular outcomes is appropriate for all students.* Carefully the student crafts his or her goals essay. Teacher and peer evaluations result in several drafts before the final copy is submitted. Acceptance to a postsecondary school and funding are the desired outcomes. *Individual students, individual traits, individual goals. Teacher facilitates investigation, working with each student to probe for understanding and determine approach. Existentialism?*

So what philosophy most closely approximates not only my beliefs about education but my practices as well? At the beginning of my career, as a traditional English teacher, it was *perennialism.* I addressed the rigorous curriculum determined by others and imparted the knowledge, dealing mostly with the classics. We covered the material primarily through lecture and direct questioning, with some self-expression periodically as a motivator.

I moved on to *essentialism* in a class called Skills Lab. Students worked to improve reading, listening, study, and critical thinking skills, all essential for success, not only in school but in the real world as well. My approach was one of *progressivism.* I prepared students to be lifelong learners. I pretested each student to determine ability level and then engaged that student in hands-on activities on that level. Although the class began with teacher-directed activities, these were followed by individual students working their way through "stations" focusing on the goals of the class. There were 24 students, each working on his or her own ability level at his or her own station improving personal skills in that area. *Individuality . . . informality of classroom procedure . . . meaningful . . . student-focused . . . teacher as facilitator . . . progressivism.*

And now, although there are aspects of progressivism in my Senior Seminar class, I have moved on again, to *existentialism.* Why all this movement over the years? The subject matter demanded it. The needs of the students determined it. And my change in philosophy influenced it. Education is not a static field; my years of experience have prompted me to grow and change . . . shift and adjust . . . to the benefit of the students and to the renewed interest of the teacher.

2005 Colorado Teacher of the Year
Montrose High School
Montrose County School District
Montrose, Colorado

With what parts of the philosophies you have investigated do you agree? With what parts do you disagree?

The Eclectic Approach

Many people find they agree with some of the statements and premises of several of the philosophies but disagree with other parts.

If you embrace some of the tenets of two or more philosophies, you are said to be **eclectic** in your philosophical thoughts about education. Eclecticism is an approach in which you select and use what you consider to be the most appropriate portions of several different philosophies. For example, you may believe students should learn classic and other timeless concepts (perennialism) as well as the basics (essentialism) but that students should accomplish their studies through investigating, inquiring, and discovering on their own (progressivism). Or, you may believe in using group work to help students increase their academic knowledge (progressivism) and in encouraging students to make responsible choices about what to study (existentialism) but insist that their choices include topics that have an impact on society and social issues (social reconstructionism).

BUILDING BLOCK 2.8

Reexamining Your Philosophical Beliefs about Education

Take a few minutes to reexamine your philosophical tenets in education as revealed by your initial thoughts in Building Blocks 2.1 and 2.2 and refined by your studies in this chapter. Then, write your answers to the following questions.

1. What do you believe should be taught? To which of the philosophies is this the closest?
2. Who do you believe should decide what should be taught? To which of the philosophies is this the closest?
3. Why do you believe this material should be taught? To which of the philosophies is this the closest?
4. How do you believe this material should be taught? To which of the philosophies is this the closest?
5. What do you think the teacher's role should be? To which of the philosophies is this the closest?
6. What do you think the student's role should be? To which of the philosophies is this the closest?

A Continuum of Schools of Philosophic Thought

The five major philosophies of education you have explored can be placed on a continuum, with the highest amount of curriculum direction provided by teachers, educators, and society on the left and the highest amount of curriculum direction provided by students on the right (see Figure 2.3).

On the left (no political analogy implied) of Figure 2.3 is the perennialist philosophy in which society at large, through numerous citizen and political task forces, has estab-

Educational Philosophy Continuum

Perennialism	Essentialism	Progressivism	Social Reconstructionism	Existentialism
Curriculum determined by society	Curriculum determined by society and teachers	Curriculum jointly determined by teachers and students	Curriculum determined democratically by teachers and students	Curriculum determined by students

Figure 2.3
Educational Philosophy Continuum.

lished certain basic classics and truths that should be transmitted to students; this curriculum preserves the liberal arts tradition. Then comes essentialism, in which the educators have determined the basic subjects and skills all students must know and be able to do based on society's determination of basic subjects and skills.

Next is progressivism, in which the teacher and the students jointly decide what is important to learn—basic classics and truths, basic skills, and current and changing topics. This is followed by social reconstructionism, in which classes of students decide what to learn based on a democratic decision of which of the many ills in society should receive their attention. On the right is existentialism, in which the student decides what to learn based primarily on his or her perceived needs and interests.

Other philosophies, such as idealism, realism, experimentalism, and critical theory, have an impact on education, but we have focused in this chapter on the philosophies we believe are basic to education.

School Philosophy and Mission Statements

Most schools formalize their educational philosophies in written mission statements. A mission statement gives the school's basic purpose and goals and often provides insight into its prevailing educational philosophy.

Portions of actual mission statements of a few schools are given here. As you read them, try to identify their primary educational philosophies. What aspects of the mission statement lead you to that specific philosophy?

Mission Statement of a Public Elementary School
The mission of our school is to offer all students an opportunity to achieve their greatest potential by providing the highest quality of learning. We believe that with the guidance of our staff, the involvement of parents, and the encouragement of the community, all students can learn and master basic academic skills. Our mission is to provide each child with a superior education and necessary skills to lead them in becoming self-sufficient, productive citizens in our ever-changing world.

Mission Statement of a Public Middle School
Our mission is to provide a unique learning experience for all students which will be academically challenging, interdisciplinary in nature, and which will reflect the values of the local community and of society as a whole. Students will be enabled to develop individually while being given the means to recognize their own self-worth, and to achieve their role as knowledgeable and responsible members of the society of the future.

Mission Statement of a Public High School
The mission of our school is to provide each student with a safe learning environment and an equitable opportunity to develop competencies necessary to become a productive member of society.

Mission Statement of a Private School
We believe that a child learns best within an environment which supports each individual's unique process of development. We emphasize cognitive and physical development along with global awareness and peaceful conflict resolution. The teacher functions as a "guide" to help students carry out many different kinds of research following their interests, and develop their curiosity and a love of learning. Our priorities are for students to make intelligent choices, focus and concentrate, and engage in caring and purposeful interaction with the environment and with others.

Use the Internet to find mission statements of schools in your area.

- Are they consistent with what you think about education?
- Would you want to teach at these schools? Why or why not?
- How important do you believe it is that your personal philosophy of education be congruent with the written philosophy of the school at which you teach?

Philosophic Perspectives of Non-Eurocentric Cultures

The educational philosophies we have discussed so far are American in nature and are steeped in European philosophical traditions. These philosophies are the driving force behind American education. Using this Eurocentric view, you have examined what you think is important in education and how those thoughts inform the beginnings of your philosophy of education.

As you have seen, our philosophy of education is strongly influenced by who we are and what our beliefs are. Tradition and culture are very important factors in the formation of our beliefs. Many teachers grew up in non-Eurocentric cultures, and many received their education in countries other than the United States. Cultural diversity among students is the norm in the classroom, and groups that used to be considered the minority are rapidly becoming the majority in many school districts. Thus, as a teacher, your cultural heritage is very likely to be different from those of some of the students in your classes. This means your philosophy of education could be in conflict with the philosophical beliefs of some students and their families. As a teacher, you must be aware and respectful of the values of your students, their families, and the community, even if these values differ from your own convictions. Activities and teaching methodologies that are inconsistent with the value structures of any particular culture represented in your classroom may limit motivation and may precipitate conflict between what the student experiences at school and at home. You must recognize and deal with these differences to avoid misunderstandings that can interfere with your effectiveness as a teacher. In Chapter 4, you will explore in more detail cultural diversity and how it affects teaching.

© BananaStock/Alamy

An important aspect of every effective teacher's philosophy of education is an awareness of their students' diversity.

Theories of Educational Psychology

This investigation into educational thought would not be complete without a look at the basic and pervasive psychologies of education. Whereas one's educational philosophy focuses on the now-familiar questions of what should be taught, how it should be taught, and what teachers and the students should do in the teaching/learning process, educational psychologies deal with ways in which the mind actually behaves while it is learning—that is, how learning occurs. As you will see, educational psychologies exert strong influences on teaching and philosophical practices, and teaching and philosophical practices exert strong influences on educational psychologies. They help provide structures for teaching methodologies, curriculum selection, and assessment procedures. You will examine educational psychologies in detail as you progress through your teacher preparation program.

As with philosophies, there are no right or wrong psychologies. During this discussion, you will examine your *own* thoughts and form your *own* conclusions. In so doing, you are forming the platform on which you will construct your personal conceptualization of excellence in teaching. And, as you have seen, excellent teachers have many different qualities.

There are many psychologies—many ways of explaining how people learn and what motivates them to behave the way they do. In this section, we focus on four psychologies that have different understandings of the human mind and therefore different applications in school. *Humanism* focuses on the need for personalization to achieve meaningful learning. *Behaviorism* explains learning in terms of external factors and stimulation. *Information processing* explains learning through analysis of how the brain processes new and stored information. *Constructivism* holds that learning occurs by attaching new experiences to existing knowledge in meaningful ways.

Educational Psychologies

Write down a few situations in which:

1. The teacher tried to see things your way. What educational psychology does this seem to represent?
2. The teacher encouraged you to come up with your own ideas. What learning theory does this seem to represent?
3. The teacher tried to encourage you to learn by promising you rewards. What psychological theory does this seem to represent?
4. The teacher taught you how to memorize long lists of information. What learning theory does this seem to represent?

Let us examine these four theoretical approaches to learning.

Humanism

The psychology of **humanism** emphasizes people's intrinsic capacities for personal growth and their abilities and desires to control their own destinies. Humanists believe people are capable of learning through their own efforts. You became somewhat familiar with humanist principles in Chapter 1, when you looked at the work of William Glasser and Arthur Combs.

Humanism was formalized as a psychology in the 1960s. The humanist believes it is necessary for teachers to understand the perceptions of individual students—to find how things seem from the student's point of view. Humanists see two basic components of learning: (1) the acquisition of information and (2) the individual's personalization and internalization of that information. According to the humanist, teachers not only must

With which of the major philosophies of education do you suppose the humanist psychology is most compatible? With which do you suppose it is least compatible?

Have you ever had a teacher who was so wrapped up in the subject material that he or she seemed to be unaware that students were in the class? How did this make you feel?

www A direct link to the Association for Humanistic Psychology website is available on the *Building Teachers* companion website.

know their subjects and see that the material is properly organized and presented but also must help students make personal meaning out of the material.

Humanism is well represented by the work of Glasser and Combs and also by the work of Maslow and Rogers. Abraham Maslow developed a hierarchical theory of human motivation that asserts that people become self-actualized to accomplish higher motives after they have fulfilled certain basic needs. (You will investigate Maslow's hierarchy in Chapter 3.) Carl Rogers developed the "Person-Centered" approach to psychology that says if we approach a person with empathy, genuineness, and nonpossessive warmth, we can enable that person to grow and develop maximally (Rowan, 2001). Rogers believed that people have a natural desire to learn and that learning must be meaningful, self-initiated, and free from threat. To Rogers, the teacher is a facilitator of learning, acting as a guide and providing students with the needed resources.

Rather than focusing exclusively on the material to be taught, humanist educators also focus on the people who are doing the learning. They focus on people's feelings, interests, likes, dislikes, abilities, and other personal qualities. The humanist educator believes learning is an "inside job"—that people learn through their own intrinsic efforts. This contrasts with other approaches that focus on pouring the information into the student without particular regard for the individual. Humanist educators believe teachers are not essential as a condition for learning; students can learn through their own internal efforts. They believe teachers cannot "teach" something to an entire class of students and expect every student will learn it. Humanist teachers adopt a position of "facilitator" to help students find and implement their most effective ways of learning.

Behaviorism

Behaviorism is a psychology that contends that learning as exhibited by one's behavior is shaped by the environment. According to behaviorists, the behavior of an individual is formed more by the actions and reactions of other people than by the individual's own free will. The psychology of behaviorism arose in the late 1940s and was based on the work of the Russian physiologist Ivan Pavlov, who developed the concept of **classical conditioning** through his research with dogs. In Pavlov's scheme, dogs can be conditioned to salivate in response to the ringing of bells as well as the presence of food, even though bell ringing has nothing to do with actually receiving food.

B. F. Skinner (1904–1990) extended the work of Pavlov to develop his **operant conditioning** theory. According to Skinner, a person's behavior is a function of its consequences; that is, it is what happens *afterward,* not before, that influences behavior. This has come to be known as **behaviorism.** To visualize this theory, imagine a student who takes an algebra test. The teacher announces that a candy bar will be given to every student who earns a perfect score. Our student gets a perfect score on the first test, gets the candy bar, and, according to behavioral theory, studies hard for the next test because of the expected reward. As another example, suppose you begin a conversation with your neighbor during class. The instructor stops the class and reprimands you. According to behavioral theory, you will not talk with your neighbor again because you want to avoid similar consequences in the future. It is the reprimand that has shaped your future behavior. It is what happened afterward that influences your future behavior. The basic principle is that the consequences of any behavior will cause an increase, decrease, or no change in the likelihood of that behavior occurring again.

The psychology of behaviorism has wide use in the classroom. As you can imagine, numerous classroom and behavior management strategies, such as the rules-rewards-punishment approach, are grounded in behaviorism. (You will investigate methods of classroom management in Chapter 8.) Many instructional strategies are behaviorist in nature. Programmed instruction was one of the earliest educational applications of behaviorism; this has given way to computer programs, interactive CD-ROMs, computer-based tutorial programs, and other computer-assisted instruction applications. Behaviorist teachers tend to favor drill, repetition, and reward-based teaching methodologies.

A good example of the influence of behaviorism in the classroom is **programmed instruction,** a method of teaching attributed to B. F. Skinner because of his concern about the difficulty in providing suitable academic reinforcements to each student in a class. In programmed instruction, the unit or lesson is broken into a series of very small steps that are presented in sequence. Each step requires a response from the student. If the student is correct, the teacher provides some form of reinforcement, such as "Good for you!" "Yes!!!" "Great job!" and the like, and the student is permitted to move to the next step. If the student is incorrect, he is referred to material designed to teach the concept.

In the 1950s and 1960s, programmed instruction was presented in text form. When computers became available, the system was computerized. Typically, in electronic programmed instruction, a piece of information is presented on the screen and the student is asked to key a response to a question about this information. The computer gives a "Yes" or a "No" response. If the response is "Yes," the computer provides reinforcement. If the response is "No," the computer refers the student to additional screens that "teach" the information; after reviewing this additional material, the student tries a similar question.

Current applications often bypass the reinforcing and recycling features but retain the system of presenting the information in small incremental steps. Because students can work their way through the program without teacher assistance, such programs often are called **tutorial programs**. You may have used a tutorial program in school, or you may have used one to learn a new computer program.

Links to several web-based programmed instruction lessons and tutorials can be found on the *Building Teachers* companion website. Computerized tutorials are also available on CD-ROMs. Try one for yourself.

Much debate surrounds the efficacy of using a behavioral approach in motivation. Certainly there are times when rewards and punishments foster students' attainment of desired goals. We all are behaviorists to some extent. Who, for example, has not wondered how much credit would be given for certain tasks accompanying their college courses? Indeed, report cards themselves can be considered behaviorist in nature.

There is ongoing debate between those who believe humanism is the best approach to education and those who believe behaviorism is the best approach. Humanists subscribe to the idea that the most meaningful motivations are related to the internal satisfactions that come from doing well and that students learn to work for their own intrinsic feelings of accomplishment. For example, the inward uplifting feeling you get from presenting a well-prepared report is far more motivating and satisfying than receiving an external reward from the professor (although that is comforting as well). In the behaviorist classroom, students learn to work for rewards given by the teacher.

We take no sides on the humanism versus behaviorism issue. Both have strengths, and both have limitations. You will study these theories in detail in later courses, after which you can make up your own minds.

> With which of the major philosophies of education do you suppose the behaviorist psychology is most compatible? With which do you suppose it is least compatible?

Information Processing

Information processing theory focuses on how the brain processes information by attending to stimuli, receiving information, processing information, storing information in long-term and short-term memory, and retrieving information. According to the information processing approach (often called **cognitive psychology**), people have the ability to manipulate information in thinking, problem solving, and other intellectual operations by using three basic mental processes: attending to sensory input in the sensory register, encoding the attended information in the short-term memory, and retrieving information from the long-term memory.

Information processing psychology was developed in the late 1950s, when computer technology was being developed. It was formed partly as a reaction to limitations seen in the behaviorist approach to education and partly to use the computer as a model for the way people think.

According to the information processing theory, people first take information into their brains by paying attention (attending) to information coming their way. The information enters the cognitive processing system through the senses and is taken into the sensory register. If the individual does nothing with the information in the sensory register, it is lost. This occurs, for example, when the teacher is lecturing and the student is daydreaming; the teacher's words reach the student's ears and stimulate the hearing receptors, but nothing happens to them in the sensory register. On the other hand, if the person pays attention to the information, it is transferred to the short-term memory, where it can be held, processed, and transferred to the long-term memory, or, if nothing is done to process the information, it is lost. Once in long-term memory, the information is never lost (although it may be difficult to retrieve) (see Figure 2.4).

According to the information processing theory, learning takes place in the short-term memory, where new information and information retrieved from long-term memory interact with each other. The result is a change in memory. It is the teacher's responsibility to help students develop processes that support the needed changes in memory. This is carried out by employing strategies such as the following:

- Organizing information carefully
- Linking new information to existing knowledge
- Recognizing the limits of attention
- Recognizing the limits of short-term memory
- Providing encoding strategies to ensure that new information is meaningful

It is important to note that the terms *sensory register, short-term memory,* and *long-term memory* refer to processes rather than actual structures. Medical and psychological research currently is taking place to ascertain the actual physiological workings of the brain; some day we may have information processing models that show how the brain cells themselves work in attending, perceiving, storing, retrieving, and manipulating information.

With which of the major philosophies of education do you suppose the information processing theory is most compatible? With which do you suppose it is least compatible?

Diagram of the Information Processing System

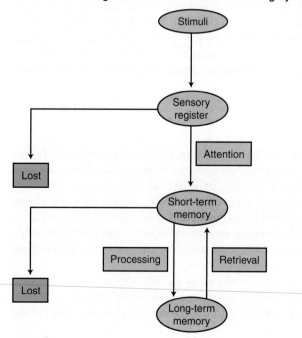

Figure 2.4
Information Processing Model.

Constructivism

Constructivism is an approach to teaching and learning that asserts that people actively construct their own understandings of information—that learners combine existing information with new information such that the new knowledge provides personal meaning. In the constructivist viewpoint, people build their own knowledge and their own representations of knowledge from their own experience. Learning does not occur by transmitting information from the teacher or the textbook to the student's brain; instead, each student constructs his or her own personal and valid understanding of this information.

Jean Piaget (1896–1980), a Swiss child psychologist, gave structure to the idea of constructivism. Piaget viewed the acquisition of knowledge as a continually developing process rather than as an end state. He viewed the mind as an aggregation of cognitive structures he called **schemata** (singular: **schema**). According to the constructivist view, schemata are opened, enlarged, divided, and connected to one another in response to the influx of information into a person's mind. Because no two people experience the same information in the same way, the schemata possessed by each individual are unique to that individual and are linked to one another in ways that represent the unique experiences the individual has had and the unique connections the individual has made between and among those experiences. In a sense, schema theory is like a set of computer files; each computer user labels files in his or her own way and groups them in folders unique to that person.

Independently, in the 1920s and 1930s, Lev Vygotsky (1896–1934), a Russian psychologist, also developed basic constructs of constructivism, but his work was not known to the Western world until much later. Whereas Piaget focused on the individual nature of constructing knowledge, Vygotsky emphasized the role other people have in an individual's construction of knowledge. In our computer analogy, Vygotsky would say that a person set up files in a unique way but used the input of other people to get started, resulting in some similarities between this person's filing system and that of others.

The constructivist teacher helps students make sense by helping each person attach the new information to information he already possesses. This process is often called constructing information, hence the term *constructivism*. The role of the constructivist teacher is to facilitate learning—to provide a variety of learning experiences that will enable each student to learn in his or her own unique way and construct the information such that it makes sense to that individual. The constructivist teacher asks students for their conclusions and their explanations rather than repetitions of what the teacher presented. To the constructivist teacher, it is far more important to listen than to tell.

As you know, this entire text is constructivist in nature. We have described the ways it is designed to engage students in Chapter 0, and you will revisit this concept periodically throughout the text.

With which of the major philosophies of education do you suppose constructivism is most compatible? With which do you suppose it is least compatible?

Educational Psychologies in the Classroom

BUILDING BLOCK 2.11

Review your responses to the questions in Building Block 2.10. Do you feel the same way? Are there any changes?

List two or three situations in which your learning was facilitated using each of the following approaches to education:

- Humanism
- Behaviorism
- Information processing
- Constructivism

Your Philosophy of Education

You have examined several basic philosophies and psychologies of education and have looked at your own thoughts. Now, you are ready to develop your own tentative philosophy of education—one that is personal to you.

My Philosophy of Education

Write a short preliminary philosophy of education. Consider these kinds of questions:

- What is the purpose of education? (What goals do you want your students to achieve?)
- What content should be taught? Why?
- How will you teach? Why?
- What are the teacher's roles and responsibilities?
- What are the students' roles and responsibilities?

Your philosophy should be a well-thought-out synthesis of your own thinking about your own teaching, *not* merely a compilation of answers to these questions. The questions are offered only to stimulate your thinking.

Compare your philosophy of education with the primary philosophies and psychologies you explored in this chapter. With which one or ones does your philosophy most favorably compare? Briefly explain why.

This activity is deliberately given at the beginning of the course to give you a chance to reflect on your own thinking and to review your thoughts as you move along. As such, your statement will not be an all-inclusive opus, nor will it be definitively refined. Rather, it will be an expression of your ideas about the teaching/learning experience as you see it now. You will use this statement to guide you in your construction and reconstruction of your thinking about quality education as you progress through the course.

Save this philosophy statement; you will use it again later.

Metaphors

One last comment dealing with your beliefs about education involves the use of **metaphors.** Researchers have looked at metaphors and teachers' latent beliefs about teaching as indicated by the metaphors they choose to characterize their role as a teacher (Bou Jaoudi, 2000; Munby, 1986; Pajares, 1992; Pittman & O'Neill, 2001; Tobin, 1990). For example, teachers characterizing themselves as "captains of their ships" may be very strong leaders, reluctant to transfer responsibility for learning to children.

Metaphors

Take a minute or two and think about a metaphor you would use to characterize your role as a teacher. Do you consider yourself the captain of your ship? A bus driver? An explorer? A scout leader? A parent?

Think about the metaphors that could be used to describe what a teacher does, and select one you believe most closely represents your current thinking about what a teacher's role is. Write it down and explain what it means.

Refer to the metaphor you choose frequently during this course; consider whether you want to change it. This may be one of the better indicators of how you are constructing the content of the course.

Conclusion

In this chapter, you have examined your current beliefs about education and have compared these beliefs with the characteristics of several different philosophies. We have suggested that educational philosophies try to answer several basic questions: what should be taught, who should decide what should be taught, why this material should be taught, how this material should be taught, and what the roles of the teacher and the student should be.

Perennialists believe schools should transmit the accumulated wisdom of past generations to today's students in a disciplined environment. Essentialists believe students should learn basic material such as the "3 Rs"; the teacher is the authority, and the students' job is to learn the material. Progressivists believe schools should develop thinking and problem-solving skills in students and should help students learn how to keep up with change; students and teachers are co-inquirers into areas of study determined by the school system and the teacher. Existentialists believe schools should teach students to make responsible choices as free individuals and should encourage them to study what is of interest to them through individual discovery and inquiry; the teacher functions primarily as a facilitator. Social reconstructionists believe it is the duty of schools to educate students to influence the reconstruction of society.

You saw that American education is driven by these Eurocentric philosophies. However, many students and teachers subscribe to non-Eurocentric perspectives, and their beliefs and expectations may differ from those governing mainstream American education.

You found there are several psychologies that describe beliefs about the way people learn. Humanists believe people are intrinsically capable and desirous of growing and learning. Behaviorists believe people's behavior is shaped by their environment and its extrinsic forces. Information processing theorists believe people learn through proper manipulation of the sensory register and short- and long-term memory functions. Constructivists believe people actively construct their own understandings by combining new information with prior experiences.

In this chapter, you saw that you already have beliefs and ideas about education, some of which are quite strong. From these prior conceptualizations and subsequent expansion and refinement, you constructed your own individual philosophy of education, which, in all probability, revealed an eclectic approach that embodies fundamental principles and concepts from several philosophies.

Trying to categorize your beliefs into a single philosophy is difficult. Do not be concerned if you were unable to put a clear-cut label on your philosophy of education. Remember that most contemporary philosophies are eclectic in nature and that you are building a philosophical foundation. You will have many experiences and will study much new information as you progress through this course and your teacher preparation program, and, indeed, throughout your professional career. Your foundation may be reinforced, or it may undergo continual revision and refinement as a result of experiences. The bricks you have laid in the foundation in this chapter are not set in cement. Keep your mind open and be willing to explore all the factors that you will experience.

The next chapter begins Part 2 of this text. In it, you will explore the source of perhaps the biggest impact on your educational philosophy—your students.

Key Terms and Concepts

Axiology, 40
Behaviorism, 60
Classical conditioning, 60
Cognitive psychology, 61
Constructivism, 63
Cosmology, 40
Deductive reasoning, 42
Epistemology, 40

Humanism, 59
Inductive reasoning, 42
Information processing
    theory, 61
Logic, 40
Metaphor, 64
Metaphysics, 40
Ontology, 40

Operant conditioning, 60
Pedagogy, 42
Programmed instruction, 61
Schemata (singular:
    schema), 63
Theology, 40
Tutorial program, 61

Construct and Apply

1. Suppose you are a sixth grade teacher and you have to teach all the subjects. How would you set up your classroom if you were a

    a. Perennialist?

    b. Essentialist?

    c. Progressivist?

2. A high school English teacher has decided to teach a 4-week unit on American poetry.

    a. Describe how this teacher would teach this material if she subscribed to the essentialist philosophy of education.

    b. Describe how this teacher would teach this material if she subscribed to the progressivist philosophy of education.

3. Fill in the columns below with the major concepts pertaining to each educational philosophy discussed in this chapter. Then, fill in the last column to represent your own philosophical thoughts.

	Perennialism	Essentialism	Progressivism	Existentialism	Social Recon- structionism	Yours
What should be taught?						
Why should it be taught?						
How should it be taught?						
What should the teacher's role be?						
What should the student's role be?						

4. Suppose you were teaching a class of fourth graders. List several things you might do in your classroom that reflect each of the following approaches to teaching and learning:

    a. Humanism

    b. Behaviorism

    c. Information processing

    d. Constructivism

Deconstructing the Standards

INTASC Principle #2 says:

> The teacher understands how children learn and develop, and can provide learning opportunities that support their intellectual, social, and personal development.

INTASC Principle #3 says:

> The teacher understands how students differ in their approaches to learning and creates instructional opportunities that are adapted to diverse learners.

For each of these two principles, write your responses to the following:

- What part(s) of this principle does this chapter address?
- How does this chapter address this principle?
- How will the concepts in this chapter help you apply this principle as a teacher?

Field Experience

- What are the governing educational philosophies of your cooperating teacher and the school to which you are assigned for your field experience?
- What are some of the ways in which your cooperating teacher approaches children of diverse cultures?
- What does your cooperating teacher in your field experience school do that shows the use of humanistic methods? What does your cooperating teacher do that shows the use of behaviorist methods?

Your Portfolio

In this chapter, you have considered many factors dealing with several philosophies and psychologies of education. Select two or three pieces of evidence that show your mastery of this topic and put them in your portfolio. This evidence could include your statement of your educational philosophy and other work done in class, work done out of class, or field experiences where you have had the opportunity to demonstrate your philosophy by implementing some aspect of classroom activity based on your philosophy.

Technology Resources

 Check out the *Building Teachers* companion website—http://www.education.wadsworth.com/martinloomis1—for more information about philosophies and psychologies of education, including links to the following resources:

- Complete texts of *A Nation at Risk* and *The No Child Left Behind Act Executive Summary*, as well as a link to the Core Knowledge Foundation established by E. D. Hirsch, Jr.
- "Who Owns the Zebra?" deductive logic puzzle
- A summary of Paulo Freire's *Pedagogy of the Oppressed*
- American Association for Humanistic Psychology
- Biographies of prominent philosophers: Mortimer Adler, Robert Hutchins, William Chandler Bagley, A.S. Neill, and George Counts

 See video footage of effective teachers in action on the *Building Teachers* CD-ROM that accompanies your textbook.

 Also link to InfoTrac College Edition through the *Building Teachers* companion website. Use InfoTrac College Edition to search for articles to enhance your study.

PART II

Student

In Part I you saw that many characteristics of effective teachers affect student achievement, and you saw that many different types of effective teaching are consistent with these characteristics. You saw your self and your beliefs about effective teaching as a primary influence on your understanding of the most effective ways of teaching. You added new experiences and understanding to your original beliefs and predispositions, building your preliminary philosophy of education.

In Part II you will explore the most important element of education—the students.

We hear a lot about the many ways in which students are different. Phrases such as these permeate discussions about education:

- "*All* students must learn."
- "Individualize your instruction."
- "Teachers must meet the needs of *every* student."

Certainly students differ from one another in many ways. The concept of student uniqueness, however, has received so much emphasis that we tend to forget there also are ways in which students are alike.

It is important to understand differences among students so that you can tailor their education to meet their needs. It is equally important to understand commonalities among students, so that you can provide suitable motivation and learning experiences for all your students. The three chapters of Part II invite you to look at how students are alike, how they are different, and how you can accommodate *all* students in your classroom. In Chapter 3, you will investigate students' common needs and how these needs are related to motivation. In Chapter 4, you will investigate the unique perspectives students bring to school, and in Chapter 5, you will investigate students' unique abilities.

The Student: Common Needs

Student learning and memory are closely tied to motivation. Students will learn what they want to learn and will have great difficulty learning material that does not interest them. Students are not poor learners; nor are they unmotivated. They are learning all the time—new dance steps, the [school] status hierarchy . . . , football strategy, and other more or less complex things—but the sort of learning for which students are motivated is not always that which contributes to attaining the goals of our [classes].

W. J. McKeachie, Professor Emeritus, University of Michigan

Other than yourself, your experiences with school, and your beliefs about education, the most significant influence on your teaching is—and should be—your students. Students bring with them many different characteristics that affect their academic achievement. Yet they are alike in many ways and have common needs.

This chapter is devoted to the exploration of needs shared by all students. Students have several fundamental needs. Among these are basic human needs, cognitive needs, and psychosocial developmental needs. You will investigate each of these categories from the viewpoint of your own experiences and understandings and through the theories and conclusions of researchers. You will find ways these common needs can be satisfied for all students in your classroom.

Because motivation is a primary concern in teaching, and because motivation is closely linked to needs, you will investigate ideas about the relationships between needs and motivation. You will consolidate what you already know about students with the work of others to construct your own conceptualizations of students' common needs, how students are alike, and how they are motivated in school. What does the quotation that opens this chapter indicate to you about motivation? What implications does it suggest for you as a teacher?

CHAPTER GOALS

As a result of your work in this chapter, you will:

1. Investigate theories of basic human needs and how these needs relate to student motivation.

2. Inquire into the nature of cognitive development, its relationship to student needs, and its influence on academic motivation.

3. Explore commonalities of psychosocial development, its relationship to student needs, and its influence on academic motivation.

4. Form conclusions about needs common to all students and how these needs relate to academic motivation and excellence in teaching.

What Do Students Need?

If you ask teachers, "What is the problem with our students today?" you are likely to hear answers such as "They're not responsible," "They're not disciplined," or "They're not motivated to learn." Often, teachers place the responsibility for student difficulties in the laps of their parents or on their environments. "Her parents just don't care!" "He's from the bad part of town; what do you expect?" However, when students are in classrooms, it is up to the teacher to provide engaging instruction and motivate them to learn. But what affects student motivation to learn? To answer this question, let us investigate what motivation entails.

Your Motivation

What would it take to get you to put down this book, stand up, find a crowd of people, step out in front of them, and cluck like a chicken? Would $5 do it? How about $10? Maybe $50 or $100? What semi-outrageous act would you perform for $100? Why would you do it? What would *motivate* you to do such a thing?

You might do this act for the money, assuming that the amount of money was enough to make the action desirable. Maybe you even said you *need* the money. Whatever the reason, you would not perform this outrageous act unless you were motivated to do it.

What motivates student learning? For some students, awards encourage student learning and achievement.

© David Young-Wolff /PhotoEdit

The concept of motivation includes the perception of a need and an action taken to meet that need. As Slavin (1997) says, ". . . motivation is what gets you going, keeps you going, and determines what you are trying to do" (p. 345). If you perceived a need for extra money, that need would give you the drive to do whatever you had to do to get some money. Your behavior would be driven by your need, with the money acting as a motivational force. Similarly, the drive to meet a need motivates students to exhibit particular behaviors, including the behaviors associated with learning.

We want our students to be motivated to learn. But motivation can occur only after certain needs common to all students are addressed. These needs include basic human needs of survival and self-fulfillment, cognitive needs, and psychosocial needs. Basic needs are those people need in order to live satisfied and happy lives. **Cognitive needs** are those people need in order to think and solve problems. **Psychosocial needs** are those people need in order to get along with themselves and with others. The nature of these needs changes with development, but these needs are essentially the same for all students at given developmental stages.

Basic Needs

All learners have the same basic needs, regardless of their differences in beliefs, interests, and goals. Whether and how these needs are met for any student affects that student's motivation to learn. Let us try to identify some of the common basic needs students bring to the classroom.

Basic Needs

1. Imagine yourself as a 3-year-old child. What are your needs?
2. Next imagine yourself as an early teenager. Do you still have the needs you identified as a 3-year-old? Have any gone away? Are there any new needs?
3. Then think about yourself at your current age. How have your needs changed? Which, if any, have remained?
4. Finally, anticipate your needs as a senior citizen. Identify new needs and needs that will no longer exist.

Maslow's Hierarchy of Needs

In Chapter 2 you saw that people become actualized to accomplish higher motives only after they have fulfilled certain basic needs. What needs did you identify in the Building Block 3.2? Which are associated with survival? Which are associated with protection? Which are associated with learning?

Psychologist Abraham Maslow identified seven categories of basic needs common to all people (1968):

1. Physiological needs (needs for food, water, and shelter)
2. Needs relating to safety and security
3. Needs relating to love and belongingness
4. Needs relating to self-worth and self-esteem
5. The need to know and understand (cognitive needs)
6. Aesthetic needs (needs relating to creativity, beauty, or art)
7. Self-actualization needs (needs relating to the ability to fulfill one's potential)

Maslow represented these needs as a hierarchy in the shape of a pyramid (Figure 3.1). A **hierarchy** is an arrangement that ranks people or concepts from lowest to highest. Ac-

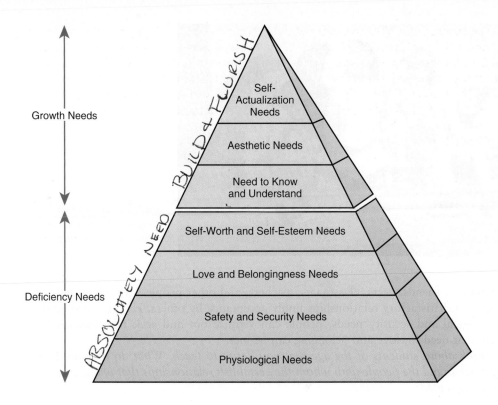

Figure 3.1
Maslow's hierarchy of needs.

cording to Maslow, individuals must meet the needs at the lower levels of the pyramid before they can successfully be motivated to tackle the next levels. The lowest four levels represent **deficiency needs,** and the upper three levels represent **growth needs.**

Physiological Needs

Notice that the physiological needs are the foundation of the pyramid. Why do you suppose these needs occupy this position?

Maslow suggested that the first and most basic need people have is the need for survival: their physiological requirements for food, water, and shelter. People must have food to eat, water to drink, and a place to call home before they can think about anything else. If any of these physiological necessities is missing, people are motivated above all else to meet the missing need. Have you ever had a hard time paying attention to what the professor is saying when you are hungry? Some of your future students may not have had breakfast—or even dinner the night before. Free and reduced breakfast and lunch programs have been implemented in schools to help students meet some of their physiological needs.

Safety and Security Needs

After their physiological needs have been satisfied, people can work to meet their needs for safety and security. (But the physiological needs must be met first.) Safety is the feeling people get when they know no harm will befall them, physically, mentally, or emotionally; security is the feeling people get when their fears and anxieties are low. How does this relate to students in school? What threats to their physical, mental, or emotional security might students perceive in school? (You will investigate safety and security in the classroom more thoroughly in Chapter 8.)

Love and Belongingness Needs

After the physiological needs and the needs for survival and for safety and security have been met, an individual can be motivated to meet the needs represented at higher levels of the pyramid. The third level of the pyramid are needs associated with love and belonging. These needs are met through satisfactory relationships—relationships with fam-

What might you do to provide for students' physical, mental, and emotional safety and security in your classroom?

Students can meet each other's need for love and belonging by sharing and talking.

How might you provide for students' love and belonging needs in your classroom?

ily members, friends, peers, classmates, teachers, and other people with whom individuals interact. Satisfactory relationships imply acceptance by others. Having satisfied their physiological and security needs, people can venture out and seek relationships from which their need for love and belonging can be met.

Think about students of the age that you desire to teach. What do they need from their teacher and the people with whom they establish relationships that will assure them they are accepted?

Self-Worth and Self-Esteem Needs

Once individuals have satisfactorily met their need for love and belonging, they can begin to develop positive feelings of self-worth and self-esteem, and act to foster pride in their work and in themselves as people. Before they can work toward self-esteem, however, they must feel safe, secure, and part of a group such as a class in school. In a study by Yamamoto et al. (1996), more than 1,700 children in grades 2 through 9 reported that the most stressful events in their lives were those that threatened their security and those that threatened to embarrass them, thereby challenging their developing sense of love and belonging. As a teacher, you need to find ways you can help students in your classes develop positive feelings about themselves and thus begin to satisfy their needs for self-worth and self-esteem.

How might you help students meet their needs for self-worth and self-esteem in your classroom?

The Deficiency Needs

The first four levels of Maslow's hierarchy of needs are essential for a person's well-being and must be satisfied before the person is motivated to seek experiences that pertain to the upper levels. If a student cannot meet any of these needs, that student will not be motivated to pursue any of the needs in the succeeding levels. Because of this, the first four levels of needs are called **deficiency needs.** After a deficiency need has been satisfied, a person's motivation to satisfy it lessens. Fortunately, many students come to school with the deficiency needs of physiology, safety and security, love and belongingness, and self-esteem already met—at home; in peer groups; in church, scouting, athletic, or music groups; in other groups; or in some combination of these. However, some students who come to school are not having these needs met elsewhere and look for ways to satisfy these needs in school. And *all* students must meet these deficiency needs before they can successfully work at learning.[1]

Why does the motivation to meet deficiency needs decrease as the needs are met?

The Need to Know and Understand

The fifth level of Maslow's pyramid represents an individual's need to know and understand. According to Maslow's hierarchy, this motivation cannot occur until the deficiency needs have been met to the individual's satisfaction. As you can imagine, the need to know and understand is a primary area of focus for education and is a topic on which we will concentrate. One of our primary jobs as educators is to motivate students so they will want to know and understand.

Aesthetic Needs

Aesthetics refers to the quality of being creatively, beautifully, or artistically pleasing; aesthetic needs are the needs to express oneself in pleasing ways. Decorating your living room, wrapping birthday presents attractively, washing and waxing your car, and keeping up with the latest styles in clothing are all ways of expressing your aesthetic sense. People are motivated to meet this need only after the previous five needs have been met. *In what (desirable) ways might your students express themselves aesthetically in your classroom? In what ways might you express yourself aesthetically in your classroom?*

The Need for Self-Actualization

At the top of the pyramid is the need for **self-actualization,** which is a person's desire to become everything he or she is capable of becoming—to realize and use his or her full potential, capacities, and talents. This need can be addressed only when the previous six have been satisfied. It is rarely met completely; Maslow (1968) estimated that less than 1% of adults achieve total self-actualization.

The Growth Needs

The upper three levels of the pyramid constitute a person's **growth needs.** Growth needs can never be satisfied completely. Contrary to the deficiency needs, for which motivation diminishes when a need is satisfied, as growth needs are met, people's motivation to meet them increases. The more these needs are satisfied, the more people want to pursue them. For example, the more one comes to understand, the more one's motivation to learn more increases. Have you experienced this yourself? In what situation? We hope you are experiencing this increased motivation to learn in your introduction to education course.

> **www** Direct links to several online personality tests are available on the *Building Teachers* companion website. Use these sites to find tests that assess your motivation to meet deficiency needs and tests that assess your motivation to meet growth needs.

> Why does the motivation to meet growth needs increase as the needs are met?

Maslow's Hierarchy of Needs

BUILDING BLOCK 3.3

Look at the needs you identified at various ages in Building Block 3.2. For each need, identify one or more categories of needs from Maslow's hierarchy with which it can be associated.

- How does the pattern of needs change as age increases?
- What other patterns can you notice?
- For each of Maslow's needs, list some actions you could take to help you meet these needs yourself.

BIOGRAPHY

© Bettmann/CORBIS

Abraham Maslow, psychologist (1908–1970), was one of the founders of the humanist psychology movement. He is most widely known for his view that people are motivated by successive hierarchical needs.

Born in Brooklyn, Maslow studied at the University of Wisconsin, where he received his B.A., M.A., and Ph.D. degrees in psychology. He taught psychology at the University of Wisconsin and later at Brooklyn College, where he came in contact with many European intellectuals, such as Adler, Fromm, and other European psychologists. Maslow moved to Brandeis University in Waltham, MA, where he served as chair of the department of psychology until his retirement in 1969.

Other Basic Needs Theories

Maslow's hierarchy of needs is common to all people and is widely accepted as a model for understanding and explaining motivation. However, other researchers and theorists also have identified human needs common to all people.

Noted psychologist William James, whose work Maslow studied, developed a theory that organizes basic human needs into three categories (Myers, 1992):

1. Material needs, including physiological and safety needs
2. Social needs, including the needs for belongingness and esteem
3. Spiritual needs

Mathes (1981) proposed three levels of motivational needs: physiological, belonging (including security and self-esteem), and self-actualization.

Alderfer (1972) developed a hierarchy based on Maslow's work, called the existence, relatedness, and growth (ERG) theory. In the ERG view, individuals must satisfy their requirements for existence (physiological and safety/security needs) and relatedness with other people (love/belonging and self-esteem needs) before they can grow in the areas of learning and self-accomplishment.

Alderfer correlated the needs in his hierarchy with actions typically required to meet these needs and ways people typically work to satisfy the needs. For example, to meet existence needs, Alderfer says individuals place a priority on acquiring material and psychological necessities, even if resources are limited. To meet relatedness needs, individuals participate in relationships with others in which they share ideas and feelings. For the growth needs, individuals act upon themselves or the environment to solve problems, leading to a creative product. These efforts engender a sense of accomplishment and contribution. Details of Alderfer's hierarchy of needs are shown in Table 3.1.

As noted in Chapter 1, Glasser (1993) identified five basic needs common to human beings:

1. Love (to care for and be cared for by others)
2. Power (to respect and be respected by others)
3. Freedom (to be allowed and encouraged to think for oneself)
4. Fun (to be able to laugh with others)
5. Survival (to make life secure)

In his Choice Theory, Glasser (1998) states that people are genetically predisposed to act to satisfy these five needs. In fact, Glasser argues, people choose how to behave partly as a result of this genetic influence.

TABLE 3.1 Alderfer's Hierarchy of Needs (ERG Theory)

Need	Action Required	How Met
Existence	Acquire material and physiological necessities	Attain what is needed, which becomes a priority, even if resources are limited
Relatedness	Participate in relationships with others	Share ideas and feelings, give and receive respect, understand, accept, and validate acceptance by others
Growth	Act upon self or environment to make creative products	Solve problems, leading to a sense of accomplishment and contribution

Another group that has expanded on the basic needs described by Maslow and others is The Search Institute, which describes sets of "developmental assets" of healthy and well-adjusted young people. Forty separate developmental assets divided into *external assets* and *internal assets* have been described for several age- and grade-levels, including early childhood, middle childhood, and adolescence (Search Institute, 2005).

A direct link to The Search Institute home page is available on the *Building Teachers* companion website. Find the developmental assets associated with the level of students in your field experience assignment and compare these assets with the students' behavior.

Basic Needs: Putting It All Together

You can see that commonalities exist in the basic needs theories and principles we have presented. What can you conclude from this? What are the basic needs common to all people?

Basic Needs Revisited

BUILDING BLOCK
3.4

Look again at people's basic needs identified by Maslow, James, Mathes, Alderfer, and Glasser.

- What are the commonalities? Which needs (if any) are addressed by only one researcher?
- How do students meet these needs?
- How does school help students meet these needs?
- How does the teacher help students meet these needs in the classroom?

Cognitive Needs

Maslow's fifth level (and first growth need) is the need to know and understand. As mentioned earlier, teachers focus primarily on this need; it is the one we are most prepared to help students meet. To do this, we must be aware that a student's potential for achievement is strongly influenced by the levels of cognitive development that all students go through (American Psychological Association, 1997) and that motivation is promoted by giving students tasks that are within the learner's cognitive capabilities.

Cognitive development is the intellectual development of the mind. As people grow and mature, they progress through several increasingly sophisticated stages of cognitive development, representing increasingly complex abilities to think and process information. People progress through the stages in the same order, but individuals move through the stages at different rates. Thus, at certain ages, most students tend to be at certain cognitive stages, and they need to be taught with strategies that are appropriate for their cognitive level. Older students have more highly developed abilities to think and reason than young children do. Accordingly, you would not try to teach algebra to first graders, and you probably would not require high school seniors to memorize nursery rhymes; these tasks normally are inappropriate for the cognitive levels of the students at those ages. Instead, you would teach algebra to older students and you would teach nursery rhymes to kindergartners to align the activities with the students' levels of cognitive development.

Let us consider the differences in people's cognitive development as they grow and mature. To get an idea of cognitive growth, compare the reasoning ability of a 3-year-old with your own reasoning as you think about the concepts presented in Building Block 3.5.

Cognitive Readiness

Look at this magnificent second-grade riddle: Which weighs more, a pound of feathers or a pound of lead?

Did you catch yourself? You have a *pound* of each, of course! They weigh the same. The riddle is a trick question that might make a 7-year-old slip up because, based on experience, children of that age "know" that lead weighs more than feathers.

Let us try something else. Suppose you have two empty glass containers like those labeled *A* and *B* in the illustration. You also have a pitcher holding 500 ml of water. If you pour half of the water in container A and the other half in container B, which container has more water?

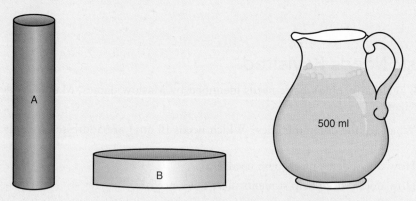

What was your answer? In fact, both containers hold the same amount of water: 250 ml. However, a 3-year-old would have told you that container A holds more water. Why would the young child say that? Even if you measured the amount of water in front of the child and poured the same measured amount into each container, the child would say that container A holds more water and would give the same answer when the demonstration was performed again. Why? What is different about your cognitive abilities from those of the young child?

How would it affect the child emotionally if you, the teacher, kept performing this demonstration, asking the same question, and insisting that the volume of water in each container was the same? What *needs* does this child have with regard to instruction that are influenced by his or her stage of cognitive development?

The concepts demonstrated in Building Block 3.5 deal with conservation. **Conservation** is the ability to recognize that the amount of material does not change when its volume or shape changes. Young children are not able to reason that the different shapes of the containers make the volumes only appear to be different. There are many such examples of young children's reasoning abilities. Young children believe a nickel is worth more than a dime because the nickel is bigger. Young children believe there are more pennies in a row if there are spaces between the coins than if the pennies touch each other. Young children believe there is more clay in a cigar-shaped cylinder than there was in the ball from which the cylinder was made—even when they see the ball rolled out into the cylindrical shape.[2]

According to Swiss biologist and psychologist Jean Piaget, all students progress through the same series of cognitive developmental stages as they get older. Piaget identified four stages, which progress from infancy through adulthood (Piaget, 1972). These stages, in the order in which students progress through them, are as follows:

1. Sensorimotor
2. Preoperational
3. Concrete operational
4. Formal operational

TABLE 3.2 Piaget's Stages of Cognitive Development

Stage	Approximate Age	Characteristics
Sensorimotor	Infancy	Information obtained through physical interaction with objects
Preoperational	Toddler and young child	Information obtained from increased use of symbolism and language Limited logic Egocentric perspective
Concrete operational	Elementary and early adolescence	Information obtained from manipulation of concrete objects Logical and reversible thinking Concept of conservation develops
Formal operational	Adolescence and adulthood	Information obtained through manipulation of symbols generalized to abstract concepts

The stages and the basic characteristics associated with each are shown in Table 3.2. Each stage represents more advanced capability (not accomplishment) for cognitive processing than the previous stages. Look at the characteristics associated with each level. How does your students' level of cognitive development relate to their basic needs? How does the level of your students' cognitive development affect your decisions about how to teach?

The earliest stage, the sensorimotor stage, is characteristic of children in infancy. During this stage, children's thinking abilities consist largely of interacting with their environment—what is around them. It is crucial to the intellectual development of children that they be given the opportunity to act on their environment in unrestricted (but safe) ways to start building the richest experiential bank they can. In later years, they will draw upon these experiences to make sense of what they are learning.

The second stage is the preoperational stage, characteristic of toddlers and young children. During this stage, children begin to develop an understanding of symbols such as letters, words, numerals, pictographs, and the like. Perhaps the most significant area of development during this stage is the acquisition of language. Preoperational children are egocentric in perspective; their thought is based on what *they* see or experience, not on what someone else has done. They cannot put themselves in someone else's shoes and tell, for example, what Janie probably saw with the magnifying glass; they can only tell what *they* saw. They are not able to reverse operations. For instance, they can learn that 6 plus 2 equals 8, but they are not able to make the reverse operation spontaneously that 8 minus 2 equals 6. Preoperational children also lack the maturity of thought that allows for conservational thinking, as you saw in Building Block 3.5.

We adults continue to be preoperational in our thought processes to a certain extent. How many people turn the map upside down when driving south? How many can follow directions to someone else's house but have difficulty finding their way back? And, to see how good you *really* are at conservation, go to an aquarium store and ask to see the various aquariums with, say, a 10-gallon capacity. It can be very difficult for us to believe that all the shapes hold the same amount of water.

Piaget's third stage is the concrete operational stage, characteristic of elementary-school and early adolescent children. During this stage, children must see, hear, feel, touch, smell, taste, or in some other way use their senses to *know.* "Seeing is believing" for concrete operational students. They can reverse thinking, and they gain increased ca-

We have indicated that adults spend much of their time thinking at the concrete operational stage. Why do you think that is?

pabilities of conservation. Many adults remain at this stage, never fully developing their formal operational thinking powers. (Remember that a cognitive stage represents the *capability* of intellectual development. It does not represent the accomplishment of that level.)

The fourth and uppermost stage is the formal operations stage, characteristic of adolescents and adults. In this stage, people have the ability to think and reason abstractly without requiring concrete examples. For example, a person in the formal operations stage will be able to imagine what it would be like if there were no gravity. However, this stage is not limited to older people; many younger students in the concrete operational stage are capable of some formal operational thinking. In Piagetian theory, formal operations is the ultimate achievement in human intellectual development.

Lawson (1978) identified five basic aspects of formal operational thought to help clarify what is meant by formal operations:

- *Proportional reasoning.* (What are the proportions of boys and girls in your class?)
- *Isolation and control of variables.* (If you are sick and take an aspirin, eat a bowl of chicken soup, and go to bed early, which made you feel better?)
- *Probabilistic reasoning.* (What are the chances you will win the lottery?)
- *Correlational reasoning.* (To what extent do people's heights correlate with the grades they earn in school?)
- *Combinatorial reasoning.* (How many different words can you make from the letters in the word *mountains*?)

Although students may arrive at each stage at different times and may take different amounts of time before they are ready to reason in the following stage, students go through these stages in the same order.

BUILDING BLOCK 3.6

Cognitive Developmental Stages and Needs

Go back to that 3-year-old child and the water demonstration you thought about in Building Block 3.5. Using Piaget's stages of cognitive development, explain why the child would give the same incorrect answer again and again, even when you carefully explain that it is wrong. Recall the emotions you said the child would feel as you were attempting to explain this demonstration. How would the child's lack of understanding affect his or her motivation? As a teacher, what do you need to know about the cognitive development of the students in your class?

BIOGRAPHY

© Farrell Grehan/CORBIS

Jean Piaget (1896–1980), a biologist and psychologist, was born in Neuchâtel, Switzerland, the son of a professor of medieval literature. At age 11, he wrote a short paper on an albino sparrow; that paper is considered the start of his brilliant scientific career. In high school, he narrowed his scientific interest to mollusks, and he maintained his interest in this area for the rest of his life. He received his doctorate in science in 1918 and worked in European psychology labs, where he questioned the "right-or-wrong" nature of intelligence tests and began to ask how children reason.

Piaget watched children at play, talked with them and recorded the conversations in detail, and conducted research with them to try to discover their reasoning processes and how their minds develop. His research focused on the child's concepts of space, time, number, causality, and perceptual and moral development. His work led to the now-famous four stages of intellectual development. Less known, but perhaps more important, are his theories of schema, equilibration, and personal constructivism developed from his exacting and thorough investigations.

The Influence of Cognitive Needs on Academic Motivation

Recall your thoughts on how a student's level of cognitive development influences the kind of learning opportunities he or she needs. How does this need affect your instructional decisions? Motivation is a precursor to learning, and preparing activities and materials that are appropriate for the cognitive levels of development of your students is necessary for both motivation and learning. Asking students to work beyond their abilities will frustrate them. Asking them to work at levels below their abilities will bore them. Either of these emotions will crush any motivation students may have had.

Psychosocial Needs

A third way in which learners are alike is their progress through the stages of psychosocial development. **Psychosocial development** refers to the growth people experience in forming self-concepts, their ways of interacting with others, and their general attitudes toward the world. The development is both personal and social, and thus is termed *psychosocial*. Remember that a basic need of all people is to feel loved and to have a sense of belonging. Schools and classrooms are social places. Individuals go through developmental stages of psychosocial development, just as they go through stages of cognitive development. You have found that students' motivation and their potential for academic achievement are strongly influenced by both their basic needs and their level of cognitive development. The same is true of their level of psychosocial development.

BUILDING BLOCK 3.7

Some Psychosocial Predicaments

Consider how you would respond in each of the following situations. Also consider how different responses might encourage or discourage future behavior in the student. Are these behaviors the kind you would want a learner in your classroom to exhibit?

Suppose a 4-year-old reports that last year's teacher told her she must have grown a foot over the summer vacation. She then shows you a self-portrait with three feet, complete with shoes and socks on each. What will you say? What message will this send to the child? What behaviors will be encouraged and discouraged?

Suppose this same 4-year-old child tells you her mother "goed to the store." What will you say? What message will this send to the child? What behaviors will be encouraged and discouraged?

Now imagine the child is in fourth grade and is hanging upside down on the playground's jungle gym. Alarmed, you yell at her, telling her to be careful and to hold on with her hands. What message will this send? What behaviors will be encouraged and discouraged?

Finally, imagine the child as a middle school student asking a question such as "Why is the sky blue?" Perhaps this question is a little off the topic being discussed, or perhaps the student has caught the teacher off guard. Suppose the teacher says, "Why don't you find the answer to that question for us and share it with the class tomorrow?" What message is the student receiving? Or suppose a student asks a question about something the class has already covered and is met with laughs and taunts from the other students. What message is this student receiving? What behaviors will be encouraged and discouraged?

Stages of Psychosocial Development

Erik Erikson (1968) proposed that, at different ages, individuals must address certain psychosocial predicaments or life crises, and that other people play a large role in how individuals deal with these predicaments. Depending on how the individual is encouraged in his or her attempts to resolve a crisis, that individual's needs for continued development are either met or not met, and motivation is correspondingly increased or decreased.

For example, the psychosocial predicament prevalent in toddlers' lives is to develop a firm sense of autonomy—the certainty that they can control their environment. Toddlers want to try ideas for themselves (think of the so-called terrible twos) without always having to depend on others. It is essential that parents, teachers, and other adults permit toddlers to explore freely but safely and do things for themselves, while providing guidance and encouragement. Children who discover they *can* perform by themselves develop a sense of autonomy. Those who are discouraged, ignored, scolded, or punished develop a sense of shame for having demonstrated what they think is bad behavior, and they develop a feeling of doubt that they have the wherewithal to make things happen. For the child's healthy progression to the next stage of life, this dilemma must be resolved such that the child develops autonomy. Thus, this stage is identified as the autonomy vs. shame and doubt stage.

The feelings that are identified in Erikson's stages are fostered by the reactions of other people and thus are psychosocial in nature. Eriskon's psychosocial stages are shown in summary form in Table 3.3.

TABLE 3.3 Erikson's Stages of Psychosocial Development

Stage	Age	Expected Resolution
Trust vs. mistrust	Infancy	Learns to trust that needs will be met by constants in the environment (parents, physical objects) *or* Will mistrust and will react to get needs met
Autonomy vs. shame and doubt	Toddler	Learns to control environment and self *or* Will experience shame and/or doubt regarding perceived inappropriate self-control
Initiative vs. guilt	Early childhood	Learns to explore and initiate activities and tasks *or* Will feel guilt regarding inappropriate actions
Accomplishment/ industry vs. inferiority	Childhood	Learns to measure success by comparison to a standard *or* Will feel inferior when performance is below that standard
Identity vs. role confusion	Adolescence	Learns to identify a concept of self by associating with certain groups of others *or* Will vacillate between several roles, never forming a definitive association or conviction
Intimacy vs. isolation	Young adult	Learns to commit to long-term relationships with others *or* Will seek isolation
Generativity vs. stagnation	Middle adulthood	Learns to contribute to or affect the environment so as to affect future generations *or* Will feel that work and efforts are leading to no significant contribution
Ego identity vs. despair	Older adulthood	Looks back on life as well lived with little regret *or* Will feel life has been wasted

© Bettmann/CORBIS

Erik Erikson (1902–1994) was born in Germany. In high school he focused on becoming an artist; after graduating, he wandered around Europe visiting museums and sleeping under bridges, living a carefree and rebellious life. When he was 25, Erikson taught at an experimental school for American students, one of the early Montessori schools. While there, he developed his interests in psychology and sociology. In 1928, he began psychoanalytic training at the Vienna Psychoanalytic Institute, where Anna Freud was his analyst. Soon after graduating in 1933, Erikson left for the United States. He started a psychoanalytic practice in Boston, began research at Harvard, and later moved to the University of California at Berkeley.

At Berkeley, Erikson studied the Lakota and Yurok Indians, whose children and adolescents faced difficulties finding their place in the world because of conflicts between the very strong native traditions taught by their families and the instruction of the teachers in the American schools they attended. The children's white teachers found them difficult to work with, and their parents believed they had been corrupted by a foreign culture. Erikson's studies led him to analyze the conflicts people go through on their way to adulthood.

In 1960, Erikson took a position as a professor at Harvard, and he stayed there until his retirement in 1968. He is best known for his epigenetic principle, which says people develop through the unfolding of their personalities in eight stages, each of which involves certain developmental tasks that are psychosocial in nature.

The Influence of Psychosocial Needs on Academic Motivation

How do the ways in which students resolve their psychosocial needs influence their motivation to succeed in school? First, think about the questions presented in Building Block 3.8.

BUILDING BLOCK 3.8

The Psychosocial-Sensitive Classroom

In this activity, you will pay special attention to the psychosocial stages of initiative vs. guilt, accomplishment/industry vs. inferiority, and identity vs. role confusion; these are the stages most children encounter while they attend school.

First, consider young children whose psychosocial struggles are with initiative vs. guilt. How might you provide opportunity for your students to take initiative in your classroom without feeling guilty?

Next, consider elementary school children whose psychosocial struggles are with industry vs. inferiority. How might you provide the opportunity for your students to be industrious in your classroom without suffering feelings of inferiority?

Finally, consider high school students whose psychosocial struggles are with identity vs. role confusion. What kinds of classroom interactions could you provide to help students form their sense of identity? What effect would discouraging adolescents from social interaction have during this stage of development? What basic needs does forming a sense of identity through the establishment of relationships address?

Young children 3 to 6 years old are in the psychosocial stage of initiative vs. guilt. As we have seen, children at this stage seek to improve their language skills and to explore their environments to learn what they can about what they live with every day. According to Erikson, those who are encouraged to explore and who succeed in their efforts develop positive feelings of initiative. Those who are discouraged, severely corrected, or punished for their explorations and language exploits develop negative feelings of guilt—guilt for having attempted something they believe they should not have tried. Success breeds motivation, and lack of success thwarts motivation.

Did you conclude that children in this stage of development need to be given multiple and varied opportunities to explore? These explorations can occur in the schoolyard, on field trips, at school assemblies, through play, in hundreds of interesting classroom activities, and at home.

Children of elementary school age are in the psychosocial stage of accomplishment/ industry vs. inferiority. Their primary goal in life is to *do*—do anything. They want to learn all about everything, and they want to learn how to do everything, from swimming the breast stroke to playing chess to reciting the names of the constellations and identifying models of cars that go by. Successful accomplishment of these tasks fosters a desire to do even bigger and better things, resulting in feelings of accomplishment and industry and good feelings about themselves and their abilities. On the other hand, children who are discouraged from these extremely important developmental activities or who are criticized and scolded for doing them will develop feelings of inferiority—feelings they are not as good as others.

Did you conclude that elementary school children need to perform activities at which they can be successful? There are many different ways students can get involved, and there are many different activities students can use to learn basic concepts. These activities range from reading and writing to drawing, play-acting, and even composing rap songs and producing mini-operas. When a student's desire for industry is encouraged, that student will feel competent and capable, will be motivated to accomplish bigger and better feats, and will increase his or her expectation for success. However, if a student is made to feel inferior, he or she will experience a sense of failure and incompetence, leading to low motivation.

Adolescents have quite a different but equally difficult predicament in their lives: identity vs. role confusion. The adolescent constantly asks the question, "Who am I?" Physical changes, coupled with cognitive changes and a growing sense of wondering about their identity, causes adolescents to turn away temporarily from their parents and to try out different roles among people of their own age to see what "fits." Concurrently (and often surreptitiously), adolescents look to parents and other adults, including teachers, for positive role models. At this age, students experiment with various educational, sexual, recreational, and occupational roles in their attempts to find and become themselves. Those who are successful in their search discover their personal identities; those who are not successful develop feelings of role confusion that must be addressed before they can progress through subsequent stages and live happy, successful, and contented lives.

Did you decide it is important to encourage multiple relationships in high school? These can be fostered through classroom-based interactions, group projects, participation in extracurricular activities, and a host of other means. When a student is helped to form a positive self-identity, that student develops the virtues of loyalty, commitment, self-reliance, and independence. But if they do not know which group to affiliate with or commit to, adolescents can find themselves spread so thin they become burdened with feelings of not belonging to *any* group. With which of Maslow's basic needs do you associate this level of psychosocial development? Is it a deficiency or growth need? What does that mean?

In Eriksonian psychology, each stage must be resolved successfully in some manner before resolution of the successive stages can be achieved. Motivation depends largely on successful resolution of the predicament in each stage. Effective teachers work with their students to foster these resolutions.

General Academic Needs

Let us put all of this together. You have made some important inferences about common needs of students. We hope you have found that all students have the same basic human needs and all students have needs that are affected by their levels of cognitive and psychosocial development. It is time to focus on how these needs are represented academi-

Peer relationships in middle and high school help students form positive self-identity, which encourages progress through the other stages of psychosocial development, according to Erickson.

© Catherine Ledner/Getty Images

cally. We will start by imagining the first day of school or class. What needs must be met? What can the teacher do to alleviate concerns and ensure these needs are satisfied?

The Scary First Day of School

Take a moment to remember the first day of school. It doesn't matter what grade level you focus on; it probably isn't too hard to recall the anxiety you may have felt. Make a list of the questions or concerns you had in your mind at that time.

Then think of the first day of the class in which you are using this textbook. What were you worried about? What did you need to know? Why did you need to know it? Did your teacher help you relax your anxieties? If so, how?

Now consider a student entering *your* classroom on the first day of school. What do you think that student needs? How do these needs affect the student's incentive to learn? How can you help meet those needs?

BUILDING
BLOCK
3.9

Other pre-service teachers have reported that, on the first day of school, they were concerned about being in the right place, understanding what they were expected to do, and not being embarrassed. They wanted to be reassured that they were indeed in the right classroom with the right teacher, and they wanted to know how to behave in the classroom so that they fit in and didn't stand out from everybody else. Their teachers helped make them more comfortable by sharing their expectations, explaining classroom procedures, and establishing personal relationships with the students.

Even when you entered your college classroom, you may have had some of these same questions, concerns, and anxieties. These concerns are basically the same for students of all ages. Brooks (1985) identified seven classroom questions students need answered on the first day of school:

1. Am I in the right room?
2. Where am I supposed to sit?
3. What are the rules in this classroom?

CHAPTER THREE • The Student: Common Needs   **85**

4. What will I be doing this year?

5. How will I be graded?

6. Who is my teacher as a person?

7. Will the teacher treat me as a human being?

Did the needs you listed in Building Block 3.9 sound like these questions? Were the seven needs met in this class? How about in other college classes? How will you respond to these concerns (most of which are never spoken aloud) with your future students?

Try to link these questions to the needs identified in Maslow's hierarchy. Many of them have to do with the needs for safety, love and belonging, and self-esteem.

From this exercise, you can tell that students share basic concerns when they begin a school year or a new class. These concerns stem from anxieties that their classroom needs might not be met—that the teacher might minimize or misinterpret students' basic human needs, cognitive needs, and psychosocial needs. Will the teacher make all students feel accepted and valued? Or is the teacher inclined to ridicule those who don't think as he or she does? Are the teacher's academic expectations appropriate for the students' age and experience levels? Or are those expectations too difficult or (equally disturbing) too easy? Will the teacher foster independence or require conformity to the rules?

Familiarity with these concerns helps us understand how we must structure our teaching and our interactions with students to satisfy their fundamental needs, thereby motivating students to maximum achievement. For, as you have seen, meaningful learning cannot take place unless the basic human needs, cognitive needs, and psychosocial needs of each student have been recognized and addressed.

The application of these fundamental needs in school settings can be combined into a few central principles of teaching. Jones and Jones (1998) listed 12 academic needs basic to all students. Their list offers a good summary of where this chapter has been leading us. To meet their academic needs, students must do the following:

- Understand and value learning goals.
- Understand the learning process.
- Be actively involved in the learning process and relate subject matter to their own lives.
- Take responsibility for their own learning by following their own interests and setting goals.
- Experience success.
- Receive appropriate rewards for performance gains.
- See learning modeled by adults as an exciting and rewarding activity.
- Experience a safe, well-organized learning environment.
- Have time to integrate learning.
- Have positive contact with peers.
- Receive instructions matched to their learning style.
- Be involved in self-evaluating their learning and effort.

How do these academic needs relate to the three categories of needs you have been investigating in this chapter? In Building Block 3.10 you will associate the academic needs listed by Jones and Jones with Maslow's needs hierarchy, Piaget's stages of cognitive development, and Erikson's psychosocial ladder.

BUILDING BLOCK 3.10 — Academic Needs

The academic needs identified by Jones and Jones are shown in the left column of the following table. Read through the list and show how each might be related to Maslow's hierarchy of needs, Piaget's stages of cognitive development, and

Erikson's psychosocial ladder. Use the questions in the right column to guide your discussions; they are the kinds of questions competent teachers constantly ask themselves to be sure they are meeting their students' needs to maximize motivation and achievement.

What are the implications of this competed chart for you as a teacher?

According to Jones and Jones, Students Need to...	Maslow's Hierarchy of Needs	Piaget's Stages of Cognitive Development	Erikson's Psychosocial Ladder	Questions to Foster Discussion
Understand and value learning goals.				How could you help a student understand learning goals and attach value to them?
Understand the learning process.				What could you do to help a student understand his or her learning?
Be actively involved in the learning process and relate subject matter to their own lives.				Why is being actively involved important? Why is it important for subject matter to be relevant?
Take responsibility for their own learning by following their own interests and setting goals.				How does giving students responsibility help meet some of their basic needs?
Experience success.				How will the experience of success affect expectations?
Receive appropriate rewards for performance gains.				How will motivation be affected if a reward is meaningful to the student? What kinds of rewards are most meaningful?
See learning modeled by adults as an exciting and rewarding activity.				What basic need does the reward of learning and understanding fulfill?
Experience a safe, well-organized learning environment.				How does a well-organized classroom lead to a feeling of security?
Have time to integrate learning.				What emotions does feeling rushed lead to?
Have positive contact with peers.				How is peer contact important to psychosocial development?
Receive instructions matched to their learning style.				How does this relate to cognitive development?
Be involved in self-evaluating their learning and effort.				Why would having the opportunity to self-evaluate be motivating to a student?

from the
TEACHER Brenda Zabel

Courtesy of Brenda Zabel

Effective teachers create opportunities for students to take control of their own learning. By designing lessons that allow students to explore a concept at a level and pace that is appropriate and accommodates individual learning styles, teachers empower students to achieve in the classroom and beyond. Students who perceive they have choices in the classroom are much more motivated to become engaged and persevere in the face of challenge than are students who perceive their education as being force-fed as if from an already established, prescribed procedure.

When students are empowered to learn, rather than instructed to learn, they take ownership in the quantity and quality of the products they produce, whether those products be written documents, oral presentations, simulated models, or electronic multimedia performances. Students who feel they have some control over where, how, and how much they learn about a subject have a greater vested interest in the amount and quality of time and energy they are willing to devote to important curricular topics both inside and outside of the traditional classroom and the traditional school day. One of the most important things teachers do is provide opportunities for students to discover and communicate ways in which key instructional outcomes are relevant and applicable in the students' daily lives.

In the high school zoology and human physiology classes I teach, one nontraditional tool that I use to empower students is music. Music is a highly motivational medium for most teenagers. Early in the school year, my teaching colleagues and I provide a theme song to accompany each new learning unit. For example, prior to beginning a learning unit on reptiles, we might play Elton John's "Crocodile Rock" for all 300 of our students in a "concert hall" setting prior to a large group class meeting. It usually doesn't take long for the students to begin suggesting their own theme songs for upcoming units. We honor these requests by playing the students' choices and reward their efforts to find real-world connections for the topics we deal with in class. The students take special pride in finding a song that is some-how connected to one of our more technical topics, such as roundworm parasites or the human respiratory system.

Another way in which I attempt to empower my students to learn is by providing them different options about how to demonstrate their understanding of an important learning objective. During a project that occurs in a unit on human histology, students first select a team of students with whom they want to work to research one specific type of human tissue selected by the team. The team members divide up the work of finding out what the characteristics of the tissue are, how the tissue functions when it is healthy, and how it functions when it is diseased, and they prepare a group presentation to share their information with other teams of students who did not research the same tissue. All through the project, the students have choices and control over their progress. The group presentation usually mirrors the individual and collective strengths of the members of each group. For example, a team of students with dramatic skills might choose to perform a short one-act play, while another team with more musicianship could compose and perform an original musical score. A team with an artistic flair might create an elaborate poster painting or three-dimensional model while a different team might choose to deliver their information as a television newscast. Regardless of the format of the final product, students appreciate and respond positively to being given the opportunity to show what they have learned in a variety of ways, determined by them, rather than in one standard pattern way determined by the teacher.

2005 Nebraska Teacher of the Year
Westside High School
Westside Community Schools
Omaha, Nebraska

Self-Fulfilling Prophecy

A principle that has been validated numerous times throughout the past half-century is the *self-fulfilling prophecy*. This principle says, essentially, that if we expect children to perform at certain levels, they will.

The self-fulfilling prophecy as applied to education came from the work of Rosenthal and Jacobson (1968). In their classic experiment (which would never be approved today because of the possible detrimental effects on students), they separated the students in an elementary school randomly into two homogeneous groups. The researchers gave the teachers the names of several students who had been randomly chosen from each group, telling the teachers that these students had scored in the top 20% on an intelligence test they had administered to all students in the school. (In fact, the "high potential" students identified to teachers had not scored higher than any other students.) They alleged these students were "about to bloom" (Rosenthal & Jacobson, 1968, p. 70). The researchers noted, "The difference between the children earmarked for intellectual growth and the undesignated control children was [only] in the mind of the teacher" (p. 70). After one year of instruction, students who had been identified as "about to bloom" made significantly higher gains on intelligence test scores than students in the control groups. The researchers concluded, "When teachers expected that certain children would show greater intellectual development, those children did show greater intellectual development" (p. 83). The prophecy of the teachers—that superior students would achieve well and that less capable students would achieve poorly—had been fulfilled.

We have said many times in this textbook that teacher expectations are of great importance in motivating and fostering student achievement. For this reason, it is critical that you examine thoroughly any thoughts you might have concerning the characteristics and perspectives brought by students into the classroom so you can develop the expectation of high achievement for *everyone*.

Instruction that Addresses Student Needs

You have found that students are alike in many ways, possessing common basic, cognitive, and psychosocial needs. You have seen there are many successful approaches to teaching based on people's feelings, ideas, beliefs, and philosophical views. And you have identified characteristics of excellent teachers and effective teaching. Recognizing that numerous factors influence teaching and learning, you might ask, "How do we implement these factors in our classrooms?" To answer that question, let us correlate the characteristics of excellent teachers and effective teaching with the fundamental student needs discussed in this chapter.

Putting Together What You Know—Basic Needs

BUILDING BLOCK 3.11

Divide a blank sheet of paper into thirds horizontally by drawing two lines from top to bottom (see diagram). At the top of the middle column, write *Attributes of Excellent Teachers and Effective Teaching*. In this column, write the primary attributes you decided are characteristic of excellent teachers and effective teaching in Chapter 1.

Next, make a heading for the left column of your paper: *Students' Basic Human, Cognitive, and Psychosocial Needs*. List the basic needs you have found in this chapter to be common to all students.

Students' Basic Human, Cognitive, and Psychosocial Needs	Attributes of Excellent Teachers and Effective Teaching	

Draw lines from each of the basic needs in the left column to one or more attributes of excellent teachers and effective teaching in the middle column that might help address that need.

What does your paper look like? Are there many lines, all crisscrossing each other? Or are the connections few and far between? Can you modify or add to the list in the middle column to let you make more connections to the list in the left column? If so, make those modifications or additions and connect them to the appropriate needs.

What teaching skills might accompany the connections?

Save this paper to use in the next building block.

What are the connections between effective teaching and students' academic needs? As you have seen, the general academic needs represent an amalgam of basic human, cognitive, and psychosocial needs applied to the classroom.

BUILDING BLOCK 3.12

Putting Together What You Know— General Academic Needs

Retrieve your paper from the Building Block 3.11. Label the right column *Students' General Academic Needs*. List the general academic needs you have found in this chapter to be common to all students.

Students' Basic Human, Cognitive, and Psychosocial Needs	Attributes of Excellent Teachers and Effective Teaching	Students' General Academic Needs

As before, draw lines to connect the academic needs in the right column to the attributes of excellent teachers and effective teaching in the middle column.

What does your paper look like? Can you modify or add to the list in the middle column to let you make more connections to the list in the right column? If so, make those modifications or additions and connect them to the appropriate needs.

What are some teaching skills that might accompany the connections?

In Building Blocks 3.11 and 3.12, you related basic student needs and basic academic needs to characteristics of excellent teachers and effective teaching. Now that you've done that, what do you believe are the most valuable attributes of good teachers? Which of these do you currently possess? Which do you believe you need to develop or refine?

As you continue your explorations in this course, keep in mind that students are alike in many ways, including their basic human needs, their cognitive characteristics, and their

In this chapter, you have identified needs that are common to *all* students. It is important for teachers to acknowledge these needs and meet them in their classroom environments and instruction. Teachers can use technology in addressing many of these needs.

Let us review Brooks's list of questions that students have on the first day of school:

_____ 1. Am I in the right room?

_____ 2. Where am I supposed to sit?

_____ 3. What are the rules in this classroom?

_____ 4. What will I be doing this year?

_____ 5. How will I be graded?

_____ 6. Who is my teacher as a person?

_____ 7. Will the teacher treat me as a human being?

Now, consider some of the technologies that were introduced in Technology & Education in Chapter 1:

A. The Internet, used by teachers as a resource for content and for instructional and management ideas, and by students for content area information
B. Television and DVDs for educational programs
C. Electronic slide shows with color, graphics, sound, video, and animation
D. Content area software on CD-ROMs
E. Word processing programs to create neat and colorful handouts, worksheets, signs, and bulletin boards

How do the technologies match up with the questions? How can these technologies help teachers answer these student questions effectively and efficiently? Write the letter of a technology in the blank by any question that technology might help answer. You may have more than one letter per blank. You may not have any letters in a blank. You may be able to think of some technology that is not listed. By all means, write it in! There are myriad other technological applications we have not mentioned.

Most of the students' first-day-of-school questions have to do with a need to know. Teachers can use word processing programs to create signs and posters informing students of the room number, the teacher's name, the subject(s) taught, and the bell schedule. Word processing and publishing programs often contain templates for newsletters, which teachers can use to inform students and parents of classroom events and activities. Teachers can develop and maintain a class website with the information, or can email the information to students and their families. (Keep in mind, however, that not all of your students will have Internet access at home.) This initial communication with students and parents is invaluable in establishing an effective learning environment that will set the tone for the rest of the year.

What about the last question: "Will the teacher treat me as a human being?" The technologies a teacher uses to introduce himself or herself to the class can do the same for students. Students would welcome the opportunity to introduce themselves by writing a paragraph, sending an e-mail, or drawing a picture to give the teacher information about them beyond what is contained in student records. (Drawing packages are available for young students to use on the computer.)

How can technology help meet some of students' common needs? Using the technologies described earlier contributes to a safe and well-organized learning environment. Computer-assisted instruction allows students to be actively involved with their own instruction, often controlling the pace of their learning. Given guidelines and broad topics, students can search the Internet for information or use appropriate content area software. This technology appeals to several learning styles, and can be visual, auditory, and tactile all at once. As the teacher models the use of technology to find and present content information, students will feel comfortable and will be motivated to do the same.

Is technology absolutely necessary to meet needs you have learned about in this chapter? Of course not. But technology can help.

---

psychosocial development. Look for specific examples of ways in which students are alike, and look for how you can provide instruction and classroom environments that meet the needs common to all students.

Conclusion

In this chapter, you have investigated ways in which students are alike. Maslow developed a pyramidal hierarchy of seven basic needs common to everyone. According to Maslow, all people have these same basic needs, and people must fulfill these needs to some degree in order to exist as human beings. People must satisfy needs that are lower on the pyramid before they can be motivated to satisfy needs at higher levels. Other researchers' basic needs theories are similar to Maslow's hierarchy and to each other.

Piaget theorized that people pass through four increasingly sophisticated stages of cognitive development. Each stage represents higher levels of people's capacities to think, reason, and solve problems.

Erikson theorized that people pass through several phases of psychosocial development. Each phase is characterized by a crisis that must be resolved; how a crisis is resolved may either foster or hinder a person's continued healthy development.

You saw that these theories are related to motivation. All students have fundamental, common needs, and the fulfillment of these needs is prerequisite to successful motivation. Through your work in this chapter, you were able to relate general needs to classroom and academic needs. Your final task was to recall characteristics of excellent teachers and effective teaching, and to correlate these characteristics with students' needs. Having completed this exercise, you can see why you must learn teaching skills and strategies that are effective for all students.

Although all students are alike in that they have similar needs, they are *un*like in that they bring unique perspectives and characteristics to these needs. These unique perspectives heavily influence how basic needs are met. This is the subject of Chapter 4. Remember, however, that no matter how different those faces look and how unlike those abilities are, excellent teaching addresses the basic needs common to *all* students.

■ Key Terms and Concepts

Aesthetic, 75
Cognitive development, 77
Cognitive needs, 72
Conservation, 78

Deficiency needs, 74
Growth needs, 75
Hierarchy, 72
Psychosocial development, 81

Psychosocial needs, 72
Self-actualization, 75

■ Construct and Apply

1. Think back to the teachers you identified in Chapter 1 as your favorite and your least favorite. Identify several reasons why you chose these teachers. Which of these reasons relate directly to increasing or decreasing your motivation? What emotions did you experience in your interactions with these teachers in their classrooms? How were your needs met or not met in the classrooms of these teachers?

2. How do Glasser's five basic needs and Maslow's seven hierarchical needs relate to each other?

3. Suppose you have a student in your class whose parents have just divorced. What needs will this student most likely express in the classroom? What can you do in an academic situation that would help to meet these needs?

4. Consider your experience in higher education. How have your professors met or not met your academic needs? What suggestions do you have for them?

5. Because behavior is driven by needs, students may display unacceptable or inappropriate behavior if their needs are not being met. Describe the kind of behavior you might observe in your classroom if the following needs were *not* being met. Then describe what the teacher might do to alleviate these concerns.

   a. The student needs to know he is in the right place.

      If he is unsure, he might _____.

      The teacher can solve this anxiety by _____.

   b. The student needs to know who you are and whether you're a nice teacher.

      If she doesn't know, she might _____.

      The teacher can solve this anxiety by _____.

   c. The student needs to know what he is expected to do in this class.

      If he doesn't know what the teacher's expectations are, he might _____.

      The teacher can solve this anxiety by _____.

   d. The student needs to know that she is not going to be embarrassed in this class.

      If she is afraid she will be embarrassed, she might _____.

      The teacher can solve this anxiety by _____.

e. The student needs to know how to act and behave in this class.

If he doesn't, he might _____.

The teacher can solve this anxiety by _____.

Deconstructing the Standards

INTASC Principle #2 says:

> The teacher understands how children learn and develop, and can provide learning opportunities that support their intellectual, social, and personal development.

- Which part(s) of this principle does this chapter address?
- How does this chapter address this principle?
- How will the concepts in this chapter help you apply this principle as a teacher?

Field Experience

1. How do your cooperating teacher and the school to which you are assigned for your field experience accommodate the students' needs identified in Maslow's hierarchy?
2. How does your cooperating teacher in the school to which you are assigned accommodate students' academic needs identified by Jones and Jones?

Your Portfolio

For your portfolio, include evidence that shows you understand the basic needs of students. You may have been able to address specific students' basic needs at some time. If so, add a narrative of what you did and why you did it. You may wish to use the material you prepared in Building Block 3.12.

What activities have you been involved in that help students experience a sense of love or belonging? In what ways have you helped students satisfy the need to know or understand? How have you helped a particular student see his or her own potential and talent? Do you have evidence of these interactions? Reflect on your experiences and use them as evidence in your portfolio.

Technology Resources

 Check out the *Building Teachers* companion website—http://www.education.wadsworth.com/martinloomis1—for more information and resources about common student needs, including access to the following websites:

- Personality tests that assess your motivation
- The Search Institute

 See video footage of real teachers addressing student needs in the classroom. Check the *Building Teachers* CD-ROM that accompanies your textbook for additional resources.

Also link to InfoTrac College Edition through the *Building Teachers* companion website. Use InfoTrac College Edition to search for articles to enhance your study.

Notes

1. Madeline Cartwright, principal of a North Philadelphia elementary school, dramatically describes how she helped children in her school meet their deficiency needs in *For the Children: Lessons from a Visionary Principal* (Berger-Cartwright, 1999).
2. Piaget developed several tasks to assess children's cognitive development. All the classic tasks are given in Appendix A of Charlesworth and Lind, *Math and Science for Young People*, 4th ed. (Albany, NY: Delmar Publishers, 2003).

CHAPTER 4

The Student and the Teacher: Acknowledging Unique Perspectives

"Students learn what they care about . . . ," Stanford Ericksen has said, but Goethe knew something else: "In all things we learn only from those we love." Add to that Emerson's declaration: "The secret of education lies in respecting the pupil," and we have a formula something like this: "Students learn what they care about, from people they care about and who, they know, care about them . . ."

BARBARA HARRELL CARSON

Carson's quotation has strong implications for you as a teacher. For your students to learn, they must know that you care about them. In Chapter 3, you found that all students have common basic needs. Yet every student has a unique perspective and is different from every other student in many ways. How can you demonstrate to *all* your students that they are important?

Among students' basic needs are the need to feel a sense of belonging, acceptance, respect, and self-esteem and the need to feel loved. Students need to know you hear them, see them, care about them, and recognize them as human beings. Child psychologist and adolescent literature author Chris Crutcher has said, "All any kid wants is a witness" (Crutcher, 2000). How are Crutcher and Carson (in the opening quotation) saying the same thing?

For your students to know that you really care about them, you must recognize and honor the unique characteristics and perspectives each individual brings. These characteristics and perspectives influence how each student's needs can be met. Students need to see relevance and purpose in the tasks and activities you ask them to do. They need input into and control over their learning, and they need to interact with information in accordance with their academic abilities. All students need to feel challenged yet have the opportunity to be successful. For this to happen, we must affirm the unique perspectives students bring to the classroom.

Students come to our schools with tremendously diverse backgrounds, experiences, strengths, limitations, cultural settings, religions, environments, and preferences. They are different in countless ways, some of which are easier to identify than others. Some of these differences have been shown to influence achievement. In this chapter, you will investigate **diversity**, including several unique perspectives that influence learning. You will investigate these perspectives to gain a sense of understanding of what they are like and to identify special learning needs of students with these perspectives. And you will investigate how you can teach to accommodate these needs, so that each student feels accepted, respected, and motivated to learn.

CHAPTER GOALS

As a result of your work in this chapter, you will:

1. Investigate the nature of diversity.

2. Explore several ways in which students exhibit diversity.

3. Describe the characteristics and challenges of teaching culturally and ethnically diverse students, English language learners, students of different religious backgrounds, students from differing socioeconomic backgrounds, both genders, and students with different sexual orientations.

4. Look at the ways in which students' unique characteristics influence how they work to meet their basic and academic needs.

5. Explore teaching methods that affirm student diversity.

The Nature of Diversity

Let us begin by investigating what you already know. The following activities and simulations will help you reflect on your knowledge and beliefs about diversity and draw conclusions about the diversity represented in classrooms.

The Shoe-Teacher and Shoe-Students

BUILDING BLOCK 4.1

Try exploring the diversity you find among the shoes in your closet.

Consider every pair of shoes you own. Go to your closet and have a look. Select one shoe from each pair you own and put the shoes you selected in a pile. Also gather one of each pair of shoes belonging to each of your family members; add these shoes to the pile.

Separate the shoes in your pile into two groups. What characteristics did you use to separate them?

Then separate the shoes in each of the two groups into two subgroups. What characteristics did you use to separate them?

One more time: If you have enough shoes in the four piles, separate each into two piles. This should give you eight piles of shoes. Name each group with a descriptive name such as *sports shoes, brown shoes, canvas shoes, high-heeled shoes, children's shoes,* and so on.

What if each shoe were a student? Each student would have the characteristics of the shoe, complete with the material it is made of, its color, its size, its purpose, and whether it is a right or a left shoe. Each shoe-student would be in a group with a label that describes the group's purpose or characteristics. None of these can be changed; they are who they are.

Look at the shoes you have on. Suppose the shoes you are wearing represent the teacher. This shoe-teacher has the purpose, the looks, and the characteristics of your shoes, and none of these things can be changed. You, the shoe-teacher, are who you are.

Now suppose you, the shoe-teacher, plan a unit for your students, the shoe-students. The lessons are to be active, requiring student participation. Suppose the first lesson includes a 5-mile hike on rocky terrain. Which of your shoe-students can participate easily in this lesson? Which will give it a fairly good try? Are there shoe-students for whom you would need to make special accommodations? What would these accommodations be?

Suppose day 2 involves walking 10 miles. Which of your shoe-students can participate easily in this lesson? Which will give it a fairly good try? Are there shoe-students for whom you would need to make special accommodations? What would these accommodations be?

Suppose the final day of your unit has your shoe-students going on a job interview. Which of your shoe-students can participate easily in this lesson? Which will give it a fairly good try? Are there shoe-students for whom you would need to make special accommodations? What would these accommodations be?

Finally, consider your own shoes. If you make the assumption that the shoe-students in your classroom have the same preferences you have and learn in the same way you do, what assignments would you, the shoe-teacher, make to your shoe-students based on the footwear you have on at the moment? Is it fair or appropriate for teachers to make assignments based on their learning or teaching preferences? What could you do as a teacher to accommodate all your shoe-students within a unit of study? Would it be possible to accommodate all the shoe-students within a single lesson?

From the activity in Building Block 4.1, you can infer that everyone in a classroom, including you, is unique and has a unique set of characteristics that affects how he or she approaches learning. This applies to students in all classes (including the students in your introduction to education class). Hopefully, you also discovered that accommodations can be made so *everyone* can participate in the lessons.

Now, let us look at ways in which you, yourself, are different from other people.

To effectively teach all children, teachers must recognize their own assumptions and beliefs about diversity.

Your Diversity

BUILDING
BLOCK
4.2

Identify something about yourself you think might distinguish you from everyone (or almost everyone) else in your class. This could be a unique characteristic, an experience, or even a fact such as the kind of car you drive or the kind of dog you have.

Pretend that whatever you have identified is tattooed on your forehead for all to see.

What kinds of judgments might people make of you if the first thing they see is your tattooed forehead? What assumptions might they make about you based on what they see, such as who you are, what you are like, or where you came from? Would these assumptions be accurate?

Now, think of something about yourself that may surprise others. (You do not have to share this information if you would rather not.) What incorrect assumptions might this information lead others to make about you?

It is easy to make assumptions about people based on their outward appearance. These assumptions may be correct, or they may be incorrect, but they are always dangerous to make! Meeting your students for the first time may trigger some assumptions on your part. To see what these assumptions might include, look at the Building Block 4.3.

Classroom Diversity

BUILDING
BLOCK
4.3

Suppose you have been given your first teaching job and it is the first day of school. You have been assigned a class of 29 students.

You already have looked through student records to get some background information about your students, and you now spend some time watching your students and talking with them as they interact with you and with each other. You make the following observations:

- There are 15 boys and 14 girls in your class of 29 students.
- Of the boys, two seem indifferent to team sports.
- There is one girl who seems to be a bit of a bully or tomboy.
- Seven students are Hispanic.
- There are six African Americans.
- Four students are Vietnamese.
- Twelve students are white.
- One student wears a yarmulke (a skullcap worn by Jewish males).
- The special education coordinator has identified several students as having special needs: Four of your students have a learning disability and two students are gifted.
- One student has muscular dystrophy and is in a wheelchair.
- Your examination of the school records tells you that 14 of your students come from single-parent homes.
- One student comes from a home with single-sex parents.
- Ten students are considered "middle class," and 19 are identified as "working class" or "poor."

Just as you separated your shoes, categorize and label these 29 students based on their observed characteristics.

What assumptions and expectations might you make for these students based on what you know about them on the first day of school?

From these activities, you have seen that numerous qualities of any person might give rise to particular assumptions and expectations.

Students' Unique Perspectives and Characteristics

Students differ from one another in a great many ways. We have been discussing diversity. Many factors contribute to this diversity. Some individual characteristics are readily apparent; others are more subtle. All these characteristics affect how students approach learning—and therefore how you should teach them.

The goal of education is that *all* children learn, regardless of their differences. A primary goal of your teacher preparation program is for you to learn ways to accommodate these distinctive variations as you motivate students in your classroom. To this end, you should explore your own experiences and beliefs. To be able to teach in ways that acknowledge student diversity, you must first acknowledge your own experiences and beliefs that may have given rise to assumptions, expectations, **stereotypes**, and even prejudices.

Cultural Diversity

When we consider cultural diversity, many of us think of **race**. But a person's **culture** includes much more than race. The dictionary defines *culture* as "the customary beliefs, social forms, and material traits of a racial, religious, or social group . . . the set of shared attitudes, values, goals, and practices" (Merriam-Webster, 2003). An individual's culture is composed of several attributes, including race, **ethnicity**, social aspects, and religion. Let us look at some aspects of the wide cultural diversity present in our world.

On October 12, 1999, the world's population reached 6 billion people, and it is expected to reach 7 billion as early as 2011 (Population Reference Bureau, 2002). If we could shrink this population to just 100 people, keeping the existing ratios the same, we would have the following information (Smith, 2002):

- Sixty-one of the 100 are Asian.
- Thirteen are from Africa.
- Thirteen are from the Western Hemisphere (North, Central, and South America).
- Twelve are from Europe.
- Twenty-two speak Chinese.
- Nine speak English.
- Eight speak Hindi.
- Seven speak Spanish.
- Thirty-two are Christian.
- Nineteen are Muslim.
- Thirteen are Hindus.
- One is Jewish.
- Fifteen are nonreligious.
- Sixty are always hungry.
- Twenty-four always have enough to eat.
- Thirty-one go to a school staffed by a single teacher.
- Seventeen cannot read.
- The 20 richest people earn about $25 per day each.

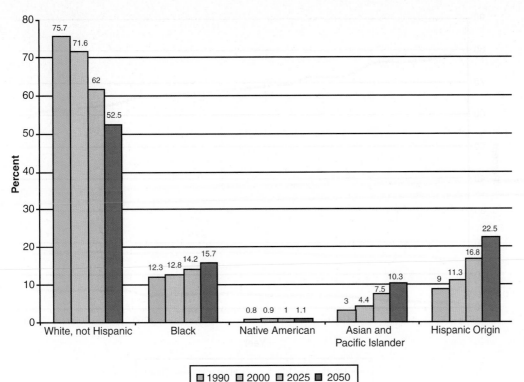

Figure 4.1
U.S. population trends by race and ethnicity, 2000–2050. (From data in Day, 2001.)

▪ The 20 poorest people earn less than $1 per day each.

▪ Seventy-six have electricity.

▪ Of those who have electricity, 42 use it for radios, 24 use it for televisions, 14 use it for telephones, and 7 use it for computers.

Where do you fall in this representation of the world's population? Are the majority of global inhabitants like you? Or are they different from you? In what ways?

The population of the United States is growing rapidly and is becoming more and more diverse. Figure 4.1 shows forecast trends in the cultural and ethnic makeup of the U.S. population from 2000 to 2050.

Similarly, the population of students in American schools is becoming increasingly multicultural. In 2003, the enrollment in U.S. public schools was 58.3% white, 16.1% black, 18.6% Hispanic, and 7.0% other (U.S. Department of Education, 2005). Figure 4.2 shows the trend in racial makeup of schools since 1972; you will notice that the percent of white students has steadily been declining and the percentage of black students has remained relatively constant while the percentage of Hispanic students has been steadily increasing, with the percentage of Hispanics overtaking the percentage of blacks in 2000. If this trend in the ethnic makeup of public school students were to continue, when would the so-called minorities of today overtake the white students in school population?

The United States Bureau of the Census predicts that, by the year 2010, as many as one of every 10 children in the United States will be **foreign-born** (Franklin, 2001). Furthermore, it has been predicted that, by the year 2025, the proportion of **students of color** (a collective term that refers to students of any non-Caucasian race, including black, Hispanic, Asian, and Native American) will increase to approximately 50% of the student population (McFalls & Cobb-Roberts, 2001). Based on your analysis of Figure 4.2, do you agree with this forecast? What, if any, modifications would you make to the forecast?

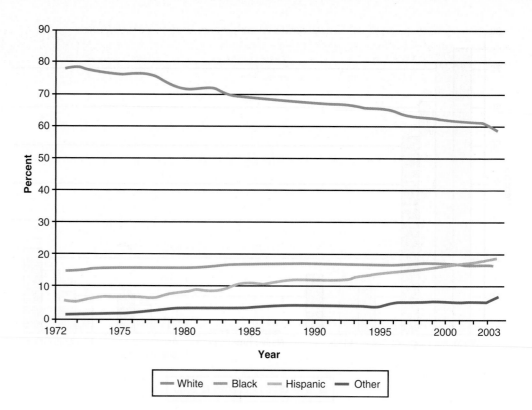

Figure 4.2
Percentages of public school students by race, 1972–2003. (From U.S. Department of Education, 2005.)

Diversity and Educational Perspectives

Philosophies of education often are based on cultural heritage and vary greatly from one cultural group to another. Some feel that education is a joint endeavor among school, community, teacher, students, and family; others feel that education is the professional purview of the teacher and that families need to stay out of teachers' way. The educational philosophy of some African Americans emphasizes that students must learn to be responsible for themselves. Hispanic culture often holds the family as the most important cultural factor. Native American educational philosophies often embrace a holistic view of teaching and a profound respect for ancestors, elders, and nature. Many Asian American families view teachers as authorities whose job is to ensure that students learn. The predominant educational philosophy of European Americans is that school is a joint venture between the parents and the teacher.

What do these perspectives mean to the academic needs of these cultural groups? How might an African American parent who subscribes to the philosophy of self-responsibility perceive a highly structured, teacher-dependent classroom? Why might some teachers feel "abandoned" when seeking collaboration or input from Asian American parents who see teachers as authoritative? These are broad, generalized questions, but it is important to realize that parents and students from different cultural groups may value different aspects of schooling, teaching, and learning.

Teaching That Acknowledges Cultural Diversity

In the early 21st century, the Multicultural Consensus Panel, a university-based interdisciplinary group of specialists, reviewed and synthesized the research related to cultural diversity. The panel issued a set of 12 essential principles that "describe ways in which education policy and practice related to diversity can be improved"

(Banks et al., 2001, p. 197). These essential principles were organized into five categories as follows:

1. Teacher learning
2. Student learning
3. Intergroup reactions
4. School governance, organization, and equity
5. Assessment

It is not by accident that teacher learning heads the list; for any progress to be made in the area of multicultural education, teachers must first uncover and identify their own biases and prejudices, working to eliminate any preconceived negative attitudes they discover. Teachers' attitudes toward diversity exert a strong influence over all aspects of education, from lesson planning to teacher–student interactions to interactions with colleagues, parents, and the community.

It is absolutely essential that teachers acquire cultural sensitivity. To do this, you must first examine your own beliefs, similar to what you did when you were identifying qualities of effective teaching and your philosophy of education. There are several ways to accomplish this self-examination. One way is to take a self-test dealing with your feelings about diversity. Several such tests can be found on the Internet.

Another way to explore your own awareness, tolerance, and bias is to participate in activities such as the one described in Building Block 4.4.

 Direct links to several multicultural awareness self-tests are available on the *Building Teachers* companion website. Check out these sites, which are designed to promote cultural awareness.

Identifying Assumptions and Expectations

Think about your grocery store. What types of people frequent the store? Can you recall your last trip there and the kind of people you saw? Are they the types of people you would expect to find? How well do the people who go to your grocery store represent your community? How well do they represent the kind of person you are? Do you see children in the store? By looking around your grocery store, could you tell which of the children you see there are probably good students and which are probably troublemakers?

Think about a shopping mall you visit. What are your favorite stores? What kinds of people would you expect to see in those stores? How are they like you? How are they different from you? How are the people who patronize the higher-priced stores like you or different from you? What about the people in the lower-priced stores? Do you think they went to college? Why or why not?

Are there some neighborhoods where you can only dream of living? What kinds of people live there? What do you suppose their children are like? What kinds of students would you expect these children to be? What do you think the children will do when they grow up?

Are there some "bad" neighborhoods where you can't imagine living? What are the people like who live there? What do you suppose their children are like? What kinds of students would you expect these children to be? What do you think these children will do when they grow up?

As you doubtless have inferred, we teachers make plenty of assumptions and hold many expectations. Some of these assumptions and expectations may reflect prejudices and biases that we need to address. Do you *really* believe that everyone can learn? Or is the notion lurking somewhere that there will always be one or two students who, for whatever reason, simply will not succeed in school? You might, for example, feel that adolescent students who are unkempt and show signs of drug or gang activity will not be able to achieve because they have other things on their minds. Or you might believe that young children who come from broken homes, who have a parent in prison, or whose parents seem disinterested in their education will have serious difficulties with academic achievement because the cards are stacked against them. Do you believe all ethnic groups and races are equally capable of learning? Or do you feel deep down inside there are some groups that just won't make it?

Perhaps the most effective way to discover your beliefs is to talk face-to-face with people who are different from you. Although such conversations may be uncomfortable at first, they can reveal both misunderstandings and congruence. Education professor Sonia Nieto says, "The unfortunate thing is when people walk on egg shells, afraid to talk about diversity ... part of it is that they fear it will bring up conflicts. And perhaps it will, so all of us ... need to be more tolerant, to learn to talk frankly with one another" (Kitagawa, 2000, p. 162).

BUILDING
BLOCK
4.5

Talking Culture

Have a conversation with a person whose ethnicity is different from yours. Explore various topics, even though the conversation may be a bit uncomfortable. Try to find the other person's point of view on such issues as intelligence, talent, motivation, family life, work ethic, success, failure, and so on.

Later, write down a few notes from this conversation.

Once again, the first, and perhaps the most important steps in multicultural education are the acceptance of students of all cultures, races, and ethnicities, and the development of the belief that *every* student can and will succeed. Examine your own cultural, ethnic, and racial beliefs to discover any biases you might have. With this information, you will be able to change the way you act, and then the way you believe. By resolving any concerns you have about multicultural settings, you can make your classroom a warm and receptive environment for all students. With such an encouraging environment, you will be well on your way to forming positive and meaningful relationships with your students, increasing the likelihood they will find the material relevant and meaningful. This in turn increases the likelihood they will learn.

Students of different cultural backgrounds have had different life experiences and thus bring different perceptions, understandings, and characteristics to the classroom. These characteristics greatly affect the achievement of students in their respective cultures and must be taken into consideration by teachers.

Banks and colleagues (2001) identified four approaches to multicultural education:

The contributions approach. A teacher using this approach includes appropriate information about other cultures and representative individuals on holidays and other events. During black history month, for example, a teacher might create a special bulletin board featuring prominent African American inventors and their inventions. The teacher might read to the class about Mexican history on Cinco de Mayo and share traditional songs, food, and dances.

The additive approach. In this approach, a teacher integrates relevant information from other cultures at appropriate places in the curriculum. For example, it might be part of the curriculum for students to learn about the events that led to the first Thanksgiving. Including a Native American perspective on Thanksgiving would be an additive approach to multicultural education. The curriculum itself is not modified; rather, it is supplemented with multicultural information. The dominant culture is still the focus of the learning.

The transformation approach. As its name implies, this approach transforms the curriculum. An investigation of multicultural perspectives is an objective of the study as students consider multiple points of view.

The social action approach. In this extension of the transformation approach, students not only explore topics but participate in activities that intend social change as an outcome. Students might investigate a social issue such as poverty and then take action on the issue, such as writing letters to political figures or undertaking a charity drive.

As you consider these approaches to multicultural teaching, how does the philosophy of multicultural education move toward the social reconstructionist philosophy (Chapter 2)?

English Language Learners

With the increasingly multicultural complexion of America's population, it makes sense that the number of languages spoken in schools also is increasing. **English language learners** (ELLs) are students whose native language is other than English, the primary language normally spoken in the school. Although most students in our schools speak English, it has been estimated that, in the 2003–2004 academic year, 10.3% of the students enrolled in schools were English language learners, an increase of 40.7% since the 1993–1994 academic year (Padolsky, 2005). In the 2000–2001 academic year, more than 400 different languages were spoken by students; besides English, the most common was Spanish (Padolsky, 2002).

This proliferation of languages, of course, is to be expected. Except for a decline in the early 20th century and another decline in the late 20th century, the number of immigrants to the United States has increased regularly (see Figure 4.3).

Predominant languages vary greatly by region in the United States, but there may be many different languages spoken in any one school. For example, at John C. Diehl Elementary School in Erie, Pennsylvania, students speak Bosnian, Vietnamese, Polish, Kurdish, Spanish, Arabic, Albanian, Russian, Ukrainian, Sudanese, and Chinese (John C. Diehl Elementary School, 2004). At Long Branch Elementary School in Arlington, Virginia (across the Potomac River from Washington, D.C.), students represent more than 25 countries and speak languages such as Urdu, Arabic, Vietnamese, Bengali, Amharic, Chinese, Tagalog, Hindi, Russian, Korean, Punjabi, Thai, Bulgarian,

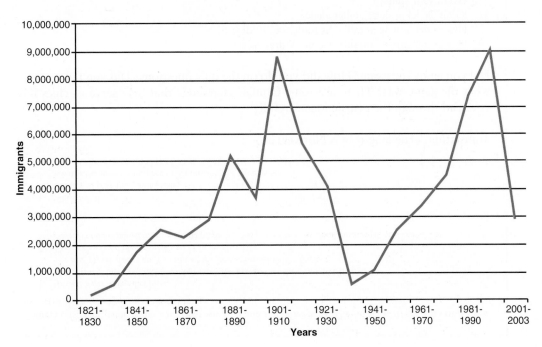

Figure 4.3
Number of immigrants to the United States, 1821–2003. (From U.S. Department of Homeland Security, 2003.)

Japanese, and Gujarati (Arlington Public Schools, 2004). So it is evident that there is great diversity in the native languages spoken by U.S. students. As Nieto says, "All the language varieties that we speak are really part and parcel of multiculturalism" (Kitawaga, 2000, p. 162).

Teaching students for whom English is a second language presents unique challenges. Not only must teachers help their students acquire the knowledge and skills required in the curriculum, they also must help them do so in a language whose familiarity ranges from none to some. Because of language difficulties, teachers cannot be sure whether any academic problems students have represent low achievement or limited English proficiency. Given this predicament, it is tempting for teachers to view English language learners as low achievers. It is correspondingly tempting for teachers to "water down" the curriculum to accommodate these students. This is "a simply indefensible solution" (Gersten et al., 1998, p. 70), because this practice denies English language learners "access to quality instruction and, ultimately, academic opportunity" (p. 70).

To help you imagine the challenges of learning in an American classroom if you do not speak English, do the activity in Building Block 4.6.

BUILDING BLOCK 4.6

A Second Language

Below are the instructions to play a simple game. Following the instructions is a short quiz. Read the instructions, complete the game, and take the quiz.

Instruksjoner: Spillet er for 2 spillere: en som er X og en som er O. Objektet får 3 Xs eller 3 Os i et vertikalt, horisontal, eller diagonal ledning.

1. Tegn 2 vertikal parallell linjer.
2. Nå tegn 2 flere parallell linjer det krysset det for det første i den grad at de ligne denne: #.
3. Det for det første spilleren merkene en X inne ettall av boksene dannet av det linjer.
4. Så , sekundet spilleren merkene en O inne en annen bokse med.
5. Spillerne fortsette tar dreier til ettall spilleren har Xs eller Os inne en vertical, horisontal, eller diagonalt line.

Prøve:

1. Hvem vant spillet?
2. Kunn De leker dette spillet alene?
3. Hva er det største antallet Xs mulig om O drar først?
4. Hva er det største antallet Xs om X drar først?

Did you enjoy the game? How did you do on the quiz questions? Did you figure out what the game was? There are some familiar characters that may serve as clues if you read through the instructions carefully.

Translation: (The language is Norwegian.)

Directions: This game is for 2 players: one is X and the other is O. The object is to get 3 Xs or 3 Os in a vertical, horizontal, or diagonal line.

1. Draw 2 vertical parallel lines.
2. Now draw 2 more parallel lines that cross the first so that they look like this: #.
3. The first player marks an X in one of the boxes formed by the lines.
4. Then, the second player marks an O in another box.
5. Players continue taking turns until one player has 3 Xs or 3 Os in a vertical, horizontal, or diagonal line.

Quiz:

1. Who won the game?
2. Could you play this game alone?
3. What is the greatest number of Xs possible if O goes first?
4. What is the greatest number of Xs if X goes first?

Teaching That Acknowledges English Language Learners

In an effort to accommodate students whose primary language is not English, teachers wonder whether they should study foreign languages so they can communicate with the children in their own languages. But with students in our schools speaking more than 400 different native languages, it is impossible for teachers to become familiar with all languages they might encounter. In fact, Gersten (1998) indicates that, in schools he studied, only 2% of teachers communicated in both English and another language with English language learners, and fewer than 1% spoke mostly in a non-English language. Yet these schools are considered exemplary relative to achievement of their students.

In 1968, Congress passed the Bilingual Education Act, which created services for limited English proficient (LEP) students. More recently, the No Child Left Behind Act has augmented the Bilingual Education Act to require states to develop English language proficiency standards that are tied to the state academic standards and require students to take English language proficiency tests.

Bilingual education is education that includes instruction in the student's native language and instruction in English. Teachers have approached bilingual education in four basic ways:

Immersion. LEP students are immersed in English-speaking classes, where teachers attempt to use very basic language so students can learn the content and the language at the same time. Note that immersion does not really fit the definition of bilingual education because no instruction is offered in the student's native language.

In this New Mexico school, teachers instruct students in both English and a Native American language.

English as a Second Language (ESL). ESL is similar to the immersion approach, except students may receive some instruction in their native language. ESL classes typically consist of students with many different primary languages. Students may attend only one ESL class per day, which focuses on developing their English skills, or they may attend up to a full day of classes that work on both English and content.

Transitional bilingual education. Students receive some instruction in their native language and also instruction in how to speak English in concentrated classes. The intent is for students to become proficient enough in English so that they can make the transition into English-speaking classes in a matter of a few years.

Developmental bilingual education. Students receive instruction in their own language as they learn English as a second language.

The National Association for Bilingual Education (2004) reports that bilingual education programs that focus on developing students' skills in their native language lead to increased achievement in English. As with any educational program, however, bilingual education must be well designed, well implemented, and well taught.

Bilingual education is not without controversy. Some people believe that non-English speakers in the United States should learn to speak English and that no special and expensive bilingual education programs should be necessary. Proponents of bilingual education note that students should be encouraged to maintain contact with their native language and culture, and that providing some instruction in the native language facilitates English language and content area acquisition in the long run. Others say that providing instruction in the native language means students may graduate without the necessary English skills. Another concern is that teachers need to be qualified to teach ESL; there is a great need for these teachers as the population of ELL students grows (Gandara, 1999).

Immigrants are divided on whether or not they believe their children should be taught in English immersion or in bilingual education programs. Sixty-three percent of those surveyed believed that all classes should be taught in English, whereas 32% believed that students should receive some instruction in their native languages (Public Agenda Online, 2003).

Bilingual education is such a controversial issue that some states have adopted legislation that virtually eliminated bilingual programs. Proposition 227 was approved by California voters in 1998 and resulted in English language learners being placed in immersion programs. Arizona passed a similar measure in 2000, as did Massachusetts in 2002. Colorado voters, however, did not approve similar propositions.

The effectiveness of English immersion and bilingual education programs has been studied in several research projects. For the most part, results have been inconclusive. Gandara (1999) notes that this finding is probably due to the fact that most ELL students do not participate exclusively in either immersion or bilingual programs but in a mix of the two.

If you are bilingual or have some familiarity with a foreign language, by all means, use it with your future students. However, a person does not need to speak other languages to be an excellent teacher. As is the case with culturally diverse students, attitude is the first and foremost consideration in providing effective education for students with emerging or limited proficiency in English. Teachers must develop the same positive attitude toward ELL students that they have for *all* students—the attitude that all students can learn and can achieve their high expectations.

English language learners are very much like other students in all respects except native language. What special needs do these students bring to the classroom in addition to the basic and academic needs we have already discussed? How much harder is it for them to feel they belong and have a chance at successful learning? What can you do to help them learn?

www Direct links to the websites of *English First* and the *National Bilingual Education Association* are available on the *Building Teachers* companion website. These sites offer different perspectives on English as a second language learning.

More than Words

Pretend that you have a student who does not speak your language. It is your job to teach this person how to prepare a gourmet meal, and you must do this without speaking or writing any words because of the language barrier. How will you instruct him or her to follow directions? How will this person show you, without speaking or writing words, that he or she understands how to prepare the meal?

Now think of a concept central to your favorite content area. For example, if you would like to be a history teacher, you might consider the American Revolution. Or, if you are studying to teach language arts, you might consider the parts of speech. How could you teach this concept to a student who does not speak your language? And how could this student show you that he or she understands this concept?

Religion

Just as there are differences in ethnicity and native language, there are differences in religious beliefs among the students in our schools. Can you think of instances in which religion has affected education? Some examples include the legal issue barring prayer from schools and the controversy over studying the theories of evolution and creationism in science classes. But how would a student's individual religious beliefs affect his or her learning or perspective on an ordinary educational task? Why is it important to be aware of your students' religious beliefs?

There are some 10,000 distinct religions in the world, of which approximately 150 have a million or more followers. Within Christianity, there are more than 33,000 different denominations (Barrett et al., 2001). Major religions by number of members in the world and in the United States are shown graphically in Figure 4.4.

Today, schools in the United States educate students from all ethnic, cultural, racial, and religious groups and backgrounds.

© Sally and Richard Greenhill/Alamy

Courtesy of Tamara Steen

They were a class straight out of hell. After eight or nine years of academic failure, largely due to limited reading ability, the majority the 13-year-old students in my English class had convinced themselves they were too stupid to learn. Because they thought they were too stupid to learn, they believed there was absolutely no point in wasting any time trying. With behavior that seemed to be goaded into malfeasance by the devil himself, they tied my guts into knots so tight each day that it took the rest of the day and most of the evening to untie them. Then one day in January, they did something right in my classroom, and since I thought that might be my only chance to compliment them all year, I concluded the class period by saying, "You were my best class today."

None of them heard the word "today." I guess no teacher had ever said they were the best at anything—and for good reason—but their reaction astonished me, as it became apparent within a few weeks that they believed being my best class meant they must be my favorite. And that belief transformed them. Starving for an adult to love them unconditionally, they gradually began to behave as if they deserved to be my favorite class—and by the end of the year they had indeed become what they believed they were.

I teach in a small rural community where 93% of our students are Latino and 86% qualify for free or reduced lunch. We are a bilingual culture where Spanish is the primary language in a great many homes. Which Mexican state each student's family claims as its home constitutes diversity in my classroom. Today, 20 years after that class from hell taught me that students see themselves through the teacher's eyes, my Advanced Placement English students are 90% Latino, with 50% classified as migrants. They are defying all the stereotypes and statistics about their ethnicity in a way that makes it an honor to know them. These teenagers take my English classes because they dream of becoming lawyers, doctors, teachers, and psychologists. They know the abilities to read and write well are necessary to succeed in college, and that college is the key to unlock the doors of their chosen careers.

If I inspire these young people, they in turn inspire me. If any student has the guts to take my advanced class, I feel I must have the guts to teach that student, no matter how low his or her initial reading and writing abilities. Every year, I have a few seniors reading at a level as low as fifth grade, largely due to English being a second language for them. Yet, at the end of the fourth quarter, when I ask my students which literary works were their favorites out of all that we studied, *Beowulf* tops the list almost unanimously, with *Hamlet, Oedipus Rex,* and the *Iliad* following closely

behind. These students are very much capable of understanding and appreciating the same difficult texts taught in any other high school across the nation— they just need different instructional strategies, strategies suitable for English Language Learners (ELLs). Remarkably, what works well with ELLs also works well with everyone else. All learners—regardless of ethnicity, gender, or language—need to talk in order to process new information. Therefore, I employ multiple ways to involve students dynamically in their own learning as they create meaning with their peers:

- We hold poetry coffee houses, where students take turns reading and analyzing poetry aloud with their classmates in a candlelit room.

- We divide the class into teams, each team dramatizing one of Hercules's labors.

- We have daily opportunities for the students to turn and talk to each other about an answer to an interpretive question based on literature we're studying.

- We hold Socratic seminars.

- We play games with our vocabulary words.

- We create documentaries about issues that connect Mabton, Washington, to the global community, which they then show to their parents at an evening presentation.

I tutor students after school for as many afternoons they need to understand how to write a college-level essay; no essay is ever finished until I can give it an honest B or it is the end of a quarter.

It is my desire that no door in the future will be closed to any of my students, except for the doors they choose to close themselves. In everything I do and say, they must know that I do not doubt their intellectual capacity. No matter how dysfunctional their home life, no matter how much they think they hate to read or write, no matter how limited their English may be, and no matter what excuse they hide behind, it is my job to find what will open their minds to the myriad possibilities that surround us all. That is my job and my passion.

2005 Washington Teacher of the Year
Mabton Junior Senior High School
Mabton, Washington

Major Religions in the World

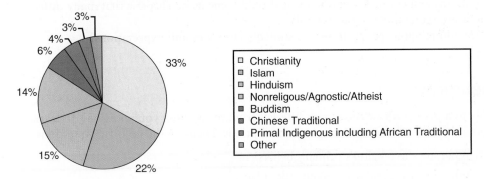

- Christianity
- Islam
- Hinduism
- Nonreligous/Agnostic/Atheist
- Buddism
- Chinese Traditional
- Primal Indigenous including African Traditional
- Other

3%
3%
4%
6%
14%
15%
22%
33%

Major Religions in the United States

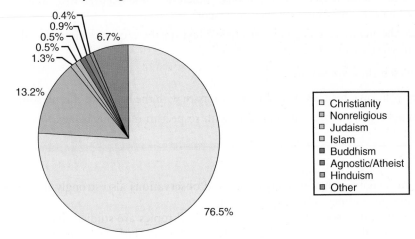

- Christianity
- Nonreligious
- Judaism
- Islam
- Buddhism
- Agnostic/Atheist
- Hinduism
- Other

0.4%
0.9%
0.5%
0.5%
1.3%
6.7%
13.2%
76.5%

Figure 4.4
Major religions of the world and in the United States by membership.

Major religions with membership in multiple countries include the following (listed in descending order of membership; adherents.com, 2002):

1. Christianity (including Protestantism, Catholicism, and Orthodox churches)
2. Islam
3. Hinduism
4. Buddhism
5. Sikhism
6. Judaism
7. Baha'i
8. Jainism
9. Shinto

Confucianism, Taoism, and Zoroastrianism also have large numbers of followers, and many people consider themselves secular, nonreligious, agnostic, or atheist.

The 10 largest Christian denominations in the United States follow (in descending order of membership; adherents.com, 2002):

1. Southern Baptist
2. United Methodist
3. Catholic
4. Church of Christ
5. Presbyterian
6. Assembly of God
7. Lutheran
8. Church of Jesus Christ of Latter-Day Saints (Mormon)
9. Jehovah's Witnesses
10. Episcopal

With this great diversity of religions, coupled with students' great diversity of national origins and ethnic backgrounds, it should come as no surprise that many different religions are represented in our schools.

How do religious beliefs influence students' attitudes and expectations?

Religions

Talk to a person whose religion is different from the religion you know best to learn about their basic beliefs, rituals, and observations. Focus on the following questions:

- What are the religion's primary beliefs?
- Where and when does worship take place?
- What are the required rituals? What do they represent?
- What are the major feasts or celebrations? When do these occur? How do adherents observe them? What do they represent?
- What are the major fast days or periods? When do these occur? How do adherents observe them? What do they represent?

Now ask yourself these questions:

- What are your own beliefs? How do they compare with the beliefs of this person?
- Can you assume a position of neutrality with respect to religious beliefs?

How do religious beliefs influence students' attitudes and expectations toward school?

As you might imagine, religious convictions and observations also strongly influence students' expectations and performance at school.

During the course of a school year, events occur and topics are studied that may be inconsistent with the values of certain religions. The study of evolutionary theory is a major example. Some religious groups object strongly to this theory, saying that it directly contradicts the Bible's account of the creation of Earth and humanity. What does this mean to the science teacher planning a unit of study on evolution, as may be required in the state curriculum? You will investigate the controversy surrounding the teaching of evolution versus the teaching of creationism in Chapter 11. As another example, in the United States it is common to celebrate holidays such as Valentine's Day, Halloween, Thanksgiving, and Christmas. However, not all students celebrate the same holidays, nor do they celebrate religious holidays at the same time. In fact, some students do not celebrate any holidays at all—not even birthdays. Individual schools and school districts establish policies concerning observance of religious holidays in school, and teachers are expected to adhere to these policies.

Happy Holidays?

To what extent do you believe it is appropriate to observe and celebrate religious and secular holidays in school if doing so may be objectionable to certain students and their families? What accommodations might teachers make to promote and assure mutual respect? Use your own experience and the conversation you held in Building Block 4.8 to help you form your own informed opinion.

You must become sensitive to the fact there will be several different religions represented in your classroom, and you must recognize and honor them all. Referring to the basic human needs outlined by Maslow (Chapter 3), you can see that doing so helps foster the positive feelings of safety and security, belongingness, and self-esteem that must be satisfied before students can focus on learning.

However, it is neither desirable nor possible to advance the beliefs of all the religions you will encounter in your classroom. Unless you will be teaching in a religious school, the most appropriate attitude to adopt concerning religion is one of neutrality. (Constitutional and legal aspects of religion in U.S. schools are discussed in Chapter 13.)

Socioeconomic Status

We often consider that people who are financially very well off or who are financially struggling belong to their own cultures. As a society, we even use terms such as *upper class, middle class,* and *lower class* to denote financial categories of individuals and families. Break the word *socioeconomic* into its parts. What do you think the word means? What do you think the term **socioeconomic status** (SES) means? What characteristics or qualities make up a person's socioeconomic status?

According to Demarest et al. (1993), a family's socioeconomic status is based on family income, parental education level, parental occupation, and social status in the community. The following demographic characteristics are used as descriptors of socioeconomic status in America (Woolfolk, 2001):

- Household income
- Parents' occupation
- Parents' education
- Parents' attitude towards education
- Parents' aspirations for their children
- Intellectual activities of the family (including trips to educationally stimulating locations such as museums, zoos, historical sites, and so on)

BUILDING BLOCK 4.10

Socioeconomic Status

Suppose you were asked to describe the socioeconomic status of a family and its environment. Using the characteristics listed previously, describe a high SES family and a low SES family. How would the environments you described for high and low SES families affect a child's educational "readiness" to enter school with a set of experiences that would form a foundation upon which to build? How would the environments you described affect a student's attitude toward learning and education?

As you saw in Chapter 3, all students have basic human needs, and the most basic of these needs are the survival and safety needs represented in the foundational levels of Maslow's hierarchy. You also saw that these basic needs must be met before a student can turn his or her attention to learning and pursue self-actualization. For families identified as having a low socioeconomic status, priority often must go to fulfilling the deficiency needs of survival and safety.

In 2004, the **poverty** rate in the United States was 12.17%, up from 12.5% in 2003 (U.S. Census Bureau, 2005). Statistics concerning children indicate that the poverty rate of children has been reduced by more than 25% since 1993. However, in 2003, 17% (up from 16% in 2002) of America's children still lived in poverty (defined as an annual income of $18,810 or less for a family of four), with African American and Latino children having the highest rates (Federal Interagency Forum on Child and Family Statistics, 2005).

Active, stimulating learning experiences in preschool can promote future academic achievement for students.

Numerous studies have shown a high correlation between low socioeconomic status and low achievement (Hodgkinson, 1995). Some lower SES parents value discipline over success in school or creativity, and this affects the value their children place on education and therefore their achievement (Campbell et al., 1991). This research suggests that programs aimed at parental attitudes may contribute to the achievement gains of low SES students (Datcher-Loury, 1989).

Home environment has been shown to affect how students function within their learning environments (Brooks-Gunn et al., 1994). Whereas children from middle and high SES families might have trips and educational toys available to them, the parents of lower SES families are forced to place precedence on housing, food, and other necessities. The result is that children from lower SES households have less exposure to experiences that prepare them for the educational environment. Being "ready" for school contributes greatly to initial success. And, as you have observed, success is vital for motivating students to achieve.

Much has been done to reduce child poverty, and much remains to be done. Reducing child poverty will result in more children entering school ready to learn, greater student academic achievement, and lower dropout rates. Meanwhile, teachers must consider the unique factors that affect fulfillment of basic needs and motivation to learn among the children of poverty in their classes.

Teaching That Acknowledges Socioeconomic Status

Students of different economic and social backgrounds have different expectations and career goals, which are influenced by their parents and communities. You, the teacher, also may have different expectations of students, depending on your beliefs about the SES group they come from. Recall Building Block 4.4, where you thought about neighborhoods in which you dream of living and neighborhoods in which you cannot imagine living. Was there a difference in your expectations when you were thinking about the students who live in these neighborhoods?

You have seen that students' motivations often vary according to social classes, which affects achievement. You also have seen that the extent to which young children are prepared to enter school correlates with their achievement in school. Because of this, federal and state programs have been initiated to help prepare young children to enter school. Examples include Head Start, Early Head Start, the Perry Preschool project, and other preschool intervention programs intended for students of low SES groups. Campbell & Ramey (1995) found that students who were exposed to a stimulating and active learning environment, such as that found in Head Start programs, exhibited higher achievement levels.

Ruby Payne's research on children of poverty (1998) offers insight into working with students of the low socioeconomic group, which, as a class, has been shown to have low

Direct links to the websites of Head Start, Early Head Start, and the Perry Preschool project are available on the *Building Teachers* companion website.

achievement levels. Payne suggests a number of principles and strategies to help low SES students increase their achievement levels, which include the following:

- Helping students establish specific goals
- Using graphic organizers such as charts and diagrams
- Helping students associate content with their personal experiences
- Helping students utilize what they already know in the learning process
- Using "hands-on" approaches
- Helping students evaluate their own performance
- Teaching students how to ask questions dealing with the content
- Helping students sort relevant information from irrelevant information

How do these strategies help students fulfill their basic and academic needs? Remember, students of poverty are likely to need reinforcement in the most basic needs such as physiologic needs, safety, security, and love and belonging.

Teaching Students of Poverty

BUILDING BLOCK 4.11

Review the strategies suggested by Payne for teaching students of poverty. Can you suggest additional strategies from previous lists you have created? How do these strategies foster heightened relationships between student and teacher? How do they help students meet their basic and academic needs?

Payne's work has made major contributions to the understanding of economic classes and students from poverty. Swan (2004) found that the use of Payne's instructional framework in a widely diverse school district was associated with an increase in student achievement. However, many in the field of multicultural education believe her work actually contributes to classism in schools instead of promoting class equity because of her emphasis on the difference between the lower and upper classes (Gorksi, 2005).

Gender

It has been said that males and females speak different languages. Maybe you have felt this way when trying to communicate with someone of the opposite sex. Because the behavioral differences between genders seem so pronounced, you might even consider them to be separate cultures. Of course, genders are not separate cultures, but there certainly are generalizations associated with being male or female. What are some of these generalizations? To what extent do you fit them? Are there any general impressions about your gender that do not apply to you? What impact, if any, do you think gender has on learning? Do you think boys are better than girls at some subjects? Do you think girls are better than boys at some subjects?

Activities for Boys and Girls

BUILDING BLOCK 4.12

The following activities are listed on various websites constructed by troops of the Boy Scouts of America and the Girl Scouts of America. Can you guess which activities came from which sites? Mark the activities you think came from the Girl Scout sites with a *G* and those which you think came from the Boy Scout sites with a *B*. Be sure to record your immediate, initial response.

B: Archery, Axe throwing, Woodcraft, Bedding materials, Bicycle maintenance, Bird houses, Homemade compasses, Cooking contests, Deduction in tracking, Fire building, Hiking, Insect collecting, Knot tying, Loom and grass mats, Map and compasses, Measurement and estimation, Night tracking, Rope making, Sign language, Snakes, Stalking and observation, Story telling, Teepee building, Tomahawk throwing, Weather wisdom

G: Tie-dying, New ways to wear a bandana, Oil changing, Acting, Surfing, Sailing, Rock climbing, Photography, Animals, Creative composing, Food fun, Safety, Sounds of music, Space Explorer, Sports and games, Science wonders, Art to wear, Math fun, Puppets, dolls, and plays

Look again at the activities. Which did you associate with girls? Which did you associate with boys? Based on these associations, which gender do you suppose would be better at math? At language? At science? At social sciences?

Many of the activities in Building Block 4.12 can be easily assigned to one gender or the other based on our stereotypical notions of traditional gender roles. However, it might surprise you to learn that some of the activities we traditionally associate with boys, such as computers, tying knots, and archery, can be found on Girl Scout websites. Making an upside-down cake in a can and participating in a songfest were activities suggested on Boy Scout websites.

Why is it that we so readily associate certain activities and subjects with gender? Are there really gender-specific differences in academic aptitudes? Are girls really better readers and writers? Are boys really better at math? Consider some findings of Dr. Janese Swanson, founder of GirlTech, Inc. (Swanson, 1996):

- Until adolescence, the physical development of boys and girls is nearly the same. This suggests that differences in their physical abilities are probably caused by practice and opportunity.
- The reading, writing, and mathematics abilities of boys and girls are essentially the same.
- Boys and girls both perform better academically when they are expected to do well and are given opportunities to succeed.
- Boys and girls performed roughly equally in mathematics, but fewer girls than boys feel they are good at the subject.
- Eleven- and 12-year olds tend to have strongly sex-stereotyped career goals; however, at this age, differences in boys' and girls' abilities are small, and the differences are declining.

Children often exhibit stereotypical, gender-specific roles very early in their development.

© Sean Justice/Getty Images

- Both boys and girls are aware that boys are valued more highly in society.
- Physical appearance and peer acceptance have the greatest influence on the adolescent self-esteem of both boys and girls.
- Boys, on average, are more aggressive than girls.
- More girls than boys lose self-esteem at the beginning of adolescence.

The gender roles of boys and girls begin to be differentiated very early in life. Boys and girls learn at an early age what their gender roles are, and they learn that the genders are treated differently. Male infants are handled more actively than females (Hensel, 1989). Boys are rewarded for risk-taking and exploration, whereas girls are rewarded for exhibiting caring and kind behaviors. Toys given to boys encourage action and creativity; those given to girls foster language development and nurturing skills. Boys tend to participate in (and are rewarded for) activities such as playing sports, outdoor games, and video games, which promote the development of spatial skills. Girls, however, are provided with toys that orient them toward taking care of the home and children (Bussey & Bandura, 1999). Parents and adults respond more positively to children who exhibit stereotypical gender-appropriate behavior (Fagot et al., 1985).

Thus strong social influences contribute to gender bias in the classroom. These influences seem to encourage girls toward "softer" subjects, such as reading and social studies, and boys toward mathematics and science. In classrooms and in society, girls are discouraged in both subtle and overt ways from participating in activities and studies traditionally associated with being male, and boys are discouraged from activities traditionally associated with being female.

However, recent research suggests there may be genetic factors that predispose males to act in masculine ways and females to act in feminine ways (Blum, 1999; Kreeger, 2002). Thus it appears masculine and feminine behaviors result from a combination of genetic inheritance and socialization.

Teaching That Acknowledges Gender

How does this translate into academic achievement? Remember that one of our basic human needs is to feel loved and have a sense of belonging. Conforming to gender roles can earn the fulfillment of this need. Boys' early orientation toward exploration gives them experience interacting with concepts associated with science and mathematics. In science and mathematics classes, therefore, many boys approach the content with more experience and confidence than some girls. Similarly, girls' early orientation toward caring and kindliness gives them experience and confidence in the "softer" behaviors many girls bring into their school years.

Thus, there have been considerable gender gaps in achievement. In the 1980s and 1990s, girls consistently performed better than boys in reading and writing, and boys consistently outperformed girls in mathematics and science. However, recent studies show that girls may have bridged the divide in mathematics and science achievement while holding on to their advantage over boys in reading and writing skills (Benfer, 2002). Some say that the historical gender gap has been eradicated entirely; others assert that the gap remains (Benfer, 2002).

Let us look at some representative data. The Program for International Student Assessment (PISA) is a system of international assessments that measure capabilities of 15-year-olds in reading, science, and mathematics every 3 years. The result of the 2003 mathematics test showed that boys scored higher than girls in mathematics literacy, but there was no significant difference between boys and girls in problem solving (Lemke et al., 2004). The National Assessment of Education Progress (NAEP), also known as *The Nation's Report Card,* administers subject-matter assessments annually to randomly selected schools in the United States. The results of the 2005 tests show that boys outscored girls in mathematics in both fourth grade and eighth grade (Perie, Grigg, & Dion, 2005) and that girls outscored boys in reading in both fourth grade and eighth grade (Perie, Grigg, & Donahue, 2005).

One of the challenges facing teachers is to foster the achievement of both boys and girls in *all* areas. Understanding the nature and development of gender-based stereotypical roles and the value placed by students and adults on these roles is a good first step toward reducing gender-based expectations in school.

Before you start drawing conclusions about methods that make content accessible to both genders, it might be useful to explore your own assumptions and expectations regarding gender.

BUILDING BLOCK 4.13

Your Gender Biases

Take the test for gender bias at the Implicit Association Test on the Internet. Use the direct link to this battery of tests on the *Building Teachers* companion website. Select the Gender-Science IAT.

Reflect on your results. What do the results tell you about stereotypical gender biases you may have?

From Building Block 4.13, can you tell what you *really* believe about gender roles? Do you really believe that males make better scientists than females? Do you really believe that females make better writers?

Schools have tended to promote stereotypical gender behaviors and beliefs that may contribute to or hinder student achievement. In a 1992 report (American Association of University Women, 1992), the AAUW found that male students not only demanded but also received more attention from teachers of both sexes, especially in mathematics and science classes. Another study found that males use their perceived power to "silence" girls, often interrupting them while the girls were speaking, and sometimes even resorting to statements and actions that can be considered sexual harassment (Claire & Redpath, 1989). The researchers noted that teachers and other school officials often ignored these actions, thereby offering tacit approval.

What would *you* do to ensure gender inequalities do not exist in your classroom? Consider the following findings reported by Hall (1982) that continue to exist in our classrooms, and reflect on the questions associated with each:

Finding: Males answer questions quickly, giving confident answers they formulate while speaking. Females wait longer to answer, choosing their words carefully before responding. Females are interrupted more often than males when answering questions.

Questions: What messages are males getting from this type of environment? What messages are females getting from this type of environment? What needs are being affected (positively or negatively)? What could you do in your classroom to provide equity for answering questions?

Finding: Girls tend to take passive roles in mixed-gender groups such as those used in lab situations and hands-on activities.

Questions: What messages are males getting from this type of environment? What messages are females getting from this type of environment? What needs are being impacted (positively or negatively)? What could you do in your classroom to provide equity for active participation?

Finding: In general, students perceive scientists as being male. In a study by Gardner et al. (1989), students were asked to draw scientists. The majority of pictures depicted the typical "nerd" scientist—a man with wild hair and thick glasses, wearing a lab coat and a pocket protector.

Questions: What does this tell you about what students believe about science and scientists? What could you do in your classroom to dispel this stereotyping?

www Direct links to websites devoted to "Draw-a-Scientist" activities are available on the *Building Teachers* companion website.

Teaching for Gender Equity

BUILDING BLOCK 4.14

Consider the basic and academic needs of each gender, as well as the special perspectives each gender brings to the classroom.

What teaching strategies would foster girls to be motivated to learn? What teaching strategies would foster boys to be motivated to learn? Make a list of these strategies.

How are they like the strategies you already have considered? How do they help students meet their basic and academic needs?

Do you see what is happening? By comparing the strategies, you are identifying some just plain "good ideas" for teaching all students—ideas that also happen to subsume specific strategies for teaching students who bring unique qualities to our classrooms.

Sexual Orientation

As you survey your classroom, many of the student perspectives and characteristics we have discussed so far may be apparent, but you may not be able to discern a student's sexual orientation. Indeed, some students go to great lengths to hide this attribute. Nonetheless, a student's sexual orientation can have a profound impact on his or her motivation to participate in your classroom.

There are several sexual orientations, including heterosexual, homosexual (gay and lesbian), bisexual (sexual orientation toward both sexes), and transgender (having the characteristics of the opposite sex). Although most people are heterosexual, many, including students in our schools, identify with alternative orientations. Of these, homosexuality predominates. Homosexual people have been called the "invisible minority." Not only is their orientation not readily discernible, they are also unlikely to disclose it, largely out of fear of others' reactions. Recall the basic needs of all students: love, security, belonging, and self-esteem. What unique issues do gay students bring to getting these needs met by teachers and other students?

Some individuals are less accepting of homosexual orientation than others, so students with nontraditional sexual orientations may have good reason to keep their orientation secret. The 2003 National School Climate Survey (Kosciw, 2004) reports the following about lesbian, gay, bisexual, and transgendered (LGBT) students:

- Ninety percent of LGBT students frequently hear derogatory comments toward homosexuality in the halls and classrooms.
- Fewer than 25% of LGBT students reported that teachers intervened when such remarks were made.

- Thirty-nine percent of LGBT students reported being verbally assaulted, physically assaulted, or both.
- Seventy-five percent reported feeling unsafe due to their sexuality or gender expression.
- One out of three LGBT students skipped school during the month preceding the survey out of fear.

The Gay, Lesbian, and Straight Education Network (GLSEN) highlights additional findings of the survey (Snorton, 2005):

- LGBT students who report significant verbal harassment are twice as likely to report they do not intend to go to college and exhibit significantly lower academic performance, with average GPAs of 2.9 versus 3.3.
- Only 10% of LGBT students who can identify supportive staff at their schools report they do not intend to go to college.

www Direct links to the Parents, Families, and Friends of Lesbians and Gays (PFLAG) association website and the Gay, Lesbian, and Straight Education Network (GLSEN) are available on the *Building Teachers* companion website. PFLAG and GLSEN answer common questions about alternative sexualities and offer information and resources that may help you in the schools.

Teaching that Acknowledges Sexual Orientation

As with religion, people's beliefs about sexual orientation are strongly influenced by the environment in which they were raised. As with gender, society has exerted strong influence on perceptions of alternative sexual orientations. And, as with culture, language, religion, SES, gender, and other individual differences, teachers have an obligation to students with nontraditional sexual orientations to demonstrate positive regard in meeting their needs as students and as human beings. Recall the characteristics of effective teachers you identified in Chapter 1. Chances are that you agreed with the researchers and others that tolerance for *all* people is a desirable characteristic—one that is normally found in effective teachers. Does your tolerance extend to people with alternative sexual orientations?

BUILDING BLOCK 4.15

Your Sexual Orientation Biases

Take Sexuality Implicit Association Test available on the Internet. The Sexuality IAT assesses for sexual orientation bias. Access the test via the *Building Teachers* companion website.

Reflect on what your results tell you. What do you think contributed to the beliefs you hold that contributed to your score? If you have discovered that you hold certain biases toward people with alternative lifestyles, what can you do to neutralize those biases and be an effective teacher?

Review the strategies you have identified that contribute to the creation of an effective learning environment for *all* students. How do these strategies serve to meet the needs of homosexual students or those students who are questioning their sexuality? Of course, there is no specific list of strategies to teach gay students. The strategies you have already identified help meet the needs of each and every student in your classroom.

Putting It All Together

You have examined many aspects of diversity, including culture, language, religion, socioeconomic status, gender, and sexual orientation. You have investigated each of these issues and attempted to identify your own personal beliefs, predispositions, biases, and prejudices. As a teacher in today's pluralistic society, it is essential that you maintain a diverse perspective in your classroom. This may mean thinking differently about what is ac-

Technology & Education   Different Strokes for Different Folks

In this chapter, you have learned that although students have common needs, each student brings a different perspective to the classroom. It might seem challenging at this point to acknowledge all the different perspectives in any one classroom, but technology can assist teachers in meeting this challenge effectively.

Using instructional technology can help teachers understand and acknowledge different cultures, religions, and languages. Several cultures and religions may be represented in the population of a classroom. The teacher can use the Internet to research these cultures and religions to gain a better understanding of students' perspectives. Imagine the validation a student might feel knowing that the teacher cared enough to learn about his or her culture or religion! When a teacher does this, what basic needs is the teacher helping to meet? Which of Brooks's questions does the teacher's action help to answer? Keep in mind that other students could also access the same information to learn more about their classmates and themselves. Take the time to educate yourself about other unique perspectives you have learned about in this chapter, taking advantage of the Internet's vast resources.

Technology affords teachers many resources to help teach English Language Learners (ELLs). We all know that a picture is worth a thousand words. Technology provides teachers with access to countless images and diagrams that can be projected or printed when giving instructions or illustrating an idea. And what you cannot find, you can draw. Don't worry if you are not an artist. Software is available to help you draw anything from a straight line to a complex diagram.

Software for language learning is also available. ELL students can use such packages to help them learn English, and English-speaking students can learn other languages. Online language courses exist, some of which are free. Translation software and websites let teachers translate work they produce for students, as well as letters to and from parents. Again, some online translation sites are free; others charge a fee. What kind of online language courses or translations sites can you find?

For younger ELL students, packages such as the LeapFrog SchoolHouse Literacy Centers can be integrated into regular classroom activities. The LeapFrog products include the LeapPad, an interactive book system, and LeapDesks, which come with headphones so students can listen independently. The Meadow Woods Elementary School in Orlando, Florida, used LeapFrog Literacy Centers with their students, 49% of whom speak Spanish. The administrators and teachers reported that when students used the LeapFrog Centers individually or in groups, not only did students acquire English language literacy, they had fun doing so. The instruction and guidance provided by the LeapPads was fast-paced and gave students visual and audio feedback, well suited to the kind of stimulating environment, as from television and video games, that surrounds today's students. Teachers noted that a valuable feature of the software package was the ability to print progress reports, which were shared with students, administrators, and parents (Meadow Woods' ESOL Students, 2002). LeapFrog SchoolHouse contracted with RMC Research Corporation to study the effects of LeapFrog Literacy Centers on a diverse population of kindergarten and first grade students in Las Vegas, Nevada. The study found that the use of the technology-based literacy centers significantly enhanced student performance on key literacy skills (RMC Research Corporation, 2004).

Content area software frequently offers different language options. DVDs and CD-ROMs, for example, may have Spanish language tracks. Many websites are also available in two or more languages. If English-speaking students find content area websites in a language other than English, an ELL who speaks that language can translate the site and share it with other students, thereby learning and practicing both language and technology skills.

Teachers can use technology as a valuable tool to acknowledge the unique perspectives students bring to the classroom. Tools and software are available to aid in communication, understanding, and learning.

---

ceptable and what is not acceptable on the part of students and teacher alike and what cultural and diversity characteristics are promoted in the classroom.

As a teacher, you have a responsibility to be sure you are *not* contributing to racism, classism, sexism, homophobia, and other elements of diversity that may create a hierarchy and define a norm. Rather, you must see that all your interactions with students foster personal and educational equity.

Metaphors Revisited

Refer to the metaphor you selected to describe yourself as a teacher in Chapter 2. In light of the investigations you have made in this chapter, ask yourself this question: "Does my metaphor imply unconditional equity?"

Conclusion

In this chapter you investigated several differences that affect the ways students learn and, ultimately, their achievement. You defined *diversity* to include numerous ways in which people are different from each other. Some of these ways are visible and immediately recognizable. Others are less visible but just as important.

You explored cultural diversity, English language learners, religious affiliation, socioeconomic status, gender bias, and sexual orientation. For each, you looked at your own perceptions so you could begin to construct your ideas about these human attributes.

You found that the student population of America's schools is becoming increasingly diversified relative to both race and ethnicity. This diversity requires teachers to be sensitive to culture-based differences in approaches to learning. The primary difficulty of English language learners is their lack of fluency with the English language; however, teachers can minimize the impact of this disadvantage with a few appropriate instructional adjustments. Many religious beliefs are represented in our schools, and teachers must recognize this fact and assume an attitude of neutrality when it comes to religion. Students' socioeconomic backgrounds have a tremendous influence on the students' preparedness for school, their attitudes toward school, and their achievement, and different socioeconomic backgrounds present unique instructional challenges. Gender roles tend to be perceived stereotypically in schools; skillful teachers teach for gender equity. Teachers need to show tolerance and respect for students who identify with alternative sexual orientations.

You saw that biases and prejudices often exist toward people with perspectives perceived as "different." Teachers must identify their own viewpoints and work toward acceptance of *all* students, regardless of their unique characteristics and perspectives, to provide a safe, respectful, and equitable classroom environment that allows students to focus on learning.

You observed that the learning strategies you have identified seem to be useful in meeting the needs of *all* students, not only the needs of single groups. It is not necessary to provide separate lists of specific ways of teaching to acknowledge the unique learning needs presented by each different perspective or characteristic. Although certain strategies can be identified for managing certain perspectives, all students have similar needs. Teachers must show students that the material being taught connects to their individual lives. This connection arises largely from the teaching and learning relationships developed in the classroom.

Crutcher (1998) said, "Whether you know it, like it, or want it, you, the teacher, will have a significant relationship with each of your students." This relationship may range from elaborate with some students to minimal with others, but it will be present. It may or may not be consistent with your own perceptions or intentions. But rest assured, there will be a relationship. Your relationships with students enable you to help them find relationships with what they are learning. These relationships are developed through respect for the perspectives brought by each student. Through these relationships, teachers must establish connections to each student's "self" to promote interest, relevance, and learning.

Many factors bear on students' ability to learn, and the factors discussed in this chapter represent selected examples. By now you can see that no two people are the same and no two people learn in precisely the same way. You will continue this exploration into the next chapter, where you will consider cognitive differences.

Key Terms and Concepts

Bilingual education, 106
Culture, 98
Diversity, 95
Ethnicity, 98

Foreign-born, 99
English language learner, 104
Poverty, 111
Race, 98

Socioeconomic status, 111
Stereotype, 98
Student of color, 99

Construct and Apply

1. List five factors you consider to be "identifiers" about yourself. These can be physical charac-teristics, information about your history or background, or a role you occupy as a citizen or family member. Which factors indicate a difference between you and most other people?
2. Why do you suppose traditionally minority populations cite their minority characteristic as defining?
3. For each unique student characteristic and perspective you investigated in this chapter, describe how these students can be expected to provide for their basic need of love and belonging and how you would expect them to motivate *themselves* to learn. Are your expectations reasonable for the age you wish to teach?
4. Make a list of teaching strategies effective for teaching *everyone* in all groups discussed in this chapter.

Deconstructing the Standards

INTASC Principle #2 says:

> The teacher understands how children learn and develop, and can provide learning op-portunities that support their intellectual, social, and personal development.

- What part(s) of this principle does this chapter address?
- How does this chapter address this principle?
- How will the concepts in this chapter help you apply this principle as a teacher?

Field Experience

1. What kinds of diversity do you see in your field experience classroom? Are these traits associ-ated with students, teachers, or both?
2. How does your cooperating teacher teach to affirm students of different cultures, socioeco-nomic statuses, genders, and sexual orientations and to promote equity in the classroom?
3. Are there English language learners in your field experience classroom? What teaching strate-gies does your cooperating teacher employ to foster maximum success on the part of ELLs?
4. What is the policy of your field experience school about religious and secular holidays?
5. How does your cooperating teacher demonstrate positive regard for all the students in his or her classroom?

Your Portfolio

Use your work in the activities suggested in this chapter to show your developing awareness of the differences among students in our schools.

Re-examine the philosophy of education you wrote in Chapter 2. Make any revisions or addi-tions that seem appropriate as a result of your work in this chapter, highlight these changes, and re-place your former philosophy with your new one in your portfolio.

To enhance your increasing awareness of diversity, try a few enrichment activities. Here are some suggestions:

- Some colleges offer language courses specifically designed for teachers. Check one out.
- Immerse yourself in a cultural experience. Attend services at a synagogue or church. Vol-unteer to tutor underprivileged kids.
- If there is an International House on your campus, visit it and pick up some literature to in-clude in your portfolio.

- Go to a Chinese restaurant where Chinese people eat or a Mexican restaurant where Mexican people eat or an Indian restaurant where Indian people eat. Write a reflection of your experience and include it in your portfolio, along with a copy of the menu.

- Refer to a newspaper or the Internet to examine the population demographics of the school systems in your area. Include the material you find in your portfolio.

- Find a student on campus or at your field placement school who identifies with a culture different from yours. Talk with the student about his or her educational experience. Write a brief reflection to include in your portfolio.

- Find out if the software in your campus or in your field placement school (or both) is available in languages other than English.

▨ Technology Resources

 Check out the *Building Teachers* companion website—http://www.education.wadsworth.com/martinloomis1—for more information and resources about student diversity and education, including access to the following websites:

- Multicultural Awareness Self Tests
- English First and the National Bilingual Education Association
- Head Start, Early Head Start, and the Perry Preschool Project
- "Draw-a-Scientist" activities
- Parents, Families, and Friends of Lesbians and Gays (PFLAG)

 See video footage of real teachers addressing student needs in the classroom. Check the *Building Teachers* CD-ROM that accompanies your textbook for additional resources.

Also link to InfoTrac College Edition through the *Building Teachers* companion website. Use InfoTrac to search for articles to enhance your study.

CHAPTER 5

The Student and the Teacher: Acknowledging Unique Abilities

Every child is an artist. The problem is how to remain an artist once he grows up.

PABLO PICASSO

There are children playing in the streets who could solve some of my top problems in physics, because they have modes of sensory perception that I lost long ago.

J. ROBERT OPPENHEIMER

We all know every student has unique abilities. Some of these abilities are expressed artistically; others may be expressed intellectually. Like the unique perspectives students bring to class that are influenced by culture, race, ethnicity, language, religion, socioeconomic status, and sexual orientation, these abilities also contribute to diversity in the classroom. Step into any classroom and you will encounter a broad spectrum of physical, sensory, cognitive, and behavioral differences. As a teacher, you always strive to create a learning environment and effective instruction that will allow *all* students to use their unique abilities to succeed.

What do you suppose Picasso and Oppenheimer were saying about the unique abilities of children and how teachers can acknowledge them?

This chapter asks you to familiarize yourself with some unique abilities and learning styles and investigate the nature of these abilities. You will infer ways of teaching to foster maximum achievement for students with diverse abilities. You will explore some of the ways in which learning abilities can be classified, beginning with the categories of exceptionality covered by the Individuals with Disability Education Act. You will examine how students with unique abilities are served by special education, with a special focus on students with learning disabilities. Although teachers and schools frequently focus on traditional measures of intellectual ability, such as IQ, you will investigate some alternative (but influential) views of intelligence. You also will explore additional categories of differences among learners that have been shown to have pronounced influences on student achievement.

CHAPTER GOALS

As a result of your work in this chapter, you will:

1. Investigate ways in which variations in ability are classified.

2. Examine how cognitive abilities and learning preferences differ among students.

3. Explore how these characteristics affect learning.

4. Infer best teaching practices to help all students learn by acknowledging their unique cognitive characteristics.

5. Identify characteristics of constructivist teaching and learning.

Exceptional Children and the Individuals with Disabilities Education Act

No two children are identical, but **exceptional students** are those who differ from societal norms to the extent that they require some form of modification to a standard educational program. These differences can vary from physical impairments to emotional and behavior disorders to intellectual giftedness. **Special education** refers to instruction specially designed to meet the unique needs of students who are recognized as exceptional (Gargiulo, 2006).

Students with exceptionalities have not always been well served by our nation's public schools. Before the mid-20th century, it was common practice to bar children with disabilities from attending school. However, the rise of the civil rights movement in the United States marked a turning point for securing the rights of citizens with disabilities. In the past 50 years, the federal government, in a series of landmark pieces of legislation, has helped to define the current special education policies and practices of our schools.

In 1975, Congress passed Public Law 94-142, the Education of All Handicapped Children Act, which required each state to develop and implement policies that assure a free and appropriate education for all students with disabilities. In 1986, Congress passed amendments to include children attending preschool. In 1990, the Individuals with Disabilities Education Act (IDEA) was passed into law to amend the 1975 law; this act was amended in 1997 and reauthorized in 2004.

The IDEA requires states to provide services for all children with disabilities so these children can receive a "full and appropriate education." The law extends to many differ-

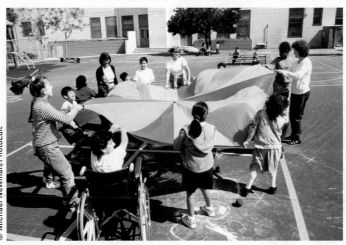

© Michael Newman/PhotoEdit

According to federal law, children with special needs must receive full and appropriate education and be educated with their typical peers in the least restrictive environment possible.

ent types of disabilities, including cognitive disabilities and physical disabilities. Among the categories covered under the IDEA are the following:

Do you know someone with a disability? What special arrangements were provided for this person at school?

- Learning disability
- Mental retardation
- Emotional disturbance
- Autism
- Speech or language impairment
- Visual impairment
- Hearing impairment
- Physical impairments, including orthopedic impairments, multiple disabilities, and traumatic brain injury

IDEA Disability Categories

Nearly 6 million students aged 3 through 21 received services for various disabilities in 2001 (U.S. Department of Education, 2003). The following list shows these disabilities and the percentage of students for each (U.S. Department of Education, 2003):

• Specific learning disabilities	41%
• Speech or language impairments	15%
• Mental retardation	11%
• Emotional disturbance	14%
• Hearing impairments	1%
• Visual impairments	less than 1%
• Orthopedic impairments	1%
• Other health impairments	12%
• Autism	2%
• Traumatic brain injury	less than 1%
• Multiple disabilities	2%
• Deaf–blindness	less than 1%

The law requires that schools provide all students with disabilities with at least the following (U.S. Department of Education, 2003):

- A full and appropriate education
- Education in the least restrictive environment
- An individualized education program (IEP)
- Due process
- Nondiscriminatory assessment
- Parental participation

The least restrictive environment provision means that students with disabilities must be educated to the greatest extent possible in general education classrooms. We can think of the least restrictive environment concept as an inverted tree that depicts a cascade of special education services, as shown in Figure 5.1.

As you can tell from the diagram, the degree of services provided for students with disabilities varies from inclusion in traditional classroom programs with some special assistance, to homebound with no school attendance at all. At some point in your own

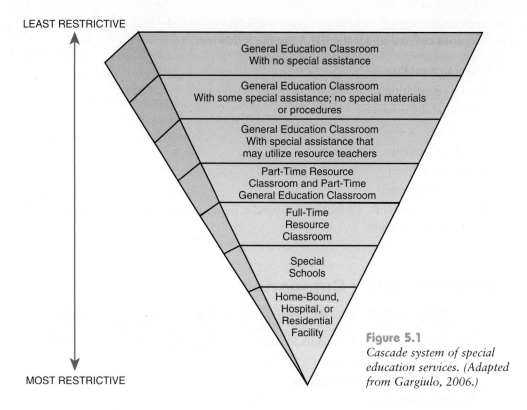

LEAST RESTRICTIVE

General Education Classroom
With no special assistance

General Education Classroom
With some special assistance; no special materials
or procedures

General Education Classroom
With special assistance that
may utilize resource teachers

Part-Time Resource
Classroom and Part-Time
General Education Classroom

Full-Time
Resource
Classroom

Special
Schools

Home-Bound,
Hospital, or
Residential
Facility

MOST RESTRICTIVE

Figure 5.1
Cascade system of special education services. (Adapted from Gargiulo, 2006.)

educational experience, you may have heard the terms **mainstreaming** or **inclusion.** Mainstreaming is a now-outdated term that was used to describe the integration of children with disabilities into general education classrooms. The word *inclusion,* a more current term, suggests that schools are getting closer to total integration of children with disabilities. In practice, inclusion may occur in varying degrees:

Regular classroom with no special assistance. This situation may be most appropriate for students with very mild disabilities that do not prevent them from pursuing challenging work, although advocates of **full inclusion** believe that all children with disabilities should be served in general education classrooms.

Regular classroom with some special teaching assistance but no special materials or procedures. Teachers of these students expand their repertoire of teaching techniques to include all students in their classes. This situation may be appropriate for students with mild disabilities who require some special treatment, either in the form of accommodation of physical handicaps (vision-impaired, hearing-impaired, and so on) or special teaching techniques.

Regular classroom with assistance from special education teachers or other specialized teachers. The classroom teacher may rely on resource teachers to deliver special instruction on the topics being studied. Special materials often are provided. This situation may be appropriate for students who can attend traditional classes but who need special planning and special instruction to accommodate their disabilities.

Regular classroom some of the time and special classroom (usually taught by special education teachers) some of the time. The traditional classes the students attend are those in which the student is believed to be able to succeed. The services provided in the traditional classroom can be any of those described previously. This situation may be appropriate for students who can succeed in traditional classrooms for some academic studies, but who need special programs and special teaching for other areas.

Resource classroom full time, with no time spent in traditional classrooms. A special education teacher normally teaches these classes. This situation may be appropriate for students who are unable to attend and succeed in traditional classes but who can attend school.

Special schools with no attendance in a traditional school or classroom. This situation is reserved for handicapped students who cannot function in a traditional school in spite of any accommodations that can be made.

Homebound, hospital, or residential facility. This situation is reserved for students with severe cognitive and functioning limitations.

Special Education Controversies

There is a great deal of controversy over the concept of inclusion in education. Some believe that inclusion helps to minimize perceived differences between students who have disabilities and those who do not. Others believe that inclusion can result in an inferior education for students with disabilities because they are required to keep up with the rest of the class.

What do you think are the benefits of inclusion for students with special needs? What are the benefits for "regular" students? What potential drawbacks exist for both groups of students? What are the challenges for the classroom teacher?

A great deal of controversy also surrounds the labeling of students. In Chapter 4, you investigated labels for yourself and for students based on unique perspectives; this chapter shows that students with different kinds of disabilities are labeled. Some believe that labeling helps educators prepare the most appropriate educational programs. Others believe that labels can be stigmatizing or even penalizing and misrepresent the true nature of individuals.

What do you think about labeling? Remember that the goal of education is to provide the best possible learning opportunities for each student to maximize his or her achievement.

Inform and support your opinion with information from your own experience and from appropriate resources, such as the Internet, newspapers, periodicals, and journals.

A second major provision of the IDEA is the requirement of an individualized education program (IEP) for each student with disabilities. The IEP is a detailed plan for a student's education that will meet the student's unique educational needs. The IEP normally is prepared jointly by the special education teacher, classroom teachers who will be involved in the student's education, the student's parents or guardians, and someone who can interpret the results of the assessment tests, such as the guidance counselor or school psychologist.

Another major provision of the IDEA is the assurance of due process. This means parents or guardians

1. have the right to examine all of their child's school records,
2. must be given notice before any change in placement or classification is made, and
3. must give their consent before their child is evaluated or placed.

The nondiscriminatory assessment provision of the IDEA requires students to be evaluated using several types of assessments that have been shown to be free of bias. The parental participation provision requires that parents or guardians participate fully in the decision-making process.

Adapting instruction for students with learning disabilities includes clearly specifying learning objectives, presenting lessons in a step-by-step format, and providing frequent assessments of student learning.

Learning Disabilities

Learning disabilities are the most commonly occurring handicapping condition. The term **learning disability** (LD) refers to a disorder in one or more of the basic processes involved in understanding or in using language (spoken or written), which may manifest itself in an imperfect ability to listen, think, speak, read, write, spell, or perform mathematical calculations. Students with learning disabilities are included among those who qualify for special education services. As of 2001, almost 2.9 million, or approximately 5% of school-age children attending public schools in the United States, were classified as having a learning disability (National Center for Learning Disabilities, 2001). The most common disabilities are seen in basic reading and language skills.

Learning disabilities are hard to diagnose but usually are suspected when there is a gap between a student's ability and his or her performance. Some signs that a student may have a learning disability include coordination problems, difficulty with concentration, and consistent problems with handwriting, remembering newly learned information, staying organized, or speaking so that he or she is understood. It is important to note that most students with learning disabilities are of average or above average intelligence (National Center for Learning Disabilities, 2001); in fact, some are considered gifted and talented.

Learning disabilities are as individual as the students who have them. **Dyslexia** is one example of a learning disability with which you may be familiar. Students with dyslexia have severe difficulties with reading comprehension, failing to understand the relationship between sounds and letters. They often sequence letters incorrectly in words while they are reading or writing, and they interchange words and numerals. To begin to understand what a dyslexic person sees while reading, try to read the passages in Figure 5.2.

Thew ord sare n otsp aced cor rect ly.

We spell wrds xatle az tha snd to us.

Sometimesallthelettersarepushedtogether

The translation of above passage is:

3. Sometimes all the letters are pushed together.

2. We spell words exactly as they sound to us.

1. The words are not spaced correctly.

Figure 5.2
What a dyslexic student might see. (Adapted from kidshealth.org.)

A link to a web site that features dyslexia self-tests is available on the *Building Teachers* companion website. Several tests are available on this site, including dyslexia tests for young children and adolescents.

From your investigations into ways to accommodate students with other unique characteristics and perspectives in the classroom, you can probably think of some effective strategies to accommodate students with disabilities.

Teaching Students with Disabilities

Select a specific student disability, such as mental retardation, hearing impairment, physical impairment, or other disability you might encounter among the students in a class you would teach.

- What teaching strategies would foster these students' motivation to learn?
- How are the strategies similar to those you have suggested for students with other unique characteristics and perspectives?
- How do they compare to teaching strategies you observed in your precollege educational experiences?
- How do they foster heightened relationships between the students and the teacher?
- How do they help students meet their basic and academic needs?

People with disabilities have special learning requirements that teachers must provide. Understanding the unique characteristics and perspectives of students with disabilities helps teachers tailor their classrooms to meet the needs of these students, as well as all the others. Here are some specific instructional strategies teachers use to adapt instruction for students with special needs:

1. Identifying the specific competencies students are to achieve
2. Ensuring that students have previously achieved the skills and understandings they need for success in the lesson
3. Modifying reading levels to meet students' capabilities
4. Preparing explicit and specific introductory and summary activities
5. Delivering introductory and summary activities in small pieces
6. Providing the information of the lesson in small pieces
7. Identifying and defining any new vocabulary words that may come up
8. Assessing student achievement frequently and being aware of students' progress and understanding
9. Developing alternative forms of assessment
10. Providing an assortment of methods students can use to demonstrate their understanding
11. Adapting physical facilities (furniture, storage areas, and other facilities) for use by all students
12. Ensuring that everyone works on the lesson's activities
13. Modifying equipment and materials as needed so all students can use them
14. Enlarging aisles and areas of movement to accommodate all students
15. Providing assistive and adaptive forms of technology resources

Compare the preceding strategies for adapting instruction for students with special needs with those you listed in Building Block 5.1. Are there similarities?

As you have seen, the IDEA identifies specific categories of disability. Some of these designations are based on assessments of intellectual ability. But what exactly is intelligence, and how is it measured?

Cognitive Abilities

You have seen that characteristics such as race, ethnicity, language, gender, socioeconomic status, and sexual orientation can affect how—or even whether—a learner approaches a learning task. Certainly these differences affect classroom climate and how we teach. However, if we were to ask, "What single student characteristic most accounts for differences in student achievement?" your first inclination might be to reply "intelligence." Intelligence is "the ability to learn or understand or to deal with new or trying situations" (Merriam-Webster, 2003). When teachers say "intelligence," they normally are referring to a student's cognitive (or intellectual) ability.

Aptitude tests, such as the Otis–Lennon School Ability Test (OLSAT), the Cognitive Abilities Test (CogAT), and intelligence quotient (IQ) tests like the Stanford–Binet and Weschler IQ tests, are used to measure **cognitive ability**, aptitude, and potential for success of students in school. These tests gauge linguistic, mathematical, and spatial abilities by posing questions that require linguistic, mathematical, and spatial thinking, together with memory skills.

Educational decisions are made partly on the basis of student IQs as measured by the tests. How valid are these tests?

Do you remember taking IQ or aptitude tests? What were your feelings about these tests?

BUILDING BLOCK 5.2

Intelligence Tests

Access two short IQ self-tests via the *Building Teachers* companion website. Take one of the tests.

- Look at the questions. What background knowledge do they presuppose you have? Are there any ambiguous questions (questions that can have more than one meaning)?

- How did you score? Do you believe that this score accurately reflects your intellectual ability? Why or why not?

- How valid do you believe the IQ score is? Why do you think so?

Measuring Cognitive Ability

Some people have concerns about IQ tests and, therefore, about decisions made on the basis of IQ scores. Primary among these concerns is the cultural bias that seems to be embedded in many IQ tests, and which may result in inaccurate scores for individuals whose experiential and cultural backgrounds differ from those that govern the tests' development. For example, a test question might ask when people are most likely to go swimming. Students whose experiences with swimming primarily deal with the school swim team might answer *winter* rather than the "correct" response of *summer*. Did you find questions with experiential or cultural bias in the sample tests you took in Building Block 5.2?

Also, some IQ tests do not allow for creative thinking and therefore may not represent the full extent of a student's ability to solve problems. In fact, some of the greatest thinkers of our time, such as Thomas Edison and Albert Einstein, did not perform well on traditional measures of intelligence.

Nevertheless, educational decisions continue to be made using IQ scores. Among those decisions is the categorization of students into intellectual ability groups. IQ scores between 70 and 130 represent normal intelligence. You can expect most of the students in your classroom to fall in this range. IQ scores below 70 indicate mental retardation, and IQ scores above 130 represent exceptional intelligence.

Naturally, the further away from the normal range an IQ score is, the fewer people have that IQ. The complete distribution of IQ scores can be represented by a graph in the shape of a bell, called the **bell-shaped curve** or the **normal curve**. On the normal curve, IQ is represented on the horizontal axis, and the number or percentage of people is rep-

In an article written for *THE* (Technological Horizons in Education) *Journal,* Margaret Bowerman shares several ways in which she integrates technology into her teaching and classroom management to meet the needs of her students with different abilities. Ms. Bowerman teaches a class of 25 third graders in Arizona. Her class includes two gifted students and seven with special needs. Most of the work in her classroom happens in learning centers and in small groups, where technology is integrated as appropriate.

Ms. Bowerman has several computers in her classroom, along with projection equipment, an interactive white board, speakers, web cams, and microscopes connected to the computer. She uses this technology in a variety of ways and for a variety of purposes, including tailoring instruction to ability, assessment, and multiple intelligences. For a math unit, she uses the interactive white board to demonstrate and practice problem solving and to play web-based math games. A learning objective for this unit is to develop definitions of geometric terms based on observation, measurement, construction, and classification of models and figures.

Students can use technology to express their understanding. They write "information cards" for the geometric definitions, create posters in Microsoft Publisher with definitions and drawings, or make a Microsoft PowerPoint electronic slide show to present information.

For her lower-ability students, Ms. Bowerman creates PowerPoint tutorials that ask them to fill in the blanks. Her higher-level students do not receive as much prompting from the PowerPoint slides. Sometimes, she has her higher-ability students create the tutorials. She notes that the technology makes it easy to alter the amount of structure provided in accordance with the students' skills.

Ms. Bowerman also uses technology to manage her classroom. By using a spreadsheet to keep track of student names and the skills students need to work on, she can sort students by skills and group them appropriately. She often groups students who have mastered a skill with students who need to work on the skill. By giving each student certain responsibilities for the group, Ms. Bowerman explains, students can express their individual talents. She reports that one student with has become the group expert at integrating "bells and whistles," such as graphics, sounds, and animation, into PowerPoint slide shows.

Ms. Bowerman uses technology as a tool to meet the learning needs of students with unique abilities. Besides aiding instruction, technology is also extremely beneficial for students with physical and health disabilities. Assistive and adaptive technology facilitates communication, mobility, learning, recreation, and personal care. Examples of assistive and adaptive technologies include the following:

- Adapted keyboards with large-print keys
- Augmentative communication devices for individuals who are deaf or hearing impaired
- Computer screen enlargers
- Speech synthesizers
- Braille embossers and Braille translation software
- Speech recognition systems

Courtesy of Bill Lisenby

Students with physical disabilities and other special needs can use technology to facilitate classroom learning. To complete her assignment, this student is using an adapted keyboard.

---

resented on the vertical axis. The normal curve for IQ is shown in Figure 5.3. Study this graph and familiarize yourself with the distribution of IQs.

Although you can expect most of the students in your classes to have IQs that fall in the normal range, you also can expect to have individuals from all other IQ ranges (except the extreme left group, which represents students who are unlikely to be included in general education classrooms).

figure 5.3

Normal curve showing relative percentages of the general population in each major cognitive ability group.

Normal Curve Showing IQ Ranges

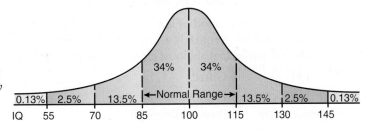

| 0.13% | 2.5% | 13.5% | ←Normal Range→ | 13.5% | 2.5% | 0.13% |

34% 34%

IQ 55 70 85 100 115 130 145

Inclusive environments encourage interaction between students with special needs and their peers. Full and appropriate educational opportunities for students with disabilities might not be possible if not for legislation like the IDEA.

Persons Who Are Gifted and Talented

Students who are **gifted and talented** have potentially outstanding abilities that allow them to excel in one or more areas. As of 2000, 6.3% of students in public elementary and secondary schools were categorized as gifted or talented (U.S. Department of Education, Office of Civil Rights, 2003). The U.S. Department of Education report, *National Excellence: A Case for Developing America's Talent* (1993), characterizes gifted and talented students as follows:

> *Children and youth with outstanding talent perform or show the potential for performing at remarkably high levels of accomplishment when compared with others of their age, experience, or environment.*
>
> *These children and youth exhibit high performance capability in intellectual, creative, and/or artistic areas, possess an unusual leadership capacity, or excel in specific academic fields.*
>
> *Outstanding talents are present in children and youth from all cultural groups, across all economic strata, and in all areas of human endeavor. (p. 8)*

Giftedness normally is recognized in the following areas (ERIC Clearinghouse on Disabilities and Gifted Education, 1990):

- *General intellectual ability:* Normally defined in terms of IQ scores of 130 and above or by students' broad general knowledge, high vocabulary, memory, and ability to employ higher-order thinking skills and abstract reasoning
- *Specific academic aptitude:* A student's outstanding talent and achievement in a particular academic area, such as mathematics, language arts, or science
- *Creative and productive thinking:* A student's ability to produce significant new and novel ideas through the synthesis of known information
- *Leadership ability:* A student's ability to direct individuals or groups through the use of negotiation and other leadership skills
- *Visual and performing arts:* A student's special talents in visual arts, music, dance, drama, and similar areas
- *Psychomotor ability:* A student's extraordinarily dexterous use of motor abilities in practical, spatial, mechanical, and physical skills

The most common method of identifying students who are classified as gifted is the use of tests. Since giftedness frequently is dependent on high intelligence, schools often use IQ scores to label the intellectual ability of gifted and talented students. The ranges are as follows:

130–144	Gifted
145–159	Highly gifted
160 and above	Profoundly gifted

Although tests of intellectual ability often are used to identify intellectual giftedness, general intellectual ability is just one dimension of giftedness and talent. As you have seen, giftedness also manifests itself in other ways and thus depends on other factors. Consequently, a greater variety of assessment tools is used to identify students who are gifted and talented in one or more areas, thereby reducing the likelihood that minority students who are gifted and talented are overlooked (as may be the case when identification depends largely on traditional intelligence tests).

Often, students who are gifted stand out from other students as being really smart, maybe even being labeled as "nerds." Students and teachers alike may make certain assumptions about students who are gifted based on their exceptional intellect, talent, or both. Some myths and truths about students who are gifted are given in the box below.

Common Myths about Students Who Are Gifted

- Students who are gifted are a homogeneous group, all high achievers.
- Students who are gifted do not need help. If they are really gifted, they can manage on their own.
- Students who are gifted have fewer problems than others because their intelligence and abilities somehow exempt them from the hassles of daily life.
- The future of a student who is gifted is assured: A world of opportunities lies before the student.
- Students who are gifted are self-directed; they know where they are heading.
- The social and emotional development of the student who is gifted is at the same level as his or her intellectual development.
- Students who are gifted are nerds and social isolates.
- The primary value of the student who is gifted lies in his or her brainpower.
- The family of the student who is gifted always prizes his or her abilities.
- Students who are gifted need to serve as an example to others, and they should always assume extra responsibility.
- Students who are gifted can accomplish anything they put their minds to. All they have to do is apply themselves.
- Students who are gifted are naturally creative and do not need encouragement.
- Children who are gifted are easy to raise and a welcome addition to any classroom.

Truths about Students Who Are Gifted

- Students who are gifted are often perfectionist and idealistic. They may equate achievement and grades with self-esteem and self-worth, which sometimes leads to fear of failure and interferes with achievement.
- Students who are gifted may experience heightened sensitivity to their own expectations and those of others, resulting in guilt over achievements or grades perceived to be low.
- The chronological age, social, physical, emotional, and intellectual development of a student who is gifted may be at different levels. For example, a 5-year-old may be able to read and comprehend a third-grade book but may not be able to write legibly.
- Students who are gifted may be so far ahead of their chronological age mates that they know more than half the curriculum before the school year begins. Their boredom can result in low achievement and grades.
- People who are gifted make up as much as 20% of the prison population.
- Students who are gifted are at high risk for dropping out of school; 20% of high school dropouts have tested in the gifted range.
- Children who are gifted are problem solvers. They benefit from working on open-ended, interdisciplinary problems, such as how to solve a shortage of community resources. Students who are gifted often refuse to work for grades alone.
- Students who are gifted often think abstractly and with such complexity that they may need help with concrete study- and test-taking skills. They may not be able to select one answer in a multiple-choice question because they see how all the answers might be correct.
- Students who are gifted who do well in school may define success as getting an A and failure as getting any grade less than an A. By early adolescence, these students may be unwilling to try anything if they are not certain of guaranteed success.

(Adapted from Berger, 1998; Culross, n.d.; Davidson & Davidson, 2004)

How do you suppose teachers could work to meet the basic needs of love and belonging, respect, and self-esteem of gifted and talented students? How might giftedness influence students' desire to learn? How might the label "gifted" affect the social aspects of school for gifted students?

BUILDING
BLOCK
5.3

Teaching Students Who Are Gifted and Talented

Review the myths and truths about students who are gifted and talented. What teaching strategies would provide motivation for these students to learn? How would they foster student perception that the material being studied is meaningful and relevant? How would they foster heightened relationships between student and teacher? How would they help students meet their basic and academic needs?

Why do you suppose people who are gifted are overrepresented in the high school dropout and prison populations?

---

www A direct link to the Jacob K. Javits Program for students who are gifted and talented is available on the *Building Teachers* companion website.

Although detailed federal mandates exist to provide services for students with disabilities, there is no federal legislation specific to students who are gifted and talented. Each state adopts its own definitions, laws, and policies concerning the nature and services provided for students who are gifted and talented (Stephens & Karnes, 2000). At the federal level, however, the Jacob K. Javits Gifted and Talented Students Education program awards grants to help students who are gifted develop their abilities and reach high levels of achievement.

Depending on state and local policies, special programs may be offered to students identified as gifted or talented. These programs may take the form of special learning environments and experiences offered at special times on certain days, often in special classrooms. Or they may take the form of the inclusion model in traditional, general education classrooms, similar to the inclusion model used for integrating students with exceptional needs.

State Legislation for the Education of Students Who Are Gifted and Talented

Forty-seven states have enacted legislation dealing with students who are gifted and talented. Legislation ranges from full mandate for services (including identification of students, special programs, and assigned personnel) to recognition of the educational needs of students who are gifted and talented. As of 2005, the only states without formal legislation dealing with students who are gifted and talented are North Dakota, Vermont, and New Hampshire (National Association for Gifted Children, 2005). (See Figure 5.4.)

Most states offer special endorsements for gifted and talented teaching specialists. These specialists provide special programs for qualifying students. However, traditional classroom teachers can expect to have students who are gifted and talented in classrooms for much of the school day. Teaching students who are gifted and talented requires presenting them with challenging work, building on their interests, allowing large blocks of time for them to pursue their projects, and encouraging continued work in out-of-school arenas.

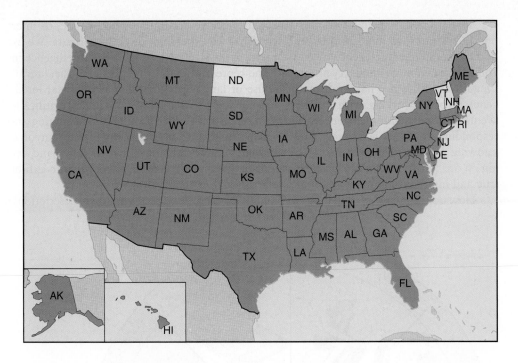

Figure 5.4
States with legislation addressing gifted and talented students. (From Council of State Directors and Programs for the Gifted and National Association for Gifted Children, 2005.)

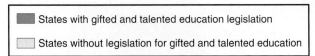

States with gifted and talented education legislation

States without legislation for gifted and talented education

Multiple Intelligences

Perhaps you have heard the assertion that instead of asking, "How smart are you?" we should ask, "How are you smart?" Howard Gardner has argued that humans have at least eight distinct intelligences, not only the two or three measured in traditional IQ tests. The eight intelligences are spatial, bodily–kinesthetic, musical, linguistic, logical–mathematical, interpersonal, intrapersonal, and naturalistic. Gardner also is investigating whether a spiritual or existential intelligence may satisfy his criteria for individual intelligences (Gardner, 2003).

BUILDING BLOCK 5.4

Your Primary Intelligences

What are your strongest intelligences? A direct link to a multiple intelligences inventory is available on the *Building Teachers* companion website. Complete the inventory; then plot the suggested bar chart.

- Where is your highest peak? Does it surprise you?
- Where is your lowest peak? Does it surprise you?
- Perhaps you had high scores in more than one section. What were they? Do you think this inventory adequately portrays your intelligences?

Review the names of each of the eight intelligences identified by Gardner. From these names, infer what people with each predominant intelligence are probably good at doing. For example, you might infer that people with a strong musical talent might be good at playing musical instruments.

Spatial intelligence involves our ability to perceive accurately what we see, to interpret this in our own mind, and to represent what we experience in visual formats. We use bodily–kinesthetic intelligence when we perform physical actions. Musical intelligence involves hearing music almost continuously and representing our thoughts in musical terms. Linguistic intelligence has to do with the use of language. Logical–mathematical intelligence involves working with numbers and solving problems logically and scientifically. We use interpersonal intelligence when we interact with other people, understanding and responding to them accurately and appropriately. Intrapersonal intelligence involves knowing ourselves, knowing who we are, being comfortable in our own skins, and acting on our knowledge of ourselves. Naturalistic intelligence is used by people who exhibit true and internalized appreciation of and sensitivity to the natural world.

How do the inferences you made in Building Block 5.4 compare with these descriptions?

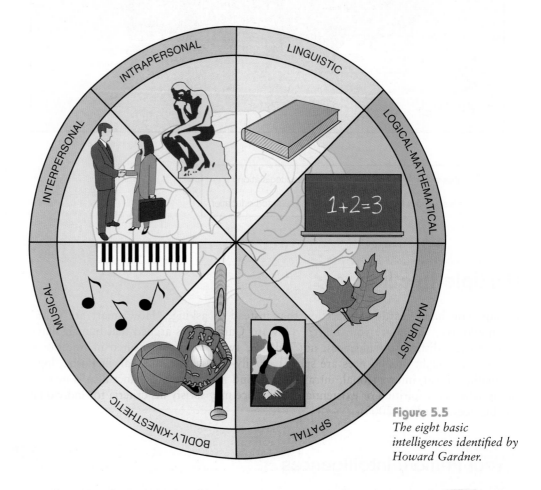

Figure 5.5
The eight basic intelligences identified by Howard Gardner.

Gardner's identification of different intelligences has brought about **multiple intelligence (MI) theory.** This theory suggests that all people have all eight intelligences; the strength of each intelligence varies from person to person. For example, one person may be an absolute whiz at mathematics (strong logical–mathematical intelligence) but unable to "carry a tune in a bucket" (weak musical intelligence). Another individual may be terrific at understanding other people (strong interpersonal intelligence), understands herself and who she is (strong intrapersonal intelligence), and inquires logically into scientific problems (strong logical–mathematical intelligence), but has difficulty in writing reports and compositions (weak linguistic intelligence).

Although you might have one predominant intelligence, you probably use all of the intelligences at one time or another to learn. You can strengthen any of the intelligences by using it more and more. Furthermore, your predominant intelligence can change over time.

J. Gardner, copyright 2003

Howard Gardner's Biography in His Own Words

I was born in Scranton, Pennsylvania, in 1943, the son of refugees from Nazi Germany. I was a studious child who gained much pleasure from playing the piano; music has remained very important throughout my life. All of my post-secondary education has been at Harvard University. I was trained as a developmental psychologist and later as a neuropsychologist. For many years, I conducted two streams of research on cognitive and symbol-using capacities—one with normal and gifted children, the second with adults who suffered from brain damage. My effort to synthesize these two lines of work led me to develop and introduce the theory of multiple intelligences in my 1983 book *Frames of Mind.* Since the middle 1980s, I have been heavily involved in school reform efforts in the United States. In 1986, I began to teach at the Harvard Graduate School of Education while continuing my long-term involvement with Project Zero, a research group in human cognition that maintains a special focus on the arts. With colleagues, I have begun a study of the nature of interdisciplinary work as it is carried out in precollegiate and collegiate settings, and in research institutions, and a study of the role of trust and trustees in contemporary American society.

(Courtesy *Project Zero, Harvard* University)

Teachers should become sensitive to the idea that students can learn through different intelligences and use this sensitivity in their interactions with students.

Teaching That Encompasses Multiple Intelligences

MI theory asks teachers to recognize the several intelligences students have and to develop a repertoire of instructional approaches that capitalize on each of the eight intelligences to "help students use their combinations of intelligences to be successful in school" (Checkley, 1997, p. 10). According to MI theory, students do not learn just through the written word and mathematics. Learning can occur through each of the other six intelligences, and teachers must teach to their students' strongest intelligences. The primary idea behind the theory of multiple intelligences is to respond to the needs of every student by making alternative learning strategies available based on the eight different intelligences. The goal is *not* to teach each concept using each of the eight intelligences or to ensure every student develops every intelligence.

MI theory has caused some controversy. Most of this controversy centers on the lack of tangible proof to back up the eight intelligences. Gardner defends the theory by saying that it is a scientific theory and needs to be evaluated on the basis of the science on which it draws. The issue, according to Gardner, is not whether the theory has been proved; after all, it is a theory. The issue is whether implementation of MI theory has produced better student learning—and the answer, based on numerous research projects, is yes.

But there is no controversy over the notion that different people learn in different ways. MI theory has made a significant contribution to education, and students whose teachers use MI theory are the winners.

Table 5.1 summarizes characteristics, examples, and ways to acknowledge each of the eight intelligences in education settings.

Multiple Intelligences

BUILDING BLOCK 5.5

Select an area of content you plan to teach, and describe an activity pertaining to that lesson you might develop specifically for each intelligence.

How would designing classroom activities and lessons in a way that gives students opportunities to use their primary intelligences help to motivate them by meeting their needs?

TABLE 5.1 Characteristics, Examples, and Teaching Strategies to Accommodate Multiple Intelligences (Adapted from Martin, 2006.)

Intelligence	Characteristics	Frequently Found in...	Teaching and Learning Strategies
Spatial	Ability to perceive the visual–spatial world accurately and represent this in one's own mind	Architects Artists Sculptors Cartographers Anatomists Boy Scouts and Girl Scouts Examples: Michelangelo Frank Lloyd Wright Salvador Dali Georgia O'Keefe	Draw maps Study maps Make models Draw pictures Solve mazes Do activities in graphics arts
Bodily–kinesthetic	Ability to use one's body or body parts, such as hands and fingers, to solve problems and express ideas	Athletes Dancers Actors Mimes Examples: Tom Hanks Meryl Streep Magic Johnson Michael Jordan Mia Hamm	Dance Pantomime Play act Play with blocks Work with construction materials Play sports
Musical	Ability to think in music, hear music almost continuously, and recognize musical patterns, remember them, and transform them	Musical performers People who love to play musical instruments People who love to sing People who enjoy listening to music Examples: Ludwig van Beethoven Duke Ellington Ray Charles Joni Mitchell Barbara Streisand	Sing songs Learn tunes Write tunes Write rap songs Engage in rhythmic games and activities Dance Play musical instruments Create rhymes Play classical music in the background (the so-called Mozart effect)
Linguistic	Ability to use language effectively, either in oral or written form, to express ideas to others	Writers Poets Storytellers Lawyers Editors Journalists Examples: Ernest Hemingway Maya Angelou	Read Write Send e-mail Play board or card games Listen to recordings Participate in discussions and conversations Use computers Search the Internet Write poetry, news reports, fiction

TABLE 5.1 Characteristics, Examples, and Teaching Strategies to Accommodate Multiple Intelligences (Adapted from Martin, 2006.)

Intelligence	Characteristics	Frequently Found in...	Teaching and Learning Strategies
Logical–mathematical	Ability to use numbers and operations mathematically and to reason logically	Mathematicians Accountants Statisticians Scientists Computer programmers Examples: John Forbes Nash, Jr. John Glenn Marie Curie Steve Wozniak Sally Ride	Argue points successfully Classify and sequence Play number and logic games Solve puzzles Draw and interpret cognitive maps Draw graphs Interpret graphs Express conclusions in mathematical formats Search the Internet
Interpersonal	Ability to understand other people, to interpret their verbal and nonverbal behavior correctly, and to exhibit sensitivity to their moods and feelings	Teachers Clergy Salespeople Politicians Examples: Ronald Regan Bishop Tutu Mother Teresa Mahatma Ghandi Eleanor Roosevelt You	Lead discussions Participate in discussions Participate in cooperative games Participate in group projects and discussions Participate in dramatic activities Role play Ask clarifying questions Study with a partner
Intrapersonal	Ability to understand oneself, know who one is, know one's own strengths and limitations, and act in accordance with this self-knowledge	People who exhibit self-discipline People who exhibit personal authenticity Examples: The Dalai Lama Martin Luther King, Jr. Deepak Chopra Karen Horney	Participate in independent projects Read books Write in journals Lead discussions Be a friend Help resolve quarrels Organize games Direct play activities Work in cooperative groups Find quiet places for reflection
Naturalistic	Ability to discriminate among living things and exhibit sensitivity to one's natural surroundings	Botanists Zoologists Ecologists Explorers Farmers Hunters Examples: Charles Darwin Jack Hanna Dian Fossey	Explore nature Group according to natural surroundings or environment Find origins Study objects found in nature Collect objects from nature Mount and label specimens from nature

Learning Styles

As you might suspect from your explorations of multiple intelligence theory, people learn more and retain it longer when the material they are learning is taught in a manner that is comfortable to them. To demonstrate this to yourself, do the activity in Building Block 5.6.

BUILDING BLOCK 5.6

Your Comfort Zones

Sit with your body relaxed and your hands folded in your lap or on your desk. Then, unfold your hands and refold them the other way—so the other thumb is on top.

Which way was more comfortable?

Do the same thing with crossing your legs and folding your arms. Is one way more comfortable to you than the other?

You can do the same for choosing which ear you bring the telephone to, which shoe you put on first, and other habitual actions.

In Building Block 5.6, you demonstrated to yourself you have strong personal preferences for a number of things you do. These preferences often are so strong (such as folding your arms one way) that it is difficult—perhaps nearly impossible—to do these simple tasks differently from the way you are used to doing them.

The same principle is true of learning: Learners have distinct preferences for the ways they learn most comfortably.

It has been shown there are several fundamental ways people take in information to process it. These ways are called **learning modalities**, and generally one modality is stronger than the others (Dunn, 1988). There are three main learning modalities: visual, auditory, and tactile–kinesthetic. People for whom the visual learning modality is strong are termed *visual learners;* people for whom the auditory learning modality is strong are termed *auditory learners;* and people for whom the tactile–kinesthetic learning modality is strong are termed *tactile learners* (referring to touch) or *kinesthetic learners* (although the term *kinesthetic learners* [referring to movement] often is used to include both the kinesthetic and tactile modalities).

To understand how people use learning modalities, let us explore them in action in Building Block 5.7.

BUILDING BLOCK 5.7

Exploring Learning Modalities

The following activity will help you discover what it is like to have each of the three primary learning modalities.

Find a friend, classmate, or family member. Looking into the eyes of your partner, secretly record the direction your partner's eyes move as you ask him or her the reflective questions that follow. Use *U* for up, *SA* for straight ahead, *S* for toward the side, *DL* for down toward your partner's left, and *DR* for down toward your partner's right.

1. What is your favorite television program?
2. What is your favorite movie from the past year?
3. Who is your favorite relative?
4. What is your favorite song or piece of music?
5. What is your favorite sport to watch?
6. Who is your favorite actor?
7. Who is your favorite actress?

If your partner's eyes moved upward or were focused straight ahead as he or she reflected on the answers, the individual probably is a predominantly visual learner. If the eyes moved to either side or down to the partner's left, the individual probably is a predominantly auditory learner. If the eyes moved down toward the partner's right, the individual probably is a predominantly tactile–kinesthetic learner (Laborde, 1984; Bandler and Grinder, 1979). See Figure 5.6.

Ask your partner to describe what he or she thought of when deciding on the response to each question. What memories were recalled? Because the way people recall information is congruent with the way they perceive and process information (the way they learn), these descriptions reveal the ways in which visual, auditory, and tactile–kinesthetic individuals learn.

How would you describe a visual learner? An auditory learner? A kinesthetic learner?

People often process information in two or even all three modalities at the same time. Thus, some people may report that two or three modalities operate at the same time. However, one of the three tends to be stronger—in many cases, much stronger than the others. For example, a student may be listening intently to someone describe how the Grand Canyon was formed (auditory learning) but also is reinforcing that information by looking at the pictures and video clips of the Grand Canyon the teacher is providing (visual learning). The teacher may also pass around samples of different rocks that came from the Grand Canyon for people to feel (tactile learning) and look at (visual learning).

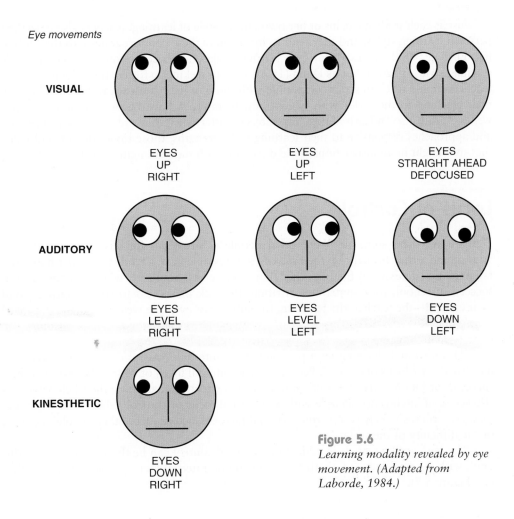

Figure 5.6
Learning modality revealed by eye movement. (Adapted from Laborde, 1984.)

However, this student is getting most of the information through the spoken descriptions. Others may rely mostly on pictures and video clips for their information and will daydream during verbal presentations.

Teaching That Includes the Primary Learning Styles

When teachers use strategies compatible with students' primary learning modalities, achievement is fostered (Dunn, 1988; Ebeling, 2000). Students learn and process information in different modalities. However, because it is not always possible to tell which modality is the strongest for each student in a given situation, teachers must teach in a manner that accommodates all the modalities. Effective teachers combine all three modalities in their lessons to the extent possible by ensuring that appropriate stimuli are present.

BUILDING
BLOCK
5.8

Learning Styles in the Classroom

Review the visual, auditory, and tactile–kinesthetic learning styles you investigated. Select an area of content you plan to teach, and describe an activity you might develop specifically for each modality.

How do these strategies foster heightened relationships between the student and the teacher? How do they help students understand that the material being studied is meaningful and relevant? How do they help students meet their basic and academic needs?

> www A direct link to a website with suggestions for accommodating student needs in each of the learning styles is available on the *Building Teachers* companion website.

Just as each student has his or her own unique style of learning, teachers also have their personal learning styles, and they tend to incorporate these comfort zones into their teaching. Ebeling (2000) writes, "Our own learning style often becomes our most comfortable teaching style" (p. 247). But as Dunn (1990) says, in seeking to foster student achievement, teachers should teach in styles compatible with those of their students, rather than limiting their teaching to the styles with which they, themselves, have become comfortable. She writes, "Students can learn almost any subject matter when they are taught with methods and approaches responsive to their learning style strengths; those same students fail when they are taught in an instructional style dissonant with their strengths" (p. 18).

Locus of Control

Did you ever hear someone blame other people or situations for misfortunes which, in your opinion, they brought on themselves? Some people have a tendency to attribute their failures and successes to factors other than themselves. Similarly, when students do not succeed in school, they sometimes attribute the lack of success to some factor beyond their control—the teacher, the teaching, the subject, or even the weather. **Locus of control** is a human characteristic that pertains to "whether people attribute responsibility for their own failure or success to internal factors or to external factors" (Slavin, 1994, p. 355). Individuals have either a predominantly internal locus of control or a predominantly external locus of control. People with an internal locus of control believe that their successes or failures largely result from their own efforts and abilities: their behavior, persistence, and intelligence. People with an external locus of control believe that their successes or failures largely result from external factors, such as luck, other people's actions, or the difficulty of the situation.

Like many other factors in education, locus of control can be thought of as a continuum, with external locus of control at one end and internal locus of control at the other (see Figure 5.7).

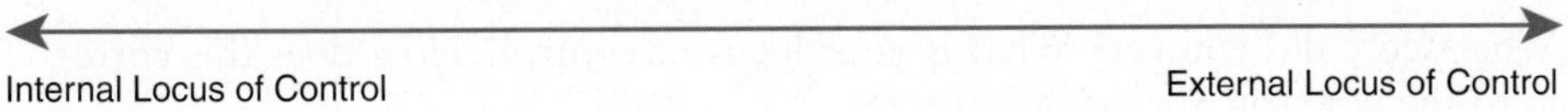

Figure 5.7
Locus of control continuum.

Internal Locus of Control ⟵——————————————⟶ External Locus of Control

The attributes discussed above represent ends of the continuum. Most of the time, an individual is somewhere between the two extremes, and the person perceives both external and internal factors as influencing the situation at hand. Nonetheless, one tends to be the dominant factor.

Your Locus of Control

Pettijohn (1998) has developed the following self-test to help people reveal their personal locus of control. Mark whether each statement is true (*T*) or false (*F*) *for you.* (Remember, there are no right or wrong answers.) This survey will give you a general idea of where you stand on the locus of control continuum.

____ 1. I usually get what I want in life.
____ 2. I need to be informed of news events.
____ 3. I never know where I stand with other people.
____ 4. I do not really believe in luck or chance.
____ 5. I think I could easily win the lottery.
____ 6. If I do not succeed on a task, I tend to give up.
____ 7. I usually convince others to do things my way.
____ 8. People make a difference in controlling crime.
____ 9. The success I have is largely a matter of chance.
____ 10. Marriage is largely a gamble for most people.
____ 11. People must be the master of their own fate.
____ 12. It is not important for me to vote.
____ 13. My life seems like a series of random events.
____ 14. I never try anything that I am not sure of.
____ 15. I earn the respect and honors I receive.
____ 16. A person can get rich by taking risks.
____ 17. Leaders are successful when they work hard.
____ 18. Persistence and hard work usually lead to success.
____ 19. It is difficult to know who my real friends are.
____ 20. Other people usually control my life.

Scoring: Give yourself 5 points each time you answered *T* to numbers 1, 2, 4, 7, 8, 11, 14, 15, 17, and 18.

Interpretation:

0–10	Very strong external locus of control
15–20	External locus of control
25–30	Both external and internal locus of control
35–40	Internal locus of control
45–50	Very strong internal locus of control

(From *Psychology: A ConnecText 4/e* by Terry F. Pettijohn. Copyright © 1999 by the McGraw-Hill Companies, Inc. All rights reserved. Reprinted by permission of McGraw-Hill Contemporary Learning Series.)

What score did you get? What is your locus of control? How does this correspond to the way you approach learning?

Reread statements 1, 2, 4, 7, 8, 11, 14, 15, 17, and 18. Knowing that they represent statements of individuals with a strong internal locus of control, what would you say such individuals believe about who or what is responsible for success? For failure? How might these people work to meet their basic needs? How might people with a strong external locus of control work to meet their basic needs?

How might individuals with a strong internal locus of control work to meet their basic needs?

How might individuals with a strong external locus of control work to meet their basic needs?

How can you help students who blame someone else for their difficulties see how they, themselves, may have contributed to their own difficulties?

How can you help students who credit someone else for their successes see how their own efforts contribute to their successes?

An internal locus of control is a very strong predictor of academic achievement (Brookover et al., 1979). It has been shown that students with an internal locus of control demonstrate significantly higher achievement than students with an external locus of control. This achievement is because students with an internal locus of control believe that their success or failure is a result of their own efforts, so they work hard to achieve success. Students with an external locus of control, however, believe that they have little or no control over their performance or achievement. They attribute whatever success or failure they experience to outside factors, so they fail to see any point in trying. They are likely to think, "What's the use? I can't do anything about it, anyhow!"

Teaching That Fosters Change in Locus of Control

People with a predominantly external locus of control can develop a more internal locus of control, but such change must be fostered deliberately. As a teacher, you can contribute to this change by encouraging students to take ownership of their own learning through becoming aware of the influence they can exert on various situations and the outcomes that occur as a direct result of their actions. To facilitate this, teachers provide activities that involve direct student manipulation and engage students in discussions that help them see their roles. Teachers ask "no-risk" questions where all responses are equally valid, such as "What do you know about …?" No matter how a student responds, that response is correct, for it indicates what the student knows—and that was the question in the first place. When teachers employ such methods, students begin to take ownership of their investigations and internalize that they do have some control over their actions and can influence results.

BUILDING
BLOCK
5.10

Fostering the Internal Locus of Control in the Classroom

Look at the teaching strategies suggested above. Describe some specific strategies you might use to encourage students of the age and grade level you plan to teach to develop the internal locus of control.

How do these strategies foster heightened relationships between the student and the teacher? How do they show students that the material being studied is meaningful and relevant? What basic and academic needs do these strategies address?

Hidden Figures

How field dependent or field independent are you? Look at the illustration below. Sixteen measurement tools are hidden in the picture. Some are used at home and some in science laboratories. Find them all. The faster you can find them all, the more field independent you are. What do you suppose being "field independent" means about learning?

From The National Institute of Standards and Technology

Hidden Tools:

Light bulb
Oscilloscope
Graduated cylinder
Blood pressure cuff
Medical syringe
Protractor
Atoms
Micrometer
Microscope
Measuring spoons
Laser
Electric meter
Thermometer
Scale
Compass
Meter stick

Field independence describes a person's ability to recognize camouflaged information easily. You probably have seen other "hidden figures" puzzles in publications like *Highlights for Children*. There may be, for example, a drawing of a farmyard, trees, and a barn with several common objects—such as a fish, a hat, and a baseball—hidden in the drawing. The field-independent student can spot the objects in the picture quickly, much to the consternation of the field-dependent student (or adult) who sees the barn, barn doors, tree trunks, cows, horses, and flower garden, but little else. The field-independent person has the ability to ignore the surrounding camouflaging field, whereas the field-dependent person is less able to do so.

Another example of field dependence/field independence comes from quiz shows such as "Jeopardy!" Many questions include related but nonessential information. Consider this question:

What president of the United States changed his name, endured drinking problems, and became commander of the Union armies before he was elected the 18th president and served two terms?

How would a field-independent person deal with this question? Would this question be easy or difficult for a field-dependent person? Why?

The field-independent person can separate what is important from what is not important and bore directly to the core of the question. (What is superfluous in the previous question?) Field-dependent people have difficulty extracting essential information from complex situations and tend to rely on external factors to achieve solutions.

A Mathematical Problem

Consider the following mathematical problem:

> The school playground is 10,000 square feet. It contains two slides, five swings, a set of monkey bars, a teeter-totter, a merry-go-round, and a sandbox. It is completely covered with grass that must be mowed every 2 weeks. Playground planners allowed 200 square feet of space for each child. How many children can this playground accommodate?

What is the solution? What information is essential to solve the problem? What information is superfluous?

How would field dependence or field independence affect a student's ability to solve this problem?

Field dependence/field independence has been associated with child-rearing practices and culture. Children whose parents or cultural groups strongly emphasize conformity are more likely to be field dependent than children whose autonomy was encouraged from an early age by their parents and their society (Witkin & Goodenough, 1981). Can you tell why? Can you see the relationship between field dependence/field independence and Erikson's stages of psychosocial development?

Studies have shown that individuals who are field dependent exhibit lower levels of achievement than those who are field independent (Lawson, 1985). Thus, it is desirable to encourage field-dependent students to operate in a more field-independent manner. The methods used to foster a more field-independent manner of thinking primarily involve helping students focus on key patterns and issues. Careful observation helps field-dependent students learn to spot characteristics closely associated with the background, which they might otherwise overlook. For example, field-dependent students may become so engrossed in examining the wholeness of a rock sample that they do not see its texture, layering, or variegations in color.

Studies continue to investigate relationships between field dependence and learning. For example, Hall (2000) investigated field dependence/field independence in computer-based geography instruction, and Dwyer & Moore (2001) investigated the relationship between field dependence/field independence and student achievement of several educational objectives.

Field Dependence and Field Independence in the Classroom

Review the inquiries you made into the nature of field dependence/field independence. Select a content area that you plan to teach. Describe an activity pertaining to that area you think might help students with a predominately field-dependent nature develop greater field independence.

How do these strategies help students focus on key patterns and individual components of larger scenarios? How do they help students meet their basic and academic needs? How do they foster heightened relationships between the student and the teacher? How do they foster student awareness that the material being studied is meaningful and relevant?

A Final Word about Unique Perspectives and Abilities

In Chapter 4 and in this chapter, you investigated ways of teaching students with unique perspectives and abilities. In the teaching strategies you considered throughout this chapter, you sought to accomplish several objectives:

- Motivate students
- Enable students to develop a relationship with the teacher, thereby fostering their relationship with the academic material
- Enable students to reinforce and satisfy their basic and academic needs

You have investigated how the teaching strategies suggested for one group of students are similar to those suggested for other groups. Now it is time to put this all together.

BUILDING BLOCK 5.14

Teaching All Students in the Classroom

Prepare a grid. Across the top, list the characteristics of students you investigated in Chapter 4 and in this chapter. Down the left side, list various teaching strategies you suggested. A few examples of teaching strategies are provided to help you get started. The grid will look something like the example that follows.

Teaching Strategy	Cultural Diversity	English Language Learners	Religion	Socioeconomic status	Gender	Sexual Orientation	Students with Disabilities	Gifted and Talented Students	Multiple Intelligences	Learning Styles	Locus of Control	Field Dependence/Field Independence
Ensure topics relate to students' lives												
Slow down the pace of the class												
Provide hands-on activities												
Use the Internet												
Prepare charts and diagrams												

Constructivism

You have investigated many characteristics and perspectives that students bring to the classroom. You have wrestled with ways of teaching to accommodate each of these exceptionalities. You have seen that numerous strategies apply to all students, regardless of exceptionality, and that certain strategies seem appropriate for given situations. With so many differences in students and so many different ways to teach them, it may seem that the teacher has an impossible and complex job.

In your investigations, you have sought ways to meet students' basic needs and academic needs and ways to help students relate content and material to their own lives, thus making the material meaningful to them and increasing their chances of learning.

This brings us to what we believe is the bottom line in teaching.

David Ausubel wrote, "The single most important factor influencing learning is what the learner already knows" (Ausubel et al., 1978, p. iv). In other words, effective teachers do in their classes exactly what you have been doing in this course: help students relate new material to what they already know.

As we indicated in Chapter 2, Piaget, Dewey, Vygotsky, and numerous others have concluded that knowledge cannot be transmitted from one person to another; people must construct their own understandings and their own knowledge. Learners construct this knowledge as they wrestle with new information and integrate it into their existing knowledge framework. When students are encouraged to relate new information to what they already know, the self is recognized, relevance is established, and learning occurs. This is **constructivism**. Each activity suggested in this textbook, and indeed this textbook itself, is constructivist in orientation.

To see at first hand what constructivist teaching and learning are all about, look at how you have been approaching this course. In all instances, you have brought your own knowledge, thoughts, and prior information to the surface before you looked at what others have said. You then combined your existing understanding with new information to form refined, revised, and sometimes new conceptualizations.

BUILDING
BLOCK
5.15

Constructing Information

Review the work you have done so far in this course. In what ways were you asked to bring your existing knowledge, ideas, and understanding to the surface of your mind? In what ways was new information provided? In what ways were you asked to combine the new information with information you already had to form new and refined conceptualizations?

How is the work you have done so far constructivist in nature?

Constructivist educators, including the authors of this textbook, believe that each learner must construct meaning for himself or herself—that learning can take place only when it is connected to the individual's already existing knowledge, experience, or conceptualizations. What students learn in school is not a copy of what they observe and hear in class; it is the result of their own thinking and processing.

In an address to the Holmes Group in 1987, Judith Lanier, then dean of the College of Education at Michigan State University and president of the Holmes Group, made these remarks:

Competent teachers jump into the heads of their students to see how they are constructing information.... Competent teachers combine content knowledge with a flexible and creative mind, constructing and reconstructing subject matter in multiple ways as they teach the children. They get inside the children's heads. They listen to them. They remain alert to students' interpretations and the ways they are making sense. (Lanier, 1987)

This is the essence of constructivism. Teachers who want to ensure learning teach in this way.

■ BUILDING
■ BLOCK
■ 5.16

My Philosophy of Education Revisited

Part I of this textbook dealt with yourself as a future teacher. Part II has dealt with students.

Revisit the philosophy of education you prepared at the end of Chapter 2. Do you still have the same beliefs? Would you like to make some changes?

Rewrite your philosophy to reflect your thinking at this point in your investigation of American education.

Conclusion

Good teachers are continually aware of the learning that is taking place among their students and are constantly searching for ways to optimize all students' learning in their classrooms. In this chapter, you investigated several factors that influence students' ability to learn.

Human intelligence ranges from low to high, and most students can be taught in the regular classroom regardless of their basic intelligence, although a few adjustments in teaching strategies may be appropriate. According to Howard Gardner, people have several different kinds of intelligences, the relative strengths of which strongly influence how they learn and achieve. People have different learning styles. Some people are internally oriented, but others look to external factors to explain their successes and failures. Some people can see the whole of a situation better than the parts, whereas others see the individual parts better.

Basic needs and fundamental academic needs are the same for everyone, regardless of any differences students may exhibit. Although a few specific teaching techniques apply to specific student needs, the techniques of teaching are essentially the same for everyone if teachers seek to foster relevance. Constructivist teaching meets this principle in that learning experiences are tailored to meet the needs of each individual student.

Effective teachers keep several principles in mind:

■ Students must satisfy their basic needs before they can be motivated or successfully challenged to learn.

■ Teachers must ensure that their teaching is developmentally appropriate to the age and grade level of their students.

■ Teachers must develop professional student–teacher relationships to foster student learning, by ensuring that each student perceives the material as meaningful and relevant.

- Teachers must treat each student as an individual; there are no cookie-cutter approaches in effective teaching.
- Teachers must uncover and deal with their own personal biases about students' perspectives and abilities and provide classroom environments that are equitable.

We trust you will always bear in mind that the best teachers are those who can tailor the instruction to meet the needs of *all* their students—no matter who those students are.

Key Terms and Concepts

Bell-shaped curve, 131
Cognitive ability, 130
Constructivism, 148
Dyslexia, 128
Exceptional students, 124
Field dependence/field
   independence, 145
Full inclusion, 126

Gifted and talented
   student, 132
Inclusion, 125
Learning disability, 128
Learning style, 123
Learning modality, 140
Locus of control, 142

Mainstreaming, 125
Multiple intelligence
   theory, 136
Normal curve, 131
Normal distribution, 131
Resource classroom, 126
Special education, 124

Construct and Apply

1. Referring to your investigations of humanism in Chapter 2 and Chapter 3, would Rogers and Maslow approve of your suggested strategies for meeting the needs of students with unique perspectives and abilities? Why or why not?
2. How might your own learning preferences affect your teaching style?
3. What common teaching strategies have you identified that would help *all* students achieve in your classroom?
4. Consider this scene: A student in a traditional classroom approaches his teacher. He says, "The gifted students are going on a field trip to the zoo. The special education kids are having a party where they get to dress up like jungle animals. I get to come in here and take notes." What is the implication? To what degree are the methods used for gifted and special education students appropriate in the traditional classroom?

Deconstructing the Standards

INTASC Principle #3 says:

The teacher understands how students differ in their approaches to learning and creates instructional opportunities that are adapted to diverse learners.

- What part(s) of this principle does this chapter address?
- How does this chapter address this principle?
- How will the concepts in this chapter help you apply this principle as a teacher?

Field Experience

1. How does your cooperating teacher facilitate the achievement of students with many different cognitive abilities and learning styles in his or her classroom?
2. How does your field experience cooperating teacher teach to acknowledge:
   - Specific learning disabilities
   - Students who are gifted and talented
   - Multiple intelligences
   - Visual, auditory, and kinesthetic learning modalities
   - Internal and external locus of control
   - Field dependence and field independence
3. Investigate the different levels of accommodations for students with special cognitive and physical needs in your field experience school.

■ Your Portfolio

Use your work in the activities suggested in this chapter to show your developing awareness of best practices in teaching.

Summarize one or more instances from your field experience where you or your cooperating teacher used certain teaching techniques to accommodate the needs of students with unique abilities.

Volunteer to tutor a student with special needs and reflect on your experiences.

■ Technology Resources

 Check out the *Building Teachers* companion website—http://www.education.wadsworth.com/martinloomis1—for more information and resources about students with special needs and abilities, including access to the following websites:

- Dyslexia Self-Tests
- IQ Self-Tests
- Jacob K. Javits Program for Gifted and Talented Students
- Thinkquest, Inc., includes strategies for teaching students according to their learning style
- A Locus of Control questionnaire

 See video footage of real teachers addressing special needs and abilities in the classroom. Check the *Building Teachers* CD-ROM that accompanies your textbook for additional resources.

 Also link to InfoTrac College Edition through the *Building Teachers* companion website. Use InfoTrac College Edition to search for articles to enhance your study.

PART III

School

In Part I, you investigated your *self*, your experiences with teaching and learning, and your thoughts about excellence in teaching and learning. Your ideas and beliefs informed your initial philosophy of education. You saw that there are several different ways of looking at education, depending on the expected outcomes. Part II helped you to see that all students have common personal, cognitive, and social needs, and that teachers must consider the unique characteristics and perspectives each student brings to the classroom to identify effective teaching strategies that facilitate equality and achievement.

In Part III, you will broaden your sphere of inquiry to include the schools themselves. You will investigate the purposes of schools, how schools are structured to fulfill their purposes, how students work within these structures to fulfill their needs, and how teachers work within these structures to meet the needs of the students they serve.

Purposes of Schools

The ability to think straight, some knowledge of the past, some vision of the future, some skill to do useful service, some urge to fit that service into the well-being of the community—these are the most vital things education must try to produce.

VIRGINIA GILDERSLEEVE, DEAN EMERITA, BARNARD COLLEGE

Chapter 6 invites you to explore the purposes of different kinds of schools. Schools can have many different purposes, depending on several factors. You will identify factors that influence schools' purposes, and you will examine how these factors influence the stated purpose of the place we call "school." What do you suppose are the primary purposes of schools envisioned by Gildersleeve in the quotation that begins this chapter?

On the surface, it might seem that schools all have the same underlying purposes—that they all have the same basic goals. But do they? Just as students have common academic needs, schools have common purposes. However, as each student brings unique characteristics and perspectives to the classroom, each school also has unique characteristics and perspectives. In this chapter, you will explore these factors and the ways in which they determine the basic purposes of schools.

CHAPTER GOALS

As a result of your work in this chapter, you will:

1. Identify factors that influence schools' purposes.

2. Explore common and unique purposes of several kinds of schools.

3. Construct conceptualizations about advantages and disadvantages of special kinds of schools.

4. Describe the purpose of what you consider to be an ideal school.

Questions about the Purposes of Schools

Consider the age group of students you wish to teach. What are the primary purposes of sending these children to school? Bear in mind that there are many ways to think about this issue. Try not to rely too heavily on personal experiences and thoughts; kinds of schools exist in addition to the kinds you attended, and there are many personal experiences other than the ones you have had.

From your list of primary purposes, write a statement of what you believe are the major purposes of schools.

Compare your responses with those of other students in your class. What are the commonalities? What are the differences?

Common Purposes of Schools

Schools serve communities, and the purpose of a school reflects the community it serves. The community is made of businesses, industries, services, government, residents, families, and friends, in addition to the faculty, administration, and students in the school. In deciding on the purpose of its schools, a group comprising representatives from all parts of the community, including educators, debate several important questions, ultimately resolving these issues into a singularity of purpose.

Purposes of Schools as Seen by Government Agencies and Noteworthy Individuals

Many government agencies, blue-ribbon panels, and educators have described what they believe are the fundamental purposes of schools.

Purposes of Schools as Seen by the Federal Government

The federal government has officially been in the education business since 1953, when President Dwight D. Eisenhower established the Department of Health, Education and Welfare and named Ovela Culp Hobby its first secretary. In 1979, President Jimmy Carter formed the first cabinet-level Department of Education and appointed Shirley Mount Hufstedler its secretary.

One noteworthy attempt to identify the purposes of schools is GOALS 2000. In 1989, President George H. W. Bush and the nation's governors met, for the first time in the history of the United States, to discuss national educational policy. Their discussion was summarized in the now-famous GOALS 2000, which comprised six national goals for public education. Two additional goals—one dealing with teacher education and professional development and the other with parental participation—were added to the original six goals, resulting in an expanded Goals 2000: Educate America Act that was passed into law in 1994.

As listed in the act, the goals are as follows:

1. *School readiness.* By the year 2000, all children in America will start school ready to learn.
2. *School completion.* By the year 2000, the high school graduation rate will increase to at least 90%.

3. *Student achievement and citizenship.* By the year 2000, all students will leave grades 4, 8, and 12 having demonstrated competency over challenging subject matter, including English, mathematics, science, foreign languages, civics and government, economics, arts, history, and geography, and every school in America will ensure that all students learn to use their minds well, so they may be prepared for responsible citizenship, further learning, and productive employment in our nation's modern economy.

4. *Teacher education and professional development.* By the year 2000, the nation's teaching force will have access to programs for the continued improvement of their professional skills and the opportunity to acquire the knowledge and skills needed to instruct and prepare all American students for the next century.

5. *Mathematics and science.* By the year 2000, U.S. students will be first in the world in mathematics and science achievement.

6. *Adult literacy and lifelong learning.* By the year 2000, every adult American will be literate and will possess the knowledge and skills necessary to compete in a global economy and exercise the rights and responsibilities of citizenship.

7. *Safe, disciplined, and alcohol- and drug-free schools.* By the year 2000, every school in the United States will be free of drugs, violence, and the unauthorized presence of firearms and alcohol and will offer a disciplined environment conducive to learning.

8. *Parental participation.* By the year 2000, every school will promote partnerships that will increase parental involvement and participation in promoting social, emotional, and academic growth of children.

From these statements, what do you suppose were the federal government's ideas about the purposes of school?

One principle of the No Child Left Behind Act of 2001 is increased accountability for states, school districts, and schools for students' achievement (see Chapter 1). This provision calls for challenging state standards and annual testing for all students in grades 3–8 in reading and mathematics, and will include testing in science in 2007 (U.S. Department of Education, 2002a). Standardized achievement tests that have been implemented in response to the accountability provision of No Child Left Behind, and the pressure for students to perform well on these tests is tremendous. Indeed, the consequences of children's failure to perform on these tests are so serious that many teachers and schools do not want to stray too far from emphasizing the basic skills the tests assess. As a result, most elementary schools have the common goal of emphasizing the so-called three Rs: reading, writing, and arithmetic.

Concerns exist about this emphasis:

1. Other subjects, such as science, social studies, art, music, and physical education, take a secondary position or are left out completely because of the time devoted to the three Rs.

2. There is little consideration for adapting teaching to individual needs; the pressure for success on standardized achievement tests appears greater than the need to accommodate children's individual needs.

3. There is little consideration for the development of social skills.

---

www A direct link to the full text of Goals 2000, progress reports, and supplemental material is available on the *Building Teachers* companion website.

Which of the school purposes outlined in Goals 2000 are the same as the school purposes you identified in Building Block 6.1?

BUILDING BLOCK 6.2

No Child Left Behind

Although No Child Left Behind primarily addresses the accountability of schools in achieving their purposes, you can still infer what those purposes are from the act's principles. Based on the No Child Left Behind legislation, what are the primary goals of schools, as envisioned by the federal government?

With what provisions of the act do you agree? What provisions cause you to pause and ask questions? What seems to be the educational philosophy underlying this act?

The purpose of schools, according to the federal government, includes teaching students the 3 Rs—reading, writing, and arithmetic, as demonstrated in legislation like the No Child Left Behind Act and Goals 2000.

© Bob Daemmrich/PhotoEdit

Many people see the No Child Left Behind Act as challenging schools' independence, stifling teachers' creativity and teaching abilities, and placing tremendous pressure on schools and teachers to demonstrate increasing standardized achievement test scores. Thus the term *high-stakes testing* has risen to prominence in educational discussions. This issue is multifaceted, and you will have the opportunity to examine it more completely in Chapter 11.

www Direct links to the No Child Left Behind Act home page and a website that has the full text of the act, progress reports, and supplemental material are available on the *Building Teachers* companion website.

Purposes of Schools as Seen by Prominent Individuals

Many prominent individuals have sought to articulate their beliefs about the general goals of schools. Here are a few:

Linda Darling-Hammond (1994), a prominent educational researcher and spokesperson for educational reform sees two fundamental purposes of schools: talent development in the context of developing the whole person, and empowering people to pursue their views of the good for themselves and for society.

John Goodlad (1984) listed four goals he considered basic to American education: academic goals; vocational goals; social, civic, and cultural goals; and goals for personal well-being.

Theodore Sizer said, "A school is prizeworthy if inside every single head—adult and child, producer and consumer—there is a clear reference to principles in every decision and a determination to do the best thing" (cited in Smith, 2002).

Lew Smith (2002), a former high school and middle school principal, believes that schools must rethink their purposes and missions in the aftermath of the September 11, 2001, attacks on the World Trade Center and the Pentagon. Basic purposes schools must consider include involving students in their own education, citizenry, and accountability, and ways of conveying the message, "We care about you and we care about each other" (p. 6).

Even Garrison Keillor of *Lake Wobegon* fame has written about the purpose of schools: "The purpose of schools is to help each child achieve his full potential, whether that potential is to become a physicist, a conductor of a symphony orchestra, an opera star, a novelist, or to be able to dress and feed himself" (Keillor, 1996, p. 1).

Famous Quotations

Following are some quotations about the purposes of schools written by individuals with great interest in education:

- The function of education is to help you from childhood not to imitate anybody, but be yourself all the time (J. Krishnamurti, spiritual philosopher).

- We are born weak, we need strength; helpless, we need aid; foolish, we need reason. All that we lack at birth, all that we need when we come to man's estate, is the gift of education (Jean-Jacques Rousseau, French philosopher and author).

- A good education is not so much one which prepares a man to succeed in the world, as one which enables him to sustain a failure (Bernard Iddings Bell, chaplain, University of Chicago).

- The object of education is to prepare the young to educate themselves throughout their lives (Robert Maynard Hutchins, president, University of Chicago).

- Education is the ability to listen to almost anything without losing your temper or your self-confidence (Robert Frost, American poet).

- Education's purpose is to replace an empty mind with an open one (Malcolm Forbes, American publisher).

- There are two types of education.... One should teach us how to make a living, and the other how to live (John Adams, second president of the United States).

- Education is not the filling of a pail, but the lighting of a fire (William Butler Yeats, Irish poet).

- The illiterate of the 21st century will not be those who cannot read and write, but those who cannot learn, unlearn, and relearn (Alvin Toffler, futurist).

- Education is the transmission of civilization (Ariel and Will Durant, authors, philosophers, and historians, winners of the Pulitzer Prize and the Medal of Freedom).

- The aim of education is the knowledge not of fact, but of values (William R. Inge, dean, St. Paul's Cathedral).

- Education is a process of living and not a preparation for future living (John Dewey, American philosopher, psychologist, and educational reformer).

- Establishing lasting peace is the work of education; all politics can do is keep us out of war (Maria Montessori, educator).

- Education is for improving the lives of others and for leaving your community and world better than you found it (Marian Wright Edelman, founder and president of the Children's Defense Fund).

- Education either functions as an instrument which is used to facilitate integration of the younger generation into the logic of the present system and bring about conformity or it becomes the practice of freedom, the means by which men and women deal critically and creatively with reality and discover how to participate in the transformation of their world (Paulo Freire, Brazilian educator).

- The first duty of a lecturer: to hand you after an hour's discourse a nugget of pure truth to wrap up between the pages of your notebooks, and keep on the mantelpiece forever (Virginia Woolf, English novelist).

If you were asked to write your own statement about the purpose of schools, what would it be?

BUILDING BLOCK 6.3

The Purposes of Schools

You have seen many different thoughts about the purposes of schools from the federal government and from a number of prominent individuals. Look at the purposes you identified in Building Block 6.1 and make any changes you think are appropriate. Write a revised school purpose statement.

Purpose of Schools as Seen in Mission Statements

Mission statements can inform us about the purposes that individual schools see for themselves.

A school's mission statement is a short document that describes the school's purpose, focusing on what the school wants to be, what it wants to do, and what its values and principles are. It reflects the shared **vision** and values of the learning community, including the faculty and administration. It becomes the criterion by which everything that happens in the school is measured. A mission statement is a living document that the learning community continually reviews, refines, and keeps up to date, to reflect current thinking about the school.

Anyone reading a school's mission statement can learn the school's primary goals, how these goals are implemented, and what the school expects its students and graduates to know and be able to do. Although there may be some discrepancy between a school's mission statement and its actual practice, the mission statement specifies why the school exists and establishes the scope of its activities (Dottin, 2001). It provides a description of the present and a direction for the future.

In Chapter 2, you read the mission statements of several schools to infer the philosophies that guided those schools' operations. Now you will look more carefully at several school mission statements to infer the fundamental purposes of those schools.

School Mission Statements

Find the mission statements of two or three public and private elementary, middle, and secondary schools in your area. Use the Internet to search for the name of the school you have in mind, and then look for its mission statement. Sometimes this document is called a *mission* or a *mission statement*; sometimes it is called a statement of *vision*, a *philosophy*, *values*, or a similar term. You may wish to examine the mission statement of a school you attended so you can compare that mission statement with your actual experiences at that school. (Of course, the time difference may be a factor if the mission statement was written since you attended the school—but the school's essential mission probably has not changed significantly.)

In the mission statement, look for these factors:

1. The school's predominant educational philosophy or approach.
2. What the school expects of its students as a result of attendance.
3. How the school provides for students' basic and academic needs.
4. Any special population mentioned.
5. Any particular curriculum mentioned.
6. Any particular instructional methods mentioned.
7. Attention given to the needs of the community the school serves.

From your investigations, determine the school's primary purpose. If you found the mission statement of a school you attended, how does that statement compare with your experience at that school?

How do the purposes of the schools you investigated compare with the purposes you cited in your revised school purpose statement?

The purpose of a school is the reason it exists. Schools have many purposes, which may range from developing students so they will fit in with existing society to providing students with the skills needed to change **society**, from mastering basic skills and concepts to keeping up with the times, from preparing to enter the work force to preparing to affect culture and society.

Some purposes seem to be common to all schools, even though individual schools may go about accomplishing these goals in different ways. Your explorations thus far have enabled you to identify some common goals or purposes of schools and schooling. Did you find that some of your ideas were different from those of your classmates and those cited in the preceding literature and the quotations? What influences your ideas? How strongly do your personal experiences and philosophy of education influence your ideas about the purposes of school? You bring your own unique perspectives to your ideas.

Courtesy of Bev Abrams

It was December 1993 and Santa Barbara Charter School had opened 3 months earlier. I was the sixth person hired to teach a first–third grade class in this open structured, constructivist public school. Teachers left as quickly as they were hired, and over fifty percent of the original families had abandoned the school. Some of the parents wanted a progressive, alternative program; others wanted a Waldorf education; others expected an accelerated academic program; and still others wanted a traditional, workbook-based school program. All had invested tremendous energy into getting the doors open for the start of school, but there was no coherent educational vision or definition of staff and parent roles.

Within days of my hire, the small staff sat down to draw up a document that defined the role of teachers in our school; within months, we also wrote a mission statement. Both statements were readily adopted by the school community because all parties were having trouble living in the programmatic vacuum that existed. The school's founding teacher provided our initial inspiration with her passion for teaching academics through the arts. The other two teachers lent our deep commitment to progressive education and love of wordsmithing to the process. Once we articulated the school's mission, conflict dissipated. By the third year, families were choosing our school with some understanding of what we offered. We found it easier to focus our limited resources on the things that mattered.

The mission statement reveals Santa Barbara Charter School's core values. The school was begun as a parent–teacher cooperative, hence the statement that the school would build the interests and skills of both students and their families. As progressive educators, we believe that good education is an ongoing process, rather than a moment in time during which students demonstrate their mastery of a collection of facts, so we stated that we would "nurture lifelong learners." Finally, we consciously chose to list "arts, academics, and relationships" in that order because we wanted "arts" and "relationships" to stand out. All schools strive to teach academic skills, but our emphasis on arts and relationships makes us unique. In light of the standardization of American education during the past 13 years, our articulated commitment to arts, academics, and relationships has kept us from being swept along with the radical narrowing of public school curriculum.

Our mission statement provides coherence, both in individual classrooms and to the school as a whole. Decision making about the use of classroom time, hiring of specialists, and purchase of supplies often refers to our mission. Though some arts opportunities vary year to year, all elementary students participate in a fiber arts program and all students are part of an annual class play. Visual arts and music are part of the weekly curriculum, and dance and recorder are taught in some grades. Arts are taught both for their own sake and to develop other

Factors Influencing Schools' Purposes

Let us now explore the effects specific influences and unique perspectives have on schools' purposes.

BUILDING
BLOCK
6.5

Unique Perspectives and Purposes of Schools

What influences the purposes of schools? Take a moment to brainstorm, listing as many factors as you can think of that might influence a school's stated purpose. Write these down to compare to those considered in this chapter.

Influence of Grade Level on School Purposes

One factor that influences the purposes a school sees for itself is its grade-level span. When we think of grade levels, we often think in terms of elementary, middle, junior high, and secondary schools. Elementary schools normally encompass the lower grades, typi-

academic understandings. At times, an art activity is done by the entire class; at other times just a few students are engaged. Art experiences are initiated in the classroom by teachers, students, and parents.

Time is devoted to cultivating relationships and building community. Communication and conflict resolution skills are facilitated based on schoolwide policy and curriculum. Class meetings are held in the lower school program, and students meet in councils in the middle school program. The first thing that visitors notice about our school is that "both children and adults are very kind." Many families have found that family dynamics shift as they use the communication strategies that children and parents learn at Santa Barbara Charter School. The school recently received a grant based on the work that we do in this area.

We have had several opportunities to revisit our mission. The first time was in 1997, as we planned our expansion to middle school. At this time, the expansion committee insisted on writing a mission statement for the new middle school program. All of the stakeholders were involved, and a committee member who was a professional writer drafted the final statement. This statement faded into oblivion because it was too long to remember or use when making daily decisions or promoting the school. Additionally, we found that having a separate mission statement distracted from creating a cohesive kindergarten-through-eighth-grade program. Subsequently, we looked at the match between the mission and implementation during our authentic assessment process in 2003. At that time, we ex-amined each area of the mission and evaluated how well the school was implementing its mission based on a parent survey, observation by an outside evaluator, teachers' plan books, and student feedback. Happily, we found that there was a high degree of consistency between the mission and the education our students were receiving. Most recently, a financial crisis forced us to look once again at our program in light of both finances and our mission during a process of long-term strategic planning (LTSP). Ultimately, the rec-ommendations of the LTSP committee reflected a commit-ment to the values stated in the mission, and these were taken into consideration planning the budget.

Our mission statement has served as the organizing principle at Santa Barbara Charter School. Other docu-ments, such as our education plan, further articulate our vi-sion. Although our mission doesn't really convey the inten-sity with which we work to keep children at the center of all decisions, it does help us plan the program and provision the school to best meet their needs and enrich their lives.

Santa Barbara Charter School Mission Statement Santa Barbara Charter School nurtures lifelong learners by cultivating the interest and building the skills of both students and their families in the arts, academics, and re-lationships.

Santa Barbara Charter School
Santa Barbara, California

cally preschool through fifth or sixth grade. Junior high schools usually include grades 7 and 8. Middle schools normally include grades 6, 7, and 8, and secondary schools ordinarily include grades 9 through 12. Figure 6.1 depicts the general structure of education in the United States.

How do the purposes of schools reflect the grade levels they include?

Purposes and Goals of Elementary Schools

BUILDING
BLOCK
6.6

Recall some of the activities in which you participated while in elementary school. What were the purposes of these activities? (You may wish to refer to Building Block 6.1.)

- What do you think was the basic purpose of your elementary school?
- What do you think are the basic purposes of a typical elementary school?
- How does the elementary school meet the needs of the students who attend it?
- What does the typical elementary school expect of its students as a result of attending school?

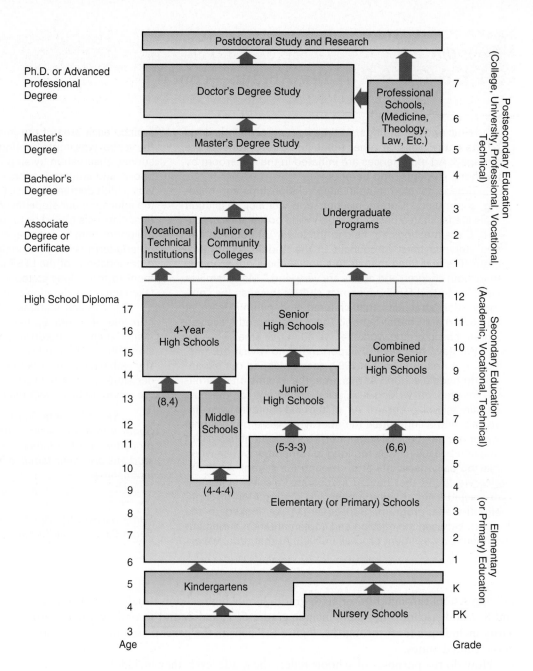

Figure 6.1
General structure of education in the United States. (Source: National Center for Education Statistics, 2001.)

Elementary Schools

Historically, elementary schools were established to teach children the three Rs: reading, writing, and arithmetic. Children needed to know how to read so that they could read the Bible. They needed to be able to write and do basic mathematics so that they could carry out their future livelihoods of farming or managing a small business.

As the American colonies expanded, towns, cities, businesses, and transportation all grew. The need for educated citizens also grew, and the country needed more and better educated individuals to promote social progress. Therefore, secondary schools and colleges were established to provide education at higher levels. Accordingly, it became the primary purpose of most elementary schools to prepare children for success in these higher grades, teaching them how to think and readying them for a useful and productive life of citizenship in the society in which they would live. (See Chapter 10.)

These purposes of typical elementary schools seem to be the same today: namely, to prepare children for success in higher grades, teach them how to think, and equip them for a useful and productive life of citizenship in the society in which they will live. Among the skills children master in the elementary school are reading, writing, and mathematics. These skills are considered paramount today, and children's success in these areas has become the number-one priority in elementary schools. As you have seen, the No Child Left Behind legislation of 2001 requires that all public school students achieve grade-appropriate proficiency in reading and mathematics.

How does the above description of the primary goals of elementary schools compare with your thoughts in Building Block 6.6? What do you think is the purpose of elementary schools?

BUILDING BLOCK 6.7

Purposes and Goals of Middle Schools

Think of some of the activities in which you participated while in middle or junior high school. What were the purposes of those activities?

- How were these activities different from those of elementary school?
- What do you think are the basic purposes of a typical middle school or junior high school?
- How does the middle school or junior high school meet the needs of the students who attend it?
- What does the typical middle school or junior high school expect of its students as a result of attending school?

Middle Schools

In Building Block 6.7, we do not differentiate between middle schools and junior high schools. However, the two are fundamentally different and have fundamentally different purposes. Junior high schools first appeared in the early 1900s in response to overcrowding in high schools. At that time, elementary schools consisted of grades 1 through 6, and secondary schools consisted of grades 7 through 12. The first junior high schools took over grades 7 and 8 and functioned essentially as high schools did, but with a younger population of students. The main purpose of junior high school was to bridge the gap between elementary school and high school.

The middle school, on the other hand, recognizes that the early adolescent learner has unique needs unlike those found in either elementary school or high school. The middle school was developed to align the educational environment with these unique needs.

Effective middle schools provide adolescent students with rich learning environments customized according to students' unique physical, emotional, social, and cognitive needs.

© Tom Stewart/CORBIS

The 1989 Carnegie report *Turning Points: Preparing American Youth for the 21st Century* (Carnegie Council on Adolescent Development, 1989) identified the unique characteristics of young adolescents and described this population as one struggling with tremendous opportunities for social, intellectual, and psychological development, and also with vulnerability and uncertainty. The report concluded that existing junior high schools did not meet the needs of young adolescents and that radical reform was needed, suggesting a purpose and direction for this reform:

> *The middle grade school proposed here is profoundly different from many schools today. It focuses squarely on the characteristics and needs of young adolescents. It creates a community of adults and young people embedded in networks of support and responsibility that enhance the commitment of students of learning. (Carnegie Council on Adolescent Development, 1989, p. 36)*

The middle school became the preferred school concept for the education of young adolescents, almost completely replacing the junior high school. In a position statement, the National Middle School Association (2001) expanded the original concept of focusing on student needs by suggesting a set of specific educational objectives to guide the development of middle schools' purposes and missions. The position statement recommends that the middle school provide learning experiences for adolescents that achieve the following goals:

- Address adolescents' varied intellectual, physical, social, emotional, and moral development.
- Help them make sense of themselves and the world around them.
- Be highly integrated and connected to life.
- Include adolescents' questions, needs, developmental issues, and ideas.
- Involve them in rich and significant knowledge about the world.
- Open doors to new ideas that evoke curiosity, the desire to explore, and at times, awe and wonder.
- Challenge students and encourage them to take maximum advantage of educational opportunities.
- Develop caring, responsible, and ethical citizens who practice democratic principles.

As you can see, much of what is advocated as the purpose of the middle school recognizes the unique needs and characteristics that accompany being an adolescent.

BUILDING BLOCK 6.8

Adolescent Needs

Think about students in grades 6, 7, and 8.

- What are their ages?
- Name some characteristics that you associate with these young adolescents.
- What activities—desirable and undesirable—interest young adolescents?
- How do you think these characteristics and interests could affect academic needs?
- Recall Piaget's cognitive and Erikson's psychosocial developmental stages. What are some unique characteristics and needs of adolescents?
- What implications do these adolescent developmental stages have for teaching and learning?
- What do you suppose would be the primary purpose of a school designed with young adolescents in mind?

Purposes and Goals of Secondary Schools

Recall some of the activities in which you participated while in high school. What were the purposes of those activities?

- How were these activities different from those in junior high school or middle school?
- What do you think are the basic purposes of a typical secondary school?
- How does the secondary school meet the needs of the students who attend it?
- What does the typical secondary school expect of its students as a result of having attended school?

Secondary Schools

High schools as we know them—free, public, and open to all—have been around since the 1800s. Recall what you know about American society at that time. What happened to industry and the economy in the 19th century? What would people need to know and do to live and thrive during that time? How might this affect the purpose of education beyond elementary school?

After the Civil War, a demand arose for workers who possessed the knowledge and skills needed to work in a society marked by industrial growth. There was also an influx of immigrants who needed education in the ideals of the United States, their new country, in addition to the knowledge and skills needed for the marketplace. High schools responded to these needs with practical curricula whose purpose was to educate the masses (Webb, Metha, & Jordan, 2000).

Today's high schools serve a more comprehensive purpose, addressing a variety of educational goals and representing all aspects of society. As a nation, we regularly examine the purpose of our secondary schools and often engage in debates about whether these schools should prepare students for college or careers. The secondary school is the last level of schooling for students who do not continue to college or who do not complete some other postsecondary education, such as a trade school. As such, most secondary schools have two purposes: one for students who will go to college, and one for those who will not go to college. Most high schools have curricula that include a college preparatory program, a basic education program for those choosing not to continue their education past high school, a vocational or industrial education program, and programs that prepare support personnel for business (Webb et al., 2000).

How does the above description of high schools compare with your thoughts in Building Block 6.9? What do you think is the purpose of high schools?

Influence of School Location on Its Purpose

Another factor that influences a school's purposes is school location. The location of a school has a great influence on its purpose, as envisioned by its community, faculty, and administration. For example, consider the school system in Oak Ridge, Tennessee. Oak Ridge is the home of the Oak Ridge National Laboratories, established in 1943 as a site of the Manhattan Project and charged with producing the fuel for the first atomic bomb. As you might imagine, many of the students in the local schools have at least one parent with an advanced degree in science. How do you think this context affects the purposes the Oak Ridge schools see for themselves?

The National Center for Education Statistics (2002a) has identified eight general locations of public schools:

- *Large city:* A city with a population of 250,000 or more.
- *Midsize city:* A city with a population of less than 250,000.
- *Urban fringe large city:* A **suburban** area near a large city.
- *Urban fringe midsize city:* A suburban area near a midsize city.
- *Large town:* A town with a population of 25,000 or more that is not included in a metropolitan area.
- *Small town:* A town with a population between 2,500 and 24,999.
- *Rural:* An area designated as "rural" by the U.S. Bureau of the Census and that is not included in a metropolitan area.
- *Rural urban fringe:* A rural area within a metropolitan area.

In 2002–2003, there were 92,330 public schools in the United States (National Center for Education Statistics, 2005a). The schools were distributed by location as shown in Figure 6.2.

BUILDING BLOCK 6.10

Location of Your High School

Think about the community in which you attended high school. Answer the following questions about your high school experience:

- What was your school's location category?
- What were your goals as a student?
- What were your parents' goals for you?

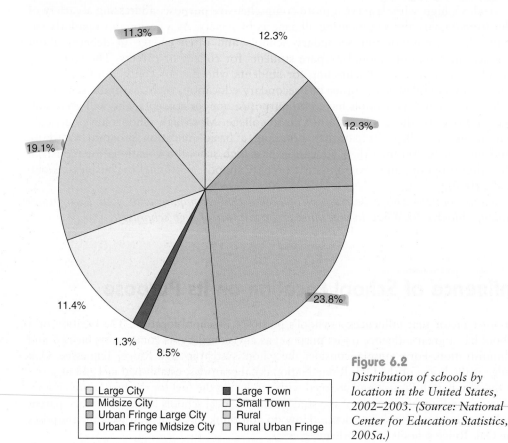

Figure 6.2

Distribution of schools by location in the United States, 2002–2003. (Source: National Center for Education Statistics, 2005a.)

☐ Large City	■ Large Town
■ Midsize City	☐ Small Town
▨ Urban Fringe Large City	☐ Rural
☐ Urban Fringe Midsize City	☐ Rural Urban Fringe

- What were the goals of most students' parents?
- What were the community's expectations for its high school students and graduates?
- Did most graduates of your high school go to college? Or did they stay in the local area to begin jobs and careers?
- Was there a vocational track at your high school?
- How extensive were the school's elective courses?
- Were college preparation courses or programs available?
- To what degree were the community's expectations represented in the school curriculum?

As you have seen, a school's mission or purpose reflects the desires and needs of the community it serves. Consider a school in an urban fringe or midsize city. What population would this school serve? What needs would the population have? The federal report, *Urban Schools: The Challenge of Location and Poverty* (National Center for Education Statistics, 1996), showed that urban schools tend to have larger enrollments and a higher concentration of students from low-income families than rural schools. Many of these students have difficulty speaking English and are thought to have less supportive home environments and less positive school experiences than students from other schools. However, urban schools' larger enrollments and greater student diversity enable these schools to offer a wide variety of programs and specialties, helping to offset student disadvantages. What do you suppose are the primary purposes of schools in urban communities?

Enrollments are smaller in rural schools than in urban schools (Stern, 1994). Many rural areas are experiencing population loss, and schools in such areas find it difficult to provide students with the opportunities for higher-education preparation that are available in urban schools. What value do you think rural schools place on preparation for higher education? DeYoung (1995) notes that although statistics may portray rural areas as disadvantaged, rural populations tend to place a higher value on keeping family members nearby than on their leaving the area for high-paying jobs or careers. Indeed, Seal and Harmon (1995) noted that in rural areas, the school may become a focal point for the town, suggesting that the community may value extracurricular activities more than academic achievement. From this, what can we conclude about the comparisons of basic purposes of urban and rural schools?

School location can influence the school's purpose. In small rural areas, the schools often serve fewer students. What might the purpose of this rural school be? In larger urban area schools, more students are served and the purpose may be dictated by the community. Would this urban school provide more academic opportunities than its rural counterpart? Why?

Nontraditional Schools

A third factor that influences a school's purposes lies in the school's basic function. In addition to the traditional elementary, middle, and secondary school configurations, many specialized schools have become prominent. These specialized schools are particularly attractive to people who have specific goals or needs. Examples include the following:

- Charter schools
- Magnet schools
- For-profit schools
- Home schools
- Alternative schools
- Vocational schools
- Private schools

Charter Schools

Charter schools are public schools that operate with freedom from one or more of the regulations that apply to traditional public schools. Charter schools enjoy a degree of autonomy not available to other schools; in return, they are accountable for producing positive academic results. Charters, granted by state educational agencies, typically last for 3 to 5 years and are renewable. These are the primary goals of charter schools:

- To realize a specific educational vision, such as focusing on a particular subject or focusing on interdisciplinary curricula without regard to subject-matter boundaries.
- To gain autonomy so faculty and administrators can provide educational services they believe best serve the needs of their school's specific population.
- To serve a special population in curriculum, methodological approaches, or both.

In the 2002–2003 academic year, there were 2,757 charter schools in the United States, equivalent to 3.0% of the total number of public schools (National Center for Education Statistics, 2005a). States with provisions for charter schools are shown in Figure 6.3.

What are the provisions for charter schools in your state? (Go to the website of your state Department of Education or your local school system.) If your state does not yet recognize the charter school concept, what steps are being taken in this direction?

What are the advantages of charter schools? What are their disadvantages? Would you want to teach in a charter school? Why?

Magnet Schools

Magnet schools focus on specific curricular areas to attract students with special aptitudes and interests that the school can foster (hence the term *magnet* school). Magnet schools represent "options so that parents . . . or students themselves will have the opportunity to choose the programs best suited to them" (Waldrip, 2000, p. 5). The primary purpose of magnet schools is to provide students with the opportunity to acquire the knowledge and skills that will enable them to realize their full potential. In magnet schools, students explore their special talents and interests while concentrating on strong academics. In the 2002–2003 school year, there were 1,719 magnet schools in the United States, equivalent to 1.9% of the total number of public schools, serving 2.9% of the total public school population (National Center for Education Statistics, 2005a).

Magnet schools exist at elementary, intermediate, and secondary levels. Although they offer a complete curriculum, each magnet school has a particular theme, focus, or emphasis that is integrated throughout the curriculum. Themes may include science,

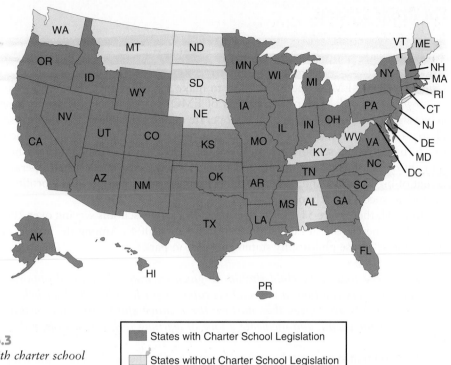

Figure 6.3
States with charter school legislation.

States with Charter School Legislation

States without Charter School Legislation

mathematics, technology, music, visual arts, performing arts, computers, or any of a number of other areas of concentration. For example, in 2005 the magnet school system in Hillsborough County, Florida (which includes Tampa) was structured as follows (School District of Hillsborough County, Florida, 2005):

Elementary magnet schools
 Computers and technology
 Environmental studies
 Foreign languages and global studies
 International Baccalaureate* and
  international studies
 Math, science, and technology
 Visual, performing, and communi-
  cation arts
 World studies
Middle magnet schools
 Engineering
 Environmental studies
 Health professions
 International Baccalaureate* and
  international studies
 Language exploration and global
  studies
 Law studies and public service

Middle magnet schools—cont'd
 Math, science, and technology
 Visual, performing, and communi-
  cation arts
Magnet high schools
 Accelerated curriculum
 Architecture and environmental
  design
 Culinary arts
 Engineering
 Health professions
 International Baccalaureate*
 International studies
 Mathematics, science, and
  technology
 Technology
 Visual, performing, and communi-
  cation arts

*The International Baccalaureate Program is a program headquartered in Geneva, Switzerland, that assists schools worldwide in developing and implementing challenging international education curricula to facilitate their graduates' admission to colleges and universities. Students who complete this program are awarded the International Baccalaureate diploma. Many of the courses they take carry college credit.

www A direct link to the International Baccalaureate Organization website is available on the *Building Teachers* companion website.

What are the advantages of magnet schools? What are their disadvantages? Would you want to teach in a magnet school?

For-Profit Schools

For-profit schools are schools operated by education management organizations (EMOs), which assume responsibility for all facets of school management, including curriculum, instruction, building maintenance and operation, administration, and other aspects of running schools. EMOs operate schools to make a profit; hence their schools are known as *for-profit schools*. The primary goals of EMOs for their schools are to raise student achievement and to make money. They operate on the principle of free enterprise that emphasizes competition as a way of improving performance, and they accept the challenge to "turn the public schools around" (Ediger, 2001, p. 3). An EMO-run school can be thought of as a business: students and parents are the customers. Their operating model is that of big business, and, accordingly, planning focuses on optimizing profits as a result of student success in school.

In 2004, there were 51 EMOs operating 463 public schools serving over 200,000 students (Commercialism in Education Research Unit, 2004). Among the leaders is the Edison Schools, whose philosophy statement says, in part:

> *We believe that every child should be given exciting educational opportunities and that every child has a tremendous capacity for learning. And we believe that great schools are places that nurture the creative spirit, prize the beautiful as much as the useful, and inculcate a love of learning (Edison Schools, n.d.).*

Based on that statement, how would you describe the predominant philosophy of the Edison Schools?

EMOs' business practices have received mixed reviews. For-profit schools tend to have longer school days and school years; they also tend to be high-tech. (For example, Edison Schools place computers in the homes of every student in third grade or higher.) However, because the bottom line of these schools is profit, they may find it necessary to reduce the number of teachers and support personnel to minimize costs. Further, supporters of traditional government-controlled schools suggest that there is little in either the instructional–managerial model or the high-tech emphasis of for-profit schools that is innovative or unique (Kaplan, 1996).

Reviews of the achievement of students who attend for-profit schools are also mixed. Student achievement data has been questioned, and comparisons with student achievement in traditional schools are inconclusive (Cardman, 2002; Ediger, 2001; GAO, 2002; Holloway, 2002; Miner, 2002). Moreover, several researchers have voiced concerns that EMOs fail to respond adequately to the needs of special students, such as **at-risk students** and students with special needs. (Ramanathan & Zollers, 1999; Zollers & Ramanathan, 1998). However, a recent review of the 20 schools Edison took over in Philadelphia shows that the rate of gain in student achievement has more than quintupled in the 2 years since the implementation of for-profit management (Whittle, 2005).

How is a school like a business? How is a school different from a business?

What are the advantages of for-profit schools? What are their disadvantages? Would you want to teach at a for-profit school? Why?

For-Profit Schools

Use the Internet to find information about a for-profit school—one in your area, if possible. (Go to your state Department of Education website.) See if you can answer the following questions to gain a good understanding of for-profit schools:

- What is the school's curriculum?
- How much does it cost to attend?
- How is it funded?
- What is the length of the school day? What is the school calendar?
- Are there admissions criteria? What are they? What does the application process require?

Home Schools

Home schooling is an educational alternative in which children learn under the general supervision of their parents at home rather than attend a conventional school. As of 2003, approximately 1.1 million (or 2.2%) of America's children were being home schooled in grades K–12 (National Center for Education Statistics, 2005b). Home schooling is legal in all states, and most require regular reports of curriculum taught, days attended, evaluations, standardized test results, and other data required from schools.

People choose to home school their children for many different reasons. Among these reasons are religious beliefs, lack of safety in regular schools, a poor fit between regular schools and their children, desire for increased family time, desire to supervise the content of their children's education, desire to provide education more suitable for their children's special needs or learning styles, and many others. Figure 6.4 shows the top reasons why people elect to home school their children.

Although students who attend school at home study a rigorous curriculum, there are concerns about home schooling, including limited access to equipment and materials, teaching parents' lack of required professional education background, limited access to enriching events, and questionable development of healthy social skills. To address these concerns, home schooling parents often work with other parents in large, well formed groups to provide their children with maximum advantages. In addition, numerous publications, curriculum programs, and instructional ideas and aids are available in print and on the Internet to help parents provide the best possible education for their children.

A direct link to the American Home School Association is available on the *Building Teachers* companion website. This association maintains a great deal of information about home schooling.

What are the advantages of home schooling? What are its disadvantages? Would you consider home schooling your child? Would you send your child to a neighbor or friend to participate in home schooling? What factors would influence your decision?

Home Schooling

Use the Internet to find information about home schooling in your state. (Go to your state Department of Education website.)

- What are the requirements for parents who wish to home school their children?
- What reports does your state require?
- Does your college or university have the same admission requirements for home-schooled students as for traditionally schooled students?
- How can students who have been home schooled through high school satisfy your college's or university's admission requirements?

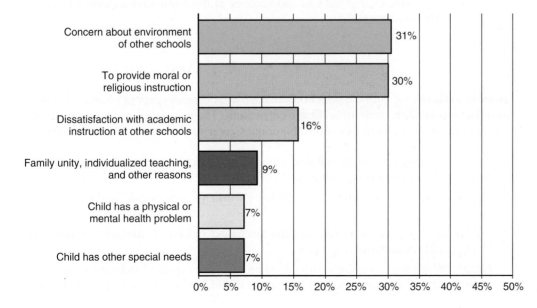

Figure 6.4
Top reasons for homeschooling. (Source: National Center for Education Statistics, 2005b.)

Alternative Schools

Alternative schools are schools whose purpose is to educate students who, for one reason or another, do not thrive in traditional schools. Alternative schools often see their missions as dropout prevention for at-risk students—students who are considered at high risk for failing or dropping out of high school before graduation because of poor grades, truancy, suspension, pregnancy, or any of a number of other reasons. In 2000–2001, 39% of public school districts had alternative schools, serving 613,000 (1.3%) of public school students (National Center for Education Statistics, 2003a).

Most alternative schools provide numerous services to students, including academic counseling; coursework that will lead to a regular high school diploma; preparation for the General Educational Development (GED) exam, a high school equivalency exam; and vocational skills.

The following are some major benefits of alternative schools:

■ More responsive and flexible environment
■ More curricular options
■ Smaller class sizes
■ More informal teacher–student relationships
■ High standards for attendance, behavior, and performance
■ Flexible scheduling

Alternative schools operate within the school district of the students they serve and are financed by the district, like the other schools under district control.

> **What are the advantages of alternative schools? What are their disadvantages? Would you want to teach in an alternative school? Why?**

Alternative Schools

Visit your state's Department of Education website or the website of your local school system to find information about alternative schools in your area. Use what you find to answer the following questions to gain a better understanding of alternative schools:

- What grades do the schools encompass?
- What are their rules and regulations?
- How are the curricula of these schools different from those of other schools in your area that encompass the same grades?
- Are there statistics that indicate the success of the alternative schools in your area? What do they show?

Vocational Schools

Vocational schools are public high schools that provide various types of vocational education programs in addition to an academic curriculum. The vocational programs are classified into the following main categories (National Center for Education Statistics, 2002b):

■ *Technical occupations* including drafting, computer technician, computer graphic designer, and computer programmer.
■ *Service occupations* including chef, childcare worker, teacher's aide, and paralegal assistant.
■ *Mechanical occupations* including auto mechanic; machinist; and air conditioning, heating, and refrigeration mechanic.
■ *Health and life sciences occupations* including emergency medical technician, veterinary assistant, dental assistant, medical laboratory technician, and agriscience technician.

- *Business occupations* including bookkeeper, secretary, sales associate, and restaurant manager.
- *Building trades* including welder, carpenter, electrician, mason, and plumber.

The number of students in vocational education programs declined between 1982 and 1990, and the number of students has remained relatively constant since then (National Center for Education Statistics, 2003b). Reasons for the decline include replacing the vocational education program concept with individual vocational courses, increased student attendance at local postsecondary regional vocational institutions, increased cost of vocational education programs, declining public perception that vocational education is desirable, and fewer rural schools offering vocational programs.

Nevertheless, vocational schools offer an attractive alternative to students who desire both skills to enter the world of work and a high school diploma.

> What are the advantages of vocational education schools? What are their disadvantages? Would you want to teach in a vocational school? Why?

Vocational Schools

Use the Internet to find any vocational schools in your area. (Go to your state Department of Education website.) Answer the following questions to understand the purpose of these schools.

- What programs does the vocational school offer?
- What facilities enable it to offer these programs?
- How does the faculty at a vocational school differ from the faculty at a more traditional school?
- What are the school's requirements for a high school diploma?
- How do these requirements differ from other high school diplomas with which you are familiar?
- What is the school's success rate in placing its graduates?

Private Schools

Private schools restrict their population of students to those who meet certain, specific criteria established by the school. These schools must meet the demands of two masters:

1. The government, with its emphasis on testing, the three Rs, and student achievement.
2. The school foundations that give the schools their reasons for existence and the finances they need.

Numerous kinds of private schools exist; each has its own specific purposes, goals, and objectives.

Types of Private Schools

BUILDING
BLOCK
6.11

Take a moment to list as many types of private schools you can think of. Think about movies you have seen or private schools in your region. Perhaps you or someone you know attended a private school. What are some possible reasons for attending a private school?

- For each school you listed, what is its primary purpose?
- What purposes are common to all the private schools?
- How do these common purposes compare with the common purposes of schools you listed earlier in this chapter?
- What purposes are unique to specific kinds of private schools?

Educating students according to a religious philosophy, according to gender, or according to a college preparatory curriculum are the purposes of some private schools.

Students in classes like yours listed the following types of private schools:

- Boarding schools
- All-male schools
- All-female schools
- College preparatory schools
- Schools with religious affiliations
- Montessori schools
- Military schools

Did you list these? Did you list any others?

In 2003, more than 6 million students (11.5% of all U.S. students) were enrolled in 27,223 private schools (23% of all U.S. schools) (Council for American Private Education, 2004), and the number is growing. Parents send their children to private schools because they believe that private schools:

1. generally provide a better education than public schools,
2. do a better job of teaching academic skills,
3. do a better job of maintaining discipline and order, and
4. do a better job of teaching students to get along with people from different backgrounds (Council of American Private Education, 2004).

> What are the advantages of private schools? What are their disadvantages? Would you want to teach in a private school? Why?

Your Hypothetical School

Now it is time to pull together the ideas you have thought about in this chapter. What do you consider to be the most important purposes of schools?

BUILDING BLOCK 6.12

Mission of a Hypothetical School

Suppose you had to write a hypothetical mission statement for a school of your choosing. Consider your current thinking about yourself as the teacher, the students with their common and diverse needs, and the purposes of schools.

Write an abbreviated mission statement for the school you conceive. Be sure to include references to the school's primary goals, how you envision the implementation of these goals, and what you expect for the students and graduates of your school (that is, what you expect them to be able to do while they are students in your school and after they leave it). Keep this statement for use in later chapters.

Retrieve the philosophy statement you wrote in Chapter 2 and updated in Chapter 5. Compare this philosophy statement with your mission statement. In what ways are the two statements alike? How are they different? If you wish, update your philosophy statement again to show the progression of your thinking so far.

Technology & Education

Technology offers students (and teachers) more opportunities to learn and build knowledge. Certain factors—such as distance, location, and financing—might prevent a school from providing its students with specific learning experiences, but technology can help fill the gap. Consider a school that does not have a teacher certified to teach chemistry, a group of students interested in advanced placement courses who attend a school at which AP courses are not offered, or a remote area in which many students live too far away from the school to get there. Virtual field trips, distance education, and virtual schools are three ways technology might help students in these situations.

Virtual field trips are structured online experiences that help students increase their knowledge of a subject or concept. A teacher who is teaching a lesson on the Grand Canyon, for example, might assign a virtual field trip. To deter students from searching aimlessly for websites about the Grand Canyon, the teacher must structure this part of the lesson by providing students with an explanation of the task (or "trip"); a list of websites or places to visit; an "itinerary;" things each student must do at the virtual destination; and list of artifacts or "souvenirs" for each student to collect at each website. Students on virtual field trips freely explore to enhance the teacher's instruction and their learning, and they do so despite of distance or expense.

Distance learning can provide students with specific opportunities to learn what they might not otherwise have. Distance learning (or e-learning, as it is sometimes called) is a learning situation in which the students are in one place and the teacher is in another. Technology facilitates the transfer of information.

Distance learning often involves transference of data on CD-ROMs, audio over phone lines, and live or recorded video via cable TV or DVDs. The Internet is also an efficient, effective way to transmit information for distance learning: web cams, e-mail, websites, chat rooms, and video and audio streaming all facilitate e-learning. Online courses are an example of Internet-based distance education.

Distance education can take many shapes and forms. A group of students might meet regularly at a remote location while a teacher in a distant classroom explains a topic. In this case, the distance learning is *synchronous*, meaning that the students are "tuned in" at the same time the instruction is taking place. In another form of distance learning, students might use individual workstations (or a home computer) to access the teacher's discussion and accompanying information at their leisure. This is an example of *asynchronous* distance learning. Of course, many online courses are a mixture of both synchronous and asynchronous instruction. For example, students might access information the teacher has posted on the Internet and then be required to log in to a chat room on a certain date and time. Academic chat rooms provide real-time interaction among students and between students and the teacher. Schools that are completely online are called *virtual schools* and have course offerings for all grade levels. Often, home-schooled children attend virtual schools.

A report released by the National Center for Education Statistics (2005c) noted that 36% of public school districts had distance education courses during the 2002–2003 school year. According to this report, distance education courses were more prevalent in rural school districts than in suburban or urban districts; these courses were also more prevalent in high schools than in middle grades or elementary schools, although distance learning was used in all these settings.

Rapid City Academy is an alternative high school in South Dakota. Researchers asked its students and teachers about their experiences with the school's online learning program (Podoll & Randle, 2005). According to participating students and teachers, the online program's advantages include flexibility and convenience, interactivity of online instruction and learning, the opportunity to reflect on lessons, and the extent to which instruction engaged students. The group cited lack of Internet access, computer failure, and lack of face-to-face interaction as disadvantages.

Distance learning and online courses certainly offer students opportunities to take courses and have educational experiences they might not otherwise have. How effective is distance learning in producing student achievement? One of the most comprehensive reviews of research on distance learning reports that students in distance learning classes tend to do neither better nor worse than students in traditional classes (Russell, 1999). Other studies have found, however, that the students who use technology for learning outperform their counterparts in the classroom (Shachar & Neumann, 2003).

To use distance education effectively, teachers must be able to organize information and design instruction to make it suitable for transmission and for student-centered learning. Teachers must also be familiar with the technology, not only to create the courses but also to troubleshoot and solve problems. Students must also contribute to their learning and the learning environment.

Can you imagine teaching your favorite content to your favorite age of student online? Why do you believe online teaching would or would not be effective?

Conclusion

Schools have many different purposes. These purposes are reflected in a school's mission statement and depend on the school's basic philosophy, the grade levels it serves, its location, its special interests, the special expertise it offers, and numerous other factors. Government agencies and noteworthy individuals have studied, written, and published various judgments about what the purposes of schools *ought* to be. Nonetheless, you have seen that all this input can be summarized into a few major purposes that are common to all schools.

You have investigated the nature of the elementary, middle, and high schools. You have looked at specialized public schools and private schools, and you have explored the advantages and disadvantages of different kinds of schools. In doing so, you have come to your own informed conclusions and applied the acid test: *Would you want to teach at this school?*

Finally, you have synthesized the results of all your inquiries in this chapter into a single, succinct mission statement for your hypothetical school of excellence.

Although a school must have a stated mission as a foundation on which to build, it must also have the resources, facilities, personnel, and organization to carry out that mission. In Chapter 7, you will identify what schools and teachers need to carry out their mission effectively. You will examine various school structures, and resources from personnel to materials and equipment to schedules, and draw conclusions about how a school's organization relates to its effectiveness.

Key Terms and Concepts

At-risk student, 170
Mission, 158
Rural, 166

Society, 159
Suburban, 166

Urban, 166
Vision, 159

Construct and Apply

1. The primary purpose of any school is to provide its students with the opportunity to learn. What other factors might influence a particular school's stated purpose?
2. Consider where you currently live. What do you suppose are the purposes of your neighborhood schools? What influences these purposes? How do you suppose the purposes of your neighborhood schools have changed in the past 50 years? What may have caused these changes?
3. Some students in small, rural towns may aspire to careers that they believe are beyond the town's ability to offer. What responsibility does the school have to these students? How can the school serve them? How could you, as a teacher, assist them?
4. Prepare a chart, listing the types of schools you have investigated across the top. Below each type of school, list the primary purpose(s) of that kind of school. Look at your chart to find purposes that are common to all schools.
5. What factors might influence you to choose a nontraditional school for your child? What advantages might a nontraditional school have over a traditional one?

Deconstructing the Standards

INTASC Principle #7 says:

> The teacher plans instruction based on knowledge of subject matter, students, the community, and curriculum goals.

- What part(s) of this principle does this chapter address?
- How does this chapter address this principle?
- How will the concepts in this chapter help you apply this principle as a teacher?

Field Experience

1. What is the purpose of the school in your field experience?
2. If your field experience is in an elementary school, compare the amount of time devoted to teaching reading, writing, and mathematics with the amount of time devoted to other subjects and activities. Are standardized tests administered? Which ones? In what subjects? What does the primary purpose of the school seem to be? Is this the same as the purpose reflected in its mission statement?
3. If your field experience is in a middle school, note how the unique characteristics and needs of middle grades learners are being met. What attention do you see in classrooms, the counselor's office, interactions with teachers, and the curriculum that seems to indicate consistency with the purpose of a middle school as described previously?
4. If your field experience is in a high school, investigate the types of curricula available to students. What are the electives? How do these curricula mirror the needs of the society of the region in which the school is located?

Your Portfolio

Add a copy of your field experience school's mission statement to your portfolio. Compare the school's mission statement with your own philosophy statement. Describe how, if you were a teacher at that school, you could contribute to the fulfillment of the mission.

Building Teachers Technology Resources

 Check out the *Building Teachers* companion website, *http://www.education.wadsworth.com/ martinloomis1*, for more information and resources about the purposes of schooling and education, including access to the following websites:

- Goals 2000
- No Child Left Behind Act
- International Baccalaureate Organization
- American Home School Association

 Check out the *Building Teachers* CD-ROM that accompanies your textbook for additional resources.

Also link to InfoTrac College Edition via the *Building Teachers* companion website. Use InfoTrac College Edition to search for journal articles to enhance your study.

CHAPTER 7

Structure of Schools

I have never let my schooling interfere with my education.

ATTRIBUTED TO MARK TWAIN

In Chapter 6, you investigated the purposes of schools. As you recall, the purpose of a school represents its fundamental reason for existence. You saw that many factors influence a school's purposes, such as grade level, location, population, the community being served, any specialties offered, and the like. You also saw that a few purposes that seem to be common to all schools, such as helping students learn to read and write, develop language literacy, develop mathematical skill, prepare to live in today's society (and tomorrow's), develop technological know-how, prepare for work, and prepare for college.

To accomplish their purposes, schools require certain facilities, materials, equipment, and personnel. For example, a magnet school focusing on science needs laboratory space and equipment. Schools also need to develop routines and schedules that will meet the needs of their students and the community they serve. Yet, the quotation attributed to Mark Twain at the beginning of this chapter seems to imply that the school itself might, in fact, interfere with education. How can this be?

In this chapter, you will examine factors that contribute to the inner workings of a school. These factors include facilities, materials, equipment, technology resources, other resources, personnel, and scheduling. You will examine these inner workings from the point of view of what a school needs to fulfill its purpose.

CHAPTER GOALS

As a result of your work in this chapter, you will:

1. Identify people, equipment, and materials schools must have to fulfill their purposes.

2. Describe various structures, organizations, and resources of specific types of schools.

3. Discuss how the structures and resources of schools facilitate the accomplishment of their stated missions.

4. Identify the roles of key personnel in schools.

What Is a School?

Let us first look at what a school is. As you have found, many different types of schools exist; these schools serve many different groups of people and have many different purposes. Schools have very complex inner workings, involving both physical facilities and people. As a student who has experienced and is currently experiencing "school," you might take these intricate workings for granted, never thinking to ask how it all works.

Do you think about the parts of your car and how they all work together before you get in, start it up, and drive off? Probably not. You just want it to start and take you where you need to go. But if you stop and think about it (even with limited knowledge of car engines), an automobile is a pretty amazing machine. Let us consider schools in the same way.

We have already established that the purposes of schools are as different as the populations they serve. A school's structure and organization must be arranged so the school can achieve its purpose. If different schools have different purposes, the structure and organization of those schools must also differ. For example, schools designed to serve very young children are not the same as schools designed for high school students, and rural schools differ from urban schools.

Needs of Schools

Let us think about a school's overall structure. What parts are needed to make it work?

If you were asked, you could probably name a few parts of a car engine. But if you thought about it a little more, you might be able to get more detailed about the parts that you name, citing some smaller, less visible, but nevertheless important parts that are vital to an engine's function. Building Block 7.1 asks you to think about a typical school in the same way.

BUILDING BLOCK 7.1

Parts of a School

Think of a particular kind of school.

1. Brainstorm and list some of the necessities the school requires to fulfill its purposes. List both large and small items—everything you can think of.
2. Compare your list with your classmates' lists.
   a. How do they compare?
   b. What made them different?
3. To what extent did your list depend on the type of school you were thinking of?

Your list probably included such categories as building, classrooms, materials and equipment, teachers, administrators, paraprofessionals, specialists, and the like. Let us consider two basic aspects of school structure: physical facilities and human resources.

Physical Facilities

Physical plant refers to the school building itself. Did your list from Building Block 7.1 contain classrooms? "Of course!" you say. But this question may not be as silly as it appears. In the 1960s, some schools were built without classroom partitions to accommodate a need for flexibility in forming adjustable groups of students (Anderson, 1966). These *open classroom* schools were popular for a while, but are no longer being built.

The purpose of the school should determine its design. Based on the design, what kind of school could this be?

The great architect Louis Sullivan wrote, "Form should follow function" (in Boudreaux, 1993, p. 1). In other words, a structure's purpose should determine its design. This principle is as appropriate for designing a school as it is for designing any other architectural structure. As you investigate the elements of school structure (buildings, materials and equipment, scheduling, and personnel), keep this dictum in mind: The purpose and goals of a school determine its design.

Let us investigate this principle relative to the schools whose purposes you examined in Chapter 6.

BUILDING BLOCK 7.2

Identifying a School's Structure from Its Purpose

In Chapter 6 you investigated the purposes of several different kinds of schools, including traditional schools (such as elementary schools, middle schools, junior high schools, and high schools) and nontraditional schools (such as charter, magnet, for-profit schools, home schools, alternative schools, vocational schools, and private schools).

Select one kind of school.

■ What two or three characteristics distinguish this school from other kinds of schools?

■ How might you design the building so the school could achieve its purposes?

The Middle School as an Example

A good example of applying the "form follows function" principle can be seen in the middle school. As you recall, the purpose of the middle school is to align the educational environment with the unique needs of the early adolescent learner. In elementary school, students spend most of each day with the same teacher and the same peers. Each grade-level classroom is usually on the same hall with others of the same grade. In high school, teachers and students change with each class and classrooms are grouped by subject. How might a school structure and organization "in the middle" of these two look?

When the middle school concept was developed, many junior high schools were converted to middle schools. Converting a junior high school required not only a change in curriculum but also a change in physical structure. As new school buildings were built, designers paid attention to developing the structure and organization that would best facilitate the middle school's purpose. The result was the now-familiar middle school building in which the rooms are arranged in "pod" form, with classrooms for each of the main subjects taught in a particular grade clustered in the same general area.

Middle school teachers work in interdisciplinary teams of four or five. A team normally comprises a social studies teacher, a mathematics teacher, a language arts teacher, a science teacher, and sometimes a reading teacher. Ideally, these teachers work in adjacent classrooms, and the team's students move from one class to the next in the same general area. Thus all students on a team have the same teachers.

BUILDING
BLOCK
7.3

Middle Schools and Junior High Schools

If you went to a junior high school, recall how the classrooms were organized. Which classes were on the same hall? Which classes were on the same hall as the science class?

If you went to a middle school, recall how the classrooms were organized. Which classes were on the same hall? Which classes were on the same hall as the science class?

Refer back to your answers for Building Block 7.2. How well do your answers represent the "form follows function" dictum?

Schools require an extensive array of classrooms: teaching space for special subjects; room for after-school programs; technology equipment and materials; and materials, equipment, and supplies to support teaching and learning. Did your list of requirements from Building Block 7.1 include trailers or portable classroom space? Or did you assume that school buildings are large enough to accommodate students? No matter how forward-thinking school-facility designers try to be, the population often grows faster than anticipated, causing overcrowded conditions. One solution to this problem has been to use portable classrooms. More than a third of America's schools use portable classrooms (Kennedy, 2001). As of 2002, it was estimated that more than 385,000 portable classrooms were in use in the United States (Roman, 2002). The primary reasons for using this temporary instructional space are overcrowding caused by a large influx of people and school district attempts to comply with state laws limiting class size.

Did your brainstorming list include rooms or areas for special offerings such as art, band, orchestra, chorus, physical education, vocational education, technology education, theater, and other specialized subjects? Did your list contain facilities for after-school programs (ASPs), extracurricular activities, and community programs? For many years, offering after-school and weekend programs and extracurricular activities—to students, families, and the community at large—has been a priority of educators and the federal government. Such activities are designed to help students, their families, and members of the community learn new skills and discover and develop new abilities. Services offered typically include tutorial services, academic enrichment activities, youth development activities, counseling and character education, and adult programs. The federal government offers support in the form of grants; the 21st Century Community Learning Centers program is one example.

Did your list for Building Block 7.1 have provisions for technology? The National Educational Technology Plans suggest that all students and teachers should have access to information technology in their classrooms, schools, communities, and homes (U.S. Department of Education, 1999, 2000, 2005). This means schools should have a computer laboratory and at least one computer in each classroom, all with Internet access. In fact, there are so many ways of using technology to enrich students' education that it is desirable to have several computers in each classroom.

Did you include adaptive and assistive technology devices in your plan? (You investigated this technology in Chapter 5.) You also saw in Chapter 5 that the Individuals with Disabilities Education Act (IDEA) requires that all children be educated in the least restrictive environment, regardless of special need. This act extends to technology, and schools must provide students with access to technology such that *all* students can use it.

How do efforts to comply with class size limitations cause the need for increased portable classroom space?

Go to the *Building Teachers* companion website to read more about 21st Century Community Learning Centers.

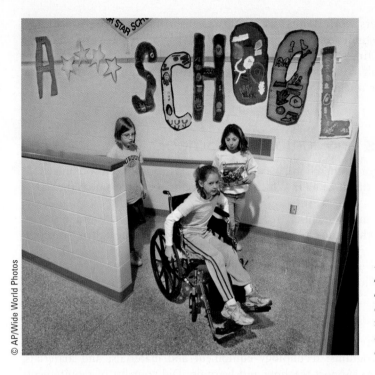

Federal legislation requires all school buildings be accessible to students with disabilities. Accessibility ramps, elevators, and other building modifications are examples.

Did your list contain facilities for students with special needs? What kinds of disabilities did you consider? What provisions for these disabilities did you list? Such provisions can range from wheelchair ramps, to space and equipment accommodations in regular classrooms, to special rooms with special facilities for students with severe handicaps.

Perhaps you took the time to consider those smaller—though no less important—requirements of a school, such as supplies for teachers, students, administrators, and custodial staff. Did you remember that all the people in a school typically eat lunch there each day? What resources are required for the formidable task of feeding everyone associated with a school? And did you remember that most schools need gymnasiums and auditoriums?

How do the physical requirements needed by a school vary according to its location, level, and basic purposes?

Personnel

Next, let us consider human resources.

Recall our analogy of the car engine from earlier in this chapter. What happens if one of the parts does not work quite right? Perhaps it does not fit well, or is the wrong size or shape, or is old and worn. What does this mean for the engine? Perhaps the part works well enough that the engine starts but runs jaggedly or unevenly. Eventually the engine could stall, refuse to restart, and bring everything to a complete halt.

For your car to run smoothly, the parts must be in good shape and must all work together in a well oiled machine. What is necessary for a school to run smoothly? Sure, there are glitches in any school year and even in every school day. But for the most part, schools succeed extremely well in carrying out their functions and achieving their purposes. To do so requires that all parts of the school you have considered—those that make up the structure and resources of the school, including personnel—be organized effectively.

Review the list you made in Building Block 7.1 What human resources did you see as necessary for the school to fulfill its purpose?

Schools require many different kinds of personnel. Of course, different kinds of schools and schools with different purposes require different kinds of personnel. Regardless of a school's nature and purpose, however, all schools require people with certain qualifications.

Teachers

Probably the predominant person you listed as necessary to a school was teacher. How many teachers should a school have? During your own experience of school, perhaps you have been in some very small classes, and perhaps you have attended very large classes, such as the lecture courses often found in colleges and universities. An important consideration in the organization of a school is the **student–teacher ratio,** the number of students assigned to one teacher in a class, on average. For example, a student–teacher ratio of 21:1 means that, on average, there are 21 students in each class assigned to a teacher.

Optimal Class Size

Based on your experience, what do you think is the optimal student–teacher ratio for each of the following classes? Why?

- Preschool class
- High school trigonometry class
- Chorus
- Middle-grades physical education class
- Third grade
- High school study hall
- High school science laboratory
- Special education class for students with moderate disabilities
- College-level introductory literature class

What do you think is the optimal class size in general? What factors are important to decisions about student–teacher ratio?

What is the maximum class size for your school system or state?

Do local school systems provide information about the general student–teacher ratios in their schools? What is the range of these ratios? Would knowing this ratio be important to you in deciding whether to accept a teaching position? Why?

Student enrollment in public schools increased steadily in the 20th century, except for a slight decline during the 1970s and 1980s. The number of teachers also has increased steadily. However, the increase in teachers has occurred faster than the increase in student population. This has resulted in a steadily decreasing nationwide average student–teacher ratio from 32:1 in 1920 to 15.9:1 in 2004 (World Almanac, 2005). Note that all instructional staff are included in this ratio, even those who have few students because of their specialties. The individual state ratios vary from a maximum of 21.8:1 in Utah to a low of 11.7:1 in Vermont. Figure 7.1 shows the national average of student–teacher ratios since 1955; the ratio has decreased regularly from a ratio of 27.4:1 in 1955 to 15.9:1 in 2001, except for a slight increase during the mid-1990s (National Center for Education Statistics, 2003).

How do the national averages of student–teacher ratios compare with the classes you attended in elementary school, middle school, and high school? What might account for any discrepancies? Note that the national average was 15.9 to 1 in 2001, a substantial reduction from the ratios in the 1950s, 1960s, and 1970s. Can school planners consider the reduction of class size an effort that has been accomplished? Or do you think there still is work to do?

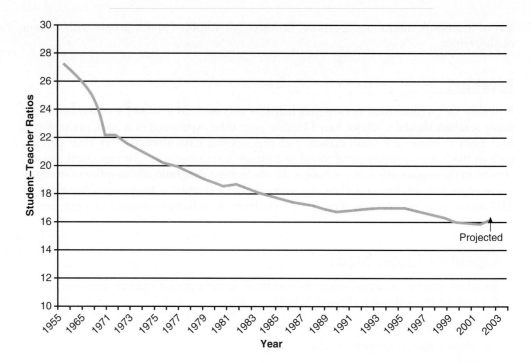

Figure 7.1
Student–teacher ratios: national averages from 1955 to 2003. (Source: National Center for Education Statistics, 2003.)

A direct link to the Project STAR website is available on the *Building Teachers* companion website.

For research and other information about student class size, access the National Education Association website using a direct link available on the *Building Teachers* companion website.

Many studies have shown that reducing class size improves student achievement, although some disagree with the interpretations of the research findings (Wenglinsky, 1998). Smaller class sizes enable teachers to spend the time and energy needed to help each child succeed, and enhance safety and discipline in the classroom. Much of the research about how class size affects achievement comes from Project STAR (Student Teacher Achievement Ratio), an experiment that took place in Tennessee (Illig, 1996; Nye, Hedges, & Konstantopoulos, 2004). In this experiment, kindergarten students were randomly assigned either to small classes of 13–17 students or to large classes of 22–26 students; students stayed in these classes for 4 years through the third grade. A follow-up study of several thousand students found that those in the small classes made better academic gains, especially in reading, and were more likely to graduate from high school than those who had been in the large classes. However, the effect was seen only in students who had attended the small classes for all 4 years; 1 or 2 years were not enough to make a difference. The researchers attributed the higher success rate of students in the small classes to increased individual attention and the inability to avoid teacher attention (Sparks, 2005).

Many states legislate class size limits to improve student achievement. For example, California Governor Arnold Schwarzenegger has proposed a class-size reduction plan for his state, whereby low-performing schools would receive enough funding to enable them to lower class sizes to a maximum of 20 students per classroom (Governor Proposes, 2005). Texas has established a student–teacher ratio of 22:1 (Magnuson, 2004). Florida has amended its state constitution to limit class size to 18 for kindergarten through third grade, 22 for fourth grade through eighth grade, and 25 in high school classes (Albright, 2005).

The National Education Association (NEA) has set a class-size goal of 15 students in regular programs and smaller class sizes in programs for students with exceptional needs (National Education Association, n.d.). However, smaller class sizes require more teachers and more money. Many states and school districts experience difficulties in implementing smaller class sizes because of limited funding. In addition, finding highly qualified teachers and appropriate classroom space makes it difficult to reduce class size.

How do the optimal student–teacher ratios you established in Building Block 7.4 compare with the optimal class sizes just discussed?

More individual attention for students, more classroom space, and increased student achievement are benefits of smaller class sizes. In which of these classrooms would you prefer to teach?

We all have had experience with "regular" or "general" classroom teachers, but in Building Block 7.1 you probably also identified other types of professional personnel who are present in schools. Some may be specialized teachers, some may have responsibilities that extend throughout the school rather than in a particular classroom, and some may have administrative responsibilities. In addition, you may have identified some nonprofessional personnel.

Teachers with Specialties

There are many different teaching specialties. The higher a school's grade levels, the more specialized the teachers are relative to subject matter. Teachers in elementary schools generally are prepared to teach all subjects, whereas middle school and high school teachers specialize in one or two subjects. However, special teachers are found in most schools. Elementary schools generally have art, music, and physical education specialists. These teachers are responsible for teaching their subjects to large numbers of students in a school—often all the students. Middle schools and high schools employ specialty teachers to implement specialty programs, such as band, chorus, orchestra, art, computers, business, shop, and others. In the upper levels, the presence of specialty teachers directly reflects the school's purpose and mission statement.

One example of teachers with specialties is the special education teacher. Special education teachers are found in most schools: elementary, middle, and high schools. Some teach students in their own self-contained classrooms; others work in conjunction with regular classroom teachers to accommodate the needs of learners with exceptionalities who can be included in regular classrooms. The United States is currently experiencing a critical need for special education teachers, due to increased enrollment of special education students, teacher retirement, and legislation that broadens the scope of special education and extends it to very young children. Also, as more and more students with special needs are included in regular classrooms, schools need more special education teachers to work with these students. Teachers who specialize in special education typically complete a focused program in which they learn to facilitate the teaching and learning of students with special needs.

Another example of teachers with specialties is the bilingual educator. Bilingual educators not only work with students to help them learn English, they also assist students with the translation of books and other materials and with understanding information presented by regular teachers, and they help teachers design instruction to make information more accessible to all students. Bilingual education programs are known by several names, including TESL (Teaching English as a Second Language), TEFL (Teaching

A direct link to a website where you can find historical and current teacher shortage areas for each state is available on the *Building Teachers* companion website.

English as a Foreign Language), TESOL (Teaching English to Speakers of Other Languages), ESL (English as a Second Language), EFL (English as a Foreign Language), and ESOL (English for Speakers of Other Languages). To earn the bilingual education specialty, teachers study specialized programs.

Many classroom teachers develop interests in other areas and can earn specialized endorsements or add-ons to their teaching certificates. Examples include early childhood special education specialists, technology specialists, reading specialists, and gifted education specialists. Others specialties are available; these vary from state to state.

Use the Internet to find which endorsement programs in education are recognized by your state. Which are offered by your college or university? What are the requirements for these endorsements? What endorsement programs do neighboring institutions offer? This information may be available online.

Administrators

Did your list include school administrators? When you think of the school principal, what comes to mind? Many people think of discipline, because when we went to the principal's office, it usually meant we were in trouble.

Depending on its size, a school may have a principal and one or more assistant principals, each of whom has a specific role and set of responsibilities. The principal is the administrative head of the school—the person to whom teachers and other school personnel report and who is ultimately responsible for the operation of the school. Indeed, the principal and the administrative staff have many responsibilities that help maintain the school's function and achieve its stated purpose. What do you think a principal's responsibilities are?

BUILDING BLOCK 7.5

The Principal's Jobs

Imagine it is early on a Monday morning and you are the school principal just arriving at work. List the items you need to do for the day. Be sure to include time for scheduled meetings or appointments. Suppose you find you have an hour of uncommitted time in your day. What would you do with it?

Next, list items you have to do for the week.

Look at your lists and generate some categories for a principal's responsibilities.

Many sources list school principals' roles and responsibilities. The U.S. Department of Labor uses the term "educational administrator" to describe someone who provides direction, leadership, and day-to-day management of educational activities in schools. The department lists the following duties and responsibilities for educational administrators (U.S. Department of Labor, 2003):

- Sets educational standards and goals
- Establishes policies and procedures to carry them out
- Supervises personnel
- Develops academic programs
- Monitors students' educational progress
- Trains and motivates teachers and other staff
- Manages guidance and other student services
- Administers record keeping
- Handles relations with parents and the community

School principals are responsible for supporting student learning and providing leadership to teachers and other school personnel. As a new teacher or student teacher, the principal together with an experienced teacher can provide you with career guidance and advice based on their extensive experience as educators.

© Michael Newman/PhotoEdit

How does the list of principal's duties you made in Building Block 7.5 compare with this list of responsibilities?

The principal traditionally has been seen as the school's leader, who supervises faculty and staff, interacts with students, makes discipline decisions, and oversees everything from student achievement, faculty performance, and staff development to building maintenance and the purchase of materials and supplies.

However, the principal's role is changing. Whereas principals formerly were considered school managers, they are now being asked to function as educational leaders. Principals seem to agree with this shift in emphasis. According to a survey released by the National Association of Secondary School Principals, high school principals view the following activities as their top three responsibilities (National Association of Secondary School Principals, 2001):

■ Establishing a supportive learning climate

■ Dealing with personnel issues

■ Providing curricular leadership, including spending time teaching in the classroom

The National Association for Elementary School Principals (NAESP) urges principals to focus on the following specific goals (National Association of Elementary School Principals, 2001):

■ Putting learning at the center of school activities

■ Promoting the academic success of all students

■ Creating rigorous content and instruction that ensures student progress

■ Creating an adult learning climate

■ Using multiple data sources for diagnosing learning progress

■ Engaging the community

Regardless of how you currently view the school principal's role, as a teacher you will want to avail yourself of your principal's expertise. After all, he or she has been in education for a long time and has solved many problems. Principals want to help; they especially want to help new teachers. The principal evaluates your performance, but it is also the principal who provides much needed assistance and advice.

Professional Support Personnel

Schools employ many people besides teachers and administrators. These individuals possess experience and special degrees or endorsements that allow them to fulfill their roles within the school building. The **library media specialist** (LMS), for example, knows about library science and various media, including computer technologies. In the Information Age, the job of library media specialist has changed significantly from that of librarian.

The **instructional lead teacher** (ILT) and the **learner support specialist** (LSS) provide curricular and instructional help to teachers and special instruction to groups of students selected on the basis of some common need. Technology specialists provide much-needed support in maintaining technological equipment and instructing teachers and students in the use of technologies. Curriculum specialists help interpret the system-mandated curriculum in terms of its most appropriate application for the students in individual schools.

Guidance counselors and school psychologists have various duties, which depend on the needs of the school and its students. They are found in all levels of schools, from elementary school through high school. As their titles imply, they are available to counsel students, advising them on issues such as personal and academic problems and postsecondary or vocational plans. These professionals also administer and interpret tests to help identify students with special needs and assist in developing Individualized Education Programs.

You can probably think of other professional support personnel whose areas of expertise meet the needs of some special students. These personnel might include speech therapists, nurses, social workers, truant officers, and police officers. As you know, it is the school's responsibility to meet the needs of *all* students. Sometimes, meeting those needs requires the collaboration of a staff with qualifications as varied as the students they serve.

Nonprofessional Personnel

Teacher's aides, or **paraprofessionals,** often provide assistance in the classroom. Paraprofessionals typically assist the classroom teacher with a variety of instructional and noninstructional tasks. Under the teacher's guidance, paraprofessionals may provide large group, small group, or individual instruction, including assisting students with special needs or English language learners. They may supervise laboratory activities, computer lessons, and other activities, including lunch and recess. In addition, a paraprofessional might assist in record keeping. Based on what you have already observed in your field experience, you can probably see just how valuable a paraprofessional might be in the busy life of a classroom teacher.

Parent and community volunteers provide teachers with instructional support, and provide students adult supervision in class. What is this volunteer doing to help in the classroom?

Parents or other community members sometimes volunteer to work in the schools. Classroom volunteers provide another set of hands, ears, and eyes that can help teachers give more students individual attention. With another adult in the room, teachers can incorporate activities that require close adult supervision, such as dissections, outdoor lessons, or activities that require the use of many different materials.

Other support personnel include the front office staff, the custodial staff, and cafeteria workers. You may also find volunteers in the front office answering phones and monitoring the comings and goings of students. Some teachers will argue that the school's staff is what keeps the place up and running.

As you have observed, a school contains many different adults with many different responsibilities. It may be surprising to learn just how many people can be at work in a school. Remember that people like those described here contributed to your own schooling experience. And soon you will be one of those people, working in a collaborative and cooperative environment to help your students and your school achieve.

Scheduling

Have you ever heard anyone say that a car engine's timing is off? In an automobile, "bad timing" might mean that the car stalls at a stop sign or races when it idles. Sometimes, a car with bad timing lurches or lags. A car engine's timing must be adjusted for the car to run smoothly. Can you apply this analogy to organizing the schedule that governs the students, personnel, and resources in a school? When people talk about school scheduling, they may be referring to the times school is in session during the year or to the time periods of the school day.

Annual Schedule

Let us first consider ways of scheduling the school year. Schools typically operate on a schedule that requires students to be in school for 180 days during the fall, winter, and spring, but not during the summer. This scheme was developed in the 19th century so that school-aged children could be at home and help on the farms during the busiest time of the year.

For students, the primary advantages of a nine-month school year include summers off for rest and regrouping, the ability to attend summer camps, and the possibility of gaining significant workplace experience. Primary advantages for teachers include summers off for rest and regrouping and the ability to take summer courses for professional development, certification renewal, or the pursuit of an advanced degree. Primary disadvantages include discontinuity of education because of the long summer vacation (students have three months to forget what they learned during the preceding year) and the need of some teachers to find summer work.

Many states and school districts have been experimenting with new and creative scheduling plans that include year-round education. There are many ways to implement year-round education. One example is the trimester system, in which students go to school for three months, have one month off, and repeat this cycle three times a year. Another method involves devising several tracks in which sequencings of school time and vacation time differ for different students and teachers, all within the same school (California Department of Education, 2001). Primary advantages of year-round systems include increased school capacity, relief from overcrowding, an enhanced instructional pace, and flexible vacation options. Primary disadvantages include increased need for faculty, staff, materials, and storage facilities; more "start-ups" and "endings" to the academic year; and a nontraditional calendar.

Among those who oppose year-round school are the owners of resorts and summer vacation attractions. These people fear that year-round school could cause them to lose business and revenue. These businesses also pay taxes to support education.

BUILDING
BLOCK
7.7

Yearly School Schedule

Which type of annual school schedule is best? Take the position of a teacher and describe the kind of annual school schedule you feel would be best for a teacher and tell why.

Do the same from the viewpoints of a parent, an elementary school student, and a high school student.

Daily Schedule

Next, let us look at ways of scheduling during the day. Your outlook on this topic will depend on the level of school at which you are planning to teach. Each level has it own unique situation and its own unique ways of solving scheduling problems.

Schools typically meet five days a week, with the same classes meeting on the same schedule every day for an academic year. In high school, a typical student attends seven different classes in discrete periods of 50–55 minutes, attending these same classes every day for a full academic year, although some courses meet for only one semester and half-day release time may be provided for certain work and apprenticeship programs. High school teachers typically teach five classes and deal with 125 or more students each day.

In an effort to provide more flexibility in using the time students are in school, innovations such as **block scheduling** have been implemented by many high schools (Irmsher, 1996). There are numerous variations to the concept of block scheduling. In one of the more common models, a school's daily schedule is organized into large blocks of time—so that students schedule four 90-minute classes per day for the first semester in the school year and four 90-minute classes per day during the second semester. This allows students to take eight classes per year instead of the traditional seven, and gives teachers the flexibility to pursue topics in greater depth than is possible in the shorter class period.

Middle schools are also moving to block scheduling, citing the same reasons for doing so as high schools.

Elementary schools typically have all-day scheduling in which students stay in their assigned classrooms for a full day all year long, except for those times when they go to other rooms for music, art, physical education, and other special subjects. The day's scheduling within a particular classroom may be determined by the teacher. Some flexibility is available to elementary school teachers in the form of **cooperative teaching, loop-**

ing, and **multi-age education**. Cooperative teaching allows individual teachers to teach subjects that they prefer and in which they have expertise, while other teachers take responsibility for subjects in their areas of expertise. This arrangement maximizes teachers' strengths and provides flexibility in forming groups. Several cooperative teaching models exist. In one, teachers of a particular grade or cluster of grades form teams; different teachers in the teams teach those subjects in which they have particular interest or expertise. In another model, subject matter specialists are responsible for teaching their subject to all children in a grade level or group of grades; this model is close to the subject specialists' model used in the middle schools and high schools. In a third model, teachers plan together in an interdisciplinary and cooperative manner, and each assumes the responsibility for a portion of the unit being taught.

In looping, the same teacher is assigned to the same group of students for 2 or 3 years. Looping has been used with increasing frequency in elementary schools and in some middle schools. This practice has the advantage that the teacher gets to know his or her students deeply. It allows the teacher to challenge the students in ways a teacher less familiar with students' capabilities may not, and it enables the teacher to provide remedial work for those who need it without having to wait for assessment results.

In multi-age education, students of several ages are clustered together in one class. Groups are formed on the basis of ability and professed interest, helping teachers provide appropriate classes because all students have approximately the same ability.

School Schedules

BUILDING BLOCK 7.8

If you were in charge, would you make changes to school scheduling? What would these changes be? Why would you make them?

Which type of daily school schedule do you believe is best for elementary schools? Which type do you believe is best for high schools? Describe the schedule and tell why you believe it is the best schedule.

Putting It All Together

You have been investigating schools' purposes and various complex factors that enable schools to achieve their purposes. Now it is time to put these elements together.

Structure of Your Hypothetical School

BUILDING BLOCK 7.9

In Building Block 6.12, you developed a hypothetical mission statement for a hypothetical school. What would your hypothetical school need in order to function?
Answer the following questions:

1. What kind of school (urban or rural; elementary, middle, or high school) is your hypothetical school?
2. What are its basic purposes?
3. What physical facilities will this school require? Think of materials and equipment and the physical structure your school will need.
4. How will your school building be laid out?
5. What personnel will your school require? What are their duties? How many of each type of professional and nonprofessional worker will your school need?
6. What requirements are specific to this school? How do they help the school fulfill its basic purpose? How do the requirements for this school differ from the requirements for other schools?

Conclusion

You have seen that schools have many different purposes, which are reflected in a school's mission statement and depend on the school's basic philosophy, the grade levels it serves, its location, its special interests, the special expertise it offers, and numerous other factors. Government agencies and noteworthy individuals have studied, written, and published various opinions about what the purposes of schools *ought* to be. All this input can be summarized into the schools' major purpose of educating all students.

You have thought about the nature of elementary, middle, and high schools, as well as specialized public schools and private schools, coming to your own well-informed conclusions about the purpose of each type of school and the various factors that influence it.

You considered these same factors in constructing a list of the facilities, personnel, and resources needed for schools to fulfill their common and unique purposes. The design and nature of the building or campus depends on the purpose and function of the school and is developed in accordance with the dictum that "form follows function." Schools need materials, equipment, and personnel to carry out their functions. Some people and equipment are common to all schools, and some are specific to certain kinds of schools. But all are needed for individual schools to fulfill their purposes.

Personnel in schools include teachers, administrators, other professionals, and non-professional employees. The student–teacher ratio is declining, but it is important to look at optimal ratios. The principal is the leader of the school, but the role of the principal is shifting from manager to instructional leader.

Often, the principal and assistant administrators are responsible for organizing the students and personnel with a schedule that optimizes resources and time. School schedules have remained constant for a century or more, but new approaches, including flexibility in daily schedules and year-round schooling, are becoming prominent.

This chapter asked you to think about the place called school. In previous chapters, you have thought about teachers, teaching, and students. In the next chapters, you will look at the relationships among all three elements: teachers, students, and the school. You will examine how the school serves the common and unique needs of its students, learn what the school expects from its teachers, and discover what you can expect from the school where you decide to teach.

■ Key Terms and Concepts

Block scheduling, 190
Cooperative teaching, 190
Instructional lead teacher
  (ILT), 188

Learner support specialist
  (LSS), 188
Library media specialist
  (LMS), 188

Looping, 190
Multi-age education, 191
Paraprofessional, 188
Student–teacher ratio, 183

■ Construct and Apply

1. How would you feel if your classroom were in a trailer? What are some of the advantages and disadvantages of teaching in a trailer? Do you believe having a class in a trailer can affect learning? How? Why?
2. How do the structure and organization of the following schools help them accomplish their purposes:
   a. Elementary school
   b. Middle school
   c. High school
3. Many people with many different kinds of responsibilities interact in a school, and the number of people in a given role varies with the type of school. How many people in each role would you expect to see in different schools?
   a. Look at the following chart of schools and personnel. Indicate on the chart the extent to which the various personnel would be present in a school. Use a double check mark (✓✓) if many are present, a check mark (✓) if some are present, and a dash (—) if none are present.
   b. What is the relationship between these roles and the school's mission?
   c. Look at each column. What accounts for the different numbers of personnel in different types of schools? (For example, why would there be more music teachers in a magnet school for the arts?)

	Elementary School	Middle School	High School	Private School	Alternative School	Vocational School
Teacher						
Principal						
Assistant principal						
Lead teacher						
Learning support specialist						
Library media specialist						
Counselor						
Paraprofessional						
Special education teacher						
Technology specialist						
Volunteer						
Nurse						
Custodial staff						
Cafeteria staff						
Other (write in)						

4. Do you believe planners should continue to try to reduce the current teacher–student ratio? Why? What do you believe is the optimal student–teacher ratio?

Deconstructing the Standards

INTASC Principle #4 says:

> The teacher understands and uses a variety of instructional strategies to encourage students' development of critical thinking, problem solving, and performance skills.

INTASC Principle #7 says:

> The teacher plans instruction based upon knowledge of subject matter, students, the community, and curriculum goals.

- What part(s) of these principles does this chapter address?
- How does this chapter address these principles?

How will the concepts in this chapter help you apply these principles as a teacher?

Field Experience

1. Explore the structure and organization of the school where you are doing your field experience. Obtain or draw a sketch of its floor plan. Why are the rooms and areas arranged as they are?
2. Use the "Technology Inventory" activity in your *Field Experience Companion* to assess the technology resources available in the school where you are doing your field experience.
3. What schedules for the school year and school day are followed in the district where you are doing your field experience? What are some advantages and disadvantages of these schedules?

Your Portfolio

1. Add a copy of your field experience school's mission statement to your portfolio. Provide a reflection that compares the school's mission statement to your own philosophy statement. Describe how, if you were a teacher at that school, you could contribute to the fulfillment of its mission.
2. Add a copy of the floor plan of the school where you are doing your field experience to your portfolio. Provide a reflection of how the school's physical structure enables it to carry out its function.

Building Teachers Technology Resources

 Check out the *Building Teachers* companion website, http://www.education.wadsworth.com/martinloomis1, for more information and resources about the structure of schools, including access to the following websites and information:

- 21st Century Community Learning Centers
- Historical and current teacher shortage areas, by state
- Recent research and statistics about student class size, from the National Education Association (NEA)
- Project STAR (Student Teacher Achievement Ratio)

 Check out the *Building Teachers* CD-ROM that accompanies your textbook for additional resources.

 Also link to InfoTrac College Edition via the *Building Teachers* companion website. Use InfoTrac College Edition to search for journal articles to enhance your study.

CHAPTER 8

The School and the Student

> "It's a little childish and stupid, but then again—so is high school."
>
> FERRIS BUELLER (PLAYED BY MATTHEW BRODERICK), TRYING TO JUSTIFY MALINGERING TO SKIP SCHOOL, IN FERRIS BUELLER'S DAY OFF, PARAMOUNT PICTURES

So far, you have considered yourself, the student, and the purposes and structures of schools. It is in this place we call *school* that the relationship between you (the teacher) and your students must be established and nurtured. In this environment, all the participants in the educational experience have certain expectations of each other. As a student, you have expectations of your teacher and your school. As a teacher, you can probably think of expectations that you might have of your students and the school in which you will work. Let us take the opportunity to explore these expectations and how schools meet them.

Students spend about a third of their day in school. In fact, "aside from their sleeping hours, most children spend more time in the presence of their teachers than they spend in the presence of their parents" (Eisner, 2002, p. 648). Students bring more than their bodies to school; they also bring their individual thoughts, feelings, experiences, backgrounds, and beliefs.

As you have seen, for your students to succeed academically, they must resolve whatever issues they bring with them to school. They must learn to function effectively and congenially in the school atmosphere. In terms of Maslow's hierarchy, this means they must have satisfied their physiological, safety, love and belonging, and esteem needs so they can focus on school work. In terms of Piagetian cognitive theory, this means students must have their thinking processes challenged at appropriate levels. In terms of Erikson's psychosocial developmental stages, this means they must have resolved at least the first two or three predicaments, including the trust, autonomy, and initiative issues.

Students can hardly be expected to devote their attention to school work if these needs and issues have not been satisfied and resolved.

When students go to school, they become part of the complex system you investigated in Chapter 7, which consists not only of physical facilities but also of other students and a whole host of adults. If you add to this mix the influences of local businesses, industries, service sectors, governments, parents, and friends—all of whom have a stake in the products of education—you get an idea of the complexity of the institution we call *school*. Within this multifaceted community, teachers must teach and students must learn.

What do you think of the quotation that opens this chapter? Is its attitude prevalent among students? Does it represent your attitude toward school when you were a student? Perhaps your attitude changed from your early childhood years, when you may have enjoyed school, to your teenage years, when liking school probably wasn't "cool."

In this chapter, you will explore the responsibilities and relationships that exist between the school and the student. You will investigate how students, teachers, and others in the school work together to create an environment that is inviting, comfortable, and maximally conducive to student learning. You will investigate the three major components of education: curriculum, instruction, and assessment. As in previous chapters, you will integrate your personal experiences with the theories and thoughts of others to enable you to draw some important conclusions and construct your understandings of how the school helps students learn.

CHAPTER GOALS

As a result of your work in this chapter, you will:

1. Describe life in school as the student experiences it.
2. Explain the responsibility of the school and its personnel to ensure the physical, intellectual, and emotional safety of each student.
3. Describe how schools help students meet their basic needs.
4. Describe effective methods for classroom and behavior management.
5. Discuss how curriculum, instruction, and assessment can be made meaningful, interesting, and engaging for students.

Student Life in the School

What is school life like for students? We all have definite ideas about this question, based on our own experiences. Certainly Ferris Bueller, of the opening quotation, had his own idea. What is yours?

How can we make students feel comfortable in school? What can we do so they will enjoy their stay?

BUILDING BLOCK 8.1

My Life in School

Did you attend a nursery school or a preschool? Can you recall what you expected when you got to school? What needs did you expect the school to meet? How did these needs and expectations change as you got older? Do you feel that your needs and expectations were met? Write a few descriptive words for each level of school: preschool, early elementary, upper elementary, junior or middle, and high school. Use the template that follows to organize your thinking. Share your answers with others in your class. How are your answers alike? How are they different? What caused the differences?

	Nursery School or Preschool	Early Elementary	Upper Elementary	Junior High or Middle School	High School
What I needed					
What I expected					
How well my needs and expectations were met					

This activity points out that differences in personalities, perspectives, values, teachers, teaching styles, available classes and electives, and many other factors influence students' expectations about their schools and their views of their educational experiences.

Students bring themselves to school, complete with their common needs and unique abilities and perspectives. Similarly, teachers, administrators, and other personnel bring themselves to school, complete with *their* common needs and unique abilities and perspectives. Yet, all these people must function as an educational community, working toward the common purpose of maximizing student learning. Let us look at some of the factors that must exist in a school to achieve that purpose.

Safety in School

We have said the primary purpose of schools is to help students learn. Before students can be motivated to learn, their basic needs must be met. One of these basic needs is the need for safety and security. This need includes not only physical safety but also intellectual safety and emotional safety. Bouchard (1998) writes that for an environment to be safe, it must be free of both physical and verbal threats. It is essential that schools provide for *all* aspects of the safety and security of their students.

Physical Safety

It is obvious that students should be assured of their physical safety at school. Building codes, inspections, and many other measures ensure that schools are safe. Fire drills, tornado drills, hurricane preparedness, and the like become part of students' lives so they can react in an orderly way if a natural disaster occurs. However despite this need for physical safety, some individuals, for whatever reason, wreak havoc in schools by theft, violence, terrorist acts, assault, or other criminal actions. Such actions threaten the safety of students and adults in schools.

Who can forget the tragedies that occurred in schools in Jonesboro, Arkansas; West Paducah, Kentucky; Edinboro, Pennsylvania; Springfield, Oregon; Littleton, Colorado; and

School staff, as well as city and state personnel can help ensure student safety on school premises. Did the schools you attended take extra precautions to ensure your safety?

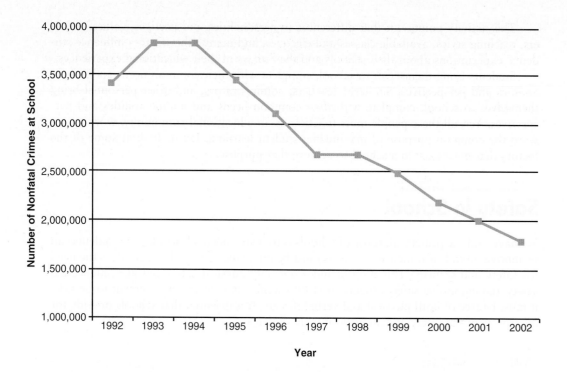

Figure 8.1

Number of nonfatal crimes committed at school against students ages 12–18 between 1992 and 2002.

Red Lake, Minnesota? Students enrolled in these schools caused multiple homicides and extensive injuries to both students and teachers. Between 1993 and 2000, 48 students were killed and 91 students were injured in school shootings (Schneider, Walker, & Sprague, 2000).

Less dramatic criminal acts can seem commonplace in our schools. Although heightened security measures have resulted in a decrease in the number of nonfatal crimes committed at school during the past decade, in 2002 more than 1,750,000 nonfatal crimes, including rapes, sexual assaults, robberies, aggravated assaults, simple assaults, and theft, were committed against students ages 12–18 while those students were in school (Figure 8.1). This represents 5.1% of all public school students in this age group (National Center for Education Statistics, 2004). Nonetheless, the National Education Association (NEA) reports that "*statistically, schools continue to be one of the most secure places for our children* [italics added]" (National Education Association, 2003, p. 1).

Why do you think the level of criminal activity in our schools has declined during the last decade? Look at the graph in Figure 8.1. Do you think school crime will eventually be eradicated? Do you think our schools are "secure places for our children," as the NEA says?

Safe Schools

None of us is a stranger to media reports of school violence. Perhaps you have thought about possible threats to your personal safety as you consider a career in teaching. School officials are responsible for assuring the safety of their students and personnel. This responsibility, of course, includes taking measures not only to thwart heinous attacks such as those we hear about in the news, but also to protect against natural hazards such as fire and severe weather, provide for the security of students' and staff's personal belongings, and ensure safety in the school buses that transport students to and from school.

- What are some of the ways school officials work to ensure the safety of students and personnel?

- How are these efforts different from those taken by your school when you were a student?

Violence in our schools is of great concern. Public response to weapons and terrorism has been swift and strong, and has included two basic approaches.

The first approach is to intensify existing security measures through the use of such procedures as the following:

- Surveillance cameras and video cameras
- Door and key controls
- Locked doors
- Metal detectors
- On-campus police officers
- ID cards
- Communications devices
- Warning codes
- Duress alarms
- Hotlines
- Video cameras on school buses
- Profiling and identifying students who may have a higher than normal risk of committing violent acts and keep track of their activities

The second approach is for schools to employ more counseling, conflict-resolution programs, and increased communication between school and home.

Did the list you compiled in Building Block 8.2 contain these measures? Should it? Many of these measures are controversial and do not fully address less spectacular threats to safety and security.

Safe schools meet the needs, interests, and special requirements of all students.[1] Schneider, Walker, and Sprague (2000) have found that schools with a high degree of long-lasting safety are well led, have a positive climate and atmosphere, ensure that *all* students are included, and are academically effective. The NEA (2003) believes that schools must address the root causes of violence among students through developing and implementing strategies to achieve the following goals:

- Reduce and eliminate bullying and harassment
- Expand access to counseling, anger management, and peer mediation
- Provide ways for students to communicate with adults about rumors and threats
- Develop instruction that teaches such values as respect and responsibility

A direct link to the National School Safety Center is available on the *Building Teachers* companion website.

Are popular methods of reducing school violence, like school police and metal detectors, enough to prevent school violence against students, teachers, and school staff?

© AP/Wide World Photos

As you continue to explore issues of school safety, refer to these NEA recommendations to see how they are being implemented.

Among the deterrents to school violence is the slogan, "It's okay to tell." This slogan has emerged to give students confidence in helping schools prevent violent behavior by reporting real or potential harmful acts. Students often know what is going on in a school before adults do, but they can be reluctant to tell anyone because of their code of silence, their sense of loyalty to their peers, and their fear of repercussions if they tell an adult about suspicious behavior. But, if a student feels that someone at school is acting differently than they normally do, and their behavior is bothering that student, they should know it's okay to tell someone. If they feel unsafe or think someone is thinking about hurting them or someone else, they should know they are not tattling by telling an adult. Addressing the concept "it's okay to tell," the Parkway School District in Chesterfield, Missouri, sent the following statement to parents in 2003:

Teach your child that reporting a threat or previous act of violence is the right thing to do. It may save a life. In all the major school incidents involving violence, someone knew the event was going to happen. In less volatile incidents such as thefts and threats, someone knew who committed the act. Children grow up with an inherent code of silence. And out of loyalty or fear, they are reluctant to tell on another student. Your child must know that reporting real acts or potential acts of malice is the right thing to do, and that it may keep other students from harm.

Many states and school districts have set up special telephone hotlines, which students can call anonymously to report suspicious or dangerous activities. These reports are investigated by the proper authorities and have prevented numerous violent incidents at schools.

Is a student hotline available in your area? What is its telephone number? How does it work? How is anonymity assured? Write down the number and share it, together with the slogan, "It's okay to tell," with school-age students you know.

How Far Should Schools Go?

Many schools have installed metal detectors at entrances and employed armed police to monitor the premises. A great deal of controversy exists over the use of these measures for school safety. What are the good points and the bad points of metal detectors and armed police in schools?

Should school officials and law enforcement officers develop profiles in an attempt to identify students at high risk for committing acts of violence?

What other measures do you think schools should take to ensure the physical safety of their students and personnel?

Intellectual Safety

A second type of safety that schools must provide is intellectual safety. Have you ever spoken up in class with what you thought was a good answer, only to have it dismissed as wrong? Although your answer made perfect sense to you, it was devalued because it was not the response the teacher sought. After several such incidents, you are likely to start believing that your thinking is not good. You find you must respond in a way that pleases the teacher, rather than expressing your own thoughts. Your intellectual safety has been compromised. You no longer feel safe to express your thoughts.

As teachers, we must preserve not only the physical safety of our students, but also their intellectual safety. This means we must seek, respect, and value our students' thinking as much as our own. How do we do this?

Intellectual Safety

1. Look at Figure 8.2 and describe what you see.
2. Select one of the following words, and note the *first* concept that comes to mind when you see it.

    FAN   FLAG   PLANT

3. What are two of your favorite foods?

Compare your answers with others in your class. Are there differences? Why?

Figure 8.2
What image do you see in this drawing?

In Building Block 8.3, you found that different people perceive the same stimulus in different ways. Is one way right, and are the others wrong? Is one way more correct than the others?

People's thoughts depend on their prior experiences. For example, in number 1 of Building Block 8.3, some people see a young lady, whereas others see an old woman. When people look at the word *FAN* in number 2, some think of a hot summer, others think of paint drying, and still others think of ball games or rock stars. What are some thoughts associated with *FLAG?* With *PLANT?* In number 3, you probably found that different people prefer different foods.

Because people's thoughts depend on their prior experiences and different people have different experiences, it is highly likely that students will interpret the same academic situation in different ways. A student may solve a geometry problem in a way the teacher did not expect. Some students may interpret Shakespearean plays differently from others. Some small children may cringe at the thought of having to pet an adorable cocker spaniel puppy. Their responses are different from what we might expect. But are those responses wrong? Or are the responses simply *theirs*?

We believe it is a fundamental principle of excellence in teaching that teachers *listen* to students. By listening to students' responses and discussions, teachers must seek to understand how their students are learning and how they are constructing their conceptualizations. Teachers must create a classroom in which students feel comfortable taking the risk of saying what they are thinking. Teachers who do this ensure students' intellectual safety.

Emotional Safety

A third type of safety is emotional safety. Emotional safety is what we feel when we know our emotions are understood and accepted by others. When others, such as students, teachers, or parents, fail to validate a student's emotions, the student learns to distrust his or her own feelings. Teasing, ignoring, judging, or diminishing another's feelings may cause this invalidation. The ensuing distrust may lead to anxiety, depression, and the repression of individuality, confidence, and creativity.

Ways in Which Emotions Can Be Invalidated

The following list shows different situations in which emotional safety is at risk (Hein, 2003):

- We are told we shouldn't feel the way we feel.
- We are told we are too sensitive, too "dramatic."
- We are led to believe there is something wrong with us for feeling how we feel.
- We are "ordered" to feel differently with phrases such as these:
  - "Lighten up."
  - "Get over it."
  - "Deal with it."
  - "Give it a rest."
  - "Stop whining!"
- Our feelings and emotions are minimized with comments such as these:
  - "It can't be that bad."
  - "Other people have it so much worse than you do."
  - "Time heals all wounds."
  - "Every cloud has a silver lining."
  - "Everything happens for a reason."
  - "You're just going through a phase."
- Our feelings are judged by comments such as these:
  - "You're a crybaby."
  - "You're too sensitive or thin-skinned."
  - "You're overreacting."
  - "You always make a big deal about little things."

Emotions are personal. When someone's feelings are validated and understood by other people, that person feels emotionally safe. As a result, he or she feels safe telling others about feelings of enthusiasm, excitement, fear, elation, worry, anger, devastation, or shame. But when a person fears criticism or ridicule of his or her feelings, that person feels emotionally unsafe.[2] He or she still has feelings but hides them. It is important that people's feelings be validated and that they not be criticized, corrected, or condemned by others for their emotions. Have you ever been bothered when someone told you should not feel the way you do? If so, your emotional safety was being threatened.

Many researchers have found a close correlation between harbored negative feelings and violent acts at school. For example, a study jointly conducted by the National Threat Assessment Center (a division of the U.S. Secret Service) and the U.S. Department of Education reported that in many of the incidents of school shootings investigated between 1974 and 2000, the attackers felt "persecuted, bullied, threatened, attacked or injured" (Vossekuil et al., 2002, p. 20). When students develop negative feelings and negative emotions and cannot express these feelings or obtain validation of them from peers and adults, they are inclined to express their feelings in inappropriate and sometimes dangerous ways.

A direct link to a website that deals with emotionally safe schools is available on the *Building Teachers* companion website.

What threats are there to students' emotional safety in school? What can teachers do to foster emotional security and safety?

Students have the ability to reach their full potential in a safe and structured classroom environment. It is important that families and communities expect and demand a safe classroom and safe school.

Most people equate a safe school and a safe classroom with physical safety. While I agree this is very important, when I say *safe school* and *safe classroom,* I am thinking of an environment where children know they can take academic risks and they will not be embarrassed by peers or an insensitive teacher. Teachers must provide this safe learning environment, where students are prepared and can take risks that let them demonstrate their skills and knowledge successfully.

I began my career as a special education teacher in a middle school. Students would have to leave their classrooms for math remediation. I can still see them coming to my room very upset and with tears in their eyes because their teachers had embarrassed them in front of their classmates by telling them they were not smart. I immediately made up my mind that each and every child placed in my classroom would always have a successful experience.

Charlie came into my life on Valentine's Day. His mother dropped him off at school with nothing. We were having Valentine parties that day and he came with no valentines to share. I hurriedly scrambled and got some construction paper and we cut and pasted valentines throughout the day, with some student helpers helping him finish.

After seeing how Charlie handled that day, I had a special place for him in my heart. I knew he had been disappointed many times in his young life and he really didn't expect anything. How sad it must be to be eight years old and not let yourself get excited about things because you know they will never come true.

I was having difficulty getting Charlie to take risks in his learning. He seldom volunteered an answer, and if he did he would always preface it with the comment, "I know this is wrong . . ." One day I was teaching a science lesson and was preparing to show a video when the remote control wouldn't work. I started to do something else when Charlie spoke up and told me he could fix it. He fiddled with it a minute, and it was working! The class started to clap and cheer and Charlie just beamed. I knew I could use this experience to help with his self-esteem.

The next day before science, I stood up in front of the class and asked the children if they remembered how Charlie had fixed the remote. They cheered again. I told them I had discovered that Charlie had turned the remote into a magical one. I had Charlie's attention! I then made the statement, "A habitat is the environment..." and I pointed the remote at the students and said, "Rewind and replay." The class immediately caught on and repeated the statement. Charlie loved it and we often used "Charlie's Magic Remote" to review for tests and lessons.

Charlie stayed with me for the rest of the year. He came to summer school that year, and I would often see him helping the slower children, repeating words or phrases I had used with him.

Charlie moved on after summer school and I truly missed him the following year. He had felt so comfortable in our school and I imagine he had to start all over again at a new school until he felt secure and safe with his learning. I wish the best for him and hope to see him again.

Teachers must do all they can to make each child's year in their rooms a safe and successful one. All students come that first day of school wanting to learn. I have never seen a year start without that energy and potential. Ineffective and insensitive teachers must be weeded out and removed. They cannot be allowed to affect students adversely.

Gabby was a small girl in my room who came from a complicated family life. Her mother was in prison and the father figure in her home was not of her choosing. She wanted to belong to someone so badly. I tried to provide this continuity and stability in my classroom. She often came in and ran her fingers over my clothes or through my hair, or traced my jewelry. She loved school and often stopped me several times during the day and asked, "Can I have a hug?" We were rehearsing for a play one day, and I noticed Gabby saying all the lines to herself. I called her forward and had her read through several of the parts. She was fantastic! I arranged for her to be in more plays throughout the year. I often used Gabby's acting ability to help the class review for tests. By noticing her talent, using it, and providing Gabby with a safe classroom where she could use her originality, I was able to give her some much needed recognition, and she gained a prominent role in our room.

When a teacher creates that safe learning environment, the rewards for the students and the teacher are immeasurable. In the classroom, I have been thrilled to observe a student reading an entire sentence without one mistake for the first time. The joy expressed on this student's face was indescribable. On one occasion, a student who had been struggling for weeks with multiplication finally looked up from his paper and said, "I get it!" The entire class broke into spontaneous applause. These are exciting moments in my profession, and I have contributed to them by creating that learning environment where students feel comfortable about taking academic risks. I cannot envision a more important task than for a teacher to create an emotionally and intellectually safe classroom.

Linda L. Eisinger
Missouri Teacher of the Year, 2004–2005
West Elementary School
Jefferson City, Missouri

Bullying

There are many sources of negative emotions, but among the more powerful and far-reaching are bullying and harassment.

BUILDING BLOCK 8.4

Bullies and Bullying

Do you remember any bullies at your school? Maybe you were picked on at one time or another, or perhaps you witnessed some students ganging up on another student.

- How would you recognize bullying if you saw it in the hallway or on the playground of a school in which you were teaching?
- What makes a person a bully? What characteristics does a bully have?
- What are some different types of bullying? When does teasing become bullying? Can spreading rumors be bullying?

Bullying is a situation in which one individual or group negatively uses its power over another individual so that the victim feels threatened or unsafe. Typically, bullying occurs repeatedly over a period of time (Olweus, 1996). The National Mental Health Association states that acts of bullying include "name-calling, making faces, obscene gesturing, malicious teasing, threats, rumors, physical hitting, kicking, pushing, and choking," as well as exclusion (National Mental Health Association, 2003, p.1). Boys tend to participate in direct physical bullying (Batsche & Knopff, 1994). In contrast, girls tend to use indirect tactics such as exclusion and gossip (Ahmed & Smith, 1994). Did your responses in Building Block 8.4 include these factors?

Did you think of cyber-bullying? The Internet has become a setting for this practice, also called virtual bullying. Students have created websites devoted to humiliating classmates and have used instant messages and chat rooms to harass individuals. These activities are largely unmonitored by adults and represent a new concern for school officials and parents.

© Yellow Dog Productions/Getty Images

Bullying and harassment can detrimentally affect the victim's social and emotional well-being. What might a teacher do to deter bullying like this against other students?

On any given day, approximately 160,000 children stay home to avoid being bullied at school (Coy, 2001). Brewster and Railsback (2001) reported that 30% of school-aged children say they have been exposed to bullying, either as the victim or as the perpetrator. These same investigators reported that teachers seem to be mostly unaware of the problem or that no serious action is taken. Bullying has led victims to depression, anxiety, delinquency, vandalism, fighting, truancy, and even suicide. Further, it is believed that constant victimization by bullies may contribute to school violence and shootings.

Long ignored by teachers, administrators, parents, and other students, bullying is now being met head on. A great deal of information and many programs are available to combat bullying. Professional organizations such as the NEA have developed antibullying programs and curricula suitable for all grade levels. There also are many seminars that train teachers and administrators to spot, intercede in, and report incidents of bullying. Some schools are implementing measures to increase teacher awareness of bullying and to reduce bullying incidents. For example, an action research project undertaken at W. F. Boardman Elementary School in Oceanside, New York, shows that increased teacher attention to students' needs and emotional well-being helped reduce bullying (Siris & Osterman, 2004). Chelwood Elementary School in Albuquerque, New Mexico, has reduced the incidence of bullying by 50% with a program that encourages everyone to stand up against bullies. Students begin each day with an action pledge (Waters, 2003, p. 145):

We will not bully other students.

We will help others who are being bullied by speaking out and by getting adult help.

We will use extra effort to include all students in activities at our school.

Some states have passed antibullying legislation and encourage students to report bullying on special, confidential phone lines. "It's okay to tell" applies to many kinds of safety threats.

Harassment

Harassment means "to annoy persistently" (Merriam-Webster, 2003). Harassment can take many forms, but sexual harassment is among the most disquieting. Other forms of harassment usually are treated as aspects of bullying.

Sexual harassment is illegal, whether it is student-to-student or adult-to-student, and whether it involves members of opposite sexes or members of the same sex. Sexual harassment is any unwanted or unwelcome behavior of a sexual nature. This includes "sexual insults, comments about a person's body, whistling, catcalls, spreading sexual gossip, exerting pressure for sexual activity or dates, staring or leering with sexual overtones, and pinching or touching buttocks, genitals, or breasts" (DeAndrade, n.d., p. 1). According to the American Association of University Women (2001), 81% of students in school report having experienced some form of sexual harassment during their school lives, with girls more likely to experience sexual harassment (83%) than boys (79%). Sexual harassment may be seen as early as kindergarten. (There is controversy as to whether sexually inappropriate behavior with students at this age can be categorized as sexual harassment, because kindergarten-aged children do not have well defined concepts of sexually appropriate behavior.) Figure 8.3 shows major kinds of sexual harassment and the percentages of boys and girls in grades 8 through 11 who reported they experienced each in the 2001 survey.

Sexual harassment is always wrong, and students should be encouraged to tell an adult if they are victims. Adults and other school officials can take the necessary actions to stop such harassment. School districts are required to have clear policies and procedures that address the sexual harassment of both students and employees, whether the harassment is committed by students or by employees (Walsh, 1999). Schools activate these procedures as needed.

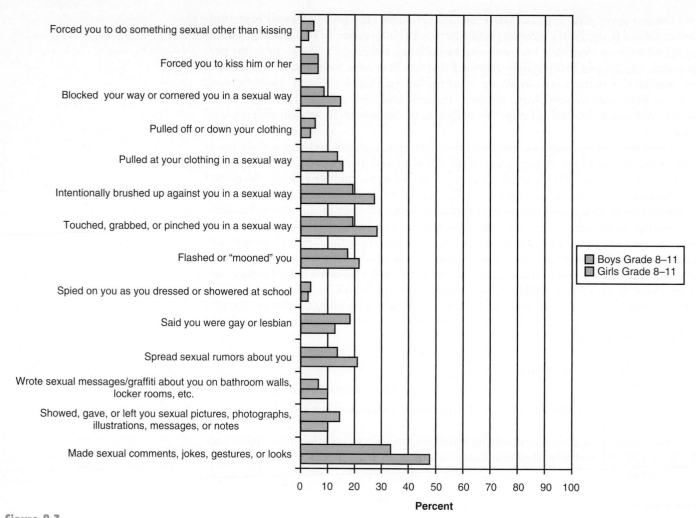

Figure 8.3

Percentages of boys and girls who experienced sexual harassment by type of harassment. (From a survey conducted by The American Association of University Women, 2001.)

School Responses to Safety Issues

Besides the operational procedures you investigated in previous sections of this chapter, schools have responded to issues of physical, intellectual, and emotional safety by implementing zero tolerance policies and character education curricula. These programs can have both positive and negative effects on the school atmosphere.

Zero Tolerance

Zero tolerance efforts across the country entail strict and swift disciplinary response to students or school personnel who engage in violent activities such as fighting, who bring or use weapons such as firearms and other dangerous objects to school, or who bring or use controlled substances such as alcohol, tobacco, or other drugs. Zero tolerance policies apply not only to students, but also to teachers. According to a 2000 report issued by the federal government, in 1996–1997, 79% of all public schools had zero tolerance policies against violence, 94% had policies against firearms, 91% against weapons other than firearms, 87% against alcohol, 88% against drugs, and 89% against tobacco (National Center for Education Statistics, 2002b).

Zero tolerance policies are not without their critics. Although it is hard to imagine a legitimate reasons for a student or adult to bring a firearm or a controlled substance such as alcohol to school, some criticize the policy's strict interpretation. For example, the American Civil Liberties Union (ACLU) provided legal representation for a middle school student in Georgia who was suspended for carrying a key chain depicting the cartoon character Tweety Bird, which school officials believed could be used as a weapon (Gaus, 2000; American Civil Liberties Union, 2000). Consequences of zero tolerance vary with the offense but usually entail some degree of suspension from school, expulsion, or the involvement of law enforcement agencies.

Despite episodes such as the one in Georgia, zero tolerance policies have the very positive effect of keeping weapons and other dangerous items out of the school. As a result, schools are becoming increasingly safe.

Use the Internet to find out whether your local school system has implemented a zero tolerance policy. Go to your state's department of education website to learn whether your state has zero tolerance laws. What are the policies and laws? What are the consequences of violating them?

Character Education

School systems are beginning to implement character education curricula to help students become more accepting of others and handle conflict and anger with more appropriate responses than outbursts, fights, and violence. Such programs may help students treat each other with kindness and control their own emotions better. Character education programs are designed to teach students values such as honesty, responsibility, courtesy, and respect. Such values cut across ethnic, cultural, and religious lines. Often, time is set aside in the school day or school week for classroom teachers to address character education topics. Typical topics include citizenship, trustworthiness, anger control, integrity, and caring. The lessons often include interdisciplinary activities and opportunities to take learning into the community.

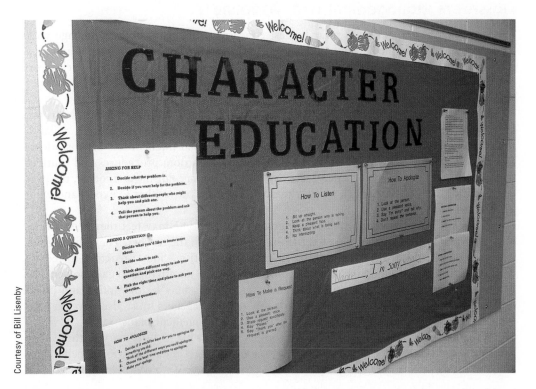

Courtesy of Bill Lisenby

School-based character education programs encourage fair, responsible, honest, and respectful student behaviors toward each other, school personnel, family, and community.

The Teacher's Role

The efforts to ensure student safety in schools discussed so far have primarily been school-level policies and procedures. As a teacher, you also have a big part to play. Of course, your responsibility as a teacher extends beyond addressing student safety. You are also responsible for your students' learning! Let us take a look at what the student can expect from the teacher.

BUILDING
BLOCK
8.5

Helping Students Feel Safe

Think of the following needs for students at the age level you plan to teach:

- Safety and security needs
- Love and belonging needs
- Cognitive needs
- Psychosocial needs

For each, list two or three *specific* actions you could take with regard to instruction and classroom climate that would strengthen your relationship with students and help them help meet these needs. (Compare these actions with the qualities of good teachers you identified in Chapter 1 and the instructional strategies you suggested in Chapters 3 and 4.)

Reduce your list to the four or five most important actions teachers can take to build positive and supportive relationships with students.

From Building Block 8.5, you can see that teachers can do a lot to help their students meet their needs and feel comfortable in school.

Classroom Management and Discipline

As a teacher candidate, one of your biggest concerns probably is how to manage your students' behavior. Implementing a fair and firm classroom management plan is among a teacher's most important activities. Often, students act out because they feel a lack of security that comes from not knowing what is expected of them or where the boundaries are. As a teacher, you can help students by providing structure and routine.

You will develop structures, procedures, and routines as a part of your classroom management plan. These are meant to help the classroom run as a cooperative, collaborative learning community and prevent the misbehavior that might result when students feel unsure of what is expected of them. Well-defined classroom procedures and routines help satisfy students' need for safety, security, and belonging. For most students, the procedures and routines are enough to meet these needs; they know what to expect and what is expected of them.

Other students, however, might have greater needs. Some may feel they need an extraordinary amount of attention, either from peers or from the teacher. They might go to extraordinary—and disruptive—lengths to get this attention. Some, reacting to feeling controlled, might act out against these authority figures in an attempt to gain power. The behavior that results from attempts to satisfy such needs may be disruptive and unacceptable in the classroom environment. For this reason, teachers must also develop consequences as well as rules as part of their classroom management plans.

Students sometimes refer to life in school as "prison-like." Why do you think they feel this way? Might it be because, as in a prison, they feel their behavior is being controlled? Surely rules and regulations are necessary at school. We have them in our general society, and we need them at school. This is partly because of legal considerations (see Chapter 13), and it is partly because schools must keep order. Structure is necessary in the school environment to enable the day and the teaching to run smoothly. Having rules, policies, and procedures is part of life in school and helps students know what is expected of them and where the boundaries are.

The teacher's method of maintaining order in the classroom is known as *behavior management*. Behavior management has two fundamental goals:

1. To permit the teacher to teach
2. To provide each student with the maximum opportunity to learn

Unfortunately, there is no magical plan that will ensure golden behavior from all of your students all of the time. However, you can examine some strategies and methods and observe the behavior management system used in your field experience classroom to gain insights on how to manage behavior effectively.

Discipline in the Classroom

Have you ever been in a class in which there seemed to be no discipline?

- What was it like?
- How did it make you feel as a student about the classroom environment?
- What did you think about the teacher?
- How did this lack of discipline affect your attitude toward the content you were supposed to be learning?

Have you ever been in a class in which the discipline was so strict that nobody dared to do anything the teacher might not like?

- What was it like?
- How did it make you feel as a student about the classroom environment?
- What did you think about the teacher?
- How did such strict discipline affect your attitude toward the content you were supposed to be learning?

There are many ways to manage behavior in the classroom, and these depend on the classroom climate the individual teacher wants to maintain. To gain an idea of the kind of behavior you expect in the classroom, do the activity in Building Block 8.7.

Classroom Behavior Expectations

Different teachers have different ideas and expectations about order in the classroom. To learn your own basic conception, take the inventory that follows. Mark each statement in accordance with the following scale:

4 = True all or almost all the time.

3 = True much of the time.

2 = True less than half the time.

1 = Never or almost never true.

1. _____ Students should be assigned seats in the classroom—often in alphabetical order.

2. _____ Seating assignments in the classroom should be negotiated between students and the teacher.

3. _____ Students should be given opportunities to make choices.

4. _____ Students must follow teacher directions, whether they like it or not.

5. _____ Students should remain quiet in the classroom except when the teacher calls on them to respond to a question.

6. _____ Students should be allowed to talk to each other, providing their discussions deal with the topic under study.

7. _____ "Controlled chaos" is okay in the classroom.

8. _____ The best way to get an unruly class to quiet down is to yell at them.

9. _____ The teacher makes the classroom rules, and students should follow them.

10. _____ If a student falls asleep in class, the teacher could bang a book on the desk to wake up that student.

11. _____ Teachers must not show any weaknesses lest their behavior management systems collapse.

12. _____ During the first week or two of class, teachers should work at negotiating rapport and mutual respect with the students.

13. _____ Teachers should nurture students' own creativity and self-expression as much as possible.

14. _____ It is okay for a teacher to laugh at himself or herself in front of the class.

15. _____ When a student violates rules, the teacher should punish that student appropriately and immediately.

16. _____ When a student violates rules, the teacher should threaten the student with punishment.

17. _____ When a student violates rules, the teacher should ignore this behavior because there really isn't anything the teacher can do about it, anyhow.

18. _____ If a student doesn't turn in homework on time, the teacher should record a zero.

19. _____ The teacher should keep the invitation open for students to do homework, even if it is late.

20. _____ The goal of effective discipline is obedience.

21. _____ The goal of effective discipline is for students to be responsible.

22. _____ Really bad students need to be put in their place.

23. _____ The teacher should ignore the behavior of really bad students; not much can be done about it, anyway.

24. _____ Students need to have the freedom to let off steam and express themselves.

25. _____ Teachers must always treat students with dignity, regardless of students' behavior.

26. _____ Students can usually be expected to ignore class rules.

27. _____ Students don't have a right to get angry in school.

28. _____ There are always a few students whose behavior cannot be controlled by the teacher.

29. _____ The teacher should post crystal-clear limits and behavior expectations on the classroom wall and enforce them.

30. _____ Teachers can expect that students will behave in class; after all, students have been brought up to respect authority, respect peers, and behave properly.

31. _____ Teachers need to keep a tight rein on the students in their classes; bending the rules only encourages further infractions.

32. _____ When a whole class decides to be unruly, there is nothing the teacher can do about the situation.

33. _____ It is okay for students to interrupt the teacher and each other if they have legitimate comments.

34. _____ The teacher is always right.

35. _____ It is good to let students win arguments when they have valid points.

36. _____ Students should never argue with the teacher.

37. _____ The teacher should reprimand students for huffing and puffing, rolling their eyes, and similarly disagreeable behaviors.

38. _____ It is fine to enforce classroom rules some days and ignore them on other days; after all, teachers are human, too.

39. _____ Students should develop the class rules by themselves; after all, it is *their* class.

Scoring: Put the number you placed by each question in the corresponding blank below, and find the total for each group. The results will show you what your current thinking is about behavior management in schools.

Group I	Group II	Group III
1. _____	2. _____	8. _____
4. _____	3. _____	10. _____
5. _____	6. _____	13. _____
9. _____	7. _____	16. _____
11. _____	12. _____	17. _____
18. _____	14. _____	23. _____
20. _____	15. _____	26. _____
22. _____	19. _____	28. _____
27. _____	21. _____	30. _____
31. _____	24. _____	32. _____
34. _____	25. _____	33. _____
36. _____	29. _____	38. _____
37. _____	35. _____	39. _____

Totals: _____   _____   _____

Chart the totals on a bar graph using a template such as the one that follows.

	Group 1	Group 2	Group 3
55			
50			
45			
40			
35			
30			
25			
20			
15			
10			
5			
0			

Group I consists of statements that represent the autocratic teacher. How would you describe an autocratic teacher's management style?

Group II consists of statements that represent the collaborative teacher. How would you describe a collaborative teacher's management style?

Group III consists of statements that represent the permissive teacher. How would you describe a permissive teacher's management style?

- In what group is your highest score?
- In what group is your lowest score?
- Is there any group in which you scored a total of 52 (the highest score possible)?
- Is there any group in which you scored a total of 13 (the lowest score possible)?

(Adapted from Wolfgang & Glickman, 1986)

Figure 8.4

Continuum of classroom behavior management styles.

Autocratic Teacher	Collaborative Teacher	Permissive Teacher

A teacher's expectations about classroom behavior management can be placed on a continuum that ranges from autocratic on the left to permissive on the right (Figure 8.4). The center of the continuum represents a collaboration between student and teacher. Based on the inventory you took in Building Block 8.7, where do you put yourself on the continuum?

The far left represents the classroom of the autocratic teacher. The teacher sets rules and expects students to obey them. No debate, bending, or negotiation is allowed. Students are expected to be quiet except when responding to teacher questions. Nobody moves around unless the teacher grants permission. Students must be in their assigned seats on time and must stay there until the teacher dismisses them.

The far right represents the teacher who is so permissive that students can do anything they want. Students talk when she is trying to teach, disturb other students, move about the room at will, do things totally unrelated to the instruction. The teacher tries tactics such as:

- Discipline-related questions that have no answers, such as "Why are you touching her?", "How many times do I have to tell you …?", or "What am I going to *do* with you?".
- Yelling: "Stop that right now!"
- Cajoling: "Oh, c'mon—I know you can be better than this."
- Begging: "Puhleeze, won't you try to be a little quieter when I'm talking?"
- Bargaining: "If you do your work you can have half an hour to do whatever you want."
- Making threats that cannot be carried out: "Do that one more time and you'll stay after school every day for a year!"

None of the teacher's actions produces any positive results. The students are running the class.

Somewhere in the middle is the teacher who relies on teacher–student collaboration to develop and maintain good order and discipline in the classroom. The teacher respects his or her students and treats them with respect (not permissiveness)—even the worst students. This teacher has a few rules of classroom behavior designed to enable the teacher to teach and the students to learn. Often, this teacher solicits student input for the design of classroom procedures, rules, and consequences. This teacher enforces the rules fairly and consistently; when a student violates a rule, the teacher makes the appropriate correction right away. This teacher is never sarcastic, never makes idle threats, and does not cut students down. This teacher is honest and authentic. This teacher knows what he or she wants, expects it, and gets it. This teacher is a collaborative teacher.

Canter (1985) uses the term *assertive* to describe the teachers who are most successful in managing classroom behavior. He says that assertive teachers take this stand about classroom management:

1. I will not tolerate behavior problems in my class. There is *no* excuse good enough for you to stop me from teaching. I will not tolerate you stopping me from teaching for any reason. You *can* behave and you *will* behave in my classroom.
2. I will not tolerate you stopping someone else from learning. Every student in my class has the opportunity to learn—free from disruptions.
3. No student will engage in behavior that is not for the good of themselves and each other. You will not threaten, bully, or attack other students.

How well does this description fit with the description of an autocratic teacher's management style you made in Building Block 8.7?

How well does this description fit with the description of a permissive teacher's management style you made in Building Block 8.7?

How well does this description fit with the description of a collaborative teacher's management style you made in Building Block 8.7?

Where would you locate Canter's assertive teacher classroom management style on the continuum of classroom behavior expectations?

You must set your own discipline program to suit yourself and the students in your class. However, your discipline plan must be congruent with the school's discipline code. Any discipline plan you set must include the overarching schoolwide rules. For example, suppose you don't care whether students chew gum in class, but the school discipline plan says that students are not allowed to chew gum in school. Your personal plan must include a "no gum chewing" clause.

No single classroom management formula works for everyone. However, the most successful teachers are those who are collaborative, assertive, respectful, and consistent, and who have high expectations and low fear that students will behave appropriately in their classrooms.

As you prepare to enter the classroom, be sure to study Canter's propositions and internalize their full implications. Work to eliminate any worries you might have that children will not behave in your class. If you have any lurking reservations, work at getting rid of them now. The self-fulfilling prophecy—the concept that people act out their predetermined ideas about themselves—is in full force when it comes to behavior management (see Chapter 3).

You probably found from the inventory in Building Block 8.7 that your classroom management beliefs reflect each of the positions on the continuum. However, you probably also found that your beliefs cluster around one of these positions. We do not like to assert that only one approach to behavior management is right and the others are wrong. There are times when you will want to invoke systems other than your preferred system. For example, you might prefer to be collaborative in your overall approach, but sometimes you will have to be autocratic and at other times you will want to be more permissive. Use the classroom management system that works best for you. The only criteria are that you can teach and your students can learn—free of disruptions.

Finally, let us mention the practice of sending misbehaving students to the principal. As you know, one of the school administration's duties is to deal with students who exhibit unacceptable behavior. But the vast majority of discipline problems can and should be handled by the teacher in the classroom. Reserve requesting the principal's intervention for only the most serious cases—cases that are potentially harmful to the student, to other students, or to you. You want to become known in your school as a teacher who can handle his or her own discipline. Then, if you send a student to the office, the principal will know that the student presents a serious problem.

Involving the principal in discipline problems should be reserved for serious behavioral issues, like those in which the teacher or other students are in danger.

Behavior Situations

How might the collaborative teacher handle the following behavior situations?

- A student talks out of turn.
- A student whispers to her neighbor while you are talking.
- A student gets out of his chair and starts to wander around the room.
- A student lays her head on her desk during your class and apparently falls asleep.
- A student repeatedly does not turn in her homework.
- A kindergarten student throws a tantrum on the floor.

A direct link to a website that deals with classroom management, behavior management, and discipline in the classroom is available on the *Building Teachers* companion website.

---

from the
TEACHER   Christie Daniels

Courtesy of Christie Daniels

Becoming a Classroom Manager

From the first day that I stepped into a public school classroom, the concept of classroom management has been drilled into my head as the single most important factor in determining a teacher's success in the classroom. After nine years of teaching the most challenging students available, I have learned that classroom management is not about discipline. It's not about organization. It isn't a methodology. Effective classroom management is, purely and simply, the process of creating an environment in which students want to learn. A teacher's classroom management skills are directly proportional to the extent to which they are willing to go to great lengths to capture and maintain their students' attention.

While serving as a mentor to a first-year teacher, I was asked the question, "Dr. Daniels, do you ever wonder if you are *really* making a difference with these kids?" I laughed as I remembered the many times that I drove home thinking and asking out loud, "Why did I even get out of bed today?" I no longer ask that question. When those nagging doubts arise, I simply close my eyes for a moment and think about Michael. Michael is a former student who helped me realize that I had finally become an effective classroom manager.

I will always remember the date—Friday, October 17, 2003. I was a behavior modification teacher at the Picayune, Mississippi Center for Alternative Education. My students had all been referred to my class as a result of having exhibited severe behavior problems in their regular classrooms. Many of my students had experienced very little, if any, success at their "home" schools.

On this particular day, Michael, one of my fifth-grade students, did not show up for school at the expected time.

This was unusual because he was the only student in my class who had not missed a single day of school. I walked into the principal's office and asked whether his mom had called to let us know he was going to be absent. My principal told me that there had been an accident. I immediately panicked, but she assured me that Michael was unharmed. She explained that Michael's bus had had a minor accident on the way to pick him up, and that by the time the bus reached his stop, he was not there. We both assumed that his mother had probably gone to work and that he had, most likely, simply decided to stay at home for the day.

At about 9:45 a.m., as my students were getting ready to take a class picture, Michael walked in soaking wet and out of breath. I looked at him incredulously and asked him if it was raining outside. He looked at me and said, "No, I walked." Michael had walked approximately six miles from his home to our school. I asked him "Why?" and he smiled and said, "I just couldn't miss one single day of your class." My principal and I cried together that day, our hearts swelled with pride for the progress Michael had made and by his newfound commitment to learning. Yes, October 17, 2003, was an important day for me. It began a new era for me—one in which I no longer question my commitment to teaching.

Christina Ross Daniels
2005 Mississippi Teacher of the Year
Picayune Center for Alternative Education
Picayune, Mississippi

Curriculum, Instruction, and Assessment

Probably the best way to keep students' attention and reduce or eliminate discipline problems is to have interesting and meaningful lessons that engage students. Under these conditions, students don't have time to misbehave, and they don't want to because they are so wrapped up in learning. There is no substitute for a good lesson.

In school, students expect to obtain knowledge and skills that are meaningful and interesting. What they learn should help them achieve and succeed—not only as they progress in their education, but also in their chosen career and in life. They expect to be taught in ways that are effective and engaging so that they may achieve learning objectives. And they expect to be given the opportunity to demonstrate their learning in authentic ways.

Education can be viewed as a three-legged chair (Tyler, 1949). These legs are

1. curriculum
2. instruction
3. assessment

In the sections that follow, let us consider how to make the curriculum, instruction, and assessment meaningful, interesting, and engaging.

Curriculum

The curriculum is the material taught in a school. Often it consists of a prescribed set of courses, with a scope and sequence for each. The scope of a course is the breadth and depth of the concepts covered, and the sequence is the order in which these concepts are introduced. The curriculum is usually prescribed by the state; individual school districts and schools normally interpret state-prescribed curricula.

BUILDING BLOCK 8.9

Meaningful Curriculum

John Dewey said, "Since there is no single set of abilities running throughout human nature, there is no single curriculum which all should undergo. Rather, the schools should teach everything that anyone is interested in learning."

- What does Dewey's statement imply about deciding what students should learn?
- How do you think curricular decisions are made?
- What do you remember learning in school? At the time, were you interested in learning these concepts and skills, as Dewey proposes?
- Consider the grade level and subject you plan to teach; what do you think most students are interested in learning? Do you think that what they are interested in learning is the same as what your state's curriculum prescribes that you teach them?
- How could you motivate students to learn about topics that do not really interest them?

You probably felt that some of the curriculum of the schools you attended was interesting, meaningful, and relevant, but some seemed meaningless, irrelevant to your life, and maybe even boring. It might have seemed that schools do not care whether the curriculum suits their students—but this is not true. After all, a school establishes goals, purposes, and a mission to ensure it provides its students with the best possible education within its set of educational beliefs.

In Chapter 14, you will investigate current trends and issues in curriculum, understanding that much work and input goes into developing curriculum. However, is the curriculum sufficiently flexible to respond to the needs of individual students? As you have seen, each student has a unique set of experiences and needs. The best teachers are those who meet students' needs by engaging them in meaningful and stimulating studies. We leave this question for you to ponder. You will spend time and energy in your teacher preparation program investigating curriculum. We hope you will focus on ways to ensure that the curriculum is interesting, relevant, and meaningful.

Instruction

The second leg of the educational three-legged chair is instruction. We have said it is up to the teacher to make the prescribed curriculum interesting, relevant, and meaningful. Is this possible? Is it possible to present a topic described by the curriculum that students may not like in a way that makes it interesting and excites students about studying it?

BUILDING BLOCK 8.10

Most Memorable Lessons

Think back to your school days. Which lessons in your precollege school years were the most memorable? Why? How did the teacher teach?

We have asked countless college students in teacher preparation programs the questions in Building Block 8.10 , and we always hear the same response. The lessons students remember are those in which they *did* something. They dissected a frog, wrote a song, acted in a play, went on a field trip, collected leaves, looked at the stars through a telescope, painted a mural, made a video, built a website, and so on. Student involvement is key to long-lasting memories. Let us look at an example of teaching to see the impact of student involvement on learning.

BUILDING BLOCK 8.11

Hands-on Teaching

A middle-grades science teacher taught a lesson on weathering and erosion. The objective was for students to discover what happens to mountains as a result of rain water and rivers. She divided the class into groups of four or five students, gave each group a set of materials, and asked them to build a mountain in the plastic bin she provided using sand, sticks to represent trees, and pebbles to represent rocks. Using small sprinkling cans with holes of various sizes, the students poured water on the sand mountain to see what would happen. They did this activity several times, using a different approach each time.

- What was the teacher's role in this lesson?
- What was the students' role?
- How was this lesson made interesting to the students? Meaningful? Relevant?
- Do you think the students found themselves engaged?

The activity you envisioned in Building Block 8.11 can be called a *hands-on* activity. The teacher selected the topic to be studied and encouraged students to branch out on their own to explore the topic in ways that were meaningful and relevant to them. Depending on students' age and degree of independence, they may receive different levels of guidance and support from the teacher. For example, students who can be thought of as independent learners (and who are in a well managed classroom) may receive directions on how to set up the equipment and be told only to explore and observe. Other students who need more support may receive step-by-step instructions, with the teacher pausing and asking questions at appropriate times. The point is that the teacher considers students' individual needs and designs instruction to meet those needs. Instruction that is tailored to the different needs of individual students is often called **differentiated instruction.** Lessons such as this are not only "hands on" but also "minds on."

We hope you will prepare and implement lessons that students find meaningful, interesting, and engaging and that you encourage students' greatest possible involvement.

What are some advantages of hands-on teaching? What are some disadvantages?

BUILDING
BLOCK
8.12

Teaching for Student Involvement

Look at the following teaching situations. For each, describe what you could do to foster the greatest student involvement.

1. Students learn the fire drill procedure.
2. Students solve a geometry proof.
3. Students determine whether a heavy ball falls faster than a light ball.
4. Students cite the basic reasons for the Civil War.
5. Students interpret a passage from *Romeo and Juliet*.
6. Students learn multiplication tables.
7. Students determine how much area a wolf pack needs for its territory.
8. Students learn the parts of speech.
9. Students identify the parts of a short story.
10. Students explain the advantages and disadvantages of various social structures such as democracy, communism, and socialism.

Assessment

Assessment is the third leg of the educational three-legged chair. Through assessment, students can demonstrate their understanding. Let us look at the assessment that goes on in the classroom.

BUILDING
BLOCK
8.13

Testing, Testing

- Name as many different kinds of tests as you can.
- Which of these are tests that are taken with paper and pencil?
- What methods *other* than a paper-and-pencil test could let students demonstrate their knowledge?
- What could students do to show they had learned the following skills and concepts?
  - How to add
  - The parts of a flower
  - The plot of an American novel
  - The main theme of Beethoven's Fifth Symphony
  - The difference between the dependent clause and the independent clause in English
  - Conversational facility in French
- Which of these assessments absolutely must be conducted with paper and pencil?
- Which of these assessment measures give students the opportunity to demonstrate fully what they have learned?

In previous chapters' Technology Boxes, you have investigated how teachers integrate technology into their instruction. In this chapter, you have focused on the student's experience in school. As a student, you probably had the opportunity to use technology to learn. When teachers use computers to help present information, it is called computer-enhanced instruction (CEI) or computer-assisted (or computer-aided) instruction (CAI). However, students may participate in CAI independently, using the computer along with other materials. CAI is also sometimes called computer-based instruction (CBI). What do you suppose a distinction between CAI and CBI might be?

Consider also that there is computer-managed or -mediated instruction (CMI) or learning (CML). There are also computer-based learning (CBL), computer-based laboratories, and computer-based testing (CBT). Don't let all the acronyms confuse you. You will learn more throughout your teacher education program. For now, simply know that students use technology in various ways to learn.

Students using technology receive content information in different formats. Basically, students can use the Internet and software to learn content in the form of tutorials, drill-and-practice exercises, games, simulations, problem-solving exercises, or demonstrations (Teaching and Learning with Technology, 2004).

Tutorials generally introduce new material to students. Typically, this material is covered in some order. For example, you follow certain steps to solve a long division problem. Tutorial software shows the student these steps sequentially, guiding him or her through the process. (An excellent tutorial would also help a student understand *why* the steps that you take to solve a long division problem actually work, thereby providing the student with the opportunity to understand the *concept* as well as the *process*.)

Once a student understands the process of solving a long division problem, a drill-and-practice program can test the student's knowledge and skills. As the name indicates, drill-and-practice programs drill the student by providing many opportunities for practice.

The drill-and-practice program might take the guise of a game, using colors, animation, and sound to present the practice problems. Many software packages provide students with a game-like environment within which to practice their skills.

Remember that technology also can be used ineffectively. For example, students may be able to solve the practice problems presented in the drill-and-practice game without truly understanding why the process works. How meaningful is that knowledge? Has the student been given the opportunity to construct any knowledge if he or she is merely taught a series of steps to repeat?

Using a simulation may offer the student opportunities to learn at deeper levels. Simulations provide real-world contexts and often incorporate problem-solving skills. For example, suppose that a simulation program puts the student in the role of commander of space mission that has crash-landed on a desolate planet and awaits rescue. A known stock of supplies is available to the crew, but these supplies must be rationed. How will the commander distribute supplies over time if he or she knows that rescue will arrive no sooner than 30 days? What if some of the crew has special needs? What if the crew must move from the crash site and carry the supplies? How will the weight be distributed? This simulation contains opportunities for students to use their skills in division as they solve the problems that may arise. In fact, given the information, students can probably figure out the process of division without having to be told. Notice that this type of content delivery allows students to use higher-order thinking skills. Simulations are often used to demonstrate or present learning experiences when the experience itself might be too dangerous, expensive, or time consuming.

Software packages that present content information as computer-based instruction (CBI) can also give students the opportunity to demonstrate their knowledge and skills. Some programs even keep track of student input so that the students and teacher can retrieve it for assessment purposes. Many textbooks come with accompanying materials for creating tests from the book chapters—the chapter tests that students take in school may have been constructed using these electronic test banks.

We have been discussing commercially available software and websites that students may use to access content. By the time you graduate from your teacher education program, you will be well versed in instructional technology (if you are not already). You can create electronic slide shows that are tutorials or drill-and-practice programs. You can construct WebQuests that guide students in searching the Internet for information to solve problems and construct new knowledge. Almost unlimited resources await you. Keep in mind that you are not limited to what you can find in educational software catalogs or on the Internet. Once again, using your professional knowledge and skills, you can tailor your instructional materials to the needs of your students.

Have you ever faced a situation in school where you knew the material but were not given the opportunity to demonstrate your understanding? For example, you may have had an American history class that dealt with causes of the Great Depression; you thoroughly understood this topic, but you were required to demonstrate your understanding through a multiple choice test. Although you had studied the material thoroughly, it may have seemed that you had never seen the information addressed in some of the test questions. Students can sometimes walk away from a test feeling that they never had the opportunity to express what they know. How would you have felt if you had been given an opportunity to demonstrate your understanding in other ways, such as creating a picture portfolio or constructing a website or a concept map?

Although you may teach interesting, relevant, and engaging lessons, you still must provide valid ways for students to demonstrate how well they have grasped the material. Students can demonstrate their learning in various ways, such as answering questions; contributing to class discussions; and completing homework, quizzes, and tests. They can also demonstrate their learning in other ways, such as those you explored in Building Block 8.13. Methods of assessment that give students the opportunity to demonstrate their understanding fully are called alternative or **authentic assessment** methods.

What would be an authentic assessment method for people to demonstrate their ability to swim? Play basketball? Play a clarinet?

Which of the methods of assessment you listed in Building Block 8.13 could be considered authentic assessments?

Sometimes it is not the type of test that causes students trouble, but the act of taking the test itself. Test anxiety is an emotional reaction that torments some students. The emotions a student brings to a testing situation can be so overwhelming that they affect the student's ability to remember what he or she learned in preparation for the test. Perhaps you, yourself, experience or have experienced test anxiety. The American School Counselor Association (2005) suggests the following strategies to help students curb test anxiety:

- Breathe easily and try to calm down.
- Do not attend to the "what if" questions that might start running through your mind. Try to think positive thoughts.
- Be prepared. Do not cram for the test the night before; instead, spend a bit of time on several consecutive days in advance covering information and testing yourself. Collect all the materials you will need to take the test—paper, pencils, calculators, etc.—the night before and get them ready to go on test day.
- Get enough sleep the night before the test—at least 8 to 10 hours.
- Eat a good breakfast on test day.

Curriculum, instruction, and assessment are the three main parts of students' school experience. These three facets must be compatible with and complement each other. With skillful development and implementation, you can use these tools to make each student's educational experience interesting, meaningful, relevant, and engaging—thereby enabling all students to maximize their achievement.

Conclusion

A school is a complex system designed to foster maximum student learning. To learn, students must become an integral part of that system. They must have their basic needs met by the school and have the freedom to express their individuality within conventional boundaries; at the same time, students must conform to safety and behavior standards set by the school and its teachers.

Safety considerations include physical safety, intellectual safety, and emotional safety. The school, with the help of its students and outside agencies, can provide reasonable assurance of students' physical safety. Some measures, such as the presence of uniformed police and profiling, are controversial. The slogan, "It's okay to tell" urges students to play a role in assuring their own safety. Intellectual and emotional safety arise from positive interpersonal interactions between student and teacher. Emotional safety is fostered through positive teacher–student interactions and through the reduction or elimination of bullying and harassment. All of these strategies require student actions to work.

Effective classroom management happens when teacher and students treat each other with dignity and respect, and when the teacher implements carefully devised personal behavior management plans.

Students' educational experience falls into three main categories: curriculum, instruction, and assessment. Competent and successful teachers ensure that these aspects of education are meaningful, relevant, interesting, and engaging to all students.

When the school personnel–student system provides for students' safety and security, cognitive, and psychosocial needs; insists on behavior that allows the teacher to teach and students to learn; and undertakes academic challenges that engage all students—then students can aspire to their highest levels of achievement.

Key Terms and Concepts

Authentic assessment, 219
Differentiated instruction, 217

Construct and Apply

1. Address Erikson's stages of psychosocial development as they relate to students' needs for individuality and acceptance. How can the school not only accept but also protect students' expressions of individuality? How can you, as the teacher, foster this healthy development?
2. Imagine you are assigned to a debate team focused on one of the issues discussed in this chapter. Choose a pro or con position and write a paragraph supporting your choice. Suggestions include the following:

   a. Metal detectors, searches, campus police

   b. Zero tolerance policies

   c. Character education

3. Explain how too much discipline in the classroom can be as ineffective as too little in creating an environment conducive to learning.
4. A common adage given to new teachers regarding classroom behavior management is, "Don't smile before Christmas!" Is this good advice? Why or why not?
5. You are currently a student in college. What is your favorite way to be taught? Think carefully. Is the method you cited your favorite because you learn the material best that way? Or is it because it helps you perform well on traditional tests? Or is it both? Explain.
6. What responsibilities does the school have to the student? What responsibilities does the student have to the school?

Deconstructing the Standards

INTASC Principle #1 says:

> The teacher understands the central concepts, tools of inquiry, and structures of the discipline(s) he or she teaches and can create learning experiences that make these aspects of subject matter meaningful for students.

INTASC Principle #8 says:

> The teacher understands and uses formal and informal assessment strategies to evaluate and ensure the continuous intellectual, social, and physical development of the learner.

- What part(s) of these principles does this chapter address?
- How does this chapter address these principles?
- How will the concepts in this chapter help you apply these principles as a teacher?

Field Experience

1. How does your field experience school address safety issues?
2. Have you seen evidence of bullying behavior at your field experience school? What has that school done to address bullying?
3. What are the schoolwide rules and regulations for students in your field experience school? What are the rules for your field experience classroom? How do the rules for your classroom compare with the school's overall rules?
4. What techniques does your field experience teacher use for effective behavior management?
5. Does your field experience teacher implement lessons that engage students? How?

Your Portfolio

1. Include a copy of the information students and parents are given regarding school policies and rules and a copy of the classroom rules where you are doing your field experience. Write your reflections on these rules' necessity for the safety of the students and school personnel. Relate your reflection to meeting students' needs for safety and belonging.
2. Include resources from your community that help students build character, such as Boys' Clubs, Girls' Clubs, YMCA or YWCA, Boy Scouts, Girl Scouts, volunteer programs, and the like. Include a list of these resources in your portfolio.
3. Begin to design your own classroom management plan, including room arrangement, routines and procedures, and classroom rules. Include your plan in your portfolio to show that you are aware of what an effectively managed learning environment might be.
4. Start a list of curriculum, instruction, and assessment ideas that make student learning interesting, relevant, meaningful, and engaging.

Building Teachers Technology Resources

 Check out the *Building Teachers* companion website, www.education.wadsworth.com/martinloomis1, for more information and resources about student safety and classroom management, including access to the following websites:

- Emotional Intelligence (EQ) Informational Site
- National School Safety Center
- Center for Prevention of School Violence

 Check out the *Building Teachers* CD-ROM that accompanies your textbook for additional resources.

 Also link to InfoTrac College Edition via the *Building Teachers* companion website. Use InfoTrac College Edition to search for journal articles to enhance your study.

Notes

1. For a complete treatment of the subject of school safety from a combined education and law-enforcement perspective, see Schneider, Walker, and Sprague, 2000.
2. For a detailed description of emotional safety and emotionally safe schools, see *Creating Emotionally Safe Schools* (Bluestein, 2001).

CHAPTER 9

The School and the Teacher

Concerning a teacher's influence: I have come to the frightening conclusion that I am the decisive element in the classroom. It's my personal approach that creates the climate. It's my daily mood that creates the weather.

As a teacher, I possess tremendous power to make a child's life miserable or joyous. I can be a tool of torture or an instrument of inspiration. I can humiliate, hurt, or heal. In all situations it is my response that decides whether a crisis will be escalated or de-escalated, and a child humanized or dehumanized.

HAIM GINOTT

In Chapter 8, you investigated the role of the student in the complex relationship among school, teacher, and student. You saw that students can expect to receive much from the school, including fulfillment of basic needs and the opportunity to learn. You also saw that students are expected to give to the school in such areas as helping to ensure safety, adhering to school rules and regulations, and respecting the classroom management systems of individual teachers. The school has responsibilities to the students, and the students have responsibilities to the school.

Similarly, the school has responsibilities to the teacher and the teacher has responsibilities to the school.

In this chapter, you will investigate the relationship between the school and the teacher, including the teacher's actions, the teacher's responsibilities to the school, and the school's responsibilities to the teacher. You will find that the teacher's primary responsibilities are instructional. You have already investigated the teacher's instructional responsibilities in this textbook, but teachers also have other responsibilities, some of which you also have previously identified. What is the importance of a teacher's responsibilities suggested by Ginott in the quotation that begins this chapter?

In this chapter, you will focus on two basic questions:

1. What does the school expect of the teacher?
2. What does the teacher expect of the school?

As a result of your work in this chapter, you will:

1. Describe teachers' instructional and noninstructional duties.
2. Detail your institution's requirements for your teacher preparation program and your state's requirements for the teacher certification you are planning to seek.
3. Describe opportunities for teachers' professional development.
4. Explain the professional behavior expected of teachers.
5. Describe teacher salary administration and the nature of tenure.
6. Describe the resources and support teachers can expect in their working environment.

The School's Expectations of the Teacher

Let us first look at the professional life of a teacher. What tasks are teachers expected to do? Certainly, they teach their classes. But what else do they do?

BUILDING
BLOCK
9.1

A Teacher's Life in School

Think back to your earliest years in school—as far back as preschool or nursery school if possible. What do you remember your teacher doing? Think of what a teacher does during the school day and throughout the school year. Which of these activities were routine? Which occurred periodically or only from time to time? Which occurred only once or twice? Similarly, recall what your teachers did in the lower elementary grades, upper elementary grades, middle school or junior high school, and high school. Use the table that follows to list some activities.

	Nursery School or Preschool	Lower Elementary	Upper Elementary	Junior High or Middle School	High School
Routine activities					
Periodic activities					
Rare activities					

What trends did you notice in the general thrust of teachers' activities as you progressed through the grades? Does it seem that teachers of young children spend a lot of time dealing with children's personal needs, whereas teachers of older students focus more on the subject matter?

Teachers' Tasks

You have tried to recall the activities of the teachers you had in school, and you have been observing the activities of your cooperating teacher in your field experience. Now, try to get more specific about what is expected of teachers from day to day.

Make a list of the tasks and activities that a teacher in the grade level that you are interested in teaching might do during a typical 24-hour day. Categorize each task as either instructional or noninstructional in nature.

Then, estimate the approximate percentage of a teacher's time in school that is spent on **instructional duties** and the approximate percentage spent on **noninstructional duties**. Does the amount of time teachers spend on noninstructional tasks seem reasonable?

In Building Block 9.2, you may have encountered some difficulties in separating instructional from noninstructional activities, because many of these activities are interdependent. For example, parent conferencing, often considered a noninstructional task, and assessing student work, an instructional task, support each other. Being the advisor or coach of a club, team, or some other extracurricular activity is a noninstructional task when compared to the daily teaching load, but it can be an instructional task when considered as a part of overall student learning.

The specific duties of teachers are established by states, school districts, and schools. Use the Internet to find the duties of teachers in your location. You may have to look for a statewide teacher assessment instrument and infer the duties from rubrics used to assess teacher performance.

Does your finding accurately reflect what, in your experience, teachers do?

Instructional Duties

First and foremost, schools expect teachers to teach. Depending on the grade level, teachers can be responsible for teaching all the academic subjects, or just one or two. They can teach an average of 23 students in the public elementary schools, or they can teach an average of 150 students per day in public secondary schools (National Center for Education Statistics, 2001).

The actual act of teaching takes up most of the teacher's day. But many tasks lead up to and follow teaching. Perhaps you thought of some of these tasks in the Building Blocks

Courtesy of Bill Lisenby

Teaching not only involves instruction time, but also time spent planning instruction and evaluating student learning. These co-teachers are planning instruction for their elementary class.

you completed earlier. Teachers must organize and sequence objectives and lessons for the day, the week, the grading period, and the school year. They must design assessments appropriate for the instruction. Few nonteachers realize the time that goes into planning and evaluating.

Did your list of teacher duties include work done at home? Teachers do a great deal of the planning, preparation, and evaluation work needed for successful teaching during evenings, weekends, and holidays. They bring work home because the school day is so filled with tasks related to students that there is not enough time to finish planning and grading as well. Elementary school teachers are particularly challenged because they normally do not have built-in planning time—they have the occasional period of free time when their students go to art, music, physical education, and other special classes, but even then they are responsible for walking their students to the special classroom. Teachers in middle school and high school typically have one or two periods built into their schedules for use in planning, grading, and report writing. But, due to meetings, parent conferences, paperwork, and other tasks that require their attention, often they are not able to use their planning time for its intended purpose: planning and grading.

The need to bring work home is especially acute for new teachers while they are developing and refining efficient routines. As you gain experience, you will find efficient ways to accomplish the teacher's tasks so you can provide rewarding educational experiences for your students while preserving your personal time. But probably you never will be able to do everything during school hours. There will always be work to do when students are not around, and this will have to be done after school or at home.

Noninstructional Duties

Besides teaching, schools expect teachers to perform noninstructional duties. Noninstructional duties are those duties not directly associated with the instruction and supervision of students. You listed several examples above. Noninstructional responsibilities assigned to teachers differ markedly between states in which teacher unions are strong and states with little or no union influence. Teacher unions work to keep teachers' noninstructional supervisory duties to a minimum. Union states insist that teacher contracts define precisely which duties are assigned to teachers and require school districts to provide extra pay for duties not stipulated in the general contracts. This can be both a benefit and a hindrance. For example, in Pennsylvania, a teacher wanted to start an after-school garden club on her own time and without remuneration. She reasoned that students could profit from the motivation, satisfaction, and intellectual stimulation they would get from participating in the garden club. But the local union had established a policy of "no extra pay, no extra work," and she was forced to abandon her idea.

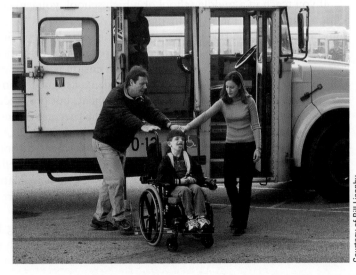

Bus duty is a noninstructional teacher responsibility. If bus duty were not required of teachers, how would students with physical disabilities manage getting from the school bus to the classroom every morning?

Courtesy of Bill Lisenby

In some schools, the less desirable noninstructional duties may fall to new teachers. In some states, however, unions and teacher associations have written policies stipulating that the majority of these duties should *not* be assigned to new teachers because these teachers need all the time they can get for planning, discussions with experienced teachers, and professional development. For example, the North Carolina Association of Educators (2003) has stated that assigned noninstructional duties are considered part of employees' responsibilities but should be minimized, especially for beginning teachers who need opportunities to develop and to interact with experienced teachers who can mentor them.

BUILDING BLOCK 9.3

Union? Or Nonunion?

Is your state a union state or a nonunion state? What are the guidelines and requirements for noninstructional supervisory duties? What are the rules or procedures for compensation for noninstructional duties?

> What other noninstructional duties have you seen teachers perform that you can add to this list?

Some noninstructional duties typically assigned to teachers in the elementary and secondary schools are shown in Table 9.1.

Many people feel that noninstructional supervisory duties, although necessary to ensure safety and order, could be performed by lower-paid, nonteaching personnel. Some schools are moving in this direction by requiring paraprofessionals to take on many of these tasks; using other nonprofessional personnel, such as bus drivers, in monitoring capacities; and hiring personnel specifically for these tasks.

In addition to noninstructional supervisory duties, teachers normally are asked to perform many other noninstructional functions. Parent conferences are among these duties. How did you classify parent conferences—as an instructional or a noninstructional activity? There are good reasons for either classification. Parent and family conferences are common in elementary school and middle school and occur frequently in high school. They are an occasion for the exchange of information between family and teacher about the student. The parent conference is viewed as a necessary supplement to the report card. Preparing for and holding conferences with all the parents of students in a class takes a great deal of time. But the value of these conferences is so high that teachers allow for conferences and the effort needed to prepare and conduct them. Strictly speaking, the parent conference is a noninstructional duty. But the courts have consistently held that parent conferences are part of normal school operations and it is reasonable to expect teachers to hold them (*Fox v. Board of Education*, 1977).

If you teach in a middle school or a high school, you can count on being assigned detention duty. Detention is normally assigned to students by school administrators as a punishment for some rule infraction. In some schools, detention is an after-school affair of silence; in others, the time is used to help students with their homework and to provide extra tutoring assistance. In-school suspension is a form of detention that occurs in a designated room during school hours. Students assigned to in-school suspension are removed from their regular classes as a punishment, but they receive assistance as required to complete their assigned work during the time they are on in-school suspension.[1] Some schools assign full-time teaching professionals to this duty; others require that teachers give up some of their planning time to staff the designated room.

Participating in professional development or continuing education, being a reflective practitioner, and implementing the rules, policies, and regulations of the school system and state department of education may also be considered part of a teacher's noninstructional duties.

Reconsider the list of activities you generated in Building Block 9.2. Would you recategorize any of the activities as instructional (associated with planning, instruction, and evaluation) or noninstructional (not directly associated with instruction of students)?

TABLE 9.1 Noninstructional Duties Typically Assigned to Teachers

	Elementary Schools	Middle Schools	Secondary Schools
Outside of the classroom	Monitoring car riders during morning drop-off and afternoon pick-up Bus duty Lunchroom duty Club sponsor Science fair judge In-school suspension duty Chaperone at school functions Volunteer at school fairs, concession booths, etc. Serving on committees	Monitoring car riders during morning drop-off and afternoon pick-up Bus duty Lunchroom duty Club sponsor Yearbook, school newspaper sponsor Science fair judge Detention duty In-school suspension duty Chaperone at school functions Volunteer at school fairs, concession booths, etc. Emergency coverage for another teacher during planning periods Serving on committees	Monitoring car riders during morning drop-off and afternoon pick-up Monitoring student parking lot Bus duty Lunchroom duty Club sponsor Yearbook, school newspaper sponsor Freshman, sophomore, junior, or senior class sponsor Science fair judge Detention duty In-school suspension duty Chaperone at school functions Volunteer at school fairs, concession booths, etc. Emergency class coverage for another teacher during planning periods Serving on committees
In the classroom	Taking attendance Managing money for lunch, field trips, etc. Managing paperwork, such as permission slips, student records, etc. Accompanying students as they move from class to gym, other classes, lunch, etc. Parent conferences	Taking attendance Managing money for field trips, yearbooks, etc. Managing paperwork, such as permission slips, student records, etc. Accompanying students as they move from class to gym, other classes, and lunch Parent conferences Advising	Taking attendance Managing money for field trips, yearbooks, etc. Managing paperwork, such as permission slips, student records, etc. Parent conferences Advising

Extracurricular Activities

BUILDING BLOCK 9.4

Think back to your days as a student—in elementary school, middle or junior high school, or high school. What extracurricular activities were available to you? Which were available during school hours? Which were limited to after-school hours? In which extracurricular activities did you participate?

Now consider how teachers might get involved in these extracurricular activities. Do you think teachers should be required to participate in these activities? Should they volunteer for such duties? Should they be paid for extracurricular duties?

What opportunities for involvement in extracurricular activities did you suggest? Teachers may coach sports teams or collect tickets at games, concerts, or plays. They may sponsor clubs or chaperone field trips or school dances. Most extracurricular activities occur before or after regular school hours and outside the regular instruction of students, but some may occur during the school day. Teachers normally are paid a stipend for sponsoring certain extracurricular activities such as team sport coaching. For other types of activities, however, teachers may be expected to volunteer. Some state policies limit the number of extracurricular activities in which new teachers can participate. In cases of compelling need, however, such as lack of adequate personnel to carry out the school's commitments, the administration may require teachers, including new teachers, to take on extracurricular responsibilities.

Which extracurricular activities would you like to be involved in at your future school? To make a positive impression during an interview, let the principal or personnel director know that you are willing to work with students and support them outside of your classroom. In hiring, school administrators look for qualified people who not only can teach well, but who also can bring other activities to the students.

Schools expect teachers to teach and to be accountable for their students' learning. They also expect teachers to carry out noninstructional duties and participate in extracurricular activities. Teachers must be well educated, highly qualified individuals to live up to these expectations.

Certification

Schools expect their teachers to be certified. Students in our schools deserve to have competent teachers as much as they deserve competent doctors and dentists. **Teacher certification** is a state's official recognition that a person has met the requirements to be a professional teacher in that state. Each state sets its own requirements for teacher certification, and these vary significantly from state to state. However, most states have the following minimum requirements:

- At least a bachelor's degree; some states require a master's degree
- Completion of an approved and accredited teacher preparation program
- A major or minor in education for elementary education majors
- A major in the subject area in which the student plans to teach for middle or high school teachers
- Passing scores on state licensure examinations

In Chapter 1, you investigated your state's certification requirements for the grade, age, and subjects you plan to teach. What routes are available to people to acquire the desired teaching certification?

Several routes to teacher certification exist, depending on your state's regulations. Many people choose the university preparation route. However, there are other routes to certification: the post-baccalaureate route, the master's degree route, and alternative routes that are especially appealing to individuals seeking to change careers.

Regardless of your route to certification, you must build solid constructions and understanding of the teaching profession. The material in this textbook and the constructions you make while investigating this material are vital for every preservice teacher.

University Certification Route

The university route to teacher certification typically entails a 4-year program of study leading to a bachelor's degree. The program includes core courses required by the college or university and content and professional education courses prescribed by the college, school, or department that offers your major.

A unique university path leading to initial certification is based on the Holmes Partnership's five-year teacher preparation program. The Holmes Partnership is a major force in educational reform. It is a "consortium of research universities dedicated to improving teacher education and the profession of teaching" (The Holmes Partnership, n.d.). Students in Holmes Partnership schools study a regular baccalaureate curriculum in a subject area for four years and concentrated pedagogy in the fifth year. At the end of this program, they are awarded both the bachelor's and master's degrees, and are eligible for state teacher certification, thereby entering the teaching force with a master's degree. Other universities that are not part of this partnership also offer five-year programs that result in both bachelor and master's degrees.

A direct link to a list of universities that are members of the Holmes Partnership is available on the Building Teachers *companion website.*

Post-Baccalaureate Certification Route

The post-baccalaureate route to teacher certification is designed to enable students who already have a bachelor's degree to earn teacher certification at the undergraduate level. If you hold a bachelor's degree in a specific content area such as mathematics, a science (biology, chemistry, physics), English, or history, it is often only a matter of taking professional education courses and participating in field experiences to receive certification at the secondary level. More coursework may be required to obtain certification at the elementary or middle grades level and even more may be required if your bachelor's degree is in an unrelated content field such as accounting, nursing, communications, psychology, or economics. Some post-baccalaureate programs lead to a second bachelor's degree, in addition to qualification for state certification. Some lead only to state certification.

Master's Degree Certification Route

Some states and institutions have developed graduate-level programs that lead to initial certification at the master's degree level. In these programs, an individual with a bachelor's degree who does not have teacher certification can earn it together with a master's degree. Students who pursue this path find they must spend a great deal of time in field experiences during their programs, and may not be able to have an outside job (except in cases where the field work can be combined with on-the-job experience). For this reason, the professional education coursework and the field experience work may be compressed into two semesters, sometimes with summer sessions added, resulting in relatively rushed class work and intense field work when compared to the university route or the post-baccalaureate route. Because of this compression, students may not have sufficient time to construct their own conceptualizations.

What are your thoughts about the master's degree initial certification program? What are some advantages and disadvantages of the master's degree route compared with the university route and the post-baccalaureate route?

Alternative Certification Route

In response to teacher shortages, numerous alternative teacher preparation programs have sprung up in the last several years. Although the post-baccalaureate and master's degree routes technically are forms of alternative teacher preparation, the term *alternative certification* more commonly refers to highly compressed teacher certification programs in which students undergo brief, intensive teacher training, and then complete a supervised teaching internship, often during their first year of professional teaching.

Such alternative routes provide opportunities for people from various educational backgrounds and walks of life to become teachers, usually specializing in the subject or area of their prior education and experience. Each state has its own version of these programs. Critics of alternative certification programs argue that teachers who complete these programs may lack adequate pedagogical skills; supporters point to the superior subject matter knowledge and experience these teachers can bring to the classroom (Otuya, 1992). In a recent national study of alternative teacher preparation programs, Humphrey and Wechsler (2005) found that, in order to prepare teachers fully, alternative programs need to focus on strengthening the mentoring component, establishing systems to help struggling participants, and linking coursework to the on-the-job training participants receive. What are your thoughts about the preparation teachers receive in alternative programs?

Troops to Teachers

www A direct link to the Troops to Teachers website is available on the *Building Teachers* companion website.

Troops to Teachers is a federal government initiative that helps eligible military persons become certified teachers. The program's primary focus is to recruit teachers for schools that serve low-income families, especially in high-need areas such as science, mathematics, and special education. Troops to Teachers is not a teacher preparation program; rather, it provides participants with financial assistance, logistical assistance, counseling, and job placement services. Participants earn their teacher certification through one of the established teacher preparation programs in their state.

Temporary, Provisional, and Emergency Certification

Some states offer temporary, provisional, or emergency teaching certification that authorizes people to hold professional teaching positions provided they pursue regular certification through an accredited teacher preparation program. These certificates normally are granted for teaching high-need subject areas, such as mathematics, science, or special education, and for teaching in high-need geographic areas, such as urban schools, schools that serve children of poverty, and remote rural schools. The regulations governing temporary and emergency certificates vary from state to state and the certificates are limited in the length of time for which they are valid. Depending on the region, it can be difficult to complete an accredited teacher education program while you are teaching full time. If you are considering a provisional certificate, you should ensure that there are reasonable options and opportunities for completing permanent certification requirements.

Teacher Certification Examinations

www A direct link to the Educational Testing Service website, where you can preview the teacher certification exams required by your state, is available on the *Building Teachers* companion website.

In addition to completing an approved teacher preparation program, candidates for teaching credentials must pass the teacher certification examinations prescribed by the state in which they are seeking certification. Most states require the appropriate Praxis exams; different states have different passing scores. The Praxis tests have been developed and are assessed by Educational Testing Service (ETS). State requirements and *Test at a Glance* publications that give the objectives and topics covered in some of the tests are published on the ETS website.

Reciprocity

Most states have reciprocal teacher certification agreements with other states. In these reciprocity arrangements, a person who has earned a teaching certificate in one state can qualify for a similar certificate in another state, providing he or she meets certain additional requirements. These requirements normally include passing the new state's teacher certification test and taking special courses. To find the reciprocity agreements and requirements for each state, talk with the teacher certification officer at your institution or access the National Association of State Directors of Teacher Education and Certification website.

A direct link to the National Association of State Directors of Teacher Education and Certification reciprocity website is available on the *Building Teachers* companion website.

Professional Development

Teachers are expected to keep up with the latest developments in education, just as physicians must keep up with the latest developments in medicine. You would not want a doctor to treat you based on the medical practices of the 1970s, and you would not want your child to be taught using curriculum, methodologies, and assessment strategies of the 1970s.

Today's schools differ from earlier schools in many respects. Curriculum has been updated to reflect new knowledge. Methodology has been updated to foster student construction and ownership of knowledge rather than memorization of information presented by the teacher. Contemporary education places greater emphasis on students' development of thinking and problem-solving skills. Assessment includes student-constructed responses and evaluation of student-focused activities rather than solely fact-based, objective tests. Technology is used to assist in instruction and help teachers in their administrative tasks.

Because of frequent and rapid changes in education, most states require a certain amount of formal professional development work to maintain teaching certification. This work can involve taking college courses, taking in-service programs offered by your school district, or completing other programs approved by the state. Some of these programs can lead to certification add-ons, and some can lead to advanced degrees. But all help you to keep up with the latest developments in education.

Besides formal work, a teacher has numerous informal options for keeping up to date. Workshops are offered by schools, school districts, colleges, universities, private and governmental agencies, or professional organizations; these workshops can last from an hour or two to a week or two. Schools receive professional journals that are available for teachers. There are professional societies for all areas of education that publish journals and hold state, regional, and national conferences.

Keeping up with your profession is crucial. You have made a good start in this course, and you need to keep the momentum going throughout your teaching career. As a school superintendent once said, "There are two kinds of teachers who have been in the business for 20 years: Those with 20 years of experience, and those with 1 year of experience 20 times." Which do you want to be?

What professional development opportunities are available at your institution? Keep your eye out for announcements. You can pursue these opportunities after you finish your program or, in some cases, while you are studying to become a teacher. Be sure to check out the student education associations that may have a chapter at your school. Ask around!

Examples of professional development include attending school-sponsored workshops and discussion groups and earning college credit toward an advanced degree.

© Spencer Grant/PhotoEdit

Technology & Education

One of the most sweeping changes occurring in education is computer-based instructional technology. It is essential that you become familiar with this technology. You will be expected to use technology to teach your students effectively, find resources and information, produce classroom materials, and manage student records and grades. This textbook offers numerous opportunities for you to use and apply technology, especially the Internet. Most states require teachers to become technologically proficient as a condition of obtaining or renewing teaching licenses. In 2001, the National Council for Accreditation in Teacher Education (NCATE) began requiring that candidates in teacher preparation programs demonstrate technological proficiency ("Technology Training," 2000). The standards for technology training are established by the International Society for Technology in Education (ISTE), which has worked with many partners to develop the National Educational Technology Standards (NETS).

The federal government has worked to support the implementation of educational technology in our schools. One area of support has been the development of technology plans for the nation. The first *National Education Technology Plan* was released in 1996 and was supplemented in 1999 with five national education technology goals (U.S. Department of Education, 1999):

1. All students and teachers will have access to information technology in their classrooms, schools, communities, and homes.
2. All teachers will use technology effectively to help students achieve high academic standards.
3. All students will have technology and information literacy skills.
4. Research and evaluation will improve the next generation of technology applications for teaching and learning.
5. Digital content and networked applications will transform teaching and learning.

The second *National Educational Technology Plan* was released in 2000 to reflect the growing sense "that there is a critical mass of opportunities to make tremendous strides in improving the nation's schools" (U.S. Department of Education, 2000, p. 1). The third *National Education Technology Plan* was unveiled in early 2005. The plan reflects the input of thousands of students and centers on seven action steps that will "help states and districts prepare today's students for the opportunities and challenges of tomorrow" (U.S. Department of Education, 2005, p. 1). The seven action steps are:

1. Strengthen leadership.
2. Consider innovative budgeting.
3. Improve teacher training.
4. Support e-learning and virtual schools.
5. Encourage broadband access.
6. Move toward digital content.
7. Integrate data systems.

How do the three national education technology plans reflect the growth in technology and the growth in teacher familiarity with technology?

Individual states use the national standards and the national educational technology plans to develop their own statewide standards for teacher preparation in educational technology. In 2005, 40 states had technology standards for teachers. The map in Figure 9.1 shows the states that have technology standards for teachers. Some states even offer special certification in instructional technology.

Begin developing your technological expertise now; if you already are well versed in technology, now is the time to begin expanding your expertise. You should be skilled in a variety of computer-based programs, such as word processing programs, spread sheets, presentation software, databases, e-mail programs, and web browsers, as well as programs specific to the subjects and grade levels

BUILDING BLOCK 9.6

Technology Requirements

Use the Internet or other resources to find the technology requirements for teachers in your state. If your state does not have specific technology standards for teachers, use the National Educational Standards, mentioned earlier. Find the answers to these questions:

- What are the technology requirements for teachers?
- What are the technology requirements for initial teacher certification? For certification renewal?
- What resources are available for learning this technology?
- What does your college or university offer?

of the students you plan to teach. As a teacher, you must develop an extensive understanding of how you can use technology as an integral part of your instruction. In today's educational world, it is the teachers skilled in the use of computer technology who are the most successful.

Direct links to the National Educational Technology Standards and the National Educational Technology Plan of 2005 are available on the *Building Teachers* companion website.

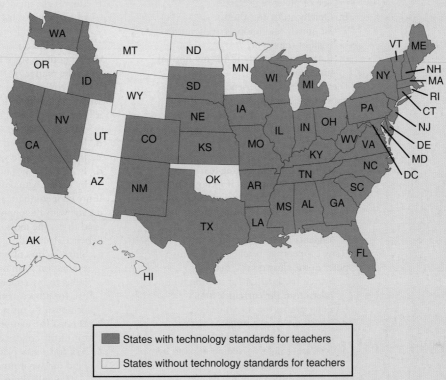

States with technology standards for teachers

States without technology standards for teachers

Figure 9.1
States with Technology Competency Standards for Teachers

- What does the state offer?
- When, where, and how will you be able to satisfy these requirements in your teacher education program?

Professionalism

Schools expect teachers to act professionally and ethically. Both kinds of actions are included in the term **professionalism.** Professionalism refers to your entire demeanor as a teacher—your appearance, your behavior, your punctuality, your respect for others, and many other characteristics. To gain a better idea of professionalism, take the inventory in Building Block 9.7. Believe it or not, all the questions in the Building Block are based on actual situations that involved preservice and in-service teachers in field experiences, resulting in breaches of professionalism.

Professionalism

What kinds of professional behaviors are expected of teachers? Choose the best available answer to each of the following questions. (More than one answer may be correct.) We will start with a few items about expectations for professional behavior in your field experience.

1. As long as I am only observing in my field placement classroom, I may
   a. Dress as I would if I were going to one of my college classes.
   b. Quietly study for a test.
   c. Sit quietly and unobtrusively in the back of the room.
   d. Eat a snack quietly if it is my normal lunchtime.

2. During my field experience, it would be appropriate for me to
   a. Initiate involvement by asking my cooperating teacher how I can help.
   b. Request the opportunity to teach a class by myself.
   c. Correct my cooperating teacher in front of the students if I know he or she has given them misinformation.
   d. Correct my cooperating teacher in private if I know he or she has given students misinformation.

3. If my cooperating teacher has a computer in the classroom, I may
   a. Search the Internet for information relevant to the current lesson.
   b. Enter grades for the students.
   c. Check my cooperating teacher's e-mail account to rid it of spam.
   d. Not use it unless given permission by the cooperating teacher.

4. If I am dissatisfied with my field experience situation, the best option for me is to
   a. Go to the school principal.
   b. Discuss my placement with others in my class.
   c. Talk with the instructor of my college class.
   d. Move to another teacher in the school who has a better classroom.

5. If I suspect a student in my field placement classroom is being abused, the best option for me is to
   a. Report my suspicions to the school counselor.
   b. Report my suspicions to the instructor of my college class.
   c. Report my suspicions to my cooperating teacher.
   d. Do nothing since I have no authority in the matter.

6. If I see my cooperating teacher behaving inappropriately toward a student, I should
   a. Report the incident to the principal.
   b. Report the incident to the instructor of my college class.
   c. Ask other students in my class what they would do.
   d. Do nothing since I have no authority in the matter.

7. When arriving at my field placement school, I should park my car
   a. In a spot reserved for the teaching staff.
   b. In a spot reserved for visitors.
   c. In any available spot.
   d. In an open spot not likely to be used by others who come to the school.

8. If my cooperating teacher is not providing me with the opportunities I believe I need to get the most out of my field experience, I should
   a. Show a copy of my field experience evaluation form or the course syllabus to my cooperating teacher and ask for advice as to how I can demonstrate my achievements.
   b. Discuss the matter with the instructor of my college class.
   c. Ask for a new placement.
   d. Find out what other students in my class would do in my situation.

9. Professional school dress for women includes
   a. Shorts and a halter top.
   b. A skirt and a long-sleeved blouse.
   c. A skirt and a tight-fitting sweater.
   d. Jeans and a t-shirt.

10. Professional school dress for men includes
   a. A shirt, tie, and jacket.
   b. Shorts and a t-shirt.
   c. Jeans and a t-shirt.
   d. Sports running wear.

11. When a student disagrees with me, I should
   a. Tell him, "Shut up!"
   b. Threaten him.
   c. Ask him to elaborate.
   d. Ignore him.

12. When a student is disruptive, I should
   a. Talk with the student.
   b. Report her to the principal.
   c. Tell other teachers in the teachers' lounge.
   d. Tell my next-door neighbor.

13. When a student does something really funny but inappropriate in my class, I should
    a. Keep quiet about it.
    b. Relate the incident to my friend in the grocery checkout line.
    c. Laugh about it in the teachers' lounge.
    d. Share it with other students.
14. If I decide to go to a nightclub with my friends for an evening, I should choose one that is
    a. Close to school.
    b. Close to home.
    c. In town.
    d. In a different school district.
15. If I decide to have a drink at a restaurant and the parents of one of my students stops by to say "Hello," I should
    a. Push the drink away.
    b. Hide the drink.
    c. Act normally.
    d. Say the waitress must have brought the wrong order.
16. If school starts at 8:05 A.M., I should be there at
    a. 8:05 A.M.
    b. 7:30 A.M.
    c. 8:30 A.M., providing I call in late.
    d. 6:00 A.M.
17. If I go to a late party Sunday evening and feel under the weather Monday morning, I should
    a. Go to school anyway.
    b. Call in sick.
    c. Show up late.
    d. None of the above; I shouldn't go to late-night parties on school evenings.
18. When I am exasperated with a student, I should
    a. Complain about this student in the teachers' lounge.
    b. Complain to my best friend.
    c. Ask another teacher confidentially for advice.
    d. Keep quiet about the situation.
19. When a mother asks me in the grocery store how her child is doing in my class, I should
    a. Tell her.
    b. Suggest she arrange for a parent conference.
    c. Refer her to the principal.
    d. Say, "I have no idea!"

20. When I disagree with a school policy, I should
    a. Discuss my concern with the principal.
    b. Complain about the policy in the teachers' lounge.
    c. Bring up my concern at a PTA meeting.
    d. Bring up my concern at a school board meeting.
21. When a kindergartener comes up to a male teacher and gives him a big hug around his knees, the teacher should
    a. Return the hug.
    b. Gently disengage from the hug.
    c. Tell the child *never* to touch an adult!
    d. Nothing—he should shake the child's hand *before* the child has the chance to hug him.
22. When a student in my first grade class shows affection to me in a public place, I should
    a. Return the affection to the child.
    b. Recognize the child in a businesslike manner.
    c. Turn away.
    d. Pretend I don't know the child.
23. When I am responsible for collecting lunch money and I decide to go to the rest room while my class is at art, what should I do with the money?
    a. Put it in my pocket and carry it with me.
    b. Put it in my purse and leave it in my room while I am gone.
    c. Hide it in my desk drawer.
    d. Deposit it in the office on my way to the rest room.
24. When a high school teacher is asked to tutor one of her students in the same subject she teaches, she should charge
    a. Nothing.
    b. The going rate for tutoring.
    c. Half the going rate for tutoring.
    d. None of the above—she should *not* tutor one of her own students on a private basis.
25. When a high school teacher is asked to tutor one of his students in a subject that is different from the subject he teaches, he should charge
    a. Nothing.
    b. The going rate for tutoring.
    c. Half the going rate for tutoring.
    d. None of the above—he should *not* tutor one of his own students on a private basis.

Discuss these situations and your responses with others in your class. Suggested "best" answers are given below.

1. c; 2. a & b; 3. d; 4. c; 5. c; 6. b; 7. d; 8. a & b; 9. b; 10. a; 11. c; 12. a; 13. a; 14. d; 15. c; 16. b; 17. d; 18. c; 19. b; 20. a; 21. b; 22. b; 23. d; 24. d; 25. d.

As you saw in Building Block 9.7, professionalism has many faces. As a professional, you are expected to model good behavior to your students and exhibit highly professional behavior at all times. In Chapter 13, you will find that the U.S. Supreme Court and lower courts have consistently held that, because of their influence on young people, teachers can and should be held to higher standards of behavior than other adults.

You can start exhibiting high standards of professional behavior in your current field experience. If you have any questions or uncertainties about professionalism in the field, you should discuss these with your professor or university supervisor. Normally, it is *not* appropriate to discuss issues of professionalism with your cooperating teacher, and it is *never* appropriate to discuss them with other teachers in the building. The following list contains professional behaviors you need to be especially concerned with in your field experience, taken from instruments used to evaluate preservice and in-service teachers.

To demonstrate professional behavior, you should:

- Demonstrate leadership and initiative.
- Demonstrate flexibility.
- Participate in positive interpersonal relationships with students, peers, parents, and administrators.
- Dress appropriately.
- Follow school rules, procedures, ethical and legal regulations.
- Respect the confidentiality of conversations and records concerning students, teachers, parents, and administrators.
- Communicate effectively.
- Cooperate and collaborate with others willingly.
- Accept and respond positively to constructive criticism.
- Accept responsibility for action and inaction.
- Be punctual and regular in attendance.
- Meet deadlines.
- Demonstrate willingness to become a lifelong learner.
- Demonstrate respect for family, community, and cultural values.

Most professions have a code of ethics to guide professional behavior, and education is no exception. The National Education Association (NEA) has issued a *Code of Ethics of the Education Profession* that governs the ethics of teachers throughout the nation (National Education Association, 1975). The code is divided into two parts:

1. Ethics involving the teacher's commitment to the student
2. Ethics involving the teacher's commitment to the profession

Each state also has a code of ethics for teachers. You should become familiar with both the NEA code and your state's code of ethics.

> A direct link to the NEA *Code of Ethics of the Education Profession* is available on the *Building Teachers* companion website.

Legal Requirements

Teachers are subject to certain legal requirements, with which you must become familiar. You will investigate these thoroughly in Chapter 13, but two of them are so important they are included here:

> *Suspected child abuse.* You must report to school authorities any instance of suspected child abuse. The suspicion can come from a student telling you about abuse, from noticeable but unexplained bruises, from other students telling you, and the like. This is not to say that you should look for evidence of child abuse in every student you see. But if you have reason to suspect that a student has been the victim of child abuse, you must report your suspicion. Failure to do so is a felony, and teachers can and have been prosecuted for trying to protect students and respect their confidences.

Drugs, alcohol, and firearms. You must report to school authorities any student who brings drugs, alcohol, or firearms to school. Teachers are required by law to report students who bring these items to school, and you must uphold the law regardless of your personal feelings.

Schools have procedures for reporting these and other infractions and require that you submit these reports in writing. Be sure to keep a copy of any written form or correspondence so you can demonstrate that you have acted in accordance with school policy and the law, should the need arise.

The Teacher's Expectations of the School

You have been investigating what schools expect of teachers. Now let us examine what teachers expect of schools.

BUILDING BLOCK 9.8

The Teacher's Expectations

Why are you thinking about becoming a teacher? We suspect it is not for the money, although educators can earn reasonable salaries, especially as they gain experience. There are other advantages to being a teacher, and it is reasonable to expect that these will be provided by the school in which you work.

What do you expect of the school? Brainstorm your responses to this question and share them with others in your class.

Teacher Salaries

It is said that teachers are underpaid and overworked. How true! Yet we *do* expect to be paid for our labors. How much can we expect to be paid? How does this compare with other professions? How are raises administered? As with certification and program requirements, teacher pay and its administration are state functions and vary greatly among states.

Normally, teachers are paid on the basis of degree held and prior experience. Each school district establishes the actual pay scale for that district; this pay scale should be available either on the Internet or from the district central office. Within a state, district salaries vary greatly. The state pays a certain base salary, and the district adds a supplement to that base. The amount of the supplement is determined independently by the district and is funded by local property taxes and, in some cases, sales taxes (see Chapter 11). Districts in less wealthy areas normally add lower supplements than wealthier districts. Why do you think that is?

What are you worth? What do you think is a reasonable starting salary for a teacher with the certification you are seeking? How much do you think the location of the school system affects salary?

BUILDING BLOCK 9.9

School Salary Scales

Select several school districts in which you might like to teach. Or, if you have no preference at present, select the school district in which you are doing your field experience. Obtain copies of the district's salary schedules from either the district offices or the Internet. Make it a habit to update this information annually.

- What is the salary for a beginning teacher with a bachelor's degree and no experience?
- What is the salary for a beginning teacher with a master's degree and no experience?

- What salary increase is awarded for each year of experience or service?
- Is there a top salary? What is it? What are the requirements to earn this salary?
- What salary do you think is reasonable for you to earn after you have gained some experience?
- How long would it take you to earn this salary in the school district you are investigating?

The traditional method of teacher salary administration in the United States is to use a salary scale such as the ones you just investigated. A beginning teacher with no experience can expect to earn the salary associated with the degree he or she has at the salary scale step of 0 years of experience. For each year of experience, the salary increases by a certain amount in a step-like fashion—usually the same dollar amount for each year. The entire salary scale may or may not increase to keep up with inflation and provide salary incentives. Often the pay increases teachers receive depend on the state's economy. Thus, although teachers can expect their salaries to increase to the next step in the salary scale each year, they do not always get cost of living or other general increases, unless the state or school board increases the scale.

An applicant's experience is discussed when a teacher is first employed by a school district; once agreed upon, this experience establishes the entry salary step. Thus, someone with a bachelor's degree who has taught successfully for three years at one school can expect a salary at the fourth step at the bachelor's degree level at a different school. However, school districts often factor in other experiences when deciding salary offers—such as military experience, classroom paraprofessional experience, experience in the business world, or other experience that would enhance that teacher's performance. In addition, signing bonuses often are offered to applicants for teaching in poor districts or low-performing schools and for teaching high-need subjects such as mathematics, science, and special education. A typical salary scale is shown in Table 9.2.

TABLE 9.2 Sample Teacher Salary Schedule (Courtesy Washington State Office of the Superintendent for Public Instruction)

Years of Service	BA+0	BA+15	BA+30	BA+45	BA+90	BA+135	MA+0	MA+45	MA+90 or PhD
0	30,383	31,204	32,054	32,906	35,640	37,401	36,426	39,161	40,924
1	30,792	31,624	32,485	33,375	36,137	37,889	36,831	39,594	41,345
2	31,181	32,022	32,892	33,850	36,605	38,375	37,239	39,994	41,764
3	31,583	32,431	33,311	34,299	37,049	38,861	37,626	40,373	42,187
4	31,977	32,862	33,747	34,770	37,536	39,361	38,031	40,796	42,623
5	32,384	33,273	34,167	35,247	38,002	39,864	38,442	41,199	43,061
6	32,802	33,672	34,596	35,729	38,472	40,344	38,864	41,607	43,478
7	33,536	34,420	35,356	36,551	39,334	41,258	39,655	42,437	44,362
8	34,612	35,543	36,502	37,796	40,616	42,611	40,899	43,720	45,714
9		36,707	37,713	39,054	41,940	44,002	42,156	45,044	47,106
10			38,938	40,376	43,301	45,432	43,479	46,405	48,535
11				41,737	44,726	46,900	44,840	47,830	50,003
12				43,055	46,189	48,428	46,255	49,292	51,532
13					47,688	49,993	47,720	50,791	53,096
14					49,194	51,618	49,227	52,396	54,721
15					50,474	52,961	50,507	53,758	56,144
16 or more					51,483	54,019	51,517	54,833	57,266

My Hypothetical Salary Scales

Suppose you were to apply for a teaching position in a district that followed the salary scale shown in Table 9.2.

- What would your salary be if you had just obtained your teaching license with a bachelor's degree and had no prior experience?

- What would your salary be if you had a master's degree (30 hours beyond the bachelor's degree) and no experience?

- What would your salary be if you had a master's degree and 6 years of experience?

- What maximum salary could you earn according to this schedule? What would you have to do to earn this salary?

Teacher salaries are higher than they used to be. But the NEA reports that, although the average salary of a U.S. public school teacher increased slightly between the 2002–2003 school year and the 2003–2004 school year, salaries have remained essentially flat for the preceding 10 years when adjusted for inflation (United Press International, 2005). According to an NEA report, the national average teacher salary for 2003–2004 was $48,402, an increase of 2% from the previous year (National Education Association, 2005). However, although salaries have increased, so has inflation. The graph in Figure 9.2 shows average teacher salaries between 1988 and 2003 in current dollars and the same average teacher salaries in 2001–2002 dollars with an adjustment for inflation. The graph for current dollars shows the increase in the actual amount of money teachers were paid. You can see that this amount increases steadily. However, we have to factor in inflation, which means a dollar had less buying power in 2002 than it did in 1998. Taking inflation into consideration produces the graph labeled "Constant 2001–2002 dollars."

What can you infer from Figure 9.2 about the progression of teacher salaries?

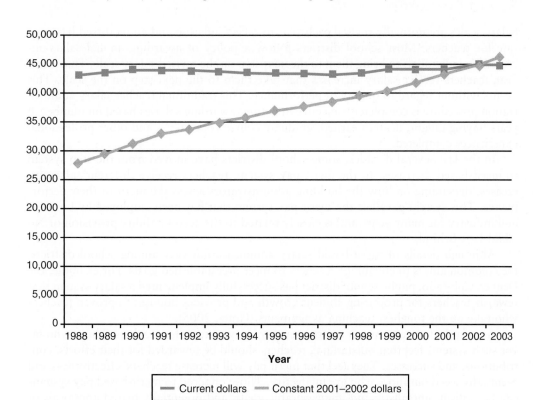

Figure 9.2

Average annual salaries for U.S. teachers in real dollars and in 2001–2002 dollars. (From the National Center for Education Statistics, 2004.)

TABLE 9.3 Average Monthly Salaries
(Including Board) of Teachers in 1847
(from Eakin, 2000)

State	Men	Women
Connecticut	$16.00	$6.50
Indiana	$12.00	$6.00
Massachusetts	$25.44	$11.38
Michigan	$12.71	$5.36
New Hampshire	$13.50	$5.65
New York	$14.96	$6.69
Ohio	$15.42	$8.73
Pennsylvania	$17.02	$10.09
Vermont	$12.00	$4.75

Just for fun, compare the salaries in Figure 9.2 with those offered by the District 1 Old Center School in Burlington, Vermont. In 1813, teachers in this school were paid $6 to $9 per week, and in 1910, almost a century later, they were paid $11 to $15 per week (Miller, 1999). Compare these salaries also with the average monthly salaries in 1847 of teachers in several states as shown in Table 9.3.

As you have seen, considerable differences can exist between the state base rates and the district scales. As you look for your first teaching job, keep in mind that different districts offer different pay scales. Many sources compare teacher salaries among all states. To gain an idea of where your state stands in the nation, check one of the many surveys published on the Internet.

www Direct links to several Internet sites that list beginning and average teacher salaries by state are available on the *Building Teachers* companion website.

Salary Increases

Salary scales are normally revised each year to reflect inflation and an increased base pay rate for teachers. Most school districts follow a policy of awarding annual salary increases to individuals to bring them to the next step on the revised salary scale. Thus, each year, teachers receive salary increases that take them to the next step on the scale. This occurs without regard to quality of performance. This traditional teacher salary administration procedure is completely objective in nature, awarding salaries based on number of years having taught, degrees earned, graduate coursework taken, and other professional experiences completed.

In the last several decades, some school districts have moved from the step system to merit-based increases. In the merit pay system, teachers receive different salary increases, depending on how the building administrators assess the merit of their performance. This system parallels the merit pay system that has been employed by business and industry for many years and is closely related to the accountability provision of No Child Left Behind.

Although details of merit-based salary administration vary among school districts, the common aim is to encourage teachers to meet preestablished goals. For example, the Denver, Colorado, public school district has successfully implemented a salary system that rewards teachers for producing student growth and provides bonuses to proven teachers who take on the toughest teaching assignments (Gratz, 2005).

A great deal of controversy exists over merit pay systems for teachers. Those who favor such systems feel that outstanding teachers should be rewarded for their efforts, contributions, and successes. They feel that merit pay will increase teachers' effectiveness and eventually weed out those who are ineffective. Those opposed to merit-based pay systems cite favoritism, unrealistic and immeasurable goals, and potentially biased appraisals of teachers' performance. Opponents feel that all teachers do fundamentally the same job and should be paid on an objective, not a subjective basis.

Tenure

Like other workers, teachers want job security. This security is provided through the vehicle of **tenure**. Tenure represents a teacher's status when that teacher is considered a permanent member of the faculty in a school district. Tenure is granted by state law, and the type and amount of protection vary from state to state. Tenure is awarded to individuals by the school board upon the individual's successful completion of a probationary (nontenured) period, normally two or three years. The primary purpose of tenure is to provide teachers with job protection by permitting them to request school board hearings if their administrators do not renew their contracts. Tenured teachers can be transferred within a school district; it is the district and not the individual school that awards tenure. If a teacher transfers to a different school district, he or she must earn tenure all over again.

Many people are under the impression that tenured teachers cannot be dismissed. This is incorrect. Districts that want to dismiss tenured teachers for incompetence can do so, but typically they must undertake a lengthy process of hearings and appeals, the results of which may be challenged in court. District personnel are reluctant to go through this potentially expensive and drawn-out procedure, and do so primarily when the evidence is clear and rapid decisions can be expected. Thus, it often is assumed that once a teacher has been awarded tenure, that teacher can keep his or her job in the school district for life, regardless of quality of performance.

Tenured teachers have the advantage of full due process of law if their contracts are not recommended for renewal. This is not true for nontenured teachers. A school district may choose not to offer a nontenured teacher a contract for the following year, without citing any particular cause. Nontenured teachers do not have the right to school board hearings and appeals (although they always can pursue their grievances through legal channels).

As late as the mid-1990s, all states had some form of tenure in place. However, this teacher security mechanism is being eroded. The state of Georgia eliminated teacher tenure altogether in 2000, leaving teachers open to termination without the guarantee of due process hearings before school boards ("Georgia Ends," 2000). Neither Nebraska nor South Dakota has tenure. Other states are considering the elimination of tenure or have eliminated it already. The primary reason cited for eliminating tenure is to reduce the difficulties involved in terminating incompetent teachers. Many school districts find the process to fire a tenured teacher so costly and time-consuming that dismissal is used only in cases of criminal conduct or gross negligence. Because the statutes defining competence in teaching are vague, ambiguous, and subject to multiple interpretations, the elimination of the tenure protection makes it easier for school districts to dismiss incompetent teachers, and, thus, raise the quality of the teachers they provide for the education of the students in their district. Tenure is thoroughly explored from a legal standpoint in Chapter 13.

Teachers fear that the job security once afforded by tenure is gone in states where tenure has been eliminated. What do you think? Does your state have tenure for public school teachers? Should it retain the laws currently on the books? What do you think about tenure? Select either a pro or a con position, and cite the arguments for your position.

Working Conditions

In Building Block 9.8, did you list factors that contribute to positive working conditions? How would you define positive working conditions? What working conditions do you feel your school should provide?

Let's Get Specific: What Do You Need?

This textbook has focused a great deal of attention on how teachers and schools meet student needs. But, as a teacher, what do *you* need? If schools and society expect you to be accountable for your students' learning, what must you have to be able to meet that expectation? Consider such factors as class size, students, other teachers, support personnel, the administration, the building and physical plant, equipment, materials, and supplies, and working hours.

- What items on your list are specific to grade level?
- What items are specific to content area?

Materials and Resources

You probably indicated that you would need a well ventilated building with good-sized classrooms, navigable hallways, and adequate cafeterias, gymnasiums, art and music rooms, playgrounds, athletic fields, and other physical attributes. You probably also said you would need textbooks with teachers' editions; student workbooks; general classroom materials; computers; supplies such as paper, pencils, folders, chalk, markers, and other office supplies. You investigated some of these material needs in Chapter 7. You may have felt, however, that you need more materials than are ordinarily supplied. After all, although it is possible to be an effective teacher with a paucity of materials, it is far easier to teach if you have what you need. There is a lot of "stuff" associated with being a teacher. As a matter of fact, some people feel one of the advantages of being a teacher is that you get abundant "stuff" to work with—books, office supplies, posters, markers and pens, mathematics and science gadgets, maps, charts, and globes—the list goes on.

The school will meet most of your needs for paper, copies, and other office supplies. Often, however, teachers invest their own money in materials they feel they need for their students or for themselves that are not provided by their school. They buy materials for seasonal activities, supplies for science and social studies activities, materials to use in making mathematics manipulatives, software for computer-based activities, and materials for many other activities. The National School Supply and Equipment Association (2001) reported these figures:

- Seventy-five percent of teachers reported they spent their own money on school supplies. The average amount spent was $589 per year.
- Pre-K and kindergarten teachers spent the most, an average of $1,794 per year.
- Teachers of grades 1 through 4 spent an average of $609 per year.

Teachers can minimize the amount of their own money they spend on materials for school. In the spring, schools normally ask teachers for a list of the equipment, materials, and supplies they will need for the following year, and they attempt to meet everyone's needs equitably and within budget. If there still is a need (and there probably will be, especially for unanticipated events), teachers can ask the PTA for donations, ask students' parents to donate materials (not money), create holiday "wish lists" to share with parents in a class newsletter, take advantage of free educational materials available to teachers, and write grant proposals. Many small grants are available for teachers to purchase equipment and materials for use in class projects. Some grants also pay for teachers to participate in professional development activities.

Support

Did you include support in your list of needs? Many teachers will tell you that they will make do with the materials they have as long as they have cooperation, collaboration, and support from their colleagues and administration. Of course, some of this support provides supplies and needed resource personnel. However, teaching is a tough job and we also need other kinds of support.

Recall that as a teacher, you are responsible for ensuring your students' safety—physical, intellectual, and emotional. As a teacher, you also have the right to expect your physical, intellectual, and emotional safety to be ensured. Schools employ policies and strategies to address the physical safety of students; these policies apply to teachers, as well. What do you think intellectual and emotional safety for teachers entails?

Teachers spend a great deal of time developing lessons designed to involve and excite students. You have explored many teaching methods in previous chapters. Some of these methods stray from tradition and may earn the teacher who practices them some strange looks or critical comments from other teachers or parents. No teacher should feel pressured or threatened by the criticism of others, as long as he or she knows, and can show, that students are learning. Teaching is an intellectual process, and its product should be protected. In what ways can a school provide for the intellectual safety of its teachers?

Not only is teaching an intellectual process; it is also emotional. Just as teachers expect their methodologies, curricular innovations, and assessment methods to be respected by others in the school, they have the right to expect they will be respected as people. How might a teacher's emotional safety be compromised? Who is in a position to threaten a teacher's emotional safety? As with students, the emotional safety of teachers can be threatened when a teacher's feelings are invalidated. Teachers expect and need support from colleagues who will respect the feelings they take into and out of the classroom.

Interactions with students can engender feelings of excitement, disappointment, hope, and anger. A teacher's biggest fear is that he or she will encounter an unmanageable class of students, the kind where students hurl insults and behave so badly the teacher is driven (sometimes literally) to tears. You can prevent this through effective classroom management techniques, such as those you explored in Chapter 8. However, the administration and other teachers will assist you in any way possible. You expect this support from the school; it is necessary to ensure your emotional security. Remember, you are seeking respect from your students, not popularity. When this respect is earned, your emotional well-being relative to students is assured.

It is often necessary for teachers to share their feelings safely. Sometimes a teacher shares his or her emotions with the steering wheel on the drive home. Sometimes, a spouse or friend becomes a sounding board. Often, a teacher's best resource is another teacher—someone who really understands, or at least someone who has chocolate!

Perhaps the most important support a teacher can have within the school building comes from the administration. Teachers make hundreds of decisions every day. They need to know they have the trust and backing of the administration in these decisions, and they have the right to expect this backing.

Teachers are responsible for supporting and nuturing students in school. How can schools support and nuture teachers? How are teachers' emotional needs met in school?

Courtesy of Bill Lisenby

Learning is a social activity and, therefore, so is teaching. Talk about teaching with others, sharing the excitement and the setbacks, and learn from your experiences and those of other professionals.

Among the advantages of being a teacher is the teacher's ability to fulfill the highest levels of personal development. Recall Maslow's hierarchy from Chapter 3. You surely have met your physiological needs when you go to work. Your safety and security needs, your love and belonging needs, and your esteem needs are met at school through your interactions with students and adults. You are satisfying your need to know and understand during your teacher preparation program, and you continue to meet this need through your implementation of best teaching practices in your school, continued professional development, and personal and collaborative reflections of your practice. You have the opportunity to satisfy your aesthetic needs in your own classroom, which you will decorate, arrange, and personalize. It is the self-actualization level in which teachers work. As you have found, the teacher's responsibility is to facilitate student learning. To do this successfully requires self-actualization. No one is going to teach for you. A day when you feel you have been in concert intellectually with your students is an extremely satisfying day, and it occurs because of you, the teacher, and your implementation of teaching practices that work.

The teacher is working toward resolution of Erickson's generativity vs. stagnation stage of psychosocial development. If you stagnate, it is virtually impossible to be an effective teacher. Teaching is exciting, and it requires much originality, imagination, and creativity to succeed. Teachers, therefore, are in the ideal position to nurture their generativity aspects.

Schools provide for teachers' physical, intellectual, and emotional safety through procedures, respect, and support. In addition, schools are the ideal venue for teachers to work at the highest levels of personal development, thereby achieving the highest levels of personal satisfaction.

Conclusion

In this chapter, you have explored the teacher's life in school. You have seen that schools have expectations of teachers and that teachers have expectations of schools. Schools' expectations of teachers include instructional and noninstructional activities, certification, professional development, expertise in educational technology, and professional and ethical behavior. Noninstructional duties vary from school to school and state to state; some are compensated financially and some are not. In either case, noninstructional duties are part of teaching. Once a teacher is certified, he or she is expected to grow professionally through professional development activities. These activities are offered by many sources and are available to all teachers in nearby locations.

Expectations teachers have for schools include reasonable salaries; job security; good working conditions; material support; and physical, intellectual, and emotional safety.

Teachers are busy, held to high expectations, and accountable for student learning. They are, themselves, lifelong learners. Effective teachers achieve these lofty goals, and you can, too. First, finish this book and the class in which you are using it. Then, complete your teacher education program. Your assignments and field experiences will help you gain knowledge and skills to bring to your classroom. Although teaching may be one of the few professions in which you are expected to have all the knowledge and skills on the first day (think about being the only teacher in a class of students), the more experience you acquire the more you can expect to benefit. Wong (2001) identifies four stages of teaching:

1. Fantasy: The stage when new teachers believe that to be successful all they need to do is relate and be a friend to their students
2. Survival: The stage when teachers do whatever is necessary to make it through the day

3. Mastery: The stage when teachers know how to achieve student success through employing effective practices

4. Impact: The stage when teachers know how to make an impact on their students through employing best practices. (p. 5)

During your first year or two of teaching, you will develop a repertoire of management strategies, lessons, and instructional methods. As you gain experience and confidence, and if the school meets your expectations for support, you will reach the later stages that Wong identifies; at the same time, you will meet the school's expectations of you.

Key Terms and Concepts

Instructional duties, 224
Noninstructional duties, 224
Professionalism, 233
Teacher certification, 228
Tenure, 241

Construct and Apply

1. Reflect on the "gray line" that exists between instructional and noninstructional duties. What tasks do teachers undertake that might be instructional but do not necessarily occur in the presence of students? Compare the teacher's instructional and noninstructional duties to the rehearsal and the opening night of a play.

2. Compare and contrast the different routes to teacher certification. What are the advantages and disadvantages of each?

3. Why is it important for teachers to stay current? Describe the classroom of a teacher who is "still in the dark ages."

4. Comment on teacher salaries. Consider that teachers are paid for 9–10 months of work. What would a monthly paycheck be before taxes? What would the monthly starting salary be for a teacher in your local school system if pay were distributed over 12 months? How does the teacher's annual salary compare to other professions?

5. What are advantages and disadvantages of tenure? Should tenure be retained in today's schools? Why or why not?

6. Recall the basic and academic needs of students that teachers and the school must meet. What are teachers' basic and academic needs? How does the school meet these needs?

Deconstructing the Standards

INTASC Principle #5 says:

> The teacher uses an understanding of individual and group motivation and behavior to create a learning environment that encourages positive social interaction, active engagement in learning, and self-motivation.

INTASC Principle #6 says:

> The teacher uses knowledge of effective verbal, nonverbal, and media communications techniques to foster active inquiry, collaboration, and supportive interaction in the classroom.

- What part(s) of these principles does this chapter address?
- How does this chapter address these principles?
- How will the concepts in this chapter help you apply these principles as a teacher?

Field Experience

1. At your field experience school, what are the expectations for faculty regarding extracurricular activities?

2. What does your cooperating teacher wish for more than anything else to improve his or her life in school?

■ Your Portfolio

1. Add copies of the NEA *Code of Ethics of the Education Profession* and your state's code of ethics for teachers to your portfolio for frequent reference.
2. Collect the information you have gathered throughout this chapter on professional development opportunities and teacher resources. Include them as appropriate in your portfolio.
3. Utilize technology whenever and wherever appropriate to complete assignments and activities and to make presentations to peers and professors. Include evidence of your technology-related knowledge and skills in your portfolio and reflect on how you will use these as a teacher to manage your work and instruct your students.
4. Make a special effort to collect evidence of your professional behavior as you progress through your program.

■ *Building Teachers* Technology Resources

 Access the *Building Teachers* companion website, http://www.education.wadsworth.com/martinloomis1, for resources and information about the teaching profession, including access to the following websites:

- American Federation of Teachers
- National Education Association
- Family Education Network
- NEA *Code of Ethics of the Education Profession*
- National Education Technology Plan of 2005 and National Educational Technology Standards
- National Association of State Directors of Teacher Education and Certification
- Educational Testing Service
- Troops to Teachers
- Holmes Group and the Holmes Partnership

 See video footage of real teachers. Check the *Building Teachers* CD-ROM that accompanies your textbook for additional resources.

 Also link to InfoTrac College Edition through the *Building Teachers* companion website. Use InfoTrac College Edition to search for articles to enhance your study.

■ Note

1. In Olympic Heights High School in Boca Raton, Florida, students who are late to school are required to spend the day in an austere room with straight-backed chairs and no desks. This makes it difficult for students to sleep or to do the homework they are required to do during the detention, and has reduced the number of tardies significantly (Patrick, 2000).

PART **IV**

Society

Society

School

Student

Self

In Part I, you investigated your *self* and your ideas and beliefs about education. In Part II, you investigated students and their common and unique needs and talents. In Part III, you investigated the nature of schools and the complex relationships among the school, students, and teachers.

Part IV extends your investigations of American education to the larger sphere of social influences. You will investigate the historical foundations of American education, ways in which schools are managed and financed, some social issues that affect teaching and schools, legal issues that impact American education, and current reform activities relative to curriculum, assessment, and teaching.

CHAPTER 10

Historical Perspectives

History, faced with courage, need not be lived again.

MAYA ANGELOU, POEM READ AT THE INAUGURATION OF PRESIDENT BILL CLINTON, 1993

Schools are social institutions. They are profoundly affected by historical developments, governments, legislation, sources of finance, diverse goals set by diverse populations, religious beliefs, social mores, folkways, expectations, and much more.

In previous chapters, you investigated the complex school system. You saw that schools have definite and specific purposes and are structured to fulfill these purposes. Today's schools result from the continuous evolution of educational thought. American schools began in colonial times, and today's schools resonate with the purposes, goals, structures, and teacher–student interactions as they have changed over time. These changes have responded to society's needs and the thinking of prominent educators. What does Maya Angelou's remark in the opening quotation imply for schools?

The current concept of K–12 schools is one with which you are intimately familiar. You probably could trade tales out of school with friends, classmates, and new acquaintances, finding similarities in your stories and experiences. We all have our own definite ideas of what school is, and you have begun to articulate your beliefs about what schools should be. However, we cannot ignore what schools have been in the past. Studying the history of education and schools helps us to understand the past and offers insights into both the present and the future.

In this chapter, you will explore schools in various historical contexts to develop your understanding of how we got where we are and why schools are the way they are. In Chapter 14, you will explore where schools should go from here.

CHAPTER GOALS

As a result of your work in this chapter, you will:

1. Describe the changes in school populations as they reflect changes in society.

2. Explain the influence of society on the purposes of school over time.

3. Discuss changes to the curriculum taught in American schools, and identify incidents in American history that have caused these changes.

4. Discuss the changes and innovations in instruction and teacher preparation and qualifications throughout the history of American education.

5. Identify influential individuals and describe their contributions to education.

Basic Educational History Considerations

There are many ways to divide the history of education into manageable pieces. In this chapter, we focus on the following time periods:

- Colonial period (1620–1750)
- Young nation period (1750–1900)
- Progressive nation period (1900–1950)
- Postwar period (1950–1980)
- Modern period (1980–present)

You will explore the history of U.S. education in the context of questions similar to those you considered in developing your philosophy of education in Chapter 2. For each time period, you will consider several questions:

- What was happening in America?
- Who went to school?
- What was taught?
- Who decided what should be taught?
- Why was this material taught?
- How were students taught?
- What were the schools like?
- Who were the influential educators and what were their contributions?

The answers to these questions have changed over time in response to the social needs of our nation as it developed into a world power. These needs have resulted in changes in legislation; changes in how schools are funded; changes in skills needed by graduates; changes in the expectations of local, regional, and national communities; changes in religious beliefs; and changes in the ways prominent educators and others view education, its curriculum, and its methodology.

To begin, read the account of an educational dilemma provided in the box.

A young boy goes off to school. He is called on for an oral recitation covering his written assignment. He breaks for lunch. In the afternoon his class practices written exercises. At the close of the day he returns home and is greeted by his father, who inquires how he did in school. The boy proudly recites what he has learned and shows off samples of his work. The father is pleased. Later that evening the youth leaves a reminder that he be awakened early in the morning. He is anxious about getting to school on time.

The next day, so the account continues, the boy's mother hands him two rolls for his lunch and he hurries off to the schoolhouse. But, for reasons unexplained, he is delayed en route and arrives late for his first class. The attendance monitor is waiting at the door and orders the boy to report to the principal. Heart pounding in fear, the youth complies. As it turns out, besides being tardy, he failed to complete his homework. The irate principal administers a sound thrashing.

Thereafter, matters go from bad to worse. The rest of the day is given over mainly to beatings for still other infractions: for slovenly appearance in violation of the school's dress code, for speaking out of turn, for standing at ease and leaving his assigned seat without permission, for lapsing into the vernacular during a foreign language class, and finally, for loitering about on school grounds after hours.

The boy now dreads school and begins neglecting his lessons. His teacher, thoroughly disgusted, eventually abandons all pretence of trying to teach the youth anything, and threatens his dismissal. The boy's father is distraught; his son is on the verge of becoming a school dropout. In a last, desperate effort to settle matters, he hits upon the idea of inviting the principal home for a conference.

The schoolmaster is treated royally upon his arrival. He is led to the seat of honor and wined and dined. Gifts are pressed upon him. On cue, the lad begins to recount all he has learned in school. Then the father joins in, lavishing praise on the teacher for his unsparing efforts on the boy's behalf. This stratagem proves successful. By now greatly mollified and in a mellowed mood, the principal launches into a long, windy speech, thanking his host for his generosity and parental concern. In a paroxysm of enthusiasm, he winds up with words of praise for the young student's supposed academic accomplishments. Everyone is greatly relieved and a crisis is averted.

From Lucas, C. J. (1980). The more things change. *Phi Delta Kappan, 61*(6), 414–416. Reprinted with permission.

When do you suppose this account was written? There are few clues in the text about its origin. Actually, this is a loose translation of the "Schooldays" composition restored from about 20 separate cuneiform tablets dating back some 4,300 years to the very dawn of civilization. Can you tell from this account what was taught in early Sumerian schools? Can you tell what the schools were like? Can you infer some of the characteristics of the complex interactions among school, teacher, student, and family?

Jumping ahead a couple of millennia, we find the writings of the ancient Greek philosophers. Socrates felt the primary purpose of schooling was for people to become moral beings (McCambridge, 1977). Plato and Aristotle believed the primary purpose of schooling lay in discovering what it means to be human, so that people could live a good life in accordance with their human nature. Plato wrote:

> *By education, then, I mean goodness in the form in which it is first acquired by a child. . . . But if you consider the one factor in it, the rightly disciplined state of pleasures and pains whereby a man, from his first beginnings on, will abhor what he should abhor and relish what he should relish—if you isolate this factor and call it education, you will be giving it its true name.*

Aristotle wrote:

> *Pleasure induces us to behave badly, and pain to shrink from fine actions. Hence the importance (as Plato says) of having been trained in some way from infancy to feel joy and grief at the right things: true education is precisely this.*

But education was destined to change.

American Education in the Colonial Period

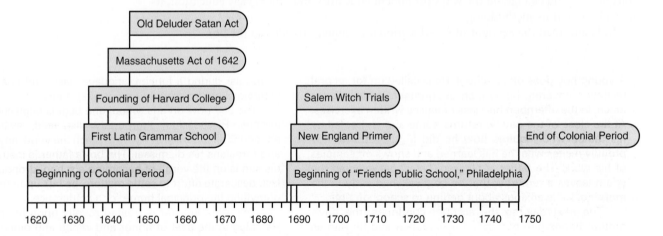

BUILDING BLOCK 10.1

Colonial American Schools

Think about what American schools must have been like in the colonial period (1620–1750).

- What was life like during colonial times? What did the colonists value?
- What was happening in the colonies during this time?

- What did people need to know and be able to do to function and thrive in their society?
- Did everyone need the same knowledge and skills?
- What do you think students were required to learn in school?
- How do you think students learned during this period?

You may recall from your studies of American history that 17th-century American colonies were settled in three different regions. The New England colonies included Massachusetts, Rhode Island, Connecticut, and New Hampshire. The Middle Atlantic colonies were centered in Pennsylvania and also included New York, New Jersey, and Delaware. The southern colonies included Maryland, Virginia, North Carolina, South Carolina, and Georgia (see Figure 10.1). Each region had its own unique characteristics, and schooling evolved differently in each.

Colonists settled in America for several reasons, among which religious freedom was of great importance. It is not surprising, then, to note that the primary purpose of education in the American colonies of the 1600s and early 1700s was to perpetuate religion. In the New England colonies, this meant maintaining Protestant religious beliefs. The Middle Atlantic colonies embraced several religious practices, although the people were

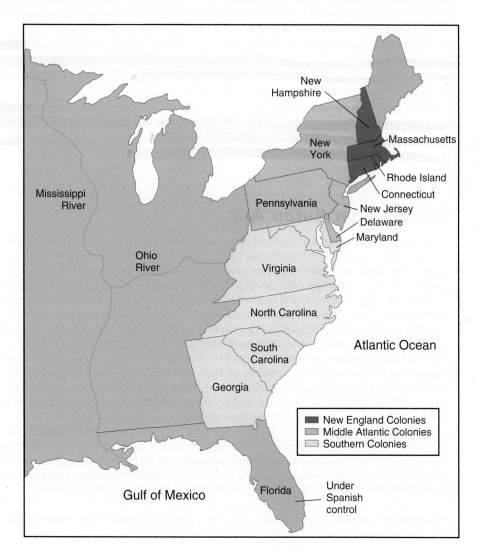

Figure 10.1
The thirteen original American colonies.

basically all Protestants. The prevailing religious practice in the southern colonies was patterned after the Anglican Church. As time progressed, different colonial regions found they needed the schools to address nonreligious challenges. As a result of their developments, colonial education became the forerunner of several practices, including:

- Public education
- Curriculum development
- Public input for school development
- Education to meet current needs
- Mandatory education for women

Because the colonies comprised three separate regions, each with its own unique thoughts about education, it is appropriate to look at each region separately.

New England Colonies

The overriding purpose of schooling in colonial America was to ensure pupils' religious salvation. The very strict Calvinist Protestant ideas embraced by the New England Puritans viewed human nature as depraved. The Puritans believed that schools should instill religious conformity and religious values. To this end, students were required to learn to read and write English, Latin, and Greek so they could pursue theological studies. Of course, the colonies were still under British rule, and the educational institutions had been transplanted from class-conscious Europe and England. Consequently there were two educational tracks, each represented in a different kind of school. One was the **vernacular school** for lower-class males that taught reading, writing, arithmetic, and religion; the other was the **Latin Grammar School** for upper-class males. These two tracks were separate; students did not move from one to the other.

The religious purpose of education was made plain in two early laws. The **Massachusetts Act of 1642** required that parents and masters see that their children know the principles of religion and the laws of the Commonwealth. The other law, the **Massachusetts Act of 1647**, was known as the Old Deluder Satan Act.

Old Deluder Satan Act

It being one chief project of that old deluder, Satan, to keep men from the knowledge of the Scriptures, as in former times by keeping them in an unknown tongue, so in these latter times by persuading from the use of tongues, that so that at least the true sense and meaning of the original might be clouded and corrupted with false glosses of saint-seeming deceivers; and to the end that learning may not be buried in the grave of our forefathers, in church and commonwealth, the Lord assisting our endeavors.

It is therefore ordered that every township in this jurisdiction, after the Lord hath increased them to fifty households shall forthwith appoint one within their town to teach all such children as shall resort to him to write and read, whose wages shall be paid either by the parents or masters of such children, or by the inhabitants in general, by way of supply, as the major part of those that order the prudentials of the town shall appoint; provided those that send their children be not oppressed by paying much more than they can have them taught for in other towns.

And it is further ordered, that when any town shall increase to the number of one hundred families or householders, they shall set up a grammar school, the master thereof being able to instruct youth so far as they may be fitted for the university, provided that if any town neglect the performance hereof above one year that every such town shall pay 5 pounds to the next school till they shall perform this order.

(From *Records of the Governor and Company of the Massachusetts Bay in New England* (1853), II: 203.)

What were the primary provisions of the Old Deluder Satan Act? What were the heads of families in towns of 50 or more families required to do for the education of their children? What were the heads of families in towns of 100 or more families required to do for the education of their children? How were these responsibilities accomplished?

To put the religious zeal of the New England colonists in perspective, one need only to look at the Salem, Massachusetts, witch trials of 1692 that resulted in a number of convictions and executions of men and women for witchcraft. Consorting with the devil was considered a felonious crime in the 17th century. The punishment for the crime was hanging. Altogether, 19 people were hanged, 17 died in prison, and one was pressed to death with rocks during torture (Salem Witch Museum, 2005). Look also at the **Hornbook** and the *New England Primer,* the primary reading books used in school. The Hornbook was not a book but a small wooden paddle with a single sheet of paper glued to it, covered with a very thin, transparent layer of cow's horn for protection. The paper had the ABCs, some pairs of letters, and a religious verse, often the Lord's Prayer, printed on it and was used to teach reading and writing. Hornbooks were used through the mid-1700s.

The *New England Primer* was first published in 1690 and combined the material of the Hornbook with religious catechism, using words, couplets, and text to teach reading. It was shorter than 90 pages and approximately 3 by 4 inches in size (see photos). The *New England Primer* was used continuously through the early 1800s.

Formal schooling was reserved for boys of European descent in the northern colonies, although some girls attended the primary schools. The boys started school at age 6 or 7 and went for 3 or 4 years. Most girls who attended school went to women's homes, where they learned housekeeping skills. These schools were called **dame schools** and served both day-care and educational purposes.

After young boys had learned to read (by age 9 or 10), there were essentially two paths available to them:

- Attendance at a Latin Grammar School to prepare them for college
- Apprenticeship or training in the father's occupation at home

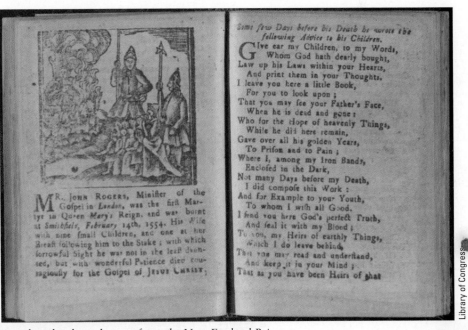

An early American hornbook, and pages from the New England Primer.

The first Latin Grammar School was established in 1635, and its purpose was to prepare upper-class boys for the entrance test to Harvard College, where they would begin their theological studies. Founded in 1636, Harvard College was the only college available. The admission requirements for Harvard College in 1642 and 1700 are shown below:

Admission Requirements in 1642
When any Schollar is able to Read Tully or such like classicall Latine Author ex tempore, and make and speake true Latin in verse and prose suo (ut aiunt) Marte, and decline perfectly the paradigmes of Nounes and verbes in the Greeke tongue, then may hee bee admitted into the College, nor shall any claime admission before such qualifications.

Admission Requirements in 1700
Everyone competent to read Cicero or any other classic author of that kind extemporaneously, and also to speak and write Latin prose and verse with tolerable skill and without assistance, and of declining the Greek nouns and verbs, may expect to be admitted to the College: if deficient in any of these qualifications, he cannot under any circumstances be admitted.

How do these admission requirements reflect the basic purpose of education in the New England colonies? What do you suppose the curriculum of the early Latin Grammar schools included?

Schools consisted of one room for 20–30 boys, where the primary motivators were praise and punishment. Teachers were required to have academic, religious, moral, and political qualifications; they were hired by boards of trustees from personal interviews and others' recommendations. Education was financed by royal donations, work and land rent, direct taxation, and some tuition.

The second path, primarily available to young boys of lower social or economic classes, was apprenticeship, which lasted approximately 7 years. As an apprentice, the boy learned all the tasks of a trade from a master and often was required to make monthly payments to him. Because of the cost, the length of time required, and the inconvenience, most boys did not take this route. Instead, most lower-class boys trained at home in their fathers' occupations; such training was free, convenient, and productive.

A colonial one-room schoolhouse. How does this sketch depict education in early America? Who is being educated, who is teaching, and what motivators for student learning are identifiable in this sketch?

Middle Atlantic Colonies

In the Middle Atlantic colonies, education took on a more practical nature than was prevalent in the north, subscribing to the principle that children should learn a useful trade in addition to reading, writing, arithmetic, and religion. Several different churches and denominations coexisted in the Middle Atlantic colonies. Consequently, instead of having a uniform system of education, as was prevalent in New England, the schools and the curriculum were established to meet local needs, including the needs of the churches, and thus were different from one area to another. Also, because of the growth of business, a middle class was emerging. The curriculum included both religious and practical subjects, and the actual program was decided jointly by the various religious groups and the teacher.

Although public schools in the Middle Atlantic colonies were meant primarily for boys, the education of girls was considered important. In fact, the Society of Friends (popularly known as the Quakers) accepted both boys and girls into their private schools, having started the Friends Public School in Philadelphia in 1689 to educate all children until they could be apprenticed to learn a trade. The school offered many kinds of classes in keeping with people's needs. The school charged tuition to those who could pay; otherwise, school was free. Teachers were paid by the parents.

By the early 1700s, many private-venture schools had arisen, and many schools became ethnically and religiously segregated as a result of the national, cultural, religious, and racial influences.

Southern Colonies

The southern colonies treated education as a private matter, separate from the state, and offered education largely to wealthy children to prepare them for college. People in these colonies believed that the most important training children could receive was in the home; there, children could be inducted into the values of their society. The purpose of education was to create a college-educated elite. There was no middle class in the antebellum south—only plantation owners, poor whites, and slaves. Poor whites who worked on farms had no access to education, and slaves were prohibited from learning to read or write.

The first southern school was founded in Virginia in 1636 and was a private free school made possible by the estate of one Benjamin Symms, who left 200 acres plus eight cows to establish a free school. Other schools followed in 1655, 1667, 1675, and 1689; all were private and paid for by individuals' contributions. One reason for the slow growth in the number of schools was that the population was dispersed; often an area held too few children to justify a school. Teachers were tutors who traveled long distances between towns to teach at town schools. The growth of schools continued at this slow pace until the founding of the College of William and Mary, America's second oldest college, in Virginia in 1693.

How do John Locke's contributions affect education today?

BIOGRAPHY

John Locke

John Locke (1632–1704) was an English philosopher and doctor. His writings greatly influenced education during the 1600s and 1700s and continue to occupy an important place in educational thought today. Unlike the early Greek philosophers, who felt people were born with all the knowledge they needed, Locke argued that knowledge is *not* innate; rather, knowledge is carried to people's minds through their sensory experiences. In his *Essay Concerning Human Understanding*, published in 1690, Locke wrote, "Let us suppose the mind to be ... without any ideas; how comes it to be furnished? To this, I answer with one word: from EXPERIENCE" (in Kreis, 2000, p. 1). Influenced by Locke's writings, school programs began to move away from the God-centered curriculum to one with secular, humanistic, and practical approaches.

Not only was Locke influential in education; his writings on social order and government strongly influenced Thomas Jefferson and the framing of the Declaration of Independence and the U.S. Constitution.

© Hulton Archive/Getty Images

Your Thoughts about Colonial American Education

- How do the inferences you made about colonial education in Building Block 10.1 compare with the descriptions you investigated in this section?

- How did colonial education mirror what was going on in the country at the time?

- Which educational philosophy or philosophies prevailed during colonial times?

American Education in the Young Nation Period

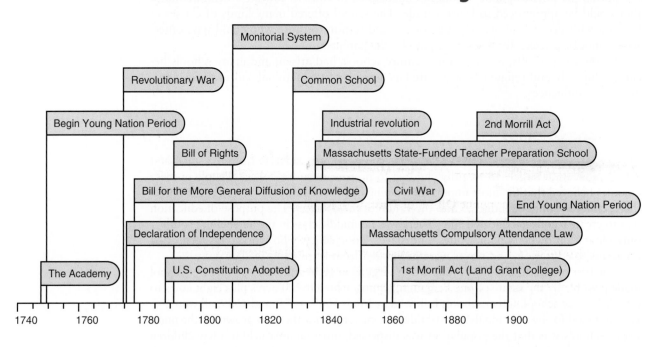

Monitorial System

Revolutionary War

Common School

Begin Young Nation Period

Industrial revolution

2nd Morrill Act

Bill of Rights

Massachusetts State-Funded Teacher Preparation School

Bill for the More General Diffusion of Knowledge

Civil War

End Young Nation Period

Declaration of Independence

Massachusetts Compulsory Attendance Law

The Academy

U.S. Constitution Adopted

1st Morrill Act (Land Grant College)

1740　1760　1780　1800　1820　1840　1860　1880　1900

Let us next consider American education from the end of the colonial period to the end of the 19th century.

American Schools in the Young Nation Period

Think about the time period from 1750 to 1900.

- What was happening in America during this time? List some major events.

- What knowledge and skills did individuals need to be able to respond to these events and to contribute to the society of a growing nation?

- Did everyone need the same knowledge and skills?

- How do you think schools and teaching changed from colonial times in response to societal changes?

- How do you think students learned during this period?

As you might expect, the American Revolution, the Declaration of Independence, the Constitution, and the Bill of Rights all had enormous influence on the purpose and nature of education during the late 1700s and early 1800s. The Civil War, immigration, reconstruction, and the Industrial Revolution had equally powerful influences on education during the late 1800s. During these times, American education expanded to include a sense of nationalism as well as preparation for a trade, in addition to the traditional studies of reading, writing, arithmetic, and the Bible. This expansion included shifts in educational goals toward occupational proficiency and the ability to participate in a democratic society. The emphasis on religion declined, and the need for job-related training became increasingly important.

Changing Purpose of Education in the Young Nation Period

To foster occupational proficiency, science—a subject new to schools—began to emerge. In 1749, Benjamin Franklin founded The Academy in Philadelphia, which later became the University of Pennsylvania, where both the classical subjects and the subjects needed for occupations were taught. Franklin felt that neither religion nor tradition should determine the purpose and character of education. The Academy was intended to cultivate trades as well as "more useful culture of young minds" (Tyack, 1967, p. 73). Franklin's Academy instituted a double track in the same school: one for vocational preparation and one for preparation for college.

In a document requesting funding for the Academy, Franklin cited four main benefits expected:

1. That the Youth of Pensilvania may have an Opportunity of receiving a good Education at home, and be under no Necessity of going abroad for it; whereby not only a considerable Expence may be saved to the Country, but a stricter Eye may be had over their Morals by their Friends and Relations.

2. That a Number of our Natives will hereby be qualified to bear Magistracies, and execute other public Offices of Trust, with Reputation to themselves and Country; there being at present great Want of Persons so qualified in the several Counties of this Province. And this is the more necessary now to be provided for by the English here, as vast Numbers of Foreigners are yearly imported among us, totally ignorant of our Laws, Customs, and Language.

3. That a Number of the poorer Sort will hereby be qualified to act as Schoolmasters in the Country, to teach Children Reading, Writing, Arithmetick, and the Grammar of their Mother Tongue; and being of good Morals and known Characters, may be recommended from the Academy to Country Schools for that Purpose; The Country suffering at present very much for want of good Schoolmasters, and oblig'd frequently to employ in their Schools, vicious imported Servants, or concealed Papists, who by their bad Examples and Instructions often deprave the Morals or corrupt the Principles of the Children under their Care.

4. It is thought that a good Academy erected in Philadelphia, a healthy Place, where Provisions are plenty, situated in the Center of the Colonies, may draw Numbers of Students from the Neighboring Provinces, who must spend considerable Sums yearly among us, in Payment for their Lodging, Diet, Apparel &c. which will be an Advantage to our Traders, Artisans, and Owners of Houses and Lands. This Advantage is so considerable, that it has been frequently observed in Europe, that the fixing a good School or college in a little inland Village, has been the Means of making it a great Town in a few Years; And therefore the Magistrates of many Places, have offer'd and given great yearly Salaries, to draw learned Instructors from other Countries to their respective Towns, merely with a View to the Interest of the Inhabitants. (From the Minutes of the Common Council: Free Library of Philadelphia, July 31, 1750.)

From Benjamin Franklin's list of purposes, what does it seem he intended the Academy to accomplish? What was the influence of the educational system in the New England colonies on the curriculum of The Academy?

In the late 1700s, Thomas Jefferson believed that the country needed a supply of college-educated people who could take leadership roles and make good decisions for the country, especially in the territories created by western expansion. Education was beginning to reflect a sense of nationalism. Schooling began to stress the scientific and practical education emphasized by Franklin and the political and civic education emphasized by Jefferson. Jefferson introduced the Bill for the More General Diffusion of Knowledge to the Virginia legislature. The bill did not pass; if it had, it would have created a system of public schools. Education thus was becoming an instrument of social and political reform and improvement.

Bill for the More General Diffusion of Knowledge: Preamble

Whereas it appeareth that however certain forms of government are better calculated than others to protect individuals in the free exercise of their natural rights, and are at the same time themselves better guarded against degeneracy, yet experience hath shewn, that even under the best forms, those entrusted with power have, in time, and by slow operations, perverted it into tyranny; and it is believed that the most effectual means of preventing this would be, to illuminate, as far as practicable, the minds of the people at large, and more especially to give them knowledge of those facts, which history exhibiteth, that, possessed thereby of the experience of other ages and countries, they may be enabled to know ambition under all its shapes, and prompt to exert their natural powers to defeat its purposes; And whereas it is generally true that that people will be happiest whose laws are best, and are best administered, and that laws will be wisely formed, and honestly administered, in proportion as those who form and administer them are wise and honest; whence it becomes expedient for promoting the publick happiness that those persons, whom nature hath endowed with genius and virtue, should be rendered by liberal education worthy to receive, and able to guard the sacred deposit of the rights and liberties of their fellow citizens, and that they should be called to that charge without regard to wealth, birth or other accidental condition or circumstance; but the indigence of the greater number disabling them from so educating, at their own expence, those of their children whom nature hath fitly formed and disposed to become useful instruments for the public, it is better that such should be sought for and educated at the common expence of all, than that the happiness of all should be confided to the weak or wicked. . . .

(From the document library at TeachingAmericanHistory.org.)

From the preamble, what do you believe was Jefferson's purpose in proposing the Bill for the More General Diffusion of Knowledge?

BUILDING BLOCK 10.4

Educational Thought in the Middle Atlantic and Southern Colonies

Benjamin Franklin came from the Middle Atlantic colonies and Thomas Jefferson came from the south. How did the traditions established in each of those regions in the 1600s influence thinking about education in the next century?

Expansion

The 19th century saw many changes in the face of America. The country was expanding westward. Industrialization brought such innovations as coal-gas lamps, electric lights, the phonograph, the steam engine, the transcontinental railroad, dynamite, the telegraph, the telephone, and the development of the Standard Oil Company. Increasing numbers of immigrants settled in America. All of this activity resulted in the expansion of America's schools to accommodate more students and to prepare these students for life in the growing industrialized nation. Consequently, all school children were taught basic knowledge, the virtues of patriotism and morality, and the skills they would need in life.

Because of growing immigration, schools began to emphasize civics, citizenship, history, geography, and moral development. Because of growing industrialization, subjects dealing with science, mathematics, thinking abilities, and vocational education appeared in the curriculum. Additionally, reading, writing, spelling, penmanship, arithmetic, and the classics continued to be prominent areas of study. In the larger towns, schools added algebra, American history, bookkeeping, geometry, and surveying to their programs; students took these courses in addition to Latin, Greek, general history, rhetoric, and logic. For many students in the mid-19th century, **McGuffey's Readers** were the primary texts for reading instruction. Each book in the McGuffey series was graded according to reading level. Not only did each book in the series provide an eclectic mix of poetry and prose; the books also stressed moral, ethical, and religious principles.

The **common school** was an elementary or primary school that came into existence in the period between 1830 and 1850, reflecting the common school movement that began in the early 19th century. This movement was based on the belief that free education would strengthen America and that all children had the right to a free, public education. The common school movement represented the beginning of compulsory education for everyone, although "everyone" was interpreted to mean primarily white boys, with a few girls and a few black children. Mary Lyon (1797–1849) worked hard to provide women with the same opportunities for education that were available to men, founding Mount Holyoke College, which became a model for women's colleges.

The first general law legislating the attendance of children at school was enacted in Massachusetts in 1852. This law required that children between the ages of 8 and 14 attend school for at least 3 months out of each year. Three weeks of this 3-month period had to be consecutive. Enforcement was loosely provided by individual cities. It took another 20 years to form enforcement procedures and hire truant officers to check absentees. By 1918, all states had passed **compulsory attendance laws**.

During the 1800s, public schools started to be funded through state and local taxes, making schools free to all students. School system superintendents were introduced to manage everything from curriculum and teaching methodology to hiring and firing personnel, maintaining the school buildings, and ensuring attendance.

The Loomis-Chaffee School

An example of a 19th-century school that disregarded the restrictive educational traditions of the time is the Loomis-Chaffee School. The Loomis Institute, as it was originally called, was chartered in 1874 by five Loomis siblings, who had lost all their children and were selflessly determined to found a school as a gift to the children of others.

The roots of the school go back to 1639, when the Loomis family (from which this textbook's coauthor Kim Loomis descended) settled in Windsor, Connecticut. The Loomis Institute was built on the original Loomis homestead. It offered both vocational and college preparatory courses, had no religious or political admission criteria, and admitted both boys and girls; each of these practices represented a major departure from tradition. In the early 20th century, the girls' division was named the Chaffee School. In 1970, the boys' and girls' divisions reunited and the school acquired its present name.

The original Loomis homestead on the campus of the Chaffee School.

Courtesy of Kimberly Loomis

Teacher Preparation in the Young Nation Period

Around 1810 to 1820, the **monitorial system** of providing training for teachers, which had been developed in England by Joseph Lancaster, was introduced in the United States. Monitors were older and better students, who were taught by experienced teachers and who instructed younger pupils. This system provided low-cost education, helped train children for future jobs, and provided hands-on experience for the monitors, many of whom went on to become teachers themselves.

The first state-funded teacher preparation school was established in Lexington, Massachusetts, in 1839. Before this time, teachers in the primary schools were selected largely on the basis of their knowledge of the subjects they were to teach and their demonstrated morality. Schools devoted to teacher preparation were known as **normal schools.** These schools focused on teaching methodologies, especially the humanistic and individualistic approaches developed by Pestalozzi (discussed later in this section), which represented a radical departure from the existing method of learning by rote memorization. Normal schools were based on a belief that teaching was a "science" that could be taught and could be learned, emphasizing the psychology of child development.

The course of teacher preparation in normal schools lasted from a few months to 2 years but dealt only with teaching in the primary grades. Preparing teachers for the academically more rigorous secondary schools was left to liberal arts colleges.

During this time, teachers were expected to do literally everything connected with the school, and students were expected to be obedient. Rules for teachers and rules for students thought to have been in effect in 1872 are shown in the box.

1872 Rules for Teachers

1. Teachers will fill the lamps and clean the chimney every day.
2. Each teacher will bring a bucket of water and a scuttle of coal for the day's session.
3. Make your pens carefully. You may whittle nibs to the individual tastes of the pupils.
4. Men teachers may take one evening each week for courting purposes, or two evenings a week if they go to church regularly.
5. After ten hours in school, the teachers may spend the remaining time reading the Bible or other good books.
6. Women teachers who marry or engage in improper conduct will be dismissed.
7. Every teacher should lay aside from each day's pay a goodly sum of his earnings. He should use his savings during his retirement years so that he will not become a burden on society.
8. Any teacher who smokes, uses liquor in any form, visits pool halls or public halls, or gets shaved in a barber shop will give good reason for people to suspect his worth, intentions, and honesty.
9. The teacher who performs his labor faithfully and without fault for five years will be given an increase of twenty-five cents per week in his pay, providing the Board of Education approves.

From Kalman, 1947, p. 42–43.

1872 Rules for Students

1. Respect your schoolmaster. Obey him and accept his punishments.
2. Do not call your classmates names or fight with them. Love and help each other.
3. Never make noises or disturb your neighbors as they work.
4. Be silent during classes. Do not talk unless it is absolutely necessary.
5. Do not leave your seat without permission.
6. No more than one student at a time may go to the washroom.
7. At the end of the class, wash your hands and face. Wash your feet if they are bare.
8. Bring firewood into the classroom for the stove whenever the teacher tells you to.
9. Go quietly in and out of the classroom.
10. If the master calls your name after class, straighten the benches and tables. Sweep the room, dust, and leave everything tidy.

Land Grant Colleges

The **Morrill Act of 1862,** also known as the Land Grant College Act, gave every state a grant of 30,000 acres of public land, to be used for colleges, for every senator and every congressman in its congressional delegation. The states were to sell this land and use the proceeds to establish colleges in engineering, agriculture, and military service. This act resulted in the establishment of more than 70 colleges and universities. The second Morrill Act, signed into law in 1890, expanded the land grant system to southern states to include black institutions. Many liberal arts colleges and universities in the United States still stressed the classical Greek and Latin language and literature curriculum. But the Morrill acts made college education available to people in all social classes, improving the lives of millions of Americans. Although conceived as technical and agricultural schools, many of the original land grant institutions have grown into large public universities, sponsored by increasing state funds.

> Did your institution start as a land grant college?

Influential Educators in the Young Nation

Several individuals, both in the United States and abroad, made highly significant contributions to educational thought and procedure during the 18th century.

© CORBIS

Johann Pestalozzi

During the 18th century, Johann Pestalozzi (1746–1827) first wrote about the importance of children learning through their senses and through concrete situations, stressing that schools should show love and acceptance of children. A Swiss educational reformer, Pestalozzi continued to influence schools well into the 19th century. He advocated sympathetic understanding of students, rather than harsh punishment. He stressed creating learning environments conducive to the maximum development of every child's natural talents, believing that students' natural intellectual powers develop from within. He reacted against the memorization/recitation method of teaching by grouping students into classes so that everyone in the group could receive the same instruction. In his view, the curriculum should include not only reading, writing, and arithmetic, but also music, geography, and nature study to help students develop their mental, moral, and physical talents. He considered preparation for life the primary purpose of education (Binder, 1974).

Pestalozzi emphasized the use of concrete objects, which were to be analyzed according to their form, number, and name. From their experiences with objects, students were led to drawing and tracing, and then to writing.

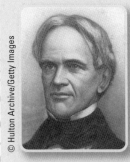

© Hulton Archive/Getty Images

Horace Mann

Horace Mann (1796–1859) has been called the father of American public education. He was appointed secretary of America's first state board of education, created by the Massachusetts legislature, and he toured the state to collect best practices and diffuse this information. Mann was a zealous advocate of free public education, nonsectarian education, teacher training schools, and the abolition of corporal punishment. He strongly supported the normal school for teacher preparation, and, with Henry Barnard, saw the development of many such schools throughout the country.

As secretary of the Massachusetts State Board of Education, Mann wrote a series of 12 annual reports. Following is an excerpt from Annual Report number 12, written in 1848.

Education then, beyond all other devices of human origin, is a great equalizer of the conditions of men—the balance wheel of the social machinery. I do not here mean that it so elevates the moral nature as to make men disdain and abhor the oppression of their fellow men. This idea pertains to another of its attributes. But I mean that it gives each man the independence and the means by which he can resist the selfishness of other men. It does better than to disarm the poor of their hostility toward the rich: it prevents being poor. Agrarianism is the revenge of poverty against wealth. The wanton destruction of the property of others—the burning of hay-ricks, and corn-ricks, the demolition of machinery because it supersedes hand-labor, the sprinkling of vitriol on rich dresses—is only agrarianism run mad. Education prevents both the revenge and the madness.

Johann Friedrich Herbart

Johann Friedrich Herbart (1776–1841) was a German philosopher who advocated a well organized curriculum and a five-step teaching method as follows:

1. Preparation for new lesson
2. Presentation of new lesson
3. Association of new material with ideas learned earlier
4. Use of examples
5. Assessment

Herbart's ideas came to the United States and were used in the normal schools. His five-step teaching method was a forerunner of today's lesson planning.

Together with Horace Mann, Henry Barnard (1811–1900) became a leader in the movement to reform U.S. common schools. He served as secretary of the Connecticut board of commissioners of common schools and, later, worked with educational reform in Rhode Island. Barnard was instrumental in increasing the number of normal schools in the United States in the latter half of the 19th century.

How do the contributions of Pestalozzi, Mann, Herbart, and Barnard affect education today? What do you think each of these early educators saw as the primary purpose of education?

BUILDING BLOCK 10.5

Your Thoughts about American Education in the Young Nation Period

- How did the inferences you made about 19th-century American education in Building Block 10.3 compare with the descriptions you investigated in this section?

- How did education mirror what was going on in the country?

- What do you think was the primary goal of education during this time?

- Which educational philosophy seemed to predominate?

American Education in the Progressive Nation Period

BUILDING BLOCK 10.6

American Schools in the Progressive Nation Period

Use the Internet, the library, and other reference materials to find information about American schools during the progressive nation period (1900–1950).

- What was happening in America during this time?

- Think about developments in industry and technology that occurred as a result of war. What knowledge and skills do you think people needed to function and to contribute to society during this period?

- Who was expected to go to school to gain this knowledge and these skills?

- What do you think school was like?

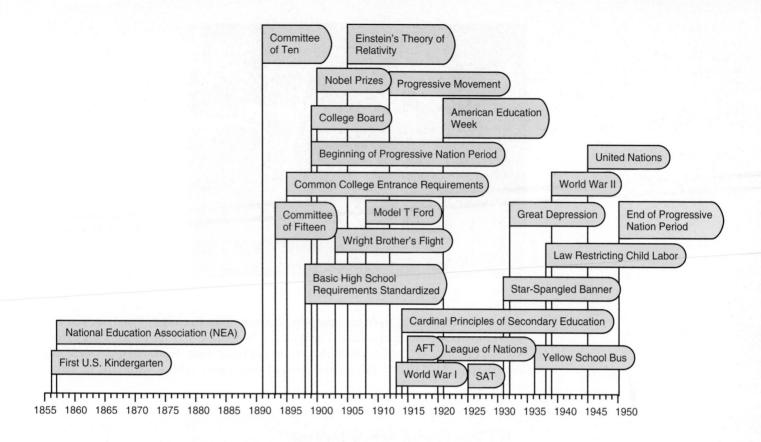

A number of events affected U.S. education during the first half of the 20th century. World War I, the economic boom of the Roaring Twenties, the Great Depression, and World War II all influenced education. During this period, the horse and carriage were replaced by the Model T Ford. The yellow school bus appeared for the first time in 1937. This now-familiar mode of transportation helped to solve the problem of students who quit school rather than having to travel long distances, and they allowed school systems to consolidate widely scattered schoolhouses into central locations. The first Nobel prizes were awarded in 1901. The Wright brothers made the first flight in 1903, the same year that baseball's first World Series was played. Einstein proposed his theory of relativity in 1905. The League of Nations was established in 1919 and was replaced by the United Nations in 1945. Babe Ruth hit 60 home runs in a single season in 1927, establishing a record that stood for 34 years. America adopted *The Star-Spangled Banner* as its national anthem in 1931. Throughout the period, America was establishing itself as an industrial nation, propelled by science and technology and operated by factories.

The increasing number of factories required an increasing amount of manpower to operate them. This need affected both school attendance and curriculum. Many children dropped out of school at an early age so that they could work and contribute to family income. It has been estimated that, in 1900, at least 18% of American children ages 10–15 were employed in industry; in the south, 25% of cotton-mill employees were below the age of 15, with half of these children below the age of 12 (Yellowitz, n.d.). Education was considered less important than money. Child labor organizations and individuals such as Mary Harris "Mother" Jones (1830–1930) fought for children's rights, saying that children must be freed from the workshops and sent to school. However, despite the fiery efforts of Mother Jones, child labor laws were slow to appear. The first federal law restricting child labor was passed in 1938 as part of the Fair Labor Standards Act and was amended in 1949. Meanwhile, the Depression saw a tremendous decrease in available jobs, and children found themselves out of work. Consequently, they were put back in school, causing increased class sizes and severely strained facilities.

Children at work in a cotton mill circa 1900. Before child labor and compulsory education laws were established, children often worked instead of attending school.

© CORBIS

In the early 1900s, over half the school population was rural. Conditions in early rural schoolhouses were primitive. The typical schoolhouse may have been a log cabin, a wooden building, or a sod house with a crude and leaky door. Windows often were small slits without glass and, in the winter, covered with paper rubbed with lard to make it translucent.

BUILDING
BLOCK
10.7

A One-Room Schoolhouse

Look at the photo of the inside of a one-room schoolhouse.
How was the school heated?
Which children were cold in the winter? Which were too hot?
What do you suppose children did if the wind howled through the building?

Library of Congress

The one-room schools typically housed 30 to 40 students of all ages and levels, taught by one teacher. As more and more children attended school, the one-room shacks could no longer handle the demand. This led to the construction of new buildings with numerous classrooms; some even had additional facilities such as lunchrooms and gymnasiums. School officials tried to determine the best way to group the children according to their ages, levels, and needs. The solution was to combine children of approximately the same age in one classroom, a system still in operation today.

Most teachers were women. In 1870, 65% of all classroom teachers were women. By 1900, the number of female teachers had grown to 75%, and the peak occurred in 1920, when 86% of all teachers were women.

Standardization of Education

By the end of the 19th century, schools had widely varying curricula, widely varying student populations, and widely varying community needs. Little consistency existed in the education of students across the country. Many students sought admission to universities, but admission officers had a very difficult time deciding who was eligible.

Two national movements emerged to address problems with education. One, the National Education Association (NEA), focused its attention on curriculum and other educational concerns. The other, the American Federation of Teachers (AFT), focused its attention on labor.

The NEA had been founded in 1857 in Philadelphia as a forum in which educational leaders would meet and discuss common concerns. By the early 20th century, the issues of a standardized school curriculum and college entrance requirements were at the forefront of the NEA's agenda. To address these issues, the NEA sponsored several major committees, described in the sections that follow.

Committee of Ten

In 1891, the Committee of Ten was formed to establish a standard high school curriculum. The committee was chaired by Charles Eliot, president of Harvard University, and included the U.S. Commissioner of Education, university administrators, and public school personnel. The committee determined that the purpose of high school was to prepare intellectually capable students (usually assumed to be white boys) for higher education. The committee recommended that education in the United States comprise 8 years of elementary school and 4 years of secondary school. (Does this sound familiar?) It recommended that high schools offer both classical and contemporary programs. The classical track included Latin and Greek classical studies; the contemporary program included studies of modern languages and English and was considered inferior to the college-preparatory track. The subjects of art, music, physical education, and vocational education were ignored. The committee decided that the goal of high school was to prepare all students, regardless of track, to do well in life, contributing to their own well-being and to society's good, and to prepare some students for college. The curriculum tracks established by the committee still exist in many of today's schools and are viewed the same way with regard to academic vs. vocational programs.

A direct link to the full report of the Committee of Ten is available on the *Building Teachers* companion website.

Committee of Fifteen

The NEA's next task was to look at elementary education. In 1893, the organization convened the Committee of Fifteen, also chaired by Charles Eliot. The committee also proposed reducing elementary school from 10 grades to 8, and recommended that the curriculum include grammar, literature, history, and geography in addition to the 3 Rs. The committee recommended that elementary schools teach hygiene, culture, vocal music, and drawing once a week for an hour, and that they teach manual training, sewing and cooking, algebra, and Latin in the seventh and eighth grades. The committee rejected the ideas of reformers who asserted that children's needs and interests should be considered when developing curriculum, and they rejected the idea of including kindergarten in elementary school.

Committee on College Entrance Requirements

The Committee on College Entrance Requirements, chaired by Chicago's superintendent of high schools, was formed in 1895 to standardize college entrance requirements. Before this time, college applicants had been interviewed by a college's president to test the candidate's knowledge of classical languages, specific readings, and moral character. The basic high school course requirements recommended by the committee consisted of a 4-year course of 16 units. A unit was defined as a full year's work in a subject taught four or five periods a week. This same idea was accepted by the Carnegie Foundation for the Advancement of Teaching, giving rise to the term **Carnegie unit.** The committee recommended the following standard requirements for admission to college:

How do the college entrance requirements of 1899 compare with the college entrance requirements of today?

- Four units of a foreign language
- Four units of mathematics
- Two units of English
- One unit of history
- One unit of science
- Four units of electives

College Entrance Examinations

The College Entrance Examination Board, now known as the College Board, was formed in 1900 to foster uniformity in college preparation by administering examinations in which candidates could demonstrate their understanding of specific subjects. Thus, both the high school curriculum and the university entrance examinations became uniform across the country. The Scholastic Aptitude Test (SAT) was first administered in 1926 to test college applicants' ability to succeed in college. Based on the principles of Binet's IQ test, the SAT assessed aptitude, whereas earlier college entrance examinations had assessed subject matter understanding.

Seven Cardinal Principles of Secondary Education

In 1915, the Commission on the Reorganization of Secondary Education issued the Seven Cardinal Principles of Secondary Education to be used as the primary guide for education throughout America. The Seven Cardinal Principles are as follows:

How do the standardization recommendations made for education resonate in today's schools? How do the Seven Cardinal Principles of Education compare with the goals of education you investigated in Chapter 6?

1. Health
2. Command of fundamental principles (reading, writing, and mathematics)
3. Worthy home membership
4. Vocation (knowing oneself to be able to choose from a variety of potential careers)
5. Civic education
6. Worthy use of leisure
7. Ethical character

Working Conditions of Teachers

Another major issue addressed in the early 20th century was the labor practices and working conditions of teachers, an issue on which the American Federation of Teachers focused. Founded in 1916, the AFT sought to improve teaching conditions, increase wages, and provide benefits for teachers.

One of the founders of the AFT was John Dewey. Dewey, the philosopher and progressive educator, stressed that worker and employer should serve each other; he was concerned that teachers were left out of the decision-making process. The AFT was formed, in part, to remedy that situation, and it continues to uphold the right of teachers to help form school policies.

Kindergartens and Nursery Schools

The first **kindergarten** ("children's garden") was established in Germany by educator Friedrich Fröbel in 1837. The concept was imported to the United States by immigrants such as Margarethe Schurs, who founded the first U.S. kindergarten in Watertown, Wisconsin, in 1856. The kindergarten concept captured the attention of American educators such as Elizabeth Peabody, who founded a kindergarten in Boston in 1873. Fröbel's kindergarten was based on free self-activity, creativity, social participation, and motor expression.

The 1920s saw the development of the nursery school, an extension of the kindergarten. Very few day nurseries existed in the United States before this time, and these were primarily operated by charity groups as day care centers to assist poor mothers who needed to work (Jacobson, 1999). In the 1920s and 1930s, nursery schools were developed to serve as laboratories for the child-study movements. Their focus was similar to the focus of the kindergartens: promoting happier and healthier children. During the Depression years, the federal government provided subsidies to establish and maintain nursery schools, causing these schools to become more widespread. With the manpower and employment demands for women during World War II, the nursery school became an integral part of the public school system (Kandel, 1957).

Literacy

Of the men who were drafted into military service during World War I, some 25% were illiterate. Alarmed about the low literacy rate of America's young men, the NEA, in conjunction with the American Legion, decided to act to raise public awareness of the importance of education. One of their first actions was the declaration of American Education Week, first observed in 1921. This led to steps to improve how schools teach and handle the curriculum and, ultimately, to increased literacy. American Education Week is celebrated annually to this day during the first full week before Thanksgiving.

> Why do you think many young men were illiterate at the time of World War I?

Teacher Preparation

In 1900, there were fewer than 50 normal schools in America. However, institutions of higher education, such as liberal arts colleges, teachers' colleges, state universities, and private universities, began to offer teacher preparation courses and programs. Teacher education went from being the subject of a course to departments, schools, and entire colleges within universities. Teacher education had arrived as a profession.

Progressivism

In the early 20th century, the United States saw a progressive movement in political and educational thought. During the presidency of Theodore Roosevelt (1901–1909), the nation was determined to industrialize and become a world economic leader. As a result of the emphasis on industrialization, American factories needed better-educated workers. This led to a restructuring of education, which occurred under the leadership of John Dewey.

The early 1900s were a time of reform, when efforts were made to control the corporate trusts and monopolies and to prevent corrupt politicians from running schools. Progressives, mainly from the middle class, were political, social, and educational reformers.

John Dewey was a key player in the progressive movement, especially in education. Considered the father of progressivism in education, Dewey subscribed to the following ideas:

- Education must foster the participation of all of society's members on equal terms and put students in a place of primary importance.

- The purpose of education is to prepare students to be lifelong learners in an ever-changing society.
- The emphasis of education is on the role of the child in a social setting.
- The teacher is the facilitator.
- The student's role is to learn and develop new understandings continually, through his or her own discoveries.
- Schools should encourage collaborative work and the use of new technologies.

Dewey thought that learning is a process that begins at birth, builds unconsciously, and comes from the demands of society (for example, the need to learn a new language). He said that education must begin with insights into the children's capacities, interests, and habits. He believed that students should be given opportunities to solve problems using a scientific method of complete thinking. According to Dewey, the school should be a form of community life and a representation of realistic life. (See Chapter 2 for details about progressive educational philosophy.)

How has Dewey's progressivism movement influenced today's thinking about education?

BUILDING
BLOCK
10.8

Your Thoughts about American Education in the Progressive Nation Period

- How do the inferences you made about American education in the progressive nation period in Building Block 10.6 compare with the descriptions you investigated in this section?
- How did education mirror what was going on in the country?
- What do you think was the primary goal of education during this time?
- Which educational philosophy seemed to predominate?

American Education in the Postwar Period

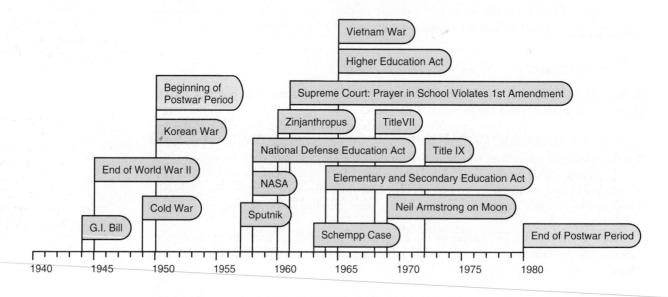

American Schools in the Postwar Period

Think about American society and schools during the postwar period (1950–1980).

- What was happening in America during this time?
- On what major concerns and goals was society focused?
- What knowledge and skills do you think students needed to learn in school to help address these concerns and meet these goals?
- Who was expected to go to school to gain this knowledge and these skills?
- What do you think school was like?

Many events during the postwar period shaped the nature of education in the United States. World War II ended in 1945, but the Soviet Union's successful atomic test in 1949 ushered in the Cold War. The Korean War began in 1950 and lasted until 1953, and the involvement of U.S. troops in the Vietnam War lasted from 1965 to 1975. In 1957, Russia successfully launched Sputnik, the first artificial satellite. NASA was founded in 1958. In 1962 John Glenn became the first American to orbit the earth, and in 1969 Neil Armstrong became the first man to set foot on the moon. In 1960, Louis Leakey found the skull of *Zinjanthropus* (called *Nutcracker Man* because of its giant molars), suggesting that human evolution began in Africa, not in Asia as previously thought.

The kinds of schools we attend, the curriculum we study while we are there, and the diversity of students' faces we see in the classroom all reflect this period's changes in social and cultural life, politics, law, and technology.

> How did post–World War II events affect American education?

Federal Involvement in Education

The emergence of federal involvement in education may have been one of the most important post–World War II developments in American education.

Servicemen's Readjustment Act

The first major federal aid package for higher education was the Servicemen's Readjustment Act of 1944, better known as the **GI Bill.** This act provided funds for returning World War II veterans to attend college. The current version of the bill is called the Montgomery GI Bill and provides up to 36 months of education benefits for college, business, technical, correspondence or vocational courses; apprenticeship or job training; or flight school. It provides assistance for members of all U.S. armed service personnel, including those on active duty and those in the selected reserve.

> www A direct link to the Montgomery GI Bill is available on the *Building Teachers* companion website.

National Defense Education Act

In 1958, President Dwight Eisenhower signed the **National Defense Education Act (NDEA)** to provide federal aid for education in the United States at all levels, public and private. The launching of Sputnik the year before pointed to urgent needs for advances in U.S. science and mathematics education. The bill was primarily intended to stimulate the advancement of education in science, mathematics, and modern foreign languages, and it specifically prohibited federal direction, supervision, or control over curricular matters, administration, or personnel. Furthermore, the United States was in a Cold War arms race that represented an atomic threat to the country. The education of America's youth supported by the NDEA was considered vital to the national security. Can you explain why?

> Why is the launching of Sputnik considered a major turning point in American education? Why was the education of America's youth in science, technology, and foreign languages considered vital to America during the Cold War era?

Elementary and Secondary Education Act

In 1964, President Lyndon Johnson declared a nationwide war on poverty and the causes of poverty. In 1965, as part of this war on poverty, Johnson signed into law the **Elementary** and Secondary Education Act (ESEA), which provided federal guidance and funds to school districts with large numbers of disadvantaged students. The ESEA helped to establish continuing expectations concerning the federal government's responsibility in supporting education. The act has been reauthorized every 5 to 7 years; the latest reauthorization was passed by Congress in 2001 and is known as the No Child Left Behind Act of 2001.

The ESEA provided funds for a wide spectrum of educational programs. One of the key programs is **Title I,** which allocates financial resources to meet the needs of students in high-poverty schools. Another is **Project Head Start.** Head Start was launched to provide preschool children of low-income families with a free, comprehensive program to meet their emotional, social, health, nutritional, and psychological needs. Children between the ages of 3 and 5 who are from families that meet the federal poverty guidelines are eligible for Head Start services. However, up to 10% of the enrollment opportunities may be filled by children whose families exceed the low-income guidelines, and 10% of enrollments should be offered to children with disabilities.

ESEA was amended in 1968 with **Title VII,** which provided federal aid to local school districts to help them address the needs of students with limited English ability, stressing language development for students in both English and their native languages. It helped to address the needs of the children of the numerous immigrants, especially people from Asia, who began flowing into the United States after the Korean and Vietnam wars. This act has been replaced by the English Language Acquisition Act under the umbrella of the No Child Left Behind Act of 2001, passed by Congress in 2002, stressing that schools should focus on English only (Crawford, 2002).

Higher Education Act

Recognizing the challenges that educationally and economically disadvantaged students face in pursuing higher educational goals, the **Higher Education Act** was enacted by Congress in 1965 to provide funds for loans, work study, and institutional aid in postsecondary institutions. Approximately 95% of the funds goes to student aid in the form of Pell Grants for economically disadvantaged students. The act has undergone reauthorization approximately every 5 years since its original passage, but Pell Grant funding has not grown as rapidly as college costs, so the grants pay far less of today's college costs than originally intended (Baum, 2003).

Title IX

Title IX of the Education Amendments of 1972 to the Civil Rights Act of 1964 was signed into law by President Richard Nixon in 1972. It provides for equal athletic opportunities regardless of gender: "No person in the United States shall, on the basis of sex, be excluded from participation in, denied benefits of, or be subjected to discrimination under any education program or activity receiving Federal assistance" (DeBray, 2003, p. 837).

Curriculum

Education in the 1950s and 1960s was influenced by many theorists and psychologists, many of whom you have investigated elsewhere in this textbook. Education was especially affected by the emphasis on inquiry-oriented, problem-based curriculum and on the development of higher-order thinking skills. Lessons were designed to foster reconciliation of new material with students' prior knowledge; multiple textbooks were used instead of the traditional single textbook; and the use of multimedia became standard in classrooms. Television, which evolved into educational technology, made its way into American classrooms; in the early 1960s, entire high schools would crowd into an auditorium with one small TV set on a stage to watch important world events unfold before them. Inquiry-based curriculum was emphasized through such innovative programs as SCIS (Science Curriculum Improvement Study) science, whole language writing, modern math, BSCS (Biological Science Curriculum Study) biology, issue-centered social studies, and other hands-on, inquiry-based programs.

Direct links to the home pages of Head Start, the National Head Start Association, and the Early Head Start National Resource Center are available on the *Building Teachers* companion website.

A direct link to the text of Title IX is provided on the *Building Teachers* companion website.

How does Title IX affect your college? There is discussion about extending this law to high schools and even lower grade levels. What do you think?

The *curriculum reform movement,* as it came to be known, gave students subject matter choices, flexible scheduling, individualized instruction, and nongraded schools. However, college entrance test scores began to drop, school enrollments began to fall, and public confidence in teaching began eroding. By the 1970s, there was a general feeling that the education system had lost sight of its basic purpose. As a result, American thinking returned to the pursuit of traditional academic studies in the liberal arts, mathematics, and sciences.

Education and Religion

The question of the influence of religion in education has a long history. The First Amendment of the U.S. Constitution states that "Congress shall make no law respecting an establishment of religion, or prohibiting the free exercise thereof . . ." This declaration was in response to the religious persecution Americans felt in England from the state-established church and says that the government will not proclaim a national religion. It insures religious freedom, protecting the church from governmental influence.

"Separation of church and state" is a phrase originated by Thomas Jefferson in his "Wall of Separation" letter to the Danbury Baptist Association of Connecticut written January 1, 1802. Jefferson wrote:

> *Believing with you that religion is a matter which lies solely between man and his God, that he owes account to none other for his faith or his worship, that the legitimate powers of government reach actions only and not opinions, I contemplate with sovereign reverence that act of the whole American people which declared that their legislature should make no law respecting an establishment of religion, or prohibiting the free exercise thereof, thus building a wall of separation between Church and State. Adhering to this expression of the supreme will of the nation in behalf of the rights of conscience, I shall see with sincere satisfaction the progress of those sentiments which tend to restore to man all his natural rights, convinced he has no natural right in opposition to his social duties. [Italics added.] (From USConstitution.net.)*

What do you think Jefferson meant in his letter?
How is the First Amendment interpreted today?

The interpretation of "separation of church and state" by the public and by the courts has had a major impact on schools. In 1961, the Supreme Court ruled that prayer in schools was a violation of the First Amendment. And in the 1963 Schempp case, the Superior Court ruled that it is unconstitutional to read the Bible and recite the Lord's Prayer as part of the regular program of exercises in public schools. As a result, public schools discontinued the practice of classroom or school-wide prayer, and many replaced prayer with a moment of silence at some point during the day, during which students may pray silently if they wish. It may be hard to keep students from prayer, however. A popular bumper sticker reads, "As long as there are tests, there will be prayer in schools."

Another challenge came in 2002 when a California father, an atheist, filed a suit that contended that the Pledge of Allegiance was unconstitutional. In 1954, Congress had added the phrase, "under God" to the pledge in an effort to distinguish our nation from atheist and communist Russia during the Cold War. In 2002, the father brought suit, alleging that having to recite the pledge each morning, as most students do, forced a religion upon his daughter. In 2004, the case was dismissed on a technicality, with the Supreme Court not ruling on the constitutionality of the pledge (Branigin & Lane, 2004). Still, the challenge continued to cause a great deal of public controversy, and schools wondered what accommodations they might have to make for students who choose not to recite all or part of the pledge.

The principle of separation of church and state and the courts prohibit religious instruction in the public schools. However, the George W. Bush administration established a Center for Faith-Based and Community Initiatives that provides federal grant funding to faith-based and community groups "to ensure equal access to education and to promote educational excellence for all Americans" (U.S. Department of Education, n.d.). The complex and emotionally charged problem of the relationship between religion and education in America is still debated today.

Education of Catholics

During the 19th-century industrialization boom, great numbers of people immigrated to the United States. Many of these immigrants were Catholic. Catholics had different religious beliefs than the Protestant majority, and many feared that their children's support for the Roman Catholic Church would diminish if the children attended public schools. This concern, augmented by the vocal and sometimes violent discrimination against Catholics, led to the establishment of Roman Catholic parochial schools. The Church tried to obtain government money to support its schools but was unsuccessful because such requests went against the principle of the separation of church and state. However, government support for parochial schools in the form of busing and support services has been allowed since the1970s.

There is much debate over the use of federal funds to support religious schools. Have you been in a situation touched by these debates? What are your thoughts about this topic? Why?

BUILDING BLOCK 10.10

Your Thoughts about American Education in the Postwar Period

- How do the inferences you made about postwar American education in Building Block 10.9 compare with the descriptions you investigated in this section?
- How did education mirror what was going on in the country?
- What do you think was the primary goal of education during this time?
- What educational philosophy seemed to predominate?
- What factors during postwar times have influenced contemporary education? Which do you feel have had positive influences? Which do you feel have had negative influences?

American Education in the Modern Period

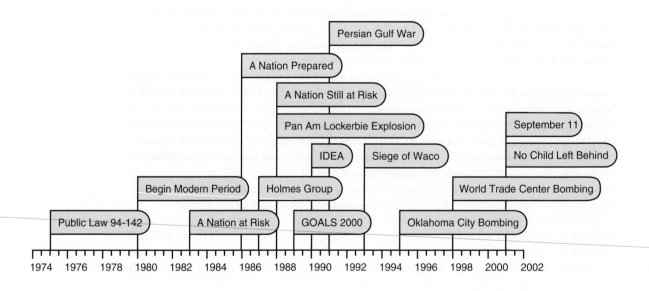

American Schools in the Modern Period

Consider the period from 1980 to modern times. Perhaps this time frame encompasses most or all of your lifetime. Think about what has happened in our country since 1980.

- What were some significant events during this period?
- On what concerns and goals has society focused?
- What knowledge and skills were necessary for people to function, thrive, and contribute to society in the 1980s? The 1990s? Beyond 2000?
- To what extent do you think Americans believe that *everyone* should have this knowledge and these skills?

Let us reflect on some of the events that have occurred since 1980. To an extent, violence has characterized this period. In 1988, a Pan Am Boeing 747 passenger jet exploded from a terrorist bomb over Lockerbie, Scotland, killing all 259 people aboard. The Persian Gulf war began in 1991 and lasted $3\frac{1}{2}$ months. The siege in Waco, Texas, ended in tragedy in 1993. The Oklahoma City bombing occurred in 1995 and the World Trade Center bombing occurred in 1998. On September 11, 2001, terrorist-flown planes crashed into the World Trade Center, the Pentagon, and a field in Pennsylvania, killing some 3,000 people, about 2,800 at the World Trade Center. Combat operations began in Afghanistan shortly thereafter to rout the seat of Al Qaeda, the terrorist group responsible for the attacks of September 11. The United States invaded Iraq in 2003.

World population reached 6 billion in 1999.

How do you suppose these events have affected who and what is taught in American schools? You have explored many modern developments in education elsewhere in this textbook. Let us look at the highlights. (You will investigate details of the modern era of education in the United States in Chapter 14.)

As you may have gathered, education in the United States has become increasingly available to all children. Remnants of midcentury segregation linger, but black activist and other groups are working to foster opportunities for African Americans that are equal to those of whites. However, there has been nationwide sentiment against allowing children of illegal aliens to attend our free public schools.

Elementary education has begun to include public preschools for children 4 years old or even younger. Middle schools are replacing junior high schools, and secondary schools are phasing out much of the former vocational track in favor of college-preparatory programs (see Chapter 7). President George W. Bush has made it a national priority that students obtain at least 2 years of college (Bush, 2005).

Public Law 94-142 was enacted in 1975 to assure that all handicapped children receive a free and appropriate public education in the least restrictive environment. This law was replaced in 1990 by the Individuals with Disabilities Education Act (IDEA), which was renewed in 1997 and again in 2004. (The law and its implications are discussed in Chapter 5.) The reauthorization of the IDEA has focused national attention and resources on ensuring that all children receive the best possible education. It is not unusual to see two teachers in one classroom, one working with children with special needs, or to see a signer translating for a student with a hearing impairment, or to hear a Braille typewriter clicking as students with vision-impairments take notes.

Educational Reform during the Modern Period

In 1983, the National Commission on Excellence in Education issued its report, *A Nation at Risk* (see Chapter 2). The commission was composed of 18 members, including university presidents, college professors, teachers, school board members, school administrators, business leaders, and even a Nobel prize winner in chemistry. The report began, "Our nation is at risk. Our once unchallenged preeminence in commerce, industry, science, and technological innovations is being overtaken by competitors throughout the world. . . . Our society and its educational institutions seem to have lost sight of the basic purposes of schooling" (National Commission on Excellence in Education, 1983, p. 1). The commission felt schools must develop not only the scientific and technological talents of American youth, but also their facility in English, mathematics, history, geography, economics, and foreign languages.

The report essentially endorsed the traditional academic model of the college-preparatory high school, and made five recommendations for attaining excellence in education:

1. "Five new basics" should be added to the curriculum of America's secondary schools:
   Four years of English
   Three years of mathematics
   Three years of science
   Three years of social studies
   One-half year of computer science

2. More rigorous and measurable standards should be adopted.

3. The school year should be extended to make the time needed to learn the "new basics."

4. The teaching should be improved through enhanced preparation and professionalism.

5. Accountability should be added to education.

A direct link to the full text of *A Nation at Risk* is available on the *Building Teachers* companion website.

How have the recommendations of *A Nation At Risk* affected education as you know it?

As a result of this report, many states strengthened their high school graduation requirements. Do the recommendations of *A Nation At Risk* sound familiar?

Despite intense nationwide reform efforts, another educational summit was held in Washington, D.C., in 1988 to discuss continued concerns over the state of education in America. Its findings were summarized in *A Nation Still at Risk: An Education Manifesto*. The summit was attended by William Bennett, then Secretary of Education, prominent educators from universities and public schools, and prominent business leaders. The manifesto asserted that, whereas our nation did not currently face imminent dangers of economic decline or technological inferiority, the state of our children's education still was far from where it should be.

President George H. W. Bush hosted a governors' summit in 1989; this summit launched a follow-up initiative to strengthen the curriculum of public school education and to increase the accountability of schools. The nation's governors identified six sweeping national goals in a document called GOALS 2000. You can find the full list of goals and their measurable targets in Chapter 6.

Because GOALS 2000 was a federal law, the federal government awarded grants to universities and professional organizations to develop standards in most curriculum areas and developed an Office of Assessment to measure progress toward meeting the goals. Thus, the development of national standards and educational accountability became a major undertaking in the 1990s. Each discipline convened task forces to develop standards. Results included national standards in all subject areas and grade levels. The standards were intended as guides and were intentionally written to provide the flexibility needed to accommodate the needs of individual students and the environments of individual communities. (See Chapter 14.) Nonetheless, there is concern that national standards could be perceived as a national curriculum, and that such a curriculum would work in opposition to programs designed to meet individual and local needs.

The most recent nationwide development in education is the No Child Left Behind Act of 2001 discussed in Chapter 1 and elsewhere in this textbook.

Improvement of Teaching

The improvement of teaching was another major educational focus of the late 1980s and 1990s. In 1986, the Carnegie Forum on Education and the Economy released the report *A Nation Prepared: Teachers for the Twenty-First Century*. The report called for stronger preparation of teachers in both subject matter and pedagogy and recommended the formation of the National Board for Professional Teaching Standards (NBPTS) and national board certification for exemplary teachers. The NBPTS was formed in 1987 with a primary goal of establishing standards for teaching and certifying exemplary teachers at the national level. NBPTS standards are listed in Chapter 1.

In 1987, the Holmes Group, a consortium of research universities with teacher preparation programs, set out to change the way teachers are prepared by strengthening connections between colleges of education and other colleges in the universities and also strengthening partnership school arrangements. Among the lasting contributions of the Holmes Group are the 5-year teacher preparation program discussed in Chapter 9 and the professional development school concept, in which teacher education is provided jointly and equally by the university and the local partner schools.

Technology

One of the major advances in American education during the modern period is the use of educational technology. Educational technology has two primary functions in schools. It is used in actual classroom teaching to help students learn, and it is used to help teachers and other school personnel in their administrative tasks. Educational technology and its applications in the classroom are discussed extensively throughout this textbook.

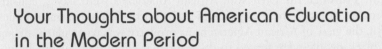

BUILDING BLOCK 10.12

Your Thoughts about American Education in the Modern Period

- How do the inferences you made about modern American education in Building Block 10.11 compare with the descriptions you investigated in this section?
- How does education mirror what is going on in the country?
- What do you think is the primary goal of education during this time?
- Which educational philosophy seems to predominate?

Education of Minorities

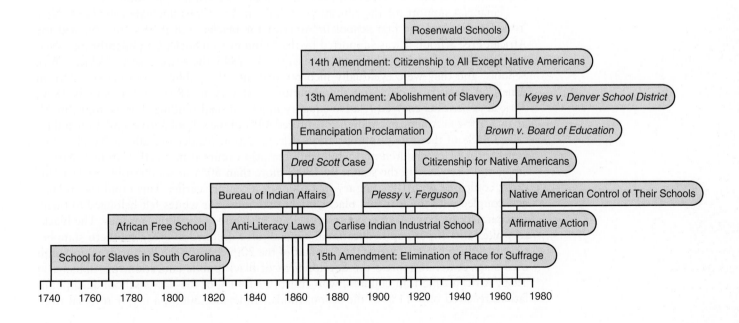

The education of minorities has been slow to arrive in America. African Americans, Native Americans, Hispanic Americans, Chinese Americans, Japanese Americans, and other ethnic groups were not afforded educational opportunities equal to those of the white population until the mid-20th century, and some still do not have equal educational opportunities.

Education of African Americans

The road to the education of African Americans has been long, arduous, bumpy, and often violent.

Educating African Americans

Reflect on the history of African Americans in the United States. List a few major events that signaled positive steps toward their education and a few major setbacks that impeded their education.

From colonial times through the Civil War, African Americans were slaves, considered property, not people. Although there were slaves in the northern and central colonies as well as in the south, the view of African Americans as property was particularly strong in the south, where black people were forced to do work that supported various industries, especially cotton.

In general, slaves were not educated, largely out of fear that slaves who could read would demand freedom. In the mid-1700s, however, religious groups in Virginia, believing that literacy was a prerequisite for baptism, began to teach slaves to read. A school for slaves was opened in South Carolina in 1743, but the legislature, concerned about the consequences of literacy movements, enacted a law prohibiting any person from teaching slaves to read or write. In 1829, Georgia enacted a similar law, and this was followed rapidly by antiliteracy laws in Louisiana, North Carolina, Virginia, and Alabama. In 1834, South Carolina enacted a law prohibiting slaves from being taught to read or write, but Quakers of the Society of Friends of North Carolina urged that this law be repealed (Lewis, n.d.), saying that "religion should be taught to the colored population to lead to kindness of the masters and faithfulness of the slaves, promote the morality of the white population, and furnish slaves with light and hope" (Lewis, n.d., p. 386).

Financial support for the education of African Americans fluctuated. In 1794, New York City opened the first school in America for blacks, and it was free. Named the African Free School, it was supported by the Manumission Society, a philanthropic organization devoted to the abolition of slavery. By 1843 there were seven African Free Schools, and they were eventually incorporated into the public school system (African American Registry, n.d.). After the abolition of slavery in 1865, and as late as 1890, African Americans enjoyed relative equality in educational funding. For example, in Alabama, African American children constituted 44% of the school-aged population and received 44% of the state's appropriations for education (Anderson, 2003). Nearly equal benefits for black children and white children also occurred in North Carolina, Mississippi, and elsewhere in the south. By 1900, more than 50% of southern blacks were literate, compared with 10% literacy in 1800, just a century earlier. This rapid rise in literacy, coupled with the fear that blacks might take jobs that whites felt belonged to them, precipitated the reversal of equality in the late 19th and early 20th centuries. The black-to-white ratio of per-pupil educational expenditures declined in every southern state between 1890 and 1910. During the first half of the 20th century, the dominant white south used state power to repress the development of black public education. In Alabama in 1930, African American children, who constituted 40% of the state's school-aged population, received only 11% of the school funds (Anderson, 2003), a major reversal from

Prior to significant school desegregation, African-American children in the South attended segregated schools, like these students attending Annie Davis School in Tuskegee, Alabama, circa 1902.

Library of Congress

just 40 years earlier. One after another, southern states enacted legislation to pay teachers on the basis of the certification they held, enabling, for example, the state of Mississippi to pay $55 a month to white teachers but only $25 per month to African American teachers in the early 20th century, partly because black teachers taught only black students. In 1910, Mississippi budgeted only 20% of its annual school budget for African Americans, who constituted 60% of the school-aged population.

Discriminatory state budgets did not deter southern blacks from educating their children. In 1917, Julius Rosenwald, president of Sears, Roebuck, & Company and a friend of Booker T. Washington, initiated a school-building program to help solve the problem of educational opportunity for African American children. Over the next 15 years, Rosenwald contributed more than $4 million, and the black community raised a matching amount, to build more than 5,000 elementary schools, called *Rosenwald schools*, across the south. By the time the school-building program was discontinued in 1932, 90% of elementary school–aged black children attended school, compared with 91% of white children of the same age. This was an increase of 54% in a single generation—in 1900, only 36% of black children and 55% of white children attended school. However, unlike the schools for white children, which focused on academics, the Rosenwald schools focused on vocational education.

Southern blacks were largely excluded from secondary education. Between 1904 and 1916, the number of secondary schools in Georgia, for instance, increased from 4 to 122, but these were schools for whites. There were no 4-year public secondary schools for blacks, even though African Americans constituted 46% of the state's secondary school–aged population. The same situation was true in the other southern states, and held true even at the beginning of World War II, when 77% of the high school–aged southern black population was not enrolled in high school.

The challenges of African American education were not limited to the south. Blacks were considered inferior to whites in the northern colonies, and this adversely affected African Americans' education.

The free and equal education of African Americans could not take place until the African American population was, itself, freed from past bondage. Key 19th-century decisions are shown in Table 10.1.

The **Brown v. Board of Education of Topeka** decision, which required desegregation of schools across the United States, was issued in 1954. In this decision, the Supreme Court ruled unanimously that separate schools for whites and blacks were inherently unequal and thus violated the 14th Amendment. In the Court's decision, Chief Justice Earl Warren wrote, "In the field of public education, the doctrine of 'separate but equal' has no place. Separate educational facilities are inherently unequal" (*Brown v. Board of Education,* 1954, p. 5).

TABLE 10.1 Key 19th-Century Decisions Affecting the Education of African Americans

Date	Decision
1857	In the *Dred Scott* decision, the U.S. Supreme Court ruled that a slave was *not* a citizen.
1863	President Abraham Lincoln issued the Emancipation Proclamation, freeing all slaves.
1865	The 13th Amendment, abolishing slavery, was ratified.
1868	The 14th Amendment, granting citizenship and civil rights to all persons born or naturalized in the United States, including blacks but *not* Native Americans, was ratified.
1870	The 15th Amendment, eliminating race as a bar to voting, was ratified.
1896	In *Plessy v. Ferguson*, the Supreme Court ruled that "separate but equal facilities" were constitutional under the 14th Amendment. This case dealt with Homer Plessy, who rode in a railroad car designated for whites, breaking Florida law. He was arrested and found guilty by Judge John Ferguson. Plessy argued that the separate car law violated his civil rights, but the Supreme Court upheld Judge Ferguson's decision. The concept of "separate but equal" was to remain the law of the land until 1954, when the Court reversed the decision.

Desegregation was difficult. In 1957, President Eisenhower sent the National Guard to Little Rock, Arkansas, to force desegregation of public schools by escorting nine African American children into a white high school. In 1961, President John F. Kennedy sent federal troops to enforce integration at the University of Mississippi after riots occurred. In 1965 Affirmative Action became law; in 1967, a federal court ordered that governors and state boards of education integrate all schools that year. In 1971, the Supreme Court upheld a measure to bus children in order to force integration in public schools.

Despite these constitutional advances, much opposition arose to awarding equal rights to African Americans. Notable among the dissenters was the Ku Klux Klan, which was first formed secretly in Tennessee in 1866 to terrorize blacks.

Among the many early civil rights leaders, two names stand out for their contributions to education: W. E. B. DuBois and Booker T. Washington. W. E. B. DuBois was the first African American to receive a Ph.D. from Harvard. Founder of the National Associ-

> Busing for integration still occurs in many school districts. How about yours?

© Bettmann/CORBIS

W. E. B. DuBois

© CORBIS

Booker T. Washington

ation for the Advancement of Colored People (NAACP), DuBois believed that African Americans needed intellectual training to prepare for leadership positions, and his many books written during the early 20th century helped make great strides in the African American community. Booker T. Washington, born a slave in Virginia in 1856, founded the Tuskegee Normal School for Colored Teachers, which later became the Tuskegee Institute. Washington headed the Tuskegee Institute and taught the newly freed African Americans to be teachers, craftsmen, and businessmen, preparing African Americans for employment with practical skills. DuBois fostered solid academic preparation of African Americans, and Washington fostered their vocational education.

Education of Native Americans

Native Americans were used as slaves during the colonial period in the north. During the 19th century, Native Americans were taught farming, mechanical skills, and domestic chores, and they were taught religion to ensure their salvation and to "civilize" them. Native Americans were not granted citizenship until 1924, almost 60 years after all other residents (including African Americans, Hispanics, Asian Americans, and other immigrants) had been granted that privilege.

The education of Native Americans was controlled from Washington, D.C., by the Office of Indian Education, a branch of the Bureau of Indian Affairs organized in the late 1800s. It was established to "carry out the federal government's commitment to Indian tribes" (Office of Indian Education Programs, n.d.). Under the control of the Bureau of Indian Affairs, Native American children were placed in boarding schools taught by white teachers to acculturate Indian youth into "American" ways of thinking and living. For example, the Carlile Indian Industrial School was opened in Pennsylvania in 1879 by Brigadier General Richard H. Pratt, who wanted to educate Native Americans rather than subjugate them. The school's most celebrated student was Jim Thorpe, an Olympic gold medalist. The school's goal was the assimilation of Native Americans into white culture; it taught the Native American students how to be American citizens and provided education in basic academic subjects and vocational training.

In 1965, Native Americans demanded control of the schools that taught their children, and they created tribal schools, where Native American cultures were taught to preserve those cultures and their traditions. These schools were federally funded. Today, schools for Native Americans are locally controlled but are operated by the Office of Indian Education. Besides core subjects, the curriculum often includes instruction in native languages, English as a Second Language, and tribal history and culture.

Apache children on arrival at the Carlisle Indian School in Pennsylvania wearing traditional clothing (left), and Apache children at the Carlisle School four months later (right).

Education of Hispanic Americans

From the mid-18th century to the early 20th century, Hispanic Americans were discriminated against, along with African Americans, Native Americans, and people from other ethnic groups. Hispanic students were taught religion, but neither the English language nor American or Hispanic cultures. Although they often had freer access to schooling than blacks or Native Americans, they were frequently segregated into the predominantly black urban schools. In 1973, the Supreme Court decided, in the case of *Keyes v. Denver School District* (Howard University School of Law, 2004), that Hispanic students have a right to attend desegregated educational facilities and a right to bilingual education to help them become proficient in English. However, whereas African American students have become mostly desegregated over time, Hispanic students often continue to be segregated. This is partly because of high concentrations of Hispanic population in large metropolitan cities and other locales, and partly because of culture. Many Spanish-speaking immigrants in the United States do not mind that their children go to school largely with other Hispanics; such families feel more comfortable dealing with schools in which the majority of parents share their common culture, language, and values (Wells, 1989).

---

from the TEACHER — Burt Saxon, Ed.D.

Courtesy of Burt Saxon

Remembering Lawrence Cremin

Lawrence Cremin came along just when I needed him most—or perhaps I should say his ideas came along just when I needed them most. Then again, it is often impossible to separate a man from his ideas, which was certainly the case with Professor Cremin.

The year was 1975 and I had just finished my fifth year of teaching at Lee High School, a desegregated school in New Haven, Connecticut. I was completely exhausted, but also somewhat discouraged. Most of my Jewish students were generally doing great, but most of my African American students were not doing nearly as well. I had been reading *Schooling in Capitalist America* by Samuel Bowles and Herbert Gintis, which argued that public schools essentially assure the reproduction of the socioeconomic patterns in America. What I had seen at Lee High School seemed to fit this framework. I had tried as hard as I could to help all my students acquire the academic skills they needed, but it seemed that most of my African American students lagged fairly far behind.

I needed to regroup for a couple years. Teachers College of Columbia University had numerous doctoral programs. I found the most flexible one, called Family and Community Education. I was allowed to take any course in the curriculum and was encouraged to take Lawrence Cremin's History of American Education course.

Lawrence Cremin is, without a doubt, the greatest historian of American education ever. He was not only one of the great professors at Teachers College, he was also the president. He had taken the presidency only on the condition that he would be allowed to continue teaching his History of American Education course. That impressed me quite a bit.

When I walked through the front door of Teachers College to register, I saw a massive portrait of John Dewey and a distinguished-looking man walking by carrying a cup of coffee. The man asked, "May I help you?' and pointed me toward the auditorium. Later I realized the man was Lawrence Cremin. That impressed me even more.

I was not so sure how I would react to Professor Cremin's ideas. Somehow I believed he was a celebrationist, extolling the virtues of public education in America without seeing any flaws. But his lectures presented a slightly different perspective. Lawrence Cremin believed that, historically, American public education had become more democratic, more tolerant, and more responsive to all minorities. He believed this was similar to the historical trend in America in general, but he also observed that public schools caused this trend as much as they reflected it. He certainly did not see the public schools as flawless, but he did see them as one of the key institutions in our democracy.

Professor Cremin encouraged questions at the end of his lectures and he invited his students also to leave questions under his office door. Although there were 130 students in the course, I noticed that I asked as many questions as the other 129 combined. Perhaps this was because I was looking for a rebuttal to the ideas of Bowles and Gintis, Michael Katz, and other radical historians. Once I left this question under his door:

Professor Cremin, you mentioned in passing that your own ancestors were poor eastern European Jewish peasants. Now you are president of

The number of Latino children in the United States is steadily increasing and is expected to reach 25% of the K–12 population by 2025 (White House Initiative on Educational Excellence for Hispanic Americans, 1999). How do you feel schools should react to the rising number of Latino students? Some of these students are illegal immigrants or the children of illegal immigrants. What do the laws in your state say about providing free education to illegal immigrants? Do you agree? What should schools do about the situation in your state?

Education of Asian Pacific Americans

The Asian Pacific American population is the largest growing minority group in America today (Marshall, 2002) and is often referred to as the "model minority" group. The Asian Pacific community is comprised of three general, broad, and distinctive ethnic groups: (1) Pacific Islanders (Hawaiians, Samoans, and Guamanians); (2) Southeast Asians (Vietnamese, Thais, Cambodians, Laotians, Burmese, and Filipinos); and (3) East Asians (Chinese, Japanese, and Koreans) (Huang, 1994). Each group is characterized by its own dis-

---

from the TEACHER   Burt Saxon, Ed.D.—cont'd

Teachers College. Is it possible your own personal experiences have led you to overestimate the amount of social mobility in America directly due to public education?

Professor Cremin seemed to like my question. He answered it honestly to start the next class. He said he had never thought about this issue. He then noted that historians must be very aware of their own biases and that he would think seriously about this matter.

That was more than good enough for me. I needed to do some serious thinking about this matter myself. My own ancestors, like Professor Cremin's, were eastern European Jewish peasants. None of my four grandparents went past the sixth grade. Yet my father, born in America, became a lawyer, and his brother became a doctor. My mother's family was even more remarkable. My grandmother bore 17 children, nine of whom died before their fifth birthday. My mother was the second surviving child born in the United States. Like her sisters, she almost finished college. Her two brothers did finish college. One became an auditor, the other an engineer. The engineer became president of his company a year before he retired. My brother, a surgeon, called me one day to say that Uncle Bud's company was on the Fortune 500 list. We had always thought it was a Mom-and-Pop operation.

In other words, my own family history provided a stark refutation to the thesis of the radical educational historians that social mobility through education was very unlikely in this country. Larry Cremin's restrained analysis of American educational history started to make more sense to me intellectually.

Professor Cremin's ideas affected me on levels far more important than the intellectual. His ideas helped restore my faith in public education. Faith was what Larry Cremin was really about. For many Americans, faith in the opportunities offered by public education has become a secular religion. I am one of those Americans. I know the public schools in America are not perfect, but they provide more hope than the schools we find in most other parts of the world.

I returned to the New Haven schools in 1977, and I have taught there ever since. My students are now almost all African Americans. My hopes for them are still great, but I realize that it will take a long time to rectify all the unfairness with which their ancestors were treated. We still have more than just vestiges of institutional racism. Some of the historical results of racism are societal, others psychological. But Lawrence Cremin was right. The long-term trend in America is positive. There is still hope, even though it is easy to become discouraged if you choose to spend your life in the urban classroom. To young teachers I would say, "Always choose hope over despair." Hope is what keeps us teachers going every single day.

Burt Saxon, Ed.D.
Connecticut Teacher of the Year, 2004–2005
James Hillhouse High School
New Haven, Connecticut

tinctive customs, philosophy, and cultural and religious backgrounds, which are decidedly different from those of the others.

Asian Pacific Americans suffered discrimination in the United States both in society and in the schools. Great numbers of Chinese immigrated to the west coast of the United States in the last half of the 18th century to work in the new gold mines and on the transcontinental railroad. But, responding to prejudices and concerns that the Chinese were taking jobs from white Americans, in 1882 Congress enacted a series of laws lasting until the mid-20th century that prohibited further Chinese immigration (Tamura, 2003). Soon after, San Francisco built segregated "Oriental schools" that Chinese students were required to attend (Chan, 1991). In the early 20th century, Japanese and Koreans replaced the Chinese in immigration to the American west coast. Their children were enrolled in regular schools, but were segregated from other students, often being required to attend all-Asian classes in separate areas of the school buildings. In 1906, the San Francisco school board required Japanese and Korean students to attend the segregated Chinese schools, an order that was rescinded 2 years later as a result of diplomatic efforts (Tamura, 2003).

Institutionalized discrimination against Asian Pacific Americans continued until the end of World War II, when the federal government granted naturalization rights to resident Asians and relaxed immigration restrictions.

Education is extremely important to many Asian Pacific Americans, and parents go to great lengths to ensure that their children attend the best schools with the highest test scores and the highest concentration of Asian Pacific American students, so their children feel supported rather than embarrassed by their academic endeavors (Wang, 2005). Asian Pacific American students are stereotypically viewed as a high-achieving group with little need for help. However, although twice as many Asian Pacific Americans obtain bachelor's degrees as the general population, the educational progress of the Pacific Islander and Southeast Asian groups is less expeditious than the East Asian group (Sandham, 1997). Thus, the stereotype is not applicable to all Asian Pacific American students, and affirmative action efforts are being undertaken, largely within the Asian Pacific American community, to provide the educational support needed by the lower-achieving groups and to debunk the notion that the Asian Pacific community is a "model minority."

> A direct link to a Web site that contains many Asian Pacific American Community links is available on the Student Book Companion website.

Conclusion

Today's schools are the result of the continuous progression of educational thought from earliest times. American schools began in colonial times with a primary purpose of teaching children religion and literacy. The independence and early development of America resulted in the expansion of education to include occupational proficiency and the ability to participate in a democratic society. After the Civil War, the subsequent period of reconstruction and industrialization, and World War I, education again shifted its emphasis to teach the skills and dispositions required for an increasingly industrialized country. World War II and the subsequent Cold War underscored the need for heightened scientific and technological education; in response, the United States developed supportive federally funded educational initiatives. After the launching of Sputnik, education focused even more on science, mathematics, and technology than before. Curriculum and instruction were constructed to make learning as meaningful as possible, but heated discussions continued about the direction education should take—issues that continue to be debated to the present day.

As you saw in this chapter, today's schools are the result of the purposes and goals of schools as they have changed over time. Truly, the more things change, the more they stay the same.

Key Terms and Concepts

Brown v. Board of Education of Topeka, 277
Carnegie unit, 266
Common school, 259
Compulsory attendance laws, 259
Dame schools, 253
Elementary and Secondary Education Act (ESEA), 269
GI Bill, 269

Higher Education Act, 270
Hornbook, 253
Kindergarten, 267
Latin Grammar School, 252
Massachusetts Act of 1642, 252
Massachusetts Act of 1647, 252
McGuffey Readers, 259
Monitorial system, 260
Morrill Act of 1862, 261

New England Primer, 253
Normal schools, 260
Old Deluder Satan Act, 252
National Defense Education Act (NDEA), 269
Project Head Start, 270
Title I, 270
Title VII, 270
Title IX, 270
Vernacular schools, 252

Construct and Apply

1. How was education in colonial times similar to education today?
2. How was education in the young nation period similar to education today?
3. How was education in the progressive nation period similar to education today?
4. How was education in the postwar period similar to education today?
5. Complete the following table:

	Colonial Period	Young Nation Period	Progressive Nation Period	Postwar Period	Modern Period
Major events					
Who went to school?					
Curriculum					
Reasons for this curriculum					
Methodology					
Purposes of schools					

6. For each period considered in this chapter, answer the following questions:
   a. What factors during that period have influenced contemporary education?
   b. Which do you feel have had positive influences? Why?
   c. Which do you feel have had negative influences? Why?

Deconstructing the Standards

INTASC Principle #4 says:

> The teacher understands and uses a variety of instructional strategies to encourage students' development of critical thinking, problem solving, and performance skills.

INTASC Principle #6 says:

The teacher uses knowledge of effective verbal, nonverbal, and media communication techniques to foster active inquiry, collaboration, and supportive interaction in the classroom.

- What part(s) of these principles does this chapter address?
- How does this chapter address these principles?
- How will the concepts in this chapter help you apply these principles as a teacher?

Field Experience

1. What accommodations have schools made for students who choose not to recite part or all of the U.S. Pledge of Allegiance in your field experience school?
2. What is the history of your field experience school? When and why was it started?

Your Portfolio

1. For your portfolio, write a reflection about how your field experience school mirrors elements of the history of education.
2. If possible, interview someone who attended a one-room school. Ask what it was like, how the teacher accommodated the different levels of the students, what nonacademic duties students and the teacher had to perform, and the like. Write up the results of this interview to add to your portfolio.

Technology Resources

 Check out the *Building Teachers* companion website, http://www.education.wadsworth.com/ martinloomis1, for more information and resources about the history of schooling in the United States, including access to the following websites:

- Committee of Ten
- Montgomery GI Bill
- Head Start, the National Head Start Association, and the Early Head Start National Resource Center
- Title IX
- *A Nation at Risk*

 Check out the *Building Teachers* CD-ROM that accompanies your textbook for additional chapter resources.

 Also link to InfoTrac College Edition via the *Building Teachers* companion website. Use InfoTrac College Edition to search for journal articles to enhance your study.

CHAPTER **11**

School Governance and Finance

Education is too important to be left solely to the educators.

FRANCIS KEPPEL, AMERICAN EDUCATOR

In Chapter 10, you examined some questions about American education, and you investigated how the answers to these questions changed through history. The questions were similar to those you considered when you were formulating your personal philosophy of education. Who should go to school? What should students learn in school? How should they be taught? You now know that the answers to these questions have changed with time.

Here are some more questions: At any point in time, *who* had the answers to the questions you have been investigating? *Who* had the power to determine the answer? *Who* made decisions about the curriculum? *Who* made instructional decisions? On what were these decisions based? And *who* paid for all this?

In this chapter, you will explore how schools are governed, controlled, and financed. How are these topics important to you as a teacher? Knowledge of governance and finance is essential for you to understand how schools work. With this understanding, you can become a participant in school affairs, rather than being a teacher who focuses exclusively on the classroom and students while others control what happens in the school. To get involved, you must know how the school conducts its business, how it is managed (governed), and how it is financed. What do you suppose Keppel meant in the quotation that begins this chapter? Why? Do you agree with it?

CHAPTER GOALS

As a result of your work in this chapter, you will:

1. Identify the stakeholders in education.

2. Describe the influence of these stakeholders on the processes and policies of education.

3. Describe the structure of educational governance at the school, local, state, and federal levels.

4. Explain how American public schools are financed.

5. Identify and discuss issues pertaining to the governance, control, and financing of education.

6. Describe issues of equity and how these issues affect the use of instructional technology.

7. Explain the importance of governance, control, and financing to teachers.

The Stakeholders in American Education

Let us start, as always, by exploring what you already know.

Who Is in Control?

Think about a school you attended and answer these questions:

- Who was in control of the instruction in the *classroom*?
  - To what extent did this person make decisions about what was taught (curriculum)?
  - To what extent did this person make decisions about instructional methods?
  - Were these decisions left to the sole discretion of the person you identified? If not, who else in the school had input into these decisions?
- Who was in control of the instruction in the *school*?
  - To what extent did this person make decisions about what was taught (curriculum)?
  - To what extent did this person make decisions about instructional methods?
  - Were these decisions left to the sole discretion of the person you identified? If not, who else had input into these decisions?

Maybe you have been in some classrooms where it seemed that the students were in control. In other classrooms, it may have seemed that the teacher had so much control that the students saw the teacher as the "warden." Still other classrooms may have seemed to promote a democratic learning community, with teachers and students both contributing to curricular and instructional decisions.

When the bell rings, the teacher starts the class and teaches. But to whom is the teacher accountable? Who else has an impact on what happens in the classroom? In Building Block 11.1, could you identify a single person in the *classroom* who makes curricular and instructional decisions? Could you identify a single person in the *school* who makes these decisions? Maybe you initially thought of the principal as the school's decision-maker. But, you know there are many individuals involved in running a school and that these individuals function at different levels within the school. The principal might be the ultimate person in charge, but there are also assistant principals, lead teachers, staff personnel, and department chairs in middle and high schools, all of whom have a stake in decisions that are made at the building level.

Teachers, principals, and school support staff all strive to positively influence and impact education.

© Chip Henderson/Index Stock Imagery

You also may have identified outside influences as decision-makers in a school. Certainly the standards and mandates of state agencies and organizations affect the curriculum and instruction in a school. Who else has a stake in the decisions that affect school operations? Ah! The students! But do the students really have an impact on decision making?

The people and institutions with an interest in education are called **stakeholders**. This word often refers to people or agencies outside the school with a particular interest in the school. However, no one can doubt that teachers and students have a real interest in the school. Consequently, *stakeholder* refers to interested parties both inside and outside of the school.

When considering the stakeholders in education, it might be useful to divide them into two groups based on the level at which each group functions:

- Those who are in control of school decisions
- Those who are not in control but who are affected by the decisions

Control and the Stakeholders

Which individuals or categories of individuals are interested in a single school? List as many as you can think of. Categorize your list into *Individuals or Categories of Individuals in Control* and *Individuals or Categories of Individuals Who Are Affected*. (You may want to use a table like the one shown here to help organize your thoughts.) Next, add to your list people or categories of people interested in the entire school system. Again, identify those in a position of control and those who are affected by decisions. Finally do the same for people or categories of people interested in the statewide school system.

	Individuals or Categories of Individuals in Control	Individuals or Categories of Individuals Who Are Affected
Building level		
System level		
State level		

Whom did you put in the table? Where did you list students, teachers, administrators, parents, workers, bosses, business owners, service providers, professionals, citizens, and politicians? Maybe you got to the point where it seemed you were listing everyone in the nation as a stakeholder in education. That's pretty powerful! How does the number of stakeholders who are affected by the schools compare with the number of people in control of the schools? From this exercise, you probably have no trouble concluding that we must be both careful and informed about the people to whom we give the power to govern our schools.

How do you suppose stakeholders who do not make decisions influence the processes and policies of education?

Governance

The **governance** of an organization refers to how the organization is controlled and who has the authority to exercise this control.

Discussions regarding organizational structures and management usually begin at the top level and then move down. However, that system contrasts with the way this book is organized. As you recall, we started our exploration of the huge topic of American education by thinking about *you* first. After all, who knows more about you than you? Since that first chapter, we have expanded our field of consideration to include the student, then the school, and now, society.

So, instead of taking a top-down approach to discuss organizational structures, we will begin with what you know best. It probably is a safe bet that most of your experience with the management of American education has been in a classroom and in a school building. (Perhaps some of us have had more experience than others with school management and policy in that part of the school building known as the principal's office.)

Building-Level Governance

Recall your previous thoughts about who is in control in any particular school building. Who controls the school? Certainly the principal can be thought of as the school's manager. If you review the principal's job responsibilities in Chapter 7, it is clear that the principal's job involves making decisions to govern the school so that the environment facilitates teaching and learning. In most schools, the principal is the head of the school. He or she is charged with the management of the school affairs; is responsible for compliance with national, state, and local school board policies; and is accountable for student achievement.

In some schools, the principal is seen as the "boss"—sometimes despotic, always reserving the final word. In others, the principal is a leader who asks teachers for input into many school decisions that affect teaching and learning. In either case, the principal is responsible to both the staff and the other stakeholders. And as you found earlier, there are many stakeholders outside the school itself.

Can the principal do this job alone? *Should* the principal do this job alone? Many members of the educational community within the school building can contribute to its governance. Principals may have one or more assistant administrators to help with building-level tasks. Teachers may serve in administrative roles as team leaders and department chairs.

Teachers and principals collaborate in numerous ways. Many schools employ a school-based management system, often called **site-based management.** As you saw in Chapter 7, the idea behind site-based management is that those who will be affected by a decision should be involved in making the decision. If teachers have input into the decisions that affect their environment and their teaching, they are more likely to support those decisions. Of course, to have input into decisions, they need to understand how schools are run.

Teachers and administrators also collaborate through jointly preparing and monitoring the **school improvement plan.** A school improvement plan is a document that identifies a school's priorities for the coming years, how these priorities will be implemented, and how the results will be assessed. It guides resource allocation, staff development, instructional content and practice, and student assessment. The school improvement plan has a great effect on the school's operation and the teachers' expectations; it requires the collaboration of the teaching staff in its development.

As you have seen, parents and other members of the community are affected by what happens at a school. But how can they provide input into school decisions? What role do parents and other members of the community play in school governance? Of course, the parents or guardians of an individual student can influence decisions made about that particular student's education at the school, but parents can have input into the bigger issues related to school governance by becoming involved in organizations such as the **Parent Teacher Association (PTA)** or the **Parent Teacher Student Association (PTSA).**

PTA and PTSA organizations meet regularly for updates on school activities and operations and discussions regarding governance and finance. During these discussions, parents provide school decision-makers with valuable input and feedback. In addition, parents, teachers, students, staff, and administrators can serve on school-based committees that work on fundraising, planning, budgeting, support for school athletics, curriculum, and community services.

Some schools have school advisory councils. As the name implies, these groups advise schools on issues such as school policy, school improvement, and budgets. An advi-

Parent–teacher associations support parent involvement in schools and encourage home–school collaboration. Are there other ways parents can become involved in and influence education in their community, states, and nation?

© Michael Newman/PhotoEdit

sory council typically includes parents, teachers, members of the community such as business and industry leaders, and students.

As you can see, many people participate in school governance at the building level, and there are many ways teachers can (and probably should) get involved. But the head of an individual school has the ultimate decision-making authority in that individual school; this head is the principal.

How can stakeholders, including teachers, provide input into what goes on in individual schools?

System-Level and Local Governance

You have seen that a school's principal has the ultimate responsibility for everything that goes on in the school, ensuring implementation of the school district's policies and regulations. A school district normally includes several schools (see Chapter 6). Typically they have several elementary schools that feed into neighboring middle schools or junior high schools, which in turn feed into centrally located, larger high schools. School districts can be very large enterprises, employing thousands of professionals in many school buildings to educate hundreds of thousands of students. Or they can be small, with fewer than 1,000 students.

BUILDING BLOCK 11.3

Your School District

Using reports issued by your local school district or on the Internet, answer the following questions:

- How many elementary schools does the district have? How many students are enrolled in these elementary schools?

- How many middle schools or junior high schools are there? How many students are enrolled in them?

- How many high schools are there? How many students are enrolled?

- How many professionals are on the staff of this school district?

- How does the number of schools compare with the number of large businesses in the area?

- How would you characterize the governance needs for this school district?

Who has decision-making authority for a school district? Who has influence over these decisions? To whom are school principals accountable?

Local school districts are governed by a **school board** and a superintendent of schools. The school board is the official policy-making authority for the school district, with the legal authority to make decisions about the operations of schools within the district and the responsibility to ensure that the schools in the district comply with local, state, and national laws, policies, and regulations. School board members act as officers of the state. Most districts select their school board members in nonpartisan elections by popular vote; however, in some school districts the mayor or another elected official appoints citizens to the school board. The board has collective authority, and no individual board member has the power to make or change educational policy. All school board meetings (except those dealing with confidential and personal matters such as grievances and terminations) are open to the public. In this way, the people represented by the board members know what is going on in their school district and have the opportunity to express their thoughts.

Local school boards originally were conceived to oversee school administrators, whose responsibility was to manage the teaching force. But the role of school boards and district-level governance is changing, affected by national standards and the No Child Left Behind legislation, which both stress accountability. You can see evidence of this effect in the National School Board Association's list of eight key areas of action, meant to guide local school boards away from a strictly managerial role toward one that affects student achievement (National School Board Association, 2005):

 A direct link to the National School Board Association website is available on the *Building Teachers* companion website.

1. Vision:
   Create district and community consensus on achievement objectives.
   Clearly define expectations for what students should know and be able to do.
   Quantify those expectations and set agreed-upon measures for achievement.
2. Standards:
   Establish clear standards for student performance and communicate them continually.
   Base standards on an external source that has credibility in the community.
   Disseminate standards clearly and widely to students, staff and community.
3. Assessment:
   Ensure that assessments are tied to established standards.
   Use multiple, ongoing assessment measures.
   Ensure that assessments are explained to the community.
4. Accountability:
   Measure the performance of all school staff members, administrators, and the school board itself against student achievement objectives.
   Continually track progress and report results honestly.
5. Alignment:
   Align resources to ensure students meet standards.

Include the community in the review of the district budget and management process.
Ensure that resources support parents in helping their children with schoolwork.
6. Climate:
   Create a climate that supports the philosophy that all children can learn at high levels.
   Empower staff to meet the needs of all students.
   Model mutual respect and professional behavior in school board meetings and with school district superintendent and staff.
7. Collaborative partnerships:
   Build collaborative relationships with political and business leaders to develop a consensus for student success.
   Communicate regularly with federal and state officials about student achievement.
   Model behavior that emphasizes trust, teamwork, and shared accountability.
8. Continuous improvement:
   Commit to continuous education and training on issues related to achievement.
   Use data on student achievement to set priorities for allocating resources.
   Adjust strategic plan on the basis of data and community input.

BUILDING BLOCK 11.4

The Local School Board

Review the National School Board Association's eight key areas of action.

- How does the earlier managerial function of the school board compare with today's goals?
- How do the action areas require communication and collaboration between administrators and teachers at the building and system levels of education?

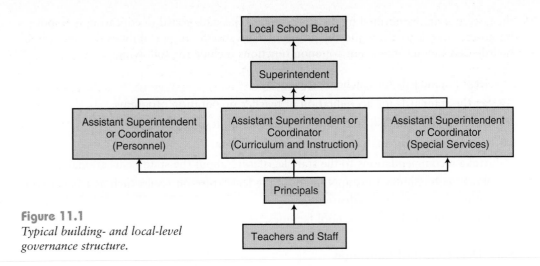

Figure 11.1
Typical building- and local-level governance structure.

The **superintendent of schools** is the head of the school district. The vast majority of superintendents are appointed by the district board of education; in a few cases, however, they are elected by the community. The superintendent's authority as head of the school district is delegated by the school board, and he or she remains accountable to the board. The superintendent is responsible for ensuring that board-approved policies and procedures are carried out in all schools in the district, and for the district's overall operational and financial management. The superintendent works collaboratively with the school board, school personnel, and the community. Superintendents of schools normally devote most of their time and effort to school management and community matters, leaving issues of curriculum, instruction, and assessment to subordinates. To this end, in larger school districts, superintendents of schools may be noneducators who come from the world of business, politics, law, or the military.

Who is the superintendent of schools in your local school district? Who is on the school board? When and where does the school board meet? What issues will the board discuss at its next meeting? How will these issues affect teachers?

In large school districts, the central office may include one or more assistant superintendents responsible for various aspects of the school district, such as elementary schools, high schools, special programs, personnel, finance, and the like. There may also be curriculum coordinators responsible for the development and implementation of subject area curriculum, and other professional personnel.

Remember that we are working our way up from the building-level of our organizational structure. Figure 11.1 shows a visual representation of how this structure looks so far.

> Should the superintendent of schools be an educator or a noneducator? Why?

> How can stakeholders, including teachers, provide input into what goes on in a school district?

State-Level Governance

To whom are superintendents and local school boards accountable? Recall that members of the school board are agents of the state. The U.S. Constitution does not specifically address education, but the 10th Amendment gives the states any powers, including education, not constitutionally delegated to the United States. Thus, each state's constitution governs how education is to be implemented in that state. At the state level, several agencies and individuals have input regarding educational policy. The educational organizational structure varies from state to state, but we can identify some positions and responsibilities that are common to all states.

State Board of Education

Each state has a state board of education. **State boards of education** establish state school policies at all grade levels, from pre-K through postsecondary years. Members of state school boards can be appointed or elected; in most states the members are appointed by the governor and confirmed by the state senate. The state board of education is responsible to the state legislature and the governor. The specific responsibilities of state school boards vary among states, but common functions include the following:

- Set the standards for teacher certification.
- Set the standards for accreditation of teacher preparation programs.
- Develop and establish statewide curriculum and testing standards.
- Collect, organize, analyze, and report school data.
- Make recommendations to the state legislature about the state's educational needs.
- Work with commissions appointed by the legislature on issues such as teacher education, financing, and redistricting.
- Formulate standards for school facilities.

State Department of Education

Each state also has a **Department of Education (DOE)**. Through the DOE, policies developed by the state board of education are put into practice. The DOE oversees all education in the state, distributes state funds appropriated for education, and monitors the use of federal education funds. The DOE also operationalizes and enforces the standards for teacher certification, teacher preparation program accreditation, and curriculum and testing developed by the state board of education. It is responsible for public relations and staff development within the state. The state Department of Education, with its subsidiary agencies, is responsible to the state board of education and the legislature.

A **chief state school officer (CSSO)** or state superintendent of schools heads the state Department of Education, although this administrator's specific title may vary among the states. Depending on the state, the CSSO may be elected or appointed by the governor or the state board of education. The CSSO often is referred to as the CEO of the state's education enterprise, which, as you have seen, is very large. The chief state school officer, the state department of education, and the state board of education all work cooperatively with the state legislature, which votes on education bills that may become laws. Gubernatorial candidates often include educational issues in their political platform. Many voters cast their vote based on the candidates' educational positions. Because the public can vote for or against potential education leaders, and because of the opportunity to become involved in special interest groups, it is easy to see that the public not only has a stake in education—but also has some influence over educational decisions.

Who is the chief state school officer (state superintendent of schools) in your state? Who is on the state board of education? How are the state board members selected?

Special Interest Groups

The public elects state legislators, but special interest groups lobby to influence the educational policies put forth in bills by the legislature each year. These special interest groups influence bills that cover such diverse topics as textbook adoption, curriculum, teacher tenure and salaries, and school calendars. Groups with a stake in decisions regarding these topics include religious and civil rights groups, parent groups, community groups, teacher unions, businesses, business associations, taxpayer associations, and colleges and universities.

One area greatly influenced by special interest groups is textbook selection. In several states, the state board of education is responsible for textbook adoption. This is a particularly contentious issue in California, Texas, and Florida, the three largest states in which textbook adoption occurs at the state level. Originally implemented so state funds could provide schools and students with free textbooks, this practice has attracted highly polarized special interest groups—and each one wants its own agenda incorporated into the adoption process. Among the more powerful of these groups are the textbook publishers,

Textbooks, Evolution, and Controversy

In March 2002, hundreds of parents in Cobb County, Georgia, signed a petition protesting the contents of the school system's newly adopted science textbooks. They claimed that the books presented the scientific theory of evolution as fact and did not address other theories, such as intelligent design. In response, the Cobb County school board approved a policy that required stickers to be placed on the covers of the textbooks stating, "This textbook contains material on evolution. Evolution is a theory, not a fact, regarding the origin of living things. This material should be approached with an open mind, studied carefully, and critically considered."

Three years later, a U.S. District Court judge heard a lawsuit filed by a group of six parents of students in the Cobb County school system. The suit claimed that the textbook stickers violated the establishment clause of the First Amendment, which states, "Congress shall make no law respecting an establishment of religion, or prohibiting the free exercise thereof." The judge ruled that the stickers violated the United States and Georgia constitutions, and that placing the stickers on the textbooks gave the impression that the Cobb County school board agreed "with the Christian fundamentalists" (Torres & Rankin, 2005). He ordered that the stickers be removed.

The lawsuit brought by the parents was originally filed in May 2002. From the time the suit was filed until the court's decision, several special interest groups spoke up in support of one side or the other. Among these were the National Academy of Sciences, which supported the removal of the stickers (MacDonald, 2002a), and a group of university professors, the Georgia Scientists for Academic Freedom, which encouraged critical examination of evolutionary theory (MacDonald, 2002b).

In a related issue, the Georgia state school superintendent came under fire for removing instances of the word *evolution* from the new state curriculum standards and replacing it with the term *biological changes over time*. The superintendent said that her intent was not to "appease Georgians who have religious conflicts with [the] scientific theory [of evolution]" but to avoid a controversial term (MacDonald, 2004a). The tactic seems to have backfired, however, as the superintendent drew criticism from science teachers, scientists, politicians, and the public in Georgia and many other states as the news story went national. The terms *evolution* and *big bang theory*, which had also been removed, were put back into the proposed state science standards, which were then approved by the state board of education (MacDonald, 2004b).

who lobby textbook adoption committees in states with large student populations, such as California, Texas, and Florida, to try to convince them to adopt their textbooks; the publishers are even willing to censor and tailor their textbooks to meet the guidelines of these states to make the huge profits involved in textbook sales. Other special interest groups also can have a great influence on textbook adoption.

What does our organizational structure look like now? We have extended our consideration from building to local to state-level governance (see Figure 11.2).

> To what extent do you believe special interest groups should influence material included in school textbooks? How can stakeholders, including teachers, provide input into what goes on in education at the state level?

The Role of the Federal Government in Education

As mentioned earlier, the U.S. Constitution makes no direct provision for education, but the 10th Amendment delegates this responsibility to the states. However, there can be no doubt that the nation has a huge stake in education. Although states assume responsibility for education and local school districts operate the school systems, the federal government is involved in education through research, reports, recommendations, legislation, and, especially, funding. Many of these activities are carried out through the U.S. Department of Education and its subsidiary educational agencies.

The U.S. Department of Education became a cabinet-level federal agency in 1979, during the Carter administration (see Chapter 4). Previously, it had been called the U.S. Office of Education and was part of the Department of Health, Education, and Welfare. The first Department of Education was established in 1837 for the purpose of collecting information about best practices in teaching and schooling to help the states establish and govern their school systems. The Office of Education gave federal aid to the states for vocational education programs in the early and mid-1900s.

Who is the secretary of education? What major programs does the federal Department of Education fund? What are the eligibility conditions for these programs? What are the impacts of these programs? What federally funded programs affected the schools you attended?

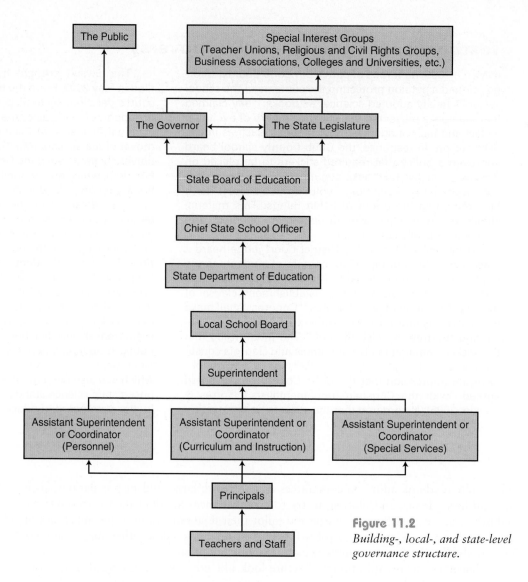

Figure 11.2
Building-, local-, and state-level governance structure.

The U.S. Department of Education has four major functions (U.S. Department of Education, 2005):

1. Establish policies relating to federal financial aid for education, administer distribution of those funds, and monitor their use.

2. Collect data and oversee research on America's schools and disseminate this information to educators and the general public.

3. Identify the major issues and problems in education and focus national attention on them.

4. Enforce federal statutes prohibiting discrimination in programs and activities receiving federal funds and ensure equal access to education for every individual.

Although the U.S. Department of Education does not make education policy, it offers much assistance and some funding. The primary influence of the federal government in educational affairs comes in the form of conditions attached to funding. States and school districts must agree to federal conditions to qualify for federal funding. For example, in order to secure Title I federal funding, schools must demonstrate that they have a significant level of students of poverty. If a school chooses not to demonstrate this demographic, it will not receive Title I federal funding, regardless of the poverty level of the community it serves.

Some people believe that the 10th Amendment should be followed to the letter. These individuals, including politicians and other influential people, believe that the U.S. De-

How can stakeholders, including teachers, provide input into the education programs of the federal government?

partment of Education should be dissolved and that the states should have full control of education and the schools. Others maintain that education is so important to the nation that the federal government must be involved.

What do you think about this issue? Perhaps you are most familiar with the federal government's involvement in education through the No Child Left Behind Act. As you know, this legislation has had a huge effect on education in virtually every state. Yet, according to the U.S. Constitution, states are responsible for their own educational policies.

Much discussion and debate centers on the No Child Left Behind legislation and, especially, the standardized testing program it requires. Many critics claim that the federal government offers insufficient funding to help states implement this federal law. But wait a minute—isn't it true that the federal government does not make educational policy? Yes, that is correct. But the federal government does provide a great deal of money to schools, districts, and states willing to abide by the federal statutes. If schools want to receive federal money, they must follow federal policies. Any state that refuses to abide by federal regulations loses the concomitant federal funding. It is possible for a state to decide that the funding is not worth compliance with the conditions imposed and choose to sacrifice federal funds in exchange for greater state control over education. That is exactly what the state of Utah did. In 2005, Utah's governor signed a measure defying the No Child Left Behind Act saying it intruded on state education priorities; the bill empowered state education officials to ignore provisions of the federal law that conflict with the state's program. In doing so, the state faces the possible loss of $76 million in federal funding ("Utah Snubs," 2005). Federal funding equals a little more than 8% of a typical school district's total educational costs (Owings & Kaplan, 2006). As of 2005, seven other states (Colorado, Connecticut, Idaho, Minnesota, Nebraska, North Dakota, and Vermont) were considering similar measures (Archibald, 2005).

What are your thoughts about federal vs. state involvement in education? Support your ideas with reasons.

You have investigated school governance at the levels of the individual school, the school system, the state government, and the federal government. Now it is time to summarize your thoughts.

BUILDING BLOCK 11.5

Control and the Stakeholders . . . Again

Look back at Building Block 11.2. Use your new understandings to revise the chart you made, this time including the federal level. Use a table like the one shown here to help you organize your thoughts.

	Individuals or Categories of Individuals in Control	Individuals or Categories of Individuals Who Are Affected
Building level		
System level		
State level		
Federal level		

■ How does this table compare with the table you prepared in Building Block 11.2?

■ How can you provide input to educational decisions at each of these levels?

Other Influences on Education and Schools

You have seen the influences stakeholders can exert on school policies and procedures. Let us consider two other factors that greatly affect schools: standardized test scores and teacher unions.

Standardized Tests

States use standardized tests to measure students' achievement to comply with the No Child Left Behind pillar of accountability (see Chapter 1). Student performance on standardized tests is of great concern not only to students and their parents, but also to states and the nation. Standardized tests have long been part of the educational fabric as a way to measure student progress toward achieving state curriculum objectives. However, the No Child Left Behind legislation mandates the use of standardized tests. According to this law, prior to the 2005–2006 academic year, states were required to use standardized tests to measure proficiency in mathematics and reading or language arts at least once during grades 3 through 5, grades 6 through 9, and grades 10 through 12. By the 2005–2006 school year, No Child Left Behind requires schools to test their students in mathematics and reading or language arts every year in grades 3 through 9 and at least once in grades 10 through 12. Effective in the 2007–2008 academic year, testing also is required in science at least once during grades 3 through 5, grades 6 through 9, and grades 10 through 12. By 2007, therefore, students will be tested annually in reading and mathematics and twice in science in grades 3 through 9, and they will be tested at least once in reading, mathematics, and science in grades 10 through 12 (see Table 11.1).

What statewide tests does your state Department of Education require? When are they taken by the students in your state?

Standardized test scores are used to judge schools' progress toward achieving state-approved objectives and meeting the adequate yearly progress (AYP) goals described in No Child Left Behind. According to the legislation, to make AYP, 95% of the students in the school and 95% of four subgroups (low socioeconomic status, racially and ethnically diverse, disabled, and language minority students) must perform at levels considered proficient by the state. Schools and states are required to make the results of their standardized tests public on so-called school report cards.

If a school fails to achieve AYP, states must provide help. Local systems must name the schools identified as "need improvement" and inform parents of their options in case the school's performance does not improve. These options include sending their children to a different school without additional costs and supplemental educational services, such as tutoring and other after-school services. If the school does not improve, it may undergo fundamental changes, such as restructuring. Schools that do

TABLE 11.1 Schedule of Testing Required by the No Child Left Behind Act (From Wenning et al., 2003)

	Before 2005			2005–2006			2007–2008		
	Grades 3–5	Grades 6–9	Grades 10–12	Grades 3–5	Grades 6–9	Grades 10–12	Grades 3–5	Grades 6–9	Grades 10–12
Mathematics	At least once	At least once	At least once	Annually	Annually	At least once	Annually	Annually	At least once
Reading or language arts	At least once	At least once	At least once	Annually	Annually	At least once	Annually	Annually	At least once
Science							At least once	At least once	At least once

well in improving student achievement may receive academic achievement awards and be designated "distinguished schools" by the state. Teachers in outstanding schools may receive financial incentives in the form of bonuses, whereas those in chronically low-performing schools may be denied their normal raises and may not be rehired for the next year, depending on how the students in their classes perform on the standardized tests.

If you can recall how many times you have seen references to No Child Left Behind in the news and have heard the term *accountability* referring to teachers and schools, you can get an idea of how strong the influence of standardized tests has been on education. Furthermore, because student performance on those standardized tests is used to measure AYP, and because schools and teachers are held accountable for student performance, you can understand the enormous influence that standardized tests have on teaching practices.

How do teachers respond to the pressures of accountability? Does the pressure for students to perform on the standardized tests affect what and how they teach? Certainly one skill teachers want their students to know is how to take a test. Some teachers prepare their students to take standardized tests by providing instruction on how to take tests. The testing atmosphere can be anxiety-ridden, and these anxieties can affect performance on the tests. By learning and applying test-taking strategies, students may feel less anxious and perform better. Teachers also may provide sample test questions for students to complete for practice. However, it is unclear whether preparation in test-taking strategies affects student performance.

There is much debate about standardized testing. Some people believe that the tests do not test what the curriculum teaches. They feel that, rather than testing the higher-order thinking skills emphasized in the curriculum, standardized tests require students to access memorized facts and concepts. As Kohn (2001) writes, "The intellectual life is being squeezed out of our schools as they are transformed into what are essentially giant test-prep centers" (p. 350). On the other hand, some people contend that standardized tests promote higher-order thinking skills in the context of the content being tested. Still others believe standardized tests can be used to help in curriculum upgrading (Franklin, 2001), and in increasing the effectiveness of education and improving instruction (Hamilton & Stecher, 2004). Some states are modifying their tests to better represent what current curriculum emphasizes.

The National Education Association, other educational organizations, and prominent educators assert that accountability should be based on more than just standardized tests. Their position is that other measures of progress such as classroom performance and graduation rates should be factored into decisions regarding overall student achievement (National Education Association, 2005a).

Standardized tests are intended to assess student knowledge acquired in the classroom. Student performance on various standardized tests influences school curriculum and federal school financing.

Standardized Testing

What are your thoughts about the standardized testing programs in effect in your state?

- Can these standardized tests provide a valid measure of student achievement? If so, how?
- Can they provide a valid measure of a teacher's effectiveness? If so, how?
- Can they distinguish "good" schools from "poor" schools? If so, how?
- Can their scores enable the public to form valid opinions about the education their children are getting? If so, how?
- Can they accomplish the goal of accountability? If so, how?

From your inquiries, you can see that the people who work with and for schools have a tremendous interest in the *what, why,* and *how* of education. We have identified teachers, administrators, and other school personnel as stakeholders in education. It matters to them what is happening not only in their school buildings, but also in their school districts, their states, and the nation.

Teacher Unions

By definition, a union is "an organization of workers formed for the purpose of advancing its members' interests in respect to wages, benefits, and working conditions" (Merriam-Webster, 2005). The largest unions in the country for teachers and other education personnel are the **National Education Association (NEA)** and the **American Federation of Teachers (AFT)**. You explored the backgrounds of these organizations in Chapter 10, and you have seen the results of some of their work throughout this textbook.

The NEA, boasting 2.7 million members, includes teachers from preschool to the college level, administrators, and other school personnel. It is the country's largest union for educators. It has chapters in every state with over 14,000 local chapters (National Education Association, 2005b). National members are influential in federal politics, and state and local lobbyists have been very influential in shaping state and national education policies and practices and in supporting candidates for school board and state education positions (Haar, 1999).

Although smaller than the NEA, the AFT asserts similar positions on educational issues and also is influential in forming educational policy (Haar, 1999). The AFT has 1.3 million members, with 43 state chapters and 14,000 local chapters. The AFT is affiliated with the American Federation of Labor–Congress of Industrial Organizations (AFL–CIO), a federation of over 50 job-specific unions (American Federation of Teachers, 2005).

The NEA is traditionally viewed as a professional organization that deals with general issues of educational policy and procedure, and the AFT is traditionally viewed as a labor union, but both are involved in collective bargaining activities as well as dealing with general education issues. The unions negotiate with school districts on behalf of teachers with respect to salaries, working conditions, transfers, staff development, and most other aspects of teacher benefits and working conditions. In many states, teachers are required to belong to a union; states in which union membership is required are often called "union states." In most union states, the unions can call for teacher strikes if they feel it is necessary to force the negotiation of teacher contract provisions, working conditions, and benefits.

Individual states have their own state education associations; many of these are affiliated with national organizations and have student chapters in colleges and universities. You might have a student education association on your campus. Usually, the dues for joining a student chapter are reasonable. There are certain benefits to student membership, such as liability insurance and free subscriptions to the association's educational journals. Not only will joining a student education organization provide you with access to important and current information and benefits, you will also have the opportunity to interact with other educators and individuals studying education.

Is your state a union or a nonunion state for teachers? What is the general opinion regarding teacher unions in your state? What would be the advantages and disadvantages of living in a state where most teachers were members of a union? What would be the advantages and disadvantages of living in a state where most teachers were not union members?

Is there a student chapter of an NEA or AFT affiliate at your college or university? What is it called? What are its activities and goals?

Financing Education

You have identified a number of stakeholders in education and have examined how these stakeholders can influence the governance and control of education. You have an idea of the complexity and enormity of the governance of education in the U.S. Can you imagine how much money is needed to operate just one school, let alone all the programs associated with it?

Adding It Up

BUILDING BLOCK 11.7

Make a list of everything you can think of in a school that requires money. Include personnel, facilities, equipment, material, and other costs associated with running a school. You might want to consider the school you used in Building Block 11.2, where you investigated who makes decisions.

Try to put a dollar figure on each person's salary and the costs of each support service item. Can you estimate a total annual cost for a school?

It is mind-boggling to try to think of everything that requires money in a single school. You probably identified teacher salaries as an expenditure. What about the cost of equipment, materials, and supplies? Electricity and water? Repairs? Landscaping? What about support personnel—administrators, nurses, cafeteria workers, custodians, bus drivers, and the like? And when you consider that in the 2002–2003 school year, the most recent year for which data is available, more than 48 million students attended more than 92,000 public schools (National Center for Education Statistics, 2005a), the numbers can be staggering.

The total expenditure for public school elementary and secondary education in the 2002–2003 academic year was $388 billion. Of this, 61.3% went to instruction (teacher salaries, textbooks, etc.), 34.6% went to support services (administration, media center, school maintenance, nurses, etc.), and 4.1% went to noninstructional costs (food service, bookstores, etc.) (Hill & Johnson, 2005). Figure 11.3 illustrates this breakdown.

Where does all this money come from? Revenues for public schools for the 2002–2003 academic year equaled $440 billion, with $388 billion going directly to edu-

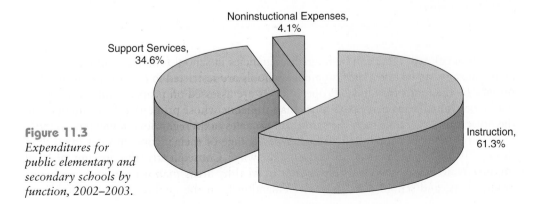

Figure 11.3
Expenditures for public elementary and secondary schools by function, 2002–2003.

Noninstuctional Expenses, 4.1%

Support Services, 34.6%

Instruction, 61.3%

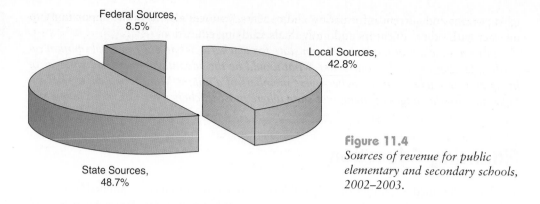

Federal Sources, 8.5%

Local Sources, 42.8%

State Sources, 48.7%

Figure 11.4
Sources of revenue for public elementary and secondary schools, 2002–2003.

cation and the remaining $52 billion allocated for school construction, debt financing, community services, and adult education programs. Local sources accounted for 42.8% of this revenue, state sources accounted for 48.7%, and federal sources accounted for 8.5% (see Figure 11.4) (Hill & Johnson, 2005).

Local Funding

Over 40% of school funding comes from local sources. But what are those local sources? Communities pay property taxes to support schools. In addition, in some areas, a portion of the sales taxes goes for school support.

Property taxes are taxes assessed on personal property, such as boats and cars, and real estate, such as homes, land, and commercial buildings. In any one community, therefore, the amount of money spent on schools depends on the value of the property in that community.

BUILDING BLOCK 11.8

Property Taxes and Equity

Think about the neighborhood where you live and its surrounding areas. Do some areas have huge, luxurious houses? Do other neighborhoods have less extravagant dwellings where middle-class people live? Have you seen lower socioeconomic neighborhoods, as well?

Now imagine that there is a school in the middle of each of those neighborhoods and suppose that the school is supported solely by a neighborhood property tax. What would the school in the luxurious neighborhood be like compared with the school in the lower socioeconomic neighborhood? What might you suggest to make the schools more equal? Would it be fair to tax the property owners in the less affluent neighborhood at a higher rate so its school could be better? Would it be fair to send some of the tax money from the luxurious neighborhood to the needy school?

Draw some inferences regarding the amount of support schools receive and the communities they are in. What are your conclusions regarding property values and school quality?

As you can tell, there can be huge discrepancies in school funding from region to region. Citizens can be taxed only so much. Schools are restricted in the education they can provide by the funds they have. Property taxes are assessed on property values; someone with more valuable property pays more than someone whose property is less valuable. On the other hand, everyone pays the same rate for sales taxes regardless of income, so those with lower incomes actually pay a higher percentage of their income in sales taxes than those with higher incomes. Can you explain why? Consequently, the amount of local funding available for schools is far greater in wealthy areas than it is in lower socioeconomic areas, and school districts vary tremendously in the quality of school buildings, amount of resources (including books), and level of teacher salaries, which include a supplement funded by local property and sales taxes in addition to the state-based salary (see Chapter 9). This disparity in funding is a very serious problem.[1]

State Funding

States provide about half of the funding for their schools. All states have sources of revenue used to finance education. In most states, this revenue comes from sales and income taxes, licensing fees, inheritance taxes, and other state sources. However, not all states have income taxes, and not all states have sales taxes.

Sources of Revenue in Your State

Does your state have an income tax?
Does your state have a sales tax? If so, what is its percentage?
What other sources of revenue does your state use to support schools?

States use several different methods to determine the educational financial aid each district receives. The most common method is based on a district's average daily membership, which is based largely on attendance. In this system, the amount of financial aid a school district receives from the state depends on the number of students who are enrolled and actually attend school in the district. Thus, large school districts receive more state aid than small districts, but they also have more students to serve.

In the 2002–2003 academic year, states spent an average of $8,041 per student on education. Of this amount, an average of $4,932 (61.3%) went to instruction, $2,780 (34.6%) went to support, and $329 (4.1%) went to noninstructional expenditures (Hill & Johnson, 2005). (See also Figure 11.14.) Table 11.2 shows a state-by-state listing of the average annual state-funded per-pupil expenditures for the 2002–2003 school year. As you can see, the per-pupil spending ranged from a low of $6,081 in Idaho to a high of $12,568 in New Jersey, a difference of $6,487.

How does the average annual per-pupil expenditure for 2002–2003 in your state compare with other states and the national average? What do you suppose are some of the reasons for these differences?

You can see there are large discrepancies among the amounts states spend on their students. What do you think causes these discrepancies? Remember that the primary sources of state funding for schools are sales tax and income tax. Therefore, the money that any particular state can allocate for education depends on the income of its residents and on the purchases made by residents, visitors, and tourists.

Some states supplement their educational funds with lotteries and other forms of gambling. Usually these revenues are intended to enhance specific educational programs, facilities, and operations. A typical example is the Florida lottery, which supports scholarships, school improvement programs, and new construction.

Why is it important for teachers to take accurate daily attendance?

Lotteries and Education

Does your state have a lottery? If not, what is the nearest state that does?

■ Are any of the state's lottery proceeds used for education? How much?

■ How does education benefit from these lottery proceeds?

(You might be able to find some of this information on the state lottery's website.)

TABLE 11.2 State-by-State Per-Pupil Expenditures (From Hill & Johnson, 2005)

State	Total	Instruction	Support Services	Noninstructional expenses
Total United States	$8,041	$4,932	$2,780	$329
Alabama	$6,300	$3,812	$2,058	$430
Alaska	$9,870	$5,740	$3,798	$332
Arizona	$6,282	$3,765	$2,221	$296
Arkansas	$6,482	$3,961	$2,196	$325
California	$7,552	$4,591	$2,678	$283
Colorado	$7,384	$4,230	$2,900	$254
Connecticut	$11,057	$7,052	$3,612	$394
Delaware	$9,693	$5,965	$3,276	$452
District of Columbia	$11,847	$6,216	$5,331	$300
Florida	$6,439	$3,786	$2,338	$315
Georgia	$7,774	$4,925	$2,459	$391
Hawaii	$8,100	$4,833	$2,839	$428
Idaho	$6,081	$3,721	$2,098	$262
Illinois	$8,287	$4,952	$3,068	$268
Indiana	$8,057	$4,932	$2,797	$329
Iowa	$7,574	$4,508	$2,511	$554
Kansas	$7,454	$4,413	$2,697	$345
Kentucky	$6,661	$4,066	$2,233	$362
Louisiana	$6,922	$4,203	$2,291	$428
Maine	$9,344	$6,269	$2,774	$300
Maryland	$9,153	$5,693	$3,042	$418
Massachusetts	$10,460	$6,656	$3,486	$318
Michigan	$8,781	$5,002	$3,509	$269
Minnesota	$8,109	$5,201	$2,536	$372
Mississippi	$5,792	$3,466	$1,966	$360

Federal Funding

The federal government contributes an average of 8.5% of all school funding. There is great variance among the states, with the New England states receiving the lowest percentage and the southeastern states receiving the highest percentage (Owings & Kaplan, 2006). Funds are provided in three main ways: categorical grants, formula funding, and competitive grants. Federal funding is overseen by the U.S. Department of Education.

Categorical Grants

Categorical grants (sometimes called *block grants*) are provided by the federal government to help fund specific elementary and secondary programs approved through federal legislation. Programs provide financial aid for eligible applicants for elementary, secondary, and college education; for the education of individuals with disabilities and those who are illiterate, disadvantaged, or gifted; and for the education of immigrants, American Indians, and people with limited English proficiency. Specific examples include the funding of arts education, bilingual education, Head Start programs, school breakfast and

TABLE 11.2 State-by-State Per-Pupil Expenditures—cont'd

State	Total	Instruction	Support Services	Noninstructional expenses
Missouri	$7,349	$4,481	$2,551	$317
Montana	$7,496	$4,606	$2,583	$307
Nebraska	$8,074	$5,151	$2,360	$563
Nevada	$6,092	$3,812	$2,080	$200
New Hampshire	$8,579	$5,569	$2,746	$264
New Jersey	$12,568	$7,424	$4,757	$387
New Mexico	$7,125	$3,953	$2,842	$329
New York	$11,961	$8,213	$3,459	$290
North Carolina	$6,562	$4,173	$2,023	$366
North Dakota	$6,870	$4,102	$2,230	$538
Ohio	$8,632	$4,956	$3,390	$286
Oklahoma	$6,092	$3,528	$2,160	$404
Oregon	$7,491	$4,438	$2,798	$255
Pennsylvania	$8,997	$5,557	$3,088	$352
Rhode Island	$10,349	$6,685	$3,396	$267
South Carolina	$7,040	$4,199	$2,464	$376
South Dakota	$6,547	$3,836	$2,361	$349
Tennessee	$6,118	$3,933	$1,885	$300
Texas	$7,136	$4,307	$2,469	$360
Utah	$4,838	$3,103	$1,461	$273
Vermont	$10,454	$6,713	$3,458	$283
Virginia	$7,822	$4,809	$2,705	$308
Washington	$7,252	$4,317	$2,582	$353
West Virginia	$8,319	$5,115	$2,742	$463
Wisconsin	$9,004	$5,566	$3,149	$289
Wyoming	$8,985	$5,381	$3,317	$287

lunch programs, and the National Writing Project. Many of these programs have been discussed elsewhere in this textbook.

Formula Funding

Formula funding refers to grants the federal government provides to schools that show need; this need often is based on the number of free and reduced-price lunches they provide to their students. Examples include Title I funding, which is directed toward raising student achievement, Title IIA funds that go toward improving teacher quality, and Title III funds that target language acquisition.

Competitive Grants

Competitive grants are provided by the federal government for specific projects and programs. States, school districts, and individual schools may submit proposals that compete with other proposals for funding for specific federal programs. An example is the National Science Foundation, which funds programs designed to improve student achievement in mathematics and science through innovative curriculum and teaching methodologies. Recipients must meet certain stipulations to receive some federal funds, and the funds are subject to restrictions.

Private Funding

Schools often obtain supplemental funds through fund-raising efforts, private grants, and commercial advertising. Fund-raising efforts raise money for specific needs, classes, or projects in individual schools. They may be sponsored by the PTA, school-based clubs, or students; examples include raising money for band uniforms, cheerleading camp, a new science center, an outdoor classroom, or any number of special projects a school could not otherwise afford. You have probably been involved in some school fundraising efforts, on either the buying or the selling side. We have all had children (maybe even your own children) come to our doors selling magazine subscriptions, candy, or fruits to raise money for a school trip, new uniforms, or some other school project. School athletic clubs often solicit funds through booster clubs that help defray the expenses incurred by athletics programs. These monies contribute to the education of the students in the community.

Money from individual benefactors, private corporations, and foundations is available through the competitive grant application process. Grant awards range from small to very large. States, school districts, schools, and classroom teachers can apply for grants targeted toward specific programs. For example, grants available from AOL/Time Warner, the Intel Corporation, and AT&T fund programs that enhance teaching and learning with technology. Toyota Tapestry grants are available for K–12 science teachers, and Verizon Communications offers funds to support literacy and English as a Second Language programs in the community. Often, such grants are awarded preferentially to schools with populations that are underserved.

Many small and large grants are available from private foundations, commercial organizations, and educational organizations, such as the PTAs, PTSAs, colleges and universities, and professional associations. Teachers can (and should) apply for these grants to fund special projects in their classrooms. Large companies often provide support for education in other ways. For example, an office supply store may post a local school's supply list or a bookstore may stock books that are on the local schools' district summer reading lists.

Some school systems have raised funds by allowing advertising on their property. You may have seen advertisements for local businesses on signs, scoreboards, and programs at athletic events. The current trend has been for schools to incorporate commercial partnerships into their potential funding. According to Alex Molnar (2004), director of the Commercialism in Education Research Unit at Arizona State University, commercial activity in schools can be grouped into eight categories:

1. Sponsorship of programs and activities.
2. Exclusive agreements: Contracts in which schools agree to sell only certain brand-name products in their vending machines.

© Mark Richards/PhotoEdit

Students and parents often initiate fundraising efforts to supplement government funding for education. Why do schools need to pursue financing outside of municipal, state, and federal funds?

3. Incentive programs: Programs in which corporations offer a reward for student achievement, such as grades, attendance, or reading.

4. Appropriation of space: The naming of or advertising in school space by corporations.

5. Sponsored educational materials: The use of privately created curricular materials.

6. Electronic marketing: The use of the Internet or other media to display advertising in schools.

7. Privatization: The management of public schools and charter schools by private corporations, called educational management organizations.

8. Fundraising.

Molnar's research has tracked commercial activity in schools since 1990. By reviewing his most recent data in Table 11.3, you can see that commercialism in schools is on the rise. For example, commercial sponsorship of school programs increased 146% between 1990 and the 2003–2004 school year, and school-based electronic advertising increased 24% in just one year.

Although commercialism in the schools is a lucrative financial resource, some find the practice problematic, believing that education should not be "tainted" with advertising. Critics claim that children are being forced to view advertising in and around their schools without parental consent and are concerned that some advertisements may market unhealthy foods or use children as subjects of market research (Larson, 2002). Others believe that students are bombarded by commercialism, anyway, so viewing advertising in school is not much different from the norm.

Some individuals have filed lawsuits that challenge the legality of contracts between schools and soft drink companies. Also, some have challenged the constitutionality of "forcing" children to watch advertising on Channel One, a daily 12-minute newscast, which contains advertisements, that is broadcast to subscribing schools (Commercialism in Education Research Unit, 2005).

The United States General Accounting Office (GAO) was asked by Congress to examine the states' responses to the increase in commercial involvement with schools. The GAO reported that 13 states have established laws addressing commercial activities in public schools, and at least 25 more states are considering such legislation. Almost all of the state legislation addresses the sale of food and beverages in school (Shaul, 2004).

TABLE 11.3 Changes in Commercial Involvement in Schools (Molnar, 2004)

Category of Commercial Involvement	Increase from 1990 to the 2003–2004 Academic Year
Sponsorship of programs and activities	146%
Exclusive agreements	858%
Incentive programs	354%
Appropriation of space	394%
Sponsored educational materials	1,038%
Electronic marketing	24% (from 2002–2003 to 2003–2004)
Privatization	−30% (from 2002–2003 to 2003–2004)
Fundraising	21% (2002–2003 to 2003–2004)

How do you feel about commercialism in schools? Is the funding gained worth exposing the students to the advertising? Or is school an inappropriate place for marketers to promote their products to students?

Issues in School Governance and Finance

As you have investigated school governance and finance, you have seen there are several issues about which educators and others involved in education have differing opinions. The degree to which the federal government should be involved in controlling and financing education, the degree to which state governments are involved, the activities of teacher unions, and the financing of education by private organizations are all controversial issues and frequent topics of debate. A few other issues warrant a closer examination.

Equality, Equity, and Adequacy

No Child Left Behind requires that states have standards to which teaching should be directed and against which student achievement should be measured. Having a set of standards for all students implies that we believe that all students can and will achieve them. For all students to achieve these standards, all students must have adequate educational opportunities. And providing adequate educational opportunities requires adequate funding. In reality, we know that not all schools and school systems receive equal funding (see above; Carey, 2004), and that the economics of the surrounding area influence the funding available to a school. Schools in areas of lower socioeconomic status do not have the funds to attract the best teachers, provide the best facilities, or purchase technology and resource materials. These schools, therefore, cannot provide the same educational opportunities, materials, and services as better-financed schools. However, the question is, "Can a school provide an *adequate* education for its students?" One school of thought says that if all students are to have adequate opportunities for achievement, schools should receive the funding from the state that is needed to provide the education their students need. This means that schools in poorer communities should receive more support from the state than schools in wealthier communities, because of their lower local tax base. This system of funding schools is known as **funding equity.**

Another school of thought says that all schools should be treated equally by the state and should receive equal funding based only on student enrollment. This system of funding schools is known as **funding equality.** Equal funding does not consider resource gaps between poor communities and wealthy communities.

As you can imagine, because of disparities between approaches to funding schools, state systems for funding public education have come under examination and dispute. In January of 2005, an *Education Week* report noted that 31 states were reconsidering their system of distributing funds to school systems, 16 states were currently in court, and in the past 5 years, 20 other states had been in court for lawsuits targeting their school funding systems ("Financial Evolution," 2005a).

BUILDING BLOCK 11.11

Equality, Equity, and Adequacy

What does the term *adequate education* mean to you? Consider the school districts in your state.

- Are some of these school districts wealthier than others?
- Do you believe the schools in your state should receive state funding on the basis of *equity* or on the basis of *equality*?
- How would you explain your decision to parents in a poor district?
- How would you explain your decision to parents in a wealthy district?

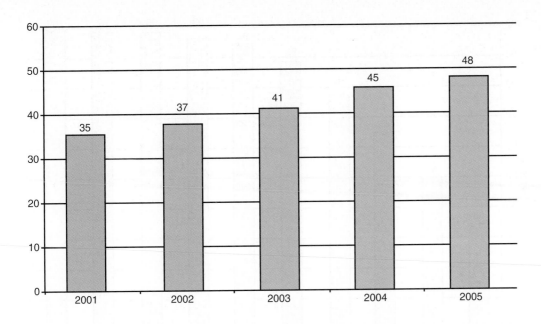

Figure 11.5
Number of states with technology standards for students, including the District of Columbia (Education Week Research Center, 2005).

Technology and the Digital Divide

You have seen the importance of technology in today's society and the importance of using technology in instruction. You have seen what the technology expectations are for teachers, and you have looked at the standards that detail these expectations (see Chapter 9). Similarly, there are technology expectations for students. More and more states have developed technology standards to guide schools in meeting their students' technology needs. Forty-seven states and the District of Columbia have technology standards for students, up from 35 states in 2001 (Figure 11.5). Minnesota, Mississippi, and South Dakota are the only states that, at this writing, do not have student technology proficiency standards in place. New York, North Carolina, and Utah actually test their students' technological knowledge and skills, and Hawaii is currently piloting a test.

To encourage technological equity for all students nationwide, availability of computers with Internet access in schools is increasing. How can schools and the government further work to decrease the digital divide that continues to exist between various student populations and groups?

Courtesy of Bill Lisenby

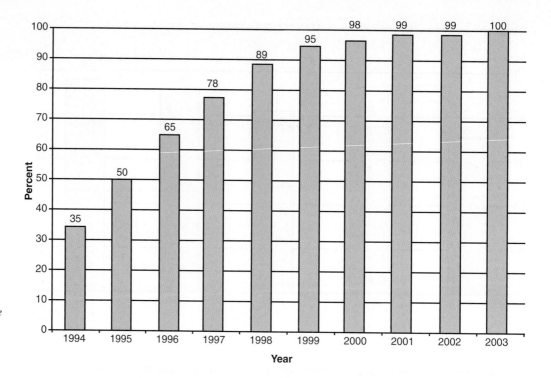

Figure 11.6

Percentage of U.S. schools with instructional computers that have access to the Internet (National Center for Education Statistics, 2005b).

Given the funding disparities among school systems, however, it should be no surprise that a disparity exists with regard to instructional materials. Technology, as you have seen, is an important instructional tool. The disparity in student access to technology, especially to computers and the Internet, is called the **digital divide.**

The Telecommunications Act of 1996 instituted a federal program to reduce the digital divide. This program, called the **E-Rate** program, provides federal funding for schools to purchase and update technology. The E-Rate is a discount schools and libraries receive to acquire telecommunications services. Eligible schools and libraries can receive discounts of 20% to 90% on telecommunications services, Internet access, and internal connections required to bring technology into the classrooms. E-Rate has cost about $2.25 billion a year, but it is currently being considered for overhaul because some argue that its primary purpose, bridging the digital divide, has been met (Trotter, 2005).

An earlier goal was to equip all schools with computers. However, the Internet's potential to aid instruction and learning has extended the technology focus: to equip schools with computers with Internet access. (See the National Educational Technology Plans, Chapter 9.) Providing Internet access in our public schools seems to be progressing well. In the fall of 2003, nearly 100% of public schools had instructional computers with Internet access, up from 35% in 1994. This applies to all schools, regardless of size, location, socioeconomic status, or percent of minority enrollment (National Center for Education Statistics, 2005b). Figure 11.6 shows the percentage, since 1994, of U.S. public schools with instructional computers that have Internet access.

A better indicator of how technology is being used in schools is the number of students per computer. In 1998, the overall ratio of students per instructional computer with Internet access was 12.1 students per computer; this decreased to an average of 4.4 students per computer with Internet access in 2003. However, this ratio was higher in schools with the highest poverty concentrations (5.1 students to 1 computer with Internet access) than in schools with the lowest poverty concentrations (4.2 to 1); it also was higher in schools with the greatest minority enrollment (5.1 to 1) than in schools with the lowest minority enrollment (4.1 to 1). Figure 11.7 illustrates the ratio of public school students to computers with Internet access from 1998 to 2003.

To help increase the access students have to computers, almost half of public schools make their technology facilities available to students outside of regular school hours,

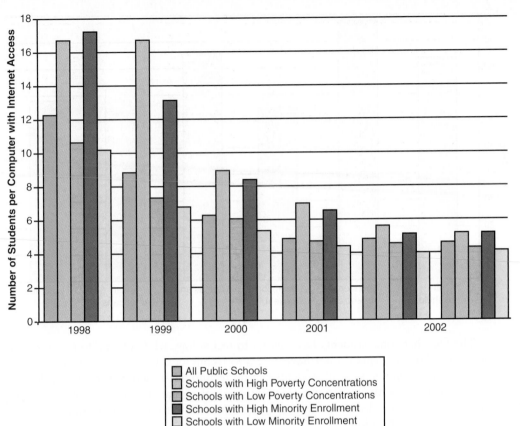

Figure 11.7
Ratio of U.S. public school students to computers with Internet access (National Center for Education Statistics, 2005b).

Legend:
- All Public Schools
- Schools with High Poverty Concentrations
- Schools with Low Poverty Concentrations
- Schools with High Minority Enrollment
- Schools with Low Minority Enrollment

mostly after school. But many students cannot stay after school because of job responsibilities, transportation issues, and the like. Consequently, some schools make their technology facilities available to students before school. But fewer schools with high minority enrollment (60%) make computers with Internet access available before school than schools with low minority enrollment (80%), and fewer schools with high poverty concentrations (54%) make technology available before school than schools with low poverty concentrations (82%) (National Center for Education Statistics, 2005b).

What are your thoughts about the narrowing of the digital divide in American public schools?

How are efforts to narrow the digital divide progressing in nonschool settings? America has made significant strides. The digital divide narrowed between 1998 and 2000 (U.S. Department of Commerce, 2000) and continued to narrow between 2000 and 2002 (Corporation for Public Broadcasting, 2003). African Americans, Hispanic Americans, and low-income families—groups that have traditionally been digital "have nots"—have made dramatic gains in computer ownership and Internet access, although they still lag behind white Americans and high-income families. A report issued by the Corporation for Public Broadcasting in 2003 provided data on the presence of computers in homes with children. The percentage of households with at least one child between the ages of 2 and 17 owning computers rose from 64% in 2000 to 83% in 2003. Although Caucasian and high-income families have the highest percentage of computer ownership, more than two thirds of African American, Hispanic American, and low-income households had computers in their homes, according to the report (see Figure 11.8).

The same basic trends can be seen for Internet access. The percentage of families with children that have access to the Internet from any location such as home, school, and libraries was 78% in 2002. Caucasian and high-income families had the highest percentage of Internet access, but African American, Hispanic American, and low-income family households have made large gains.

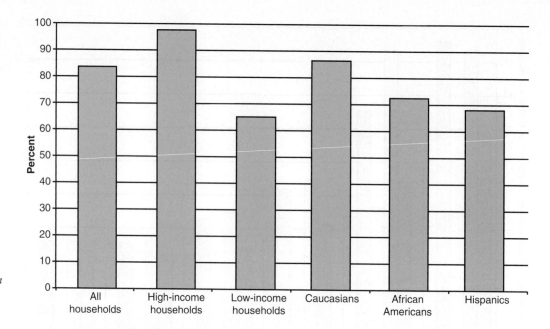

Figure 11.8
Percentage of U.S. family households owning computers in 2002 (Corporation for Public Broadcasting, 2003).

The fact that some students have access to technology while others do not is an equity issue. Many students do not have access to technology at home, and teachers must guard against assuming that all students can do technology-based projects easily. Knowing what you know about effective teaching, remember that the presence of technology alone does not ensure learning. Teachers must know how to integrate technology effectively into their instruction.

All students should have access to teachers who know how to use technology to teach effectively. This statement has direct implications for you as you progress through your teacher education program. It is not sufficient that you simply know how to turn on the computer, run some software, and surf the Internet. You must know how and when it is appropriate to utilize technology to enhance your instruction.

With everything you have read so far, you understand that the teaching and learning process is not easily quantified in such a way that its influences can be defined exactly. We know that good teachers have an impact, and so do adequate facilities and supplies. But in what proportions? Does it take more money to get lower-achieving students up to par than higher-achieving students? What technologies and how much technology will produce the greatest achievement results with lower-achieving students and students of low socioeconomic status?

Equal, equitable, adequate. There has been an evolution of thinking regarding the funding of education. Certainly this will continue to be a hot topic of debate and controversy.

School Choice and Voucher Systems

If some schools are getting more money than others, attracting the best teachers, and providing the best facilities and equipment, it would seem that a student from an underfunded, underachieving school would do well to transfer to the wealthier school. Of course, most students go to schools within their district. However, many parents choose to send their children to different schools for various reasons. This freedom to choose a school is called **school choice.**

According to Cookson (1994), there are six types of school choice:

1. Intradistrict choice: Parents choose to send their children to another school within their district.

2. Interdistrict choice: Parents choose to send their children to a school in another school district.

from the
TEACHER Kathleen Thomas

Courtesy of Kathleen Thomas

Teaching methods have changed in recent years, partially due to the explosion in microelectronics. Using technology to deliver instruction is one method that sparks the interest of students who are already accustomed to a fast-paced, interactive environment. By actively engaging students in using a variety of technology tools, a teacher can become the classroom facilitator in the learning process, allowing the students to make many of the discoveries on their own. A learning community atmosphere can be established where students and teachers interact and learn from each other. Using technology in the classroom requires students to apply upper-level thinking and problem-solving skills. This teaching method also helps students develop appropriate transfer skills to make the transition from the school environment to the workplace.

At our school, one of the goals of our school improvement plan is for 100% of our high school students to be technologically competent, as measured by a specific checklist of criteria. Our school advisory council encourages teachers in our district to apply for a number of technology grants, particularly for our at-risk populations, in addition to the funds that are appropriated by the district. We need *all* of our students to have access to up-to-date technology equipment and the Internet in order to bridge the digital divide that results from students who may not have computer access in the home. As a marketing and business teacher, I have tapped into federal Perkins funds to purchase a wireless laptop lab that my students use on a daily basis. I have also been awarded a SMART Board (an interactive white board) and interactive software through the Smarter Kids Foundation to use with my students. In order to effectively integrate technology, I have had to advance my own education by taking a number of courses in the field. I didn't want my students to have stronger technical skills than I did, but actually they have taught me just as much as I have learned in some technology classes!

I teach high school business and marketing courses. In my classroom, we use the constructivist approach, which merges what my students and I already know with the ideas of others. Many of my students have already learned so many technical skills on their own and from other courses that once we get together and work on an assignment or use the new software, we learn from each other as a team. We all help each other learn constantly. I am proud that they are learning the curriculum, applying their technical skills, and working cooperatively.

I integrate technology into most of my lessons. For example, for a marketing project, my students used the wireless laptop lab to research companies on the Internet, and design and execute a detailed electronic advertising plan for companies they researched. Students used Microsoft Word, PowerPoint, Microsoft Excel, Microsoft Publisher, Front Page, Kar2ouche storyboard software, a digital camera, a scanner, and many websites and search engines to prepare the written and visual aspects of their project. Some of the visuals they developed included websites; banner ads; television commercial storyboards; billboards; print advertisements, such as those in magazines, newspapers, or directories; and specialty or give-away items. Students were to create as realistic a campaign as possible. Some of the visual work completed for their campaigns was comparable to real advertising campaigns!

Each student then prepared a multimedia presentation using PowerPoint and other programs. They presented their advertising campaigns to their peers using an interactive white board, and then to judges at the state Association of Marketing career development conference. The students used an LCD projector so they could project their campaigns as they went over their corresponding notes. They used sound and special effects to make their presentations come alive.

In order to complete their projects, students needed to use higher-level thinking skills and apply their research to the development of an actual multimedia project. They used real websites and companies for all their research; I wanted them to make the real-world connections to see that what they are learning can lead them to very lucrative careers in marketing and advertising. Each student's learning was authentic because they were able to choose any site; it was relevant because many of my students want to major in marketing at the college level. I serve as facilitator in their learning process. I hear myself saying, "What do you think?" over and over. I work with each student every day wherever they are in their campaign, which allows each one the freedom to work on their individual outlines and visual work. Technology has been integral to this project. Using the Internet in marketing is crucial to teaching real-life marketing skills.

I want my students to be very comfortable with all aspects of technology as they prepare to enter the real world. Using technology takes a different type of mindset and planning by the classroom teacher, but the results, even in a one-computer classroom, definitely help many of our students achieve, learn, and grow.

Kathleen Thomas
Delaware Teacher of the Year for 2004–2005
Caesar Rodney High School
Camden-Wyoming, Delaware

3. Controlled choice: Parents may choose another school, but their choice is restricted so as to maintain ethnic, gender, or socioeconomic status balance.

4. Magnet schools: Parents may choose to send their children to a magnet school to focus their studies. Recall from Chapter 6 that magnet schools focus on certain areas of the curriculum, such as mathematics, science, or the arts.

5. Charter schools: Although still responsible for documenting student achievement, charter schools are free to implement innovations with reduced government control. Recall from Chapter 6 that charter schools function more independently than other schools.

6. Voucher plans: Parents may choose to send their children to private schools (including those with religious affiliations) with funds for tuition made available by the federal government.

Of these six types, voucher plans have been the most controversial. Perhaps the biggest controversy surrounds the issue of the separation of church and state. Some contend that the federal government should not supply funds for students to attend private schools with religious affiliations. Thirty-seven states have constitutions that contain clauses or amendments that prohibit the government's providing aid to any organization with a religious affiliation. However, in 2002, the U.S. Supreme Court ruled that a voucher system in Cleveland, Ohio, was "neutral with respect to religion" because the funds did not limit choice to religiously affiliated schools, but rather to any private school within the district (*Zelman v. Simmons-Harris*, 2002).

Some studies have shown that school choice helps low-income and special-needs students and families. In a study of Florida's McKay Scholarship Program, the country's second largest voucher system, Greene (2000) found that families that chose private schools using the voucher plan were overwhelmingly satisfied; this satisfaction stemmed from smaller class sizes, fewer behavioral problems, more and better services, and less victimization than in public schools (Greene & Forster, 2003). Greene (2000) makes the point that parental satisfaction does not necessarily mean that school choice promotes student achievement, but he has found an increase in achievement among students who have used vouchers to choose private schools. Nonetheless, in January 2006, the Florida Supreme Court struck down the statewide voucher system that uses taxpayer money to fund children attending private schools because the system "sets up an 'alternate system' not accountable to the state" (Romano, 2006).

Along with the advantages cited by Greene, proponents of school choice believe that the competition such choice creates among schools will force schools to become more effective. If schools want to keep their students, and therefore their federal funding, they must step up their efforts and improve their performance. Opponents maintain that allowing any school to fail hurts the educational system as a whole. If a school loses students and money, it cannot be expected to improve (Education Week, 2005).

Conclusion

In this chapter, you have investigated systems of school governance and finance. As you have seen, governing and financing American education are part of a very complex process.

Your school's governance structure has a huge impact on the working and learning environment. During your field experience and student teaching, pay attention to the teachers' general feelings about the school. Do they feel supported? If they have an idea or a concern, do they believe they will be listened to? Ask the same types of questions as you interview for professional teaching positions. Although teachers spend most of their time in a classroom with children and adolescents, remember that teaching takes place within the context of the school. If teachers feel that they are not listened to or respected, their morale declines. Teaching is a hard enough job to do every day without being unhappy in the workplace.

The governance of the school system beyond the building level also affects the teacher. You are hired by the school system, not the particular school in which you teach.

The system has its own policies and procedures with regard to salaries, contracts, benefits, and leave. As you have learned, state-level governance affects such policies as well, but states also determine curriculum, certification requirements, and ethical standards for you, the teacher. At the national level, funding and legislation affect the classroom teacher by influencing what and whom you teach.

Do not forgot that all of these policies, processes, and people must be funded. You might agree that it is safe to say that there is never enough money for education. Schools, school systems, and states depend on taxes to finance their educational efforts; many have also felt the need to try some creative funding endeavors.

School governance and finance will always be an important and controversial issue in education. The stakeholders in education you identified early in this chapter are the same ones who will argue the issues. Remember that society is the ultimate stakeholder in education. Members of society fund education and elect those who hold power over education. Because of this, it is understandable that issues of current concern to society will make their way into schools, even though these issues might not relate directly to mathematics, science, the language arts, and social sciences. Because schools serve and are supported by society, however, they must respond. In the next chapter, you will identify some current and consistent social issues and explore how the schools have responded to them.

Key Terms and Concepts

American Federation of Teachers (AFT), 298
Categorical grants, 302
Chief state school officer (CSSO), 292
Competitive grants, 303
Department of Education (DOE), 292
Digital divide, 308
E-Rate, 308

Formula funding, 303
Funding equity, 306
Funding equality, 306
Governance, 287
National Education Association (NEA), 298
Parent Teacher Association (PTA), 288
Parent Teacher Student Association (PTSA), 288

School board, 289
School choice, 310
School improvement plan, 288
Site-based management, 288
Stakeholder, 287
Superintendent of schools, 291

Construct and Apply

1. Draw a table showing the governance structure in (a) a single school with which you are familiar, and (b) a school district with which you are familiar. For each entity, list the internal and external stakeholders who might influence decision making.
2. By law, standardized tests are here to stay. Do you believe standardized test scores can adequately assess the effectiveness of teachers for purposes of accountability? If not, what other information should be used? How should it be used?
3. Describe how education is funded by local, state, and federal funds.
4. Make a list of alternative sources of revenue for schools. Think outside the box and see how creative you can be.
5. What is the difference between *equity* and *equality* in educational funding?

Deconstructing the Standards

INTASC Principle #9 says:

The teacher is a reflective practitioner who constantly evaluates the effects of his/her choices and actions on others (students, parents, and other professionals in the learning community) and who actively seeks out opportunities to grow professionally.

CHAPTER RESOURCES

INTASC Principle #10 says:

> The teacher uses fosters relationships with school colleagues, parents, and agencies in the larger community to support students' learning and well-being.

- What part(s) of these principles does this chapter address?
- How does this chapter address these principles?
- How will the concepts in this chapter help you apply these principles as a teacher?

Field Experience

1. Does your field experience school employ a site-based management system? If so, does your collaborating teacher get involved? In what ways?
2. If possible, attend a school board meeting.
   What was the agenda?
   What was discussed?
   What was decided?
   How do the discussions and decisions affect the schools?
   How do the discussions and decisions affect the teachers in the schools?
3. Does your cooperating teacher prepare his or her students for the standardized tests they will take? If so, how? Talk to your cooperating teacher about standardized testing and accountability, using the appropriate activity in your *Field Experience Companion*.
4. Access the school report card for your field experience school. What does this report card tell you about the school? Check your inferences with your cooperating teacher.

Your Portfolio

1. Prepare a diagram or flow chart showing the system of governance in your field experience school, district, and state. Include names for the positions you identify.
2. Obtain details, pictures, or other information about the unique ways your field experience school or classes in the school raise money; be sure to describe what the money will support.

Technology Resources

 Check out the *Building Teachers* companion website, http://www.education.wadsworth.com/martinloomis1, for more information and resources about school finance and governance.

 Check out the *Building Teachers* CD-ROM that may have accompanied your textbook for additional chapter resources.

 Also link to InfoTrac College Edition via the *Building Teachers* companion website. Use InfoTrac College Edition to search for journal articles to enhance your study.

Note

1. Jonathan Kozol's classic book, *Savage Inequalities* (1991), discusses the forces of equity and the extremes of wealth and poverty in the U.S. school system.

CHAPTER 12

Social Issues and the School's Response

In the schoolhouse, we have the heart of the whole of society.

HENRY GOLDEN

A primary purpose of schools is to provide students with the knowledge and skills they need not only to function in the world, but to become contributing members of society. In some cases, students may even be inspired to promote social change. In your investigations into the history of American education, you explored what was happening in society during specific time periods. You extended the influences of these events to determine who went to school, what they learned, and how they were taught. As you have discovered, society has a strong and profound influence on schools and education.

What are your thoughts about Golden's quotation at the beginning of this chapter? Do you believe that the heart of society is in the schoolhouse? How would you explain this quotation to someone? How can events happening *outside* the school building influence what goes on *inside* the school building?

In this chapter, you will explore some significant current social issues and how the school responds to these issues. You will investigate the relationship between society and the school and society's influence on you and your classroom.

CHAPTER GOALS

As a result of your work in this chapter, you will:

1. Identify current social issues that affect schools and education.

2. Explain how schools have responded to social issues and describe the controversies that often surround these responses.

Social Issues

You have heard the assertion that children are our future. As a society that recognizes this, we strive to nurture and protect our children. And, as a function of society, schools respond to issues that threaten students' well-being—emotional and physical.

Social Issues

What is the definition of a *social issue?* Break up the term. What is an issue? What issues are we, as a society, concerned about right now? List as many current social issues as you can. (A few examples to help you get started might include capital punishment, the pharmaceutical industry, and identity theft.) Keep this list; you will refer to it throughout this chapter.

While creating your list of current social issues, you undoubtedly realized that issues can change as society changes. Issues that were very important two or three decades ago have changed in importance or have been replaced by new issues. For example, capital punishment was once endorsed by the majority of Americans, pharmaceutical companies were thought of as serving society, and identity theft did not exist. Some issues seem to persist; for example, drug use by students was a concern in the 1960s and remains a concern today, but the current focus is on different drugs, their increased availability, and the ages of those abusing them. When you begin teaching, no doubt there will be issues that will affect your school and your students that do not exist today.

You have explored many social issues already in this textbook. For example, you investigated poverty in Chapter 4 and school violence, bullying, and sexual harassment in Chapter 8. Because numerous other social issues face us today, it is difficult to identify a few key issues on which to focus in this chapter. However, the chapter's purpose is for you to explore how social issues affect what goes on in schools. Therefore, we will present some prevalent issues for you to grapple with. Your investigations into the relationships between these social issues and schools can equip you to apply your understanding to new or different social issues that may arise when you are in the classroom. An important part of this chapter involves not only *what* issues affect schools, but also *how* these issues affect schools and *how* the schools respond.

Look at the list of current social issues you generated in Building Block 12.1. Which of these social issues have the potential to affect the emotional well-being of students? Which have the potential to affect their physical well-being? Which involve the entire community or segments of the community? Is it the school's responsibility to address these issues?

Social Issues That Affect Emotional Well-Being

Students struggle with a number of issues that can influence their emotional well-being, thereby affecting both their performance in school and their motivation to go to school. Pressure from divorce and nontraditional family structures as well as poverty, bullying, violence, child abuse, and other difficulties can cause some students to make a commitment to excel in school and others to drop out.

Divorce

Did the list you made in Building Block 12.1 include divorce as a social issue?

According to the National Vital Statistics Report (Munson & Sutton, 2004), the divorce rate in the United States is 3.8 divorces per 1,000 people. Given that the marriage rate is 7.5 marriages per 1,000 people, it seems that about 50% of marriages end in divorce. However, this calculation assumes that the people getting divorced in any given year are the same ones who got married during that year. In actuality, the comparison of all marriages to all divorces shows that the divorce rate is around 41% (Hurley, 2005). Regardless, about one million children are affected by divorce each year (Amato, 2001).

Students who come from divorced families tend to exhibit declining academic achievement, put less effort into doing school work and maintaining relationships, and give up when the going gets rough (Rudolph, Kurlakowsky, & Conley, 2001; Sun & Li, 2002). This is a social issue that directly affects schools, and schools find they are able to help. In the school environment, teachers can provide students from divorced homes with day-to-day intellectual and emotional support, offering intellectual structure to help these students reverse their scholastic declines (Santrock, 2004). Students from divorced families can be referred to guidance counselors and school psychologists for help in resolving issues associated with the divorce. Together, the teachers and specialists can help these students come to grips with difficulties they may be experiencing.

How does the school's providing deliberate support and structure to children of divorced families help these students to increase their academic achievement?

Schools also can take a proactive role in curbing the rate of divorce. For example, Florida requires that all high school students be taught marital and relationship skills (Sollee, 1998). Many school districts are upgrading their family life courses to include communication skills, conflict management and resolution methods, and problem-solving techniques; lack of such skills seems to be a prominent factor in divorces.

A direct link to a website that has suggestions for supporting children from divorced families is available on the *Building Teachers* website.

The Effects of Divorce

BUILDING BLOCK 12.2

What might be some of the emotional effects of divorce on a child in the age group you wish to teach?

As a teacher, what could you do to help children of divorce achieve their basic needs of safety and security, love and belonging, and self-esteem?

Family Structure

Did the list you made in Building Block 12.1 include the diverse **family structures** that exist in today's society? Studies of the family and its impact on children are both broad and deep. There are many different family structures, and each functions differently in different cultures, different ethnic groups, and with different ages of children.

According to a recent report issued by the Federal Interagency Forum on Child and Family Statistics (2005), in 2004 only 68% of children aged 0–17 lived with two married parents. Nearly one quarter (23%) lived with only their mother, 5% lived with only their father, and 4% lived with neither parent (Federal Interagency Forum, 2005). The report

The traditional family structure that once included a mother, father, and children has given way to primary caretakers who can be grandparents, extended family members, single parents, foster parents, and adoptive parents.

© LWA-Sharie Kennedy/zefa/CORBIS

classifies family structure into three categories—living with two parents, living with a single parent, and living with neither parent—as follows:

1. Living with two parents:
   Two married biological and/or adoptive parents
   One biological and/or adoptive parent and one stepparent
   Two cohabiting parents

2. Living with a single parent:
   Single mother
   Single mother with cohabiting partner
   Single father
   Single father with cohabiting partner
   Single stepparent

3. Living with neither parent:
   Grandparent(s)
   Foster parents
   Other relative(s)
   Nonrelative(s)

There are other family structures in addition to those listed here, such as same-sex parents and polygamous families. Can you identify more?

Studies have investigated effects of various family structures on student achievement in school and on student behavior, but these studies show that family structure varies so much that little direct correlation between types of family structures and student outcomes can be inferred. For example, Dunifon and Kowaleski-Jones (2002) found that single parenthood was associated with reduced mathematics scores and with juvenile delinquency, but only for white and nonminority children. These researchers did not find negative effects of single parenthood on African American children. De-Laire and Kalil (2001) found that teenagers living in nonmarried families were less likely to graduate from high school or attend college, but cautioned that not all nonmarried families are alike; teenagers living with their single mother and at least one grandparent have outcomes that are often better than those of teenagers living in traditional married families.

Nonetheless, as you know, family background is a significant determiner of students' attitudes toward school. Thus it is important that schools and teachers extend the attitude of acceptance that you investigated in Chapter 4 to family structure.

How might teachers support children who come from diverse family structures? What can they do to help these children maximize their achievement?

BUILDING BLOCK 12.3

Social Issues That Affect Emotional Well-Being

Consider your explorations in the areas of divorce and family structure.

- How do these issues affect the emotional well-being of students in our schools?
- Is it the school's responsibility to address these issues?
- If so, who should address them? How?

School Dropouts

Pressures from divorce and nontraditional family structures can lead some students to drop out of school. Did you include school dropouts among the social issues you listed in Building Block 12.1?

Most people would agree that education is key to survival in today's technological society. Adults must be literate, know how to use mathematics in everyday situations, and be well versed in technological skills to succeed. In many businesses, the minimum requirement for employment is a high school diploma.

High school dropouts tend to have lower critical thinking skills than students who complete school. High school dropouts earn lower incomes and face higher unemployment than students who complete high school. It has been estimated that high school dropouts earn an average of $6,415 less per year than those who complete school (Bhanpuri & Reynolds, 2003). Dropouts are more likely to have health problems, engage in criminal activities, and become dependent on welfare than high school graduates.

During the 2000–2001 school year, 5% of students aged 15–24 who attended school at the beginning of the school year dropped out before the school year ended—that percentage represented more than 505,000 students (National Center for Education Statistics, 2004). Of these, more males dropped out than females, more Hispanics dropped out than African Americans, and more African Americans dropped out than whites. Asian Americans had the lowest dropout rate; the dropout rate was highest among children from low-income families (see Table 12.1).

Students give several reasons for leaving high school before graduation, the most prevalent of which are poor academic performance and a strong (but somewhat naïve) motivation to go to work and earn money.

States vary in their compulsory attendance laws; most states require students to stay in high school until age 16. Many states are considering changing (or have already changed) the compulsory attendance to age 17 or 18 in an attempt to decrease the number of dropouts.

At what age can students voluntarily drop out of school in your state? Are changes in the compulsory attendance law being considered? If so, what are they?

TABLE 12.1 2000–2001 Dropout Rate for High School Students Aged 15–24 (National Center for Education Statistics, 2004)

Characteristic	Percentage
Total	5
Sex	
Male	5.6
Female	4.3
Ethnicity	
Hispanic	8.8
African American	6.3
White	4.1
Asian American	2.3
Family Income	
Low income	10.7
Middle income	5.4
High income	1.7
Age	
15–16	3.9
17	7.8
18	6.6
19	8.4
20–24	21.2

In their daily interactions with students, teachers can help those students who are thinking about dropping out of school choose to finish high school. Strategies they can employ include helping students see positive academic results, help them overcome academic hurdles, and provide warmth, support, and encouragement.

BUILDING BLOCK 12.4

Reducing the School Dropout Rate

You have seen that some state governments are attempting to curb the school dropout rate by raising the age at which students can voluntarily drop out of school.

- Do you believe this action will lower the dropout rate?
- What specific actions can high school teachers take to encourage potential dropouts to finish school?
- What warning signs might elementary and middle school teachers see that suggest a student is a likely candidate to drop out of high school?
- What actions can elementary and middle school teachers take to lessen the likelihood that at-risk students will drop out of school?

Social Issues That Affect Physical Well-Being

Students today are exposed to a number of issues that affect their physical well-being, and some of these issues affect what is taught in the schools.

Teenage Car Accidents

Did the list you made in Building Block 12.1 include teenage driving accidents? Teenage vehicular accidents and the resulting fatalities are a very serious social issue that affects schools. In 2005, the Insurance Institute for Highway Safety reported that, in 2004, 5,610 teens were killed in automobile accidents, and that in 2002, the latest year for which data are available, 41% of all teenage deaths among 16–19 year olds were related to motor vehicles. Teenagers have a much higher rate of automobile accidents and resulting deaths than any other classification of drivers. Many teenagers die as passengers in motor vehicles. In 2004, 62% of teens killed in automobile accidents were passengers in a car in which another teen was driving.

Teens are more likely than more experienced drivers to be at fault in the automobile accidents in which they are involved. They are more likely than other drivers to be in-

© Mark Gibson/Index Stock Imagery

Teen auto accidents are quickly becoming a leading cause of teen fatalities and injuries.

volved in fatal single-car accidents. Reasons for such high incidences include the facts that teens are more likely than older drivers to speed, to drive at night, not to wear seatbelts, to take risks, and to underestimate dangers. Alcohol also plays a role in teen accidents. In 2004, 28% of all teen males and 13% of all teen females killed in car accidents were legally impaired by alcohol (Insurance Institute for Highway Safety, 2005).

Some states are responding to the high rate of teen accidents by raising the minimum licensed driving age, implementing provisional or graduated licensing programs that impose curfews on teen drivers, limiting the number of teenaged and nonrelated passengers in a teen driver's car, or a combination of these strategies.

A logical response of schools to the alarming statistics of teenagers and motor vehicles might be to reinstate driver education courses, many of which were discontinued due to budget cuts, or to reexamine existing driver ed courses. However, research indicates that driver education courses are not as effective as they were once thought to be; and that these courses may actually contribute to automobile accidents involving teenagers. By taking the driver education course, the thinking goes, teens can acquire a driver's license, and, because they took the class, they tend to overestimate their competence as drivers, when in fact they are still young and inexperienced (Robertson, 1980). Other research also has shown that most driver education courses have little or no effect on changing teens' risky driving behaviors (Mayhew et al., 1998; Society for Adolescent Medicine, 1997). Accordingly, no research clearly indicates that school-offered driver education courses help to reduce vehicular homicides. Fatal automobile accidents involving teens are a social issue that schools would like to help solve, but no clear solution currently exists.

> **What are the requirements for a driver's license in your state?**

Teenage Driving

BUILDING BLOCK 12.5

You have seen that states are attempting to curb the number of teen driving accidents by imposing license restrictions.

- Do you believe this action will lower the rate of teen motor vehicle accidents?
- Do you believe that teen driver safety is an issue schools should address?
- Is there something specific schools should do about this problem? If so, describe a possible solution.

Health Issues

Did the list you made in Building Block 12.1 include health issues? Which ones? Good health is essential to successful living. According to the National Association of State Boards of Education (NASBE), schools play an important role in addressing students' needs by helping students succeed academically and by supporting the growth that will enable them to lead successful, productive adult lives (Pecori, 2000). Today's society tends to believe that teaching the fundamental principles of good health enables students to lead successful, productive adult lives, and that (with a few exceptions) this education should be undertaken by the schools. Such factors as exercise, nutrition, sleeping habits, and cardiovascular health have been taught by schools for many years to encourage healthy living.

Take a moment with Building Block 12.6 to focus on some specific health-related issues that concern contemporary society.

Health Concerns

BUILDING BLOCK 12.6

What are some current health issues? Jot a few down.

- Which of these issues have implications for students?
- What role should the school play in teaching these health issues?

The list you made in Building Block 12.6 is probably one that you could duplicate by reading newspaper headlines or watching television news: childhood obesity, drugs, sex, violence, and so on. Certainly, schools can address students' need to become educated about health issues. Let us take a look at how schools may respond to the contemporary health issues of childhood obesity, drugs and alcohol, and sex education.

Childhood Obesity

One health issue that affects schools is **childhood obesity.** Statistics show that childhood obesity is on the rise in the United States. Several factors contribute to childhood obesity, such as junk food and limited exercise. People are calling for action to reduce childhood obesity, and schools are responding to that call.

The American Obesity Association defines an obese child or adolescent as one who is at or above the 95th percentile of his or her body mass index (BMI) (American Obesity Association, 2002). Body mass index is a relationship between height and weight that can be calculated using the following equation (U.S. Food and Drug Administration, 2001):

$$\text{BMI} = \frac{705 \times \text{body weight (in pounds)}}{\text{height (in inches)} \times \text{height (in inches)}}$$

What is a healthy BMI for children and teens? The amount of body fat a child has varies with age and gender in addition to height and weight. In general, the BMI increases as a child gets older. For this reason, BMI for individuals up to the age of 20 is reported as a percentile rather than the actual body mass. Percentile is the percent of the population at or below a given BMI. The BMI percentile for children with healthy weight ranges between the 5th and the 85th percentiles. A BMI between the 85th and the 95th percentiles indicates that the individual is at risk for obesity, and a BMI at the 95th percentile and above indicates the child is overweight. A BMI at or below the 5th percentile indicates the child is underweight.

The latest statistics from the National Center for Health Statistics, a division of the Centers for Disease Control (CDC), indicate that an estimated 16% of children and adolescents aged 6–19 years are overweight and that the number of overweight children and adolescents is increasing (National Center for Health Statistics, 2005). Table 12.2 shows the percentage of overweight children and adolescents for selected years from 1963 to 2002.

In response to this unhealthy trend, schools are reexamining their lunch and breakfast programs and their physical education programs. Several organizations have compiled resources and developed curricular materials and programs to help schools. For example, the CDC's Division of Adolescent and School Health has published the *School*

Direct links to a template where you can calculate your body mass index and charts showing the interpretation of BMI for children aged 2 to 20 are available on the Building Teachers companion website.

TABLE 12.2 Prevalence of Overweight Children and Adolescents for Selected Years, 1963–2002 (National Center for Health Statistics, 2005)

Age	1963–1970	1971–1974	1976–1980	1988–1994	1999–2002
6–11	4%	4%	7%	11%	16%
12–19	5%	6%	5%	11%	16%

According to the Centers for Disease Control, more than 15% of children between the ages of 6 and 19 are obese. Healthier school lunch options and school-based nutrition programs can address this issue, but what can individual teachers do to further manage childhood obesity?

© Baerbel Schmidt/Getty Images

Health Index for Physical Activity and Healthy Eating: A Self-Assessment and Planning Guide. This online resource allows schools to compare their own nutrition programs with other, exemplary programs. To assist schools in food planning, the American School Food Service Association provides several documents that address nutrition program policy. The National Heart, Lung, and Blood Institute has developed the *Eat Smart School Nutrition Program Guide,* which provides school food service personnel with information on how to reduce fat and sodium in school meals.

Nutritious food choices help students to maintain a healthy weight, and exercise also plays a role. However, physical education programs are being cut back across the nation. Even so, exercise, physical education, and sport activity materials are available to help schools develop and implement exercise programs. Organizations such as Human Kinetics and the American Association for Active Lifestyles and Fitness have materials about physical education and sports available for use by schools. These materials include recommendations and activities for students with special needs.

www Direct links to several websites devoted to curbing childhood obesity are available on the *Building Teachers* companion website.

www Direct links to the websites of groups devoted to exercise and physical fitness programs in schools are available on the *Building Teachers* companion website.

How are schools modifying their food and physical education programs to help reduce childhood obesity?

BUILDING
BLOCK
12.7

Childhood and Adolescent Obesity

■ Do you believe that childhood and adolescent obesity is a problem in today's society?

■ Is there something specific schools should do about childhood and adolescent obesity? If so, describe what you think would be a solution.

■ Some schools are cutting back their physical education programs. Why do you suppose they are doing so? How can this be reconciled with the increasing rate of childhood and adolescent obesity?

Drugs and Alcohol

Drug and alcohol use by students has been a concern of parents, teachers, and society for many years. Figure 12.1 presents information about drug use by U.S. students between 2001 and 2004. The data, from the Monitoring the Future study (Johnston et al., 2004), represents combined information for 8th, 10th, and 12th graders about the use of any illicit drugs (including alcohol) in the month previous to the surveys. From the figure, you can see that the overall use of illicit drugs has declined; however, the report notes that the use of inhalants by 8th graders has increased. We can probably all agree that *any* illicit teen drug use is contrary to what the National Association of State Boards of Education considers supportive of the growth that will enable students to lead successful, productive

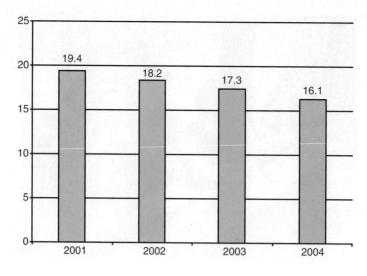

Figure 12.1
Percent of 8th, 10th, and 12th graders reporting past-month use of any illicit drug (Johnson et al., 2004).

lives. Schools can play a major role in educating youth about drug abuse. Have you seen evidence of this social issue in the schools?

In what class do students learn about drugs and their harmful effects? At which grade level? Many schools offer health courses that address these topics. In addition, several programs for K–12 students offer information outside the traditional health class.

Do you believe schools should be involved in drug and alcohol abuse prevention programs? How are they involved now? What else, if anything, should they do?

The Office of Safe and Drug-Free Schools, a division of the U.S. Department of Education, oversees federal funds for drug prevention. Drug-Violence Prevention grants are awarded to schools and other organizations to develop drug prevention activities for students. Several national organizations provide information and curricular materials about drug and alcohol abuse. For example, the National Institute on Drug Abuse (NIDA), the National Institutes of Health, and the U.S. Department of Health and Human Services offer free, science-based materials for teens, teachers, and parents. These materials help students understand the scientific basis for the harmful effects of drug abuse. NIDA hosts NIDA for Teens, which provides facts, real stories, and answers to frequently asked questions about drugs. Available for teachers are several curricular materials, including posters, CD-ROMs, modules of activities, and magazines for grades K–12. Parents can access information and activities to do at home.

You probably have seen Just Say No posters in the halls of your field experience school, you may have observed National Red Ribbon Week, and you may have seen program materials from D.A.R.E. The Just Say No campaign was mounted by former First Lady Nancy Reagan in the early 1980s to help raise awareness about the harmful effects of drug use and abuse. National Red Ribbon Week is held during the last week in October and is commemorated by individuals wearing or displaying red ribbons to signify their commitment to leading drug-free lives. The U.S. Drug Enforcement Agency sponsors National Red Ribbon Week, and the National Family Partnership coordinates activities. More than 80 million Americans participate in National Red Ribbon week each year.

D.A.R.E. (Drug Abuse Resistance Education) is a drug abuse program designed to equip students in elementary, middle, and high schools with knowledge about drug abuse, its consequences, and skills for resisting peer pressure to experiment with drugs, alcohol, and tobacco. The program is taught in regular classrooms by uniformed police officers who create a positive atmosphere for interaction between students and the police officer. The D.A.R.E. program is used in all 50 states and in 53 countries. The D.A.R.E. website reports that 26 million children in U.S. schools use the D.A.R.E. curriculum and other drug abuse prevention educational materials (D.A.R.E., 2005).

More information and programs about drug abuse are available to educators than we can list in this textbook. However, it should be clear that the social issue of drug and alcohol abuse affects schools.

A direct link to the National Institute on Drug Abuse/National Institutes of Health website is available on the *Building Teachers* companion website.

A direct link to the 2004 Red Ribbon Week website is available on the *Building Teachers* companion website.

D.A.R.E. is one of several programs developed to educate students about and prevent drug use. How might local police officers positively affect students about drug, alcohol, and tobacco use?

© James Leynse/CORBIS

Drugs and Alcohol

You have noted that the overall use of drugs and alcohol by school-aged students seems to be decreasing.

- Do you believe that schools should be involved in drug and alcohol abuse prevention programs? Why or why not?
- How are schools involved in drug and alcohol abuse prevention efforts now?
- Is there something specific schools should do about the issue of drug and alcohol use and abuse by students? If so, describe what you think they might do.

Sex-Related Issues

The education of school-aged children in matters of sex and sexuality is a huge social issue, one that schools can help address. However, unlike schools' responses to childhood obesity and the use of drugs and alcohol, their responses to sexual issues are fraught with controversy.

What are society's concerns about sex? People are troubled by the potential for teens to become pregnant or to become infected with a **sexually transmitted disease (STD)**. Some people also believe that premarital sex is morally wrong.

Teenage Pregnancy

The Centers for Disease Control has surveyed youth in 9th through 12th grade every 2 years since 1990 as part of the Youth Risk Behavior Surveillance System (YRBSS). The survey's purpose is to assess the prevalence of **risky behaviors** by young people in several categories, including sexual behavior. According to the 2003 survey, the percentage of U.S. high school students engaging in risky sexual behaviors had not changed significantly since 2001 (Centers for Disease Control, 2004). In fact, the latest statistics on teen pregnancy show that, overall, teen pregnancies decreased by about 28% between 1972 and 2000 (The National Campaign to Prevent Teen Pregnancy, 2004a), and that teenage birth rates decreased by about 42% between 1991 and 2003, the last year for which data is available (*Morbidity and Mortality Weekly Report,* 2005). Nonetheless, when compared with other industrialized countries, the United States has the highest rate of teen pregnancy (National Campaign to Prevent Teen Pregnancy, 2001).

What does a teenage girl do when she finds out she is pregnant? What does she do when she gives birth? Sometimes she continues regular school attendance until the baby is born; sometimes her options are limited to attending an alternative school or even dropping out of school altogether. A fact sheet provided by the National Campaign to Prevent Teen Pregnancy provides the following statistics (2004b):

- Parenthood is the leading cause of dropping out for teenage girls.
- Only 1.5% of women who were teenage mothers have college degrees by the time they are 30.
- The children of teen parents do poorly in school and are 50% more likely to fail and repeat a grade.

Schools around the country have responded to the social issue of teen pregnancy by hosting prevention and early intervention programs. For example, a program in Nashville, Tennessee, provides sex education, tutoring, service learning opportunities, and after-school activities for 3rd through 6th graders. Louisiana has established school-based health centers that provide care and counseling. Schools across the country have adopted the Preventing Teen Pregnancy curriculum developed by Girls, Inc., that provides skills, insights, values, personal tools, peer support, and complete information to help girls aged 9 to 18 make informed choices to prevent pregnancy (National Campaign to Prevent Teen Pregnancy, 2004b).

The National Campaign to Prevent Teen Pregnancy has noted that, contrary to what you might believe about peer pressure, students believe that guidance counselors and teachers are the second most reliable source of information about sex and sexuality—second only to their parents and families (National Campaign to Prevent Teen Pregnancy, 2004c). Teens say their parents influence their decisions about sex more than their peers (37% vs. 33%, respectively), but parents believe that their teen's friends have the greater influence (47% vs. 28%, respectively) (National Center to Prevent Teen Pregnancy, 2004c). It seems that parents might safely take an increased role in the sex education of their children.

Do you believe that teenage pregnancy is a problem schools should address? What stance should the schools take on this issue? What, if anything, do you think schools should do about this problem?

Acquired Immune Deficiency Syndrome (AIDS)

Another major social issue related to sex is sexually transmitted diseases, especially AIDS. As Figure 12.2 shows, except for a slight decline in 2000 and 2001, there has been an alarming increase in the number of teenagers diagnosed with **AIDS** since 1985. Nevertheless, according to the YRBSS survey, 88% of students surveyed said that HIV and AIDS had been addressed in school (Centers for Disease Control, 2004).

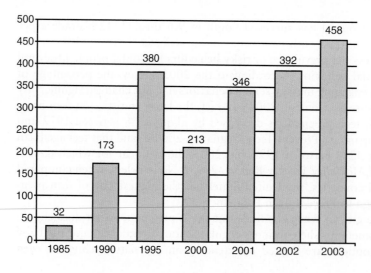

Figure 12.2
Acquired Immune Deficiency Syndrome (AIDS) cases diagnosed at ages 13 to 19, 1985–2003 (National Center for Health Statistics, 2004).

Do you believe that AIDS prevention is a problem schools should address? What, if anything, do you think schools should do about this problem?

Programs that provide students with accurate information and provides schools with educational materials have been developed in response to the AIDS epidemic. The American School Health Association (ASHA) provides information, curriculum materials, and resources for 7th through 12th graders, schools, and parents in a publication called *Health in Action*. ASHA also has student workbooks, teacher guides, and parent guides for elementary school–aged students. The student workbooks are written in a comic-book style and include activities for parental involvement. Teacher resources include classroom activities and transparency masters. ASHA also offers resource guides for schools that want to plan and develop HIV and AIDS education programs.

One extremely controversial action taken by some schools in an effort to reduce teenage pregnancies and AIDS and other sexually transmitted diseases (STDs) is the distribution of condoms in schools. The thinking behind this tactic is that having condoms available to students who decide to engage in sexual behaviors after having been educated about sex, pregnancy, and STDs will encourage them to make safe choices. On the other hand, opponents of this practice insist that students may feel free to engage in sexual behaviors simply because they can get condoms easily. However, studies have shown that the opposite may be true—that students at schools with condom-availability programs have sex less often than those at schools without condoms (Kirchheimer, 2003).

Most experts feel that comprehensive sex education and AIDS-prevention programs should be continued in schools; such programs include content information and education about such factors as the perception of peer norms, teen beliefs and personal values about sex and condom contraception, and the ability to say "No" to having sex. However, many schools are shifting away from comprehensive sex education and HIV-prevention programs because of the increased federal funding for abstinence-only programs (AIDS Alert, 2005).

> Direct links to the National Campaign to Prevent Teen Pregnancy and the American School Health Association websites are available on the *Building Teachers* companion website.

> Should schools hand out condoms to students? What are your thoughts about this controversial topic?

Sexual Orientation

Another social issue affecting schools is the controversy surrounding **sexual orientation.** Did the list you made in Building Block 12.1 include sexual orientation as a social issue? Some may argue that sexual orientation is *not* an issue and that it should not be addressed in schools. However, you will be teaching and working with gay and lesbian individuals, so this topic is one you must consider.

Gay and lesbian students are increasingly "coming out" and speaking up in schools. Currently, the average age of coming out is about 16 years old, whereas in the 1970s, it was about 20 years old. Because of this tendency to come out earlier and because of increased exposure to gay and lesbian matters through politics and the media, the younger generation is more accepting of gays in society than earlier generations. A recent *Newsweek* poll found that, among 18–29 year olds, 41% approve of same-sex marriages; the approval rate among the general U.S. population is only 28% (Rosenberg, 2004).

What are your thoughts about school-aged gay and lesbian students? (Remember the attitude of acceptance you explored in Chapter 4.) Do you think this topic presents a problem schools should address? If so, what initiatives do you think schools should take? Do you think homosexuality in school-aged children is an issue? Why?

As homosexuality has become more prominent in society and has gained greater acceptance by young people, increasing numbers of schools have responded by permitting their students to form gay–straight alliances (GSAs). The 2003 National School Climate Survey notes that twice as many students reported a GSA in their schools as in 2001 (Kosciw, 2004).

School GSAs have created controversy. Opponents argue that the existence of GSAs promotes homosexuality, with an agenda of "turning" students gay. Proponents say that homosexual students need the support of GSAs and cite safety concerns and statistics, such as those you saw in Chapter 8. (Recall that many gay and lesbian students reported feeling unsafe and unsupported at school.) The National School Climate Survey cited data indicating that the presence of a GSA contributes to students' feelings of emotional and physical safety. The data showed that, among surveyed gay and lesbian students, 68.3% of those in schools without a GSA felt unsafe, whereas 60.9% felt unsafe in schools with a GSA (Kosciw, 2004). So, even with a GSA, a significant portion of gay and lesbian students feel unsafe in their schools.

Schools have tried to respond to the controversy of having GSAs in schools in ways that satisfy anti-GSA protestors but that also meet students' needs. A case in Georgia serves as an example. After hearing about gay–straight student alliances at other high schools, a student in a rural county received permission to start a gay–straight alliance at her school. The community responded with an uproar that was heard around the nation. A conservative Christian group in Kansas sent representatives to protest, but local people—both supporters and opponents of the club—joined together and told the protesters to go home and mind their own business.

In an attempt to defuse the situation, the student organization was renamed Peers Rising in Diversity Education (PRIDE) to better represent the inclusive nature intended by the club's founder. However, a change of name was not enough to defuse the controversy. The district school superintendent opposed any sex-based club but acknowledged that students had the same right to assemble for this club as they would with any other extracurricular club. In response, the Board of Education suggested abolishing all nonacademic extracurricular clubs. At a public meeting, this idea was shot down by the reasoning that students need to show their involvement in extracurricular activities, such as service clubs and sports, when they apply to colleges (Yoo, 2005). The state superintendent of schools offered a proposal that would require students to obtain parental permission to attend any extracurricular club meetings. This proposal was not approved (MacDonald, 2005).

Because of the controversy, however, the school district decided to ban *all* extracurricular clubs (including Key Club, Interact, Students Against Drunk Driving, and the Fellowship of Christian Athletes, in addition to the newly formed PRIDE) from holding on-campus meetings. Administrators encouraged the formation of clubs outside of the school, led by adults in the community (Snorton, 2005).

Sex Education

You have investigated school-based sex education programs. Should the schools do more? Providing sex education courses in school is very controversial, mostly because of differing social mores and religious beliefs. Many parents want their children to have sex education in school, but it seems that everyone has his or her own idea of just what a sex education class should entail. Sometimes parental permission is required (even for learning facts about AIDS in science classes), but not all parents give their consent.

www Direct links to the websites of the Gay, Lesbian, and Straight Education Network and the Parents and Friends of Lesbians and Gays are available on the *Building Teachers* companion website.

What alternatives do you believe schools should provide for students whose parents do not give consent for their children to study sex education in school?

BUILDING BLOCK 12.9

Sex Education

You have seen that there are several sex-related concerns that can affect our young people.

- Do you believe that schools should be involved in sex education programs? If so, on what topics should the programs focus?

- How are schools involved in sex education now?

- Is there something specific schools should do about sex-based issues? If so, describe what you think they should do.

- Do you believe Gay-Straight Alliances (GSAs) should be permitted in schools? Why or why not?

Social Issues That Affect the Community

Did the list of social issues you made in Building Block 12.1 include community-based issues? There are hundreds of social issues that affect local communities, such as crime, gangs, illiteracy, vandalism, and many more. Students can participate in resolving many such issues by becoming involved in **service learning**.

Service learning engages students in meaningful service to their community through the integration of community issues with the school's curriculum. Service learning projects involve collaboration among teachers, students, and the community to identify, study, and propose solutions to community problems, often implementing the solutions and evaluating their results. The problems consist of social concerns that may affect small or large segments of the community.

Students have participated in a wide range of service learning projects, including tracking arsonists, working with students who have been affected by gang violence, help-

> *www* Direct links to three sources for service learning are available on the *Building Teachers* companion website.

---

from the TEACHER — Deb Perryman

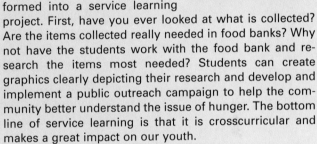

Courtesy of Deb Perryman

If we were to research the mission statements of schools across the nation, we would find some mention of "creating citizens." But when do our schools actually provide students with the opportunity to act as citizens? The No Child Left Behind legislation calls for students to meet or exceed state standards. A worthy goal, as citizens must be educated and motivated to participate in today's society. Why not use the time we have in schools to actually show our young people how learning will apply to their lives? Why not allow our students to solve community problems and act as citizens? I have found a teaching strategy that allows me to fold learning standards into community action. This strategy is called *service learning*. To me, service learning is the ultimate teaching tool in the constructivist's tool box. Service learning allows students to explore issues, formulate possible solutions, and implement and then evaluate those solutions. In the service learning model, the project students undertake is the shared responsibility of both the teacher and the student.

In service learning, students explore one or more aspects of a community issue. The teacher works to tie the exploration into a project that addresses the curriculum. For example, picking up litter near a creek on a monthly basis can be related to the Clean Water Act and therefore fits the environmental curriculum. The students are exploring a community issue (litter and its effect on creeks) while meeting state learning standards. My goal is for the students to find the source of that litter and outline a permanent solution to the litter problem. As their facilitator, I encourage them to implement their solutions and evaluate the outcomes.

Service learning is *not* community service. Although community service projects are wonderful and do provide positive student outcomes, they are not tied directly to curriculum. Take, as an example, one of America's most popular community service projects: the canned food drive. Please tell me how placing collection boxes in a central location helps students meet learning standards. Think for a moment how this community service project can be transformed into a service learning project. First, have you ever looked at what is collected? Are the items collected really needed in food banks? Why not have the students work with the food bank and research the items most needed? Students can create graphics clearly depicting their research and develop and implement a public outreach campaign to help the community better understand the issue of hunger. The bottom line of service learning is that it is crosscurricular and makes a great impact on our youth.

Planning a service learning project is as easy as planning a party. You have to think about who, what, where, when, and how. Whom do you want to be involved? What issue do you want your students to work on? Where and when will this project fit into your lesson plans? Where and when will it fit into the community? How will this fit into your curriculum, and how will the project be evaluated?

Please remember two additional tidbits. First, involve students at every stage of the project, including planning and evaluation. Second, make sure that the students are talking a legitimate community need. Projects that are token projects are doomed to fail. Kids know when you are faking, so don't! As you might imagine, the first project is the most difficult. Once you get through one, I dare you to *not* find additional projects.

Illinois Teacher of the Year, 2004–2005
Elgin High School
Elgin, Illinois

School-based service learning projects can encourage prevention of social issues like vandalism, pollution, arson, and crime. These students are involved in a service learning project that seeks to reduce vandalism in their community. How might a teacher integrate this service learning project into the curriculum?

ing illiterate adults learn to read, mapping ancient aqueducts, and proposing solutions to air pollution caused by school bus emissions (Bradford, 2005; "Learning from the Community," 2004; Touhig et al., 2005).

From this brief excursion into some of the many social issues that affect people today, you have seen that many such issues affect the children who attend our schools. Now it is time to pull everything you have learned in this chapter together.

BUILDING BLOCK 12.10

Society and the Schools

In Building Block 12.1 and Building Block 12.3, you listed some social issues that exist in today's society.

- Which of the issues on your list have prompted action by schools?
- Which issues have not prompted action by schools? Why do you suppose this is? Which of these issues do you believe schools should do something about? What should they do?
- Which issues have prompted controversy about school action? What kinds of controversy? Is there a commonality among the controversies?

Conclusion

This chapter has focused on several social issues that affect our schools. Some of these issues may be solved, but some will persist. In the future, social issues will arise that we can't even pretend to anticipate now. However, after examining some issues and the schools' responses in this chapter, you can apply the same strategies to discern how other issues affect what, how, and whom you teach.

Social issues are, by nature, controversial. And what about that phrase, "Children are our future"? Citizens expect students to address various social issues as they join society. In school, students should learn what they need to know and be able to do to solve these problems. The controversy becomes more complicated, however, because everyone has his or her own ideas not only about a particular issue, but also about what students need to learn to address the issue. Teachers stand in the middle: We are members of society, with our own beliefs regarding *what* and *how* and *whom* we teach. Remember that you are in the classroom to help students learn and to think—not to teach them what you think.

You have seen that often, when social issues involving schools arise, legislation is also involved. In the next chapter, you will explore ethical and legal issues that affect education—and especially teachers.

Key Terms and Concepts

AIDS, 326
Childhood obesity, 322
Family structure, 317

Risky behavior, 325
Service learning, 329
Sexual orientation, 327

Sexually transmitted disease
(STD), 325

Construct and Apply

1. How do issues such as divorce, family structure, and other issues that affect a student's emotional well-being influence that student's work in school?

2. Suppose you are the principal of an elementary school and you decide that health should be emphasized in all grades, but you can include only a single topic from these issues: childhood obesity, drug and alcohol abuse, and sex education. Which topic would you choose? Why? What would the topic be if your school were a middle school? A high school? Why?

3. If schools are to play a role in teaching students about sex, safety, and health issues, to what extent should teachers be held accountable for their own behavior?

Deconstructing the Standards

INTASC Principle #9 says:

The teacher is a reflective practitioner who constantly evaluates the effects of his/her choices and actions on others (students, parents, and other professionals in the learning community) and who actively seeks out opportunities to grow professionally.

- What part(s) of this principle does this chapter address?
- How does this chapter address this principle?
- How will the concepts in this chapter help you apply this principle as a teacher?

Field Experience

- What do the teachers in your field placement school do to help students from divorced homes or unconventional family structures?
- What does your school do to help reduce the rate of high school dropouts?
- What types of information and activities does your field placement school use for drug abuse education and prevention?
- What sex education programs are offered by your field experience school?
- Does your field experience school employ service learning strategies? If so, describe the issue(s) addressed and how students and teachers approach them.

Your Portfolio

1. Pay attention to the social issues and the school's response in your community. How do the schools in the area where you wish to be employed respond to these issues? Read the newspaper daily and become educated about the factors and people involved. Summarize the facts you find and write a reflection to include in your portfolio.

2. Review the philosophy of education statement you wrote in Chapter 2. Based on your investigations into the history of American education and society's expectations of schools, revise this statement to incorporate your ideas about what students should learn.

Building Teachers Technology Resources

 Check out the *Building Teachers* companion website, http://www.education.wadsworth.com/martinloomis1, for more information about how schools respond to social issues, including links to the following websites:

- American Association for Active Lifestyles and Fitness
- American School Food Service Association
- American School Health Association
- Cesar Chavez Foundation
- Children of Divorce
- Corporation for National Service
- Division of Adolescent and School Health, CDC
- Gay, Lesbian, and Straight Education Network (GLSEN)
- Human Kinetics
- National Campaign to Prevent Teen Pregnancy
- National Heart, Lung, and Blood Institute
- National Institute on Drug Abuse/National Institutes of Health
- National Service Learning Clearing House
- Parents and Friends of Lesbians and Gays (PFLAG)
- Red Ribbon Week

 Check out the *Building Teachers* CD-ROM that accompanies your textbook for additional chapter resources.

Also link to InfoTrac College Edition via the *Building Teachers* companion website. Use InfoTrac College Edition to search for journal articles to enhance your study.

CHAPTER 13

Teachers, Students, and the Law

By Linda Webb, Ed.D., Kennesaw State University

> The law's final justification is in the good it does or fails to do to the society of a given place and time.
>
> ALBERT CAMUS

Camus justifies the law in terms of whether it does good or fails to do good for a society. Do you think laws governing schools can be judged by the same standard, that is, by whether they do or fail to do good for schools and those within the schools? Elsewhere in this textbook, you have looked at a number of laws that affect teachers, students, and schools. Think back to previous chapters. Do you remember the requirements for the lengths of a school year and a school day? Do you recall the requirements of the Individuals with Disabilities Education Act (IDEA)? How would you describe the "good" those laws were enacted to accomplish? Have they accomplished their intended purpose?

You probably have heard about recent school legal issues from the media. If you have children or siblings currently in school, you have probably become familiar with still other legal issues, and you no doubt can recall legal issues from your own time in school. Think about the issues about which you have read or seen reports recently. What do you think is the purpose of each such law? What is its impact on schools? Does it have a good effect?

Schools in the United States operate within a framework of laws and regulations that seek to ensure that all children within society can obtain an education that prepares them for a successful adult life. At the same time, schools operate in a litigious society, and lawsuits are common, involving all aspects of education. The decisions made in lawsuits and other court decisions help shape the educational environment and specify the exact meaning of laws.

This chapter focuses on three basic questions:

1. What is the employment relationship between the teacher and the school board?

2. What is the legal relationship between the student and the school?

3. What are the rights and responsibilities of teachers on the job and students when they are in school?

You will examine some of the laws and regulations that affect teachers, students, and schools. Your explorations will help you gain a basic understanding of how the legal system works and a basic understanding of the legal framework for education. In turn, this will enable you to understand how to comply with the law, how to ensure your rights, and how to challenge violations of law appropriately.

CHAPTER GOALS

As a result of your work in this chapter, you will:

1. Identify the system of laws governing education in the United States.
2. Explain teachers' major rights and responsibilities.
3. Explain students' major rights and responsibilities.
4. Describe the impact of court decisions on school operations and individuals within the school.

Laws Affecting Teachers, Students, and Schools

Think again about the laws you have encountered in this course. Think also about the laws that you remember from your days in schools or that you know about from siblings, children, or the media. What are some laws affecting schools? What are the sources of these laws: local, state, or federal? Let us start by exploring some of the laws that affect students, teachers, and schools.

BUILDING BLOCK 13.1

It's the Law!

Take a few minutes to jot down some laws that affect schools. How do these laws affect teachers, students, or both? Make a chart with four columns:

■ The law.

■ Its source: Is it a local law? A state law? A federal law?

■ Its impact: Does the law require that teachers or students do certain things or refrain from doing certain things? Why?

■ The consequences of violating it: What happens if someone breaks the law?

You may wish to use a table such as the one shown here to help you organize your thinking; we give an example to help you get started.

Law	Source (Local, State, Federal)	Impact	Consequences of Violation
Be on time to school.	State	If a teacher isn't on time, no one is around to take care of the students.	The teacher's employment could be terminated if this behavior continues.

If you were to group the laws you cited in Building Block 13.1 into categories, you would find that the laws fall into several categories, such as the rights and responsibilities of teachers and students, child abuse and neglect, and the rights of students with special needs. What categories could organize your list?

You probably generated a lengthy list of laws governing school life. Let us examine whether all the items you listed are laws. Some of them might be regulations. Others might be court decisions. Are laws, regulations, and court decisions all the same? Do they affect schools equally?

Sources of Laws and Regulations Impacting Schools

Laws and regulations come from federal, state, and local sources, and from the courts which, through numerous cases, have interpreted the laws. Some laws are based on the federal or a state constitution and are known as **constitutional laws.** Some are passed by the legislature at the federal or state level and are known as **statutes.** Some result from decisions made by the courts and are known as **case law.** Rules enacted by school boards and other state agencies to ensure compliance with the laws are called **regulations.**

Federal Sources of Laws

The U.S. Constitution is the supreme law of the land. The Constitution gives Congress the power to provide for the general welfare in the United States. Although the word *education* is not found in the Constitution, Congress has used the general welfare rationale to enact legislation providing for research and support of educational programs, providing financial assistance for such functions as school lunches, and mandating safety regulations, such as the Asbestos School Hazard Detection and Control Act of 1980. In Chapter 5 you learned about the Individuals with Disabilities Education Act (IDEA). This is an example of a federal law passed that affects the day-to-day operation of schools. Think about the laws you listed in Building Block 13.1. Many of them probably concern federally controlled rights, such as employment discrimination and teacher rights. Federal legislation is a basis for many aspects of school life.

What do you think should be the role of the courts in education?

Most federal laws that directly affect education policies offer federal funds to the states but with conditions attached. For example, Title I funds must be distributed according to a formula whereby the school district gives the most money to the schools with the greatest need based on free and reduced lunch population. If the district gives more Title I money to a school with less need, all Title I money is withheld from the entire district. A state or a school that accepts federal money is bound by the conditions attached to those funds.

State Sources of Laws and Regulations

In the United States, public schools are a function of state government. The state's right to determine laws, rules, and regulations for public schools within its boundaries is derived from the 10th Amendment to the U.S. Constitution which, as you have seen, states,

"The powers not delegated to the United States by the Constitution, nor prohibited by it to the states, are reserved to the states respectively, or to the people." Because the U.S. Constitution does not specifically list education as a federal function and does not prohibit the states from regulating education, educational control is reserved for the states. Each state enacts laws and regulations determining how education functions within its boundaries.

All state constitutions specifically address public schools and provide for a uniform, efficient system of public education. Unlike the federal government, the states have the power to make laws governing education. For example, all 50 states have laws requiring students within specified age ranges to attend school.

Regulations differ from laws in that they are not enacted by legislatures and are not part of a state's legal code. But regulations often carry the force of law. You are probably familiar with regulations in your state regarding certification and curriculum. Regulations governing facilities are less well known. For example, did you know that many state boards of education in the southern United States have mandated that all schools be air conditioned?

Local Sources of Laws and Regulations

Although U.S. schools are controlled by the states, local boards of education administer the state laws, rules, and regulations. These boards often add their own local regulations, such as deciding that all teachers must attend specific staff development activities. Local boards also formulate regulations covering such issues as the district student discipline policy, teacher attendance policy, and school year calendar.

As you can see, each state has layers of rules and regulations. But state law takes precedence. Figure 13.1 shows the layers of school control within the state.

BUILDING BLOCK 13.2

Which Are Laws?

Review the laws you listed in Building Block 13.1.

- Which represent laws?
- Which represent regulations?
- Which do you think were enacted at the federal level? The state level? The local level?

The Courts

You have seen that there are two sources of law governing schools: state laws and federal laws. These laws are debated and passed by representative legislatures and do not rely on precedents. Remember the law enacted by some southern states that all school buildings must be air conditioned? This law did not rely on any previous law or precedent. There were no previous examples to be considered.

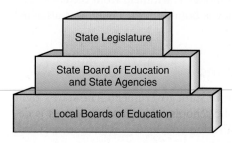

Figure 13.1
Levels of school control in states.

A third type of law mentioned earlier is case law. Case law results when judges rule on a legal dispute. IDEA, for example, has been the basis of numerous lawsuits wherein parents felt their children were not receiving the education to which they were entitled by law. When judges ruled on issues regarding IDEA, schools were required to provide specific services and act in specific ways. Thus, the determination of a court case had the impact of law.

Courts tend to use previous case law to guide them in their decisions. Case law establishes precedents that guide arguments regardless of when or where the previous decision was handed down, provided the decision was the result of a hearing held in state court, federal court, or the U.S. Supreme Court.

The Impact of Courts on the Daily Life of Teachers and Students

Since the landmark *Brown v. Board of Education of Topeka* desegregation decision in 1954, the courts have assumed a significant role in education. Although court decisions had affected schools before *Brown*, the latter half of the 20th century saw an unprecedented volume of lawsuits and resulting court opinions, affecting virtually every aspect of school life. As the impact of the No Child Left Behind act is felt across the nation, courts are certain to become involved in the new areas of accountability, school choice, and local control. Court decisions on these issues will affect the daily life of all within schools.

> Can you think of a recent court case that had an effect on the schools in your area? What was the case and what was its impact?

Teachers and the Law

Teachers are affected by state and federal laws and constitutional provisions and agreements negotiated between schools and teacher unions. Court rulings that interpret the laws have brought changes in what is required of teachers and have redefined teacher rights. Laws and their interpretations will affect almost every aspect of your professional life, starting before you are employed and continuing throughout your career.

Refer to the list of laws you developed in Building Block 13.1. Look specifically at the laws governing teachers. Do you see categories? For example, do some of the laws govern employment? Do some deal with teacher rights? Teacher responsibilities? Do you see some overlap? For example, laws that address employment may also deal with teacher rights and responsibilities.

Teacher Certification

Every state has laws and regulations that detail requirements for the certification and employment of teachers. Certification is the basic requirement for teacher employment and is based on professional preparation and other requirements determined by the state. The requirements for teacher certification have been tested in the courts and have consistently been allowed to stand. For example, in *United States v. South Carolina* (1977), the court upheld the use of the National Teacher Examinations, even though the test had been shown to disproportionately disqualify minority applicants. In *Keyishian v. Board of Regents* (1967), the court ruled that teachers may be required to sign an oath pledging support for the federal and state constitutions and promising to faithfully perform their duties. And in *Bay v. State Bd. of Educ.* (n.d.), the court ruled that finding a burglary conviction in an applicant's past was sufficient reason for the state to refuse a teaching certificate. Generally speaking, courts will not intervene in certification requirements unless a person's rights have been violated.

As you saw in Chapter 9, teaching certificates are issued for specific time periods to teach specific subjects and ages; they are usually valid for a 5- to 10-year period. Although the certification satisfies state requirements, local school districts may require additional training. To maintain a teaching certificate, a teacher must meet the state's requirements

In your opinion, what are some valid reasons for dismissing a teacher? Why do you think these reasons are valid?

and, normally, acquire additional refresher education. Failure to meet continuing education requirements results in ineligibility for certificate renewal, which, in turn, can result in loss of employment.

States may impose new conditions for certification renewal that supercede those that were in effect when the teacher was awarded the certificate. For example, the Supreme Court of Texas ruled that teachers holding life certificates could be required to pass a teacher examination as a condition of continued employment, even though the certificates were "permanent" (*State v. Project Principle,* 1987). The Supreme Court of Connecticut ruled that permanent certificates could be eliminated and replaced with 5-year certificates renewable with additional training (*Conn. Educ. Assn. v. Tirozze,* 1989). When courts rule that something "could" or "can" occur, it means that the action is legal. Thus, the state of Texas could legally require teachers holding permanent certificates to pass a teacher examination as a requirement for continued employment, and could revoke the certificate of any teacher who failed to do so.

Every state has a **code of ethics** (a list of standards for ethical conduct) for teachers (see Chapter 9) and a description of reasons for suspension or revocation of the teaching certificate. A teaching certificate may be revoked for offenses such as moral turpitude (the blatant violation of standards of moral conduct), unfitness, and felony criminal convictions. It is important to understand that revocation of a teaching certificate is not the same as loss of employment. However, because a teacher normally cannot be employed in a school without a certificate, revocation results in loss of employment. Conversely, nearly 100% of the time, the teaching certificate is revoked after a teacher is dismissed by the school board, largely because the board has requested the revocation.

BUILDING BLOCK 13.3

Revocation of Teaching Certificates

Several interesting legal cases illustrate reasons why teaching certificates can be revoked:

- In 1981, the Florida Appellate Court upheld the revocation of two teachers' certificates for growing 52 marijuana plants in a greenhouse (*Adams v. State Professional Practices Council,* 1981).

- In 1972, the California Appellate Court upheld the certificate revocation of a teacher who had performed sexual acts with another male in public view in a restroom (*Moser v. State Bd. of Educ.,* 1972).

- The Commonwealth of Pennsylvania upheld the revocation of a teacher's certificate based on a guilty plea to mail fraud (*Startzel v. Commonwealth, Dept. of Educ.,* 1989).

What basic cause of certificate revocation underlies each of the preceding decisions?

Access your state's department of education to find cases that have resulted in revocation of teaching certificates in your state. What are some of the most common reasons?

Employment

The local board of education sets the employment requirements for teachers within the school district. The authority for employment and termination of teachers is exclusively vested in the local school board and cannot be delegated to any other body or official. For the most part, contracts of employment are offered only after the board has voted to employ the applicant.

However, state laws govern teacher contracts. Most teacher contracts are not specific, other than salary and employment date information; they state only that the applicant is to be employed for a specific number of days (usually 180–185) at a specific salary. Grade, specific school, and subject to be taught are not included, because the **contract** is a document for employment in the school district and not at a specific school within that district. Contracts are legal documents, and, as such, contain the following:

- The offer and the acceptance
- The names of competent parties signing the contract
- The financial consideration
- Pertinent legal subject matter, including references to applicable state laws such as those covering tenure and dismissal

In states where teacher unions have collective bargaining rights, the local teacher union may be specified as agent for the teacher and may negotiate employment conditions on the teacher's behalf. Although job duties are not specifically outlined in the contract, they may be implied through the nature of the position.

A teacher may legally and ethically break a contract only by following approved procedures for contract release. In most states, this involves sending a written request for release. The local board then acts on the request. Failure to obtain proper release from a contract may result in monetary damages awarded to the school district (for the cost of locating and employing a replacement), loss of teaching certificate, and unemployability in other school districts. In most states, teacher applications ask whether the applicant has also signed a current contract with another district. If so, the new district will not consider the applicant for employment. If the applicant answers "no" but has in fact signed another contract, the applicant may be terminated and even prosecuted for lying on the application.

BUILDING BLOCK 13.4

Contracting for a Job

Current teacher shortages have made it possible for qualified teachers in many areas to shop around for positions best suited to them.

Consider the following scenario: Mrs. Wilson, a mathematics teacher, has signed a contract to teach in District A. Her husband has been reassigned to a job site 30 miles from their current residence, and they have decided to relocate to the new area, which is served by a different school district: District B. Not only is District B advertising for qualified mathematics teachers, this district is paying $2,500 more per year than District A for someone with Mrs. Wilson's level of experience. District B also offers a one-time signing bonus of $2,500 for science, mathematics, and special education teachers.

What are Mrs. Wilson's legal options? What is her most ethical course of action?

Noninstructional Duties

Instructional duties include the act of teaching and those actions connected to teaching, such as lesson planning. You investigated teachers' instructional and noninstructional duties in Chapter 9. You saw that the courts tend to hold that noninstructional duties, such as lunch and bus duty, are part of normal school operations and that teachers must undertake such duties because those duties constitute a significant part of the school program. However, teachers cannot be required to undertake duties that are not related either to their work or to school. In its rulings on implied obligations of teachers, a New York court stated that any teacher may be required to supervise study hall and conduct conferences; English teachers may be assigned to direct school plays, physical education teachers to coach intramural and interschool athletic teams, and band directors to ac-

What should teachers expect to do in school besides teach their classes?

Teachers may be legally required to undertake certain noninstructional duties, such as supervising the lunchroom.

company bands on trips. A mathematics teacher, on the other hand, cannot be required to coach an athletic team, and no teacher may be required to perform services such as traffic duty, school bus driving, or janitorial services (*Parrish v. Moss,* 1951).

After a teacher is employed by a school district, that teacher can be assigned to any school in the district, and the principal can assign the teacher to any grade level in the school, as long as the assignment is within the teacher's area or areas of certification. Teachers sometimes want to specify the school, grade, and/or subject they will teach, especially after they have taken a year or two off. Schools often—but not always—can accommodate individual requests. For example, in California, a teacher returning from a sabbatical leave of absence was assigned to teach fifth grade but wanted to be assigned to her previous grade level. The court ruled that she did not have a "vested right to a specific school or to a specific class level of students within any school" (*Adelt v. Richmond School Dist.,* 1967). Teachers may be transferred to different schools, but only when the decision is based on objective, nondiscriminatory reasoning, such as moving an English teacher from a school with a dwindling student population to one whose student population is growing. An example of a transfer based on discriminatory reasoning is the transfer of a teacher who had disagreed with and openly criticized school policies but still obeyed them; the courts invalidated that transfer (*Adcock v. Bd. of Educ. of San Diego Unified School District,* 1973).

BUILDING BLOCK 13.5

What Are My Assignment Options?

A principal has assigned a social studies teacher to coach the academic bowl team. The team meets twice weekly after school for two hours. Last year, the team won the state bowl and was invited to compete in the national bowl, but the national competition is held in another state. The social studies teacher has refused the assignment on the grounds that child care issues prevent her from getting home late or traveling out of state.

- What are the teacher's legal options?
- What are the principal's legal options?
- How is this case similar to the teaching assignment principles discussed previously?

Tenure

Tenure grants teachers the right to continued, permanent employment status. Many, but not all states award tenure to teachers. Teachers receive the right to tenure by state law, and tenure is awarded by local boards of education after 2 to 5 years of satisfactory teaching within a school district. Only those employed in regular, full-time teaching positions can receive tenure. Most commonly, tenure is awarded upon the successful completion of 3 years' teaching and the offer and acceptance of a fourth contract within the district. This system has been upheld by the courts. In a landmark decision, an Oklahoma school district was not compelled to award tenure to a teacher who had worked for 4 years on a temporary contract, even though the minimum requirement for tenure was 3 years in that district (*Scheer v. Independent School District No. I-26 of Ottawa County*, 1997).

Tenure has two primary advantages:

- The teacher has a reasonable assurance of continued employment.
- The teacher cannot be dismissed without cause, advance notice, and legal hearings.

Dismissal

Before achieving tenure, a teacher may be dismissed without cause at the end of the teaching year. *Without cause* means the teacher does not have to be given a reason for the decision not to reemploy him or her. Additionally, a nontenured teacher who is dismissed does not have the right to due process. The employment of nontenured teachers can be terminated simply through nonrenewal. The nontenured teacher has a 1-year contract with a beginning date and an ending date, and the school system has no obligation to reemploy the teacher at the end of the contract term. The school system's only obligation is to provide the teacher with a notice of intention not to reemploy by a specified date, which is April 15 in most states.

Teachers awarded tenure cannot be dismissed without **due process**. Due process refers to a person's right to be adequately notified of charges or proceedings involving him or her and the opportunity to be heard at these proceedings. When a school system wishes to dismiss a tenured teacher, due process includes the following:

1. Notice of charges or reasons for dismissal
2. Prior notice of a hearing
3. The right to legal counsel
4. A hearing before an impartial party
5. The right to compel supportive witnesses to attend
6. The right to confront and cross-examine opposing witnesses, and to view evidence prior to the hearing
7. The right to testify in one's own behalf
8. The right to have a transcript of proceedings to use on appeal

Once a teacher has earned tenure, the school board is required to show good cause for dismissal and must provide the teacher with all the due process rights outlined previously. Boards cannot dismiss tenured teachers without just cause. The four most common reasons for dismissing a tenured teacher are incompetence, insubordination, immorality, and criminal activity. Some of the actions that can lead to dismissal are clear violations of a code of ethics or a law. From Chapter 9, recall that each state has a professional code of ethics covering teacher behavior. When a teacher violates this code, a board may move to dismiss or reprimand the teacher. Other actions are not so clear cut and can be argued to have no effect on the teaching and learning process. When courts examine appeals by teachers who have been dismissed for cause, they generally examine whether the reason for dismissal negatively affected the teacher's performance.

You may recall from Chapter 9 that tenure has been eliminated in some states and that other states are considering its elimination. In states that have abolished tenure, teachers gain due process rights after a certain number of years of employment. In states with strong teacher unions, a specific dismissal process is usually part of the union agreement.

Incompetence

Have you ever had an incompetent teacher? What did that teacher do (or not do) that showed incompetence?

Incompetence has been broadly interpreted by the courts. It can include lack of subject matter knowledge, inability to maintain discipline, the use of unreasonable discipline, unprofessional conduct, and willful neglect of duty. It can include attitudinal deficiencies; failure to get along with colleagues, parents, and administrators; neglect of duty; and even showing too many films or videos.

As you can tell, incompetence covers numerous situations. Here are several that resulted in dismissal:

- A teacher administered excessive punishment on three occasions (*Kinsella v. Board of Education*, 1978).
- A teacher had problems communicating material effectively to her students (*Johnson v. Francis Howell R-3 Board of Education*, 1994).
- A teacher had a messy classroom and produced unplanned lessons that were poorly communicated to students (*Blunt v. Marion County School Board*, 1975).

In each of these instances, the teacher was observed, evaluated, and offered opportunities to improve prior to his or her dismissal. Most states have a clearly defined process to provide tenured teachers with ample opportunity for remediation in the areas in which they have exhibited incompetence before they can be dismissed. Thus, dismissal for incompetence usually happens after numerous instances of evidenced problems reflecting unsuccessful remediation efforts. However, a teacher can be dismissed as the result of one action showing incompetence if that action is extremely serious. Such was the case when a teacher who had exhibited weak and unreasonable discipline was dismissed for using a cattle prod with high-amperage batteries to discipline students (*Rolando v. School Directors of District No. 125,* 1976).

As you can see, incompetence is a somewhat vague term that covers a range of behaviors. But in spite of its broad interpretation by courts, incompetence is not the most frequent cause of teacher dismissal. One reason it is not used more often is the lengthy process required. Another reason is that incompetent teachers generally exhibit other behaviors that result in dismissal before incompetence is documented enough to withstand legal challenges. In the case involving the cattle prod, today the teacher would probably be arrested on charges of cruelty to a child, suspended while charges were pending, and dismissed for criminal behavior if convicted, instead of going through the time-consuming process needed to show incompetence.

BUILDING BLOCK 13.6

Is This Incompetence?

Mr. Jones has been teaching mathematics at Broadview Middle School for 10 years and was voted Teacher of the Year 3 years ago. During the 7 months of this academic year, Mr. Jones has been habitually tardy and has submitted incomplete lesson plans. Numerous parent complaints suggest that his lessons are disorganized and that students have difficulties as a result. Observations of his teaching confirm this.

- Based on this scenario, do you believe Mr. Jones is exhibiting incompetence? What is your reason?
- What are Mr. Jones's legal options?
- What are the principal's legal options?

Teaching performance is observed and evaluated by administrators. Teachers who demonstrate incompetence are often given opportunities for remediation and to correct their teaching practices.

Insubordination

Insubordination is "a willful disregard of express or implied directions of the employer and a refusal to obey reasonable orders" (*School District No. 8, Pinal County v. Superior County 102 Ariz.*, 1967). As with incompetence, dismissal for insubordination most often occurs after a series of actions. However, a single, sufficiently serious incident may be good cause. Here are several instances of dismissal for insubordination that were upheld by the courts:

■ A teacher took a vacation with her husband after being denied permission to be absent from school (*Fernald v. City of Ellsworth Superintending School Committee*, 1975).

■ A teacher obtained a substitute and attended a 5-day conference after being ordered not to go (*Christopherson v. Spring Valley Elementary School*, 1980).

■ A shop teacher refused to report to a new school because he felt his tools would not be secure (*Stephens v. Alabama State Tenure Commission*, 1993).

As you can tell from the preceding cases, courts have looked at willfulness as the determinant of insubordination. Additionally, the courts look to see whether harm resulted, whether the punishment is appropriate to the insubordinate act, and whether the rule or order broken was reasonable and within the authority of the person making it.

BUILDING
BLOCK
13.7

Is This Insubordination?

Jim Evans is a music teacher working at two schools. He is at each school only two or three days a week and does not have a homeroom. Teachers report to School A at 7:30, and the homeroom period at that school is from 7:55 to 8:20. Jim routinely reports to School A around 8:15, and a new principal reprimanded him for it. Jim responded that he has worked there for 7 years and has always been allowed to report late because he doesn't have a homeroom.

■ What are Jim's legal options?
■ What are the principal's legal options?
■ What do you believe is the solution to this conflict?

Immorality

Historically, teachers have been viewed as an example to their students. The rules of conduct and codes of ethics governing teachers are written guides to acceptable behavior, keeping teachers' exemplary role in mind. One court decision confirming the exemplary role of teachers says, "We note that statutes from colonial days forward recognize the unique position of teachers as examples to our youth ... requiring school committees to have full and satisfactory evidence of a teacher's moral character. This special role of teachers on impressionable and not fully tutored minds distinguished them from other public officials" (*Kilpatrick v. Wright*, 1977). Another court decision defined teacher immorality as "a course of conduct as offends the morals of the community and is a bad example to the youth whose ideals a teacher is supposed to foster and elevate" (*Horosko v. Mount Pleasant Township School District*, 1939).

Today, changing lifestyles and disagreements about what constitutes moral behavior make it difficult to define proper teacher behavior. One court ruling held that, to be considered immoral, conduct must meet two tests (*Thompson v. Southwest School District*, 1980):

1. It must be immoral under the standards of the particular community involved.
2. It must be found to impair the teacher's ability to teach.

Generally, any act or behavior that substantially interferes with students' learning and impairs the teacher's fitness to teach serves as a basis for charges of immorality. Teacher immorality can be exhibited in unprofessional conduct, criminal activity, and certain types of sexual activities.

Unprofessional Conduct

Examples of unprofessional conduct that may be deemed immoral are numerous and varied. Two cases demonstrate where lack of professionalism becomes immorality:

- The court upheld dismissal for immorality of a teacher who, after having been denied permission to attend a conference, did so anyway, and claimed upon her return that she had been absent due to illness (*Bethel Park School District v. Drall*, 1982).
- Dismissal for immoral conduct was upheld when a teacher tampered with student test results to raise reported scores to exceed state goals (*Hanes v. Board of Education of City of Bridgeport*, 2001).

Other examples of unprofessional conduct can include suggesting answers to standardized test questions, plagiarism, swearing at students in class, dressing inappropriately, and writing inappropriate e-mail.

BUILDING BLOCK 13.8

Is This Unprofessional Conduct?

On the first really warm day of spring, two teachers called in sick. A parent spotted them picnicking in a local park. When the principal learned they were in the park during the school day, he recommended their dismissal, and the board approved it. The board also reported the action to the state certification body and asked that both teachers' teaching certificates be revoked.

- What cause do you think the board gave for the teachers' dismissal?
- Do you think a court would uphold the dismissal? Why or why not?
- Should the state revoke the teaching certificates? Why or why not?

Criminal Activity

The courts view commission of a felony (a serious crime such as armed robbery or possession of drugs for resale) or even an arrest and being charged with a felony or a misdemeanor (a lesser crime such as public intoxication or shoplifting) as just cause for dismissal on grounds of immorality. For example, one court upheld the dismissal of a teacher who was charged with theft, assault and battery, and fleeing a police officer (*Gary Teachers Union, Local 4, American Federation of Teachers v. School City of Gary*, 1975). The courts have also upheld dismissals of teachers for attempting to fight and displaying a gun (*Williams v. School District No. 40 of Gila County*, 1966), possession of cocaine and marijuana (*Dominy v. Mays*, 1979), and failure to take appropriate action in response to a spouse's use of the family home for growing and selling marijuana (*Kari v. Jefferson County School District*, 1993).

Teacher dismissal cases can be based on charges of criminal activity and even circumstances in which the teacher is not formally charged; a school district does not have to wait for a conviction to initiate proceedings. For example, the court upheld a dismissal based on allegations that a teacher stole a teapot used as a prop in a school play, took 20 dollars from a basketball game's receipts, and stole a set of the school's books (*Kimble v. Wroth County R-III Board of Education*, 1984). Dismissal also was upheld in a case in which criminal charges of shoplifting were pending against a teacher (*Gillett v. United School District No. 276*, 1980).

Sexual Activity

Although court decisions have been inconsistent, there has been a trend toward providing teachers more freedom in their private lives than has been the case historically. Community mores regarding morality vary, however; for example, activities that are acceptable in a metropolitan area may be viewed as immoral in a smaller, more rural area. Immorality decisions from the courts rely on individual case circumstances.

Sexual activity cases revolve around three issues: heterosexual activity, homosexual activity, and improper relationships with or actions toward students. In instances of the first two activities, greater latitude for teacher behavior has come with changing lifestyles in the larger society.

When examining reasons for dismissal involving sexual activity not related to students, courts try to determine whether the behavior has impaired the teacher's fitness to teach and whether the action was public or private. For example, the court ruled in favor of a teacher who had been dismissed for allowing male nonrelatives to stay overnight in her apartment (*Sullivan v. Meade Independent School Dist. No. 101*, 1976). A different ruling was handed down when a teacher's lifetime certificate was revoked after a plea bargain led to her conviction on charges of "outraging public decency" (committing an act so bad that the public's sense of decency is outraged); an undercover police officer had arrested the teacher at a private nightclub after watching her commit three separate sexual acts, a violation of the state's penal code. The court ruled that her behavior "certainly reflected a total lack of concern for privacy, decorum, or preservation of her dignity and reputation" (*Pettit v. State Board of Education*, 1973).

The circumstances under which a teacher may be dismissed for heterosexual activity have broadened significantly in recent decades. Out-of-wedlock pregnancy is no longer a legally defensible reason for dismissal. For example, the dismissal of an unwed pregnant teacher was overturned because there was no evidence of an adverse effect on students (*Avery v. Homewood City Bd. of Educ.*, 1982). The court held that the U.S. Constitution protects out-of-wedlock pregnancy, so the burden was on the board to show that the teacher would have been discharged if she had not been pregnant.

As with heterosexual activity, and despite the disparity in rulings by the different courts, decisions regarding dismissal for homosexual activity have increasingly centered on whether the acts in question were public or private. As gay rights have become more recognized, court rulings over teacher dismissal cases based on homosexual behavior have become less restrictive. The courts have ruled that homosexual people "are entitled to at least the same protection as any other identifiable group which is subject to disparate treatment by the state" (*Glover v. Williamburg Local School District Board of Education*, 1998). In this basic gay rights case, the court ruled that a gay teacher could not be dismissed because of rumors that he had held hands with his partner during a school holiday party. A recent Supreme Court case heard the appeal of two men who were charged and convicted of vi-

While teachers cannot legally be dismissed for being pregnant and unwed, should they be allowed to continue teaching their classes? Or should they be reassigned for the duration of their pregnancy?

olation of a Texas statute that makes it a crime for two persons of the same sex to engage in certain sexual conduct. The court found that there was no legitimate state interest in the private sexual conduct of the two men (*Lawrence v. Texas*, 2003). This ruling brought private sexual conduct into the realm of liberty rights. For school districts, this means that the central issue in dismissing homosexual teachers must be whether the act was public or private and whether it makes the teacher ineffective in discharging duties.

As you have seen, the court decisions have made it clear that public behavior and impact on ability to teach determines in large part the legality of dismissal for sexual activities, whether heterosexual or homosexual.

BUILDING BLOCK 13.9

Is This Immorality?

Mrs. Jackson, the cheerleader advisor, and Mr. Hughes, the football coach, were spotted one Saturday morning coming out of a motel room together in a town 35 miles from where they teach. The principal, who saw them on his way to visit a relative, confronted them. They admitted they had been having an affair for several months. The principal asked the board to dismiss Mrs. Jackson and Mr. Hughes and to request revocation of their teaching certificates.

- On what basis do you believe the principal is seeking the teachers' dismissals? Why do you think so?
- Do you think a court would uphold the dismissal? Why or why not?
- Should the state revoke their teaching certificates? Why or why not?

Sexual Activity Involving Students

The courts have been consistent in insisting that teachers be above reproach in their dealings with students. Not only do the courts generally uphold dismissals for sexual activities involving students, they also uphold publication of the dismissals and place no time constraints on when the impropriety occurred. The following rulings against teachers dismissed for sexual misconduct involving students illustrate the courts' strong position in this area:

- A teacher had female students sit between his legs, kissed them on the cheek, and touched one student's breast (*Lombardo v. Board of Education of School District No. 27*, 1968).
- A teacher made repeated offensive sexual statements toward female students and placed his hand on a student's back and snapped her bra strap (*Knowles v. Board of Education*, 1993).
- A junior high school teacher was dismissed for sexual misconduct with a 15-year-old male student. The court upheld the dismissal despite her plea that she was acting under the influence of either mental illness or medications associated with that illness (*Howard v. Missouri State Board of Education*, 1996).
- A teacher was dismissed for sexual misconduct that had occurred 24 years earlier, and his conviction was publicized. The court held that the public had an interest in protecting school children from a sexual predator and that interest outweighed the teacher's interest (*DeMichele v. Greenburgh Central School District No. 7*, 1999).

What legal issues involving teachers have recently made the news in your area? Why were those issues newsworthy?

The courts have also upheld dismissal of teachers for sexual activities involving minors who were not their students, for involvement in activities that give the appearance of impropriety, and even for inappropriate behavior of students toward the teacher. For example, the courts upheld a Florida teacher's dismissal for performing a sexual act with his 9-year-old stepdaughter (*Tomerlin v. Dade County School Board*, 1975).

Teacher Rights

Teachers are held to high standards because of their exemplary role in relation to students. But teachers also enjoy the constitutional rights afforded all citizens. The basic rights guaranteeing freedom of speech, freedom of the press, freedom to assemble, and due process are afforded teachers, along with equal protection provisions safeguarding property and liberty interests. Teachers who have felt that their constitutional rights were violated have sued their board of education. Resulting court decisions have established a substantial body of common law, clarifying teachers' rights and responsibilities.

Freedom of Speech and Expression

The First Amendment to the U.S. Constitution provides that the exercise of free speech cannot be restrained. The seminal case establishing teacher rights to **freedom of expression** involved a teacher's dismissal for having written a letter to a newspaper criticizing school officials' fundraising practices. In this case, the Supreme Court ruled that, even though the letter contained inaccuracies, there was no evidence that the teacher inserted these inaccuracies knowingly or recklessly, so he could not be dismissed for exercising his right to speak on important public issues. The court recognized that the rights of individual teachers must balance with the rights of the state to maintain an orderly educational process, stating, "The problem in any case is to arrive at a balance between the interests of the teacher, as a citizen, in commenting upon matters of public concern and the interest of the state" (*Pickering v. Board of Education*, 1968).

However, the Supreme Court has ruled that a teacher who otherwise does not deserve to be rehired cannot retain employment solely on a claim of the right to free speech (*Mount Healthy v. Doyle*, 1977). In this case, a teacher had called a local radio station and criticized the dress and appearance code established by school administrators. But the teacher also had been involved in a fight with another teacher, argued with cafeteria employees, and sworn and made obscene gestures at students. Speech that is not protected and that can legally result in dismissal includes racial slurs made about or to students, vulgar remarks made to a school principal, and abusive language that consistently denounces school officials to teachers and other school employees.

Academic Freedom

Academic freedom is an area of expression that deals with such responsibilities as teaching methods and materials and specific subject matter. Although teachers have rights in determining what and how they teach, the courts have made it clear that teachers must follow the curriculum and exhibit professional behavior. The courts have upheld dismissals in the following cases:

- A teacher showed a violent and sexually explicit movie after she had been warned that it was inappropriate (*Fowler v. Board of Education of Lincoln County*, 1987).
- A teacher allowed excessive profanity in her students' projects (*Lacks v. Ferguson Reorganized School District R-2*, 1998).
- A teacher reneged on a promise to administrators that he would not assign a specific novel (*Harris v. Mechanicville Central School District*, 1978).

Political Activity

Political activity is another area of freedom of expression; teachers' rights as citizens must be balanced against the competing interests of the schools. Teachers have much the same political rights and freedoms enjoyed by other citizens. In most states, they may run for public office, campaign for others, and engage in political debate.

Like all rights, however, the right to political activity is not unbridled. The courts have upheld the right of states to mandate leaves when teachers gain office or to prohibit public employees from participating in partisan politics. A teacher must not use his or her position to promote a particular political view, use the classroom for political purposes, or be involved in political activities that disrupt the classroom in any way. Basically, teachers may legally engage in political activities that are conducted off school premises and do not interfere with their teaching.

Teachers cannot be punished for legal individual political activities. School districts cannot demote, transfer, or nonrenew a teacher because of political activity. Districts may restrict political activity or employment when political activity is incompatible with teaching. For example, the courts have held that teachers cannot serve on the school board in the district in which they teach (*Jones v. Kolbeck*, n.d.).

Personal Appearance

Personal appearance also falls within freedom of expression. School boards have established dress and grooming codes for teachers, based on a belief that proper appearance promotes professionalism and assists in maintaining students' respect. Teachers have challenged such codes on the grounds that they violate free speech and expression, liberty, and privacy. Cases have revolved around such issues as skirt length and modesty of clothing for women and beards and neckties for men.

The courts have established a significant body of case law upholding the legality of establishing teacher dress and grooming codes. For men, such codes may require a necktie, address hair length, or prohibit beards; for women, they may dictate skirt length. The rationale behind these rulings was clearly stated in the *Miller* case: "If a school board should correctly conclude that a teacher's style of dress or plumage has an adverse impact on the educational process, and if that conclusion conflicts with the teacher's interest in selecting his own life style, we have no doubt that the interest of the teacher is subordinate to the public interest" (*Miller v. School District*, 1976).

Freedom of Religion

Freedom of religion is a First Amendment right and includes all aspects of religious observance and practice. The Civil Rights Act of 1964 requires employers to make reasonable accommodations for an employee's religious practices and observances. For example, teachers must be allowed to use personal leave for religious purposes, such as observing a religious holiday. After all available personal leave (normally two to three days per year) has been used, teachers must also be allowed to take additional days without pay for religious observances. However, the religious observance must be part of the teacher's religion, and the teacher may not claim simply any day as his or her Sabbath.

The issue of religious dress has attracted a great deal of litigation in recent decades. Decisions have varied in the different courts, but there is a trend toward prohibiting teachers from wearing religious attire in the classroom. For example, the court ruled against a Sikh whose teaching certificate was revoked after she continually wore white clothes and a white turban to teach her sixth- and eighth-grade classes (*Cooper v. Eugene School District No. 41*, 1987). Another court ruled against a Muslim woman who sought to dress in traditional attire that covered her entire body except for her hands and face (*United States v. Board of Education for the School District of Philadelphia*, 1990).

Another aspect of religious freedom deals with participation in activities. For example, teachers may refuse to participate in the Pledge of Allegiance, even when reciting the pledge is a routine part of the school day. On the other hand, a teacher may not refuse to comply with curriculum requirements because such requirements violate personal religious beliefs (*Russo v. Central School District No. 1*, 1973). In this case, the teacher refused to teach the Pledge of Allegiance or to celebrate holidays such as Abraham Lincoln's birthday, because she believed that teaching about Abraham Lincoln was excessive devotion to an individual, which violated her Jehovah's Witness religious beliefs.

Teachers cannot use the classroom to proselytize or disseminate their religious beliefs. The courts upheld dismissal when a teacher encouraged students to accept her beliefs and become involved with a religious group (*LaRocca v. Board of Education of Rye City*

School District, 1978), and when a teacher began the school day with prayer and a bible story (*Fink v. Board of Educ. of Warren County School Dist.*, 1983).

The courts have been careful to protect teachers' religious rights. At the same time, they have recognized a compelling state interest in educating children in an atmosphere that does not promote religion. The limitation of teacher religious freedom was clearly stated in *Palmer*, in which the justices wrote that education "...cannot be left to individual teachers to teach the way they please" and that teachers have "...no constitutional right to require others to submit to their views and to forego a portion of their education they would otherwise be entitled to enjoy" (*Palmer v. Board of Education of the City of Chicago*, 1980).

BUILDING BLOCK 13.10

Celebrating the Teacher's Religion

Each day, Elaine wears a necklace with a cross on it. Her principal has asked her to stop wearing the cross to school. She has refused, saying that she has a right to wear the cross that was given to her by her late father.

- Do you think Elaine has a legal right to wear the cross?
- What legal arguments could she use?
- What are the principal's options?

Right to Privacy

As you saw earlier, the courts have upheld the idea that teachers are exemplars. At the same time, however, teachers enjoy the right to privacy in their personal lives. Yet those rights end when a teacher's behavior adversely affects the teaching and learning process.

Many court cases centering on the right to privacy involve teacher dismissal and/or revocation of teaching certificate based on immorality charges stemming from sexual improprieties. However, as noted earlier, sexual impropriety alone does not necessarily serve as a legally defensible cause for punitive action. In overturning the revocation of one teacher's certificate, a court ruled that the teacher's private acts, because they did not negatively affect his teaching, were his own and not subject to employer scrutiny (*Erb v. Iowa State Board of Public Instruction*, 1974). The right to privacy was not supported by the courts, however, when a school administrator engaged in sexual activities during school hours. In that case, the court ruled that the administrator's behavior resulted in gross neglect of duty. For this reason, the court ruled that he did not deserve protection based on the right to privacy (*Schedule v. The Capitol School District*, 1976).

When the courts view issues of teacher privacy, they seek to determine whether the conduct directly impairs the teacher's performance in the school and whether the conduct is the subject of such notoriety that it significantly limits the teacher's ability to meet his or her responsibilities.

A modern concern involving the right to privacy is electronic mail (e-mail). Nearly all teachers have e-mail available at their school. That e-mail facilitates communication with parents and with others in the school system. Although many school systems do not prohibit teachers from using school e-mail for private communication, teachers should be aware that a school e-mail account is *not* private. Indeed, most school systems monitor e-mail, and inappropriate communication by teachers may result in disciplinary action.

Do you think a teacher's school e-mail account should be private? Under what conditions do you believe school officials should have access to it?

Search and Seizure

The Fourth Amendment to the U.S. Constitution guarantees freedom from unreasonable **search and seizure**. As drug use has become more common in our society, some teachers have been faced with random testing for drugs and alcohol. Such tests are a form of search and have been called suspicionless because there was no reason to suspect the affected teachers were guilty of drug use. Numerous court cases have examined the legality of these searches, and teachers have commonly argued that the process was an unreasonable search that violated their right to privacy. As with other issues involving teachers, the courts have examined issues in terms of effect on performance of duties.

To a certain extent, random drug testing of teachers is legal. The reasoning behind decisions that allow random drug tests was expressed by Sixth Circuit Court of Appeals: ". . . the suspicionless testing regime is justified by the unique role they play in the lives of school children and *in loco parentis* ("in the place of a parent") role imposed upon them" (*Knox County Education Association v. Knox County Board of Education,* 1998). The courts also have ruled that school systems may use drug-detecting dogs and that a teacher's refusal to take a drug test after suspicion has been established by a dog sniffing a teacher's car is a legal cause for termination (*Hearn v. Board of Education,* 1999).

Legal Liability

In today's litigious society, teachers live with the constant concern that they may be sued and held **liable** for substantial damages. In legal terms, teachers are liable for tortuous acts. Simply put, a **tort** is a wrongful act, other than a breach of contract, for which relief may be obtained in the form of damages. Torts include a variety of actionable or civil wrongs committed by one person against another, and can be committed either by overt actions or by failure to act. Thus a tort can be intentional or the result of negligence. When a tort action occurs, one person (the plaintiff) brings a suit against another (the defendant) to obtain damages. The plaintiff usually requests damages in the form of money.

The most common intentional tort is assault and battery. Assault is a threat to use force which causes fear. Battery takes place when physical contact occurs. Assault and battery lawsuits against teachers are most common in states that still allow corporal punishment; such cases generally result from a teacher's use of excessive punishment. Numerous court cases involving teachers who used excessive punishment have resulted in substantial awards to plaintiffs, but a decline in such cases has accompanied the decline in the use of corporal punishment. Whether or not a state allows corporal punishment, teachers should use force *only* to defend themselves from physical harm, and then only to the degree necessary. Other intentional torts include such acts as libel, slander, defamation, false arrest, malicious prosecution, and invasion of privacy.

By far the most common tort actions against teachers are for negligence. Within the negligence category, most actions stem from inadequate supervision. Lawsuits commonly maintain that harm occurred to students because a teacher failed to give adequate supervision. In many instances, such lawsuits are based on the idea that an accident would not have happened if the teacher had practiced proper supervision.

Teachers have been found liable for student injury based on inadequate supervision in a wide variety of cases. For example, a teacher was held liable on negligence for ignoring a boy who flipped a knife into the ground until the knife hit an object, was deflected, and destroyed another student's eye (*Lilenthal v. San Leandro Unified School District,* 1956). Another teacher was found liable when a student was injured in a game while the teacher was out of the room (*Cirillo v. City of Milwaukee,* 1967).

Although it seems obvious that a teacher should have known not to let a student have a knife at all or to leave students unsupervised, negligence is not always cut and dried. Definite elements and conditions determine whether or not a teacher is negligent. Generally, the teacher must exercise a standard of care that a "reasonable and prudent" person would exercise under similar circumstances. The standard varies with the circumstances. For example, the standard would be higher with first-grade students on a playground or with high school chemistry students in a laboratory than it would be with eleventh graders reading a short story. In all circumstances, however, the teacher

Technology & Education   I found It on the Internet!

As a student, you know it is illegal to plagiarize others' work. **Plagiarism** involves taking the ideas of others and representing them as your own, without giving the proper credit. You have probably written a few papers in which you had to compile resources, synthesize ideas, and cite references on a bibliography page. Giving authors credit for their ideas and writing is expected; not to do so is plagiarism. Schools have policies that contain stiff consequences for students caught plagiarizing.

Plagiarism used to consist of copying directly from books, encyclopedias, and other people's work, but now it includes copying directly from the Internet. Not only does the Internet contain a wealth of material, but many websites, called *paper mills,* offer essays, research papers, and the like for purchase. Some paper mills are careful to say that the materials they provide are for research only, but that does not mean that students will use the materials in this way.

Internet plagiarism has increased rapidly, according to the Center for Academic Integrity (McCabe, 2005). In 1999, 10% of students surveyed admitted to plagiarizing material from the Internet. In 2005, this number rose to about 40%. However, 77% of the students surveyed did not think that plagiarism from Internet sources was a serious concern.

Another study of 4,500 secondary students, conducted by researchers at Rutgers University, found that 72% of those surveyed admitted to cheating and over 50% said that they had copied and pasted sections of text from the Internet without providing proper citations (Schulte, 2002).

Instructors can use online services, such as those offered by Turnitin.com and iThenticate, to help them find instances of plagiarism. These services compare student work with millions of the most frequently cited resources and can search the Internet rapidly for additional sources. The results of the comparison indicate the likelihood of plagiarism.

A great deal of material on the Internet is protected by copyright. **Copyright** means that the originator of the material—words, pictures, music, etc.—maintains the right to decide who can copy and distribute the material. Not only does using copyrighted material without proper attribution constitute plagiarism, it is also a copyright violation. A lot of Internet material is available to teachers without copyright protection; indeed, many copyright holders specifically waive protection to make their material freely available to teachers. But teachers must be careful about using Internet materials. Can you tell why?

Students and teachers alike must comply with the **Fair Use Provision of the Copyright Act** of the United States of America. According to the provision, copyrighted material used for "purposes of criticism, comment, news reporting, teaching (including multiple copies for classroom use), scholarship, or research is not an infringement of copyright" (U.S. Copyright Office, n.d.); but all other uses violate copyright laws. If you are not sure whether you are using copyrighted material fairly, the Fair Use Provision of the Copyright Act advises you to consider the following (U.S. Copyright Office, n.d.):

- The purpose and character of the use, including whether such use is of a commercial nature or is for nonprofit educational purposes
- The nature of the copyrighted work
- The amount and substantiality of the portion used in relation to the copyrighted work as a whole
- The effect of the use upon the potential market for or value of the copyrighted work

When in doubt, always provide a citation and obtain permission. Penalties for copyright infractions can be up to $150,000, even if you did not know you were violating copyright.

As you adhere to high standards, be sure to require the same of your students. If you are teaching in a middle school or high school, be sure your students understand what plagiarism is and that information on the Internet is intellectual property belonging to other people. Students should also know that you are familiar with both paper mill websites and plagiarism detection sites.

---

is responsible. Students must be supervised at all times, including during the school day while they are outside the classroom, before school, and after school while they are on school property.

Examples where the courts found negligence include the following cases:

- A student died from boxing during noon recess (*Dailey v. Los Angeles Unified School District,* 1970).
- A student was injured by a paper clip thrown by another student while both were awaiting transportation to another school, unsupervised (*Titus v. Lindberg,* 1967).
- An unsupervised student was injured in a classroom after school when a piano fell on her (*Kidwell v. School Dist. No. 300, Whitman County,* n.d.).

Teachers are also required to provide supervision off the school premises during athletic events or school-sponsored outings. The courts found negligence in the following cases:

- A child was injured when a log on which the teacher had posed four children for a photograph rolled over (*Morris v. Douglas County School Dist.*, 1965).
- A student was injured in a hazing incident at a school-sponsored club when the faculty advisor was not present (*Rupp v. Bryant*, 1982).
- A student's wrist was slashed and her purse taken during a required supervised field trip to view a film (*Raleigh c. Independent School District No. 615*, 1979).

Although there are defenses against liability lawsuits and the defendant can sometimes negotiate a reduction in the degree of negligence, you should be aware that, as a teacher, you may be subject to lawsuits and held liable for large amounts of money. If you should be found liable, the award to the plaintiff could take all your assets. Even if you should be found not liable, the cost of legal representation is substantial, often running into tens of thousands of dollars. Professional teacher organizations and teacher unions provide legal representation and liability insurance as membership benefits. In some states, membership in a teacher's union or professional organization is optional. In all states, the cost of membership in an organization that provides legal representation and professional liability insurance is a small price to pay compared to the cost of defending against a single tort suit.

A direct link to the National School Board Association website, a great source of school law, is available on the *Building Teachers* companion website.

Students and the Law

The law applies to students as well as teachers, and much of the law is intended to protect students. U.S. public schools operate under the concept of *in loco parentis* ("in the place of a parent"); teachers and school officials exercise control over the students under their supervision. Furthermore, throughout much of American history, schools promulgated rules and disciplined students with the view that education was a privilege and students' rights could be routinely restricted. In 1969, however, the U.S. Supreme Court held, in the landmark *Tinker* case, that students do not shed their rights at the schoolhouse door (*Tinker v. Des Moines Independent Community School Dist.*, 1969). *Tinker* made clear that educators must respect students' rights and can restrict those rights only for legitimate reasons.

Due Process

As citizens, students are entitled to substantive and procedural due process rights. **Substantive due process** means that a valid reason must be demonstrated to justify restrictions to a student's rights, and that the way those rights are restricted must be reasonable. For example, restricting the student's right to free speech during classroom instruction and enforcing that restriction through detention represents a rule necessary to learning that is enforced through reasonable means. **Procedural due process** means that specific legal procedures are followed to ensure fair treatment of students. Over the past five decades, thousands of court cases have dealt with issues of due process. Many cases have been decided against school personnel because procedural due process was not adequate.

The basic due process requirements for dealing with students have been derived from decisions of the U.S. Supreme Court. In particular, two cases laid the groundwork for students' due process safeguards. The *Gault* case overturned the 6-year reform school sentence of a juvenile convicted of making obscene telephone calls (*In re. Gault*, 1967), because the student had not been given due process rights. The court noted that no appeal had been provided, no written charges had been presented, and protection against self-incrimination had been denied. This view of students' due process rights was strengthened a few years later when a court considered the case of a student suspended for 10 days after a disturbance in the school cafeteria. In that case, the court ruled that the right to attend school is a legitimate right and a suspended student, even when the suspension was 10 days or less, must be given notice of charges, an explanation of the evidence, and a hearing providing an opportunity to tell his or her side of the story (*Goss v. Lopez*, 1975). The court outlined informal procedures for cases of short suspensions but noted that expulsions or suspensions of more than 10 days could require the formal due process procedure. Today, most school systems provide students and parents with written discipline policies; such policies usually include an outline of student rights and a list of infractions and their consequences. By disseminating a sound discipline policy, schools protect themselves and ensure student rights.

Pregnancy and Marriage

In Chapter 12, you saw that pregnant students may have limited opportunities to attend school or continue their education. However, the courts have unanimously ruled to invalidate school rules that prohibit married or pregnant students from attending school or that cause them to be treated differently from other students. Numerous courts have issued similar rulings on these issues over a long period of time. In one of the first cases, in 1929, a court said that for a school system to ban a student based on marriage there must be a showing of immorality, misconduct, or a deleterious effect on other students (*McLeod v. State ex. Rel. Comer*, 1929). In 1966 another court ruled that a married 16-year-old had the right to attend school even though she had a child (*Alvin Independent School District v. Cooper*, 1966). The right of pregnant students to attend school was confirmed by the courts a few years later (*Ordway v. Hargraves*, 1972). Following are general guidelines for educators concerning pregnant or married students and students with children:

1. The courts have invalidated rules prohibiting married or pregnant students from attending school.
2. Married or pregnant students have the same rights as other students.
3. Only when compelling evidence of disruption, interference with school activities, or negative influence on other students is present can the school restrict married or pregnant students' attendance or participation in activities.
4. Only the student's physician can determine when the student should withdraw from and return to school.
5. Homebound instruction must be offered students who withdraw from school because of pregnancy.

Freedom of Speech and Expression

As you have seen, the First Amendment provides for freedom of speech. But constitutional rights do not mean that students can behave in any manner they choose. The school's compelling interest is to maintain a proper atmosphere for learning. Thus, students can be prohibited from expressing themselves in ways that disrupt or harm the learning atmosphere. At the same time, a student may not be deprived of speech and expression that is not disruptive or harmful.

Tinker, cited earlier in this chapter, made clear that students have the right to express themselves, but that this expression must be done in an orderly way. For example, students' right to wear black armbands was protected by the First Amendment because those involved did nothing to disrupt, or even potentially disrupt, learning. However, students who caused a disturbance by remaining in the hall talking and placing political buttons on students who did not want them were suspended. The court found the suspensions valid because the students caused a disturbance that school authorities had a right to control (*Blackwell v. Issaquena Bd. of Educ.*, 1966). Similarly, the Supreme Court upheld the suspension of a student who delivered a nominating speech that referred to the candidate with an extended sexual metaphor (*Bethel School Dist. No. 403 v. Fraser*, 1986). The court held that schools may legitimately establish standards of civil and mature conduct, and a school that tolerated "lewd, indecent and offensive" speech would find it difficult to convey those standards. Likewise, schools may prohibit students' use of "fighting words" and "true threats." **Fighting words** are those that "have a direct tendency to cause acts of violence by the person to whom, individually, the remark is addressed" (*Jones v. State*, 2002). Racial epithets are an example of fighting words that may be prohibited. **True threats** involve speech that a reasonable person could view as a serious intention to harm another. A note threatening other students is an example of a true threat.

Student newspapers, plays, and literature fall within the realm of free expression. At the same time, schools do have some control. The key to determining the legality of prohibiting a particular expression can be found in the *Tinker* ruling: "To justify a prohibition of a particular expression of opinion, school officials must be able to show that their action was caused by something more than a mere desire to avoid the discomfort and unpleasantness that always accompany an unpopular viewpoint. There must be facts that might reasonably lead school authorities to forecast substantial disruption of or material interference with school activities" (*Tinker v. Des Moines Independent Community School Dist.*, 1969).

The following guidelines are useful in determining whether students' right to free speech and expression apply:

1. When deciding to prohibit expression or punish expression, determine whether there is evidence of significant disruption or potential disruption, indecent speech, or disregard for authority. When punishment is involved, provide due process.

2. Materials may be banned that are vulgar, mock others' race, origin, sex, or religion, or if they are counter to the mission of the school.

3. The time and place of distribution of all materials may be regulated.

4. Legally defensible guidelines should be formulated regarding a school newspaper.

5. Determine whether a newspaper is to be an open forum or a curriculum-based publication. Students have greater freedom of expression in an open forum.

6. Develop a specific procedure whereby newspaper submissions must be reviewed before publication. Provide an appeals process.

Dress and Appearance

Dress is generally viewed as a form of self-expression. As such, it is a First Amendment right and schools must show a compelling reason why restrictions on dress are necessary. The courts generally strike down vague or arbitrary dress codes. The courts uphold dress codes that aim to protect safety or prevent disruption or distraction that interferes with learning.

Schools may regulate dress and appearance where health and safety issues are concerned. For example, schools may prohibit long hair and jewelry and mandate safety glasses in shop classes or laboratories. Schools may also ban clothing, jewelry, or hair styles that indicate gang affiliation. Immodest or suggestive clothing may be banned, as may T-shirts containing sexually vulgar messages. Recently, some public schools have instituted the requirement that students wear uniforms. Generally, the argument for uniforms centers on educational and disciplinary issues. The constitutionality of uniforms was upheld in a recent case in which the court wrote that a uniform policy is constitutional if it furthers an important government interest, if it is not intended to suppress student expression, and if it is no more restrictive than is necessary to facilitate the school's educational interest (*Canady v. Bossier Parish School Board*, 2002).

How could a requirement for school uniforms contribute to a school's safety and discipline?

Students in public schools may be required to wear uniforms provided there are compelling reasons. What reasons might be considered compelling?

© Bill Bachmann/Index Stock Imagery

Numerous court cases have dealt with male hair and beards, but no conclusions can be drawn yet; courts have both upheld and ruled against school regulations based on a variety of arguments from both plaintiffs and defendants. The Supreme Court has consistently declined to hear these cases.

Search and Seizure

The Fourth Amendment to the U.S. Constitution prohibits unreasonable searches and seizures. Although students enjoy rights under that amendment, school officials are less limited than police in search and seizure practices. School officials need neither a warrant nor probable cause to initiate a search. Reasonable suspicion is a valid reason for school officials to initiate a search.

As the need to eliminate weapons, drugs, and other banned items has intensified and methods of detection have become more varied, issues of search and seizure in the schools have become more complicated. The Supreme Court established a standard of reasonableness for searches in schools in a case in which a teacher caught two students smoking in the bathroom. She took both to the principal's office. One admitted smoking, and the other denied she had smoked. The principal sought evidence by examining the second student's purse, finding marijuana and evidence of drug dealing. The student's parents sued, contending that the search was illegal because the principal did not have a search warrant (*New Jersey v. T.L.O.*, 1985). The court said that reasonableness of search has two elements:

▪ Whether circumstances justified the action at its inception

▪ Whether the scope of the search was reasonable in relation to the situation

A search can be justified if a school employee has reasonable grounds to believe that the search will provide evidence that a student has violated the law or school rules. The scope of the search should be reasonable in terms of the situation and the age and gender of the students. School officials may search students' purses, book bags, lockers, packages, and automobiles parked on school property if there is reasonable cause to believe that evidence of some violation may be found.

Students themselves may be searched, although there is a higher standard for reasonable suspicion as the search process becomes more invasive. Courts have occasionally upheld strip searches of students. Personal searches and, especially, strip searches should be undertaken only when there is urgency based on a reasonable suspicion that the student possesses a dangerous object or substance.

A modern method of search is drug testing. The courts upheld the right of one school to require urinalysis drug testing for athletes (*Veronia Sch. Dist 47J v. Action,* 1995) and of another school to require the drug testing of all students who participate in any extracurricular activity (*Board of Education v. Earls,* 2002).

The courts have disagreed on the use of canines in searches. The issue focuses on whether specially trained dogs can establish reasonable suspicion for a search. Broadly speaking, courts have upheld the use of canines to establish a basis for a search when there was a reasonable belief that some illegal substance or object was present. They have similarly upheld the use of dogs to sniff lockers routinely when parents had been advised of the probability of routine locker searches. The courts have even upheld the use of dogs to sniff students when a reasonable belief existed that a particular student had drugs. The courts have not upheld mass searches by canines or searches for which there was no reasonable basis.

The following guidelines are useful for educators:

1. All searches must be based on a reasonable suspicion that a student has violated the law or school policy. A student who looks guilty is not sufficient reason for a search.
2. Schools may undertake routine searches of lockers and desks, especially when parents have been notified that this is normal procedure.
3. The more invasive the search, the closer it comes to a need for probable cause.
4. Personal searches should be done in private and only by school officials of the same gender as the student being searched. If clothing is removed, the student should remove it and should be provided with alternative garments while clothing is searched. If you are searching only pockets, have the student turn his or her pockets inside out.

What kind of evidence do you think constitutes a "reasonable belief" that a student may have an illegal substance or object?

Privacy of Records

The **Family Educational Rights and Privacy Act of 1974 (FERPA)** applies to all schools receiving federal money. Commonly referred to as the Buckley Amendment, this act guarantees parents and students confidentiality and fundamental fairness concerning the maintenance and use of student records. It prohibits the release of information about students under 18 years of age without parental consent. At the same time, it provides certain rights to parents and guardians of minor children.

Parents or guardians may legally do the following with regard to school records:

- Inspect their child's school records.
- Challenge accuracy of information.
- Have corrections made.
- Request a hearing to contest information they perceive as inaccurate.
- Place a statement of disagreement in student records.
- Determine what confidential information is released and to whom.
- Receive prior notice of records subpoenaed by the courts.
- File a complaint with the U.S. Department of Education concerning alleged violations.
- Seek relief in civil court.

Students 18 years of age or older control their own records.

FERPA applies only to identifying information about individuals. It does not apply to test data, special population data, or other general data gathered by schools. The key to the legal release of data is whether individual students can be identified. Individual students have a right to privacy.

Records of individual students can be released to the following in addition to parents and guardians:

- Other school officials or teachers in the system who have a legitimate interest
- Authorized representatives of government, including state education department personnel
- State and local officials collecting information required by state statutes
- Accrediting organizations

Students' right to privacy of records means that teachers must exercise care in revealing information. Teachers should discuss individual student grades, discipline issues, and other matters only with those who have a legitimate reason to know. Schools should have a clear procedure for releasing information, including the requirement for a written request for release of information and specific procedures ensuring timely compliance with parent requests. Schools and teachers should not post grades in any way that makes it possible to identify individuals.

Corporal Punishment

Twenty-seven states have banned **corporal punishment.** More than half the school districts in nine other states have banned corporal punishment. Figure 13.2 shows the current status of state laws and regulations regarding corporal punishment. Although the Supreme Court has ruled that corporal punishment of students is not constitutionally prohibited (*Ingraham v. Wright*, 1977), the trend in recent years has been to ban corporal punishment.

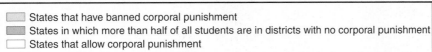

☐ States that have banned corporal punishment
☐ States in which more than half of all students are in districts with no corporal punishment
☐ States that allow corporal punishment

Figure 13.2
Current Status of state laws regarding corporal punishment. (National Coalition to Abolish Corporal Punishment in Schools, 2004.)

Was there corporal punishment in a school you attended? How effective do you think corporal punishment is in modifying student behavior?

Where corporal punishment is not banned, school officials must be certain that due process is followed, that the punishment is not of excessive force, and that it is administered only by authorized individuals (usually the principal or other administrator). Most school boards require that a second adult be present as a witness during the administration of corporal punishment.

BUILDING
BLOCK
13.11

What Are the Students' Rights?

The new principal at Mountain View High School has banned clothing with any kind of emblem or writing, including designer labels and corporate symbols. Parents have protested bitterly, and students have threatened a walk-out.

- What are the students' legal rights?
- What are the principal's legal rights and obligations?
- Should the rule be reversed? On what basis?
- If the principal did not reverse the rule, do you think a court would uphold it? Why or why not?

Conclusion

In this chapter you have investigated the system of laws governing education in the United States. You have found some important rights and responsibilities of teachers and the impact of court decisions on teachers, students, and schools. As a result, you have acquired a basic understanding of how to comply with the law and ensure your rights.

Throughout the discussion of teachers and the law, you saw that teachers are considered exemplars. The courts have repeatedly cited the legality of requiring the teacher to model exemplary behaviors for students. Similarly, you have seen that courts seek a connection between teacher behavior and effect on the teaching and learning process.

Although the teacher enjoys the rights of a private citizen, the teacher's responsibility as an exemplar who is effective in the classroom places demands and restraints on behavior that are not borne by those in other professions.

Think back to the list you compiled in Building Block 13.1. Did your examples include most of the areas discussed in this chapter? How do the impact and consequences you listed compare with the chapter's discussions? Which legal areas were new to you? How have the constructions you made in this chapter affected your view of teaching and schools?

Key Terms and Concepts

Academic freedom, 347
Case law, 335
Code of ethics, 338
Constitutional law, 335
Contract, 339
Copyright, 351
Corporal punishment, 357
Due process, 341
Fair Use Provision of the
    Copyright Act, 351

Family Educational Rights
    and Privacy Act of 1974
    (FERPA), 356
Fighting words, 354
Freedom of expression, 347
Freedom of religion, 348
In loco parentis, 350
Liable, 350
Plagiarism, 351
Procedural due process, 352

Regulation, 335
Search and seizure, 349
Substantive due process, 352
Statute, 335
Tenure, 341
Tort, 350
True threats, 354

Construct and Apply

1. In view of everything you have explored in this chapter, who do you believe really controls schools in the United States? Do parents, through their elected board of education, determine what is taught and how? Does the local board of education? Does the state board of education? The state legislature? The federal government? What influence does the court system have on local schools? Think about the schools in your neighborhood and try to decide who determines what is taught and how. What examples can you think of to support your point?

2. From your inquiries in this chapter, it should be clear that, where students are concerned, a teacher cannot be too circumspect in his or her behavior. The newspapers have provided ample coverage of situations in which teachers were accused of improper behavior with students. When a teacher was found to be innocent, what had been a front-page story became a fifth- or eighth-page paragraph. What basic principles or rules will you observe to ensure that you will not be accused of improper behavior with students?

3. Based on your explorations in this chapter, do you believe you will have to make any concessions in order to teach? Even if you don't perceive that you will have to make concessions, how will the role of teacher affect you in terms of such things as attire, personal lifestyle, etc.? What specific things can you think of that you will do to ensure that you serve as an exemplar?

Deconstructing the Standards

INTASC Principle #9 says:

The teacher is a reflective practitioner who constantly evaluates the effects of his/her choices and actions on others (students, parents, and other professionals in the learning community) and who actively seeks out opportunities to grow professionally.

- What part(s) of this principle does this chapter address?
- How does this chapter address this principle?
- How will the concepts in this chapter help you apply this principle as a teacher?

Field Experience

Interview an administrator or a respected veteran teacher at your field experience school. Ask questions such as the following:

- Have dismissals been recommended at the school? On what basis?
- What kind of example are teachers and administrators in the school expected to set for students?
- What legal issues most affect the daily lives of administrators and teachers? How do these issues affect them?

Your Portfolio

Develop a *personal* code of ethics to guide your behavior as a teacher. Include this in your portfolio.

Technology Resources

 Access the *Building Teachers* companion website, http://www.education.wadsworth.com/ martinloomis1 , for more information and resources about school law, including links to the following websites:

- National School Board Association
- FindLaw
- Supreme Court decisions
- Federal court decisions
- Landmark cases
- United States courts, for information on legal structure and court cases
- Cornell Law School

 Check out the *Building Teachers* CD-ROM that accompanies your textbook for additional resources.

 Also link to InfoTrac College Edition via the *Building Teachers* companion website. Use InfoTrac College Edition to search for journal articles to enhance your study.

References

Reading Legal Citations

This chapter cites many legal cases. A legal citation follows a standard format that lets you find cases, statutes, regulations, and law review articles.

There are three basic parts to any legal citation: the name of the case, the location where the case can be found in a multivolume set of legal materials, and a date. The case name is fairly obvious. The plaintiff's name (the person bringing the case to court) appears first. The defendant's name (the person or entity defending against the plaintiff's charge) appears last. The location is written in terms of volume number where the case can be found, work in which the case is cited, page in the work on which the case begins, and page of the exact reference. The year is the year in which the case was decided.

The following example illustrates the parts of a citation:

Brown v. Board of Education 347 U.S. 483 488 (1954).

In this example, Brown was the plaintiff, bringing a case against the defendant Board of Education. The case is reported in volume 347 of *United States Reports* (the official reporter for U.S. Supreme Court cases). The case begins on page 483, and 488 is the page referred to in our example. The case was decided in 1954.

In some cases you will see the abbreviation *cert. den.* This means that the case was appealed to the U.S. Supreme Court and the court refused to hear it.

Some other common abbreviations include the following:

- F.2d or F.3d: Reporter for the U.S. Circuit Courts of Appeal
- F.Supp or F.Supp.2d: Reporter for the U.S. Districts Courts opinions
- S.W., W.W.2d, or S.W.3d: Reporter for the highest courts in selected states (used for states in the southwestern United States)

Direct links to several sources of school law are available on the *Building Teachers* companion website. The National School Board Association has tremendous resources; you can sign up for a free weekly bulletin of court decisions impacting education. FindLaw is an easy-to-use reference on specific cases. The Supreme Court site provides U.S. Supreme Court decisions, current cases, and the cases the Court refuses to hear. Fedworld.gov provides decisions of all federal courts. Landmarkcases.org provides information about landmark cases; information can be found by name or topic; uscourts.gov provides information on federal cases and legal structure; the Cornell Law School provides comprehensive and easy-to-use source information and includes information about individual states.

CHAPTER 14

Curriculum and School Reform

> In order to transform schools successfully, educators need to navigate the difficult space between letting go of old patterns and grabbing on to new ones.
>
> TERRENCE DEAL, EDUCATOR

In this textbook, you have investigated many topics related to education, schools, and teaching. You began each inquiry with an exploration of your thoughts, feelings, and what you already knew about the topic. After some further investigation, you formulated your ideas about the best way to handle that topic today.

In Part I, you identified characteristics of outstanding teachers and investigated the meanings and implications of major educational philosophies. In Part II, you listed teaching characteristics that support students' needs and teaching strategies that seem appropriate for students with a variety of perspectives and abilities.

In Part III, you wrote a hypothetical mission statement that described your hypothetical school. You debated the best ways to achieve successful and meaningful student–school interactions and you investigated the responsibilities the teacher and the school have to each other.

In Part IV, you saw the impact of curricular and educational practices from a historical perspective and thought about the best ways to run a school. You also looked at the influence of society, social problems, and the law on school policies, procedures, and teaching.

In all these inquiries, you investigated the way things were, they way things are, and the way you believe things ought to be.

Changing education to make schooling what it ought to be is known as educational reform. Look again at the quotation that begins this chapter. What do you suppose Deal meant by it?

Educational reform involves changing and refining the education system to meet the needs of the students and the society to which they belong. You, also, are a member of society. What do *you* think is wrong with education today? What do you think should be changed? How do your views compare with those of others in society? These questions represent the topic of this chapter. You will investigate the general topic of educational reform, the views of society as a whole, and areas in which steps are being taken to align education with current needs and views.

As a result of your work in this chapter, you will:

1. Identify major educational reform thrusts.
2. Investigate curriculum reform movements in social studies, science, mathematics, and language arts.
3. Compare current curriculum guidelines with the needs of society.
4. Investigate the authentic assessment movement.
5. Identify current goals of teacher preparation programs.
6. Investigate reform activities dealing with school structure, governance, and finance.

What Is Educational Reform?

You already have investigated numerous topics in this textbook that deal with educational reform. To get an idea of what is involved in reform, look at Building Block 14.1.

BUILDING BLOCK 14.1

Educational Reform Topics

Think about some of the investigations you have made and the conclusions you have reached using this textbook. Look at the following questions in light of what you have investigated so far:

■ What *curriculum* do students study today that is appropriate and necessary for success in today's society?

■ What *instructional* activities do teachers use to help students learn the content and skills they will need?

■ What *assessment* opportunities do teachers provide that enable students to demonstrate this knowledge and these skills?

■ What *teacher induction* elements prepare teachers to enter the workforce and provide their students with the most effective opportunities?

■ How do the *structures* of new schools support today's teaching and learning environment?

■ How does school *governance and finance* support today's teaching and learning environment?

In Building Block 14.1, you previewed the main topics of educational reform. In its broadest sense, educational reform consists of examining all aspects of education—curriculum, instruction, and assessment; teacher preparation; school buildings; scheduling the school day and year; and methods of governance and finance—and modifying them to keep up with changing times. For some people, however, change is frightening, and they tend to want to hold onto their old ideas. Their schooling worked fine for them, so why should today's students need something different? Besides, educational change often reflects a change in educational goals and philosophies; and as you saw earlier, people tend to hold firmly to their philosophies and goals for schools.

People have been talking about educational reform since the first American schools opened. Recall from Chapter 10 that Benjamin Franklin's Academy added vocational proficiency to classical and religious studies because of the growing needs of the country.

Later, additional subjects were made available to reflect changing national priorities. In the late 19th and early 20th centuries, the National Education Association sponsored several committees to standardize the curriculum. Those committees made several decisions that still guide education today, such as:

- High School graduation requirements
- Elementary education curriculum
- The Carnegie unit of credit
- Daily and yearly schedules of K–12 schools
- The separation of schools into elementary, junior high, and secondary schools

In the past 25 years or so, attention to education has intensified. In 1983, *A Nation at Risk* declared, "The educational foundations of our society are presently being eroded by a rising tide of mediocrity that threatens our very future as a Nation and a people" (National Commission on Excellence in Education, 1983, p. 1) (see Chapters 2 and 10). Test scores were falling, and colleges and employers complained that high school graduates were inadequate in reading, writing, and calculating (see Chapter 2). The GOALS 2000 conference of 1989 and the resulting federal legislation passed in 1994 addressed such concerns by enumerating goals that all American schools should strive to meet (see Chapters 6 and 10).

National Educational Reform Organizations

With guidance from national professional teaching organizations and the federal government, individual states have taken steps to reform their systems of education, thereby addressing current concerns. Besides the initiatives taken by individual states, many nationwide organizations have been established to assist in U.S. educational reform efforts, such as the Center for Educational Renewal, the Coalition of Essential Schools, New American Schools, and the Center for School Change.

The Center for Educational Renewal (CER), founded by John Goodlad, Kenneth Sirotnik, and Roger Soder, in 1985, has been instrumental in developing a total reform effort. Goodlad believes that lasting and meaningful educational reform emerges from purposeful discussion among all parties and that reform must address a systemic approach that addresses all aspects of school change concurrently, considering how a proposed change in any one area may affect other areas (Goodlad, 1991).

The CER seeks to implement an educational reform agenda through its National Network for Educational Renewal, a network of school and university partnerships involving thousands of teachers and professors throughout the United States. The focus of the CER includes four areas (Center for Educational Renewal, n.d.):

Educational reforms, including curriculum, instruction, and assessment innovations aim to improve all aspects of teaching to best promote student learning. How did educational reform measures affect your education?

Courtesy of Bill Lisenby

- Fostering the skills, dispositions, and knowledge necessary for effective participation in a democratic society

- Ensuring that students have access to the understandings and skills needed for satisfying and responsible lives

- Developing nurturing educators

- Ensuring educators' competence in and commitment to serving as stewards of schools

The Coalition of Essential Schools helps individual schools and school systems develop programs that will nurture students to reach their fullest potential through "emphasizing equity, personalization, and intellectual vibrancy" (Coalition of Essential Schools, 2003, p. 1).

New American Schools (NAS) is a nonprofit organization that provides professional services to schools, school districts, state departments of education, and other education organizations to help shape, support, and sustain systemwide innovations and improvements in learning. NAS is active in fostering comprehensive school improvement through consulting services, grants, and research. More than 4,000 schools throughout the United States have been affected by the work of NAS (New American Schools, 2003).

The Center for School Change at the University of Minnesota works with educators, students, and other stakeholders throughout the United States to strengthen education.

The educational reform efforts discussed above focus on changes within schools. Berliner (2005) believes that there are factors outside of school that also must be addressed. He writes that school reform is "heavily constrained by factors that are outside of America's classrooms and schools" (p. 2), especially poverty, which is an environmentally caused problem that becomes a social problem that cannot be fixed by schools.

www Direct links to the websites of the Center for Educational Renewal, the Coalition of Essential Schools, New American Schools, and the Center for School Change are available on the *Building Teachers* companion website.

How do organizations that deal with educational reform address the questions asked in Building Block 14.1?

Main Areas of Educational Reform

There are so many items on the school reform agenda that it can be difficult to categorize them. However, let us look at the basic areas you saw in Building Block 14.1:

- Curriculum
- Instruction
- Assessment
- Teacher preparation
- School structure
- Governance and finance

Examination of these areas should provide a good overview of current reform efforts.

Curricular and Instructional Reform

One of the major reform movements involves standards. In response to the concerns cited in *A Nation at Risk* and GOALS 2000, the federal government has helped finance the development of nationwide standards for each subject taught in school. The standards detail what students should know and be able to do as a result of studying a subject. Standards also suggest the most effective methods of teaching students to achieve those ends. They are guides to curriculum and instruction, and they present concepts and skills against which to measure achievement.

Individual states use these standards to develop their own statewide curriculum, which then becomes the official curriculum of the state. To provide nationwide consistency, standardized tests, based on the standards, assess student achievement. The results of these tests provide data for judgments about achievement and program effectiveness. This thrust in educational reform has become known as the **standards movement.**

There is some concern that the standards may come to be perceived as a "national curriculum," and that a national curriculum could work in opposition to individualized programs designed to meet the needs of students, their schools, and their communities. Many people believe that students throughout the nation should study the same curriculum so that everyone has a common knowledge base and parents can relocate to another state or school district without their children having to adapt to a new curriculum. Many others believe that, to be meaningful, the curriculum must be tailored to reflect individual, school, and community needs and characteristics. For instance, the curriculum in Scranton, Pennsylvania would differ from the curriculum in Santa Fe, New Mexico because the students in each of these two communities have different needs and interests.

Do you believe there should be a national curriculum? Or do you believe curriculum should be different for different states and communities? Why?

It is difficult to separate curriculum (what is taught) from instruction (how it is taught). In earlier chapters, you investigated both curriculum and teaching methodology. This chapter combines these areas so you can investigate the current thinking about both. As you will see, curriculum and instruction are intertwined: It is difficult to consider one without the other. We focus on the four major subjects of social studies, science, mathematics, and language arts, although standards also have also been developed for all the other subjects (such as foreign language, art, music, physical education, and computer technology). Use the thinking you develop in this section to examine the other standards.

Social Studies Curriculum

Social studies, which was introduced into U.S. schools to promote citizenship and civic competence, traditionally has focused on history, civics, geography, and economics.

Learning Social Studies

BUILDING BLOCK 14.2

Think back to the social studies courses you have taken. List some of the topics you studied.

- What were you supposed to learn?
- Do you think the same topics should be taught today? If yes, which ones?
- Do you think there should be changes in the social studies topics that were taught? What should these changes be?
- Do you think there should be changes in the way social studies is taught? What should these changes be?

Chances are that you recall having had to learn names, dates, places, events, and other facts related to history, cultures, governments, civics, economics, geography, and social issues. Your study of these topics may have seemed isolated from other subjects and from your life, although topics taught in elementary school were probably less isolated from your life than those required in middle school and high school.

The goal of contemporary social studies education is "to help young people develop the ability to make informed and reasoned decisions for the public good as citizens of a culturally diverse, democratic society in an interdependent world" (National Council for the Social Studies, 1994b, p. 1). Social studies is viewed as more than a collection of facts to memorize. Today's social studies curriculum fosters understanding of how events came about and how people relate to each other, encouraging students to develop respect for different viewpoints and cultural beliefs. Today's social studies curriculum encompasses many disciplines and seeks reasons and connections rather than names, dates, and places. The following principles guide the modern social studies curriculum (National Council for the Social Studies, 1994a):

- Social studies education is *meaningful*: The curriculum focuses on the impacts of historical and current situations and events on students' lives and on the direct study of social problems and possible solutions.
- Social studies education is *integrative*: The study of any social issue, past or present, requires integration with other subjects such as science, language, mathematics, and the arts.
- Social studies education is *value based*: It encourages students to come to their own conclusions and evaluate these conclusions in light of society's and the students' own values.
- Social studies education is *challenging*: It requires students to solve problems and employ higher-order thinking skills and helps students become independent learners and responsible citizens.
- Social studies education is *active*: The primary emphasis is on real social problems that affect people today, rather than an accumulation of facts. It urges observing, role-paying, reading (especially primary source documents), and writing; it also utilizes collaborative and cooperative learning.

In 1994, the National Council for the Social Studies developed standards for social studies education in grades kindergarten through high school. These standards focus on the following 10 integrated themes:

1. Culture
2. Time, continuity, and change
3. People, places, and environments
4. Individual development and identity
5. Individuals, groups, and institutions
6. Power, authority, and governance
7. Production, distribution, and consumption
8. Science, technology, and society
9. Global connections
10. Civic ideas and practices

How can these social studies themes foster the integration of several subjects?

Courtesy San Lorenzo Middle School

Students at San Lorenzo Middle School reenact the Civil War Battle of Bull Run. How does this learning activity reflect the standards of the National Council for the Social Studies?

The National Council for Social Studies also suggests several teaching and learning strategies, including acquiring information and manipulating data; developing and presenting policies, debates, and stories; constructing new knowledge; and participating in groups.

Access the social studies standards for your state. How do they compare with the national standards?

There are concerns with the current social studies curriculum guidelines. The focus of the current curriculum is on solving problems rather than memorizing facts. How, critics wonder, will students learn factual information that everyone ought to know if they are not required to memorize these facts? For example, in a survey of Arizona's college seniors, Block et al. (2002) found that only 40% knew basic facts about American history. In another study, the American Council of Trustees and Alumni surveyed seniors at top American colleges and universities, as identified by the *U.S. New and World Reports* annual ranking of colleges, to assess the seniors' knowledge of high school–level American history. The survey found the following:

- Only half of the students surveyed could identify George Washington as an American general at the Battle of Yorktown.
- Only 42% could identify George Washington as "First in war, first in peace, first in the hearts of his countrymen."
- Less than one quarter correctly identified James Madison as the "Father of the Constitution."
- Only 28% could identify the phrase "Government of the people, by the people, for the people" as a line from the Gettysburg Address.
- Less than two thirds could identify the U.S. Constitution as establishing the division of power in American government.
- Little more than half (52%) knew George Washington's farewell address warned against permanent alliances with foreign governments.

However, 99% of these students could identify Beavis and Butt-Head, and 98% were familiar with rap singer Snoop Doggy Dogg (Neal, Martin, & Moses, 2000, p. 2).

Another concern about the contemporary social studies curriculum relates to textbooks. As you saw in Chapter 11, textbook publishers must comply with the rules laid down by state boards of education and large school districts. Critics argue that social studies textbooks may leave out important information (such as omitting certain primitive aspects of Meso-American societies), distort historical data (such as portraying the activities of the Chinese communist party and its leader, Mao Zedong, as a liberation movement), or interpret events in only one way, thereby denying students the opportunity to understand situations from multiple points of view (such as presenting only one perspective on Islam) (Thomas B. Fordham Institute, 2004). It is the responsibility of individual school districts to grapple with these contentious issues.

www You can access the national social studies standards through a direct link on the *Building Teachers* companion website.

www You can take the American Council of Trustees and Alumni history survey yourself. A direct link is available on the *Building Teachers* companion website. Correct responses and the percentage of students who chose each response are given.

How well do you know basic facts about American government?

Modern Social Studies Curriculum

BUILDING BLOCK
14.3

Pick a social studies topic and do the following:

1. Describe how a teacher might have approached this topic in the past.
2. Describe how a teacher in today's school who follows the guidelines of social studies curriculum reform might approach the same topic.

Science Curriculum

Science was introduced into American schools as "natural history," whose purpose was to instill in students an appreciation for and an understanding of the natural world.

Learning Science

Think back to the science courses you have taken. List some of the topics you studied.

- What were you supposed to learn?
- Do you think the same topics ought to be taught today? If yes, which ones?
- Do you think there should be changes in the science topics that were taught? What should the changes be?
- Do you think there should be changes in the way science is taught? What should they be?

After the launch of Sputnik, the appropriateness of the science curriculum began to be questioned. As you saw in Chapter 2, the scientific community urged that students should learn science in the same way scientists do science. This meant that science programs should focus on inquiry, exploration, problem solving, and higher-order thinking skills, rather than the memorization of facts.

A host of new science programs began to emerge, such as Elementary Science Study (ESS) and Science Curriculum Improvement Study (SCIS) for elementary grades, as well as Physical Science Study Committee (PSSC) physics, Chemical Education Materials Study (CHEM) chemistry, and Biological Sciences Curriculum Study (BSCS) biology. However, teachers were not involved in decisions to adopt these new programs, received little training, and lacked needed materials. As a result, the programs failed and teachers reverted to their former science programs, even though student achievement was higher under the new programs (Shymansky, Kyle, & Alport, 1982). Only the BSCS continues to be used in today's classrooms.

In 1990, the American Association for the Advancement of Science responded to continuing concerns about the state of science education in the United States with Project 2061, named for the year when Halley's Comet will make its next pass near the Earth. One product of Project 2061 was the publication of *Science for All Americans* (Rutherford & Ahlgren, 1990), which makes the following suggestions for teachers:

- Treat science topics using an interdisciplinary approach.
- Focus on systems and interrelationships among the disciplines, rather than isolated facts and concepts.
- Proceed from the concrete to the abstract.
- Start lessons with questions rather than answers.
- Help students access information they have previously acquired.
- Engage students in collecting evidence and answering questions.

The *National Science Education Standards* were published in 1996. These standards describe what students should know, understand, and be able to do as a result of their learning experiences in science. The standards call for inquiry-based science education programs, in which teachers facilitate learning rather than impart information, use multiple and authentic methods of assessment, provide learning environments conducive to inquiry learning, maintain high standards of intellectual rigor, and actively participate in the development and planning of their science programs.

The *National Science Education Standards* outlines eight categories of content for grades K–4, 5–8, and 9–12 (National Research Council, 1996):

1. Unifying concepts and processes in science
2. Science as inquiry
3. Physical science

Elementary students tend a class garden as part of their science curriculum. This activity promotes inquiry learning instead of rote memorization of facts.

4. Life science
5. Earth and space science
6. Science and technology
7. Science in personal and social perspectives
8. History nature of science

Access the science standards for your state. How do they compare with the national standards?

How well do current science programs work? Remember GOALS 2000 (Chapter 6). Goal 5 stated that, by the year 2000, American students would be first in the world in math and science achievement. Standardized tests of mathematics and science achievement, named the Third International Mathematics and Science Study (TIMSS), have been administered to students in several different grade levels in many countries. Equivalent versions of the test have been administered three times: in 1995, 1999, and 2003.

Results of the science sections of the tests show that U.S. students in third and fourth grades consistently perform near the top, eighth-grade students consistently perform near the middle, and high school seniors perform near the bottom of international results. Some people have pointed out that interpreting these tests can present problems, citing the difficulties inherent in interpreting standardized tests for a worldwide population. Nonetheless, according to these results, the United States has fallen short of its goal that U.S. students be first in the world in math and science achievement. Table 14.1 shows the number of countries scoring above, near, and below the United States in both mathematics and science on the three international TIMSS tests.

Access the science standards for your state. How do they compare with the national standards?

 **www** You can access the National Science Education Standards through a direct link on the *Building Teachers* companion website.

www A direct link to a website where you can find details about the TIMSS is available on the *Building Teachers* companion website.

Modern Science Curriculum

BUILDING BLOCK 14.5

Pick a science topic and do the following:

1. Describe how a teacher might have approached this topic in the past.
2. Describe how a teacher in today's school who follows the guidelines of science curriculum reform might approach the same topic.

TABLE 14.1 Comparison of the United States and Other Countries on the TIMSS Tests (Data from National Center for Education Statistics, 2001; National Center for Education Statistics, 2004; and Office of Educational Research and Improvement, 1999)

		Significantly Higher (Number of Countries)	Not Significantly Different (Number of Countries)	Significantly Lower (Number of Countries)
Fourth grade mathematics	1995 (26 countries)	7	7	12
	1999 (not tested)			
	2003 (25 countries	11	1	13
Fourth grade science	1995 (26 countries)	1	6	19
	1999 (not tested)			
	2003 (25 countries)	3	6	16
Eighth grade mathematics	1995 (41 countries)	20	14	7
	1999 (38 countries)	14	7	17
	2003 (45 countries)	9	11	25
Eighth grade science	1995 (41 countries)	9	17	15
	1999 (38 countries)	14	6	18
	2003 (45 countries)	7	6	32
Twelfth grade general mathematics	1995 (21 countries)	14	5	2
Twelfth grade general science	1995 (21 countries)	11	8	2
Twelfth grade advanced mathematics and science students taking advanced mathematics	1995 (16 countries)	11	5	0
Twelfth grade advanced mathematics and science students taking physics	1995 (16 countries)	14	2	0

Note: The term *significantly* refers to statistical significance, the likelihood that the scores are true representations of students' knowledge and understanding.

Mathematics Curriculum

As you recall from Chapter 10, mathematics (in the form of arithmetic) has been part of the curriculum of American schools since colonial times. The goal of arithmetic was for students to be able to perform basic computations, a skill they needed to succeed.

BUILDING BLOCK 14.6

Learning Mathematics

Think back to the mathematics courses you have taken. List some of the topics you studied.

■ What were you supposed to learn?

■ Do you think the same topics ought to be taught today? Why?

■ Do you think there should be changes in the mathematics topics that were taught? What should they be?

Mathematics has always been considered one of the so-called 3 Rs. People need to know how to add, subtract, multiply, and divide: At the practical level, these skills allow you to balance a checkbook, estimate the cost of groceries, prepare a family budget, choose an insurance and health plan, and the like. Similarly, people need to know how to apply numerical facts and processes to problem situations, such as calculating the cost of gas for a trip, finding the amount of carpeting needed for a house, or doubling or halving a recipe. The extension of basic mathematical knowledge to fractions, decimals, and percents is part of our daily life: Think of baseball statistics, the lottery, election results, and public opinion polls.

Have you been exposed to mathematics recently? What kinds of mathematics were involved?

The traditional method of mathematics instruction involved memorizing math facts using flash cards, computing countless pages of sums, differences, products, and quotients, going to the chalkboard to work out the answer to a problem, memorizing rules and procedures ("When dividing fractions, turn the bottom fraction upside-down and multiply"), and developing step-by-step proofs. Mathematics was taught this way from the 1600s to the mid-20th century, when Sputnik spurred the call for drastic steps to improve both mathematics education and science education. As a result, educators developed the so-called **New Math.** For several decades, this approach to mathematics permeated classrooms at all levels. Pioneered by the School Mathematics Study Group (SMSG), the study of mathematics was made more rigorous by the use of actual mathematical language and algebraic notations. As early as the first grade, missing addends were designated with letters as in algebra; for example, in the expression $3 + x = 5$, first graders were expected to solve for x. The idea was that theory would lead to understanding; to that end, the New Math virtually eliminated the use of physical objects and mathematics manipulatives. Some of us remember having to learn about sets and set theory with its fancy notations. The theoretical basis of mathematics was considered far more important than constructing personal understandings.

For a time, test scores rose, but then they began to decline, leading to a public outcry that something had to be done. The New Math was based on principles that most parents did not understand, so they could not help their children with their homework. The New Math eschewed the use of manipulatives, so it definitely was not appropriate to the cognitive developmental levels of young students who, as you saw in the theories of Piaget, need hands-on experiences, including manipulating actual materials, to be able to develop understanding—especially in the elementary school, but often in older students as well. Such problems led to the demise of the New Math.

In keeping with the standards movement of the 1980s and 1990s, K–12 mathematics standards were developed. The most recent version is *Principles and Standards for School Mathematics* (National Council of Teachers of Mathematics, 2000). This volume describes "a future in which all students have access to rigorous, high-quality mathematics instruction" (National Council of Teachers of Mathematics, 2000). The standards are divided into the following five content groups, all of which apply to mathematics curriculum in grades K–12:

1. Number and operations
2. Algebra
3. Geometry
4. Measurement
5. Data analysis and probability

In addition, there are five process standards:

1. Problem solving
2. Reasoning and proof
3. Communication
4. Connections
5. Representation

You can access the national mathematics standards through a direct link on the *Building Teachers* companion website.

The current mathematics curriculum is interdisciplinary and seeks to show how mathematics can help to explain scientific, social, and other natural phenomena. Contrary to the rejection of physical objects that characterized earlier math courses, today's mathematics urges the use of manipulatives so students can construct their own personal understandings. Examples of such manipulatives include geoboards, pattern blocks, counting blocks, and tangrams for lower grades, and relation shape forms, relational geometrical solids, Pythagorean theory manipulatives, and angle blocks for upper grades.

Access the mathematics standards for your state. How do they compare with the national standards?

How do our students fare in mathematics when compared with students in other countries? (Remember that GOALS 2000 calls for American students to be the best in the world in both science and mathematics.) As you can tell from Table 14.1, fourth graders consistently performed near the middle in mathematics, eighth graders also performed near the middle (although there was some improvement in the 2003 test), and high school seniors performed at the low end in both general and advanced mathematics. Clearly, the United States has a long way to go to be first in the world in mathematics achievement.

BUILDING BLOCK 14.7

Modern Mathematics Curriculum

Pick a math topic and do the following:

1. Describe how a teacher might have approached this topic in the past.
2. Describe how a teacher in today's school who follows the guidelines of mathematics curriculum reform might approach the same topic.

Language Arts Curriculum

The language arts consist of the commonly used forms of communication, including reading, writing, listening, and speaking. Language arts instruction in the early grades (pre-K, kindergarten, and early elementary grades) focuses on teaching children how to read, write, and convey meaning. In the later elementary grades, middle school, and high school, the focus is on developing meaningful and accurate communication, writing to learn, and reading to learn. One goal of language arts is for students to be able to read and comprehend factual material.

BUILDING BLOCK 14.8

Learning English and Language Arts

Think back to the English or language arts courses you have taken. List some of the topics you studied.

- What were you supposed to learn?
- Do you think the same topics ought to be taught today? Why?
- Do you think there should be changes in the English and language arts topics that were taught? What should these changes be?
- Do you think there should be changes in the way English and language arts are taught? What should these changes be?

In education, they say just stick around and you will see lots of changes—and everything will keep coming back around again and again. I never paid a lot of attention to that statement, because I have always felt that I needed to learn whatever was new if I thought that it could help me teach some child better. I have seen several changes that have affected education that appear to make our schools better. Throughout my years in public school classrooms, and especially over the past 26 years of my teaching career, these changes have allowed teachers to really explore the needs of students as individuals—versus teaching all students the same way.

The biggest change for math occurred when NCTM adopted new standards in the early '90s. This change was well received by many educators. Thanks to the hard work of NCTM, these standards and accompanying assessment tools have been accepted, and we are constantly learning applicable techniques that will assist our students in learning, with very few adjustments.

In Kentucky we adopted the Kentucky Educational Reform Act (KERA) in the early '90s. This act was brought about by a lawsuit regarding equity in funding for our public schools. This change has affected a lot of classrooms, teachers, and especially students. Our entire state's testing programs have changed tremendously. I now use the KERA standards as a guide for direction when planning lessons. Every lesson has a KERA goal that I must try to make sure my students attain. Some say that we teach the tests, but actually the state test assesses the concepts that we have taught. These concepts are what students should be learning.

Some say that most teachers teach the way they were taught. I was taught in the early '60s by teachers who stood in the front of the room and lectured. That was fine with me because I am not a very kinesthetic person. I listened and I wrote, and so I learned. But in my teaching, I use many techniques. I use some lecture, some cooperative group work, and some discussion. I can stand in the front and lecture; I can use hands-on materials; and I can use visual and auditory methods to reach all learning styles. I feel I am a facilitator of learning in my classroom. I am a resource in my room for my students' education.

As far as my curriculum and teaching style are concerned, I did not have to change a lot. I was a KERA teacher prior to the act. We were now encouraged to do more hands-on teaching, encourage students to think more, and explain more to make learning more applica-

ble. So I teach somewhat differently from the way I was taught. Adapting to KERA was not difficult for me. I felt validated when we implemented KERA. I tried to make a conscious effort to address all learning styles on a more regular basis than before, but that was not a new teaching technique for me. This is what is best for the children. We all know that they do not learn alike, so we have to make a conscious effort to reach as many as we can as often as we can.

Teaching by encouraging is the easiest thing to do for me as I teach middle school math. Math is a subject that lends itself to real-life application. It is easy to teach middle school students new math concepts by relating the new concept to their world. For example, one of my favorite units to teach is on using percents. What better way to show students how to use percents than to have them practice using percents? I bring in menus, and we order our meal and add the tax and gratuity. This is such a simple idea but a great way for students to see the real application. They want to do more because they can see the application. When students want to do more, it is because they are excited or empowered by what they are learning. I encourage them to think of more ways to use the math they have just learned. Other examples of activities I use include sports, games, and shopping. Students can relate to all these activities, and they can use the concepts and skills immediately outside the classroom. The students love it because they know why they are learning that particular concept or skill.

Then the ultimate happens: Students feel empowered because they know why. When the math standards and curriculum were aligned in the early '90s, the math teacher's job was made easier. We know what to teach according the NCTM standards, so we have aligned our state and district curricula with the national standards and teach our concepts accordingly. That was the goal of NCTM. I do believe that these standards are powerful. And I enjoy teaching math because I can relate math to the students' worlds. Their worlds are then validated.

2005 Kentucky Teacher of the Year
Georgetown Middle School
Georgetown, Kentucky

Whether a person is successful in life depends largely on that person's ability to read and write. Illiterate people often are restricted to a lower socioeconomic class and limited job possibilities, such as manual labor. With few exceptions, the better-paying jobs and higher-status positions go to the literate people. This is as true today as it has been throughout history. (Farris, Fuhler, & Walther, 2004, p. 48)

Reading and writing are indispensable skills. As long as schools have existed, students have been taught to read and write. In the early 1800s, students were taught using the **phonics** method, by which they learned the sounds of letters and letter groups. In the mid-1800s, this system was replaced with a methodology in which students memorized entire words. When basal readers such as the *McGuffey Readers* and the *Dick and Jane* series were introduced, students learned to read using sight cards, ditto sheets, and workbooks keyed to the stories in the reader. The 1980s saw the introduction of **whole language,** a constructivist approach to teach reading and writing in which students learned from first-hand experiences. Whole language was a holistic movement that endorsed temporary, invented spelling and sentence construction in the certainty that students would refine their skills as the need arose and they gained experience.

The whole-language approach was very popular and used materials relevant to students, who were given choices about what to read and what to write about. Teachers used interdisciplinary thematic units to aid in teaching reading and writing meaningfully; the unit's topic served as the subject. By 1990, however, leaders of business and industry questioned students' reading and writing skills, complaining that they had to teach new hires how to read and write effectively. The public became upset that students did not master reading and writing skills in the earliest stages of learning.

After extensive evaluation and analysis by committees and task forces, it was concluded that reading and writing programs in the elementary grades should achieve an appropriate balance between the whole-language inquiry approach and the more didactic phonics approach (Adams, 1990). This balanced combination of whole language and phonics is called the **interactionist approach,** or balanced approach, to teaching language arts.

In 1996, the International Reading Association and the National Council of Teachers of English published *Standards for the English Language Arts.* The document's purpose is to "provide guidance in ensuring that all students are proficient language users so they may succeed in school, participate in society, find rewarding work, appreciate and contribute to our culture, and pursue their own goals and interests throughout their lives" (International Reading Association, 1996, p. 1). The reading and language arts standards include 12 interrelated content areas shown in abbreviated form below:

1. Students read a wide variety of print and nonprint texts.

2. Students read a wide range of literature.

Courtesy of Becky Stovall

Effective reading and literacy instruction involves a balance of phonics and whole language approaches. Were you taught to read and write using phonics, whole language, or a combination of both?

3. Students apply a wide range of strategies to comprehend, interpret, and appreciate texts.

4. Students adjust their use of spoken, written, and visual language to communicate effectively.

5. Students employ a wide range of strategies in writing.

6. Students apply knowledge of language structure, language configurations, media techniques, figurative language, and genre to create, critique, and discuss print and nonprint texts.

7. Students conduct research and communicate their discoveries effectively.

8. Students use a variety of technological and information resources to gather and synthesize information and to create and communicate knowledge.

9. Students develop an understanding of and respect for diversity in language.

10. Students whose first language is not English use their first language to develop competency in English and develop understanding of content.

11. Students participate in a variety of literacy communities.

12. Students use spoken, written, and visual language to accomplish their own purposes.

Modern reading and writing programs encompass all grade levels and all subjects, from pre-kindergarten through high school. Lower grades concentrate on skills development, and upper grades focus on strategies for reading in the various disciplines, including vocabulary, methods of conceptualization, text patterns, and other reading and writing traits characteristic of the discipline. Students in today's classrooms are encouraged to write, expressing their thoughts in both sketchy and finished forms using journaling, reports, descriptions, and formal papers. Today's educators believe that the language arts are not taught in isolation but are an integral component of all subjects. Students write thoughts, summaries, and papers, and read textbooks and other reading material to become proficient at these skills.

Access the reading and language arts standards for your state. How do they compare with the national standards?

As with science and mathematics, international assessments have been conducted in reading. The Progress in International Reading Literacy Study (PIRLS) was first conducted in 2001 and is scheduled to be repeated in 2006. This test assessed reading literacy in the fourth graders of 35 countries, using both multiple-choice and written response formats. U.S. fourth graders performed close to the top, with children from only three countries (England, Bulgaria, and Sweden) recording higher performances. In all countries, fourth-grade girls demonstrated significantly higher reading achievement than boys (Mullis et al., 2003).

> Have you noticed the differences between reading a modern popular novel and reading a textbook? Have you been taught how to read a subject-specific textbook such as a biology textbook or an algebra textbook?

>  You can access the national reading and language arts standards through a direct link on the *Building Teachers* companion website.

Modern Language Arts Curriculum

BUILDING BLOCK 14.9

Pick a reading or writing activity, such as reading a contemporary novel or preparing a research paper, and do the following:

1. Describe how a teacher might have approached this activity in the past.
2. Describe how a teacher in today's school who follows the guidelines of language arts reform might approach the same activity.

Student Performance

How well do these new curricula work? You have seen the results of international assessments in science, mathematics, and reading. Many state and national assessments show student progress. Let us consider a national indicator: the nation's report card.

The National Center for Education Statistics, a division of the U.S. Department of Education, has conducted national assessments in science, mathematics, and reading since 1969 to show overall achievement levels of U.S. students. The **National Assessment of Education Progress (NAEP),** also known as the nation's report card, compiles the results.

Let us look at the long-term trends in the nation's report card in science, mathematics, and reading for elementary grade students (age 9), middle grade students (age 13), and high school students (age 17). (Social studies has not been included in the NAEP.) Keep in mind that these trends are based on standardized test scores and their interpretations are subject to the same interpretive variables as other standardized test scores. Nonetheless, the nation's report card can help answer our question, "How well do our education programs work?"

National achievement trends in science, mathematics, and reading in the United States since the early 1970s, according to the nation's report card, are shown in Figure 14.1 (science), Figure 14.2 (mathematics), and Figure 14.3 (reading). The figures illustrate the following trends (National Center for Education Statistics, 2005):

Science

- Nine-year-olds: Scores declined during the 1970s and began to rise between the early 1980s and the mid-1990s.

- Thirteen-year-olds: Scores declined during the 1970s, rose during the 1980s and early 1990s to the 1970 level, and have remained relatively unchanged since.

- Seventeen-year-olds: Scores declined during the 1970s and early 1980s, rose between 1986 and 1992, and have remained relatively unchanged ever since, although they have not caught up to the 1970 scores.

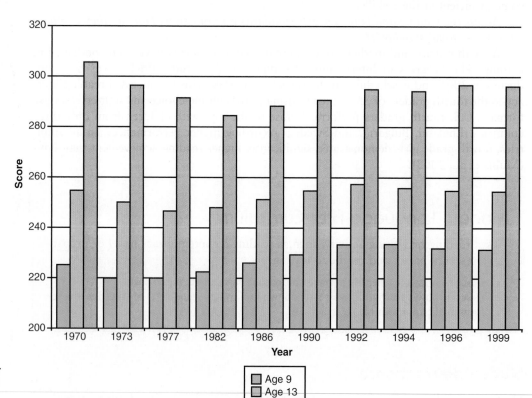

Figure 14.1
Trends in average scale scores for the nation in science, 1970–1999 (National Center for Education Statistics, 2005).

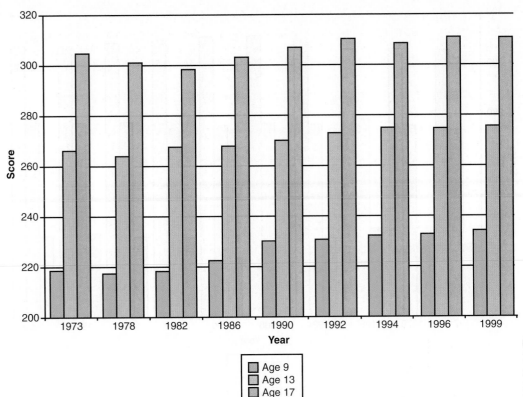

Figure 14.2
Trends in average scale scores for the nation in mathematics, 1973–1999 (National Center for Education Statistics, 2005).

Mathematics

- Nine-year-olds: Overall, scores have risen across the assessment years.
- Thirteen-year-olds: Scores have risen consistently across the assessment years.
- Seventeen-year-olds: Scores declined slightly during the 1970s and 1980s, but rose in the 1990s to exceed the 1973 mark.

Reading

- Nine-year-olds: Scores rose between 1971 and 1980 and then declined until 1990, when they began to rise again.
- Thirteen-year-olds: Despite some fluctuations, there has been little change in reading scores across the assessment years.
- Seventeen-year-olds: Scores remained constant during the 1970s, increased slightly during the 1980s, and then declined somewhat during the 1990s.

Does Curriculum Reform Work?

Examine the statistics from the nation's report card about student achievement during the past three decades in science, mathematics, and reading. Correlate the score trends with the corresponding curriculum trends for each decade.

What can you conclude about the relationship between curriculum reform efforts and student achievement? Might other factors affect the achievement trends reported in the nation's report card?

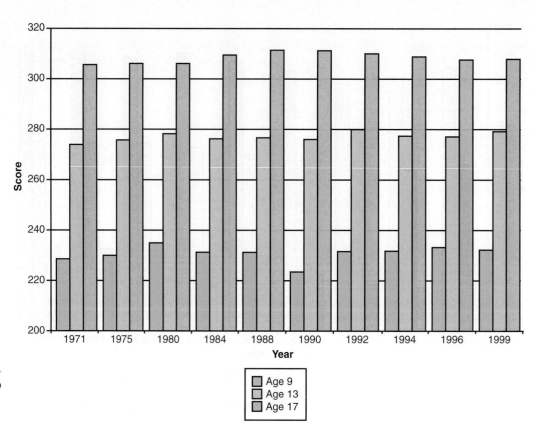

Figure 14.3
Trends in average scale scores for the nation in reading, 1971–1999 (National Center for Education Statistics, 2005).

Interdisciplinary Approaches

The prevailing approach to curriculum at all levels involves the separation of the subject-area disciplines into discrete subjects, each with its own time slot, its own textbook, and its own program of study. However, there is an emerging paradigm shift from the discipline-centered approach to an integrated approach that provides students the opportunity to investigate problems through overlapping applications of multiple disciplines. You will recall that one of the objectives in modern curriculum development is subject integration. You saw several examples of the interdisciplinary approach in the material on social reconstructionism in Chapter 2.

Interdisciplinarianism is a curricular approach that includes two or more disciplines in a single area of study (Jacobs, 1989). A good example of interdisciplinarianism is the use of graphs (a mathematics topic) to interpret experimental data obtained in a science experiment. Another example is writing a story about a person living on the moon, combining science and language arts. The more subjects that are drawn into the study of a topic, the more sophisticated the approach becomes and the more interrelated the disciplines become.

Beane (1997) distinguishes interdisciplinarianism from the **integrated curriculum,** defining integration as an approach that organizes curriculum around "significant problems and issues without regard for subject area boundaries" (p. xi). You saw examples of curriculum integration Chapter 12's section on service learning. According to Beane, in true integration, the study of individual disciplines is subjugated to the study of a problem or situation in which individual disciplines are called upon as needed to help in the selected study, not for their own sake.

It is obvious that interdisciplinary and integrated approaches are easier to develop and implement in elementary schools than in middle schools or high schools. However, many upper-level schools implement interdisciplinary and integrated approaches, resulting in education that is meaningful, interesting, and relevant, all of which are "'essential preconditions'" for building motivation" (McBee, 2000, p. 258).

You have investigated current reform trends in curriculum and instruction in the four disciplines of social studies, science, mathematics, and the English language arts. You also have investigated constructivist teaching (see Chapters 2 and 5). Building Block 14.11 will help you pull all this together.

What Would You Do with Curriculum?

Brooks & Brooks (1999) offer 12 characteristics of constructivist teaching. Some deal with curriculum, some deal with instruction, and some deal with assessment. They are listed in abbreviated form in the following chart.

Give an example of how each characteristic can be applied in the major subject areas. You may wish to use a chart similar to the one shown here.

Characteristic of Constructivist Teaching	How It Is Applied in Social Studies	How It Is Applied in Science	How It Is Applied in Mathematics	How It Is Applied in Language Arts
1. Encourage and accept student autonomy and initiative.				
2. Use raw data and primary sources, along with manipulative, interactive, and physical material.				
3. Use cognitive terminology such as *classify, analyze, predict,* and *create.*				
4. Allow student responses to drive lessons, shift instructional strategy, and alter content.				
5. Inquire about students' understandings of concepts.				
6. Encourage students to engage in dialogue, both with the teacher and with one another.				
7. Encourage student inquiry.				

Characteristic of Constructivist Teaching	How It Is Applied in Social Studies	How It Is Applied in Science	How It Is Applied in Mathematics	How It Is Applied in Language Arts
8. Seek elaboration of students' initial responses.				
9. Engage students in experiences that might contradict their initial hypotheses, and then encourage discussion.				
10. Allow wait time after posing questions.				
11. Provide time for students to construct relationships and create metaphors.				
12. Nurture students' natural curiosity.				

Assessment Reform

You have explored the concept of assessment in several parts of this textbook, and you have seen that the purpose of assessment is to obtain information about student achievement. There are many ways to assess, and educational reform efforts seek to strengthen assessment so it measures what students actually know and can do.

BUILDING
BLOCK
14.12

Assessing Your Achievement

What kinds of assessments do you remember having had as a student? Write them down.

- Did these assessments give you the opportunity to show what you knew about the topics?
- What do you believe teachers should do to find out what a student *really* knows?

The primary goals of assessment in education are to obtain and interpret information about what students know and can do and to use this information to guide instructional and educational decisions. One traditional assessment method is the **paper-and-pencil test,** in which students select among multiple-choice or "true or false" test items, supply answers to fill in blanks, or write an essay on a given topic. With the possible exception of open-ended essays, this form of assessment requires students to select which of several possible answers is the correct one. As discussed in Chapter 8, multiple-choice assessments measure a student's ability to select a response; they do not necessarily show what the student knows and can do. In a multiple-choice test, students cannot generate their own responses and do not have the opportunity to explain their reasons for choosing a response. How do your responses to Building Block 14.12 compare to this description of traditional assessment?

Learning theory holds that different people construct their understanding of material in different ways. Thus, traditional testing has begun to yield to more authentic methods that assess what students *really* know. Assessing student performance on tasks relevant to real-world activities is called **authentic assessment.** The current subject-area national standards encourage the use of authentic assessment methods. These authentic assessments methods include portfolios, journals, interviews, observations, performance assessment, and human judgment. Further, teachers often weave assessment directly into the instruction, instead of testing with end-of-unit tests, midterms, and finals given *after* the instruction.

Portfolios are folders of evidence of students' accomplishments. You are probably keeping a portfolio in this course to show evidence of your achievement of the basic course goals established by your professor or institution. **Journals** are records of a variety of information, such as reflections, descriptions of projects and laboratory inquiries, questions, answers, reports, stories, drawings, charts, tables, and many other things. Journals often are used in conjunction with other assessment methods to show what students have learned. When conducting **interviews,** teachers ask questions during a lesson to check for student understanding and to uncover alternative ways of thinking. Based on student responses to the questions, teachers can affirm student understanding or take appropriate steps to help students clarify their thinking.

Many schools have replaced traditional methods of assessment with authentic assessment, because authentic assessment provides the information they really want—what students know and what they can do.

BUILDING BLOCK 14.13

Using Assessment Data

Use your current understandings of authentic assessment and standardized testing and experiences you may have had with these forms of assessment to answer the following questions.

- What kinds of authentic assessments have you experienced?
- How are authentic assessments different from pencil-and-paper tests?
- How are authentic assessments different from standardized tests?
- Can standardized tests be authentic?
- How can educators use data from both authentic assessment and standardized tests to inform educational decisions?

One way teachers can assess student achievement authentically is to record observations.

Teacher Education Reform

Teacher preparation, a concern for many years, is a major element of educational reform. Much of what you investigated about teacher preparation and certification in Chapter 9 represents the current state of reform efforts. The No Child Left Behind legislation requires schools to place a highly qualified teacher in every classroom. The Ready to Teach Act of 2003 provides federal funding to improve teacher preparation so this goal can be accomplished (Boehner, 2003).

Teacher education reform efforts target five basic areas:

- Subject-matter knowledge
- Pedagogical knowledge and skills
- Methods of teacher preparation
- Incentives and accountability
- Teacher induction

Subject-Matter Knowledge

In general, educators agree that subject-matter knowledge is critical to effective teaching. When you investigated your teacher preparation program in Chapter 9, you probably found an emphasis on subject matter, regardless of the program you plan to pursue. In fact, some states are eliminating the undergraduate degree in education as a teacher certification requirement; instead, they require that future teachers major in a content area. However, most educators believe that the subject matter understanding needed by teachers is different from the understanding needed by traditional majors; teachers need to know their subject in ways that make it teachable to others. Thus, teachers need to know and understand the pedagogy associated with teaching the content areas.

What undergraduate major does your state require for teacher certification: a major in education? Or a major in a subject area?

Pedagogical Knowledge and Skills

Pedagogical knowledge and skills comprise the "how to teach" component of teacher education. You probably know someone who is a whiz in his or her subject area but cannot teach it. There is controversy over the relative importance of subject matter and pedagogical expertise to teaching effectiveness. The dominant view is that teachers need rigorous training in educational theory and pedagogical skills. For example, Wenglinsky (2000) found a high correlation between the performance of eighth grade students in science and mathematics and teachers who emphasized hands-on learning, higher-order thinking skills, and individualized instruction in their teaching. He concludes that "what really matters [in teaching quality] is not where teachers come from but what they do in the classroom" (p. 32). He reported that strong subject-matter knowledge is particularly essential for science and mathematics teachers in high schools and middle schools. The opposing view holds that teachers need only minimal exposure to education theory and pedagogy and that teachers best acquire their skills through on-the-job experience. (This view is championed by the Thomas B. Fordham Foundation.)

Darling-Hammond (2000) reviewed research and evidence to ascertain relationships between teacher qualifications and student achievement. She found that teachers' subject-matter knowledge is critical, but that its relationship to student performance varies depending on grade level and level of student sophistication. She also found that, regardless of grade level or subject taught, student achievement relates strongly to teachers having full certification and a major in their field. Darling-Hammond concluded that training future teachers how to teach specific subjects has the greatest impact of all on student achievement.

Teacher Preparation Methods

As you found in Chapter 1, most teacher education programs must be accredited. This means that external reviewing agencies assess programs for compliance with the reviewing agency's standards. The two primary national teacher accreditation agencies are the National Council for the Accreditation of Teacher Education (NCATE) and the Teacher Education Accrediting Council (TEAC). Both review teacher preparation programs using peers (teacher education faculty from other institutions). NCATE has adopted standards that emphasize candidate performance in all areas to demonstrate subject-matter knowledge and understanding and application of learning theories and teaching skills, as emphasized in educational reform movements. TEAC requires institutions to undertake internal evaluations in accordance with their standards and principles.

Whereas national accreditation organizations evaluate the effectiveness of teacher preparation programs according to national standards, individual states are responsible for ensuring that the programs comply with state standards and requirements; this responsibility normally belongs to the state department of education.

Standards for Teacher Preparation

BUILDING BLOCK 14.14

Review the NCATE standards in Chapter 1. How do these standards address the reform goals you identified in Building Block 14.1?

Incentives and Accountability

Incentives tend to foster a desire to do things differently, and accountability measures the extent to which goals are met. Several education programs provide both incentives and accountability to improve teacher preparation and performance.

State certification exams (see Chapter 9) ensure that teacher candidates have the knowledge and understanding of the content and pedagogy deemed essential by the licensing state for teaching the subject or area for which they are seeking certification. Some states require new teachers to demonstrate effectiveness in the classroom as a condition for continued certification. One state (Georgia) goes even further by guaranteeing that teachers who graduate from state institutions will be effective in the classroom, or the degree-awarding institution must provide remedial training at no cost to the teacher.

The National Board for Professional Teaching Standards (NBPTS) awards national-level certification to inservice teachers who demonstrate their effectiveness through portfolios, videos of their teaching, reflection, and content exams. National certification is recognized by all states and normally carries a monetary incentive.

Teacher Induction

One way to help teachers learn the pedagogical applications of subject matter is through collaboration between colleges of education and the public schools they serve. In the last decade or two, schools and colleges have collaborated in teacher induction programs, acknowledging that new teachers need mentoring so they can apply their newly acquired content knowledge and teaching skills in the classroom. When you interview for a teaching position, you should feel free to ask whether the district has a new teacher mentoring program and, if so, what the program entails. The most successful teacher induction programs have several features in common:

- They use experienced, well trained teachers as mentors.
- They are based on well articulated standards and goals.
- They are adequately funded.

- They include special and appropriate evaluation processes for new teachers.
- They extend beyond the new teacher's first year to include the second and sometimes the third years.
- They include a reduced teaching load for the new teacher.
- They provide appropriate class placements.
- They include opportunities to observe other teachers.
- They allow new teachers to participate in professional development opportunities.

Some people argue that experienced teachers, not just new teachers, can benefit from similar reforms. For example, Cohen (2002) makes the following suggestions, adding that many of these reforms are based on common sense, most cost nothing, and none requires restructuring, retraining, expensive testing, or additional personnel:

- Offer sabbaticals.
- Reallocate budgets to make more money available for books; let teachers choose them.
- Involve teachers in the evaluation process.
- Change hiring practices to attract top candidates.
- Make tenure mean something.
- Reallocate the use of time to protect teachers.
- Have administrators teach.

A recent study found that the top professional needs and changes desired by teachers were smaller class size, more planning time, support and respect as a professional, less standardized testing, adequate materials and supplies, administrative support and leadership, and time and financial support for professional development and study (Dagenhart et al., 2005).

The U.S. Department of Education has launched an initiative called Teacher-to-Teacher: Supporting Success. This initiative is designed to recognize and disseminate outstanding teacher achievements (U.S. Department of Education, 2004). And in 2005, the federal government approved a $500 million Teacher Incentive Fund that provides states with money for inservice teachers who teach in high-need schools and achieve excellent results (Spellings: Reward Teachers, 2005).

 A direct link to the home page of the Teacher-To-Teacher: Supporting Success initiative is available on the *Building Teachers* companion website.

School Structure

Schools are undergoing a number of changes to help remedy the perceived problems of education. Changes to the physical plant itself and school-day scheduling are among these reforms. As you saw in Chapter 7, during the 1960s the open classroom model of schools was developed to facilitate individualized instruction. If teachers had easy access to many students in many classrooms in many grades, the idea went, they could form the most appropriate groups, thereby individualizing instruction while maximizing the use of their time and resources.

BUILDING
BLOCK
14.15

Classroom Layouts

Describe the arrangement of the classrooms in your elementary school. Your middle school or junior high school. Your high school. Why do you suppose they were arranged as they were?

How would you arrange them differently to meet today's needs?

Building Layout and Facilities

Today's schools are built to accommodate today's educational systems. In elementary schools, grades are normally self-contained to encourage teachers to get to know their students and to implement learning opportunities that meet every student's needs. In middle schools, grades are arranged in pods, with a team of teachers made up of one teacher for each subject. Four classes of students move from class to class but stay in their pod for the major subjects. The teachers on each team meet regularly to plan the most appropriate strategies for their classes and for individual students. The middle school concept offers the individual attention of the elementary school and the subject matter expertise of the high school (see Chapter 7).

In high schools, different subjects generally are taught in their own special areas, often arranged by department. Besides maximizing learning opportunities for each subject, this arrangement maximizes the use of materials, equipment, and, in the case of science, lab space. However, this arrangement also reinforces the current subject-centered approach common to most high schools. Physical education and other special subjects, such as band, chorus, and woodworking shop, are taught in their own areas.

As school buildings age, in many areas maintenance has lagged behind need. In 2005, the American Society of Civil Engineers gave school infrastructure a grade of D based on the condition, performance, capacity, and funding for schools ("School Infrastructure," 2005). Many schools are substandard relative to current reform trends. Maintenance and renovation are the answer. Maintenance reduces a school's rate of deterioration, and renovation enables schools to modify existing structures to meet current needs, rather than abandoning those structures. State and local budgets usually do not contain sufficient money for new buildings, major maintenance, or renovations, so funding is obtained through special purpose local options sales tax (SPLOST) initiatives voted on by people in the school district. SPLOST involves adding a small amount to sales taxes; this additional tax is earmarked for school facilities and construction.

One of the more dramatic reforms in school facilities relates to educational technology. Libraries, once devoted to print material, have become media centers. Most schools now have technology labs and technological facilities installed in classrooms. Because the Internet is such an integral part of today's education, schools have installed Internet connections, both wired and wireless (see Chapter 11).

Educational reform often results in innovative and improved learning space for students. Computers and Internet access are standard additions to school libraries and media centers across the nation.

Scheduling

Many school districts are revisting the concepts of the school day and the school year. Administrators and teachers are scheduling school days to maximize instructional time. New scheduling plans include block scheduling in high schools and looping and multigrade scheduling in elementary schools. Some school systems have implemented an extended school year, which favors several short breaks throughout the year over a long summer vacation—during which time students tend to forget what they learned the year before (see Chapter 7).

Types of Schools

Another aspect of reform that deals with school structures involves the increasing array of school types and the options for school choice. You explored several nontraditional schools in Chapter 6, including the following:

- Charter schools that operate with freedom from one or more state regulations
- Magnet schools that concentrate on specific areas of curriculum
- Education management organizations (EMOs), for-profit corporations that assume responsibility for the total operation of schools
- Home schooling, where students learn under the general supervision of parents in their homes

  Can you think of other nontraditional schools?
  These issues are all part of the larger educational reform picture.

Governance and Finance Reform

The typical system of school governance is top-down. In this system, teachers receive directives from the principal, and the principal receives directives from the district. As you saw in Chapter 11, state and federal agencies outline the parameters for various aspects of education, including curriculum, assessment, educating students with special needs, and more. The school districts interpret these rules and regulations in terms of their implementation, and, in the typical system of governance, hand implementation directives down to individual teachers through the principals.

The top-down system of governance is yielding to systems in which all participants in education are seen as equal contributors, often resulting in a bottom-up approach. This system is a response to widespread concerns of teachers, parents, politicians, and community members, who see the teachers as experts who know the students in their classes and how they best learn and who should have a major voice in deciding what is appropriate for their students' education.

The bottom-up movement has influenced several new approaches to school governance. One is site-based management, which, as you saw in Chapter 11, allows individual schools to determine and control reform discussions, uniting the teachers, administrators, parents, and students to foster locally determined procedures that reflect the needs and desires of the local school and community. Site-based management requires teamwork and collaboration among school administrators and teachers, replacing the "boss management" concept with a "lead management" concept. Teachers and school administrators work together as they rethink what they do, how they do it, and how they measure it (Siu-Runyan & Heart, 1992). Of course, upper levels of administration still must function as "boss" in such areas as setting priorities, implementing state laws governing education, requiring standardized tests, requiring curriculum that will ensure highest possible performance on the tests, etc. In the final analysis, the administration is held accountable for schools' performance.

Many people question the need for large administrative structures, which characterize many large school districts. Large school districts often have many administrative staff members, such as assistant superintendents, curriculum directors, and special program directors, all of whom are highly paid. Some people question the extent to which these positions are essential in running schools. As a result, current reform efforts are streamlining the administrative structure to save money and reduce the layers of bureaucracy.

BUILDING BLOCK 14.16

Site-Based Management

Consider the site-based management system of school governance.

- How does this system aid in the implementation of curriculum reform?
- How does this system give teachers a voice in a school's operation? What kinds of helpful input can teachers provide?
- How does this system address the concerns voiced by John Goodlad about the need for reform efforts at the local school level, treating reform as a total entity rather than individual parts?

Conclusion

The reform of American education is being undertaken in response to concerns voiced by business, government, and society at large. Educational reform extends to all aspects of education, including curriculum, instruction, assessment, teacher preparation, school structures, and governance and finance. Many organizations are spearheading or assisting in reform efforts. The federal government collects data, provides funding, and acts in an advisory capacity. State governments establish policies for their state education programs. Nonprofit organizations offer various types of assistance in educational reform efforts.

Subject-specific professional education organizations have developed standards that have shaped curricular and instructional reform. States have adopted and implemented these standards to varying degrees. National and international tests reveal trends about student achievement and its relationship to curriculum. Efforts to reform assessment focus on gaining accurate information about students' achievement of knowledge and skills.

Teacher education reform aims to ensure that all teachers are experts in both pedagogy and subject matter. Changes in school structures maximize the use of school buildings and instructional time. Governance and finance are moving toward a bottom-up approach that includes teachers in the decision-making processes.

Many reformers urge viewing educational reform holistically rather than in separate components. Controversy exists over several reform initiatives, but most people would agree that American education requires systemic changes to keep up with the times and meet the demands of living in today's society.

■ Key Terms and Concepts

Authentic assessment, 381
Integrated curriculum, 378
Interactionist approach, 374
Interdisciplinarianism, 378
Interview, 381
Journal, 381

McGuffey Readers, 374
National Assessment of
  Education Progress
  (NAEP), 376
New Math, 371
Paper-and-pencil test, 380

Phonics, 374
Portfolio, 381
Standards movement, 365
Whole language, 374

■ Construct and Apply

1. What does *systemic educational reform* mean?
2. Name at least six areas of American education being looked at from an educational reform point of view. For each, summarize the reform efforts being undertaken.
3. List at least five common thrusts in the current curriculum standards that represent current directions in education.
4. Why is reforming assessment a high priority? What initiatives are today's schools undertaking to accomplish this reform?
5. What competencies do professional organizations want preservice teachers to demonstrate?
6. Describe how society influences educational reform efforts.

■ Deconstructing the Standards

INTASC Principle Number 9 says:

The teacher is a reflective practitioner who constantly evaluates the effects of his/her choices and actions on others (students, parents, and other professionals in the learning community) and who actively seeks out opportunities to grow professionally.

What part(s) of this principle does this chapter address?

How does this chapter address this principle?

How will the concepts in this chapter help you apply this principle as a teacher?

■ Field Experience

1. Find out what standards your cooperating teacher uses to guide the instruction.
2. Where does your cooperating teacher get the curriculum he or she uses?
3. What elements of educational reform do you notice in your field experience school?

■ Your Portfolio

1. Obtain a copy of your state's standards for the subject(s) and level(s) you plan to teach; include it in your portfolio.
2. Obtain a copy of the curriculum your field placement school uses for the subject(s) and level(s) you plan to teach; include it in your portfolio.
3. Prepare a document that compares the two.

■ Technology Resources

 Access the *Building Teachers* companion website, http://www.education.wadsworth.com/ martinloomis1, for more information and resources about the curriculum and school reform, including links to the following:

- Center for Educational Renewal
- Coalition of Essential Schools
- New American Schools
- Center for School Change
- National social studies standards
- National science education standards
- TIMSS (Third International Mathematics and Science Study)
- National mathematics standards
- National reading and language arts standards
- Teacher-To-Teacher: Supporting Success

 Check out the *Building Teachers* CD-ROM that accompanies your textbook for additional chapter resources.

 Also link to InfoTrac College Edition via the *Building Teachers* companion website. Use InfoTrac College Edition to search for journal articles to enhance your study.

PART V

Building a Teacher

Now we come back to the *Self*. You have explored characteristics of excellent teachers, your philosophical ideas about education, and characteristics of students including their common needs and their unique perspectives and abilities. You have investigated characteristics of schools including their purposes, structures, and the interactions among students, teachers, and schools. You have explored the influences of society on education and schools, both past and present.

So, it is time to come back to you. Do you want to become a teacher? Why?

CHAPTER 15

Your Motives for Teaching

"Why do you want to be an elementary school teacher?"

"Because I love kids!"

"Why do you want to be a high school teacher?"

"Because I love my subject!"

"Why do you want to be a middle school teacher?"

"I'm not sure!"

The conversation that begins this chapter represents the typical answers future teachers give when, on the first day of their Introduction to Education course, they are asked why they want to become a teacher.

Everyone who wants to be a teacher has had powerful experiences in school, both positive and negative, that have informed their decision to pursue a career in education. As you now know, however, there is much to consider when thinking about teaching—a lot more than just the experiences you had in school. You have also examined relevant information and constructed new knowledge as you have progressed through this textbook.

Most introductory education textbooks include a chapter on motives for teaching at the very beginning of the book. We suspect that it will not surprise you that this textbook, written in a constructivist voice, puts this chapter at the end. Certainly, your motives for teaching deserve exploration, especially in your first education class. Anyone considering becoming a teacher should carefully examine his or her motives before entering a teacher education program. But how well informed would your reasons have been in the beginning of this course— before your classes, before your investigations, and before your field experiences? Flip back to this textbook's table of contents and look at all you have explored. You knew a great deal about teaching, schools, and learning at the beginning of this course, but surely you know a lot more now than you did when you started. In this chapter, you will draw on the knowledge and experiences you have gained in this course to explore the question, "Why do you want or don't want to teach?"

CHAPTER GOALS

As a result of your work in this chapter, you will:

1. Explore your motives for wanting—or not wanting—to teach, in terms of self, students, school, and society.

2. Consider whether teaching can be called a profession.

3. Discuss how you can promote the profession of teaching and how you can continue your professional development.

Identifying Your Reasons for Teaching

Review the organization of this book. You started out by exploring what *you* already know and believe about effective teachers and teaching. Then, you moved to an examination of *students*—how they are alike and how they are different—and what that means for teaching. Next, you investigated *schools*, where learning, the act of teaching, and the teacher–student relationship takes place. Finally, you saw that a school has general and specific purposes and structures that serve the community in which it is located. Such communities are a function of *society* and its beliefs.

Self, students, schools, and society. Where do your motives for teaching lie? Let us investigate all four areas.

Self

What is it you know about your *self* that makes you believe you would be a good teacher? If you review the qualities of effective teachers and teaching you investigated in Chapter 1, you probably identify with some of them.

BUILDING BLOCK 15.1

Your *Self* as a Teacher

List your personal qualities and skills that you believe will help you to be an effective teacher. If you have decided not to teach, to what other professions might these qualities and skills be suited?

- How does this list compare with the characteristics of excellent teachers and effective teaching you listed in Chapter 1?
- How did you acquire these qualities and skills? Which ones are innate and which did you learn?

There is an age-old debate about whether teaching is an art or a science. If you believe it is an art, your motives for teaching might include your belief that you have an innate talent for it. You might think that some individuals are naturally talented teachers. Have you had a teacher who seemed naturally talented in this way? Such teachers seem to have a knack for getting people to learn. Perhaps someone has told you that you are a "natural" teacher.

Yet, as you have seen, definite teaching methods and strategies have been shown through research to affect student achievement. These are skills that can be learned.

BUILDING BLOCK 15.2

Is Teaching an Art or a Science?

Think about the characteristics of an art—what an artist does, what technique he or she uses, how much free expression comes into play, the role of talent, etc.

Think about the characteristics of a science—what a scientist does, what technique he or she uses, how much free expression comes into play, the role of talent, etc.

Then answer the question, "Is teaching an art or a science?" Explain your response.

Whether teaching is more an art or a science is a classic debate. Psychologist B. F. Skinner (see Chapter 2) believed that teachers could be trained to use educational strate-

Teaching is both an art and a science. Effective teachers know how to best assist students. To what extent are those skills based on knowledge and/or talent?

gies and materials effectively. To Skinner, teaching is truly a science, with a methodology to be practiced and followed. On the other hand, Elliot Eisner, a Stanford University professor of education, argues that teaching is more of an art. He notes that teachers must deal creatively with the unexpected in their students' learning and behavior. Rigid models, methods, and templates for instruction or management do not apply to every classroom situation. The teacher must possess the intuition of how, when, and where to use his or her skills effectively (Eisner, 1983). Gage (1978) combines the two views to assert that teaching is an art that is informed by science. Gage writes, "in medicine and engineering, where the scientific basis is unquestionable, the artistic elements also abound" and "in teaching, where the artistic elements are unquestionable, a scientific base can also be developed" (p. 18).

Some believe that certain people have a predisposition toward teaching, somewhat akin to the talents children inherit from their parents. A parent who possesses a talent for drawing, singing, or playing a musical instrument, for example, often has a child with similar artistic talent. Many teachers and future teachers will tell you that they come from a family of educators. As with doctors, police officers, and other professionals, several generations of a family may be involved in education. Perhaps you belong to such a family and count your family's teaching experience as one of your motives for teaching. Does this mean that you could have inherited a talent for teaching? Or does it mean that teachers pattern themselves after other teachers in their families? What qualities of effective teachers might you inherit or develop from being a part of a family with a history of teaching?

A teacher's attitudes toward self, content, peers, students, parents, and the community can be thought of as his or her *disposition*. It is not difficult to see how we might acquire some of the same dispositions as important people in our lives. Understanding, patience, and kindness can be learned from others who demonstrate those dispositions. These are certainly dispositions that will help a person become an effective teacher.

When considering your motives for teaching, did you think of emotions associated with a passion for teaching? One characteristic common among successful teachers is passion. These successful teachers are passionate about teaching their content and their students. These teachers may believe that teaching is a "calling" (Farkas, Johnson, & Foleno, 2000).

Look around your education class. You might see students who are coming to teaching as a second career. What motives do you think would influence someone to leave an existing career and study to become a teacher? If you are choosing teaching as a second career, what influenced your decision? Have you heard someone in your class say, "I've always wanted to teach"? Maybe you have said these words yourself. What does this statement imply about the speaker's motives for teaching?

What do you know about your *self* that makes you think you would (or would not) be a good teacher? At the beginning of this course, you knew that you were interested in teaching. Now you know that effective educators need to have certain dispositions and skills. If you have chosen to continue in your teacher education program, you believe you have some innate talent for teaching or can learn the necessary skills. Fueling this ambition might be that you are the next in a long line of educators in your family. Your learning in this course and your field experiences may have helped you identify your passion for teaching; or you may have discovered that you are not passionate about education. Either way, we hope that you have clarified your motives for teaching—or not teaching—in the context of your *self*.

The Student

The hypothetical conversation at the beginning of this chapter seems to indicate that a person's passion for teaching depends on his or her major. It seems to suggest that if you are studying to be an elementary teacher, you are passionate about children. If you are going to be a secondary teacher, you are passionate about content. And if you are pursuing a middle grades certification, you are passionate about both.

Of course, this "conversation" was meant only to introduce the chapter and to provide a bit of a laugh. All successful teachers, regardless of major, are passionate about their students. In fact, when someone asks you what you want to teach, we hope that your first answer will be "students." If you are not fond of young people in the age group you want to teach, it will not matter how much you love your content. You have seen that teachers have a relationship with each and every student, whether they want one or not. Many teachers cite this relationship as the initial source of their motivation to teach.

In Chapter 1, you recalled your favorite teacher. Did this teacher seem to like the students in his or her class? Did this teacher seem passionate about the well-being and achievement of each and every student? Did this teacher inspire you to go into education? Many future teachers saw how a certain teacher affected their lives and the lives of others—and were inspired to do the same.

We have heard teacher education students proclaim, "If I can help just one student learn, it will be reward enough." Actually, if you chose to pursue a career in education, you will help far more students than you realize. You will see evidence of this learning on tests and through other measures of achievement, but every once in a while a past student will contact you. You may be surprised that the student discusses not only the content from your class, but also the quality of your relationship with that student and how it affected his or her life.

Have you expressed your appreciation to your favorite teachers? Find out how to contact your favorite teachers and let them know how they affected you and influenced what you are doing with your life. Do it now, before you forget. It will make their day!

What are some of the ways passionate teachers inspire and motivate students?

Some individuals had a negative relationship with a teacher. Inspiration can come from bad experiences as well as good. Imagine a teacher telling a student: "You don't belong in this class. Don't count on getting into college." What choices does that student have? He could change his schedule and get out of that class. Or he could be inspired to prove the teacher wrong. He might even be inspired to become a teacher himself and make sure that other students do not have the same experience. Does this motivation apply to anyone you know?

The opportunity to work with students is a strong motive for many who desire to become a teacher. You may have thought that you want to teach because you love kids. Now you know that students are as different as they are alike. Recall from Chapters 3, 4, and 5 that the common needs, unique perspectives, and unique abilities that students bring to your classroom have significant implications for teaching. In your field experience, you may have discovered that you do not love all of your students all of the time. You may have even been relieved when you saw that a particularly challenging student was not in class one day. However, you now know that you must have what classroom management expert Harry Wong calls "positive regard" for every student (Wong, 2004). What do you think positive regard for every student means?

The opportunity to work with students is a powerful motivation to teach. However, perhaps in your field experiences, you had quite enough of being with children or adolescents each day and you have decided you do not want to work with students full time. Or perhaps your investigations and field experiences have caused you to change your mind about the age group you would like to teach. Regardless, you are now aware of the challenges and the rewards of working with students.

BUILDING
BLOCK
15.3

What Is It about Those Kids?

What do you like about children and adolescents? Answer this question in the context of the age group of students you wish to teach. What is it about students that makes you want to have the kind of relationship with them that will help them learn? Describe the characteristics you anticipate seeing in your future students.

The School

Some of us enjoyed the whole experience of school. We earned good grades and thrived in the social and academic atmosphere. Some people choose to go into education because they had very positive experiences in school. (Some even stay in school so long that they become professors of education, teaching others how to teach.) One might think that anyone who wants to be a teacher must have liked school. This is not always the case. Some students had less–than-enjoyable experiences in school but are choosing education as a career to make others' school experiences more positive and enjoyable.

Those who really enjoyed school and who seemed to work well in a structured academic environment may be motivated to teach by the atmosphere of learning. They count among their skills the ability to organize and plan well. They enjoy the daily schedule, whether it is from class to class in a middle or high school or from day to day in an elementary classroom. They enjoy the intellectual stimulation that comes with being in a school environment.

Some individuals like the control that comes with teaching, not in the sense of controlling behavior, but in the sense of designing and conducting lessons. Some teachers like the attention they get from being at the front of the class. Indeed, it has been said that teachers must be good actors. But even though most of the time, attention and effort in a school is focused on students, many people in a school must work together to make it all happen. You may be attracted by the apparent autonomy that you can have in your classroom, but you must collaborate and cooperate with myriad other individuals in the building to promote the purpose of the school.

Some say that teachers must be good salespeople. What do you think this means?

All of these other people in the school—the students, the other teachers, the administrators, and other personnel—have expectations. Now you know that teaching is more than managing your classroom, implementing the curriculum, and instructing and assessing students. Among other duties, you are responsible for student safety. You are expected to participate in noninstructional and extracurricular activities. You are expected to be certified and highly qualified. You should be current in educational research and theories, practices, and technologies through participation in professional development activities.

Would it surprise you to learn that some students are interested in teaching because they want weekends and summers off? This response may come from seeing teaching from a student's point of view. Now, however, you know that teaching requires a lot of time and effort, especially for new teachers. Maybe you are even shaking your head at the time it takes to prepare, teach, and evaluate a lesson. However, you know that with time, teachers gain experience and become more fluent in their practice, able to meet school and professional expectations while having the occasional weekend and a few weeks in the summer to rest and recuperate or participate in professional development opportunities.

The opportunities for lifelong learning and for working with others to promote a school's purpose may be a strong motivation for you to teach. Or you may have decided that it's just too much. Regardless, you have learned more about the place called school, and you understand more about the teacher's place in it.

The Place Called School

BUILDING BLOCK 15.4

Teachers work in the place called school. List some characteristics of the school that you find attractive as a teacher, and list some characteristics that you find unattractive. How does the possibility of working in a school factor into your motivation for becoming a teacher?

Society

Earlier we mentioned that some refer to teaching as a "calling." Is this true for you? The calling is an inner urge that may reflect your desire to make a contribution to society.

The Big Picture

BUILDING BLOCK 15.5

What do you hope to contribute by teaching? Do you believe that your day-to-day efforts in the classroom can produce a ripple outside the school? If so, how? Describe a chain of impact that your teaching could have on society.

In your study of the history of education in the United States, you learned that Americans have sought to educate the next generation to become conscientious citizens and contribute positively to society. Teachers can contribute to society by guiding the development of future conscientious citizens. The draw to the classroom is the power to affect society through teaching. You now know, however, that this power is not held by the teacher alone. The many stakeholders in education also have a strong influence. You now know that, beyond the people in the school building, members of society have a stake in education, with a huge investment in and influence on not only *what* is taught and *how* it is taught, but also on educational policy, procedures, ethics, and law. As a classroom teacher, you must respond to current social issues and the reforms they instigate. You now know that teachers are held accountable.

The opportunity to work with and for these stakeholders may motivate you to continue your study of education. On the other hand, you may have decided that too many

How, what, when, and where teachers teach can be influenced by external factors, such as parents, the community, the government, and the law.

people are telling you what to do and you do not wish to be held accountable for factors beyond your control. Either way, you have learned a great deal about the place that teaching and schools occupy in society.

Teaching is a noble profession. You now know that 21st-century teachers must be aware that the populations of society—and therefore of our classrooms—are diverse. Students represent many different ideas about what constitutes a positive contribution to society. As a teacher, your contribution is *not* to teach what you believe, but to guide students in acquiring the skills to make their own decisions about what *they* believe.

Are your reasons for becoming a teacher based on an adequate perception of what teaching is really like? We hope that the investigations you made using this textbook and through class and field experiences have allowed you to construct a realistic understanding of students, teaching, and schools.

What Do Teachers Say?

How do your reasons for wanting to teach compare with the reasons given by practicing teachers? Every 5 years, the National Education Association (NEA) conducts a survey of teachers, entitled *The Status of the American Public School Teacher*. The 2001 survey asked teachers why they originally chose teaching as a career and why they chose to stay in teaching. The desire to work with young people topped both lists. Table 15.1 summarizes the reasons cited in the survey.

The survey also showed that 60% of teachers would choose to teach again, and that 46% of teachers said they plan to stay in the classroom until they voluntarily retire. Sixteen percent said they will stay until they are required to retire. Five percent said that they definitely plan to leave teaching as soon as possible, and 11% said they will probably stay until something better comes along (National Education Association, 2003).

from the
TEACHER — Elizabeth Day

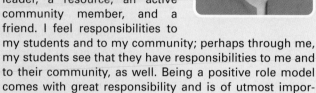

Courtesy of Elizabeth Day

A Member of the Community

Twenty-eight years ago, the phone rang at my house at eight in the evening. It was the superintendent of the school district in which I now teach, informing me that the Board of Education had decided to hire new teachers. If I accepted the sixth-grade position for which I applied, I would be teaching in the district that I had attended as a student. I was indeed excited to know that, when the new school year rolled around, not only would I have my first teaching job, but I would be able to return to my own community to be with the people I had been brought up with and had learned so much from. Along with the decision to teach in my community, I made the choice to live there, as well. I was returning to Mechanicville, New York, "The Friendly City," to see just what I might accomplish as a teacher and what I might be able to give back to my community. Because my two greatest role models, my mom and dad, gave so unselfishly to our city for so many years, I believed that this could be my chance to do the same.

As a teacher, I led by example. Nevell Bovee, an American author and lawyer, has stated, "Example has more followers than reason." Because I live in the same community in which I teach, the example I set as my students see me both in and out of the classroom gives them an opportunity to follow. I am a role model when I am a spectator at their sports events outside of school, an active participant in community bands and local theater, and a parent actively engaged in my own child's education. Through church activities, I joyously sing at former students' weddings, and I compassionately share the grief that accompanies the death of students or their family members. Whatever I'm doing, I work diligently with the members of my community in positive interpersonal relationships. My students and the community see me as a teacher-leader, a resource, an active community member, and a friend. I feel responsibilities to my students and to my community; perhaps through me, my students see that they have responsibilities to me and to their community, as well. Being a positive role model comes with great responsibility and is of utmost importance to me.

Teaching in my community and making a difference in the lives of the people with whom I work and live has held great reward for me. Reflecting back on my teaching experience, I realize that almost everyone under 40 in my town is someone who has sat in my classroom. I also know that I have influenced many people both inside and outside of my classroom. Teaching is my chance to make a positive difference in the lives of many. As my students make their journeys, I hold close to the idea that they, too, will continue to make a difference in the hearts and minds of those they encounter. If what they do can in any way be traced back to something I did, an example I set, or a role that I played, then my desire to reach out to others has come full circle, and I know that I have done my job well.

Elizabeth F. Day
2005 New York Teacher of the Year
Mechanicville Middle School
Mechanicville, New York

TABLE 15.1 Why Teachers Chose Teaching as a Career and Why They Chose to Stay in Teaching (from National Education Association, 2003).

Reason Cited	Originally Chose Teaching (%)	Chose to Stay in Teaching (%)
Desire to work with young people	73	68
Value of education in society	44	43
Interest in subject matter	36	41
Influence of a teacher	32	N/A
Too much invested to get out	N/A	30

(Note: Respondents could cite more than one reason.)

Nieto (2003) surveyed several teachers in the Boston area, each highly respected and in the teaching profession for more than 25 years, to assess why these people stayed in teaching. The teachers gave the following basic reasons for staying in the profession:

- Autobiography: The teachers are deeply involved in their teaching. Teaching has become their defining characteristic.
- Love: The teachers love their students and the subjects they teach.
- Hope and possibility: The teachers have hope and faith in their students, their abilities as teachers, and the profession of teaching.
- Intellectual work: The teachers constantly update their knowledge and teaching skills.
- Democratic practice: The teachers are committed to social justice and the ideals of democracy, fair play, and equality.
- Ability to shape the future: The teachers feel their work and actions are of greater consequence than those of almost any other profession.

How do the reasons for staying in teaching given by teachers in Nieto's sample compare with your own reasons for becoming a teacher?

As you consider your motives for teaching, you must also consider why teachers leave the profession. Some teachers believe that they made the wrong career choice. Those who took the 2001 NEA survey were asked to indicate whether they would choose teaching as a career again. Although 60% of respondents indicated that they would choose to be teachers again, 18% said that they might or might not choose teaching again, and 21% said that teaching would not be their choice (NEA, 2003). Table 15.2 shows the reasons teachers gave in the NEA survey for wanting to leave the profession before retirement.

The rate of attrition (the gradual decrease of staff due to resignation, retirement, etc.) of new teachers is of great concern. The National Commission on Teaching and America's Future (2005) found that nearly one out of every two teachers, or close to 50%, leave the classroom within 5 years. The national attrition rate of teachers during the first 5 years of service is shown in Figure 15.1.

Responding to these alarming statistics, the commission (and many other scholars and teacher support groups) recommends strengthening teacher induction programs to

TABLE 15.2 Why Teachers Want to Leave Teaching Before Retirement (From NEA Survey, 2001)

Reason	Percentage
Low salary	37
Poor working conditions	20
Lack of support systems	3
Student-related issues	4
Administration-related issues	8
Parent-related issues	5
Lack of prestige	2
Lack of opportunity for advancement	5
Other	17

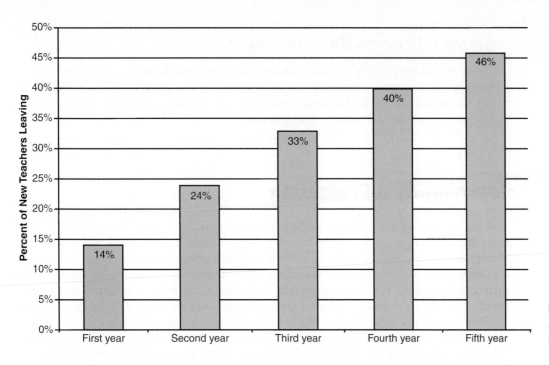

Figure 15.1
National attrition of teachers in the first 5 years of teaching.

help new teachers make a smooth and rewarding transition from the teacher preparation program to actual classroom situations (see also Chapter 14).

Is your passion for getting into education strong enough to sustain your motivation throughout your career, given what you now know about the challenges and complexities of being a teacher? Peske et al. (2001) suggest that, contrary to earlier times when people thought in terms of a single career and lifetime loyalty to a single organization, people today think in terms of several careers with several different organizations. In a large survey, the researchers found that "While there were respondents who planned to make teaching a lifetime career, they were surprisingly few in number" (p. 305). This finding suggests that some people may perceive teaching as one of several careers they will pursue. In fact, you may be one of those considering teaching as a new or different career path.

A direct link to the National Commission on Teaching and America's Future website is available on the *Building Teachers* companion website.

I'm Outta Here!

Look at the reasons teachers cited for wanting to leave the profession in Table 15.2. Which are related to the skills and dispositions required for teaching? Which have to do with students? Which have to do with the context of the school? Which have to do with society?

BUILDING
BLOCK
15.6

We hope that you have become better informed regarding the issues cited in Table 15.2 as you have explored the topics in this textbook, participated in class discussions, and completed your field experiences. Those of you who decide to continue in the teacher preparation program can do so better informed. For some, however, these issues may be significant enough for them to decide against teaching as a career. Regardless of your final decision, you now understand the teacher's role in society and the challenges that affect that role. How can you, as a member of your community, help teachers—and therefore the students who are the future citizens of your community—be successful?

So You Want to Be a Teacher?

Using the understanding you have constructed about teaching as a career, write a statement listing the reasons why you want to become a teacher. If you have decided *not* to continue in the field of education, or if you are undecided, write a statement listing your reasons for your current thinking.

Teaching as a Profession

You have reviewed the strong relationships among teaching, schools, and society. It is clear that teaching is a noble profession, but you probably have received mixed messages about how society regards teachers. Television shows, public service announcements, and awards (such as state or national teacher of the year awards) acknowledge teachers and their contributions. Yet some portrayals of teachers are less than flattering. Perhaps friends and relatives wonder about your motives for wanting to teach. Consider the nontraditional students in your class. Many of them have chosen education as a *second* career. Why do you think nontraditional students did not go into teaching in the first place?

Besides the debate about whether teaching is an art or a science, another debate exists: whether or not teaching is a profession. James Davis, a professor of higher education and the director of the Center for Academic Quality at the University of Colorado, points out that teaching involves the application of professional judgment after consideration of specific and varying situations, and that this application is characteristic of a profession (Davis, 1997). Careers that are commonly accepted as professions are doctors, engineers, and lawyers. Is teaching a profession?

Is Teaching a Profession?

Think of a profession outside the field of education.

- What does it take to become a member of this profession?
- What are the characteristics of the job?
- Are there requirements to remain a member of the profession? What are they?
- To what extent do your responses apply to teachers and teaching?

What are the major characteristics of a profession? List as many as you can think of that distinguish a profession from a field of work that is not considered a profession.

List as many characteristics of teaching as you can think of that make it a profession.

Webster's Dictionary (2005) defines a profession as "a calling requiring specialized knowledge and often long and intensive academic preparation." Does this definition of a profession fit teaching?

In his seminal work, Lieberman (1956) listed the following five characteristics of professionals:

1. A professional must offer an essential social service that depends on intellectual techniques in its performance.

2. A professional must undertake an extended period of specialized training and accept personal responsibility for his or her actions and decisions.

Teaching requires significant preparation and training, self-governance, a code of ethics, and reliance on specific intellectual techniques and methods. In what other ways can teaching be considered a profession and not a trade or a job?

© Manchan/Getty Images

3. It is generally accepted that the service rendered by the professional is of more value than the economic gain from performing the service.

4. Although they are served by professional organizations, members of a profession are self-governing.

5. A code of ethics sets standards for professional behavior.

How does your list from Building Block 15.8 compare to Lieberman's definition of a profession? Let us examine more closely the characteristics he defines.

An Essential Social Service Dependent on Intellectual Techniques

Do teachers perform an essential social service? Schools are compulsory, which indicates that society believes teaching is essential. However, remember that within society, different views exist on what constitutes essential teaching methods and curricula. There are also indicators that society might not value teachers. What might those indicators be? How does society view teachers as compared with other professionals, such as doctors and lawyers?

Public Perceptions

BUILDING
BLOCK
15.9

Review the reasons teachers gave for leaving the profession in the NEA survey summarized in Table 15.2. Which of those reasons can be linked to public perceptions? Do they make up a large or a small percentage of reasons for leaving teaching?

According to *A Sense of Calling* (Farkas, Johnson, & Foleno, 2000), under-30 college graduates hold a high opinion of teachers and teaching. However, even though some of those surveyed would consider teaching as a career, the reasons respondents cited for choosing a different career included low salary, limited opportunities for advancement, and a low public opinion of teachers. How consistent do these reasons seem to be with those cited by teachers who choose to leave the profession in the NEA survey in Table 15.2?

It might seem logical that the more a profession is valued, the larger that profession's salary would be. It seems that everyone—not just people who have chosen to become teachers—is aware that teachers' salaries are not competitive with those of other professionals. In the NEA survey of 2001, low salary was the most frequently cited factor in teachers' decisions to leave the field.

Nonetheless, research conducted by an economics professor at Ohio University for the Thomas B. Fordham Institute indicates that, relative to other comparable professions, teachers are not underpaid (Vedder, 2003). Vedder used information from the Bureau of Labor Statistics and found that, although annual salaries for teachers are lower than those of some other occupations such as accountants, scientists, nurses, editors, and reporters, teacher salaries were about the same when considered as weekly earnings.

Vedder notes that when fringe benefits are factored in, teachers' salaries plus benefits exceed those of other occupations by 10–13% (Vedder, 2003). As you know, teacher salaries typically cover 9-, 10-, or 10.5-month contracts, whereas others work year-round; this fact may affect our perceptions of teacher salaries. But remember that teachers spend a significant amount of time working at home in the evenings and on the weekends. How does this time figure in to Vedder's statistics? How do you feel about teacher salaries considering the Department of Labor statistics and Vedder's propositions?

Although low salaries for teachers are an issue, many teachers believe that increasing salaries will neither improve the quality of entering teachers nor solve the problems associated with teaching. Rather, teachers tend to believe that factors such as smaller class sizes, better-behaved students, motivated colleagues, and supportive administrators would be much stronger incentives to enter the teaching field and stay (Farkas, Johnson, & Foleno, 2000).

Although many teachers pursue advanced degrees, a teacher can enter the classroom with a bachelor's degree. On the other hand, in numerous other professions, students must attend graduate school to receive the credentials that allow them to practice their profession. Consequently, teachers may be seen as less educated than other professionals. However, No Child Left Behind mandates that all teachers be "highly qualified": held to high standards in order to complete programs and to become and remain certified. Teacher education programs require candidates to complete content area courses and courses in pedagogy while maintaining an acceptable grade point average. Some states such as New York require a master's degree for teacher certification. Teachers surveyed for *A Sense of Calling* indicated that they believe that their teacher education programs prepared them well to be successful in the classroom. In particular, they believed that their education gave them strong content area knowledge. School administrators agreed (Farkas, Johnson, & Foleno, 2000).

All states have certification requirements that include passing standardized tests in content area and pedagogical knowledge. All states also require teachers to continue their education in professional development activities. These requirements are similar to those of other professions and show that teaching is a service that does depend on intellectual techniques in its performance.

Specialized Training and Personal Responsibility

Many professions, including teaching, require specialized training. (We always challenge those who refer to teachers as being "trained" to alter their vocabulary when referring to teacher education. Saying that you train your dog is appropriate. But, as constructivists, we believe that our students are capable of more intellectual input and output than a golden retriever, with no disrespect to the dog.)

Students in teacher education programs are usually required to complete many hours of field experience. You may be completing your first field experience in this course, and you probably will have more opportunities for field experiences throughout your teacher education program. The field experiences, sometimes known as *clinical* experiences, extend preservice teachers' classroom-based education to actual teaching situations, providing highly specialized training.

How do the field experiences required of teacher education candidates compare with the clinical requirements of other professions, such as doctors, lawyers, and engineers?

Although we seem to get mixed messages about the public's regard for teachers and teaching, there is certainly no doubt that the public holds teachers responsible for student achievement. This accountability is understandable; interactions between the teacher and the student make up most of the school day. You have investigated teacher accountability elsewhere in this text. How does the concept of accountability relate to Lieberman's characteristic of a profession that includes the acceptance of personal responsibility for decisions and actions?

The Service Is More Valuable than the Economic Gain

It is clear that the service component of Lieberman's conception of a profession applies to teaching. As stated earlier, many teachers would prefer smaller classes, more administrative support, and better motivated colleagues over more money.

Teachers believe that their service is worth more than their personal economic gain. Recall that the primary motive most often cited for teaching is the opportunity to make a difference in young people's lives. Passion for their work drives teachers to continue learning, create classroom environments conducive to learning, develop effective lessons, reflect, and participate in professional development.

Of course there is value in the service of teaching. The intangible rewards—the joy of relationships with students, the knowledge of making a difference in students' lives—keep teachers in their classrooms. Perhaps this is why some teachers choose to leave the classroom for the same issues they were aware of even before they entered the profession. These teachers may have found that, for them, such intangible rewards do not sufficiently outweigh their perception of low salaries, unsatisfactory working conditions, and low social prestige.

Professional Organizations and Self-Governance

Lieberman's description also posits that professionals have organizational bodies and are primarily self-governing. Such is the case for teachers. Table 15.3 lists some national professional organizations for educators. Remember that there are also regional and state organizations.

You have investigated teacher unions in this text; the two largest are the American Federation of Teachers (AFT) and the NEA. It is clear that there is no shortage of organizations for educators! However, these organizations do not govern the actual act of teaching. As you have seen, for most of the school day, teacher and students interact within the classroom walls, where most decisions are made by the authority in that room: the teacher. However, you have also learned that many individuals, committees, and professional organizations outside of the classroom and the school building exert great influence on teachers. The local school board is an example. Although doctors, lawyers, and even real estate agents are governed by boards of their colleagues and peers (other doctors, lawyers, and agents), school boards are usually not made up of teachers. What are the advantages and disadvantages of this arrangement?

www Direct links to the websites of these organizations are available on the *Building Teachers* companion website.

Positively affecting the lives of young people is a reward of teaching that far outweighs minor challenges.

© Blend Images/Alamy

TABLE 15.3 Professional Organizations for Teachers

Discipline	Organization
Art education	National Art Education Association
Early childhood education	Association for Childhood Education International National Association for the Education of Young Children National Center for Montessori Education
English, language arts, and reading education	American Library Association International Reading Association National Council of Teachers of English
Foreign language education and teaching English to speakers of other languages	American Council on the Teaching of Foreign Languages Teachers of English to Speakers of Other Languages, Inc.
Mathematics education	National Council of Teachers of Mathematics School Science and Mathematics Association
Music education	Association for Technology in Music Instruction National Association for Music Education
Science education	American Association of Physics Teachers National Association of Biology Teachers National Science Teachers Association School Science and Mathematics Association
Social studies education	National Council for the Social Studies
Special needs and gifted education	Council for Exceptional Education National Association for Gifted Children
Physical education	National Association for Sport and Physical Education
Technology education	Association for Career and Technical Education Association for Educational Communications and Technology Computer Assisted Language Instruction Consortium (CALICO) Computer-Using Educators Consortium for School Networking Institute for the Transfer of Technology to Education International Society for Technology in Education International Technology Education Association (ITEA)
Other organizations for teachers	American Association for School Administrators American Counseling Association American Educational Research Association American Federation of Teachers American School Counselors Association Association for Supervision and Curriculum Development National Association of Elementary School Principals National Association of Independent Schools National Education Association National Middle School Association National School Boards Association National Staff Development Council

Technology & Education

The list of professional organizations for educators in Table 15.4 includes organizations that focus on the use of technology. Throughout this text you have read that teachers can and should use technology for instruction and classroom management. To be a professional, you should remain current in your technological knowledge and skills. And, obviously, teachers must work to do so, because technology advances so rapidly.

As you gain experience as a teacher, explore opportunities to learn more about technology and integrate it into your classroom. Take advantage of the information offered by organizations such as those listed in Table 15.4. In addition, several other resources are available to help you increase your level of expertise in instructional technology. Some examples are:

- Center for Applied Special Technology (CAST): CAST is a nonprofit organization that works to expand learning opportunities for all individuals, especially those with disabilities, through the research and development of innovative, technology-based educational resources and strategies.
- Center for Children and Technology (CCT): The CCT is a part of the Education Development Center, an international nonprofit organization. The CCT investigates the use of technology to improve teaching and learning. It also designs and develops technological applications that support engaged, active learning in formal and informal settings.
- Center for Technology in Learning (CTL): The CTL is part of a large research group called SRI International. The CTL's mission is to explore the use of technology to improve teaching, learning, and assessment through inquiry and innovation. In research and development, this organization focuses on the interactive environments of classrooms and teacher education programs.

Code of Ethics

As in other professions, professional organizations for educators have standards that govern members' conduct and behavior, called codes of ethics. State departments of education also have codes of ethics for teachers. You investigated codes of ethics for educators in Chapter 9. Teachers are expected to adhere to a code of ethics, so that when questions arise about appropriate behavior and actions, the code of ethics can help a teacher make the best choices. Ethical breaches can cause teachers to lose their jobs. Such breaches may even make local or national news. Teaching certainly fulfills Lieberman's criterion of having a professional code of ethics.

 Direct links to the websites of these technology oranizations are available on the *Building Teachers* companion website.

Your Chosen Profession

So far in this chapter, you have considered your motives for teaching in the context of your self, the students, the school, and society. You have seen that it is not completely clear whether teaching can be called a profession. Most individuals who choose or consider teaching as a career probably believe that teaching is a profession. But others in society may not be so sure. What can you do to raise the prestige of teachers and teaching?

One obvious answer is that if you want to be perceived as a professional, you must act like one. You looked at some elements of professionalism in Chapter 9. Your teacher education program has professionalism components on which you will be evaluated. What are these components?

Professionalism

BUILDING
BLOCK
15.10

If your professor told you that he or she would be keeping tabs on your professional behavior, what do you suppose he or she would look for? How does the professionalism you display on campus provide insight into how you would behave in field experiences and as a new teacher? What are some instances of professional behavior that you would be sure to do in schools as a field experience student, a student teacher, or a new teacher, but that might *not* be as important for you as a college student?

In which professional behaviors do you have the opportunity to demonstrate proficiency as a student teacher or in your field experience?

Factors such as tardiness, poor communication or collaboration with the cooperating teacher or college supervisor, inappropriate attire, inappropriate interactions with students, lack of preparation, and breaches of confidentiality are behaviors that warrant remediation. From the moment you complete your introductory education course and move on to other education courses, your professionalism is being scrutinized. Is this appropriate and fair? How does knowing about this scrutiny influence your thoughts about whether or not teaching is a profession?

After you have attained your first teaching position, of course you will continue to model professionalism. Not only will your behavior be observed by your colleagues and administrators, you will also be watched by your students, their parents, and the entire community. Being under the community's watchful eye also has implications for your behavior outside of school. As you have seen, teachers are held to higher standards than others in the community. You investigated elements of professionalism in Chapter 9, but let us extend the concept to the behavior of actual teachers. What might a parent perceive as he or she spots you in a local restaurant enjoying a cocktail with your dinner? What if a student saw you, just after you'd rolled out of bed on a Saturday morning, making an emergency trip to the grocery store for coffee? What if, as you were leaving a local bar, you bumped into parents with whom you had recently had a conference regarding their student's misbehavior in your class? Does it matter? After all, you are an adult. Furthermore, you are not on the job 24 hours a day. We will leave you to ponder these dilemmas. Often, it is hard to reach a definitive answer.

If you want to bolster others' perception of you as a professional, what can you do in your school? Your first two or three years of teaching will be spent polishing your skills, increasing your repertoire, and settling into the culture. Once you become fluent and established, you can consider taking on some leadership roles in your school and your community. As a teacher, you will have the opportunity to be involved in school committees that focus on issues such as textbook adoption, school policy and accreditation reviews, technology plans, and the like. You may also work with students who are involved with athletic teams, the yearbook, school newspaper, extracurricular clubs, or social functions. Choose to participate in these activities. Doing so not only demonstrates your commitment to your profession and to your students, it adds another level of reward to your professional life. (You may sincerely like your students while they are in your class, but wait until you get to know them before and after school! You might discover facets of their personalities that are more interesting, creative, and humorous than the classroom allows.) What extracurricular activities might you be interested in sponsoring as a faculty member? Seek opportunities to volunteer in these activities as you progress in your teacher education program.

You may choose to take on some administrative responsibilities. After you have gained some experience, you may pursue the opportunity to become department chair or team leader. Or you may wish to become a learner support specialist or instructional lead teacher, whose responsibilities extend beyond a department or grade level to the entire school. If you focus your required professional development activities on receiving additional endorsements and certifications in areas such as reading, ESOL, gifted and talented education, and special education, not only will you broaden your professional knowledge and skills, you may also get a pay increase. National Board Certification and graduate degrees also carry benefits and prestige.

Beyond your school building, you can promote excellence in education by being a member of some professional organizations such as those listed in Table 15.4. Select your professional organizations carefully and focus on one or two. Attending the state, regional, or national conference of an organization is a wonderful way to interact with colleagues, exchange ideas, and reinvigorate your motivation. As you gain experience, you may decide to present papers at these conferences, reaching out to a larger audience of educators by sharing your knowledge and experience. You can become more active in your professional organization by volunteering or taking on a leadership role. You can help out at a conference and serve on (or eventually chair) the organization's governing body or service committee. Again, by getting involved, not only do you serve your professional development, you also help to bolster the prestige of the profession itself.

Finally, modeling professionalism in your classroom—by exhibiting professional behavior, taking on leadership roles in your school and professional organization, and participating in lifelong learning—lets you motivate *your* students to become teachers. They will see through you what a challenging, exciting, and rewarding career teaching can be. *You* will be the teacher they mention when they are asked about their motives for becoming teachers.

Your Philosophy of Education . . . Again

Revise your philosophy of education statement to reflect your motives for teaching and the understanding you have gained in this course about teaching and education. Look again at the metaphor you chose for teaching. Do you still agree with it? Should you change it? Write down the metaphor you now believe describes you as a teacher and refer to it throughout your teacher preparation program.

Conclusion

In this chapter, you recalled the motives for teaching you had when you began this course. You considered those motives in the context of the information you have read in this textbook, and you examined whether teaching is a profession—and what you can do to promote it as such.

We mentioned early in this chapter that most introductory education textbooks place the chapter on students' motives for teaching at the very beginning of the book. Considering that this textbook is constructivist-oriented, why do you think this chapter comes at the very end?

What have you concluded about your motives for teaching or not teaching? Can you state one prevailing reason? Should you be able to? Remember the educational philosophy of eclecticism (see Chapter 2). Does it apply to your motives for teaching?

You might think it unusual for the concluding paragraphs of a textbook's last chapter to be so full of questions. Realize that this book, and the class for which you have read it, is actually the very beginning of a complex learning experience: your teacher education program. Knowing what you now know about how a constructivist-oriented lesson begins, does it surprise you that we are asking you more questions?

◼ Construct and Apply

1. Young children often say they want to be teachers when they grow up. Why do you suppose this is? What might their motives be for saying this? In what ways could these motives change as they get older? How might they stay the same?
2. People admire and trust teachers and yet are quick to point the finger of blame at teachers first when test scores drop. How do you explain this seeming contradiction in the public perception of teachers?
3. What are your thoughts regarding teacher salaries? Are teachers underpaid or are they compensated adequately for the time they spend working?
4. Define your opinion on whether or not teaching is a profession, using Lieberman's classic definition of a profession.

◼ Deconstructing the Standards

INTASC Principle 9 says:

> The teacher is a reflective practitioner who continually evaluates the effects of his or her choices and actions on others (students, parents, and other professionals in the learning community) and who actively seeks out opportunities to grow professionally.

INTASC Principle 10 says:

> The teacher fosters relationships with school colleagues, parents, and agencies in the larger community to support students' learning and well-being.

What part(s) of these principles does this chapter address?

How does this chapter address these principles?

How will the concepts in this chapter help you apply these principles as a teacher?

◼ Field Experience

1. What are the expectations about professionalism in your field experience school? How are these expectations communicated to teachers? How is professional behavior monitored? What are the consequences for breaches in professional behavior?
2. What were your cooperating teacher's initial motives for choosing teaching as a career? What are his or her motives for remaining in the profession? For what reason might your cooperating teacher consider leaving the classroom? If he or she is considering leaving, what factors will influence or have influenced this decision?
3. How do the students in your class perceive teaching as a career? Ask them a few questions to discover their thoughts.

◼ Your Portfolio

Keeping your initial philosophy of education statement intact, write another statement that represents any shifts, refinements, or additional thoughts you might have as a result of completing this textbook, your course, and your field experience. Be sure to discuss how these activities have influenced your thinking, thereby demonstrating your ability to reflect.

◼ *Building Teachers* Technology Resources

Access the *Building Teachers* companion website, http://www.education.wadsworth.com/martinloomis1, for more resources and information about the teaching profession.

See video footage of real teachers. Check the *Building Teachers* CD-ROM that may have accompanied your textbook for additional resources.

Also link to InfoTrac College Edition through the *Building Teachers* companion website. Use InfoTrac College Edition to search for articles to enhance your study.

The address, phone number, website, and e-mail address (if available) for the teacher certification office in each state are listed in this Appendix. Use this contact information to find the kinds of teaching certificates issued by each state, the requirements for these certificates, and details of the teacher preparation programs approved by that state.

Alabama
State of Alabama Department of Education
Teacher Education and Certification Office
5201 Gordon Persons Building
PO Box 302101
Montgomery, AL 36130-2101
334-242-9977
E-mail: teached@alsde.edu
http://www.alsde.edu/html/sections/section_detail.asp?section=66

Alaska
State of Alaska Department of Education and Early Development
801 West 10th Street, Suite 200
Juneau, AK 99801-1894
907-465-2831
E-mail: tcwebmail@eed.state.ak.us
http://www.eed.state.ak.us/TeacherCertification/

Arizona
Arizona Department of Education
Certification Unit
PO Box 6490
Phoenix, AZ 85005-6490
602-542-4367
E-mail: Certification@ade.az.gov
http://www.ade.state.az.us/certification/

Arkansas
Office of Professional Licensure
Arkansas Department of Education
#4 State Capitol Mall
Room 106B or Room 107B
Little Rock, AR 72201
501-682-4342
http://arkedu.state.ar.us/teachers/teachers_licensure.html

California

California Commission on Teacher Credentialing
1900 Capitol Avenue
Sacramento, CA 95814
888-921-2682
E-mail: credentials@ctc.ca.gov
http://www.ctc.ca.gov/credentials/default.html

Colorado

Colorado Department of Education
201 East Colfax Avenue
Room 105
Denver, CO 80203
303-866-6628
E-mail: Educator.Licensing@cde.state.co.us
http://www.cde.state.co.us/index_license.htm

Connecticut

Bureau of Educator Preparation, Certification, Support and Assessment
Connecticut State Department of Education
PO Box 150471, Room 243
Hartford, CT 06115-0471
860-713-6969
E-mail: teacher.cert@po.state.ct.us
http://www.state.ct.us/sde/dtl/cert

Delaware

Delaware Department of Education
Licensure/Certification Office
401 Federal Street, Suite 2
Dover, DE 19901
302-739-4686
http://deeds.doe.k12.de.us/

Florida

Florida Department of Education
Bureau of Educator Certification
Suite 201, Turlington Building
325 West Gaines Street
Tallahassee, FL 32399-0400
800-445-6739
http://www.fldoe.org/edcert

Georgia

Georgia Professional Standards Commission
Two Peachtree Street
Suite 6000
Atlanta, GA 30303
404-232-2500
http://www.gapsc.com/

Hawaii
Hawaii Teacher Standards Board
650 Iwilei Road, #201
Honolulu, HI 96817
808-586-2600
E-mail: licensing@htsb.org
http://www.htsb.org/

Idaho
Idaho Department of Education
Teacher Certification
PO Box 83720
Boise, ID 83720-0027
208-332-6880
www.sde.state.ed.us/certification

Illinois
Division of Teacher Certification
James R. Thompson Center
100 West Randolph Street, Suite 14-300
Chicago, IL 60601
312-814-8113
http://www.isbe.net/certification/

Indiana
Indiana Department of Education
Division of Professional Standards
Room 229, State House
Indianapolis, IN 46204-2798
866-542-3672
www.doe.state.in.us/dps

Iowa
State of Iowa Board of Educational Examiners
Licensure
Grimes State Office Building
Des Moines, IA 50319-0146
515-281-3245
http://www.state.ia.us/boee/

Kansas
Teacher Education and Licensure
Kansas State Department of Education
120 SE 10th Avenue
Topeka, KS 66612-1182
785-291-3678
http://www.ksbe.state.ks.us/cert/cert

Kentucky
Education Professional Standards Board
100 Airport Road, 3rd Floor
Frankfort, KY 40601
502-564-4606
E-mail: dcert@ky.gov
http://www.kyepsb.net

Louisiana
Louisiana Department of Education
Division of Teacher Certification and Higher Education
PO Box 94064
Baton Rouge, LA 70804-9064
225-342-3490
E-mail: customerservice@la.gov
http://www.doe.state.la.us/lde/tsac/home.html

Maine
State of Maine Department of Education
Certification Office
23 State House Station
Augusta ME 04333-0023
207-624-6603
http://www.maine.gov/education/cert/index.html

Maryland
Maryland State Department of Education
Certification Branch
200 W. Baltimore Street
Baltimore, MD 21201
410-767-0412
http://www.marylandpublicschools.org/MSDE/divisions/certification/

Massachusetts
Massachusetts Department of Education
Office of Educator Licensure
350 Main Street
Malden, MA 02148
781-338-3000
http://www.doe.mass.edu/educators/e_becoming.html

Michigan
Michigan Department of Education
Office of Professional Preparation Services
Michigan Department of Education
608 W. Allegan Street
Lansing, MI 48909
517-373-3324
http://www.michigan.gov/mde/

Minnesota
Minnesota Department of Education
Educator Licensing and Teacher Quality
1500 Highway 36 West
Roseville, MN 55113-4266
651-582-8200
E-mail: mde.educator-licensing@state.mn.us
http://education.state.mn.us/mde/Teacher_Support/Educator_Licensing/index.html

Mississippi
Mississippi Department of Education
Office of Educator Licensure
359 North West Street
PO Box 771
Jackson, MS 39205-0771
601-359-3483
http://www.mde.k12.ms.us/ed_licensure/

Missouri
Missouri Department of Elementary and Secondary Education
Educator Certification
PO Box 480
Jefferson City, MO 65102
573-751-0051
E-mail: webreplyteachcert@dese.mo.gov
http://www.dese.mo.gov/divteachqual/teachcert

Montana
Montana Office of Public Instruction
Educator Licensure
PO Box 202501
Helena, MT 59620-2501
406-444-3150
http://www.opi.state.mt.us/cert/index.html

Nebraska
Nebraska Department of Education
301 Centennial Mall South
PO Box 94987
Lincoln, NE 68509
402-471-0739
E-mail: tcertweb@nde.state.ne.us
http://www.nde.state.ne.us/TCERT

Nevada
Nevada Department of Education
Teacher Licensing Office
1820 East Sahara Avenue, Suite 205
Las Vegas, NV 89104
702-486-6458
E-mail: license@doe.nv.gov
http://www.doe.nv.gov/licensing.html

New Hampshire
New Hampshire Department of Education
Bureau of Credentialing
101 Pleasant Street
Concord, NH 03301-3860
603-271-2407
www.ed.state.nh.us

New Jersey
New Jersey State Department of Education
Office of Licensure and Credentials
PO Box 500
Trenton, NJ 08625-0500
609-292-2070
http://www.nj.gov/njded/educators/license/

New Mexico
New Mexico Public Education Department
Professional Licensure Bureau
300 Don Gaspar
Santa Fe, NM 87501-2786
505-827-5800
E-mail: license@ped.state.nm.us
www.ped.state.nm.us

New York
New York State Education Department
Certification Unit
5N Education Building
Albany, New York 12234
518-474-3901
E-mail: tcert@mail.nysed.gov
http://www.highered.nysed.gov/tcert

North Carolina
North Carolina State Board of Education
Department of Public Instruction
301 N. Wilmington Street
Raleigh, NC 27601
919-807-3300
http://www.dpi.state.nc.us/employment/

North Dakota
North Dakota Education Standards and Practices Board
2718 Gateway Avenue, Suite 303
Bismarck, ND 58503-0585
701-328-9641
E-mail: espbinfo@state.nd.us
http://www.nd.gov/espb/licensure/

Ohio
Ohio Department of Education
Office of Certification/Licensure
25 South Front Street, Mail Stop 105
Columbus, Ohio 43215-4183
614-466-3593
http://www.ode.state.oh.us/Teaching-Profession/Teacher/Certification_Licensure/

Oklahoma
Oklahoma State Department of Education
Professional Standards Section
2500 North Lincoln Boulevard, #212
Oklahoma City, OK 73105-4599
405-521-3337
http://www.sde.state.ok.us/pro/tcert/profstd.html

Oregon
Oregon Teacher Standards and Practices Commission
465 Commercial Street NE
Salem, OR 97301
503-378-3586
http://www.tspc.state.or.us/

Pennsylvania
Bureau of Teacher Certification and Preparation
Pennsylvania Department of Education
333 Market Street
Harrisburg, PA 17126-0333
717-787-3356
E-mail: ra-teachercert@state.pa.us
http://www.teaching.state.pa.us/teaching

Rhode Island
Rhode Island Department of Elementary and Secondary Education
Office of Teacher Preparation, Certification, and Professional Development
Rhode Island Department of Education
Office of Teacher Certification
255 Westminster Street
Providence, RI 02903-3400
401-222-4600
http://www.ridoe.net/Certification_PD/

South Carolina
South Carolina Department of Education
Division of Educator Quality and Leadership
Landmark II Office Building
3700 Forest Drive, Suite 500
Columbia, SC 29204
803-734-8466
E-mail: certification@scteachers.org
http://www.scteachers.org/

South Dakota
South Dakota Department of Education
Office of Accreditation and Teacher Quality
700 Governors Drive
Pierre, SD 57501
605-773-3134
E-mail: certification@state.sd.us
http://doe.sd.gov/oatq/

Tennessee
Office of Teacher Licensing
Tennessee Department of Education
4th Floor, Andrew Johnson Tower
710 James Robertson Parkway
Nashville, TN 37243-0377
615-532-4885
E-mail: Education.Licensing@state.tn.us
http://www.state.tn.us/education/lic

Texas
Texas Education Agency
Educator Certification and Standards
1701 North Congress Avenue, WBT 5-100
Austin, TX 78701-1494
512-936-8400
http://www.sbec.state.tx.us/SBECOnline

Utah
Utah State Office of Education
Educator Licensing
250 East 500 South
PO Box 144200
Salt Lake City, UT 84114-4200
801-538-7740
http://www.usoe.k12.ut.us/cert/

Vermont
Vermont Department of Education
Licensing Office
120 State Street
Montpelier, VT 05620-2501
802-828-2445
E-mail: licensinginfo@education.state.vt.us
http://www.state.vt.us/educ/new/html/maincert.html

Virginia
Virginia Department of Education
Division of Teacher Education and Licensure
PO Box 2120
Richmond, VA 23218-2120
800-292-3820
http://www.pen.k12.va.us/VDOE/newvdoe/teached.html

Washington
Office of Superintendent of Public Instruction
Old Capitol Building
PO Box 47200
Olympia, WA 98504-7200
360-725-6400
E-mail: cert@ospi.wednet.edu
http://www.k12.wa.us/certification

West Virginia
West Virginia Department of Education
Office of Professional Preparation
Building 6, Room 252
1900 Kanawha Boulevard East
Charleston, WV 25305
800-982-2378
E-mail: mfmiller@access.k12.wv.us
http://wvde.state.wv.us/certification/

Wisconsin
Teacher Education, Professional Development and Licensing (TEPDL)
Department of Public Instruction
125 S. Webster Street
P.O. Box 7841
Madison, WI 53707-7841
800-441-4563
http://dpi.wi.gov/tepdl/index.html

Wyoming
Professional Teaching Standards Board
1920 Thomes Avenue, Suite 400
Cheyenne, WY 82001
307-777-7291
http://ptsb.state.wy.us/

GLOSSARY

Academic freedom The freedom of teachers and students to express their ideas in school without religious, political, or institutional restrictions.

Accreditation The formal, official approval signifying that the requirements of excellence described in professional standards developed by professionals in a particular discipline have been met.

Aesthetic Creatively, beautifully, or artistically pleasing.

AIDS Acquired Immune Deficiency Syndrome, a viral infection caused by the human immunodeficiency virus (HIV) that gradually destroys the immune system.

Anthropology The branch of metaphysics in philosophy concerned with the nature of humans.

At-risk student A student considered at high risk for failing to complete high school.

Authentic assessment Education tasks that resemble the real-world applications of the skills and knowledge being assessed.

Axiology The branch of philosophy concerned with values.

Behaviorism The psychological approach that explains behavior by examining external experiences.

Bell-shaped curve See **normal curve.**

Bilingual education Instruction provided in both a student's native language and in English.

Block scheduling A scheduling system in which a school's daily schedule is organized into large blocks of time.

Brown v. Board of Education of Topeka U.S. Supreme Court decision in 1954 that required schools in the United States to desegregate.

Carnegie unit Unit of credit awarded to students for the completion of a full year's work in a subject taught 4 or 5 times a week.

Case law A law that is the result of decisions made by the courts.

Childhood obesity A condition of children being overweight.

Classical conditioning A form of learning in which an organism learns to associate a stimulus with a nonrelated response.

Code of ethics A guide to acceptable professional behavior.

Cognitive ability The ability to learn, know, and understand.

Cognitive development The intellectual development of the mind.

Cognitive needs Those needs associated with learning, knowing, and understanding.

Cognitive psychology The psychological approach that explains behavior by examining mental processes.

Common school Elementary school in the 19th century that was free and public.

Compulsory attendance laws Laws requiring children to attend school for specific periods of time.

Conservation With regard to cognitive development, the ability to recognize that the amount of material does not change when volume or shape changes.

Constitutional law A law based on the U.S. Constitution or a state constitution.

Constructivism A learning theory that proposes that students construct their own knowledge by combining information they already have with new information, so that new knowledge takes on personal meaning to the student.

Contract An agreement with specific terms between two or more persons or entities in which there is a promise to do something in return for a valuable benefit.

Cooperative teaching A method of distributing teaching responsibilities in elementary schools such that teachers assume responsibility for their areas of expertise.

Copyright The exclusive right of the author or creator of a literary or artistic property (such as a book, movie, or musical composition) to print, copy, sell, license, distribute, transform to another medium, translate, record, perform, or otherwise use (or not use) their work, and to give it to another by will.

Corporal punishment The infliction of physical pain on someone as punishment for committing an offense.

Correlation The mutual relationship between or among variables.

Cosmology The branch of metaphysics in philosophy concerned with the origin and structure of the universe.

Culture The customary beliefs, social forms, and material traits of a racial, religious, or social group.

Dame schools Colonial school for girls.

Deductive reasoning The type of reasoning that proceeds from the most general to the most specific.

Defamation Making untrue statements about another that damage his or her reputation.

Deficiency needs In Maslow's hierarchy of needs, those needs that are critical to a person's well being and that must be satisfied first and foremost. These include physiological needs, safety and security, love and belonging, and self-worth and self-esteem.

Differentiated instruction Instruction that is tailored to the different needs of individual students.

Digital divide Disparity in access to computers and the Internet among different groups of people.

Diversity The condition of being different from one another.

Due process A person's legal right to be adequately notified of charges or proceedings involving him or her and to be given the opportunity to be heard.

Dyslexia A learning disability in which an individual has difficulty with reading comprehension and writing.

Empathetic Having understanding of or participating in someone else's feelings or ideas.

English language learner A person learning to speak English whose primary language is other than English.

Epistemology The study of knowledge.

Ethnicity Affiliation with a group that has general customs, language, and social views and based on common racial, national, tribal, religious, linguistic, or cultural origin or background.

Exceptional students Students who require some form of modification to the standard educational program.

Fair use provision of the copyright act The use of copyrighted materials determined to be fair and not an infringement of the copyright act based on four factors: (1) whether the use is commercial in nature or for nonprofit educational purposes; (2) the nature of the copyrighted work; (3) the portion used in relation to the copyrighted work as a whole; and (4) the effect of the use on the potential market value of the copyrighted work.

Family structure The related or unrelated persons who share living arrangements.

FERPA The Family Education Rights and Privacy Act of 1974 (FERPA), a federal law that protects the privacy of student education records and requires institutions to adhere strictly to the guidelines governing students' rights regarding the release of student records.

Field dependence/field independence A characteristic related to an individual's ability to recognize camouflaged information.

Fighting words Words intentionally directed toward another person that are so nasty and full of malice as to cause the hearer to suffer emotional distress or incite him or her to retaliate physically (hit, stab, shoot, etc.).

Foreign-born In the United States, a person who was born in a country other than the United States.

Freedom of expression The liberty to speak and otherwise express oneself and one's opinions, guaranteed by the First Amendment to the U.S. Constitution.

Freedom of religion The right to choose a religion (or no religion) without interference by the government, guaranteed by the First Amendment to the U.S. Constitution.

Funding equality An education funding principle by which schools receive the same amount of funding, based on the size of their student populations.

Funding equity An education funding principle by which schools with the greatest need receive the greatest amount of funding.

GI Bill A federal act that provides funds to returning war veterans to attend college.

Gifted and talented student A student who has potentially outstanding abilities that allow him or her to excel in one or more areas of intellectual endeavor, creativity, leadership, and artistic pursuits.

Governance How an organization is controlled, including who has the authority to exercise this control.

Growth needs In Maslow's hierarchy of needs, the upper three levels of needs, which humans will try to satisfy after their **deficiency needs** have been met. These levels include the need to know and understand, aesthetic needs, and the need for self-actualization.

Hierarchy An order of rank.

Higher Education Act A federal program that provides grants and loans to students in college (often in the form of Pell grants).

Hornbook A single-faced wooden paddle used to teach reading in colonial times.

Humanism The psychological approach that stresses people's capacity and desire for personal growth.

In loco parentis "In place of parents."

Inclusion The practice of assigning students with below normal or above normal IQs or disabling conditions to the same classrooms they would attend if they were not disabled.

Inductive reasoning The type of reasoning that proceeds from the most specific to the most general.

Information processing A cognitive psychology that explains learning by manipulation of sensory register, short-term memory, and long-term memory.

Instructional duties Teacher duties directly associated with planning, instruction, and evaluation.

Instructional lead teacher A teacher whose responsibilities include assisting teachers in developing and implementing strategies to reach all types of learners and whose focus is on aiding teachers.

Integrated curriculum A curriculum organized around themes, problems, and issues, without regard for subject-area boundaries.

Interactionist approach An approach to reading and writing instruction that combines phonics and whole-language teaching methodologies.

Interdisciplinarianism A curriculum design that includes more than one discipline in an area of study.

Interview An assessment method that consists of a structured or open conversation between student and teacher in which the teacher asks questions relating to the objectives of a lesson.

Journal Students' writings, including what they did, what they learned, and their reflections, often used as an element of authentic assessment.

Kindergarten The year preceding first grade in elementary schools.

Latin grammar schools Schools in the New England colonies for upper-class males that taught the subjects necessary for admission to college.

Learner support specialist A teacher whose responsibilities include assisting teachers in developing and implementing strategies to reach all types of learners and whose focus is on aiding individual students.

Learning disability A disorder that interferes with the learning process.

Learning modality See **learning style.**

Learning style An individual's preference about how information is presented and taken in. Learning styles include visual, auditory, and tactile.

Locus of control A characteristic that describes whether an individual attributes responsibility for failure or success to internal or external factors.

Libel Broadcast or written publication of defamation.

Liable (legal liability) A legal responsibility, duty, or obligation; the state of one who is legally bound to do something that may be enforced by legal action.

Library media specialist Professional educator whose specialty includes library science and multimedia management.

Logic The branch of philosophy concerned with reasoning.

Looping A system of assigning students in elementary schools to the same teacher for two or more consecutive years.

Mainstreaming Placing a disabled student in regular school classes.

Massachusetts Act of 1642 An early Massachusetts law that required parents and masters to see that their children know the principles of religion and the laws of the Commonwealth.

Massachusetts Act of 1647 The "Old Deluder Satan Act" that required towns with at least 50 households to hire a schoolmaster to teach children to read and write, and required towns of 100 households or more to have a school that would prepare children to attend Harvard College.

McGuffey Reader Primary reading text in the 19th century.

Metaphysics The branch of philosophy concerned with questions of reality.

Mission A specific goal or task.

Monitorial system Teacher preparation program wherein future teachers received training in the schools they, themselves, attended.

Morrill Act of 1862 Land Grant College Act that gave land to states to develop colleges.

Multiage education A system of clustering students of different ages in elementary schools in the same class.

Multiple intelligences theory A proposition by Howard Gardner asserting that traditional measures of intelligence are limited and that individuals possess different types of intelligences. These intelligences include spatial, bodily–kinesthetic, musical, linguistic, logical–mathematical, interpersonal, intrapersonal, and naturalistic intelligences.

National Assessment of Education Progress (NAEP) The "Nation's Report Card," an annual assessment of the achievement of public school students in elementary, middle, and high schools in science, mathematics, and reading.

New England Primer A small book used to teach reading in the New England colonies.

New math A mathematics program in which students were taught the theoretical basis of mathematics through the use of actual mathematical language and notations.

Noninstructional duties Teacher duties not directly associated with instruction of students.

Normal curve The symmetrical, bell-shaped curve of a **normal distribution.**

Normal distribution The distribution of a large number of cases of a given variable, such as intelligence.

Normal schools Schools in the late 19th and early 20th century for the preparation of elementary school teachers.

Ontology The branch of metaphysics concerned with the nature of being and reality.

Operant conditioning An approach to learning in which the consequences of a behavior produce changes in the likelihood that the behavior will occur again.

Paper-and-pencil test A multiple-choice test or other assessment that requires short written responses.

Paraprofessional Teacher aide.

Pedagogy The art and science of teaching.

Perception A mental image of what one experiences.

Plagiarism Representing the writings, literary concepts (a plot, characters, words), or other original work of another as one's own product.

Portfolio An authentic assessment method consisting of a container or folio of evidence that shows a student's progress toward achieving the knowledge and skills of a subject.

Poverty The state of lacking a usual or socially acceptable amount of money or material possessions.

Procedural due process A form of due process that ensures that specific legal procedures are followed to ensure fair treatment of students.

Professionalism The ethical behavior exhibited by teachers.

Project Head Start A federal program that funds preschools for children from families of poverty.

Psychosocial development Development of psychological and social factors within an individual.

Race A group of people that possesses traits that are inherited and sufficient to characterize the group as a distinct human type.

Regulation A rule that is enacted by a state or local agency to ensure compliance with the law.

Risky behavior Behavior that may result in adverse consequences.

Rural Pertaining to the countryside rather than the city.

Schemata (sg. *schema***)** Cognitive structures.

School choice The ability to select a school other than the one to which a student has been assigned by his or her school district.

School improvement plan A plan that identifies a school's priorities for the coming years, methods to implement these priorities, and ways to assess the results.

Search and seizure Examination of a person's premises by law enforcement officers looking for evidence of the commission of a crime, and taking articles of evidence (seizure and removal).

Secondary Education Act A federal act that provides federal guidance and funds to school districts with large numbers of disadvantaged students.

Self-actualization The state of having become everything a person is capable of becoming, realizing one's full potential, capacities, and talents.

Sexual orientation An individual's primary physical and/or emotional attraction to others of the opposite or same gender, or to both.

Sexually transmitted disease A disease transmitted largely through sexual behavior.

Site-based management A system of management in which plans and decisions involve all employees in a site.

Slander Oral or spoken **defamation.**

Society A community or group defined by a common set of traditions and goals.

Socioeconomic Involving both social and economic factors.

Socioeconomic status A position influenced by a combination of social and economic factors including income, education, occupation, and place in the community.

Special education Instruction that is specifically designed to meet the unique needs of students who are recognized as exceptional.

Service learning A teaching strategy that engages students in meaningful service to their communities through integration of community issues and the school curriculum.

Stakeholder A person or institution with an interest in education.

Standards movement An educational reform movement in which exemplary performances in specific areas of education are identified, especially in curriculum and instruction and teacher preparation.

Statute A law passed by the federal, state, or local legislature.

Stereotype A standard image or idea that represents an uninformed opinion or biased attitude toward a group.

Student of color A person of any non-Caucasian race, including black, Hispanic, Asian, and Native American.

Student–teacher ratio The average number of students assigned to one teacher.

Substantive due process A limited form of due process in which a valid reason must be demonstrated to justify restrictions to a student's rights; the way those rights are restricted must be reasonable.

Suburban Pertaining to a community on the outskirts of a larger town or city.

Teacher certification A state's official recognition that a person has met the requirements to be a professional teacher in that state.

Tenure A teacher's status as a permanent member of the faculty in a school district.

Theology The branch of metaphysics in philosophy concerned with God and the relations among God, mankind, and the universe.

Title I A federal program that provides funds to meet the needs of students in high-poverty schools.

Title VII A federal program that provides financial aid for the education of students with limited English ability (also known as the Bilingual Education Act).

Title IX A federal act providing for equal athletic opportunities regardless of gender.

Tort A wrongful act, other than a breach of contract, for which relief may be obtained in the form of damages.

True threats Actions conducted with the intent to intimidate or place the victim in fear of bodily harm or death.

Urban Pertaining to a city.

Vernacular schools Schools in the New England colonies for lower-class males that taught reading, writing, arithmetic, and religion.

Vision A foresight into the possible future of a school.

Whole language A constructivist approach to teaching reading and writing in which students learn from firsthand experiences.

REFERENCES

Direct links to references marked with 🌐 are available on the *Building Teachers* companion website.

Adams, M. J. (1990). *Beginning to read: Thinking and learning about print.* Cambridge, MA: MIT Press.

Adams v. State Professional Practices Council, 406 So.2d 1170 (Fla. App.1981).

Adcock v. Board of Educ. of San Diego Unified School Dist., 10 Cal.3d 60, 109 Cal.Rptr. 676, 513 P.2d 900 (1973).

Adelt v. Richmond School Dist., 250 Cal.App.2d 149, 58 Cal.Rptr. 151 (1967).

🌐 Adherents.com. (2002). Major religions of the world ranked by number of adherents.

Adler, M. J. (1982). *The Paideia proposal.* Old Tappan, NJ: Macmillan.

🌐 The African American Registry. (n.d.). *The African Free School opens.*

Ahmed, Y., & Smith, P. (1994). Bullying in schools and the issue of sex differences. In J. Archer (Ed.), *Male Violence* (pp. 70–83). London: Routledge.

AIDS Alert. (2005). Teen sexual risk behavior news is both good and bad: Experts promote comprehensive education. *AIDS Alert, 20*(3), 32–34.

🌐 Albright, L. (2005, July 23). Jeb plays games with Florida class size. *People's Weekly World.*

Alderfer, C. (1972). *Existence, relatedness, & growth.* New York: Free Press.

Alvin Independent School District v. Cooper, 404 S.W. 2d 76 (Tex. 1966).

Amato, P. R. (2001). Children of divorce in the 1990s: An update of the Amato and Keith (1991) meta-analysis. *Journal of Family Psychology, 15*(3), 355–370.

American Association of University Women. (1992). *The AAUW report: How schools shortchange girls.* Washington, DC: AAUW Educational Foundation.

🌐 American Association of University Women. (2001). *Hostile hallways: Bullying, teasing, and sexual harassment in school.* Washington, DC: Author.

🌐 American Civil Liberties Union. (2000). *ACLU of Georgia represents student suspended from school for carrying "Tweety Bird" key chain.*

🌐 American Civil Liberties Union. (2003). A question of innocence.

🌐 American Federation of Teachers. (2005). Who we are.

🌐 American Obesity Association. (2002). *Fact sheet: Obesity in youth.*

American Psychological Association Board of Educational Affairs. (1997). *Learner-centered psychological principles: A framework for school redesign and reform.* Washington, DC: American Psychological Association.

🌐 American School Counselor Association. (2005). *Helping children overcome test anxiety.*

🌐 Anderson, D. J. (2003, September 27). *The historical context for understanding the test score gap.* Paper presented at Race, Culture, Identity, and Achievement lecture series, Wheelock College, Boston, MA.

Anderson, R. H. (1966). *Teaching in a world of change*. New York: Harcourt, Brace, & World.

Archibald, G. (2005). Utah set to reject No Child Left Behind. *The Washington Times*.

Arlington Public Schools. (2004). ESOL/HILT here at Long Branch. In *ESOL/HILT*.

Ausubel, D. P., Novak, J. D., & Hanesian, H. (1978). *Educational psychology: A cognitive view* (2nd ed.). New York: Holt, Rinehart and Winston.

Avery v. Homewood City Bd. of Educ., 674 F.2d 337 (5th Cir. 1982), cert. den. 461 U.S. 493, 103 S.Ct. 2119, 77 L.Ed.2d 100 (1983).

Ballou, D., Brewen, D. J., Finn, Jr., C. E., Goldhaber, D. D., Hickock, E. W., Kanstroroom, M., Kwiatkowski, M., Palmaffy, T., Podgursky, M., Poliakoff, M. B., Schaefer, N., Stone, J. E., Strauss, R. P., & Wilcox, D. D. (1999). *Better teachers for better schools*. Washington, DC: Thomas B. Fordham Foundation.

Bandler, R., and Grinda, J. (1979). *Frogs into princes: Neuro linguistic programming*. Moab, UT: Real People Press.

Banks, J. A., Cookson, P., Gay, G., Hawley, W. D., Irvine, J. J., Nieto, S., Schofield, J. W., & Stephan, W. G. (2001). Diversity within unity: Essential principles for teaching and learning on a multicultural society. *Phi Delta Kappan, 83*(3), 196–203.

Barrett, D. B., Kurian, G. T., & Johnson, T. M. (Eds.). (2001). *World Christian encyclopedia: A comparative survey of churches and religions in the modern world* (2nd ed.). Oxford, U.K.: Oxford University Press.

Batsche, G., & Knopff, H. (1994). Bullies and their victims: Understanding a pervasive problem in the schools. *School Psychology Review, 23*(2), 165–174.

Baum, S. (2003). College financial aid. In J. W. Guthrie (Ed.), *Encyclopedia of education* (2nd ed.), pp. 376–378. New York: Macmillan Reference USA.

Bay v. State Bd. of Educ. 378 P.2d 558 561.

Beane, J. A. (1997). *Curriculum integration: Designing the core of democratic education*. New York: Teachers College Press.

Berger, S. (1998). *College planning for gifted students* (2nd ed.). Arlington, VA: Council for Exceptional Children.

Berliner, D. C. (1985). Effective classroom teaching: The necessary but not sufficient condition for developing exemplary schools. In G. R. Austin & H. Barber (Eds.), *Research on exemplary schools*. Orlando, FL: Academic Press.

Berliner, D. C. (2005, May 15). Our impoverished view of educational reform. *Teachers College Record*. ID Number 12106.

Berliner, D. C. (2005, August 2). Our impoverished view of educational reform. *Teachers College Record*. ID Number 12106.

Bethel Park School District v. Drall, 67 Ps. Cmwith. 143, 445A 2d 1377 (1982).

Bethel School Dist. No. 403 v. Fraser, 478 U.S. 675, 106 S.Ct. 3159, 92 L.Ed.2d 549 (1986). (Case No. 117).

Bhanpuri, H., & Reynolds, G. M. (2003). *Understanding and addressing the issue of the high school dropout age*. Naperville, IL: Learning Point Associates.

Binder, F. M. (1974). *The age of the common school, 1830–1865*. New York: John Wiley & Sons.

Blackwell v. Issaquena County Bd. of Educ., 363 F.2d 749 (5th Cir. 1966).

Block, M. K., Franciosi, R. J., & Geiger, M. (2002). *What do college students know? A survey of Arizona universities*.

Bluenstein, J. (2001). *Creating emotionally safe schools*. Deerfield Beach, FL: Health Communication.

Blum, D. (1999, July). What's the difference between boys and girls? A funny thing happened when we left "puppy dogs' tails" and "sugar and spice" behind. Scientists discovered that it's not just our culture that makes rules about gender-appropriate behavior—it's our own body chemistry. *Life, 22*(8), 44.

Blunt v. Marion County School Board, 515 F.2d 951 (5th Cir. 1975).

Board of Education v. Earls, 122 S. Ct. 2559 (2002).

Boehner, J. (Chairman). (2003). Press release: House approves bills to help states put a qualified teacher in every classroom. *News from the Committee on Education and the Workforce.*

Bou Jaoudi, S. (2000). Conceptions of science teaching revealed by metaphors and by answers to open-ended questions. *Journal of Science Teacher Education, 11*(2), 173–186.

Bouchard, Jr., M. L. (1998). *Building Teacher-Student Solidarity in a More Democratic Classroom.* Capstone project for partial fulfillment of the Masters of Arts in Education degree at Hamline University, St. Paul, MN.

Boudreaux, G. (1993). *Louis Sullivan: The growth of an idea.*

Bowerman, Margaret. (2005, May). Successful strategies for meeting the needs of diverse learners. *THE Journal Online, 32*(10).

Bradford, M. (2005). Motivating students through project-based service learning. *THE Journal, 32*(6), 29–31.

Brandt, R., & Voke, H. (2002). A lexicon of learning: What educators mean when they say . . . . Association for Supervision and Curriculum Development.

Branigin, W., and Lane, C. (2004). Supreme court dismisses pledge case on technicality. *Washingtonpost.com.*

Brewster, C., & Railsback, J. (2001). *Schoolwide prevention of bullying.* Washington, DC: Office of Educational Research and Improvement.

Brookover, W., Beady, C., Flood, P., Schweister, J., & Wisebaker, J. (1979). *School social systems and student achievement.* New York: Praeger.

Brooks, D.M. (1985). The first day of school. *Educational Leadership, 42*(8), 76–79.

Brooks, J. G., & Brooks, M. G. (1999). *In search of understanding: The case for constructivist teaching.* Alexandria, VA: Association for Supervision and Curriculum Development.

Brooks-Gunn, J., Klebanov, P., and Duncan, G. (1994). Economic deprivation and early-childhood development. *Child Development, 65*(2), 25.

Brown v. Board of Education, 347 U.S. 483 (1954).

Bruner, J. S. (1965). *The process of education.* Cambridge, MA: Harvard University Press.

Bush, G. W. (2004). The essential work of democracy. *Phi Delta Kappan, 86*(2), 114, 118–121.

Bush, G. W. (2005, February). State of the Union address.

California Department of Education. (2005). Year-round education program guide.

Campbell, F. A., & Ramey, C. T. (1995). Cognitive and school outcomes for high-risk African American students at middle adolescence: Positive effects of early intervention. *American Education Association Research Journal, 32*(4), 743–772.

Canady v. Bossier Parish School Board, 250 F.3d 437 (5th Cir. 2002).

Canter, L. (1985). *Assertive discipline.* Santa Monica, CA: Canter and Associates.

Cardman, M. (2002, October 30). GAO: Foundation shaky for for-profit schools' claims. *Education Today, 36*(206), 1–2.

Carey, K. (2004). The funding gap 2004: Many states still shortchange low-income and minority students. Washington, DC: The Education Trust.

Carnegie Council on Adolescent Development. (1989). *Turning points: Preparing American youth for the 21st century: The report of the Task Force on Education of Young Adolescents.* New York: Author.

Carnegie Forum on Education and the Economy. (1986). *A nation prepared: Teachers for the twenty-first century*. New York: Author.

Cartwright, M. (1999). *For the children: Lessons from a visionary principal*. Ardmore, PA: Berger-Cartwright.

CBS News. (2002). Capital punishment reforms urged.

Center for Educational Renewal. (n.d.). *Agenda for education in a democracy*. Seattle: Author.

Centers for Disease Control. (2004, May 21). Youth Risk Behavior Surveillance: United States, 2003. *Morbidity and Mortality Weekly Report, 53*(SS-2).

Chambers, G. (2000, November 16). Distinguished Educator Series Lecture, Bagwell College of Education, Kennesaw State University, Kennesaw, GA.

Chan, S. (1991). *Asian Americans, an interpretive history*. Boston: Twayne.

Charlesworth, R., & Lind, K. K. (2003). *Math and science for young children* (4th ed.). Albany, NY: Delmar Learning.

Checkley, K. (1997). The first seven . . . and the eighth: A conversation with Howard Gardner. *Educational Leadership, 55*(1), 8–13.

Christopherson v. Spring Valley Elementary School, 90 Ill.App.3d 460, 45 Ill. Dec. 866, 413 N.Ed. 2d 199 (1980).

Cirillo v. City of Milwaukee, 34 Wis.2d, 705, 150 N.W.2d 460 (1967).

Claire, H., & Redpath, J. (1989). *Girls' & boys' interactions in primary classrooms*. Ealing Gender Equality Teams Occasional Paper No. 2. London: Elthorne Professional Centre.

Coalition of Essential Schools. (2003). *About the Coalition of Essential Schools*. Oakland, CA: Author.

Coalition of Essential Schools. (2005). *CES national affiliate schools*.

Cohen, R. M. (2002). Schools our teachers deserve: A proposal for teacher-centered reform. *Phi Delta Kappan, 23*(7), 532–537.

Combs, A. (1993, July 19). [Effectiveness of the helping professional]. From a lecture at Kennesaw State University, Kennesaw. GA.

Commercialism in Education Research Unit. (2004). *Profiles of for-profit education management companies, 6th annual report 2003–2004*. Tempe, AZ: Arizona State University.

Commercialism in Education Research Unit. (2005). *CERU Litigation Web Site*.

Cookson, P.W. (1994). *School choice: The struggle for the should of American education*. New Haven, CT: Yale University Press.

Cooper v. Eugene School District No. 4J, 301, Or. 358 (1986), appeal dismissed, 480 U.S. 942 (1987).

Corporation for Public Broadcasting. (2003). *Connected to the future: A report on children's Internet use from the Corporation for Public Broadcasting*.

Costa, A., & Liebman, R. (1995). Process is as important as content. *Educational Leadership, 52*(6), 23–24.

Council for American Private Education. (2004). *Facts and studies*.

Council of State Directors of Programs for the Gifted and National Association for Gifted Children (2001). *State of the states: Gifted and talented education report, 1999–2000*. Washington, DC: National Association for Gifted Children.

Coy, D. (2001). *Bullying*. Washington, DC: Office of Educational Research and Improvement.

Crawford, J. (2002). Obituary: The Bilingual Education Act 1968–2002. *Rethinking Schools Online 16*(4).

Crutcher, C. (1998). Personal communication.

Crutcher, C. (2000). Personal communication.

Culross, R. (n.d.). Gifted and talented: Question and answer by Rita Culross, Ph.D. *Family Education.*

Dagenhart, D. B., O'Connor, K. A., Petty, T. M., & Day, S. D. (2005). Giving teachers a voice. *Kappa Delta Pi Record, 41*(3), 108–111.

Dailey v. Los Angeles Unified School District, 470 P.2d 360 (Cal. 1970).

D.A.R.E. (2005). Media kit.

Darling-Hammond, L. (1994). The purpose of education. From *Reinventing our schools: A conversation with Linda Darling-Hammond* (video transcript).

Darling-Hammond, L. (2000). Teacher quality and student achievement: A review of state policy evidence. *Education Policy Analysis Archives, 8*(1).

Datcher-Loury, L. (1989). Family background and school achievement among low income blacks. *Journal of Human Resources, 24*(3), 528–544. (ERIC Document Reproduction Service No. EJ393255).

Davis, J. R. (1997). *Better teaching, more learning.* Phoenix, AZ: American Council on Education/Oryx Press Series on Higher Education.

Day, J. C. (2001). *National population projections.* Washington, DC: U.S. Census Bureau.

DeAndrade, K. (n.d.). Sexual harassment at school: What every parent should know. *Family education network.*

DeBray, E. H. (2003). Federal education activities [History]. In J. W. Guthrie (Ed.), *Encyclopedia of education* (2nd ed.), pp. 836–840. New York: MacMillan Reference USA.

DeLaire, T., & Kalil, A. (2001). *Good things come in 3's: Single-parent multigenerational family structure and adolescent adjustment.* Chicago: University of Chicago, Harris Graduate School of Public Studies.

Demarest, E. J., Reisner, E. R., Anderson, L. M., Humphrey, D. C., Farquhar, E., & Stein, S. E. (1993). *Review of research on achieving the nation's readiness goal.* Washington, DC: U.S. Department of Education.

DeMichele v. Greenburgh Central School District No. 7, 167 F.3d 784 (2nd Cir. 1999).

DeYoung, A. J. (1995). Constructing and staffing the cultural bridge: The school as change agent in rural Appalachia. *Anthropology & Education Quarterly, 26*(2), 168–192.

Dominy v. Mays, 150 Ga. App. 187, 257 S.Ed. 2d 317 (1979).

Dottin, E. S. (2001). *The development of a conceptual framework.* Lanham, MD: University Press of America.

Dunifon, R., & Kowaleski-Jones, L. (2002). Who's in the house? Race differences in cohabitation, single parenthood, and child development. *Child Development, 73*(4), 1249–1264.

Dunn, R. (1988). Teaching students through their perceptual strengths or preferences. *Journal of Reading, 31*(4), 304–308.

Dunn, R. (1990). Rita Dunn answers questions on learning styles. *Educational Leadership, 48*(2), 15–19.

Dwyer, F. M., & Moore, D. M. (2001). Effect of gender, field dependence and color-coding on student achievement of different educational objectives. *The International Journal of Instructional Media.*

Eakin, S. (2000). Giants of American education. *Technos Quarterly, 9*(2), 1–9.

Ebeling, D. G. (2000). Adapting your teaching to any learning style. *Phi Delta Kappan, 28*(3), 247–248.

Ediger, M. (2001, April). *Assessing for-profit schools.* [Opinion paper]. (ERIC Document Reproduction Service No. ED 458 675).

Ediger, M. (2002, November 11). GAO: For-profit schools claims on shaky foundation: Research inadequate to pass judgment on Edison Schools, others, according to report. *Education USA, 44*(23), 1–2.

Edison Schools (n.d.). *Edison Schools: Philosophic groundings.*

Education Week. (2005). Research center: Vouchers. *Editorial Projects in Education.*

Education Week Research Center. (2005). Stat of the week.

Eisner, E. W. (1983). The art and craft of teaching. *Educational Leadership, 40*(4), 5–13.

Eisner, E. W. (2002). Questionable assumptions about schooling. *Phi Delta Kappan, 84*(9), 648–657.

Erb v. Iowa State Board of Public Instruction, 216 N.W.2d 339 (Sup.Ct. Iowa 1974).

ERIC Clearinghouse on Disabilities and Gifted Education. (1990). *Giftedness and the gifted: What's it all about?* ERIC Digest No. 476. (ERIC Document Reproduction Service No. ED321481).

Erikson, E. H. (1968). *Identity: Youth and crisis.* New York: Norton.

Fagot, B. I., Hagan, R., Leinback M. D., & Kronsberg, S. (1985). Differential reactions to assertive and communicative acts of toddler boys and girls. *Child Development, 56,* 1499–1505.

Farkas, S., Johnson, J., Foleno, T., et al. (2000). *A sense of calling: Who teaches and why.* New York: Public Agenda.

Farris, P. J., Fuhler, C. J., & Walther, M. P. (2004). *Teaching reading: A balanced approach for today's classrooms.* Boston: McGraw-Hill.

Federal Interagency Forum on Child and Family Statistics. (2005). *America's children: Key national indicators of well-being, 2005.* Washington, DC: U.S. Government Printing Office.

Fernald v. City of Ellsworth Superintending School Committee, 342 A.2d 704 (Me.1975).

Financial evolution. (2005). *Education Week, 24*(17), 8–12, 14.

Fink v. Board of Educ. of Warren County School Dist. 65 Pa.Cmwlth. 320, 442 A.2d 837 (1982), app. dism. 460 U.S. 1049, 103 S.Ct. 1493, 75 L.Ed.2d 927 (1983).

Fowler v. Board of Education of Lincoln County 819 F.2d 657 (6th Cir. 1987). Cert.den. 484 U.S. 986 (1987).

Fox v. Board of Education of Doddridge County et al No. 13920. 160 W. Va. 668, 236 (S.E.2d 243 1977). In Deschaine, M. C. (2002). Can a school district assign teachers duties set outside regular classroom instruction? Graduate Student Portfolio. Grand Rapids, MI: Central Michigan University.

Franklin, J. (2001). The diverse challenges of multiculturalism. *Education Update, 43*(2), 1–8.

Franklin, J. (2001). Trying too hard? How accountability and testing are affecting constructivist teaching. *Educational Update, 43*(3), 1, 4–5, 8.

Gage, N. L. (1978). *The scientific basis of the art of teaching.* New York: Teachers College Press.

Gandara, P. (1999). *Review of research on the instruction of limited English proficient students.* University of California Minority Research Institute.

Gardner, A. L., Mason, C. L., & Matyas, M. L. (1989). Equity, excellence, and "just plain good teaching." *The American Biology Teacher, 51*(2), 72–77.

Gardner, H. (2003, April). *Multiple intelligences after twenty years.* Paper presented at the annual conference of the American Educational Research Association, Chicago, IL.

Gargiulo, M. M. (2006). *Special education in contemporary society* (2nd ed.). Belmont, CA: Wadsworth/Thomson Learning.

Gary Teachers Union, Local 4, American Federation of Teachers v. School City of Gary, 165 Ind. App. 314, 332 N.E.2d 256 (1975).

Gault, 387, U.S. 1; 875 S. Ct. 1428; 18 L. Ed. 2d 527 (1967).

Gaus, M. (2000, October 28). ACLU sues Cobb schools over "zero tolerance" policy Tweety Bird flap: Group claims education officials illegally withheld information. *Atlanta Journal and Constitution*, p. G-4.

Georgia ends teacher tenure. (2000). *State Legislatures, 26*(7), 17.

Gersten, R. (1998). The double demands of teaching language-minority students. In R. M. Gersten & R. T. Jiménez (Eds.), *Promoting learning for culturally and linguistically diverse students.* Belmont, CA: Wadsworth Publishing Company.

Gersten, R., Marks, S. U., Keating, T., & Baker, S. (1998). Recent research on effective instructional practice for content-area ESOL. In R. M. Gersten & R. T. Jiménez (Eds.), *Promoting learning for culturally and linguistically diverse students.* Belmont, CA: Wadsworth Publishing Company.

Gillett v. Unified School District No 276, 605 P2d 105 (KS S.Ct, 1980).

Glasser, W. (1993). *The quality school teacher.* New York: Harper Perennial.

Glasser, W. (1998). *Choice theory: A new psychology of personal freedom.* New York: Harper Perennial.

Glover v. Williamsburg Local School District Board of Education 20F.Supp.2d 1160 (Ohio 1998).

Goodlad, J. I. (1984). *A place called school.* New York: McGraw-Hill.

Goodlad, J. I. (1991). *Education renewal: Better teachers, better schools.* San Francisco: Jossey-Bass.

Gorski, P. (2005). *Celebrating the joys of exclusion: The internal undermining of multicultural education.* [working paper.]. St. Paul, MN: EdChange.

Goss v. Lopez, 419 U. S. 565, 95 Ct. 729, 42 L.Ed.2d 725 (1975). (Case No. 127).

Governor proposes class-size reduction plan. (2005). *Education Daily, 38*(93), 5.

Grace, M. (1999). When students create their own curriculum. *Educational Leadership, 57*(3), 49–52.

Gratz, D. G. (2005). Lessons from Denver: The pay for performance pilot. *Phi Delta Kappan, 86*(8), 568–581.

Greene, J. P. (2000). *A survey of results from voucher experiments: Where we are and what we know.* (Civic Report No. 11). The Manhattan Institute for Policy Studies.

Greene, J. P., & Forster, G. (2003). *Vouchers for special education students: An evaluation of Florida's McKay Scholarship Program.* (Civic Report No. 38). The Manhattan Institute for Policy Studies.

Haar, C. K. (1999). *Teacher unions and parental involvement.* Washington, DC: Education Policy Institute.

Hall, J. K. (2000). *Field dependence–independence and computer-based instruction in geography.* (Doctoral dissertation, Virginia Polytechnic Institute and State University, 2000).

Hamilton, L., & Stecher, B. (2004). Responding effectively to test-based accountability. *Phi Delta Kappan, 85*(8), 578–583.

Hanes v. Board of Education of City of Bridgeport, 783 A.2d 1 (Conn. App. Ct. 2001).

Harris v. Mechanicville Central School District, 45 N.Y. 2d 279, 408 N.Y.S. 2d 284 N.E. 2d 213 (1978).

Hearn v. Board of Education, 191 F.3d 1329 (11th Cir. 1999).

Hein, S. (2003). Invalidation. *EQ Informational Site on Emotions, Emotional Intelligence, Teen Suicide, & More.*

Helsep, R. D. (1969). *Thomas Jefferson & education*. New York: Random House.

Hensel, R. A. M. (1989). Mathematical achievement: Equating the sexes. *School and Science and Mathematics*. Newton, MA: Education Development Center, Inc. (ERIC Reproduction Service Document No. EJ407598).

Herek, S. (Director). (1995). *Mr. Holland's opus*. [Motion picture]. United States: Hollywood Pictures.

Hetrick, E. S., & Martin, A. D. (1987). Development issues and their resolution for gay and lesbian adolescents. *Journal of Homosexuality, 14*, 25–43.

Hill, J., & Johnson, F. (2005). Revenues and expenditures for public elementary and secondary education: School year 2002–2003. Washington, DC: National Center for Educational Statistics.

Hirsch, Jr., E. D. (1987). *The dictionary of cultural literacy: What every American needs to know*. New York: Houghton Mifflin.

Hirsch, Jr., E. D. (1988). *Cultural literacy: What every American needs to know*. Madison, WI: Turtleback Books.

Hirsch, Jr., E. D. (1991). *A first dictionary of cultural literacy: What our children need to know*. Madison, WI: Turtleback Books.

Hirsch, Jr., E. D. (1994). *What your third grader needs to know: Fundamentals of a good third-grade education (the Core Knowledge series)*. New York: Dell.

Hirsch, Jr., E. D. (1995). *What your fifth grader needs to know: Fundamentals of a good fifth-grade education (the Core Knowledge series)*. New York: Dell.

Hirsch, Jr., E. D. (1995). *What your sixth grader needs to know: Fundamentals of a good sixth-grade education (the Core Knowledge series)*. New York: Dell.

Hirsch, Jr., E. D. (1997). *What your kindergartner needs to know: Preparing your child for a lifetime of learning (the Core Knowledge series)*. New York: Dell.

Hirsch, Jr., E. D. (1998). *What your first grader needs to know: Fundamentals of a good first-grade education (the Core Knowledge series)*. New York: Dell.

Hirsch, Jr., E. D. (1999). *What your second grader needs to know: Fundamentals of a good second-grade education (the Core Knowledge series)*. New York: Dell.

Hodgkinson, H. L. (1995). What should we call people? Race, class, and the census for 2000. *Phi Delta Kappan, 77*(22), 173–176, 178–179.

Holloway, J. H. (2002). For-profit schools. *Educational Leadership, 59*(7), 84–85.

The Holmes Partnership (n.d.).

Horosko v. Mount Pleasant Township School District, 335 Pa. 369, 6 A.2d 866 (1939), cert. den., 308 U.S. 553 60 S.Ct. 101.

Howard University of Law (2004).

Howard v. Missouri State Board of Education, 913 S.W.2d 887 (Mo. Ct. App. 1996).

Huang, G. (1994). Beyond culture: Communicating with Asian American children and families. ERIC Digest 94 (ED366673).

Humphrey, D. C., & Wechsler, M. E. (2005, September 2). Insights into alternative certification: Initial findings from a national study. *Teachers College Record*.

Hurley, D. (2005, April 19).Divorce rate: It's not as high as you think. *The New York Times*, p. F7.

Hutchins, R. M. (1952). *Great books of the Western world. Encyclopaedia Britannica, Inc., in collaboration with the University of Chicago*. Chicago: W. Benton.

Illig, D. C. (1996). Reducing class size: A review of the literature and options for consideration. Sacramento, CA: California Research Bureau.

Imig, D. G. (2002, April 23). Lecture at Kennesaw State University, Kennesaw, GA.

Ingraham v. Wright, 430 U.S. 651, 97 S.Ct. 1401, 51 L.Ed.3d 711 (1977). (Case No.124).

Insurance Institute of Highway Safety. (2005, March). *Q & A: Teenagers: General*. Statistics from the website.

International Reading Association. (1996). *Standards for the English language arts*.

International Reading Association. (2003). *Standards for reading professionals: Revised 2003*.

Interstate New Teacher Assessment and Support Consortium (1992). *Model standards for beginning teacher licensing, assessment, and development: A resource for state dialogue*.

Irmsher, K. (1996). *Block scheduling*. ERIC Digest, Number 104. (ERIC Document Reproduction Service No. ED-393-156).

Jacobs, H. H. (Ed.). (1989). *Interdisciplinary curriculum: Design and implementation*. Alexandria, VA: Association for Supervision and Curriculum Development.

Jacobson, L. (1999, February 24). Changing versions of childhood. *Education Week, 18*(24), 32–34.

John C. Diehl Elementary School (2004). *About our school*.

Johnson v. Francis Howell R-3 Board of Education, 868 S. S. 2d 191 (Mo. App. E.D.1994).

Johnston, L. D., O'Malley, P. M., Bachman, J. G., & Schulenberg, J. E. (2004, December 21). *Overall teen drug use continues gradual decline; but use of inhalants rises*. Ann Arbor, MI: University of Michigan News and Information Services.

Jones, R. (2005). Head Start study suggests minimal benefits. National Public Radio.

Jones, V. F., & Jones, L. S. (1998). *Classroom management: Creating communities of support and solving problems*. Boston: Allyn & Bacon.

Jones v. Kolbeck, 119 N.J.Super. 299,291 A2d 378 (1972).

Jones v. State, 64 S.W.2d 728, 734 (Ark. 2002).

Kalman, B. (1947). *Early schools*. (The Early Settler Life Series). New York: Crabtree.

Kandel, I. L. (1957). *American education in the twentieth century*. Cambridge, MA: Harvard UP.

Kaplan, G. (1996). Profits r us: Notes on the commercialization of America's schools. *Phi Delta Kappan, 78*(3), 1–12.

Kari v. Jefferson County School District, 852 P.2d 235 (Or. Ct. App. 1993).

Keillor, G. (1996). *Education*.

Kemp, L., & Hall, A. H. (1992). Impact of effective teaching on student achievement and teacher performance: Equity and access implications for quality education. (ERIC Document Reproduction Service No. ED348360).

Kennedy, M. (2001). Creative growth. *American School & University*.

Keyes v. School District No. 1 413 U.S. 189 (1973).

Keyishian v. Board of Regents, 385 U.S. 589 (1967).

Kidwell v. School Dist. No. 300, Whitman County, 53 Wash.2d 672, 335 P. 2d.

Kilpatrick v. Wright 437 F. Supp. 397 (M.D. Ala. 1977).

Kimble v. Wroth County R-III Board of Education, 669 S.W.2d 949 (Mo. Ct. App. 1984).

Kinsella v. Board of Education, 64 A.D.2d 738, 407 N.Y.S.2d 78 (N.Y. App. Div. 1978).

Kirchheimer, S. (2003). Condoms in schools don't boost teen sex. WebMD Medical News.

Kitagawa, M. M. (2000). Profile: The light in her eyes: An interview with Sonia Nieto. *Urbana, 78*(2), 158–164.

Knowles v. Board of Education, 857 P.2d 553 (Colo. Ct. App. 1993).

Knox County Education Association v. Knox County Board of Education 158 F.3d 361 (6th Cir. 1998).

Kohn, A. (2001). Fighting the tests: A practical guide to rescuing our schools. *Phi Delta Kappan, 82*(5), 349–357.

Kosciw, J. G. (2004). *The 2003 National School Climate Survey: The school-related experiences of our nation's lesbian, gay, bisexual and transgender youth.* New York: GLSEN.

Kozol, J. (1991). *Savage inequalities: Children in America's schools.* New York: Harper Perennial.

Kreeger, K. Y. (2002). Yes, biologically speaking, sex does matter: Researchers move beyond the basics to better understand the differences between men and women. *The Scientist, 16*(1), 35–37.

Kreis, S. (2000). John Locke, 1632–1704. *The history guide: Lectures on modern European intellectual history.*

Krupnick, C. (1985, Spring). Women and men in the classroom: Inequality and its remedies. *On Teaching and Learning: Volume 1 Online Document.*

Laborde, G. Z. (1984). *Influencing integrity: Management skills for communication and negotiation.* Palo Alto, CA: Syntony.

Lacks v. Ferguson Reorganized School District R-2, 147 F3d 718 (8th Cir. 1998).

Lanier, J. (1987). From a tape recording of an address to the first Holmes Group conference.

LaRocca v. Board of Educ. of Rye City School Dist., 63 A.D.2d 1019, 406 N.Y.S.2d 348 (1978).

Larson, K. (2002). Commercialism in schools. ERIC Digest. Eugene, OR: ERIC Clearinghouse on Education Management. (ERIC Document Reproduction Service No. ED465194).

Lawson, A. E. (1978). The development and validation of a classroom test of formal reasoning. *Journal of Research in Science Teaching, 15*(1), 11–24.

Lawson, A. E. (1985). A review of research on formal reasoning and science teaching. *Journal of Research in Science Teaching, 19*(3), 233–248.

Learning from the community. (2004). *NEA Today, 23*(1), 59.

Legler, R. (2000). Alternative certification: A review of theory and research. North Central Regional Educational Laboratory.

Lewis, R. (n.d.) Up from slavery: A documentary history of negro education. *ChickenBones. A Journal for Literary & Artistic African-American Themes.*

Lieberman, M. (1956). *Education as a profession.* Englewood Cliffs, NJ: Prentice Hall.

Lilenthal v. San Leandro Unified School Distr., 129 Cal.App.2d 453, 293 P.2d 889 (1956).

Lombardo v. Board of Education of School District No. 27, 100 Ill.App.2d N.E.2d 495 (1968).

Lucas, C. J. (1980). The more things change. *Phi Delta Kappan, 61*(6), 414–416.

MacDonald, M. (2005, April 14). Board rejects after-school idea: Parental permission slip logistics, inconsistencies cited. *Atlanta Journal-Constitution,* p. C1.

Magnuson, S. (2004). Texas schools chief backs off class-size waivers. *Education Daily, 37*(208), 3.

Marshall, P. L. (2002). *Cultural diversity in our schools.* Belmont, CA: Wadsworth/Thomson Learning.

Martin, D. J. (2006). *Elementary science methods: A constructivist approach* (4th ed.). Instructor manual. Belmont, CA: Wadsworth/Thomson Learning.

Maslow, A. (1968). *Toward a psychology of being* (2nd ed.). New York: Van Nostrand Reinhold.

Mathes, E. (1981). Maslow's hierarchy of needs as a guide for living. *Journal of Humanistic Psychology, 21,* 69–72.

Mayhew, D. R., Simpson, H. M., Williams, A. F., & Ferguson, S. A. (1998). Effectiveness and role of driver education and training in a graduated licensing system. *Journal of Public Health Policy, 19*(1), 51–67.

McCabe, Donald. (2005, June). *CAI research: The assessment project.* Durham, NC: The Center for Academic Integrity.

McCambridge, T. R. (1997). *Liberal education and American schooling.* Doctoral dissertation, University of California at Los Angeles.

McDermott, P., & Rothenberg, J. (2000, April). *The characteristics of effective teachers in high poverty schools: Triangulating the data.* Paper for roundtable discussion at the annual meeting of the American Educational Research Association, New Orleans, LA. (ERIC Document Reproduction Service No. ED450353).

McFalls, E. L., & Cobb-Roberts, D. (2001). Reducing resistance to diversity through cognitive dissonance instruction: Implications for teacher education. *Journal of Teacher Education, 52*(2), 164–172.

McKeachie, W. J. (1986). *Teaching Tips* (8th ed.). Lexington, MA: Heath.

McLeod v. State ex. Rel. Colmer, 154 Miss. 468, 122 So. 737 (1929).

Meadow Woods' ESOL students leap into learning. (2002, May 1). *THE Journal Online, 32*(10).

Menendez, R. (Director). (1988). *Stand and deliver.* [Motion picture]. United States: Warner Studios.

Merriam-Webster. (2003). *Merriam-Webster's Collegiate Dictionary* (11th ed.). Springfield, MA: Author.

Merriam-Webster OnLine. (2005).

Miller, R. (1999). *District 1 Old Center School House.*

Miller v. School District, 495 F.2d 76 (1st Cir. 1976).

Miner, B. (2002). For-profits target education. *Rethinking Schools Online.*

Minor, L. C., Onwuegbuzie, A. J., & Witcher, A. E. (2000, November). *Preservice teachers' perceptions of characteristics of effective teachers: A multi-stage mixed methods analysis.* Paper presented at the annual meeting of the Mid-South Educational Research Association, Lexington, KY. (ERIC Document Reproduction Service No. ED454500).

Molnar, A. (2004). *Virtually everywhere: Marketing to children in America's schools. The Seventh Annual Report on Schoolhouse Commercialism Trends: 2003–2004.* Tempe, AZ: Arizona State University.

Morbidity and Mortality Weekly Report. (2005, February 4). Quick stats: Pregnancy, birth, and abortion rates for teenagers aged 15–17 years—United States, 1976–2003. *CDC 54*(04), 100.

Morris v. Douglas County School Dist. N. 9, 241 Or. 23, 403 P.2d 775 (1965).

Moser v. State Bd. of Educ. 22 Cal.App.3d 988, 101 Cal.Rptr. 86 (1972).

Mount Healthy v. Doyle, 429 U.S. 274, 97 S.Ct. 568 (1977).

Mullis, I. V. S., Martin, M. O., Gonzales, E. J., & Kennedy, A. M. (2003). *PIRLS 2001 international report: IEA's study of reading literacy achievement in the primary schools.* Chestnut Hill, MA: Boston College.

Munby, H. (1986). Metaphor in the thinking of teachers: An exploratory study. *Journal of Curriculum Studies, 18,* 197–209.

Munson M. L., & Sutton P. D. (2004). Births, marriages, divorces, and deaths: Provisional data for 2003. *National vital statistics reports, (52)*22. Hyattsville, MD: National Center for Health Statistics.

Myers, G. (Ed.). (1992). *William James: Writings 1878–1899: Psychology, briefer course / The will to believe / Talks to teachers and students / Essays.* New York: Collier.

A nation at risk. (1983).

A nation still at risk. (1998). Eric Digest No. ED429988.

National Association for Bilingual Education. (2004). *Does bilingual education really work?*

National Association of Elementary School Principals. (2001). NAESP redefines role of school principals. *NAESP Principal Online.*

National Association of Secondary School Principals. (2001). Priorities and barriers in high school leadership: A survey of principals.

National Board for Professional Teaching Standards. (1999) *What teachers should know and be able to do.* Southfield, MI, and Arlington, VA: National Board for Professional Teaching Standards.

National Campaign to Prevent Teen Pregnancy. (2001). *Halfway there: A prescription for continued progress in preventing teen pregnancy.* Washington, DC: Author.

National Campaign to Prevent Teen Pregnancy. (2004). *Fact sheet: Recent trends in teen pregnancy, sexual activity, and contraceptive use.* Washington DC: Author.

National Campaign to Prevent Teen Pregnancy. (2004). *Fact sheet: Why the education community cares about preventing teen pregnancy.*

National Campaign to Prevent Teen Pregnancy. (2004). *With one voice 2004: America's adults and teens sound off about teen pregnancy.* Washington, DC: Author.

National Center for Education Statistics. (1996). *Urban schools: The challenge of location and poverty.*

National Center for Education Statistics. (2000). *Vocational education.*

National Center for Education Statistics. (2001). *Digest of education statistics, 2001, Chapter 1. All levels of education.* And Table 69. Highest degree earned, number of years teaching experience, and average class size for teachers in public elementary and secondary schools, by state: 1993–94.

National Center for Education Statistics. (2001). *Highlights from the Third International Mathematics and Science Study: Repeat (TIMSS_R).*

National Center for Education Statistics. (2002). *Indicators of school crime and safety: 2002.*

National Center for Education Statistics. (2002). *Overview of public elementary and secondary schools and districts: School year 2000–01.*

National Center for Education Statistics. (2002). *Vocational education offerings in rural high schools.*

National Center for Education Statistics. (2003). *Digest of education statistics, 2003: Chapter 2: Elementary and secondary education.*

National Center for Education Statistics. (2003). *Contexts of elementary and secondary education: Special programs: Public alternative schools for at-risk students.*

National Center for Education Statistics. (2003). *Fast facts: Vocational education.*

National Center for Education Statistics. (2004). *Dropout rates in the United States: 2001.* Washington, DC: Author.

National Center for Education Statistics. (2004). *Highlights from the Trends in International Mathematics and Science Study (TIMSS), 2003.*

National Center for Education Statistics. (2004). *Indicators of school crime and safety: 2004.* Washington, DC: U.S. Government Printing Office.

National Center for Education Statistics. (2004). *Projections of education statistics to 2013 (32nd ed.).* Washington, DC: Author.

National Center for Education Statistics. (2005). *Reporting brief. NAEP 1999 trends in academic progress: Three decades of student performance.*

National Center for Education Statistics. (2005). *Public elementary and secondary students, staff, schools, and school districts: 2002–2003.* Washington, DC: Author.

National Center for Education Statistics. (2005). *Internet access in U.S. public schools and classrooms: 1994–2003.* Washington, DC: Author.

National Center for Education Statistics. (2005). *Issue brief: 1.1 million homeschooled students in the United States in 2003.*

National Center for Education Statistics. (2005). *Distance education courses for public elementary and secondary school students: 2002–03.*

National Center for Health Statistics. (2005). *Health, United States, 2005: With chartbook on trends in the health of Americans.* Hyattsville, MD: Author.

National Center for Health Statistics. (2005). *Prevalence of overweight among children and adolescents: United States, 1999–2002.*

National Center for Learning Disabilities. (2001). *LD at a glance.*

National Coalition to Abolish Corporal Punishment in Schools. (2004). *U.S.: Statistics on corporal punishment by state and race.*

National Commission on Excellence in Education. (1983). *A nation at risk: The imperative for educational reform.* Washington, DC: Author.

National Commission on Teaching and America's Future. (2005). *Induction into learning communities.* Washington, DC: Author.

National Council for Accreditation of Teacher Education (2002). *Professional standards for the accreditation of schools, colleges, and departments of education,* 2002 edition. Washington, DC: National Council for the Accreditation of Teacher Education.

National Council for the Social Studies. (1994). *Expectations of excellence: Curriculum standards for social studies.* Washington, DC: Author.

National Council for the Social Studies. (1994). *Curriculum standards for social studies: Executive summary.* Washington, DC: Author.

National Council of Teachers of Mathematics. (2000). *Principles and standards for school mathematics.* Reston, VA: Author.

National Education Association. (n.d.). Class size.

National Education Association. (1975). *Code of ethics for the education profession.* Washington, DC: Author.

National Education Association. (2003). *School safety.*

National Education Association. (2003). *Status of the American public school teacher 2000–2001.* Washington, DC: Author.

National Education Association. (2005). *Rankings & estimates: Rankings of the states 2004 and estimates of school statistics 2005.* Washington, DC: Author.

National Education Association. (2005). Accountability and testing.

National Education Association. (2005). About NEA.

National Mental Health Association. (2003). *Bullying and what to do about it.*

National Middle School Association. (2001). *This we believe: Developmentally responsive middle level schools.* Columbus, OH: author.

National Paideia Center. (2005). Paideia active learning; philosophy and methodology; columns of instruction.

National Research Council. (1996). *National science education standards.* Washington, DC: National Academy Press.

National School Board Association. (2005).

National School Supply and Equipment Association. (2001) *NSSEA releases study on teachers' shopping habits.*

Neal, A. D., Martin, J. L., & Moses, M. (2000). *Losing America's memory: Historical illiteracy in the 21st century.* Washington, DC: American Council of Trustees and Alumni.

New American Schools. (2003). *New American Schools: About us.*

New Jersey v. T.L.O., 469 U.S. 325, 105 S.Ct. 733, 83 L.Ed.2d 720 (1985). (Case No.123).

Nieto, S. M. (2003). What keeps teachers going? *Educational Leadership, 60*(8), 14–18.

North Carolina Association of Educators. (2003). *Extracurricular and noninstructional duties: Policy code 7405.*

Norton, J. L. (1997, November 13). *Learning from first-year teachers: Characteristics of the effective practitioner.* Paper presented at the Annual Meeting of the Mid-South Educational Research Association, Memphis, TN. (ERIC Document Reproduction Service No. ED418050).

Nye, B., Hedges, L. V., & Konstantopoulos, S. (2004). Do minorities experience larger lasting benefits from small classes? *The Journal of Educational Research, 98*(2), 94–100.

Office of Educational Research and Improvement. (1999). *Highlights from TIMSS, the Third International Mathematics and Science Study: Overview and key findings across grade levels.*

Office of Indian Education Programs. (n.d.). *About us.*

Olweus, D. (1996). Bully/victim problems at school: Facts and effective intervention. *Reclaiming Children and Youth, 5,* 15–22.

Ordway v. Hargraves, 323 F. Supp. 1155 (D. Mass. 1971); Mun. Separate School Dist., 338 F. Sup. 1376 (N.D.Miss. 1972).

Otuya, W. (1992). *Alternative teacher certification: An update.* ERIC Digest. (ERIC Document Reproduction Service No. ED351312).

Owings. W. A., & Kaplan, L. S. (2006). *American public school finance.* Belmont, CA: Thomson/Wadsworth.

Padolsky, D. (2002). NCELA FAQ No. 5: What are the most common language groups for ELL students? *National Clearinghouse for English Language Acquisition & Language Instruction Educational Programs.*

Padolsky, D. (2005). NCELA FAQ No. 1: How many school-aged English language learners (ELLs) are there in the U. S.? *National Clearinghouse for English Language Acquisition & Language Instruction Education Programs.*

Pajares, M. (1992). Teachers' beliefs and educational research: Cleaning up on a messy construct. *Review of Educational Research, 61,* 307–332.

Palmer, P. (1998). *The courage to teach: Exploring the inner landscape of a teacher's life.* San Francisco: Jossey-Bass.

Palmer v. Board of Education of the City of Chicago, 603 F.2d 1271 (7th Cir. 1979), cert.den., 444 U.S. 1026 (1980).

Papandreou, A. (1995). *Teaching viewed through student performance and selected effectiveness factors.* (ERIC Document Reproduction Service No. ED392760).

Parrish v. Moss, 200 Misc. 375, 106 N.Y.S.2d 577 (1951), aff. 279 App.Div. 608, 107 N.Y.S.2d 580 (1951).

Patrick, K. (2000, September 10). Boca Raton, Fla., high school institutes detention for late students. *Knight & Ridder/Tribune Business News.*

Payne, R. K. (1998). *A framework for understanding poverty* (Rev. ed.). Highlands, TX: RFT Publishing.

Pecori, J. (Ed.). (2000, December). *The future is now: Addressing social issues in schools of the 21st century*. Alexandria, VA: National Association of State Boards of Education. (ERIC Document Reproduction Service No. ED467227).

Peske, H. G., Liu, E., Johnson, S. M., Kauffman, D., & Kardos, S. M. (2001). The next generation of teachers: Changing conceptions of a career in teaching. *Phi Delta Kappan, 83*(4), 304–311.

Pettit v. State Board of Education, 10 Cal. 3d 29, 109 Cal. Rptr. 665, 513 P.2d 889 (1973).

Piaget, J. (1972). *The psychology of the child*. New York: Basic Books.

Pickering v. Board of Education, 391 U.S. 563, 88 S. Ct. 1731 (1968).

Pittman, K., & O'Neill, L. (2001). Using metaphors to evaluate ourselves. *Classroom Leadership, 4*(5), 1–3.

Podoll, S., & Randle, D. (2005, September). Building a virtual high school . . . click by click. *THE Journal Online, 33*(2).

Population Reference Bureau. (2002). *World population data sheet*. Washington, DC: Author.

Prater, G., Rezzonico, A., Pyran, R., Chischille, J., Arthur, V., & Yellowhair, B. (1995). Effective teachers: Perceptions of Native American students in rural areas. In *Conference Proceedings of the American Council on Rural Special Education*. (ERIC Document Reproduction Service No. ED381332).

Public Agenda Online. (2003). *Now that I'm here: What America's immigrants have to say about life in the U.S. today*.

Questions of quality and impact. (1999, June). American Educational Research Association.

Raleigh v. Independent School District No. 625, 275 N.W.2d 572 (Minn. 1979).

Ramanathan, A. K., & Zollers, N. J. (1999). For-profit schools continue to skimp on special education: A response to Naomi Zigmond. *Phi Delta Kappan, 81*(4), 284–290.

Reed, D. F., & Davis, M. D. (1999). Social reconstructionism for urban students. *The Clearing House, 72*(5), 291–294.

RMC Research Corporation. (2004). *The Literacy Center K–1 Las Vegas Project: A research study by RMC Research Corporation for LeapFrog SchoolHouse*. Emeryville, CA: LeapFrog Enterprises.

Robertson, L. S. (1980). Crash involvement of teenaged drivers when driver education is eliminated from high school. *American Journal of Public Health, 70*, 599–603.

Rolando v. School Directors of District No. 125, 44 Ill.App.3d 658, 3 Ill.Dec. 402, 358 N. E. 2d 945 (1976).

Roman, M. I. (2002). Help us rebuild America. *Commercial Modular Construction Magazine*.

Romano, L. (2006, January 6). Florida voucher system struck down. *Washington Post*.

Rosenberg, D. (2004, May 24). The "Will & Grace" effect: With Massachusetts leading the way, gay marriage is slowly becoming a reality—and dividing generations. *Newsweek*, p. 38.

Rosenthal, R., & Jacboson, L. (1968). *Pygmalion in the classroom*. New York: Holt, Rinehart and Winston.

Rowan, J. (2001). A guide to humanistic psychology: The person-centered approach. Alameda, CA: Association for Humanistic Psychology.

Rudolph, K. D., Kurlakowsky, K. D., & Conley, C. S. (2001). Developmental and social-contextual origins of depressive control-related beliefs and behavior. *Cognitive Therapy and Research, 25*(4), 447–475.

Rupp v. Bryant, 417 So.2d 658 (Fla. 1982).

Russell, (1999). *The no significant difference phenomenon: A comparative research annotated bibliography on technology for distance education* (5th ed.). Montgomery, AL: International Distance Education Certification Center.

Russo v. Central School District, No. 1, 469 F.2d 623 (2nd Cir. 1972), cert. den. 411 U.S. 932, 93 S.Ct. 1988 (1973).

Rutherford, F. J., & Ahlgren, A. (1990). *Science for all Americans*. New York: Oxford University Press.

Salem Witch Museum. (2005). Salem, MA: Author.

Sanders, W. L., & Rivers, J. C. (1996). Cumulative and residual effects of teachers on future academic achievement. Knoxville, TN: University of Tennessee Value-Added Research and Assessment Center.

Sandham, J. L. (1997). Educational needs of Asian-Americans highlighted. *Education Week, 16*(34), 9.

Santrock, J. W. (2004). *Educational psychology* (2nd ed.). Boston: McGraw-Hill.

Scheer v. Independent School District No. I-26 of Ottawa County 948 P.2d 275 (OK 1997).

Schneider, T., Walker, H., & Sprague, J. (2000). *Safe school design: A handbook for educational leaders*. Eugene, OR: ERIC Clearinghouse on Educational Management. (ERIC Document Reproduction Service No. EA 030 490).

School District No. 8, Pinal County v. Superior Court 102 Ariz. 478, 433 P.2d 28 (1967).

School District of Hillsborough County, Florida. (2005). *Magnet schools: The choice that fits.*

School infrastructure rates a "D," says ASCE report released in March. (2005). *School Construction News, 8*(5), 1.

Schulte, B. (2002, September 15). Cheatin', Writin' & 'Rithmetic: How to succeed in school without really trying. *The Washington Post*, p. W16.

Seal, K. R., & Harmon, H. L. (1995). Realities of rural school reform. *Phi Delta Kappan, 77*(2), 119–125.

Search Institute. (2005). What are developmental assets?

Shachar, M., & Neumann, Y. (2003). Differences between traditional and distance education academic performances: A meta-analytic approach. *International Review of Research in Open and Distance Learning, 4*(2).

Shaul, M. S. (2004, August). *Commercial activities in schools: Use of student data is limited and additional dissemination of guidance could help school districts develop policies.* Report to Congressional Requesters. Washington, DC: U.S. General Accounting Office.

Shymansky, J. A., Kyle, W. C., & Alport, J. M. (1982, November–December). How effective were the hands-on science programs of yesterday? *Science and Children*, 14–15.

Siris, K., & Osterman, K. (2004). Interrupting the cycle of bullying and victimization in the elementary classroom. *Phi Delta Kappan, 86*(4), 288–291.

Siu-Runyan, Y., & Heart, S. J. (1992). Management manifesto. *The Executive Educator, 14*(1), 23–26.

Slavin, R. E. (1994). *Educational psychology: Theory and practice*. Boston: Allyn & Bacon.

Slavin, R. E. (1997). *Educational psychology: Theory and practice* (5th ed.). Boston: Allyn & Bacon.

Smith, J. N. (Director). (1995). *Dangerous minds.* [Motion picture]. United States: Hollywood Pictures.

Smith, L. (2002, February). In the aftermath, what's the purpose? *The School Administrator Web Edition.*

Snider v. Kit Carson School District R-1, in Cheyenne County, 166 Colo. 180, 442 P.2d 429 (1968).

Snorton, R. (2005, September 1). GLSEN concerned by local school board action in White County, GA. *GLSEN News & Announcements*.

Society for Adolescent Medicine. (1997). *Driver education: A position paper of the society for adolescent medicine*.

Sollee, D. (1998). *Florida's high school marriage education bill*. Washington, DC: The Coalition for Marriage, Family and Couples Education.

Sparks, S. (2005). Study: Small classes early on can keep students in school: Sustained small-group K–3 structure has lasting effects on graduation, academics. *Education Daily, 38*(89), 3.

Spellings: Reward teachers who get results. *Achiever, 4*(8), 1–2.

Spring, J. (1986). *The American school, 1642–1985*. New York: Longman.

Startzel v. Commonwealth, Dept. of Educ., 128 Pa.Comwlth. 110 562 A.2d 1005 (1989).

State v. Project Principle, 724 S.W.2d 387 (Tex. 1987).

Stephens, K. R., & Karnes, F. A. (2000). State definitions for the gifted and talented revisited. *Exceptional Children, 66*(2).

Stephens v. Alabama State Tenure Commission, 634 So.2d 549 (Ala. Civ. App. 1993).

Stern, J. (1994). *The condition of education in rural school*s. Washington, DC: U.S. Department of Education, Office of Educational Research and Improvement.

Sullivan v. Meade Independent School Dist. No. 101, 530 F.2d 799 (8th Cir. 1976).

Sun, Y., & Li, Y. (2002). Children's psychological well-being improves after divorce, but test scores do not. *Journal of Marriage and Family, 64*(2), 472.

Swan, W. W. (2004). *Impact of Ruby Payne's* Instructional Framework *on student achievement in East Allen County Schools, Indiana, 2001–03*.

Tamura, E. H. (2003). Introduction: Asian Americans and educational history. *History of Education Quarterly, 43*(1), 1–9.

Taylor, H. (2004, March 12). *The Harris Poll #19, March 12, 2004: Teachers' job satisfaction rises to highest level in 20 years*. Harris Interactive.

Teaching and Learning with Technology. (2004). *Ways to structure the delivery of information using instructional technology*. Information Technology Services at Pennsylvania State University.

Teacher quality is most important factor (2000). Hoover Institution Newsletter.

Technology training. (2000). *Kappa Delta Pi Record, 36*(4), 189.

Thomas B. Fordham Institute. (2004). *The mad mad world of textbook adoption*. Washington, DC: Author.

Thompson v. Southwest School District, 483 F. Supp. 1170 (Mo. 1980).

Tinker v. Des Moines Independent Community School Dist., 393 U.S. 503, 89S.Ct.733 21 L.Ed.2d 731 (1969).

Titus v. Lindberg, 49 N.J. 66 228 A.2d 65 (1967).

Tobin, K. (1990). Research on science laboratory activities: In pursuit of better questions and answers to improve learning. *School Science and Mathematics, 90*, 403–418.

Tomerlin v. Dade County School Board, 318 So.2d 159 (Fla. 1975).

Torres, K., & Rankin, B. (January 15, 2005.) Disclaimers on evolution killed: Cobb schools' warning stickers in science books unconstitutional. *The Atlanta Journal-Constitution*, p. A1.

Touhig, K., Stephenson, D., Lillquist, D., Bird, J., Adler, S., & Babitz, M. (2005). Environmental health and service learning. *Academic Exchange Quarterly, 9*(1), 50–53.

Trotter, A. (2005). E-Rate: The road ahead. *Education Week, 24*(35), 30–31.

Tyack, D. B. (Ed.). (1967). *Turning points in American educational history*. Waltham, MA: Blaisdell.

Tyler, R. W. (1949). *Basic principles of curriculum and instruction*. Chicago: The University of Chicago Press.

United Press International. (2005, June 24). Teacher salaries flat, average $46,742. *UPI News Track*.

United States v. Board of Education for the School District of Philadelphia, 911 F.2d 882 (3rd Cir. 1990).

United States v. South Carolina, 445 F. Supp. 1094 (D.S.C. 1977).

U.S. Copyright Office. Copyright Act of the United States of America. Fair Use Provision of the Copyright Act. §107. Limitations on exclusive rights: Fair Use.

U.S. Department of Commerce. (2000). *Falling through the net: Toward digital inclusion*. Washington, DC: Author.

U.S. Department of Education. (n.d.). *White House initiatives: Center for faith-based and community initiatives*.

U.S. Department of Education. (1993). *National excellence: A case for developing America's talent*. Washington, DC: United States Government Printing Office.

U.S. Department of Education. (1999). *E-Learning: Putting a world-class education at the fingertips of all children*.

U.S. Department of Education. (2000). *Revising the 1996 national educational technology plan*.

U.S. Department of Education. (2000). E-Learning: Putting a world-class education at the fingertips of all children (the national educational technology plan).

U.S. Department of Education (2002). Executive summary: The No Child Left Behind Act of 2001.

U.S. Department of Education (2002). *No child left behind*.

U.S. Department of Education (2002). *Supreme Court clears the way for school choice, research suggests choice improves student achievement*.

U.S. Department of Education. (2003). *Twenty-fifth annual report to Congress on the implementation of the Individuals with Disabilities Act*. Jessup, MD: Author. Retrieved from http://www.ed.gov/about/reports/annual/osep/2003/25th-vol-1-sec-1.pdf.

U.S. Department of Education. (2004). Office for Civil Rights. OCR Elementary and Secondary School Survey.

U.S. Department of Education. (2004). Teacher-to-Teacher initiative: Supporting success.

U.S. Department of Education. (2005). *National education technology plan*.

U.S. Department of Education. (2005). *What does the Department of Education do?*

U.S. Department of Education, National Center for Education Statistics. (2005). *The condition of education 2005* (NCES 2005-094). Washington, DC: U.S. Government Printing Office.

U.S. Department of Homeland Security. (2003). *Yearbook of immigration statistics*. Washington, DC: Author.

U.S. Department of Labor, Bureau of Labor Statistics. (2003). Occupational outlook handbook, 2002–2003 edition, Educational administrators.

U.S. Food and Drug Administration. (2001). *Body mass index and health. Insight 16: March 2000. Statistical data included*. Washington, DC: Author.

Utah snubs federal No Child Left Behind act. (2005). *MSNBC News*.

Vedder, R. (2003, Summer). Comparable worth. *Education Next*, p. 14.

Veronia Sch. Dist. 47J v. Acton, 515 U.S. 646 (1995).

Vossekuil, B., Fein, R. A., Reddy, M., Borum, R., & Modzeleski, W. (2002, May). *The final report and findings of the Safe School Initiative: Implications for the prevention of school attacks in the United States*. Washington, DC: U.S. Secret Service and U.S. Department of Education.

Waldrip, D. (2000). A brief history and philosophy of magnet schools. *Magnet Schools of America*.

Walsh, M. (1999). Harassment ruling poses challenge. *Education Week on the Web*.

Wang, F. K. (2005). Education culture gap: Tugging at a few threads of truth behind the model minority myth. New Orleans, IMDiversity.

Waters, R. (2003, January). The school that stopped bullies. *Readers Digest*, 141–146.

Webb, L., D., Metha, A., & Jordan, K. F. (2000). *Foundations of American Education*. Columbus, OH: Merrill.

Weir, P. (Director). *Dead poets society*. [Motion picture]. United States: Touchstone Pictures.

Wells, A. S. (1989). Hispanic education in America: Separate and unequal. New York: ERIC Clearinghouse on Urban Education. (ERIC Document Reproduction Service No. ED316616).

Wenglinsky, H. (1998, May). The effect of class size on achievement: What the research says. Research Policy Information Center.

Wenglinsky, H. (2000). *How teaching matters: Bringing the classroom back into discussions of teacher quality*. Princeton, NJ: Educational Testing Service.

Wenning, R., Herdman, P. A., Smith, N., McMahon, N., & Washington, K. (2003). *No Child Left Behind: Testing, reporting, and accountability*. ERIC Digest. (ERIC Document Reproduction Service No. ED480994).

Westbury, I. (2003). Curriculum, school: Overview. In J. W. Guthrie (Ed.), *Encyclopedia of education* (2nd ed.), pp. 529–535. New York: Macmillan Reference USA.

White House Initiative on Educational Excellence for Hispanic Americans. (1999). *Latinos in education*. Washington, DC: U.S. Department of Education. (ERIC Document Reproduction Service No. ED440817).

Whittle, C. (2005). The promise of public/private partnerships. *Educational Leadership*, 62(5), 34–36.

Williams v. School District No. 40 of Gila County, 4 Ariz.App, 5, 417 P.2d 376 (1966).

Witkin, H. A., & Goodenough, D. E. (1981). Cognition styles: Essence and origins. Field dependence and field independence. *Psychological Issues* Monograph 51. New York: International Universities Press.

Wolfgang, C. H., & Glickman, C. D. (1986). *Solving discipline problems: Strategies for teachers*. Boston: Allyn & Bacon.

Wong, H. K., & Wong, R. T. (2001). *The first days of school*. Mountain View, CA: Harry K. Wong Publications.

Wong, H., & Wong, R. T. (2004). *The first days of school: How to be an effective teacher*. Mountain View, CA: Harry K. Wong Publications.

Woolfolk, A. (2001). *Educational psychology* (8th ed.). Boston: Allyn & Bacon.

World Almanac. (2005). New York: World Almanac Books.

Yamamoto, K., Davis, O. L., Jr., Dylak, S., Whittaker, J., Marsh, C., and van der Vesthuisen, P. C. (1996, Spring). Across 6 nations: Stressful events in the lives of children. *Child Psychiatry and Human Development*, 139–150.

Yecke, C. P., & Lazo, L. O. (2002). *Choice provisions in No Child Left Behind*. PowerPoint presentation.

Yellowitz, I. (n.d.). *Houghton Mifflin reader's companion to American history: Child labor*.

Yoo, C. (2005, May 8). Gay teens seek support and safety. *Atlanta Journal-Constitution,* p. C1.

Young, B. N., Whitley, M. E., & Helton, C. (1998, November). *Students' perceptions of characteristics of effective teachers.* Paper presented at the annual meeting of the Mid-South Educational Research Association, New Orleans, LA. (ERIC Document Reproduction Service No. ED426962).

Zellner, W. (2000, February 7). Going to bat for vouchers. *Business Week Online.*

Zelman v. Simmons-Harris, 536 U.S. 639 (2002).

Zollers, N. J., & Ramanathan, A. K. (1998). For-profit charter schools and students with disabilities: The sordid side of the business of schooling. *Phi Delta Kappan, 80*(4), 297–304.

CREDITS

Chapter 0. 3: Courtesy of Bill Lisenby 5: © Royalty-free/PhotoDisc/Getty Images 9: Courtesy Kim Loomis 10: Courtesy Dave Martin

Chapter 1. 16: Courtesy of David Ottenstein Photography 18: © Dynamic Graphics Group/Creatas/Alamy 20: Courtesy of Linda Winburn 21: © Barbara Laing/Time Life Pictures/Getty Images 22: © AP/Wide World Photos 26: © Photodisc Collection/Getty Images 27: © Stewart Cohen/Getty Images 29: bottom right, Photo Courtesy of The Field Psych Trust 29: top right, © Craig Ferre Photography/Courtesy William Glasser Institute

Chapter 2. 47: center, © ImageState/Alamy 47: bottom left, © Center for the Study of The Great Ideas 49: Courtesy Hoover Institution 50: © Hulton Archive/Getty Images 51: © Richard Hutchings/PhotoEdit 52: © Hulton Archive/Getty Images 54: Photo courtesy of the Paulo Freire's Archive of Paulo Freire Institute 55: Courtesy Kathy Heavers 58: © BananaStock/Alamy

Chapter 3. 71: © David Young-Wolff/PhotoEdit 74: © White Cross Productions/Getty Images 75: © Bettmann/CORBIS 80: © Farrell Grehan/CORBIS 83: © Bettmann/CORBIS 85: © Catherine Ledner/Getty Images 88: Courtesy of Brenda Zabel

Chapter 4. 96: © AGStockUSA, Inc./Alamy 105: © Bob Daemmrich/PhotoEdit 107: © Sally and Richard Greenhill/Alamy 108: Courtesy of Tamara Steen 112: © Michael Newman/PhotoEdit 115: © Sean Justice/Getty Images

Chapter 5. 124: © Michael Newman/PhotoEdit 128: Courtesy of Bill Lisenby 131: Courtesy of Bill Lisenby 132: © Paul Conklin/PhotoEdit 137: J. Gardner, copyright 2003.

Chapter 6. 157: © Bob Daemmrich/PhotoEdit 160: Courtesy of Bev Abrams 163: © Tom Stewart/CORBIS 167: left, © Catherine Karnow/CORBIS 167: right, © GeoStock/Getty Images 174: © Craig Witkowski/Index Stock Imagery

Chapter 7. 180: © Michael Newman/PhotoEdit 182: © AP/Wide World Photos 185: right, Courtesy of David Ottenstein Photography 185: left, © Jeff Greenberg/PhotoEdit 187: © Michael Newman/PhotoEdit 189: © Michael Newman/PhotoEdit

Chapter 8. 197: Brian Snyder/Reuters/Landov 199: © AP/Wide World Photos 203: Courtesy of Linda Eisinger 204: © Yellow Dog Productions/Getty Images 207: Courtesy of Bill Lisenby 213: © Sean Cayton/The Image Works 214: Courtesy of Christie Daniels

Chapter 9. 224: Courtesy of Bill Lisenby 225: Courtesy of Bill Lisenby 231: © Spencer Grant/PhotoEdit 243: Courtesy of Bill Lisenby

Chapter 10. 253: right, Library of Congress 253: left, © Hofstra University Libraries–Special Collections 254: © Bettmann/CORBIS 255: © Hulton Archive/Getty Images 259: Courtesy of Kimberly Loomis 261: top, © CORBIS 261: bottom, © Hulton Archive/Getty Images 262: wikipedia.org 264: bottom, Library of Congress 264: top, © CORBIS 277: Library of Congress 278: left, © Bettmann/CORBIS 278: right, © CORBIS 279: left, © Arizona Historical Foundation 279: right, © Arizona Historical Society 280: Courtesy of Burt Saxon

Chapter 11. 286: © Chip Henderson/Index Stock Imagery 289: © Michael Newman/PhotoEdit 297: © Charles Gupton/CORBIS 304: © Mark Richards/PhotoEdit 307: Courtesy of Bill Lisenby 311: Courtesy of Kathleen Thomas

Chapter 12. 317: © LWA-Sharie Kennedy/zefa/Corbis 320: © Mark Gibson/Index Stock Imagery 323: © Baerbel Schmidt/Getty Images 325: © James Leynse/CORBIS 329: Courtesy of Deb Perryman 330: © Jeff Greenberg/PhotoEdit

Chapter 13. 340: © BananaStock/ PictureQuest 343: © Michael Newman/PhotoEdit 355: © Bill Bachmann/Index Stock Imagery

Chapter 14. 363: Courtesy of Bill Lisenby 366: Courtesy San Lorenzo Middle School 369: left and right, Courtesy of Becky Stovall 373: Courtesy of Billie Travis 374: Courtesy of Becky Stovall 381: Courtesy of David Ottenstein Photography 385: © Catherine Ledner/Getty Images

Chapter 15. 392: Courtesy of Bill Lisenby 393: © Comstock Images/PictureQuest 396: © image100/Alamy 397: Courtesy of Elizabeth Day 401: © Manchan/Getty Images 402: © Blend Images/Alamy

INDEX